Educational Psychology in the Classroom

by the same author

An Introduction to Social Psychology
Contemporary Research in Social Psychology: A Book of Readings
The Psychology of College Success

with Donn Byrne

Psychology: An Introduction to a Behavioral Science

with Donn Byrne and Fredrica Lindgren

Current Research in Psychology: A Book of Readings

with Leonard W. Fisk, Jr.

Psychology of Personal Development

with Lori Fisk

A Survival Guide for Teachers

with Fredrica Lindgren

Readings in Educational Psychology

with Robert I. Watson

Psychology of the Child

Educational Psychology in the Classroom

FIFTH EDITION

HENRY CLAY LINDGREN

Professor of Psychology
San Francisco State University

JOHN WILEY & SONS, Inc.
New York / London / Sydney / Toronto

Copyright © 1956, 1962, 1967, 1972, 1976, by John Wiley & Sons, Inc.

All rights reserved. Published simultaneously in Canada.

No part of this book may be reproduced by any means, nor
transmitted, nor translated into a machine language
without the written permission of the publisher.

Library of Congress Cataloging in Publication Data:

Lindgren, Henry Clay, 1914–
   Educational psychology in the classroom.

   Bibliography: p.

   1. Educational psychology. I. Title.

LBI051.L67 1976   370.15   75-31716
ISBN 0-471-53649-0

Printed in the United States of America

10 9 8 7 6 5 4 3 2 1

to Etta and Fred

Preface

Educational psychology is psychology applied to teaching and learning processes. Inasmuch as the relationship between teacher and pupil is a social one, and both teaching and learning take place in a social setting, a good case can be made for the proposition that educational psychology is to a large extent applied *social* psychology.

Probably many students who enroll in a course in educational psychology have gained a head start in their study of human behavior through a general introductory course in psychology. If they have, so much the better. Although some of the concepts introduced in this book will already have been covered in the introductory course, their treatment here should give them a new and deeper meaning. The chief difference between educational psychology and general introductory psychology is a matter of focus and emphasis. Whereas introductory psychology has the purpose of helping students to develop a *general* understanding of human behavior through the application of the scientific method, educational psychology attempts to help the student to *apply* both the understanding and the methods of psychology to problems encountered in teaching-learning situations.

A textbook in educational psychology should not be regarded as an all-knowing oracle. It cannot provide solutions for the more or less individualized problems that teachers are bound to encounter in classrooms. But a textbook can help teachers solve such problems by preparing the way for professional understanding and insight.

To the author, such preparation means that the textbook should help teachers and prospective teachers to perceive learners and learning situations in new and different ways. In other words, he hopes that persons who read this book will develop points of view that will be different from the ones they would have had if they had not read the book.

The teacher who can react to a classroom problem from one point of view only—usually that of frustration or exasperation—is at a disadvantage. His only choice is that of repeating the methods which have already produced the difficulty or of reprimanding or otherwise punishing the children for their failure. The teacher who is able to examine a problem from a variety of aspects has the advantage of being in a position to use several different approaches. Furthermore, he is also likely to perceive himself as a factor in the situation and is thus able to see how *his* behavior contributes to or affects the problem under consideration.

An improved understanding of both human behavior and learning situations hence must imply a certain amount of self-analysis and self-understanding. It is hoped, therefore, that students who read this book will come to know and understand *themselves* better both as persons and as teachers—as individuals in learning situations. It is almost axiomatic that the understanding of the behavior of other persons (including adolescents and children) develops in direct proportion to the growth in understanding our own behavior. Furthermore, unless students are able to relate the learning that takes place in educational psychology classes to their own experience, any advantage to be gained from having taken the course and read the book will be lost once the course is over. Indeed, experience with teachers taking in-service training has led me to suspect that many of them have neither been encouraged nor helped to relate what they have learned in educational psychology courses to their personal experience. In this book, therefore, special efforts have been made to encourage students to see the relationships between the findings and hypotheses of psychologists and the events of everyday life.

I also hope that students reading this textbook will be encouraged to adopt what might be termed "the scientific point of view" with regard to the data of their professional lives. If teachers and teachers-to-be attain this point of view, it will mean that they will have developed an interest in probing into the causes and effects of classroom problems and events. It means also that they will maintain an enlightened skepticism and an open-mindedness with regard to their own findings as well as to the claims and pronouncements of professional and lay figures alike.

And, finally, I hope that readers will gain a better understanding of their roles as teacher-psychologists—as artists and scientists in the field of human relations—to the end that the inevitable frustrating experiences of the classroom will not produce cynicism, apathy, and discouragement but will instead lead to study, understanding, learning, professional growth, and an increased interest in the psychological problems of education.

The case material used at various points in this book is drawn from my own experiences, as well as from those of my colleagues, students, and counselees. I have elaborated on these incidents rather generously, changing names and situations, partly to disguise the identity of the chief figures, but also to highlight the points that the cases were selected to illustrate. Hence they are to be considered as fictional creations, rather than as clinical reports, although they are drawn from life and are as realistic as I can make them.

In this fifth edition, as in previous editions, I have stressed the importance of the teacher's functioning as a behavioral scientist. In his work, I have selected examples of relevant research and have organized and presented them in such a way as to clarify and give meaning to the problems that teachers are likely to encounter. It is my belief, supported by my experiences in teaching and working at all levels of education, that the competency and general effectiveness of any teacher can be extended if he understands the psychological implications of the events taking place in his classroom as well as in the lives of his students.

Although educational psychology can be supported and defended as an academic field in its own right, it is also my feeling that the usefulness of educational psychology as an applied science depends largely on the extent to which its activities and outcomes are shared by classroom teachers and psychologists alike. Therefore it is my hope that this textbook may help broaden the areas of mutual concern, understanding, and cooperation between teachers and psychologists.

My efforts to incorporate these objectives into this revision were aided and encouraged by my colleagues and my students at San Francisco State University. I am also grateful to Harold L. Weeks, Director of Research, San Francisco City Schools, who read and criticized the chapters on evaluation and measurement; to Lori Fisk, teacher, textbook author, and educational consultant, who did an annotated analysis of the fourth edition of this book; to Frederick C. Howe of Buffalo State University College and Doris Kraemer of Montclair (N.J.) State College, who reviewed the book at various stages of production. And finally, I thank Fredi Lindgren, who helped edit the manuscript and prepare it for publication.

Henry Clay Lindgren

SAN FRANCISCO STATE UNIVERSITY
SEPTEMBER, 1975

Contents

and anxiety / Teacher-centered versus group-centered methods / Overdwelling and other dominating habits / Getting it all together through structure and organization / The teacher as an autocrat / Communication and intercommunication / Communication as an essential skill / The increasing complexity of teaching-learning problems

11 Discipline and the learning situation 257

12 The learner-centered classroom 285

13 The evaluation of learning 315

xvi

CONTENTS

Educational Psychology in the Classroom

1

Understanding the Psychology of Teaching and Learning

IN THIS CHAPTER WE SHALL COVER

- ■ "What's wrong with education?" as viewed by its critics

- ■ "What's good about education?": what surveys show

- ■ The need for scientific evidence in understanding educational processes

- ■ Understanding the learner, the learning process, and the learning situation

- ■ What "understanding" means

- ■ Sources of understanding: psychologists' and teachers' contributions

- ■ The teacher as an educational psychologist

Education as a Storm Center

Education today is the focal point for a great deal of controversy and dissension. Everyone, it seems, has something to say about the public schools, and much of what is said is uncomplimentary.

In the recent past, the more radical reformers, such as John Holt (1964, 1972), George Leonard (1969), Paul Goodman (1966), and Edgar Z. Friedenberg (1965), have criticized the schools for stifling the free spirits of children and preventing them from developing their unique potentialities. What the reformers recommend is that adult demands, stan-dardized requirements, and penalties be reduced or eliminated altogether. Ivan Illich (1971) has gone even further. He believes that the educational establishment is past saving and proposes that compulsory schooling be abolished. Charles Silberman (1970) views such recommendations as essentially elitist and impractical, but he nevertheless sees the schools as mindless, dull, and repressive. He would like classrooms to be a great deal more "open" than they are in most school systems and looks to the British primary schools as ideal models.

This array of critics has attracted a great deal of attention during the last decade and a half, probably because the intellectual climate prevailing in the Western world has been one of freedom, permissiveness, and innovation. During the decades following World War II, however, it was the conservative critics who attracted the most attention. Mortimer Smith (1966) and his Council for Basic Education attacked the schools for being unconcerned about competence, achievement, and discipline, and being preoccupied with personal and social adjustment. Smith was supported in his attacks by eloquent and angry statements from Arthur Bestor (1956) and Admiral Hyman G. Rickover (1963), who expressed their dismay that American schools, unlike those in Europe, showed no interest in getting students to master mathematics, science, grammar, the "great books," the "great ideas of mankind," and foreign languages. Although the cries of these critics seem fainter today, their supporters are still on the march, for the feeling is widespread that the schools are too permissive and their curricula lack rigor. For example, a professor of public affairs complained recently that his daughter "comes home from the sixth grade with a glowing report card and a marvelous social experience, but tells us candidly that she hasn't been required to learn very much" (Denny, 1974).

An even larger number of critics is concerned about the immense amounts of money that are invested in public education and suspects that much of it may be wasted. The critics want to know exactly what it is that the public gets for its tax dollars and have demanded that administrators and teachers be held accountable for achieving visible results. There should be some direct relationship, these critics say, between input in the form of public funds and output in the form of knowledge and skills acquired by children. How can the schools be considered successful, they ask, when a national survey shows that 6 percent of male adolescents between the ages of twelve and seventeen are functionally illiterate? In some segments of the population, the illiteracy rate runs as high as 50 percent (U. S. Dept. of Health, Education, and Welfare, 1973).

The case against the schools seems even more damning when we consider the findings of James S. Coleman and his associates (1966) who conducted a survey of students at all social levels in schools throughout the country and concluded that one school is very much like another as far as measurable results are concerned. And Christopher S. Jencks and his associates (1972) have used data from the Coleman study and other sources as a basis for saying that the amount and kind of schooling an individual completes has relatively little effect on his eventual economic success.

The complaints and criticisms seem to be endless, and the reader often has the uncomfortable feeling that no matter how extreme or ridiculous they may sound, they all have at least the kernel of truth. At the same time, the reader wonders if there is not another side to the picture. After all, the schools have been producing graduates for some time, and some of them do seem to be responsible, competent, and even creative. Is there any evidence to show that the schools, far from being totally ineffective, actually make positive contributions to the welfare of the general public and of the individuals they educate? Fortunately for the schools and the individuals who staff them, the evidence is abundant.

Analyses of demographic data show that higher levels of school support are associated with social benefits. The more a state spends on education (and the fewer pupils it requires each teacher to instruct), the lower the rate of illiteracy among its youth. States that have lower illiteracy rates, in turn, also have lower homicide rates, using the latter statistic as an indicator of social disintegration (Walberg and Rasher, 1974). Similarly, greater educational attainment, as measured by the percentage of each state's residents who completed four years of high school, is associated with such indicators of positive social health as higher per capita income and a higher volunteer rate for the Peace Corps. States with higher levels of educational attainment are also likely to report lower murder rates and pro-

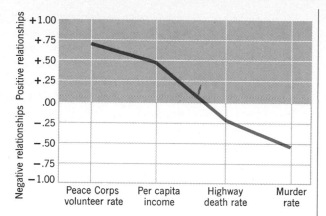

FIG. 1-1. Relationship between educational attainment and various demographic indexes, calculated for the fifty United States and the District of Columbia, 1972–1973 (Lindgren, 1974).

portionately fewer highway deaths[1] (Lindgren, 1974). (See Figure 1-1.) Such data support the widespread view that schooling has a positive influence on individual behavior.

Although everyone agrees that the policies and practices that prevail in American schools could be substantially improved, surveys of academic skills indicate that students in the United States are generally as competent as those in other countries. During the 1960s an organization called the International Association for the Evaluation of Education conducted a survey of the school achievement of children in twenty-two countries. Approximately a quarter of a million children were tested at ages ten and fourteen and in the last year of secondary school. In general, American students did very well. For example, the mean reading score of American high school seniors placed them twelfth—about at the midpoint—among the countries surveyed, and the scores made by the top 10 percent of the American seniors were higher than comparable groups in

all the other countries surveyed. About 70 percent of American adolescents graduate from high school, whereas in other countries, relatively few young people attain such a level of schooling. In Germany, only 1 percent of all eighteen-year-olds are still in school (Hechninger, 1973).

Reassuring as such findings are, they do not directly answer all the complaints about education that have been raised by the critics we mentioned, radical and conservative alike. These surveys make it clear, to be sure, that American schools generally have positive long-range effects on students, but they do not give us any indications of what kind of changes should be made in order to help those who attend school but receive few benefits, as well as those who attend school sporadically and eventually drop out, to cite two major educational problems. Those who know the schools are aware of these and other inadequacies, yet are confused by the contradictory proposals for educational reform. How can educators and others interested in making the schools more effective evaluate criticisms and suggestions?

Educational Psychology and the Search for Answers

The answer to this question lies in investigation and research. The critics of the schools are for the most part sincere, and many of them are impassioned and eloquent. Sometimes they cite statistics to support their arguments, but both the lay public and teachers are correct in their usual reaction of expressing reservations about data put forth by individuals or groups who rigorously advocate a position. What is needed to clarify and to bring matters into focus are what scientists refer to as "hard data"—information based on scientific studies that are properly designed and carefully controlled and monitored. Inasmuch as teaching and learning are forms of human behavior, it is to the behavioral scientist—especially the psychologist—that the laymen and educators turn in their search for something more substantial than opinions, feelings, and selectively culled data on which to base decisions

---

[1] The highway death rate, like the murder rate, is a demographic indicator of social disintegration and poor mental health. Police reports show that most highway deaths are the result of heavy use of alcohol and other drugs, and research studies show that repeated traffic violations are indicative of psychological problems (Huntley, 1973).

as to what needs to be corrected in the schools and what changes should be introduced.

The questions raised by critics of the schools are ones that every educator, teacher, and administrator alike must deal with from time to time, if only because he[2] is working at the storm center of an enterprise that is socially relevant and the focus of a great deal of public concern. Although these queries are of the utmost importance in determining the characteristics of schools both now and in the future, they are not the only problems that teachers must face as they go about their daily tasks. Teachers are, for example, continually asking themselves questions like these:

How can I get Frank to try harder in math?

What did I do that made the class so interested today?

How can I get my kindergarteners to put things away when they are through with finger painting?

How will the students react when they see their grades on this quiz?

Spelling drill bores me even more than it does the kids; I wonder if they would learn more if I made a game out of it?

Why did I snap at Suzie when she asked me to repeat next week's assignment?

These questions, like the monumental one of how to evaluate criticisms and proposals for reform are basically psychological in nature. They are psychological in the sense that they are concerned with highly complex processes of human behavior. Although the questions can be answered, the answers are not likely to be simple and obvious, because human behavior is not simple and obvious,

[2] The question of whether to refer to the teacher as "she" or "he" is a perplexing one. Most elementary school teachers are women, whereas most teachers in secondary schools and colleges are men. Without intending offense to either sex, I shall follow the conventional practice of using the masculine grammatical form as a way of referring to a teacher or an administrator, unless his or her sex is obvious from the context.

and there are no foolproof ways of teaching. Hence the answers to such questions are likely to vary with different schools, teachers, subjects, and classroom groups. For another, a teacher's ability to formulate valid answers will depend, at least in part, on how well he understands his students, his school, his community, and especially himself. Most of all, the success of his search for answers will depend on his insight into how students learn and the part that teachers play in stimulating, facilitating, or blocking learning. The usefulness or validity of the answers will also be determined by the extent to which they are psychologically sound—in other words, whether they are based on principles that are consistent with the way in which people can be expected to behave under certain circumstances.

Psychology is a behavioral science, that is, it is a science concerned with the study of human behavior. It is a science that is concerned, among other things, with identifying reasons why people behave as they do and developing principles that can be used to specify how likely they are to behave in certain ways and under what conditions such behavior is likely to occur. What the concerns of psychologists have led to is an *understanding* of human behavior. They have also led to the development of a number of different techniques that have been found useful in understanding specific instances of behavior. Such understanding is the chief contribution of psychologists, and the techniques they employ are valuable to the extent that they are based on or extend the understanding of human behavior. The word "understanding," as used in this way, has complex overtones, and we shall discuss them soon.

Understanding Educational Processes

Educational psychology is an applied branch of the main field of psychology, that is, it consists of the application of psychological principles and techniques to the development of educational strategies and programs and to the solution of educational problems. Its chief function is that of helping people involved in education to develop a better theoretical and functional understanding of educational processes. By "better understanding" we mean a broader, deeper, and more effective understanding, an understanding that is based on scientific research and not on popular belief or folklore, an understanding that is more realistic and will lead to more effective teaching and learning. By "educational processes" we mean the behavioral changes that take place in and result from school experiences, particularly that kind of experience we call "classroom learning."

Everyone, even the most naïve kindergartener, has *some* understanding of educational processes. Perhaps the college students who enroll in teacher-education courses have somewhat more understanding of education than most people because they must have thought about education for some time, probably years, before deciding that they wanted to become teachers. Furthermore, as they themselves participated in the educational process that preceded their entrance into the teacher-education program, they developed concepts and ideas of what education is, what it does, and how it functions. To a large extent, however, the understanding of educational processes possessed by students enrolling in courses in educational psychology is what might be termed "prescientific," that is, it is an understanding largely composed of common sense and personal impressions, all rather generously conditioned by popular belief and even folklore about the nature of those processes known as teaching and learning. We also use the term "prescientific" to indicate a kind of understanding that precedes and hopefully may be supplanted by understanding more firmly based on scientifically derived concepts. Much of this nonscientific understanding is valid and useful, but much of it is not, as we show in our discussion in Chapter 7 of popular beliefs about education. It is useful in the sense that it gives the student some point of reference in studying a professional field, like education, but it is not useful and is even detrimental when it *prevents* learning—when, for example, it keeps the student from adjusting his preconceptions to fit new facts. The great deficiency of prescientific understanding

of educational processes, however, lies in its incompleteness, for it does not take into account the psychological factors and forces that play a highly significant role in stimulating, directing, and inhibiting learning processes. It is the student with a prescientific orientation to education who is unaware of these complexities and who hopefully looks for fail-proof methods of teaching and of classroom management.

It is the special contribution of educational psychology, then, to fill in the gaps in the student's understanding of educational processes and to correct his misconceptions. If the educational psychologist is successful in this undertaking, the student will be helped to see education and its processes in quite a different light, that is, he will see possibilities, relationships, and problems he never saw before. And, by reason of having acquired these new insights, he is likely to become a more effective teacher than he would be if he had not undertaken the study of educational psychology. For instance, the person who has a good psychological understanding of educational processes is not only able to identify more problems in a given classroom situation than can be seen by persons with only nonscientific understanding of education, but he is also in a position to find more solutions to these problems. The person who has a nonscientific and consequently incomplete understanding of educational processes is more likely to encounter difficulties because he is not aware of what are the really crucial and significant problems.

Psychology and the Professional Status of Teachers

We noted earlier that social benefits are associated with the attainment of higher levels of education. The virtual universality of this association has led almost all communities and nations in recent years to make enormous investments of time, money, and human energy in developing and expanding educational enterprises. The net result is that the teacher has become a much more important figure than he was in the days when education was considered to

(Ford Button, *Phi Delta Kappan*, October 1974).

"You'll find 'Teaching Methods That Never Fail' under fiction."

be less crucial. Teachers have found this new importance to be ego-building and pleasant, especially when it has brought improved economic status, but in other respects it has made them more vulnerable, for they are also expected to be more effective. We noted in the opening section of this chapter that the public is demanding *results* and is holding teachers accountable when the results are not forthcoming.

One of the results of this rising tide of expectations is that the teacher has been forced to become more expert, more professional. There are still some who believe that "anyone can teach," but teachers are having increasing success in demonstrating that persons employed as teachers should know something about teaching, as well as the subject matter that they are teaching. What teachers know about effective teaching is to a large extent psychological. Teaching and learning are, as we have said, psychological processes, and the teacher who understands them is in a better position to develop the kind of procedures and techniques that will lead to effective learning. With this kind of understanding, he can develop expertise

and competence in dealing with educational problems in a professional way.

Whatever respect teaching has as a profession today is to a large measure due to the contributions of educational psychology. The less professional and the more amateurish the teacher, the more likely he is to be ignorant of psychological principles; the more professional and competent the teacher, the more likely he is to have an expert understanding of these principles. Indeed, one can say that the effective teacher these days is one who is in some degree a part-time educational psychologist.

FOCAL AREAS OF EDUCATIONAL PSYCHOLOGY

There are three elements or focal areas in education that concern educational psychologists and teachers: the learner, the learning process, and the learning situation.

The Learner

We begin with the learner. He is the most important of the three elements, not only because people are more important than processes or situations, but primarily because without the learner, there is no learning. As John Dewey pointed out, unless someone is learning, there is no teaching, just as there is no selling without customers.

By the word "learner" we mean the pupils or students who individually and collectively comprise the classroom group—the persons on whose behalf the educational program exists and operates. A great deal of what happens in the classroom (or is expected to happen, but does not) can be explained in terms of the personalities, developmental stages, and psychosocial problems of students who comprise the class. Educational psychology can, for example, help a fifth-grade teacher become more effective by providing him with the basis for developing a better understanding of children in general, of children around the ages of eleven and twelve, and of the particular children in his class. Educational psychologists can also help this teacher by telling him something about the patterns of behavior that commonly occur whenever individuals interact with one another in a group setting.

The Learning Process

Next in order of importance is the learning process—the process by which people acquire changes in their behavior, improve performance, reorganize their thinking, or discover new ways of behaving and new concepts and information.

By the "learning process," we mean whatever people do when they learn. What they "do" includes behavior that is not directly observable, such as perceiving, thinking, remembering, and identifying, as well as behavior that can be directly observed, such as writing, computing, attending, and talking. Learning is always going on; it is a process that begins at birth (or, perhaps, even before) and continues in some form or other throughout our lives. Most of what we learn, even as children, is not acquired in the classroom. We learn to have attitudes and feelings toward ourselves and others; we learn to be the kinds of people we become. This means that children are learning, even when we think they are not learning. To be sure, they may not be learning the subject matter of the curriculum, but they are learning something. Sometimes they learn because of what their teachers do, and sometimes they learn in spite of them. Sometimes they learn things that are irrelevant or even undesirable. The educational psychologist is interested in what happens when an individual learns, why he learns what teachers want him to learn, and why he learns what teachers do not want him to learn. This preoccupation of the educational psychologist with learning is a healthy attitude for the teacher to develop because prescientific concepts of education are likely to be concerned with *teaching* rather than with learning. In other words, there is a common tendency for teachers to be concerned with the question: "What shall *I* do in order to *teach* this subject or skill?" and to overlook the equally important question: "What do *students* do who are trying to

learn this subject or skill?" To remind ourselves of the coequality of teaching and learning in this book we sometimes refer to the "teaching-learning process" and the "teaching-learning situation."

The Learning Situation

The learning situation refers to the environment in which the learner finds himself and in which the learning process takes place. Some aspects of the environment may be immediate, such as the classroom or library in which the student is applying himself to the tasks of learning. Other aspects of the learning situation may be remote, but still relevant, such as the relationship between the school board and the superintendent of schools.

The learning situation refers to *any* factor or condition that affects the learner or the learning process. The teacher is one element in the learning situation. So is the classroom setting: the effectiveness of the ventilation system, the afternoon light that shines in the eyes of the students and makes them sleepy, the noise of the school band practicing down the hall, the arrangement of seats, and so forth. But the most significant factors involve people: the attitudes and behavior of the teacher, the morale of the class, the emotional climate of the school, and so forth. Still other significant factors are more elusive. Indeed, we might be inclined to overlook them, if educational psychologists had not identified them as important. The general attitude of the community toward education is one of these elusive but significant factors. If education and schools do not rate very high on the community's scale of values, such an attitude may serve as a powerful deterrent to classroom learning; it may even be a more potent factor than the behavior of the teacher. Even though the attitude exists "outside" the classroom, it is part of the learning situation because of its effect on the learner and on the learning process in that school.

Teachers who are aware of the intimate relationship between the learning process and the learning situation are in a position to use this awareness to develop situations that promote involvement and exploration, whereas those who are preoccupied with subject matter content may inadvertently create situations that are inhibiting and discouraging.

Mrs. Harper's class was discussing the current fuel crisis. When Mrs. Harper asked, "What is coal used for?", a boy answered without putting up his hand: "They make oil out of it and puts it in a lamp. My Grandma say they have a coal-oil lamp all the time before they move to the city."

Mrs. Harper frowned and said, "Ronald, how many times must I tell you to put up your hand and be recognized before you are called upon. Besides your answer is all wrong." Ronald hung his head sheepishly, and the rest of the children laughed and hooted at his discomfiture.

Mrs. Becker's class was also discussing the fuel problem. When she asked, "Where does energy come from?", Jill said "From Mars." "Where did you get that idea," asked Mrs. Becker. "They said so on TV that Mars is a source of energy," the girl answered. The class started snickering, but Mrs. Becker continued. "What did they mean by that—anyone?" "Maybe they mean Mars candy," suggested Ricky. "And what does a candy bar have that makes it a source of energy?" Mrs. Becker persisted. There were some wild guesses until someone suggested "Sugar?" Mrs. Becker then reminded them that last week they had burned some sugar in an experiment, and what did it look like? Yes, *coal.*

Most people think of education principally in terms of the learning situation, particularly the part played by the teacher. The teacher is seen as one who produces learning by manipulating the learning situation—by making assignments, giving grades, explaining, testing, or whatever. Such behavior, however, is *instruction,* and may or may not result in learning. It is true that of the three aspects of education we have discussed, the learning situation is the aspect that can be most directly controlled by the teacher, although he does not have as much control as is popularly thought. Furthermore, to think of education only in terms of the teacher's attempts to control the learning situation is to overlook the great importance of the part played by the learner and the learning process. In addition, such a point of view makes education appear deceptively simple—more mechanical than it actually is. It ignores the essential dynamic and vital facts of edu-

cation, namely, that learning is an ongoing, continuing process, and the learner is a growing, changing organism.

WHAT "UNDERSTANDING" MEANS

In our discussion of what is meant by the terms "learner," "learning process," and "learning situation," we have indicated what it is that the teacher needs to understand in order to carry out his professional role. The term "understanding" itself also deserves some interpretation. Teachers who do not know children very well do not relate the restlessness of children to their having been kept indoors because of bad weather. Or, to use an example cited earlier, they do not see the relationship between learning difficulties in the classroom and the existence of widespread prejudice toward education on the part of the community. They do not see that if parents think education a waste of time, children will also tend to consider it a waste of time.

A Many-sided Approach

Understanding also means being able to explain, and explaining something means describing it from different aspects, levels, and points of view. The mechanic sees an automobile not only in terms of its function as a vehicle but also as an arrangement of moving parts, as a consumer of liquid fuel, and as a producer of electrical energy. He sees it as a sensitive mechanism whose component parts must be adjusted to proper balance and harmony if it is to operate properly. He also sees it as a mechanism that has strength and power. The perceptive teacher sees a certain child as having most of the characteristics of a typical ten-year-old girl. He sees her as the product of her social environment, conforming, more or less, to the patterns of behavior prescribed by those around her. He sees her as someone who has certain individual characteristics that distinguish her from other children of her age and sex. He sees her, too, as someone who approaches learning situations in arithmetic with confidence, but who needs encouragement and emo-

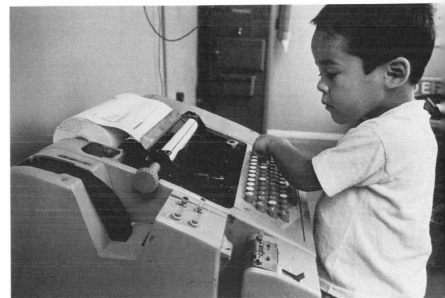

THE LEARNER, THE LEARNING PROCESS, AND THE LEARNING SITUATION

Learning is a process that has infinite variations. We can extend and deepen our understanding of the learning process and learners themselves by observing their behavior in various situations that stimulate learning.

tional support with her reading. He sees her as someone who stands a little apart from the other girls in her class, as a girl who would rather play with boys, if they would let her. He also sees her as someone who is slightly "above grade level" in math and science, and slightly "below her grade" in English and social studies. During the period this teacher has been working with this child, he has collected a great many facts and impressions about her. Some of these facts and impressions he finds helpful in explaining her behavior as a student and as a person. Because he is able to make these explanations to himself (or to others, if need be), he can understand her better.

An Awareness of Important Factors

Understanding, too, means developing an awareness of important factors. A good mechanic knows that the condition of the paint or the grill work on an automobile has nothing to do with its mechanical condition, although he has probably learned from experience that the person who does not take proper care of the exterior of his car is not likely to take proper care of its moving parts. Similarly, an experienced kindergarten teacher is not particularly disturbed if a five-year-old wets his pants the first day he comes to school. To be sure, she will take steps to prevent a recurrence, but she will recognize that the first day of school is a trying experience for five-year-olds, and that such incidents are part of the day's work for the teacher. On the other hand, she will be alert to pick up any really unusual behavior a child might display, particularly if it continues over a period of time. The behavior may not in itself be disturbing. For example, a child may simply be slow about reacting to directions or suggestions. From observing the child, the teacher may get a hunch that he is slow because he does not hear very well, and that he is watching other children for cues as to what he should do next.

Once we know what to look for, it is not too difficult to see relationships between different events in an ongoing social situation or to take notice of small but significant incidents. It is not easy, however, to be sensitively aware of important factors and simul-taneously involved in instructional duties. To do this, the teacher must first learn how to observe and then must somehow work the techniques of observing into his instructional role. This means that he must operate in a kind of bifocal way, shifting back and forth between the cognitive (thinking, intellectual) aspects of the classroom scene and its affective (emotional, feeling) aspects. The teacher thus becomes what is termed a *participant observer:* one who is an active participant but who also withdraws for brief intervals to determine what is going on with respect to his own behavior, as well as the behavior of others.

Probing Beneath the Surface of Behavior

Being able to identify the really important factors in a situation is an essential part of being a teacher, just as it is an essential part of good practice in any profession. This is a part of teaching that cannot be learned from a book, although "book learning" can often stimulate an alertness to the clues that *suggest* the presence of important factors. Furthermore, teachers who have already developed the knack of getting the "feel" of a classroom situation often find that their skill and sensitivity are broadened and deepened through reading appropriate books. Of course, there are teachers with many years of experience who have not yet developed this sensitivity to the crucial factors in a situation. These are the teachers who continue to make the same wrong moves, who seem to have a genius for developing resistance instead of cooperation among students.

Psychologists sometimes call the ability to get the "feel" of a situation "insight." Often teachers are hard put to account for hunches or feelings that later turn out to be quite accurate. Let us use the experience of the kindergarten teacher we just mentioned whose hunch that the slow-reacting child was hard of hearing turned out to be correct. We might ask her why she felt that the child was hard of hearing, instead of, say, mentally retarded. She might reply somewhat as follows: "Well, I suppose I could say that it was because he could build block trains and draw pictures which were a lot like those done by other children his age. But I think that the real reason was that he didn't *act* like a child who was really retarded or who had brain damage or anything like that. He just acted like other children I have known who had a hearing loss."

A teacher's ability to develop insight into significant factors in behavior is also dependent on his empathy—his sensitivity to and awareness of the attitudes and feelings of others. An empathic person is aware of "feeling-tone" when nothing is being said or in spite of what is being said. Like sensitivity to important factors and insight, empathy is a social skill that can be learned. A technique that has been developed in the last few years to help teachers and teacher trainees develop these skills is *microteaching*. A teacher or trainee is videotaped while he instructs four or five students for five or ten minutes. He immediately reviews the tape and gets comments from the students and a supervisor. He then replans and reteaches the same lesson to another group of students, again is videotaped, and again goes through the evaluation procedure. Although the method can be used to concentrate on aspects of instruction such as organization and clarity in the presentation of material, it can also be employed to teach skills such as "reinforcing student participation" and "probing for student understanding" (Bush, 1970). Elementary education students participated in an experiment in which they saw a thirty-minute videotape of themselves teaching the third grade. When their responses to an attitude questionnaire were compared with a group that had not had this experience, the experimental group showed a higher degree of self-acceptance, expressed more favorable attitudes toward teaching and toward children, and were more critical of conventional ideas about teaching. They also said that the experience helped allay many of the anxieties they had had about facing a class (Goldman, 1969).

Thinking Causally

Unless a teacher has a good understanding of the fundamentals of human behavior, he is likely to fall into the common trap of evaluating the behavior of children in terms of its effect on *him* rather than in terms of its probable causes. If so, his reaction may be one of annoyance and retaliation rather than that of understanding. In other words, he is likely to worsen a difficult situation, instead of improving it. Teachers who have become more sensitive to significant factors, and who have developed more insight and empathy, are also likely to think about behavior in a "causal" way. The teacher in the anecdote about the hard-of-hearing child was able to take the first step toward understanding his behavior because she was "thinking causally," that is, she reacted to his behavior with the question: "What causes him to behave that way?" The first step toward increased understanding often occurs when we ask ourselves the question: "What *causes* that?"

The fact that this teacher cannot readily put her feelings and reactions into words does not detract from their validity. Some of the most fundamental experiences of everyday life defy adequate translation into words. On the other hand, mere strength of conviction does not give validity to observations. In all likelihood, the beliefs of unsuccessful and inadequate teachers are as strong as those of successful ones. How, then, can we distinguish between valid and invalid hunches?

Making Valid Predictions

We come now to our last definition of understanding. Understanding a child means being able to make reasonably accurate predictions about his behavior. Thus the hunches of successful teachers are more likely to prove correct than the hunches of unsuccessful ones. We do not always have to base our predictions on hunches, however, and this is one of the reasons why courses such as educational psychology are a part of the professional curriculum for teachers. Psychologists and educators have been studying various aspects of education for many years in search of factors that are related to success and failure in learning. These factors include methods and techniques, personality, maturity, heredity, physical surroundings, motivation, and emotional climate, to name a few of the many dimensions that have been explored. Although there is much yet to be discovered about learning and the conditions under which it occurs, we have nevertheless been able to accumulate a respectable body of research data that is very helpful in clarifying much of what affects learning in the classroom as well as elsewhere. For example, we can predict that tenth-graders reading at the eighth-grade level are more likely to improve their reading ability if they get a chance to tutor fourth- and fifth-graders who are reading below grade level than they would if they did not have this experience and were given the usual remedial reading experience (Good and Brophy, 1973). This improvement will not come automatically, of course, for the experimental arrangement must be set up with tact and skill, but it is nevertheless an ingenious way of changing the negative and apathetic attitudes of a group of students who are usually regarded as potential school drop-outs.

Psychological tests can also predict which children will need more help with reading when they enter school, information that the first-grade teacher will find useful in organizing the class for various learning activities. At the high school and college level, furthermore, tests of a different nature can be used by counselors to help students predict their probable success in completing the training for different careers.

These are samples of the many kinds of predictions that educators and psychologists, working together, have been able to make with some degree of success. Because these predictions, as well as the data on which they are based, are available to the educational profession, we have a better understanding of the learner, the learning process, and the learning situation.

SOURCES OF UNDERSTANDING

Laymen's Concepts of Education

Education, unlike other professional specialities— medicine, law, and engineering, for examples—is more open and accessible to the general public. One of the advantages of this relationship is that educators are more responsive to community needs than are practitioners in other professions, but a disadvantage is that it has been more difficult for educators to develop a sense of expertise and professional consciousness. One survey, for example, showed that teachers are generally concerned with the recognition and appreciation they might receive from persons *outside* their profession, whereas people in other professions were more concerned with recognition by their colleagues and other members of their profession (Pasamanick and Rettig, 1959). The teacher who is continually looking to laymen for appreciation, who is overly anxious about the opinion that laymen have of him and his work, who seeks their praise and approval and is upset by their criticism, is the teacher who will be guided by lay concepts of teaching and learning. Because laymen's thinking about educational processes is almost entirely prescientific, teachers who are overresponsive to laymen's opinions are likewise going to adopt prescientific ways of thinking about their work.

What Psychologists Can Contribute

In defense of teachers, however, we should point out that it is only in the last fifty years or so that psychology (which is in itself a relatively new science) has had anything to say about educational processes. Furthermore, much of what psychologists have said in the last fifty years has had only incidental value for classroom instruction and has often been irrelevant. As E. Robert LaCrosse, Jr. (1970) has pointed out, the goals of psychologists and teachers are basically different: Psychologists are interested in developing a scientific understanding of human behavior, including learning, whereas teachers are interested in the techniques and outcomes of instruction. Psychologists also have been overready to analyze and to interpret teaching-learning behavior before they knew much about it; teachers, for their part, have tended to reject psychologists' theories and interpretations without examining them. Some teachers, according to LaCrosse, "view the psychologist-researcher as a member of an exotic foreign tribe with an unintelligible and sometimes threatening new language." It is regrettable, he notes, that the psychologist and the teacher do not collaborate more effectively, because at this point in the development of the two professions, each has much to learn from the other.

The picture is beginning to change, however. There are today a good many joint undertakings in process that involve psychologists and educators as coresearchers. Some of these projects got their start during the War on Poverty when Operation Head Start, Follow Through, and other experimental programs were initiated. The theoretical bases of these programs came from developmental, experimental, and social psychology, and measurement psychologists have also participated in their evaluation. The chief burden of the experimental ventures, however, was carried by educators—the teachers and administrators who participated in the planning stages and who provided the services that formed the heart of the programs.

Psychologists today are much more willing to leave the laboratory for the purpose of testing their theories in real-life situations and to participate in ongoing programs in the schools and elsewhere in the community. Clinical psychologists have taken a great deal of initiative in this move. They have, together with applied social psychologists, developed the field of community psychology, an area that is especially concerned with the needs of the urban poor and the problems of individuals who have more than the usual amount of difficulty in adjusting or adapting to the demands of an industrialized society.

This does not mean that the more theoretical areas of psychology are inactive, for it is from these specialities—developmental, personality, experimental, social, and measurement psychology—that educational psychologists, clinical psychologists, and other applied psychologists draw their theoretical concepts and techniques. The applied psychologist is a practitioner in the sense that he works with real-life problems, but he is primarily a scientist.

Teachers' Experiences

Probably the largest group of contributors to educational psychology as an applied science are the people who are also its most important "consumers"—the teachers themselves—for it is they who provide the impetus and stimulus that are the beginning of many a research project. Teachers question methodology, they improvise and innovate, they experiment with new methods and new curricular materials, they start chains of questioning that eventually come to the attention of the educational psychologist, and they make demands for certain kinds of surveys and studies. Not all their demands produce the results they want or expect. As a result of teacher requests, educational psychologists have done literally hundreds of studies with ability grouping or "tracking," only to find that it has no effect on achievement and produces negative attitudes on the part of students. Sometimes desired research results are favorable but slow in coming. For years, research studies failed to turn up any evidence favoring the use of smaller classes over larger ones. Only in recent years have investigators been able to confirm what teachers have always suspected, that is, that smaller groups are potentially better learning situations (for example, McDaniel and Feldhusen, 1970). The research on the effect of classroom group size turned out to be more complicated than anyone had anticipated because of problems in finding and applying the proper scientific controls, but other suggestions made by teachers for investigations have been researched with less difficulty. For example, a good many ideas for innovative instructional methods have been found, after investigation, to be psychologically sound.

Educational Psychology as Applied Science

Arthur Coladarci (1959), Dean of the Stanford School of Education, once said that educational psychology is the empirical foundation of education, that is, it represents those aspects of education that can be verified by experimentation, testing, and observation, what might be called the "*scientific* basis of education." In the final analysis, progress made in educational psychology is bound to affect the philosophical bases of education. If, for example, experimentation and observation show repeatedly that the ability of children to solve complex problems is not developed very readily in rigid, authoritarian settings, we are forced thereby to reexamine and eventually make changes in the psychological climate that prevails in classrooms. Such changes cannot occur unless they are accompanied or preceded by changes in educational philosophy.

Much of the potential effectiveness of educational psychology is lost if teachers do not, in effect, become "educational psychologists" in their own right. This means that teachers must learn to apply scientific methods to their own classroom practice and must become objective, scientific observers, as well as active participants, in the classroom setting. It also means, according to Coladarci, that they must come to think of teaching (selecting methods and techniques of presenting material, constructing curricula and courses of study, choosing textual materials, and so forth) as a process of "testing hypotheses about behavior." In other words, the teacher must adopt an "experimental attitude" toward his efforts. As he make decisions regarding classroom procedure, he should be saying, in effect: "I am betting that *this* way of organizing *this* class will help *these* pupils to achieve *these* educational objectives."

Coladarci's approach has the advantage of requiring the teacher both to seek continually for the best data on which to base his decisions and to test the adequacy of these decisions by frequent checking and rechecking. It can also provide the basis for genuine professional growth. Indeed, much of the progress made by education during the last generation or so has been due largely to the readiness of teachers to apply this extension of the scientific method of their own work. Coladarci points out that where teachers are unwilling or unable to use the methods and findings of educational psychology in their teaching, they have no choice but to teach by habit, dogma, rule of thumb, or sheer guesswork—

methods based on prescientific concepts of educational processes. As LaCrosse (1970) puts it, they can only fall back on their "articles of faith."

Throughout this book we have tried to approach the task of the teacher from two points of view, both of which are consistent with educational psychology as it is developing today: (1) that of the applied scientist who is able to select, plan, and evaluate his teaching strategies with a calm, objective eye, and (2) that of the skilled practitioner, artist, or clinician, who has a feeling for the basic elements of his work, who respects himself and respects his students, and who is dedicated and committed to making the teaching and learning in his classroom as effective as possible.

In presenting both the research and the practical-clinical side of educational psychology in this book, we will try to show how one supplements the other, how research findings of both the experimental and the social psychologist often suggest causes, relationships, and strategies that the practitioner might otherwise overlook, and how the hunches that emerge from classroom data provide hypotheses that can be checked by the more precise research methods of the experimental and the social psychologist.

Interpreting Educational Measurements

We have avoided detailed descriptions of experimental method or statistical findings in presenting this research. Instead, we have limited ourselves to a few simple statistical concepts—those of the mean or average, percentage, and correlation. Most students are already conversant with concepts of the mean or average and of percentage, but correlations may be a new idea, although the underlying principle is a simple one. A correlational coefficient is a single figure or number used to describe the *relationship* between two variables (anything that can be measured is a variable). The relationship between any two variables picked at random is likely to be zero. For example, we can expect that there will be no relationship at all (.00) between the average daily attendance (ADA) at Jedediah Smith Elementary School in San Francisco on Wednesdays and the corresponding ADA figures for the sessions of the United States Congress. These two variables have nothing in common, and there is no reason to expect that they would be anything other than zero. On the other hand, we do expect that there would be a positive relation (perhaps a correlation of +.70)[3] between the ADA at Jedediah Smith and at Bret Harte, a school in the same area, because what affects attendance at one of these schools (weather, flu epidemics, and so on) is likely to be much the same for both schools. Similarly, we expect that there will be a positive correlation (actually, about +.40) between the number of years of education completed by each of a couple of thousand adults selected at random and their annual income. The two measures, years of education and income, tend to vary in the same direction: the more education, the higher the income; the less education, the lower the income.

Correlations can be negative, as well as positive. The relationship between truancy and school performance is a good example. The correlation will vary in different schools and different communities, but we can count on there being a negative correlation, perhaps about −.50, between the number of days absent and scores pupils make on standardized tests of achievement in reading, mathematics, and other school subjects.

Some students have had unhappy experiences with math in elementary school and react to the introduction of figures into a discussion with some anxiety. In this textbook, however, we shall introduce figures only to emphasize points made in the discussion and not as concepts important in and of themselves. If we say that Method A produces better results than Method B, it helps to indicate how much better Method A is. In other words, the difference between the two methods becomes clearer if we can say that the time children spent using Method A in studying correlated +.60 with their success on a test of knowledge, in contrast with

only +.05 between time expended and success for Method B.

There are only a few graphs and tables in which we express a relationship between variables in terms of correlational coefficients. In each instance, the interpretation of the figures used will probably be obvious from the text and the description of the figure or table, but it may be well to keep this discussion in mind in case there happens to be problems of interpretation.

SUMMARY

Education has been under attack by critics of both radical and conservative persuasions, as well as by those who want evidence that taxpayers are getting their money's worth. Although there is hard evidence that schooling produces positive effects in the students it serves, and that individuals who have more education are usually better off in many ways than those who have less education, there is no doubt that education could be made more effective. Educational psychology is essentially a way of searching for answers to the question of how teaching and learning may be improved. The kinds of questions that laymen raise about the schools and that teachers ask about classroom teaching are to a significant degree psychological questions, psychological because they are concerned with human behavior.

Educational psychology, an applied branch of psychology, is concerned with helping teachers understand the problems of teaching and learning. Although most students of education have some understanding of educational processes before they begin their professional training, much of this understanding is "prescientific" in that it is composed largely of common sense, personal reactions, personal evaluations, popular beliefs about education, and even folklore. Some of this background is valid and useful, but much of it is neither valid nor useful and may actually interfere with the development of a more scientific understanding of the teaching-learning process. The teacher's social and professional status has increased in recent years partly because of the greater social value placed on his services and partly because he has become more of an educational psychologist.

---

[3] It should be noted that +.70 is not a percentage. If we wanted the proportion of communality of the two schools' ADA, we must square the coefficient of correlation: .70 squared is .49, or 49 percent.

Educational psychology is concerned with the development of an understanding of three focal areas: the learner, the learning process, and the learning situation. These three areas overlap and are interrelated. There is a tendency for teachers to be overly concerned with the learning situation and to ignore the learner and the learning process. By "understanding" we mean seeing relationships in human behavior that are not apparent at first glance, being able to explain behavior from various aspects and points of view, developing an awareness of important factors in behavior, identifying the causes of behavior, and making accurate predictions about behavior. Without understanding, a teacher is likely to fall into the trap of reacting to students' behavior in terms of its effect on *him,* instead of its background or other significant aspects.

Many ideas that teachers have about teaching and learning are picked up from laymen, whose opinions tend to rate higher with teachers than they do with most other professions. As teachers gain better understanding of their professional tasks, they are likely to discard some of their prescientific notions. Psychologists can aid in this process. Although there was a communication gap between psychologists and educators in the early years of educational psychology, today there is much more close collaboration. Psychologists and educators have worked together on innovative programs such as Operation Head Start, and many of the problems that educational psychologists work on have emanated from the classroom. For their part, teachers find that they can become more competent if they become "educational psychologists" in their own right by employing scientific methods in observing what goes on in their classrooms and by experimenting with and studying methods of teaching and learning.

Suggested Problems

1. Put yourself in the place of a child just completing the first grade. What are some of the concepts he would very likely have developed regarding the learning process and the learning situation?

2. Where does subject matter (what is to be learned) fit into the triad of the learner, the learning process, and the learning situation?

3. It has been stated that the behavioral sciences (including educational psychology) are at about the same relative point in their development at which the biological and physical sciences were a hundred years ago. What would be the basis for such a statement? What does this imply with respect to the future development of educational psychology? Why have biological and physical scientists been able to advance more rapidly than behavioral scientists?

4. What kinds of factors or problems might make it difficult for a teacher to play the role of a behavioral scientist (and "educational psychologist" in his own right) in his classroom?

5. Look over the writings of some of the critics of education—Holt, Illich, Kozol, Bestor, and Mortimer Smith, for example—and note what kind of data they supply for their criticisms. Evaluate their supportive data in terms of the extent to which it satisfies or convinces you.

Suggested Readings

Andreas, B. G. *Psychological science and the educational enterprise.* New York: Wiley, 1968.

Lindgren, H. C., and Lindgren, F. (eds.). *Current readings in educational psychology,* 2nd ed. New York: Wiley, 1972. Section 1 contains a brief history of educational psychology and a review of elementary statistics.

Tanner, L. N., and Lindgren, H. C. *Classroom teaching and learning: A mental health approach.* New York: Holt, Rinehart, and Winston, 1971.

Selections by some of the critics mentioned early in this chapter may be found in books of readings. Two of the more recent ones are:

Davis, G. A., and Warren, T. F. (eds.). *Psychology of education: New looks.* Lexington, Mass.: Heath, 1974.

Gall, M. D., and Ward B. A. (eds.). *Critical issues in educational psychology.* Boston: Little, Brown, 1974.

There are many professional journals that contain

articles exploring the various issues that we touched on briefly in this chapter and will be discussing at greater length in this book. The National Education Association's *Today's Schools* is especially good, as is the *Phi Delta Kappan*. Other useful journals are: *School and Society, Harvard Educational Review, Teachers College Record*, and *Educational Leadership*.

Learners and
Their Motives

IN THIS CHAPTER WE SHALL COVER

■ **The factors that cause learners to behave as they do**

■ **The competence drive**

■ **Basic human needs**

■ **Anxiety and its effects**

■ **The human organism as an energy system**

■ **Inherited characteristics**

■ **Self-concept and the locus of control**

■ **Motives that function beyond awareness**

As teachers carry out the various tasks of their professional role, their chief concern is that of promoting, stimulating, and guiding learning. The fact that teachers are preoccupied with learning does not necessarily mean that learning ought to be or even can be understood as a process apart from the learner, even though we may for various reasons study or analyze one or more aspects of learning, purposely ignoring, for the moment, other aspects of the learner and his behavior. At various points further along in this book, we shall in fact focus our attention on the learning process, but in this chapter, as well as the five that follow, we shall be considering the "background" of learning: those characteristics of the learner and his environment which affect the amount and kind of learning that will take place and that determine indeed whether students will learn at all. In this chapter we are especially concerned with various aspects of the moti-

vational forces that help explain why people behave as they do. A teacher's effectiveness is, generally speaking, proportionate to his understanding of the motivation of the learners he supervises. It is this motivation that provides force and direction to the behavior they display, whether this behavior be the kind of learning the teacher is trying to foster or something less desirable.

THE INSIDE (AND OUTSIDE) STORY OF MOTIVATION

Why Do Learners Behave as They Do?

Psychologists use two basic approaches in answering questions such as this: organismic and environmental. In this chapter we shall focus on the forces that operate for the most part "inside" the human organism, the forces that are often discussed by psychologists under the heading of *motivation,* in contrast to forces that are largely *environmental.* Sometimes an individual is figuratively or even literally pushed or manipulated by external forces or factors into performing a given act; sometimes there is a feeling within him that appears to be the prime source of the act; but most likely whatever he does is the result of the reciprocal interaction and interplay of many forces, both external and internal. The motivational or "inside" forces include needs, wants, drives, feelings and emotions, interests and attitudes, guilt and anxiety, and so forth. The environmental or "outside" forces and factors include not only the attractive, disturbing, or reassuring aspects of the situation in which the individual finds himself but also the attitudes and expectations of others, rewards, dangers, threats, and so on. It is ordinarily very difficult to determine where an internal pressure leaves off and an external one begins, and the differences between internal and external forces may not be very sharp or precise. For instance, Miss Everett may tell Dora Smiley to pay attention, that first-graders do not whisper when the teacher is talking. Dora stops whispering and listens, paying close attention to what Miss Everett is saying. Dora does this partly in response to external forces: the request of the teacher, the teacher's expectation that her command will be obeyed, the fact that other children are looking at her, the psychological atmosphere of the classroom, and so on. But this bit of behavior also results from forces within Dora: her respect for authority, her desire to please Miss Everett, her ambition to be a well-behaved first-grader, and her unwillingness to suffer embarrassment. To some extent these internal forces are the mirror images of external ones. Miss Everett's desire to be obeyed is mirrored in Dora's desire to obey her. The idea that teachers are entitled to respectful attention is both an internal and an external force. It is a concept or generalized feeling that is a part of the school situation, and Dora is incorporating it into her own set of values.

Although trying to distinguish between internal and external forces introduces what may seem like a note of artificiality into our attempts to understand the learner's behavior, it very often is helpful to make such distinctions in the interest of better un-

derstanding. Although any behavioral act has a completeness all its own, we can often get a better understanding of it if we split it up into sections or layers, so to speak, just as engineering students can gain a better understanding of the operation of an automobile engine by studying cross-sectional drawings. In this chapter and the one that follows we examine those forces and conditions that are largely internal in character, in Chapters 4 and 5 we consider forces and conditions that are largely external, and in Chapter 6 we take up a number of the ways in which we respond to internal tensions and external demands.

The Need to Become Competent and Effective

There are many approaches to analyzing and classifying the internal forces that result in the individual displaying the phenomenon we term "behavior." Laboratory or experimental psychologists tend to prefer systems that explain behavior in terms of what are termed "drives"—motives that are largely biological, such as hunger, thirst, and sex. In recent years, however, many psychologists have become increasingly dissatisfied with this approach to motivation, useful as it may be in the laboratory. Although a great deal of animal behavior and some aspects of human behavior can be understood in terms of primary drives, other aspects are not explained so simply. For example, the eagerness of animals to engage in activity apparently for its own sake, irrespective of any readily identifiable physical needs, raises a question as to the usefulness of primary drives as the sole basis for explaining behavior. In view of the fact that humans, unlike other animals, have an almost infinite capacity to acquire new modes of behavior, attempts made to explain on a purely physiological basis the wide range of socialized or symbolic behavior that individuals display have but limited value for the teacher or for any other professional person who is primarily concerned with working with people.

What teachers need, then, are ways of looking at human behavior that go beyond the merely biological or physical and that provide bases for a more effective understanding of behavior—more effective, that is, than the understanding that most of us have developed merely as a result of everyday observations of ourselves and others.

One of the more perceptive ways of explaining human motivation is the one devised by Robert W. White (1959) of Harvard University some years ago. After examining and analyzing a great deal of research data, White concluded that, apart from satisfying the most elementary, biological needs, most human behavior is concerned with attempts to gain some measure of *competence.* This seems to be particularly true of such behavior as exploring, investigating, communicating, thinking, attending and perceiving, and manipulating the environment. These strivings toward competence he termed *effectance,* an activity that results in a feeling of efficacy or effectiveness. According to White, the need for competence or effectiveness operates relatively independently of the physical drives and enables us to discover and invent ways of adapting ourselves to our immensely complex and continually changing environment. It is this need for effectiveness that results in most of the learning we accomplish, inside or outside of the classroom.

Conclusions similar to those of White were also reached by Carl Rogers (1951) and Arthur W. Combs and Donald Snygg (1959) as a result of their research in psychotherapy and human learning. These psychologists maintained that the basic human motive is a "need for adequacy," which they described as a "great driving, striving force in each of us by which we are continually seeking to make ourselves ever more adequate to cope with life" (Snygg and Combs, 1949). The need for adequacy has two aspects: maintenance and enhancement. From birth to death, the individual's need to maintain himself is the most important task of existence. But maintenance involves more than mere survival; it is more than merely satisfying primary drives on a here-and-now basis. The human being is a continually changing organism living in a continually changing world, and if he is to maintain any kind of continuity and psychological integrity, he cannot resign himself to an existence as a passive participant in the changes that are a part of everyday life. A human being, more than any other animal, is able to anticipate future events, and this anticipation leads him to make changes in himself and his environ-

ment in order not only to maintain himself in his present situation but also to *enhance* himself and his possibilities in such a way that he will be able to maintain himself in the future and, thus, will feel some degree of security in being able to do so. For instance, when Rick Conley came into the fifth grade in the first week of March, he asked the other boys who the captains of the softball teams were and then approached one of them to ask what positions were open. Rick was interested not only in developing his competence in the sport but also in establishing positive relationships with his classmates in order to enhance his acceptance by his peer group.

"Need" Defined

Before we continue with our discussion of the forces that produce behavior, it may be well to explain that the term "need," as used in this book, refers to a condition experienced by the individual and not to a condition attributed to the individual by others, however well-intentioned they may be. Needs experienced by an individual are "psychological needs," whereas needs attributed to him by others are "normative needs." It is important to make the distinction between psychological and normative needs because teachers are inclined to confuse the two with one another. To say, for example, that a child needs "rewarding social contacts" is to recognize a universal psychological need to obtain satisfactions from relationships with others. But to say that a child needs "an understanding of the elements of algebra" is to refer to the expectations, standards or norms (hence, the term "normative needs") that adults have developed on his behalf. A child has no choice but to respond in some way to his psychological needs; they are a dimension or aspect of the psychological factors that motivate his behavior. On the other hand, he may or may not respond to the normative needs that adults have prescribed for him.

Basic Needs

During infancy and the early years of childhood, behavior is dominated by an active concern or even a

BASIC PSYCHOLOGICAL NEEDS
Needs develop in sequential form, beginning with needs for maintenance and security and for love and attention, which appear very early in life. Social needs, especially the need to belong, appear next, and finally emerges the need for self-actualization, self-expression, and creativity.

preoccupation with physiological processes—with what might be called "maintenance needs." The newborn infant is upset when his primary drives for food, sleep, agreeable skin temperature, and the like encounter interference. Conversely, he is relaxed and happy when they are met. Within a year or two, however, he has developed needs concerned with enhancement. He doesn't want the plain red ball that he has; he wants the fancier ball that the other baby has. He flies into a rage when his mother takes one of his brothers on her lap to comfort him. He may have been happily playing with his toy automobile, but the sight of Brother on Mother's lap causes him to throw a tantrum. That lap belongs to *him;* he has first call on his mother's attention! His status has been debased, and he wants it reenhanced immediately.

The need to which this baby is reacting has nothing to do with physical maintenance. According to everyday common sense, he should be happy and contented. He has been fed; his clothing is dry; he is not tired; he has every reason to be physically comfortable; he even has a toy to play with. Yet anyone seeing his face contorted with rage and hearing his earsplitting squeals would have to admit that something is obviously lacking in his life. That something is *attention,* or, to use a word commonly applied to this need: *love.*

There is a considerable body of research to show that the need for attention or love is essential in normal human development. Some psychological workers, such as René Spitz (1945, 1946), have claimed that the need for love is so vital that, if it is not met, children will not develop normally and may even lose the will to live. Although Spitz's research was challenged on methical grounds by Samuel Pinneau (1955), the main thrust of the evidence that has accumulated over the years suggests that the normal development of children depends on their receiving some degree of attention. In one study, a group of severely mentally retarded children were transferred from a large institution to a smaller residential unit that was run on family-group lines, in which staff members made special efforts to maintain warm, personal relationships with each child. Over a period of eighteen months, these children showed twice as much gain, measured in terms of mental age, than did children in a matched group that had remained within the institutional setting (Tizard, 1964). We shall report more research dealing with the need for love and attention in the next chapter.

The need for attention or love appears at times as a need for maintenance and at other times as a need for enhancement. A child who turns to his mother for reassurance and emotional support is looking for some form of attention that will restore his self-confidence—a maintenance need. But if he satisfies this need, he also enhances his ability to cope with the pressures of his social and physical environment.

There are other needs that have dimensions of both maintenance and enhancement. As children enter the middle years of childhood, they start the long process of growing away from the home and becoming a part of the larger community. They begin to seek the company of children their own age and to discover the joys and sorrows of life in the "peer group." The "need to belong" begins to have particular significance. They learn to think of themselves as members of a family, a classroom group, a gang, a Scout troop, a church, and a community. Membership in such groups enhances the self: An individual is more competent and effective if he feels he "really belongs" and if he is able to function as a group member. This newly acquired concept of himself as a social adequate person is maintained by experiences that demonstrate his degree of acceptance by the group. Perhaps the act of becoming a functioning member of one or more groups outside the home is, initially at least, more of an enhancement need than a maintenance one, but once established, it becomes a need that requires frequent and recurring satisfaction: a maintenance need.

The needs we have described thus far are sometimes called "deficiency needs" because they are necessary for human survival. They are also basic to a need that is more obviously related to enhancement, what Carl Rogers (1951) and Abraham H. Maslow (1954) termed the need for "self-actualization": the drive to find ever-more-adequate means for self-expression, to realize one's potentialities, to develop greater degrees of effectiveness and competence, to be creative, to develop roles in life that are satisfying and worthwhile. It is here that the "growing edge" of the individual personality is invested. If this need is alternately stimulated and satisfied, continual learning and growth take place. If it is never aroused or never satisfied, the individual's psychological development tends to remain static.

The need to belong is to some degree similar to what Henry A. Murray (1938) termed the "need for affiliation," commonly designated as "n Aff," whereas self-actualization needs include what Murray called the "need for achievement," or "n Ach." Socializing, cooperation, and the seeking of friendships are motivated by n Aff, whereas n Ach is associated with persistence, striving to excel, decision making, and self-improvement (Stacey, 1969). Children rating high on n Ach also are stimulated by competitive situations and activities in which they can receive some kind of "feedback" in the form of progress reports, for instance, grades, test scores, or praise and criticism from others. Although n Aff and n Ach are both important in the normal development of both children and adults, attempts to satisfy both simultaneously are likely to produce psychological conflict. (See cartoon.) Needs for affiliation are other-centered, whereas needs for achievement are self-oriented, hence the problem.

Both n Aff and n Ach have been the subject of a great deal of research in recent years, and we shall be referring to them again at various points in this book. The two needs are of vital concern to educators, partly because they become prominent during the school years and partly because they trigger drives that may lead to cooperation, school achievement, and other forms of teacher-approved behavior but which may also lead to behavior that works at cross-purposes with teachers' objectives and values.

The behavior that is characteristic of each of the various subvarieties of the needs we have described grows increasingly complex as we follow their development from the first to the fourth level, using the scheme presented in Figure 2-1. Behavior

(Wall Street Journal)

"But why should I apply myself more? I'm very popular with the other kids just the way I am."

Needs for achievement (n Ach) and needs for affiliation (n Aff) are often in conflict.

that is related to needs at the lower, more physiological level tends to be simple and oriented to single, well-defined goals; behavior that satisfies needs at the upper, more socialized level tends to be symbolic or abstract, and oriented to complex goals. The need for oxygen can be satisfied only by breathing air containing oxygen, but the need for creativity may be satisfied by helping another person solve a difficult problem, by learning a new skill, or by repairing a leaky faucet.

Needs at the upper, more socialized end of the scale make greater demands on the maturity and intelligence of individuals. Getting and keeping a job is a far more complex form of behavior than comforting an unhappy child or falling asleep, although in our fast-moving culture it sometimes happens that we are able to learn the more complex

Basic (or normal) needs	Characteristics	Results of frustration (or anticipated frustration) of basic needs
4. Needs for self-actualization, self-expression, creativity, and feelings of general adequacy and competence (including the need for achievement, or n Ach).	Primarily concerned with enhancement, relatively complex, abstract, and other-centered.	Anxiety
3. Needs to belong (including the need for affiliation, or n Aff).		
2. Needs for attention and love.		
1. Needs concerned with bodily processes and the security or defense of the human organism.	Primarily concerned with maintenance or defense, relatively simple, and individual-centered.	Fear or anger.

FIG. 2-1. A developmental system of behavior.

skills that are necessary for job-getting and job-holding but "forget" some of the simpler ones—how to give and receive love, or even how to fall asleep at night. Sometimes frustrations at the more abstract, socialized levels interfere with our ability to meet needs at the more rudimentary levels. For example, it is not unusual for people who are having difficulty in maintaining satisfactory relations with others to encounter difficulty with processes of digestion or elimination. The reverse can also occur. Students who are preoccupied with problems of making and keeping friends and becoming accepted as members of a group (n Aff) may have difficulty in becoming involved in the kind of intellectual activity that would improve their academic status (n Ach). Such problems and dilemmas show how our inability to meet needs at one level limits our ability to meet needs at other levels, and how the various levels of needs we have described are actually different aspects of the overriding basic human need to become adequate and competent.

Anxiety, Tension, and Apprehensiveness

The psychological needs that we have been describing may serve as the basis for understanding a great deal of human behavior, particularly those kinds of behavior that are in our own best interests. But much behavior that we observe in others (as well as in ourselves, to be honest) is obviously not in our best interests and cannot easily be accounted for by needs to become competent or adequate. Here are two examples:

Howard teases George whenever they are together. George is bigger than Howard and he does not tolerate being teased. Every time Howard teases him, George pummels him unmercifully until someone separates them. This goes on day after day. It is plainly not in Howard's best interests to tease George and be beaten by him. Why, then, does he do it?

Lucy has the intelligence to get good marks—an IQ of 130—but her grades are below average. She is what educational psychologists call "an underachiever." Her parents and teacher are concerned about her inability to get grades consistent with their expectations for her, and Lucy herself is quite worried. Although she tries to do better, she always manages to sabotage her own efforts. It is against Lucy's best interests to get poor grades, just as it is against Howard's interests to pick a fight with a bigger boy. Why don't Howard and Lucy act sensibly? And why don't they respond to psychological needs for competence and adequacy?

Explaining the behavior of two individuals like Howard and Lucy would take a great deal of time and effort on the part of a person with special psychological training, but we can nevertheless come to a general conclusion about most forms of behavior that are obviously not in the best interests of the individuals concerned, that is, such behavior is motivated by, or is an attempt to cope with, a considerable degree of anxiety.

Although the term "anxiety" takes on different shades of meaning as it appears in the writing and research of psychologists in various fields of specialization, there is general agreement that it refers to a complex and sometimes chronic emotional state generally characterized by fear, apprehension, or tension. As such, it is associated with failure to meet our needs, anticipation of such failure, or even merely an awareness of the possibility of failure. We have therefore included it in Figure 2-1 on the "frustration" side of the diagram. As Figure 2-1 shows, the frustration or anticipated frustration of basic, normal needs results in emotional disturbances that take the form of fear, anger, or anxiety. The more we are concerned with our vital or biological needs, the more likely we are to experience and display fear or anger, whereas the more we are concerned with our ability to function on a socialized or intellectualized level, the more likely we are to experience some form of anxiety or tension. Fear and anger are "primitive" emotions; they are the spontaneous and sometimes dramatic accompaniment to situations involving (1) immediate or present danger to ourselves or (2) some direct and drastic interference with ongoing behavior. But frustrations that threaten needs at more abstract and socialized levels are likely to be of a more sub-

tle, indirect nature. Not only are they harder to identify, but they also involve behavior that is highly complex, behavior that is a part of the intricate web of our relations with others. Perhaps we feel irritated when someone in authority accuses us of carelessness, but our anxiety about our status leads us to swallow our anger. Or perhaps we feel that we are being left out of plans being made by our group but are really not sure and would feel silly bringing it up. Hence we feel awkward and insecure in our relations with the group; we have a feeling of emptiness whenever we think about the problem. It is a bothersome, elusive feeling, and it will not go away.

That is the quality of anxiety. It is elusive, bothersome, and hard to identify. It commonly develops within the context of face-to-face relations with others—what psychologists call "interpersonal relations." In its most intense form it can be quite painful, so painful that we are usually willing to go to great lengths to avoid it. Because anxiety is so painful, we sometimes do things that are not in our best interest in order to avoid or reduce anxiety. We do not know what the source of Howard's anxiety is, but it appears to be so strong that he is willing to suffer physical pain in preference to the pain of anxiety. For her part, Lucy is willing to suffer the disgrace of poor marks rather than face and deal directly with her anxieties.

How We Learn to Be Anxious

The observations of Harry Stack Sullivan (1947), the great psychiatrist and teacher, led him to the conviction that the initial experiences with anxiety occur in infancy, when infants sense displeasure or emotional upset in their parents, particularly their mothers. Sullivan noted that infants displayed such symptoms as restlessness, irritability, and feeding problems when their mothers were displeased or disappointed, or even when their mothers were troubled by events that had nothing to do with the child. So close is the emotional linkage between mother and infant, according to Sullivan, that negative feelings on the part of the mother are likely to disturb the infant's sense of security, that is, his need to be loved and to feel secure in his mother's love. This feeling of insecurity and psychological isolation from the mother is what Sullivan terms "anxiety." (It is understood, of course, that negative feelings and anxiety occur in the best-ordered households and are part of the normal process of human interaction. It would be as undesirable to shelter a child from all negative feelings as it would be to overexpose him to such feelings.)

The anxiety we first experience as infants continues to have an effect on our behavior throughout life. It appears whenever others criticize, snub, or disapprove of us—whenever we are "rejected." The more important the rejecting individual is to us, and the more power he has, the greater our anxiety. Our own behavior can arouse anxiety as well, whenever we find ourselves behaving in ways that are inconsistent with the concept we have of ourselves. Situations that are ambiguous or confusing may also arouse anxiety. The future is a major source of anxiety because of its uncertainty. Hence we lay plans and take precautions to make the future somewhat more predictable and thus allay our anxieties to some degree.

According to Camilla M. Anderson (1950), a psychiatrist who has developed a theory of human behavior similar to Sullivan's, *all* human behavior is based on the avoidance of anxiety: "Everything one does, every choice one makes, every reaction one gives, every item and detail of one's behavior is calculated to forestall anxiety or to deal with it if it arises." Although some psychologists would find Anderson's statement too sweeping and all encompassing, it is nevertheless likely that anxiety is directly or indirectly involved in much everyday behavior, particularly the behavior that involves our relations with others.

Although we have stressed the unpleasant features of anxiety, there is no question that it has positive values. Our wish to avoid anxiety is a major factor in our learning to be careful and considerate in our relations with others, to conform to the laws and customs of society, and to provide for the future. Anxiety that enables us to behave like civilized individuals in a civilized society is what we shall call "normal anxiety." A certain degree of normal anxiety is therefore necessary as a kind of goad or stimulus to keep us at the task of becoming more adequate. But an overabundance of anxiety distracts us from the positive direction of development and leads us to develop forms of behavior concerned solely with the avoidance or reduction of anxiety. Hence the appearance of behavior that is not in our basic interests. It should be clear, then, that our basic need to become competent and adequate and our tendencies to develop varying degrees of anxiety are both likely to have a significant effect on learning. We shall have more to say about their effects in Chapter 9.

The Human Organism as an Energy System

Psychologists have made considerable use of a theoretical model taken over from the physical sciences, a model that envisions any organism as a *system* that is acted upon by forces in the environment and, in turn, acts upon the environment. The result of this is a continuous process of interaction that continues as long as the organism survives. The environment of any of us may be considered as presenting an almost infinite array of stimuli to which we, in turn, are able to react with an infinite array of responses. The environmental features to which we attend or to which we are in some way responsive are the stimuli that become what is termed *input,* as far as the organism's energy system is concerned. In Figure 2-2 input may be ob-

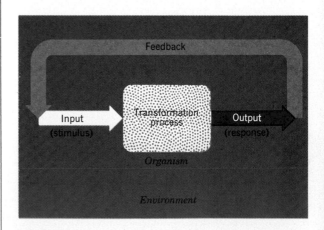

FIG. 2-2. The human organism as an energy system.

served as approaching the box designated *orga-nism* from the left side. This input is "converted" by what are called *transformation processes,* in that its reception initiates certain internal events that lead the organism to react in some way or other. This reaction becomes *output*—the *response* or behavior that occurs as a result of the transformation of the input of stimuli. The response, in turn, produces changes in the environment because its appearance introduces a new element, which becomes one of the stimuli to which the organism responds. As a result, the response or output is *fed back* into the organism, which may then react to its own response by emitting a new response that may be the same as the previous response or that may intensify it or modify it in some other way. We shall refer from time to time to this theoretical model because it has some value in describing certain aspects of teaching-learning processes.

Rewards, Reinforcements, and Benefits

Each of us is organized in such a way that we are likely to respond positively to any stimuli that may enable us to maintain and enhance ourselves—unless, of course, we happen to be preoccupied in dealing with the frustration or threatened frustration of some need. This means that under ordinary, nondisturbing conditions we are likely to react to our environment by emitting the kind of responses that enable us to gain satisfaction and to avoid disturbing, frustrating experiences. Inasmuch as satisfaction can result only from interacting with the physical and/or social environment in some way or other, it follows that our environment has the power to affect our behavior to a marked degree. Certain stimuli in the environment are naturally going to be more significant than others because they are beneficial, that is, they are more obviously related to the satisfaction or to the frustration of our needs. As we respond to these stimuli, we are more likely to emit certain responses because they, rather than others, are more appropriate to the stimuli that satisfy our needs. These more appropriate responses are said to have been *rewarded.* Because they come to dominate our general pattern of behavior

and thus crowd out unrewarded responses, we can also say that they have been *reinforced,* to use the appropriate psychological term.

Let us take as an example the experience of a first-grader learning the sequence of numbers. The teacher asks him to count from one to ten. He complies readily, having learned to count before he entered school. But when the teacher asks him what number comes immediately after seven, he hesitates and asks, "Nine?" The teacher says, "No, count from one to seven and then tell me what comes next." This time he gets the answer and is reinforced by his pleasure in being right, as well as by the teacher's approval. As the lesson continues, some of his responses are right, and some are wrong. But only the correct responses are reinforced by the teacher's saying, "That's right." Gradually, he learns to avoid the incorrect responses and to think through the sequence of numbers before giving his answer.

Learning consists of the changes in behavior that result from interaction with the environment, and reinforcement is the basic event that makes learning possible. Inasmuch as the more active part of our environment consists of other people, it is clear that a great deal of our learning results from the extent to which others reinforce our responses. We can, of course, become our own reinforcers, and this is what often happens when we work on a task purely for the pleasure we get out of doing it. This latter kind of learning figures largely in satisfying needs for self-actualization and achievement.

Stimulation, Arousal, and Excitement

If our ability to obtain satisfaction depends on the presence of the proper stimuli, it follows that we are apt to prefer the kinds of settings that are more likely to provide those stimuli. Therefore, in a very general way, environments that are rich in stimuli—that are stimulating—are more attractive than those that are poor in stimuli. We might rephrase this to say that interesting or exciting environments become preferred over those that are monotonous and dull. As Constantinos A. Doxiadis (1970), the world-renowned city planner, has observed, ". . . we do not know of any species of animals that try to increase their potential contacts with the environment once they have reached the optimum number of contacts. Man alone always seeks to increase his contacts.''

During the last two decades or so, evidence has been accumulating which suggests that there may be a basic need for stimulation, a need that is involved with the maintenance of biological processes and is thus essential for normal development. The importance of stimulation is shown by the fact that when it drops below a certain level, the human organism is likely to be disturbed. For example, volunteers who were blindfolded and placed in soundproofed rooms for extended periods experienced hallucinations and suffered impairment in problem solving (Hebb, 1955).

Research shows that stimulation also makes an important contribution to the development of animals. Young animals that are handled or otherwise stimulated by experimenters at frequent intervals during the weeks after birth develop more rapidly, are more curious, and are better at solving problems than are "control" animals, that is, their litter mates that did not receive the special treatment (Meier, 1961; Spence and Maher, 1962; Wilson, Warren, and Abbott, 1966). Furthermore, rats and mice that spend weeks prior to maturity in an environment that has a variety of stimulating objects and events—is *stimulus-enriched*—are not only superior in solving maze problems but actually develop a thicker cerebral cortex (the "thinking" part of the brain), in contrast to control animals raised either under normal laboratory conditions or under *stimulus-deprived* conditions (Bennett et al., 1964; Wallace, 1974).

We cannot, of course, do the same kind of studies with children, but experiments in which infants have been given a great deal of extra stimulation rather consistently show that the treatment has been beneficial. In one hospital study, premature infants in an experimental group were given special attention, whereas those in a control group received whatever treatment the hospital staff normally gave such infants. Staff members caring for the experimental group were told to pick them up frequently,

rock them while feeding them, and suspend colored mobiles over their cribs. At the end of four weeks the experimental group of infants had gained more weight and were in better physical and neurological condition than were the control infants. When the mother of an infant in the experimental group came to take her child home, she was instructed in ways of continuing the extra stimulation begun in the hospital. At the end of a year's period, the infants in the experimental group tested close to normal on intelligence and developmental scales, whereas the control group were found to be significantly retarded, on the average (Scarr-Salapatek and Williams, 1973).

What is good for premature infants appears to be good for normal infants as well. Yvonne Brackbill (1970, 1973) monitored the effects of extra stimulation on normal month-old infants by subjecting them to normal and increased amounts of sound, light, air temperature, and clothing. As the results reported in Figure 2-3 indicate, the more the stimulation, the more the infants relaxed and slept, and the less they cried.

Research of this type has important implications for people who work with children because it shows the significance of the degree of stimulation experienced during the early years. Much of the work that has been done recently to help children raised in environments that are variously described as "economically depressed," "culturally deprived," or "socially disadvantaged" has drawn heavily on the results of these studies. We shall have more to say on this topic in later chapters.

Genetic Aspects of Behavior and Motivation

Those aspects of behavior that are determined by biological inheritance are termed *genetic,* in contradistinction to those that are acquired through learning. Traits that are acquired genetically are most likely to be observed in an individual's appearance—his height, the color of his eyes and hair, the shape of his feet and hands, and the like. Some characteristics we inherit are universal in the human race, such as the structure and functioning of the digestive tract, the knee-jerk reflex, and the ap-

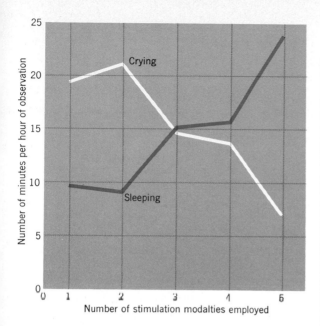

FIG. 2-3. Average number of minutes per hour of observation[1] spent by twenty-four infants in crying or sleeping under differing amounts of stimulation[2] (after Brackbill, 1970).

pearance of fear or anger in severe stress situations.

Some behavior associated with sex differences also may be genetically determined. The fact that among monkeys the males are more aggressive and the females engage in more fondling and stroking behavior suggests that tendencies among humans for males to be more adventurous and females to be more loving, supportive, and accepting are genetically determined (Harlow, 1962). Human males from childhood onward in all societies are more likely to form and remain within the context of groups than females are. Male group life also is likely to be more intense and physically active (Tiger, 1969).

The fact that certain patterns of behavior are inherited does not imply, however, that they cannot

[1] Each infant was observed for twenty minutes immediately after it had been fed.

[2] Stimulation modalities consisted of increases in sound (85 versus 62 decibels), light (400 versus 50 watts), restraint (swaddling versus nonrestrictive clothing), and room temperature (88 versus 78 degrees Fahrenheit).

be modified. One advantage that a human being has over the lower animals is his capacity to learn an infinite variety of behavior patterns. Although tendencies to react emotionally to stress are probably genetically determined, we learn, during the process of growing up, how to deal with difficult situations in ways that reduce their potential for stress. We also learn to face a certain amount of stress (for example, an examination or a minor emergency) without flying into a rage or a panic.

No one can say with any certainty how much of our behavior is determined by genetic factors. Often, when we think we have identified a characteristic or pattern of behavior that appears to be inherited, we also find evidence that it may be related to a certain social culture or a kind of personality. Furthermore, it is very likely that many of the factors that we generally think of as being biologically inherited are actually transmitted through social inheritance, rather than through biological inheritance. For example, we say: "Philip King gets that temper from his father. The Kings always have been quick-tempered people." In all probability, Philip learned a quick-tempered way of behaving by imitating his father and the other members of his family. It is possible, of course, that Philip was irritable from birth—even newborn babies differ in temperament. But whether the newborn irritable Philip becomes or remains a quick-tempered child will depend on the kind of reinforcing experiences he has. In other words, it will depend on what kinds of behavior his family encourages or discourages.

Although children's behavior is highly modifiable, we recognize the fact that there are genetically determined trends that have a significant effect and are persistent. Some consistencies in behavior appear even before birth. The rapidity with which twenty-five infants mastered certain developmental problems of behavior during the first few months of life was found by C. Etta Walters (1965) to be related to the amount of activity they had shown during their last three prenatal months. Early activity levels give important clues to the kinds of persons that infants eventually become. But how this activity is received by families and by the society into which a child is born is equally and perhaps even more significant. Clyde Kluckhohn (1949) reported, as a result of observing the development of Zuñi and white infants, that the Indian culture had the effect of lowering the level of activity in children. White babies that appeared hyperactive at birth maintained this level of activity at two years of age, but the Zuñi babies did not.

SOCIAL INFLUENCES ON PERSONALITY AND MOTIVATION

The Case of the First-born Child

In addition to cultural patterns, other combinations of social forces shape the behavior of individual children. Birth order appears to have a considerable effect on personality, particularly for persons who are first-born in their families. First-born slum children, for example, seem to have fewer psychological problems than their later-born brothers and sisters (Dohrenwend and Dohrenwend, 1966). Data from a nationwide survey of American children between the ages of six and eleven indicate that there is a tendency for firstborns to have higher IQs than only or later-born children (U.S. Dept. of Health, Education, and Welfare, 1974). Dutch army draftees who were first-born in their families also scored higher on intelligence tests than those who had been only or later-born children (Belmont and Marolla, 1973). Firstborns additionally appear to have an advantage with respect to other personality traits. To cite one example out of many investigations, a study of kindergarten children found firstborns to be more creative and also more popular than children in other birth-order positions (Laosa and Brophy, 1970).

Not all the reports of the personality traits of firstborns are favorable. Parents interviewed in a study reported by Allison Davis and Robert J. Havighurst (1947) stated that their first-born children were more inclined to be selfish and self-centered. When Helen L. Koch (1955) asked teachers to rate five- and six-year-old children on a number of behavioral characteristics, she found that the children who were first-born were described by their teachers as more intense emotionally, more upset by defeat, more inclined to offer alibis. Male college students who were first-born also appear to be more timid than other students because they were less likely to participate in dangerous sports, such as football, boxing, and wrestling (Nisbett, 1968).

Space does not permit an extensive review of the large number of research studies of birth-order effects on personality and social behavior which has appeared in the last few years, but the main finding seems to be that the individual who is or was the oldest child in his family is somewhat more likely to attain success than his siblings, irrespective of whether success is measured in social, economic, or intellectual terms. The effect seems to be strongest when the individual is male and comes from a small to medium-sized middle-class family. The effect for firstborns of both sexes is also accentuated when the next-born sibling is of a different sex (Smelser and Stewart, 1968).

Both the greater success and the personality characteristics that are likely to be the lot of the first-born child can be explained in terms of the experiences that he, rather than his younger brothers and/or sisters, is likely to have as a child. In the first place, he receives more attention than they do; in fact, he has a monopoly of it until the next-born child arrives on the scene. He also is more likely to play certain roles, such as taking care of his siblings in the absence of the parents (Kammeyer, 1967). He is held up as a model when his behavior is satisfactory, and he is shamed for letting his siblings down when it is not. Robert D. Palmer (1966) points out that the firstborn tends to turn to his parents, rather than to his siblings, in search of models on which to pattern his behavior, is exposed to greater parental expectations regarding responsibility and achievement, develops a harsher superego or conscience, and ends up by becoming more adult-oriented than his siblings. A. P. MacDonald, Jr. (1969) maintains that firstborns tend to be more highly socialized than later borns and feel more obligation to conform to authority figures. He tested this proposition in the form of an experiment that featured the possibility of receiving an electric shock and found that firstborns were more likely to keep their appointments as participants in the experiment and were more inclined to trust the experimenter.

Perception and Personality

We have selected the behavior and early experiences of the firstborn child as an example of the ways in which the social environment molds character and behavior. The firstborn happens to be a particularly good case because there are certain consistencies in their personality and social behavior. However, the fact that the example we have chosen displays these consistencies does not mean that the relationship between environment and behavior is simple or obvious. First, there are many exceptions to the general trends in firstborn behavior that we have described and, second, both firstborns and others may vary markedly in the way in which they react to environments that are quite similar. Here is a man who is a coal miner. He says that he never had a chance to get ahead in life because his family was so poor that he had to go to work in the mines before he was out of the sixth grade. But here is another man, a successful lawyer in the same town. He explains his success by saying that the poverty he experienced as a child made him determined to go to school so that his children would not have to put up with the same living conditions. One man says that he is a failure *because* of his childhood environment; another man ascribes equal importance to his childhood environment but says that he succeeded *in spite of it.*

It appears, then, that the conditions under which children grow up are not as important in determining their behavior as the way in which they react to or see these conditions. An individual may be a completely inadequate parent as far as society is concerned. He may be a criminal psychopath who ruthlessly exploits his children. But if his children see him as a parent who loves them, they will vigorously resist and resent any attempts of the authorities to interfere with their relationship, even if the proposed change means putting them in the home of a family who will give them excellent care and who will really love them. A certain teacher may be a kind and generous person, but if a child regards

her as an enemy, he will react to her and behave toward her just as he would toward an enemy. It is always important to remember that a child reacts to situations and people in terms of his *own* perceptions and points of view, not in terms of the points of view held by adults, and not necessarily in terms of the points of view of other children.

The "Self"—the Center of the Psychological Universe

The pattern of perceptions developed by the individual as he grows from infancy to childhood and maturity is what some psychologists call the "self-structure." The world appears as a confused mass of impressions to the newborn infant. He is even unaware of his physical dimensions—of where *he* leaves off and where the *world* begins. Watch a baby discovering and rediscovering the important fact that his hands and feet are really a part of himself and not playthings that someone has left lying around.

During the early years of childhood, the child begins to make differentiations out of the blur of impressions that is his world. As Carl Rogers (1951) once put it, "A portion of the total perceptual field gradually becomes differentiated as the self." Not only does the child begin to see himself as a person somehow separate from the rest of the world and from other people, but he learns to recognize and identify familiar faces, sounds, objects, and events. As he grows old enough to play with other children, he finds that certain things belong to them and certain things belong to him. In a way, the things that belong to him are a part of him, and when anyone tries to take them away, he both feels and behaves as though someone is trying to amputate a limb. He has similar feelings about the people who love and care for him. They, too, are a part of him—a psychological part of him, which is why he is disturbed when they are disturbed or why he is disconsolate if they leave him for long periods of time. As the child grows to adolescence and adulthood, he normally becomes less dependent on other individuals and less personally attached to possessions and other things in his physical environment. In other words, persons and things become less and less a part of him, because he has learned to differentiate between what *belongs* to him and what is physically and actually a *part* of him. Nevertheless, even a mature adult has a wide circle of persons, situations, creations, and possessions in which he has invested some of himself and in which he is personally involved. To some extent, they form a part of his psychological self.

How "The Self" Operates

Arthur W. Combs and Donald Snygg (1959) have developed a useful method for studying the interrelationship of various aspects of the self-structure. They call the individual's perception of view of himself his *self-concept,* the part of the environment in which he is involved or has a psychological or emotional investment his *phenomenal self,* and the rest

of the environment of which he is aware or to which he responds his *phenomenal environment.* (We shall use the term "perceived" instead of "phenomenal" inasmuch as it seems somewhat clearer and less technical.)

The self-concept is what the individual thinks of as his actual self—the part that is "really me." The perceived self, as Figure 2-4 shows, *includes* not only the self-concept but also those aspects of the environment that an individual *identifies* with himself—"my family," "my school," "my country," and so forth. Both the self-concept and the perceived self are in turn included within the perceived environment or the "phenomenal field," as Combs and Snygg call it. Other psychologists refer to it as the individual's "personal field," his "behavioral field," his "psychological field," or his "life space." Perhaps a good everyday term for it would be his "pri-

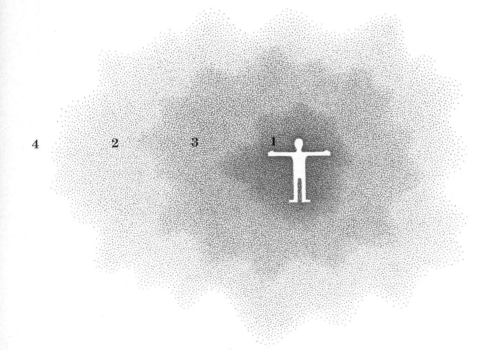

FIG. 2-4. Schematic concept of the "self-structure": Area 1 is the self-concept, at the very center of the "psychological universe"; Area 2 is the phenomenal or perceived self; Area 3 is the phenomenal or perceived environment; and Area 4 is the environment that is beyond awareness. The vagueness of the boundaries between the areas suggests that concepts and objects may shift back and forth from one area to another (after Snygg and Combs, 1959).

vate world." Therefore, to sum up what we have been saying about the process of development, the confused blur of sensations experienced by the infant becomes differentiated during the childhood years into a private world (or self-structure) consisting of himself (his self-concept); the things, events, and people with which he is personally involved (his perceived self); and the world as he sees it (his perceived environment).

Some interesting studies have been done in recent years on *locus of control*, a term that refers to the area of the psychological field in which an individual locates the major forces controlling his life (Coopersmith, 1967). Very young children are likely to locate these forces elsewhere because they see that they have little to say about what happens to them. As a child becomes older, more competent, and more responsible, he learns that he does have some freedom of choice about what he can do and cannot do; therefore he takes more responsibility for his successes and failures. He therefore perceives his locus of control as becoming more "internal" and less "external," and this process of shifting the locus of control from external to internal normally continues well into the adult years. Some individuals, however, are less able to make this shift. This is especially true of the individual who grows up in impoverished circumstances where he is literally at the mercy of his environment and has little freedom for self-determination. Some children living in more affluent circumstances may also feel that they have little to say about the events that occur in their lives and may, like many deprived children, adopt a passive attitude toward others. The perceptual stance that we call "locus of control" is very important in determining how optimistic a child will be about putting forth the effect needed to succeed in school. A child's belief that he will fail, or that there is not much use in making the effort to learn, can become an extremely potent force in determining his progress in school and in later life.

"Reality" Is How We Perceive It

We introduced this discussion of perceptual factors in behavior by saying that children react to situations and people in terms of their own perceptions and points of view, as contrasted with the perceptions and points of view of adults. The phenomenal field or private world of an individual is *reality*, as far as he is concerned. In other words, we all tend to react to the world that we perceive, not the world as perceived by others, and the way in which we perceive the world is for us "reality." What we perceive and the way in which we perceive it are governed or conditioned by our psychological needs. This helps to explain why the children of inadequate parents, mentioned previously, so often resist attempts to place them in more adequate homes. These children have a strong, and to a large degree unmet, need to be loved. The strength of this need leads them to overvalue the little attention they get from their parents. Thus we should not be critical if they overrate the little love they get because it is all they have. These children do not see being transferred to a better home as an opportunity to get more love and attention. Rather, they see it as an attempt to separate them from the only love they have ever known. Hence they are likely to resist any attempts to change their status. They simply do not see the facts that are obvious to any objective adult: that their own parents are treating them very shabbily and that their new parents will give them the love and care they need. The adult cannot understand this because they are viewing the whole situation in terms of their broader experience, in terms of *their* perceived environment and not in terms of the environment as perceived by the children. We should add, in passing, that such children can be helped by skilled psychotherapists to develop and reorganize their private worlds along more realistic lines, but any such attempts must take into account the gap between the world as they see it and the world as viewed by adults.

How Perceptions Change with Maturity

As children grow to maturity, their perceptions of self and environment change. As these changes take place, their behavior is modified accordingly. Sometimes changes do not take place as rapidly as would be desirable, whereupon maladjustments are likely to occur.

Simone was upset and unhappy the first day at kindergarten. She had looked forward to school as a pleasant and exciting experience, but instead she was confused, depressed, and anxious. During the first few days, she stayed very close to the teacher, refused to participate in the games and activities, and spent most of the time sucking her thumb, something she had not done since she was three. By the beginning of the second week, however, she began to respond to the teacher's suggestions that she might like to play house with some of the other children, and after a few more days she was enjoying kindergarten as much as any other child.

One way to interpret Simone's behavior is to say that she had some initial difficulty in developing a concept of herself as a pupil in kindergarten. It took her a few days to organize her concept of the new environment and to determine where she fit in. She stayed close to her teacher, just as she would have stayed close to her mother in a similar confusing situation. Perhaps she was afraid of what might happen to her, afraid of unknown dangers. However, once she developed an adequate concept of herself as a member of a group of kindergarteners and had satisfied herself that the situation was no more dangerous than her own home, she felt free to modify and adjust her behavior according to a more appropriate and more mature pattern. As long as she perceived school as a threatening situation, she behaved in an immature and anxious fashion, but when she was able to develop a picture of the situation that was closer to objective reality, she was able to behave more realistically and with greater confidence. Simone's teacher wisely refrained from putting too much pressure on her to participate actively with the other children because she knew that children often have difficulties during the first days of school. Furthermore, any attempts to tell Simone that she was foolish or naughty might have aroused even greater anxiety.

The point is that the behavior of children is determined by their perception of themselves and of the world around them. As this perception changes, their behavior changes accordingly. As much as they might like to do so, teachers cannot *give* con-

cepts directly to children, by insisting, for instance, that they become more mature and realistic in their attitudes. Usually such direct approaches serve only to strengthen the immature attitudes that are interfering with the development of more realistic concepts and consequent behavior. Sometimes adults, who are in a hurry and who want to get on with the business of educating, find children's resistance to change a source of difficulty and annoyance. Such adults are themselves at fault in the sense that they are unable to modify *their* private worlds to accommodate the idea that children's concepts of life may be different from those of adults and that such concepts predetermine children's behavior. In fact, this tendency of adults to force certain kinds of behavior on children and to maintain *their* private worlds at the expense of the private worlds of children underlies much of the tension, irritability, and anxiety found in classrooms today. It results in unhappiness and frustration for everyone involved: for teachers, parents, and administrators but most particularly for children. Much of this unhappiness and frustration could be obviated if adults had a better understanding of the feelings and perceptions of children. Inasmuch as adults are more mature and actually more flexible than children, it is easier for them to understand and make adjustments for the kinds of perceptions children have than it is for children to understand and make adjustments to adult perceptions.

UNDERSTANDING MOTIVES

Motives that Lie "Beyond Awareness"

There is an important point to keep in mind as we attempt to understand human behavior: We are generally unaware of the more important forces and motives that lie behind our own behavior. This point is easily forgotten or overlooked. Ofter we see others doing things that are not in their best interests and hence try to help them by showing them what they are doing that is wrong. Then we are surprised when they vigorously deny having done the very thing we have seen them doing. Whenever we try to help adults in this way and find ourselves rebuffed, we usually tell ourselves that we should have minded our own business in the first place. But with children, our attitude is different. When children deny something we have seen them do with our own eyes, we feel that they are being willful, are lying, are deliberately defying us, or are just being difficult and obstinate. It is hard to grasp the fact that children, like adults, have much difficulty in seeing their behavior as it appears to others.

Just before the sixth grade was dismissed for the day, Miss Roth asked Dick Hansen to see her after school. She tried to tell him unobtrusively, so as not to embarrass him in front of the class-room group, but she was not too successful. Dick had been such a problem in the month since school began that most of the class kept half an eye on him in order not to miss what he would do next. So when Miss Roth went over to Dick's desk and said something in a low voice, every child in the room knew he was being asked to stay after school.

When the last child had left, Miss Roth straight-ened up her desk while Dick waited sullenly. She really didn't like to keep him waiting, and the desk straightening actually wasn't very impor-tant, but she wanted to think through how she would handle this matter. Things simply could not go on as they had.

When she had things in order, she turned and faced Dick.

"Dick," she said, "what are we going to do with you?"

The sullen look faded from Dick's face, to be replaced by a perplexed frown. "I don't know what you mean, Miss Roth."

Miss Roth was firm. "I think you know what I mean."

She took a sheet of paper from under her desk blotter. "Last Friday, when you were in line at the cafeteria, you shoved the children ahead of you so hard that the little girl who was getting a bowl of hot soup spilled it over her hand and had to get first aid."

Dick started to, "Well, I didn't . . .," but Miss Roth raised her hand.

"I'm not finished, Dick. There's lots more. Monday, you put your foot out in the aisle and tripped Leonard, who was coming up to erase the blackboards for me. He didn't get hurt, but he *could* have had a nasty fall. The same day, dur-ing recess, I saw you go over to the girls' play area and take their volleyball. Mrs. Richards saw you, too, and made you return it, but not without a big argument from you. Tuesday, you inter-

rupted me four times when I was giving instruc-tions on the new history workbooks."

"I just wanted to go to the toilet," Dick mut-tered.

Miss Roth ignored his interruption. "Tuesday was also the day you brought a lizard to class. It took us twenty minutes to capture the poor thing. On Wednesday, you were half an hour late to school, the fourth time you have been tardy since school started a month ago."

She paused and looked at Dick. The sullen look was back.

"I could go on and on, but there wouldn't be any point to it. I think it should be clear that you are a real problem to me, to the class, and, I think, to yourself. What are we going to do with you?"

"I don't know where you got all that stuff," Dick said, defensively. "A lot of it isn't so, and besides I can explain some of the things. That business about Mrs. Richards. I don't know what she was raising such a big fuss about. I was walking by and one of the girls yelled: 'There's Richard the chicken-hearted!' I yelled back something and they dared me to take their ball, so I did."

Miss Roth sighed. She knew this wasn't going to be easy. "You shouldn't have been near the girls' play area in the first place, and in the sec-ond . . ."

"Yeah, I suppose I'm supposed to take all the stuff anybody wants to throw at me lying down," answered Dick angrily. "Well, I'm not going to do it. Nobody's going to push *me* around!"

Miss Roth tried another tack. "Let's see, Dick, you're about five feet eight?"

"Five, nine and a half. So what? he retorted belligerently.

"Well, you're the tallest boy in school, any-way," Miss Roth went on, trying not to show her exasperation. "The boys in the sixth grade look up to you. You're a kind of a leader. It doesn't help them get along in school when you keep doing the things I've mentioned. We want to help you, Dick. We really do."

Dick looked at her, his eyes blazing. "If you really wanted to help, you could stop picking on me. Everybody tries to shove me around—teach-ers, my sisters, my folks, and the kids at school. You say you want to help me," mimicking her tone, "but you're just like all the rest. You make me sit here so you can read me a bunch of stuff. Maybe I did those things or maybe I didn't. I don't even remember half of them. They're all little things that don't amount to much anyway, but to hear you talk, you think I was a criminal or something. Why—why does everybody have to make trouble for me?"

Dick evidently did not expect an answer to that question, for he put his head in his hands and cried bitterly.

Miss Roth sat at her desk aghast at the vehemence of Dick's attack, frustrated at not being able to make him understand, pitying him and wanting to comfort him, but not knowing how to do any of these things or *what* to do at all. . . .

One of the most frustrating things about Miss Roth's situation is that she has Dick "dead to rights." She has a list of things she has seen Dick do. The boy is annoying, impertinent, cruel, insubordinate—any and all of a long list of words that his teachers and parents and even his classmates would agree on. Yet he doggedly refuses to admit or accept these things about himself. And, worst of all, although she sincerely wants to help him, he sees her as an enemy.

There are various hypotheses that may help us understand why Dick denies Miss Roth's accusations. For one thing, the behavior she describes is apparently inconsistent with his self-concept. She paints the verbal picture of a boy who is a bully, who is against everyone, whereas the picture Dick has of himself is that of someone who is always being criticized or picked on. He is so obsessed with the idea of the world's being against him that he cannot see how much he is against the world.

There are, of course, a number of other hypotheses that could account for Dick's behavior. For example, in what way does Dick's height create problems for him? Here are some other questions that might lead to useful clues:

What kinds of basic needs are not being met for Dick, and how does his behavior constitute an attempt to meet these needs?

What kinds of "reinforcing events" experienced in Dick's early childhood may have resulted in the kind of behavior he displays?

What kinds of "reinforcing events" are probably occurring at school that aggravate Dick's problems?

The "locus of control" for Dick is clearly external. He perceives the causes of his misbehavior as "out there" in the environment and does not see how his attitudes toward others, as well as toward himself, lie at the bottom of many of his problems. This is plainly immature of him, but what is the school doing to help him become more mature? What *could* the school do to help him mature?

Think back over your own elementary school experiences. In what way would Dick have been helped by the kind of school you attended? In what way would he not have been helped?

In what way could Miss Roth's attitude help Dick? In what way is it not helpful?

Some school authorities would react to Dick's behavior by "getting tougher" with him. In what way would this help him? In what way might this worsen the problem?

Other authorities might advise "taking some of the pressure" off him. In what way would such a policy help him? What risks would such a policy run? If Miss Roth adopts such a policy, what other steps should she take?

Motive as Purpose and Goal

Dick's problems lead us to two more points about behavior: All behavior has some purpose, and all behavior results from a multiplicity of causes.

Let us take the first point. Dick's behavior is not accidental; he did not just "happen to be bad." He has become involved in this behavior as a way of coping with his anxiety. Something is bothering him, and aggressive, rebellious behavior is Dick's way of handling this bothersome feeling. Furthermore, his behavior has symbolic meaning for him. His rebelliousness may be a way of saying to the world, in effect: "You can't do this to me." Or it may be a way of saying: "Nobody likes me. How could anybody like me; I don't like myself. But look at me, look at me. If you look at me while I pull my pranks, I'll forget about you not liking me."

These are some of the many motives that might lie behind such rebellious behavior. A complete list of motives would be a long one indeed, because there are many forces, both internal and external, that bear upon each of us and contribute in some way to the behavior we display. Furthermore, each act, each bit of behavior, has the purpose of attaining some goal, meeting some need, reducing or forestalling some anxiety, or symbolizing some feeling.

Motives as Multiple Causes of Behavior

The second point—the multiple causality of behavior—is equally important. In our everyday dealing with one another, we are inclined to look for single causes for behavior, partly because it is easier to cope with the behavior of others if we assume it is due to a single cause. If a youngster misbehaves in a classroom, we assume it is due to a "need for discipline." So we prescribe punishment and go on to the next problem, assuming we have solved this one. We encounter a youngster who cannot read and assume that he has not been taught to read properly. Hence we apply ourselves to the task of teaching him properly, with the tacit assumption that we are better teachers than the ones he has had. And so we go through life, assuming single causes for the behavior we encounter and attempting to solve problems with solutions appropriate to the single causes we identify.

One of the reasons why our attempts to deal with problem behavior so often fail is that we are overlooking the complex constellation of causal factors or motives behind every act. In trying to account for Dick Hansen's behavior perhaps we might find that *all* the hypotheses or hunches we have developed have some truth in them, even though there are contradictory elements in them. If so, this would not be unusual. The chances are that some of the hypothesized causes would turn out to be more important, more crucial than others, but this would not mean that the others were invalid. There is a vast and complex network of conflicting needs, demands, and forces that we have to contend with at any given moment in our lives. We are figuratively pushed and pulled in a dozen directions at once. We therefore try to respond to the forces that seem most important to us and to satisfy as many demands as possible.

Doreen is a ninth-grader who is enrolling in first-year algebra. She is taking algebra because her parents expect her to and because she wants to go to college. But her best friends are taking a business sequence and do not plan to go to college. She feels a little lonely, taking algebra with-

out anyone she knows. She is afraid of algebra. She has heard that it is a terrifically hard subject, and she is afraid she might fail. But she cannot drop out of a course just because she might fail. That would not be proper. It would disappoint her parents, and she would be ashamed of herself. Her counselor wants her to take algebra. Her counselor thinks she is good college material and that she has the intelligence and the background to do algebra. Doreen is not so sure, but she does not want to disappoint the counselor, any more than she wants to disappoint her parents.

We have listed just a few of the many factors or forces that favor or disfavor Doreen's enrolling in algebra. She enrolls in it because the forces favoring her enrollment are stronger than the forces against it, thereby satisfying the most pressing needs at the expense of less important needs. Every behavioral act is a compromise whereby we try to satisfy as many needs and cope with as many demands as possible, but the needs and demands that are the most powerful and the most pressing at the moment are the ones with the greatest influence. For Doreen, it is more important to fulfill her parents' expectations than it is for her to conform to the expectations of her age-mates. The choice she makes involves some anxiety, of course, because it means being isolated from her friends for part of a school day. Other adolescents might be moved to make a different decision in a similar situation because the need to be with friends and to behave in ways acceptable to the group often carries more weight than the opinions and wishes of parents during this stage of development.

SUMMARY

Human behavior may be viewed from the standpoint of forces "inside" and "outside" the individual that impel his thoughts, feelings, and actions. This chapter is principally concerned with the "inside" forces—motivation. Although some psychologists prefer a system that explains behavior in terms of "primary drives"—internal forces that are largely physiological—other psychologists prefer to think of human behavior as impelled by needs to be competent and effective. These needs may be classified in a hierarchy ranging from the most simple and biological to the most abstract and complex. Needs for belongingness and self-actualization are sometimes described as needs for affiliation (n Aff) and achievement (n Ach). Both these needs are powerful motives during the school years. When needs are frustrated or threatened by possible frustration, particularly when needs at the more abstract and socialized levels are involved, we are likely to experience anxiety. Much of our behavior that appears contrary to our best interests is apparently the result of attempts to reduce or ward off anxiety. Anxiety is likely to occur in experiences involving our relations with others, that are ambiguous, or have an element of uncertainty. In spite of its negative aspects, some degree of "normal anxiety" is necessary for socialization.

The human organism can also be regarded as an energy system, existing in an environment that is composed of *stimuli.* Those stimuli that have an effect on the organism are termed *inputs,* which lead to energy changes called *transformation processes,* and result in *responses* or *outputs.* The organism may react to its own responses, in which event, they are *fed back* into the organism and are reacted to in a manner similar to that of other inputs.

Our environment has a powerful effect on our behavior because it controls the means for satisfying our needs. When our attempts to secure satisfaction are rewarded, the behavior that preceded the satisfaction is said to be *reinforced.* This reinforcement is the basis for learning of all types, including social learning, and results in the individual patterns of behavior or personality that make us the individuals we are. Environments that are rich in stimuli tend to be preferred to less stimulating types of environment because they offer a greater opportunity for satisfaction or, perhaps, because the need for stimulation is in itself a function of the basic overriding need for maintenance and survival. In any event, a reduction in stimulation is experienced as unsettling, and an increase in stimulation appears to have a facilitating or "encouraging" effect on the development of young organisms.

Genetic factors constitute another dimension of the "inside" forces that affect behavior. Some aspects of behavior, such as aggression in males and socialization in females, appear to result from genetic influences. However, the human organism's capacity to acquire varied patterns of behavior is such that genetically determined behavior may be modified drastically through learning.

The tendency of first-born children to have more successes and to develop somewhat different personality characteristics than individuals in other birth-order positions indicates the importance that social factors play during the early stages of the life span. The firstborn's preeminence may result from his being the recipient of more attention than his siblings, from the roles he plays as a supervisor and model for his siblings, and from his tendency to relate favorably to parents and other adults.

Although genetic factors and the social environment play important parts in determining behavior, the way in which we perceive ourselves and our environment is equally important. We organize these perceptions into what psychologists call the *self-structure,* which includes the *self-concept,* the *perceived self,* and the *perceived environment.* Our concepts of ourselves and our environment constitute "reality" for us, and this "reality" forms the basis for our actions, feelings, thoughts, and decisions. The child who perceives his "locus of control" as being "external," rather than "internal," is likely to behave in passive ways, avoid responsibility for his acts, and be reluctant to take initiative in classroom learning.

We are not generally aware of the ways in which our behavior is influenced by our concepts of self and environment. Furthermore, our lack of awareness of the self-structure of others leads us to misunderstand and misjudge their behavior. This difficulty becomes particularly acute when we try to work with children because we are inclined to forget that the concepts children have of themselves and their environment tend to differ markedly from the concepts adults have of the same children and the same environment.

In attempting to develop an understanding of learners and the concepts and needs that underlie their behavior, it is important to keep in mind that all behavior, however irrational it may seem, has purpose and results from a multiplicity of causes.

Suggested Problems

1. When Mr. Parchen returned to his class in civics after a brief absence, he caught Andy May-

hew throwing chalk across the room at another boy. He asked Andy to leave the room and go down to the principal's office. Andy replied: "Try and make me." Mr. Parchen walked right up to Andy, looked him in the eye, and said: "Leave the room, Andy." He did not see Andy any more that day until after school, when he looked out of the window and saw him and five other boys roaring down the street in a stripped-down old car, shouting and hooting. What internal and external forces were very likely operating to cause Andy to defy Mr. Parchen?

2. Mrs. Fritchman was somewhat alarmed when her daughter, Carrie, came home from her first day in junior high school. Carrie was not her usual cheerful self but was depressed and discouraged. She said she disliked all her teachers and hated her new school. What psychological needs do you think are involved in Carrie's behavior? In what ways does anxiety enter into the situation?

3. What are some of the ways in which your concepts of yourself and your environment (including people who play important roles in your life) differ from those you had when you were in high school? In what ways do they differ from the concepts you had in grade school?

4. In what ways do you think your concepts of yourself differ from those your friends have of you? Your instructors? Your parents?

5. Describe some of the ways in which reinforcement has shaped your behavior and made you the kind of person you are today.

6. Think of someone who has problems in getting along in school or on the job. Is there any indication that his or her problems are the result of a belief that his or her "locus of control" is "external?" How can one tell whether an individual is "internal" or "external"?

7. What are some of the ways in which n Aff and n Ach have contributed to your present status as a student? Describe a situation in which n Aff and n Ach are in conflict for you. How do you resolve such conflicts?

8. In what ways has your position in your family as a child (first, middle, last, only, or whatever) had an effect on the kind of person you are today?

9. Not only individuals can be regarded as energy systems but organizations as well. Describe an organization of which you are a member in terms of its inputs, transformation processes, outputs, and feedback.

Suggested Readings

Combs, A. W., and Snygg, D. *Individual behavior: A perceptual approach to behavior,* rev. ed. New York: Harper, 1959. A highly readable presentation of the perceptual approach to the understanding of human behavior, with special application to problems of education and learning.

Gale, R. F. *Developmental behavior: a humanistic approach.* New York: Macmillan, 1969. A textbook that treats human development in terms of self theory, along the lines of Snygg, Combs, Rogers, and Maslow.

Lindgren, H. C., and Fisk, L. W., Jr. *Psychology of personal development,* 3rd ed. New York: Wiley, 1976. The first seven chapters discuss the part played by psychological needs, self-concept, and anxiety in human behavior.

Lindgren, H. C., and Lindgren, F. (eds.). *Current readings in educational psychology,* 2nd ed. See papers in Part 2 that deal with the self-concept and with birth-order effects.

Maslow, A. H. *Motivation and personality.* New York: Harper, 1954. An integrated collection of essays on psychological factors in mental health, achievement, creativity, and self-actualization.

Rogers, C. R. *Client-centered therapy.* Boston: Houghton Mifflin, 1951. In this author's opinion, Chapter 11, "A theory of personality and behavior," is one of the clearest and most concise explanations of how personality develops and why people behave as they do. Like the treatment by Combs and Snygg, the point of view is largely perceptual.

Staats, A. W., and Staats, C. K. *Complex human behavior: A systematic extension of learning principles.* New York: Holt, Rinehart, and Winston, 1963. See chapters dealing with personality and human motivation. Treatment is largely from the point of view of reinforcement psychology.

Thelen, H. A. *Education and the human quest.* New York: Harper, 1960. See Chapter 2—"What makes Johnny tick?"—in this provocative and challenging book.

3

The Growth and Maturation of the Learner

IN THIS CHAPTER WE SHALL DISCUSS

- Evidences of development and growth
- What "maturity" means
- Aspects and dimensions of development
- Cognitive and noncognitive development
- Jean Piaget's developmental stages
- Piaget, Montessori, and the British Infant schools
- Do schools help children think?
- The effects of stimulation and arousal on deprived children
- *Sesame Street* and *Plaza Sesamo*

- Social development as an educational goal
- Lawrence Kohlberg's stages of moral development
- Social learning, modeling, and imitation
- Emotional or affective development
- Erik Erikson's developmental phases
- Physical development: Its relationship to other aspects of development
- Consistencies and inconsistencies in development
- Accelerated and retarded development
- Providing for individual differences in development

Indications of Growth and Development

When I was a boy it used to annoy me that grown-up visitors seemed obsessed with the need to comment on my growth in size. "My, but you're getting to be a big boy!" "Haven't you grown, though!" "Why, you're almost up to my shoulder!" Exclama-tions like these only aggravated my feeling of awkwardness and embarrassment, and I wished sometimes that I would stop growing so that I would be less conspicuous. *I was not conscious of having grown, except perhaps when I noticed that my clothes were not fitting as well as they used to.*

Now that I am an adult, I see things differently, of course. It is somewhat of a shock to notice suddenly that the baby who lived next door when we moved in is now in the third grade, or that the girl who came trick-or-treating in a clown's costume on Halloween is now attending college and is checking out groceries at the supermarket on weekends.

One of the reasons why we find it a little difficult to adjust to what seem to be startling changes in children is that our concepts of them tend to be rather static. Let us assume that we become acquainted with a two-year-old girl. Having made her acquaintance, we are likely to go away with a fairly accurate picture of a two-year-old girl in our minds. When we see her again after a year or so, we are startled by the contrast between the picture we had in our minds and what we see before us. Even if we see her more frequently, we have a little difficulty in bringing our mental picture up to date each time we see her. Some people have more trouble with this than others, but the tendency is for our concepts of children to lag behind their actual growth and development.

Nor is the teacher or the parent who sees the child every day usually aware of many of the changes that are taking place. To begin with, the changes that constitute growth and development usually come gradually; hence we are seldom conscious that they are occurring. Gil complains to his parents that he is having trouble with subtracting single-digit numbers, such as 7 from 9. His father tries to help him, but his methods seem different from those of the teacher, so the attempt is dropped and nothing more is said. A few months later, the parents visit Gil's classroom during Public Schools Week and, in looking over his work, are surprised to find that he is now doing a rather good job of subtracting *three*-digit numbers. Only when we have a good opportunity to compare an earlier form of behavior with current behavior are we able to see that growth has occurred.

It is not easy to develop a broad and dynamic understanding of the process of growth. We tend to single out special aspects of growth for our attention instead of trying to see it as a total and continuous process. For example, we commonly think of growth as a series of stages beginning or ending, say, at six months, eighteen months, three, six, and eight years, and the like. Such formulations make growth *appear* to consist of well-defined stages or periods, rather than as the continuous and more or less gradual unfolding that it actually is.

Growth and development express themselves not only in changes in appearance but also in changes in behavior. It is the changes in behavior that are most significant for the teacher. For one thing, most of the new behavior that appears is *learned* behavior, and the teacher, as a specialist in learning, will want to play some part in guiding or stimulating the kind of learning that is taking place. A teacher must therefore be alert and sensitive to the many ways in which the process of growth and development reveals itself, for such sensitivity is a necessary part of developing a working understanding of students and their behavior.

Here is another reason why we should be concerned with the growth and development of children. When we evaluate the learning of students (which means that we are to some extent evaluating our own work as teachers), we are inclined to direct our attention primarily to their *current* status. We see Laura as someone who is up to her grade in social studies and science but behind in English and reading. We see George as someone who does not pay attention very well and who interrupts and disturbs the other students. It is relatively easy to determine the current level of academic work or social behavior of students but relatively difficult to fit this information into some kind of historical or psychological perspective that takes into account their developmental patterns and problems. Laura *is* behind in English and reading, but did she make any progress during the last year? Does George's behavior have anything to do with his being a late-maturing adolescent? When we stop to think about the children who come to our attention and put together some of our observations, we may often be surprised to find that bits of behavior that have annoyed or perplexed us suddenly become more understandable.

Maturity: A Concept Larger than "Age"

When we say that a child is "at grade level" in reading, we are in effect making a comparison between his behavior and the behavior of other children of similar age. We are, to use the statistician's term, comparing him with the "norm" for his grade. We can use this method of comparison with many kinds of behavior other than reading, not only with educational skills and knowledge of subject matter but also general intellectual competence, social competence, emotional behavior, physical coordination, and so forth. When we make such comparisons, we are making judgments regarding a child's *maturity*. Maturity, used in this sense, refers to the extent to which a child is in step with other children his age. A boy who has started to develop secondary sex characteristics (growth of hair in the pubic and underarm regions, deepening voice, and so forth) at the age of twelve would be considered an "early maturer" or "physically advanced for his age," for such changes more commonly appear at fourteen. Another boy who first begins to show these characteristics at sixteen would be considered a "late maturer" or "physically immature for his age." The extent to which a child exceeds or lags behind the developmental norms for his age may tell us a great deal about his behavior. We shall have more to say about this later.

There are norms for social and emotional behavior, just as there are norms for physical development. A child of eight who is unable to engage in group play, and whose play pattern resembles that of a three-year-old in other respects, may be considered to be socially immature. The fifteen-year-old boy whose attempts to interact with other students consist largely of the shoving, pushing, and half-playful fighting more characteristic of preadolescents is equally immature.

Maturity is a term that may be used in one of two different ways. The first is the concept of maturity we have been describing: behavior that is appropriate to the age of the individual concerned. The second use of the term refers to the behavioral standards and expectations of adults. If we use the term "maturity" in this second sense, most of the behavior displayed by children may be considered immature. It is, of course, unrealistic to expect children to come up to adult norms, although adults frequently demand behavior from children that is more appropriate of adults than it is of children, without being aware that their demands are unreasonable.

When psychologists speak of "mature" or "immature" behavior in reference to children, they are usually referring to the kind or level of behavior appropriate to the age of the child. Although temper tantrums are "immature" according to adult standards, calling them "immature" does not help us understand the individual who displays such behavior. If the child in question is three years old, then we must keep in mind that three-year-olds commonly have temper tantrums, and that they usually outgrow them. If he is a nine-year-old, then we are more seriously concerned because temper tantrums are not common among nine-year-olds. Temper tantrums would not be considered immature for a three-year-old, but they would be for a nine-year-old.

Let us look at another example. Roger, aged four, is happily playing with building blocks in the corner of the nursery school. Felice, the same age, wanders in after a vigorous workout on the jungle gym. Her attention is drawn to the buildings and bridges that are taking shape, and she decides that the most interesting thing in the world right now is to play with blocks. As she moves into the area, Roger makes loud cries of protest and hits Felice. It may be that he is reacting to her invasion of his personal world, his life space for the moment. Observations of animals show that the concept of "my territory" is firmly established among many species, and that birds, mammals, and even certain kinds of fish will fight if their private areas are invaded. It may well be that this instinct to maintain and defend a personal area is present in humans and appears quite early.

Roger has an additional basis for his protest. Although he has been playing with the blocks for only fifteen minutes, he has "invested" something of himself in them, and they have in turn become a part of him, psychologically speaking. They are *his;*

they *belong* to him; for the moment, they are a *part of his perceived self.* To share them would be a little like losing a portion of himself. Perhaps he feels anxious at this prospect; he certainly feels psychologically threatened and proceeds to attack the source of his threat. He forgets that nursery school toys belong to all the children; he forgets that he is under the surveillance of watchful adults, who even at that moment are bearing down upon him from all directions.

When Roger is seven, he may still have a degree of possessiveness about any school equipment he happens to be playing with, but he will be less involved in it emotionally. Furthermore, requests on the part of another child that he share such equipment would probably be recognized by him as legitimate. He would be more likely to remember that one "takes turns" with school equipment and that even if he has to surrender it to another, he will eventually get his turn again. Because he is aware that what he is giving up or sharing is not really his, he is less anxious and less hostile.

Aspects and Dimensions of Development

There are at least three aspects of development in the examples we have given: cognitive, social, and emotional. Cognitive development refers to activities that involve thinking, perceiving, and/or problem solving—activities that in ordinary language might be referred to as "intellectual." Social development appears in any form of behavior that involves relations with others, while emotional development refers to feelings and attitudes, an aspect of behavior that psychologists sometimes term *affective.* Roger at age seven has attained a considerable degree of cognitive maturity because he can now discriminate between what is really his and what is community property. This ability to discriminate is basic to his willingness to accept the rights of others to use equipment that belongs to everyone. He also attained a degree of emotional maturity in his ability to restrain the expression of his irritation and hostility when the other child presents his claims to use the equipment in question, even though the temptation to resort to angry words and

blows may be quite strong. A great many four-year-olds are powerless to resist this temptation. Becoming more mature means, in part, developing the inner strength to deal with one's emotions.

A fourth type of development, physical development, is perhaps the most basic of all. This kind of development is the most visible, in the sense that its progress can be observed and measured most readily. Evidence of physical maturation includes increases in height and weight, changes in body build, the development of secondary sex characteristics, loss and eruption of teeth, and the ossification (change into bone) of cartilage in the wrist. We say that physical development is basic to all other aspects of development because the ability to engage in the kinds of activities involved in intellectually, socially, and emotionally mature behavior depends on the development of certain neurological, glandular, muscular, and skeletal structures and functions—in other words, on physical maturation.

COGNITIVE DEVELOPMENT

Of the four dimensions of growth, development, and maturation that we have mentioned, the one with which schools have traditionally been most concerned is the cognitive dimension. Families were considered to be the chief socializing agents, and schools were originally organized to enable children to acquire the kinds of cognitive skills that they could not learn at home. Although schools today have social as well as cognitive goals, the general public still considers their primary objective to be cognitive goals. Of course, this does not mean that the community and the schools can afford to be unconcerned about other dimensions of development. All four aspects of development are interrelated, and we cannot expect children to advance more rapidly along cognitive lines than they do in physical, emotional, and social ways. Because of the interrelationship between the four aspects of development, we are continually discovering that we can do a better job of helping youngsters develop intellectually by providing them with opportunities for self-development and self-expression in the emotional, social, and physical areas of life. Sometimes, of course, we find ourselves giving particular attention to the noncognitive aspects of a child's life because certain kinds of difficulties—physical, emotional, or interpersonal—are interfering with his ability to learn in the classroom.

The relationship between cognitive and physical aspects of development is not always obvious. A child is usually unable to do much thinking until he can talk, and he cannot talk until he is able to assume an erect position and to establish control over his lips, tongue, and throat. Nor can he learn to read

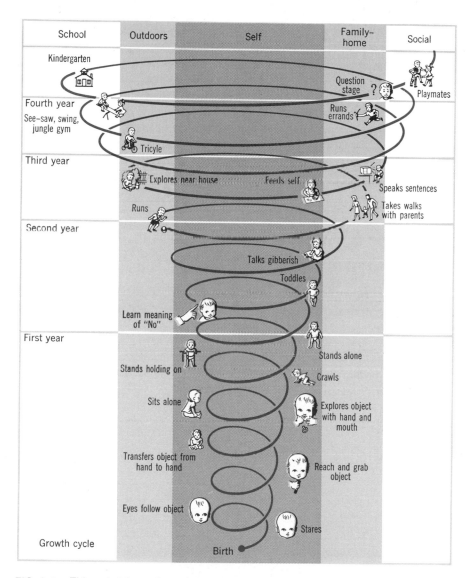

FIG. 3-1. This spiral "growth cycle" is based on the research of Arnold Gesell and his associates. It covers the first five years of life and shows how the various aspects of maturity are interrelated. (Courtesy Arnold Gesell and "Life Magazine," based on material drawn from A. Gesell et al., "The First Five Years of Life" and "Infant and Child in the Culture of Today," New York, Harper, 1940 and 1943.)

until the muscles in his eyes can accommodate the specialized kind of focusing essential to reading. Some of the work that was carried out by Arnold Gesell and his co-workers at the Gesell Institute for Child Development at Hartford, Connecticut, shows how the various kinds of maturation and development are interrelated. Figure 3-1 consists of a developmental "time schedule" covering the years between birth and age 5. Notice how the child's interests and activities move in ever-widening circles, first including only the physical self and later involving his physical and social environment.

The Responsibility of the School

The farther we get from the cognitive or intellectual aspects of growth and development, however, the less certain we are that we are involved in activities that are rightfully the responsibility of the school. There is a fairly extensive area of ambiguity that lies between the responsibility of the school to foster cognitive development and the responsibility of the community to provide welfare services for children. Here are some of the puzzling questions that stem from this ambiguity and that often have to be resolved by the school and other agencies or organizations in the community:

Should the school be responsible for the after-hours recreation of children? Or is this the responsibility of the city recreation department? When school playgrounds constitute the recreation facilities in question, problems of jurisdiction inevitably arise.

Who should teach manners and other forms of acceptable social behavior? Is this the responsibility of the school or the parents or both?

What about the building of character and the teaching of moral values? Are these functions the responsibility of the school, the parents, religious organizations, or voluntary organizations such as the Scouts?

Who should provide psychotherapy for emotionally disturbed children? Is this the responsibility of the school, the community, social welfare agencies, or the parents? An easy answer to this question is

"parents," but parents are often unwilling or unable to follow through when psychotherapy is clearly indicated and strongly recommended. In the meantime, the child in question is unable to make any progress in learning, is disturbing the other children in the class, and may be well along on the road to delinquency.

Resolving such dilemmas is never easy, and no standard formula applies. Each school system and each community deals with its constellation of problems differently. Wheresoever the lines of authority and responsibility are drawn, however, the school has a right to be involved actively or in a consultant capacity in any problem that affects children's learning. It has a right to raise questions about its own activities and responsibilities and even to prod parents and community agencies into removing the obstacles that interfere with learning. Some communities have therefore enlarged the scope of the school's services beyond those specifically concerned with the intellectual growth and development of children. Hence some schools provide after-school recreational supervision, psychotherapy, dental care, and subsidized lunches. A great many schools provide vocational counseling; special courses such as "senior problems" or "senior goals" that are concerned more with emotional and social maturity than with academic aspects of learning; and courses that are concerned principally with recreational, vocational, or artistic skills.

Piaget's Developmental Stages

The best-known student of cognitive development is Jean Piaget, a French-Swiss psychologist who was originally trained as a biologist but who has for more than fifty years observed and analyzed the behavior of children.

Piaget and his co-worker, Bärbel Inhelder, view cognitive development as being a continuous process of unfolding, but with recognizable stages or levels:

1. The *sensory-motor phase* (approximately ages 0 to 2), in which the infant in effect "creates" a personal world related to his desires for physical

satisfaction and within the scope of immediate (here-and-now) sensory experience. During the final months of this phase, the child begins to reflect about his experiences, starts to develop an awareness of the characteristics and particularly the *permanency* of objects, and obtains some glimmerings of the notion of *causality* in events. He is, however, confused by problems of differentiating between himself and his environment.

2. The *period of preparation for conceptual thought* (approximately ages 2 to 11 or 12) is further divided into the *preconceptual phase* (ages 2 to 4), the *phase of intuitive thought* (ages 4 to 7), and the *phase of concrete operations* (ages 7 to 11). During the early part of this period, the child is preoccupied with play, begins to develop language ability, learns to use imitation, and evaluates and reevaluates his perception of the environment. During the later years, he organizes systems of classifications for the perceptions and concepts that he has acquired and develops concepts of social justice and reciprocity.

3. The *phase of cognitive thought* (ages 11 or 12 and beyond). During this period, the child (now a youth) acquires the ability to think and reason beyond his own immediate world and his own beliefs. Problems are approached more systematically and less on a random, trial-and-error basis. Ideas of social justice and proper modes of social interaction become clarified and expanded (Inhelder and Piaget, 1958).

Piaget's ideas are attracting a great deal of attention on the part of American educators today. Many educators agree with him when he maintains that it is a waste of time to try to tell young children things that cannot be experienced through their senses, that is, through seeing and feeling, as well as hearing. Children, he says, must be permitted to manipulate objects and symbols, to test their questions and suppositions against reality. It is only through interacting directly with his environment that the child is able to construct within himself a schematic understanding of his physical and social world. Piaget is critical of classroom situations in which books and teachers' talking are the basic media of instruction, in which education takes place in the context of large groups, and in which paper-and-pencil tests are used as the only measures of what has been learned. In some respects, Piaget's thinking resembles that of Maria Montessori (1964), who concluded, as a result of extensive work with children in the slums of Rome more than sixty years ago, that cognitive abilities develop according to well-defined stages closely tied in with critical periods in which sensory modalities are especially active or "sensitive."

The ideas put forth by Piaget and Montessori have been incorporated into the philosophy of some of the more experimental British primary or "infant" schools, as well as the "open classrooms" and "free schools" in the United States and Canada that have appeared in the last ten years or so. There is a fundamental difference between Piaget and the majority of American educational psychologists. Piaget thinks that the elements underlying a child's knowledge of the world are inborn and do not have to be acquired through learning. This knowledge has to be "constructed" by the child as he interacts directly with his environment. Most American psychologists generally express the view that the child's understanding of the world has to be acquired, and that his success in acquiring it depends on the kind of environment he experiences. Robert M. Gagné (1968, 1970), for example, suggests that the stages described by Piaget are not necessarily predetermined by inborn developmental trends but are the result of the child's having learned sets of rules that are progressively more complex. How did the child acquire these sets of rules? Presumably because he has been "taught" them by the environment. If we follow Piaget's lead, we will assume that children will develop cognitive concepts and skills when they are neurologically and experientially "ready" for them; if we follow Gagné and other American educational psychologists, we will assume that children can acquire cognitive concepts and skills as fast as they can be taught them.

Educators who emphasize the discovery aspects of learning are likely to borrow heavily from Piaget

THE COURSE OF COGNITIVE DEVELOPMENT
Piaget maintains that children's cognitive development follows a well-defined sequence of stages, beginning with the sensory motor stage. The preconceptual, intuitive-thought, concrete-operations, and cognitive-thought follow one another, in orderly fashion, during the childhood and prepubertal years.

Piaget's writing and research has had major
influence on the direction of developmental
research with children, especially during the last
quarter of a century.
Maria Montessori, like Jean Piaget, maintained that
children's cognitive abilities develop according to
well-defined stages.

and Montessori, whereas those who see learning as produced by the child's environment, and especially by his teachers, are likely to take their cues from American behaviorists, such as B. F. Skinner, whose concepts we will examine in Chapter 8.

An American psychologist who occupies a position fairly close to that of the Europeans is Jerome S. Bruner (1961, 1964a), who strongly espouses the idea that the child learns best through discovery. Bruner has presented a system of cognitive development that is consistent with that of Piaget and has proposed that children's thinking develops in three stages, which he describes as (1) *enactive* (events represented through motor responses), (2) *iconic* (events represented through mental images of the perceptual field), and (3) *symbolic* (events represented through design features that represent remoteness and arbitrariness). These three stages, in brief, consist of the successive emergence of action, image, and word, and correspond approximately to Piaget's *sensorimotor, perceptual,* and *abstract* modes of cognitive functioning.

The difficulty with most education, according to the Piaget–Bruner point of view, is that teachers begin with the abstract—especially the verbal—modes of experience, whereas they would have better results if they would start with the more active sensorimotor aspects. According to Piaget, the child's ability to coordinate perceiving and manipulation (perceptual-motor development) underlies conceptual development. This principle appears to be supported in studies of disadvantaged children with reading difficulties, who were found to have problems in shifting their basic mode of attending to their environment from looking to listening and back again, while dealing with a problem requiring them to discriminate between auditory and visual stimuli (Katz and Deutsch, 1967). In one experiment some disadvantaged kindergarteners (the experimental group) were given special training in posture, maintaining balance, hand-eye coordination, and the like, whereas others (the control group) were not. At the end of the training period, children in the experimental group scored higher on a test of reading readiness than did those in the control group and were also more successful in learning to

read when they entered the first grade (Fisher and Turner, 1970). In another investigation, fourth- and fifth-grade children who were reading significantly below grade level were compared to other children of similar IQs who were reading at grade level or higher. The comparisons indicated that the retarded readers also lagged behind the others in their ability to make accurate perceptual discriminations. In the opinion of the investigators, the slow readers were having problems because they had been pushed beyond their maturational level (Whipple and Kodman, 1969).

As we have indicated, most American educational psychologists have tended to object to Piaget's formulations on the grounds that he places too much stress on the biological development of the organism and not enough on the environment. They also have other objections. Some psychologists have, for instance, questioned his carefully worked out stages of cognitive development on the grounds that they may be applicable mainly to children growing up in middle-class European homes and attending European schools. Others have complained that his system consistently underestimates the age at which middle-class American children can accomplish certain processes. The fact that so many children from economically disadvantaged homes have difficulty in school may result, as Piaget's thinking would suggest, from their not having had basic perceptual-motor experiences, but it may also be due to other factors, for instance, low motivation, the inability to relate to teachers and other adults, or the lack of adequate models from which to learn attitudes and skills.

Although as yet no experiment has been conducted that can be considered to be a major test of Piaget's theories, there have been a number of studies whose results raise questions about the universality of his concepts. John T. Mouw and James T. Hecht (1973), for example, tested a notion of Gagné's that cognitive skills are more dependent on learning than they are on development. The investigators trained third- and fourth-grade children (the experimental group) in a classification-type task and compared their performance with other children who had not received the special training (the control group). Results showed that the children in the experimental group were more likely to have mastered the principles involved in classifying objects. Piagetian theory would have suggested that the fourth-graders, being more mature, should have gained more through the special training than the third-graders, but results showed no significant difference between the two groups. In other studies, children have been successfully taught complex cognitive skills which, according to Piaget, they should not have been able to learn, inasmuch as such operations are presumed to be appropriate only for children at later ages and stages (Goldschmid, 1968; Anderson, 1965).

Piaget and his supporters do not attach much importance to studies like these. They maintain that only a rigid interpretation of his theories makes such experiments appear to be successful challenges. In actuality, Piaget recognizes that children may develop rapidly or slowly within the structural framework he has proposed. The fact that a child learns a concept "ahead of schedule" is not very significant. What matters is that the *general* trend of cognitive development is sequential.

Do Schools Help Children Learn to Think?

Both the followers and opponents of Piaget are agreed on one major item, namely, that irrespective of whether the child's cognitive development is or is not paced by his physiological development, the knowledge and skill he acquires depends on his environment. Members of the two groups differ on a number of points as to the kind of environment educators ought to provide for children, but few suggest that schools are unnecessary and should be abolished. For one thing, studies of the type we cited in Chapter 1 show that schooling generally has positive results as far as the competence, well-being, and even the happiness of children and adults alike are concerned. No one is exactly sure why it has this effect, but theories and speculations abound. It may be that schools teach children some of the information they must have in order to cope in a complex world, or it may be that they teach the attitudes and values that are essential in a society composed of interdependent individuals and groups. Perhaps children learn both in school.

The Piagetian concept that cognitive development is a natural process has led a few of his followers to raise the question of whether schools are irrelevant and even unnecessary. If a child is going to develop at his own pace, they say, much of what the schools do is irrelevant and may even interfere. Would not children be better off if, as Ivan Illich (1971) and his followers urge, they were not required to attend them?

Hard evidence on this question is difficult to secure. Much of it is anecdotal and is based on reports of the early experiences of famous individuals, such as Thomas Alva Edison and Winston Churchill, whose experiences in schools were unhappy and who can perhaps be said to have succeeded in spite of their formal education rather than because of it. Edisons and Churchills are, after all, very unusual people, and it is difficult to build a case against the schools based on their experiences.

What is needed to put the question to the test is some kind of comparison based on larger and less selective samples, say, between schooled and unschooled children coming from similar social backgrounds. Evidence of this kind may be found in studies of children living in fairly primitive areas, some of whom attend village schools and some of whom do not. According to Sylvia Scribner and Michael Cole (1973), who have conducted investigations of this type in West Africa, when rural children who attend school are presented with series of interrelated problems, they solve them by developing generalizations or rules that can be applied to all the problems, whereas unschooled children deal with such problems singly, treating each new problem as completely new and different from its predecessors. Once the schooled children grasp the rule, they are able to solve subsequent problems more rapidly, whereas unschooled children show little improvement. Other studies give similar results: Schooled children exhibit a considerable degree of cognitive flexibility in solving problems, even when the problems are drawn from the natural, nonschool environment, whereas unschooled children use a rigid, pedestrian approach, one based on first impressions (Greenfield, Reich, and Olver, 1966).

Scribner and Cole also showed children a group of common objects, told them to spend two minutes using any method they preferred to help them remember, and later asked them to recall what they had seen. When children attending school were asked what they had done to facilitate recall, they said they had rehearsed the names of the objects in their minds or aloud or they described other methods, whereas the unschooled children were at a loss to explain what they had done and frequently fell back on vague, nonspecific explanations, such as "God helped me." The point is that the schooled children were much more aware of the problem-solving strategies they used, whereas the unschooled lacked such insight.

The results of such investigations support neither Piagetian nor non-Piagetian explanations of cognitive development, but they do show that children must be exposed to certain kinds of experiences if they are to develop higher levels of cognitive functioning. But the most likely environment in which children are going to have such experiences is, of course, the classroom.

Intervention and Stimulation During the Preschool Years

In Chapter 2 we noted that the human organism has a need for stimulation and that, within reasonable limits, more stimulation is better than less stimulation, even for the very young. The research on this subject is extensive and the results mainly positive. In one study, investigators provided intensive daily care and cognitive training over a six-year period for children of women who lived in the Milwaukee slums and who had IQs of 75 or less—far below average. The children were taken into the program when they were three months old and were tested at regular intervals on a number of cognitive measures. This experimental group was compared with a control group of children whose mothers lived in

the same area and who also had IQs of 75 or less. A developmental measure based on use of language, IQ, and the ability to learn a variety of cognitive tasks showed that the children in the experimental program averaged consistently higher than the control group from six months onward, as Figure 3-2 shows (Heber et al., 1972).

An investigation of a somewhat different nature was conducted in England by Barbara Tizard and Judith Rees (1974). These investigators studied the cognitive development of preschool children who were living in orphanages that went to considerable pains to provide a great deal of attention to the children placed in their care. Studies usually show that children in institutions tend to score very low on intelligence tests and other cognitive measures. Wayne Dennis (1973), for instance, reported a mean IQ of 53 for otherwise normal preschool children in a Middle East orphanage where there was a low level of attention. The children in the British institutions, however, had a mean IQ of 105. This figure is considerably lower than the mean IQ of 115 that

(H. Martin in NEA JOURNAL)

"Good morning, pre-head starters. . . ."

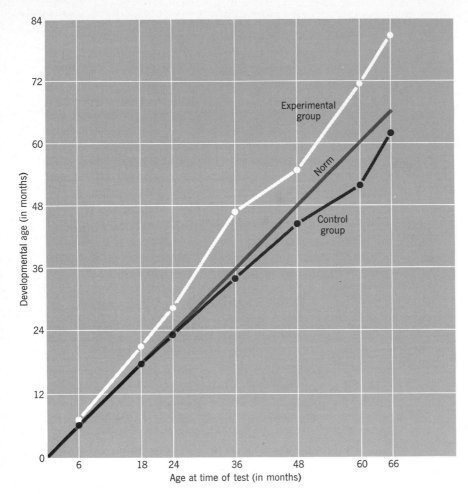

FIG. 3-2. Developmental ages (representing composite scores on various cognitive measures) of experimental and control groups of slum children who were tested at various ages (data from Heber et al., 1972).

was attained by children from these same institutions who had been adopted by middle-class parents, but it was nevertheless higher than the mean IQ of 100 for children who had been taken back from the institutions by their natural mothers, most of whom were very poor, had other children to care for, and were able to spend little time with them. It is especially interesting that the highest IQs in all these groups were attained by children who had been read to at least three times a week and who

had visited a children's library at least once a month. No child who had had these experiences had an IQ of less than 110.

The findings of the Milwaukee and the British studies are consistent with those of earlier investigations: The cognitive development of children is likely to be facilitated if they are exposed to environments that are stimulating, in which they get considerable attention, and that provide them with enriched cognitive experiences. The results of such studies were the basis of two large-scale educational programs: Project Head Start and *Sesame Street.*

The Head Start project was initiated in the summer of 1965 by the U.S Office of Education in order to provide preschool children from poverty homes with more adult attention and enriched learning experiences than they would have otherwise received. In order to accomplish these ends, the ratio of adults to children has been kept very high, and a great deal of time and money has been invested in providing games, art activities, cognitive tasks, and audio-visual materials. We shall go into greater detail in discussing preschool enrichment programs of the Head Start type in Chapter 16, but for the moment we note only that the available evidence suggests that the program has been moderately successful in achieving its goals, although it is admittedly difficult to evaluate an undertaking that has involved so many children in so many different ways. The programs in which children participated over longer time spans—a year or more—have apparently had some effect on the development of cognitive skills, but there is no evidence that participation in the summer programs only has had any effect (Ohio State University/Westinghouse Learning Corporation, 1969).

Evaluations of the effect of *Sesame Street* have been more reassuring. This televised program has been produced by Children's Television Workshop (CTW), a joint effort sponsored by the Carnegie Corporation, the Ford Foundation, the Office of Economic Opportunity, and the United States Office of Education. *Sesame Street* consists of a series of programs for three- to five-year-olds which are intended to introduce them to verbal and quantitative concepts in an entertaining manner. The series was launched in November, 1969, by National Educational Television (NET) and scheduled to appear one hour a day, five days a week. The effect of watching *Sesame Street* has been assessed by Samuel Ball and Gerry Ann Bogatz (1970) of the Educational Testing Service. Tests measuring various cognitive functions (recognition of shapes and letters, ability to sort and to solve puzzles, and so

on) were individually administered to more than seven hundred socially disadvantaged children before and after the television season. Results, as shown by Figure 3-3, indicated that the children's cognitive growth during the season was related to the amount of exposure they had to the program. These findings support one of the chief arguments put forth by *Sesame Street's* proponents before the program was launched, namely, that inasmuch as the nation's twelve million preschool children spend more than thirty hours a week on the average watching television, they might as well spend part of that time looking at something that is potentially educational. The cost of educating children by television is also quite small. CTW estimates that the cost of the program per child comes to less than one cent a day.

Equally dramatic results have been achieved by Rogelio Diaz-Guerrero and Wayne H. Holtzman (1974) who conducted an experiment using a version of *Sesame Street,* entitled *Plaza Sesamo,* completely redesigned, adapted to the Mexican culture, and presented in Spanish. The subjects were preschool-aged children from disadvantaged families. The children, who were attending day-care centers, were divided into experimental and control groups. The experimental groups saw one hundred thirty

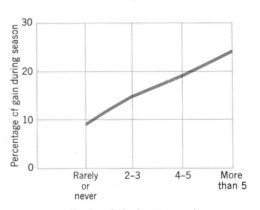

FIG. 3-3. Cognitive gains of socially and economically deprived children as related to the amount of time they spent watching "Sesame Street" during the television season, 1969–70 (Ball and Bogatz, 1970).

programs five days a week for six months, whereas the control group watched cartoons and other non-educational programs in separate rooms. Tests administered before and after the experiment showed that children in the experimental group, irrespective of their age, scored higher than the control group children on concepts taught by *Plaza Sesamo,* namely, general knowledge, understanding of numbers, and letters and words. What is especially interesting is that the experimental group also scored higher than the control group on cognitive tasks that were *not* taught by the program, namely, understanding of spatial concepts and relationships of parts to wholes, competence in sorting and classifying objects and symbols, ability to identify geomet-ric figures embedded in mazes, and oral comprehension (see Figure 3-4). The results of this experiment indicate that children who are exposed to stimuli designed to expand their understanding of their environment not only are able to learn the concepts and skills that are taught but are also sufficiently stimulated to pick up unrelated cognitive skills.

SOCIAL DEVELOPMENT

Social Competence and the Curriculum

One of the major educational trends in the last seventy years or so has been the expansion of the cur-

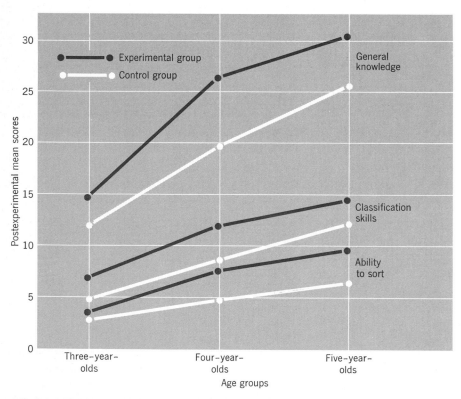

FIG. 3-4. Mean scores on a general-knowledge and two cognitive-skill tests made by two groups of Mexican preschool children: (1) an experimental group who saw televised programs of *Plaza Sesamo* for six months, and (2) a control group who saw noneducational television programs for the same period (data from Diaz-Guerrero and Holtzman, 1974).

riculum beyond the narrowly academic pattern of the nineteenth century into the area of social competence. This change has come about partly because parents, employers, and the community at large demanded that the school take some responsibility for developing social competencies in children, and partly because of a growing realization on the part of psychologists and educators that it was impractical and inefficient to separate intellectual development from social development. Thus in 1918 we find the National Education Association showing a concern for social maturity in formulating its "seven cardinal principles of education": health, command of the fundamental processes, worthy home membership, vocation, citizenship, worthy use of leisure, and ethical character. Social maturity was also an important consideration in 1938 when the Educational Policies Commission of the National Education Association set forth a series of educational objectives concerned with the capabilities, understandings, and attitudes the Commission members felt students should attain as a result of the educational process. Much of what we attempt to teach in schools today has been included in the curriculum because we feel that it will help individuals cope with the problems of life. And most of the problems of life grow out of relations with others— that is to say, they are problems of social adjustment. Hence it follows that the need to develop social maturity is to a large degree the rationale of education: It is the "why" of education.

Directions of Social Development

The word "development" means, essentially, an "unfolding," and the direction of all growth follows this pattern in its general outward movement. Arms and legs grow outward from the center of the body, and the mouth can perform the intricate motions of eating and speaking long before the fingers have developed an equal degree of dexterity. And so it is with social development. The infant is at first completely self-concerned, but with successive stages of maturity his mother, his father, and then the other members of his family become objects of concern to him. During the preschool years he becomes moderately interested in playmates outside the family, but an active interest in outsiders does not generally appear until he is well into the primary grades. During the school years he acquires some new models for his behavior: Teachers and classmates assume an importance that sometimes rivals that of his family. By adolescence, many youngsters are more likely to take their cues from their peers than they are from their family. The adolescent also becomes involved in a number of different worlds outside the family and school: the employment world, the world of informal groups, the world of organized recreation, and so forth.

We can see this outward direction of development by contrasting the kinds of moral judgments made by children at different ages. At the age of seven, for example, there are two easily discernible modes of judging misbehavior. The less mature one, which Piaget (1948) terms *objective responsibility,* leads children to judge misbehavior in terms of the amount of material damage that results. The more mature mode, *subjective responsibility,* leads children to take into consideration the intentions of the misbehaving individual. A child who accidentally causes minor damage while engaged in taking some cookies would be judged more harshly according to judgments based on subjective responsibility, whereas the child who inadvertently causes major damage while engaged in some innocent type of behavior would be judged more harshly according to judgments based on objective responsibility.

Lawrence Kohlberg (1969) has conducted a large number of investigations over the last two decades and has further elaborated Piaget's concepts of children's moral stages. Like Piaget, Kohlberg views the child's moral development as proceeding from the specific to the general, from self-centered and immediate concerns to concerns about the welfare of others that are grounded on general principles. His interviews of children and adolescents have led him to conclude that the course of moral development takes place in the following stages:

PRECONVENTIONAL STAGES

Stage 1. Punishment and obedience orientation. At this stage, the child is primarily concerned with keeping out of trouble and thus avoiding pain, restriction of freedom, and anxiety. This stage corresponds to Piaget's objective responsibility.

Stage 2. Instrumental-relativist orientation. The child is still preoccupied with his own needs but realizes that others have rights as well. Hence he is sometimes willing to "make a deal" which attempts to meet the needs of all parties in an equitable fashion.

CONVENTIONAL MORALITY

Stage 3. Nice-girl/good-boy orientation: the "golden rule." At this stage the child has learned to enjoy the good will of others and now seeks to gain their approval and please them. He conforms to stereotyped versions of social norms and takes the intentions of others, as well as his own, into consideration in making judgments. Piaget's "subjective responsibility" appears in this stage.

Stage 4. Law-and-order orientation. The child recognizes that social order depends on the willingness of individuals to "do their duty" and to respect properly constituted authority.

POSTCONVENTIONAL STAGES

Stage 5. Social-contract orientation. Right actions tend to be defined in terms of standards, requirements, and rights that society has agreed upon. With proper procedure, these regulations may be changed, hence judgments made at this stage are more flexible than those made at Stage 4. Most emotionally mature adults are able to function at this stage, at least on occasion.

Stage 6. Universal-ethical-principle orientation. In making choices, the individual not only considers the rules of society but also the extent to which universal ethical principles apply. In extreme instances, the individual may permit himself to be publicly humiliated or even martyred in order to stand up for these principles. Relatively few individuals attain this stage of development.

Kohlberg's investigations, which have been undertaken in a number of different cultures, convince him that individuals go through these stages in in-

variant order, that is, a child cannot begin with Stage 2 but must first experience Stage 1. Furthermore, most individuals, adults and children alike, irrespective of their stage of maturity, make their decisions according to a number of orientations. An eight-year-old, for example, may make most of his moral decisions at the nice-girl/good-boy stage but under stress may revert to Stage 2 or even Stage 1. Figure 3-5 shows the modes of moral judgment that prevail at various ages during childhood and adolescence.

Morality and Social Learning

Social learning, as conceptualized by Albert Bandura (1969), is based on what we would call "imita-

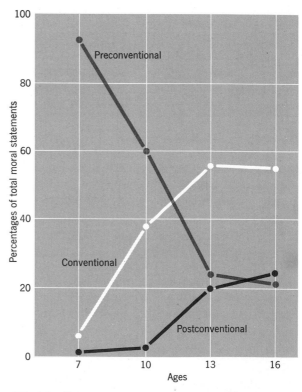

FIG. 3-5. Percentages of children and adolescents at various stages making moral judgments categorized according to preconventional, conventional, and postconventional modes (after Kohlberg, 1963).

tion'' in everyday language. The individual whose behavior is imitated becomes a *model* for the imitator, and Bandura therefore uses the term *modeling* to describe the social learning process. The more conservative behaviorists, such as B. F. Skinner, maintain that individuals learn acceptable forms of social behavior when certain acts meet with the approval of others and hence are reinforced. Social learning theorists, such as Bandura, maintain that if this were the only way that social behavior were acquired, a child would have to attempt various kinds of actions until he happened to hit on one that would meet with the approval of an adult or a peer, whereupon it would be reinforced. Bandura points out, however, that such a concept of learning is unrealistic because it does not indicate how the child happened to express the new behavior in the first place. The explanation of the new behavior, according to Bandura, is imitation or modeling. The child therefore acquires more mature forms of making moral judgments by copying them from models—from adults or from other children who have some degree of status.

In an experiment to show the significance of models in the acquisition of social behavior, Bandura and Frederick J. McDonald (1963) had children aged five to eleven participate in one of several types of experimental situations. The children had first been tested in order to determine whether they were using an objective or a subjective mode of judging moral conduct according to Piaget's classification. In one experimental situation, the children observed an adult model who expressed moral judgments contrary to the mode that they were using. Some of the children were reinforced (praised) for adopting the same style of judgment as the model, whereas others were not and merely observed. A third group had no contact with the model but were reinforced for making judgments counter to their usual mode of judgment. Results showed that children who were exposed to the behavior of the model showed the most change, and it hardly mattered whether they were reinforced or not. Those who were reinforced only, and who did not observe the model, showed only small changes.

The study suggests that as far as moral judgments are concerned, children are more likely to be influenced by the behavior of others, particularly those whom they respect, than they are by reinforcement of their behavior. Although the study was concerned only with the learning of modes of moral judgment, it has implications for a wide range of children's behavior. It suggests that the learning of more mature modes of social behavior is more influenced by the models to which children are exposed than by the extent to which children are reinforced. In other words, the ''Do as I say, not as I do'' approach is likely to have little lasting influence on children's behavior because they are more inclined to attend to what the adult does, rather than to what he says.

Another attempt to reverse children's modes of moral judgment was made by William G. Le Furgy and Gerald W. Woloshin (1968) whose subjects, aged eight to sixteen, heard the voices of what they thought were other children in the experiment making judgments contrary to their own. The method was found to be exceedingly effective in getting children to adopt more mature modes of moral judgment, but it was less effective in getting them to revert to less mature modes. These children, however, were considerably older than the children in the study by Bandura and McDonald and were probably more sophisticated. In any event, the Le Furgy and Woloshin experiment shows that the modeling process continues to operate throughout childhood and adolescence and that peers play a significant role as models for social learning.

EMOTIONAL OR AFFECTIVE DEVELOPMENT

Emotional Maturity

We used to believe, when we thought that education was purely an intellectual or cognitive experience, that emotions and feelings had no place in the classroom, but the evidence that the affective side of life—emotions and feelings—cannot be excluded is now overwhelming. A child will not learn as long as he does not want to learn, sees no sense in learning, or is preoccupied with other problems. It is, of course, possible for skillful teachers to help children develop the feelings and attitudes that are vital prerequisites to learning, and this is what effective teachers actually do, often without being consciously aware that they are dealing with children's emotions. The necessity to consider the affective aspects of learning, group behavior, and individual behavior is discussed at greater length and in various contexts throughout this book, since everything that happens in the classroom is in some way related to the emotions of persons participating in the learning situation. Everyone, including the teacher, brings his feelings into the classroom.

Boaz Kahana and Eva Kahana (1970) have pointed out that all developmental theorists, including Piaget and Freud, emphasize the interrelationship of affective and cognitive processes. Thinking cannot develop unless a child has been able to establish control over his impulses and has learned how to delay gratification, that is, has learned to wait his turn, to plan for future rewards, and to accept the reality of a world in which instant fulfillment of wants and wishes is usually impossible.

To test the theorized relationship between impulse control and cognitive functioning, Kahana and Kahana compared scores on intelligence and problem-solving tests with the willingness of second-grade boys to choose a larger reward to be given after a delay of several days, in preference to a smaller reward to be given immediately. Results showed that boys who were willing to accept the delay functioned on a higher cognitive level than those who behaved more impulsively. Results of other tests, however, showed that too much impulse control interfered with abstract thinking.

One characteristic that is associated with emotional immaturity is dogmatism, or the rigid adherence to a certain viewpoint, coupled with an unwillingness to consider other points of view or contrary data. Inasmuch as the learning of complex concepts requires a degree of openness and flexibility on the part of the student, it is obvious that tenden-

cies to be dogmatic would seriously impede his academic progress. Popular belief ordinarily holds that children are more teachable than teenagers and adults because their minds (hence their attitudes) are as yet unformed. Teenagers, on the other hand, have the reputation of being negativistic, rigid, and arrogant—attitudes characteristic of dogmatism. Some research by C. C. Anderson (1962) of the University of Alberta, however, shows that there is actually a decline in the amount of dogmatism during the teen years (see Figure 3-6). The relationship between dogmatism and cognitive ability is further demonstrated by Anderson's finding that the dogmatism of the more intelligent students declines more sharply than that of the less intelligent ones.

Phases of Emotional Development

Erik Erikson, a psychoanalytic writer, has undertaken a classification of the way in which emotional stages of development are correlated with cognitive and social development (see Table 3-1). He identifies each stage of emotional development by the kind of psychosocial crisis which is likely to occur and which, if handled successfully, enables the individual to deal adequately with the kind of crisis and problem that he will encounter at the next stage of development. Each crisis is described in terms of both the favorable and unfavorable outcomes of dealing with the problems that occur. For example,

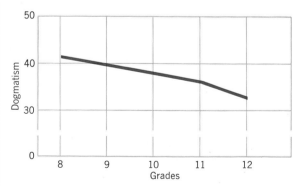

FIG. 3-6. Decrease in dogmatism during the high school years (Anderson, 1962).

TABLE 3-1. Outline Presentation of Erikson's Eight Developmental Phases[a]

Periods	Psychosocial Crises	Relationships with	Experiences, Decisions, and Choices
Infancy	Trust versus mistrust	Maternal person	To get; give in return
Early childhood	Autonomy versus shame, doubt	Paternal person	To hold (on); to let (go)
Play age	Initiative versus guilt	Basic family	To make (= going after); to "make like" (= playing)
School age	Industry versus inferiority	Neighborhood; school	To make things (= completing); to make things together
Adolescence	Identity and repudiation versus identity diffusion	Peer groups and outgroups; models of leadership	To be oneself (or not to be); to share being oneself
Young adult	Intimacy and solidarity versus isolation	Partners in friendship, sex, competition, cooperation	To lose and find oneself in another
Adulthood	Generativity versus self-absorption	Divided labor and shared household	To make be; to take care of
Mature age	Integrity versus disgust and despair	Mankind; my kind	To be, through having been; to face not being

[a] After Erikson, 1959.

during the play-age period, which occurs before the child enters school, the child may develop a degree of initiative about undertaking activities, or he may learn to feel guilty about doing things on his own. The family is the model and the reinforcer in this kind of learning. Some families encourage and reward initiative; others look upon it with disfavor and may raise the question of whether the child is trying to be "different" or "better" than the other members of the family. The child who feels guilty about initiating activities is also likely to experience failures during the school age. Instead of becoming productive and learning to work together with classmates, he will be inclined to be plagued by feelings of inferiority and self-doubt and consequently will withdraw from activities involving achievement or cooperation.

Adults tend to be far more concerned about the need to help children establish emotional controls than they are about helping them to find socially acceptable ways of *expressing* their emotions. Yet the two problems are interrelated. The child who does not have an adequate outlet for his emotions, who cannot tell others how he feels, is the child who will create difficulties for himself and those around him. This is why school teachers and administrators today think it important to introduce students to free, rather than rigidly prescribed, art experiences, to provide for a variety of supervised playground activities, and to give students opportunities to talk about things that are important to them, either in group discussions in the classroom or in private conferences with counselors. We are just beginning to recognize that an important part of growing up is learning how to cope with the things that are troublesome, rather than pretending that they do not exist. Nor is emotional maturity entirely negative, for it is equally important to find ways to express positive feelings.

PHYSICAL DEVELOPMENT

Adaptation of the School to Differences in Levels of Maturity

A parent once told me that the thing that caught his eye when he visited his son's fourth-grade classroom during Public Schools Week was the fact that the desks in the room were of different heights. The children had been divided into reading groups of six, two to a desk, and three desks had been brought together so that the members of each group were facing one another. It occurred to him that the working spaces were not very efficient because some of the desks in each group were at different heights. He was wondering whether the variation was for artistic effect or whether it had happened accidentally, when the children all stood up to go out on the playground. Then he noticed that the children, too, were of different heights and that the shorter children were assigned to the lower desks and the taller children to the higher ones. He was quite impressed by the willingness of the school to adjust the furniture of the classroom to the height of each child. It was a marked contrast to the classrooms of his childhood, where all desks were of a uniform height.

Varying the height of desks is, of course, only one of the ways in which we have learned and are still learning to adjust and adapt the school program to the physical needs of children. Programs of recreation and physical education also are obvious attempts to meet the physical needs of youngsters by giving them opportunities to engage in vigorous play and to learn gracefulness and smooth hand-eye coordination. However, our chief concern with physical maturation is to see that the school program does not run counter to the normal physical needs of children. The greater restlessness of small children has led us in the primary grades, for example, to prescribe a shorter school day, punctuated with frequent recesses.

The school does not play as active a role in aiding students to attain physical maturity as it does in aiding them to attain intellectual, social, and emotional maturity. Normal physical growth and development will occur regardless of the content of the school curriculum. However, understanding of child and adolescent behavior is incomplete without some knowledge of patterns of physical maturation. Indeed, as we indicated in our discussion of early- and late-maturing adolescents, the development of emotional and social behavior is to a large degree paced by the rate of physical maturation. The physical changes of puberty are accompanied by new interests and attitudes. Boys and girls who were figuratively at swords' points a few months earlier now find each other's company attractive and enjoyable. During this stage of development they become more conscious of their appearance and size. On the one hand, these changes make for self-consciousness and embarrassment, but on the other, they are used to support demands for greater freedom, independence, and autonomy. As the teenager attains the height and begins to take on the appearance of an adult, he also asks for more of an opportunity to play adult roles. Such demands seldom fail to put adults on the defensive, a position which makes it difficult to be objective and sympathetic in understanding the behavior in question.

Sex Differences in Physical Development

Variations in maturational rates also create problems for the teacher, particularly during the junior high school years. The average girl reaches puberty approximately two years before the average boy, but differences in the age of attaining puberty may run as high as four years within the same sex. Thus a seventh-grade class may contain one or two boys who have already attained puberty and one or two who will not attain it for another four years. Figure 3-7 presents some of these differences in graphic

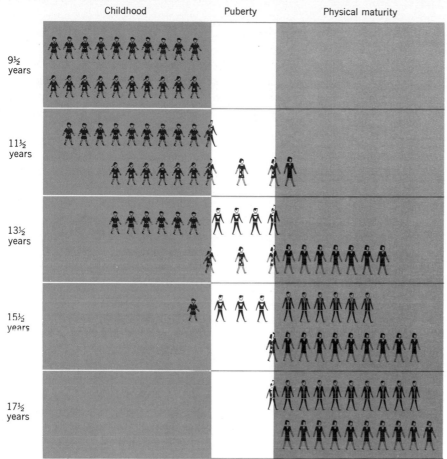

Childhood   Puberty   Physical maturity

9½ years

11½ years

13½ years

15½ years

17½ years

Each boy represents 10 percent of all boys of given age measured
Each girl represents 10 percent of all girls of given age measured

FIG. 3-7. When boys and girls mature (Keliher, 1938; U. S. Public Health Service, 1973).

form. Although these wide gaps in physical maturity are both obvious and important, we sometimes forget that they exist, particularly when we see the same children day after day. But what is even more important, we tend to forget that variations in physical maturity are related to and accompanied by variations in social, emotional, and intellectual maturity. It is therefore unreasonable to have the same expectations for a boy of thirteen who is short and slight and who speaks with a childish soprano that

we have for a girl the same age who could pass for eighteen.

Relationship with Other Types of Development

Although we have focused our attention on significant aspects of physical maturity during the last few paragraphs, what we have said should not be interpreted as indicating that patterns of physical development are more crucial than any other phase of development in determining the pace of intellectual, social, and emotional maturity. Physical changes are but one of the forces that have an effect on behavior, and, in a complex, highly socialized society like ours, other forces may have an even greater impact on behavior. The importance of the nonphysical factors is indicated by a study of the self-concepts of boys twelve to fifteen, conducted by Walter D. Smith and Dell Lebo (1956). Although the researchers found that social maturity was more affected by physical maturity than by chronological age as such, they also found that attitudes relating to interest in girls and emancipation from parents were more affected by chronological age. Smith and Lebo suggested that chronological age was a significant factor because older boys had more opportunities for experience. It is very likely, too, that the groups in which boys participate have a significant effect on their attitudes and other forms of behavior. A number of studies of group behavior has shown that the expectations that group members have for one another may serve as very powerful forces in initiating, directing, or inhibiting behavior patterns.

Nutritional Deficiencies

We should not leave this section without discussing some of the more recent work on the relationship between nutrition and all aspects of development. This area in the past has been somewhat neglected by psychologists, who have been more concerned with cognitive and affective aspects of development. Although common sense would suggest that deficiencies in nutrition would have deleterious effects on all kinds of development, the relationship has not always been clear. This is partly because it is not always easy to determine where the level of malnourishment begins in a relatively prosperous country, as well as how widespread it is, and partly because opportunities for research are, for obvious reasons, not easy to come by. After all, no one wants to set up a controlled experiment in which children are deliberately undernourished in order to determine what effect this would have on their future development! Furthermore, when we discover malnourished children, our natural tendency is to feed them, rather than to maintain them in their underfed condition in order to see how it affects their cognitive functioning.

In recent years, however, a number of studies have appeared that point to a relationship between nutrition and cognitive development. These studies, as reviewed by Henry N. Ricciuti (1970), have dealt with children from poor families in Latin America, India, South Africa, and Colorado who had been undernourished during early childhood. Much more research has been done in correlating nutritional and developmental deficiencies than in finding solutions to the problem. Some early tentative work reviewed by Ricciuti, however, suggests that administration of thiamine (vitamin B_1) brings about improvement in cognitive functioning.

Better nutrition also seems to be at the bottom of a phenomenon that has puzzled physiologists for some time, namely, the downward trend in the age at which girls have their first menstrual period—the *menarche*.[1] Recently, correlations between body weight and menarche show that increases in weight apparently trigger this adolescent event (Frisch and Revelle, 1970). The fact that each succeeding generation of Americans (and Europeans as well) is taller and heavier than the last would thus account for a decline in the age at which puberty occurs.

INDIVIDUAL DIFFERENCES IN GROWTH AND DEVELOPMENT

Consistencies and Inconsistencies Within Individuals

Thus far in this chapter, we have described some of the general trends and sequences of events that characterize the various kinds of maturity and maturation. There are, of course, individual variations that occur within the limits of these trends. This individuality is not, however, haphazard, since there

[1] Since 1840, the age of menarche has declined about four months per decade (Tanner, 1972).

tend to be basic consistencies that identify each individual's pattern of development, as well as his behavior in general. These consistencies appear even at birth. Beverly Birns (1965) found that newborn infants tended to respond not only to certain stimuli (soft tone, loud tone, cold disk, pacifier) with differing degrees of intensity, but that the intensity of their responses also tended to be consistent over a period of several days. In other words, children who reacted sharply to a cold disk also tended to have strong reactions to pacifiers and the other kinds of stimuli that she presented.

Studies of such consistencies in behavior can produce important information for students of human growth and development and for teachers as well. If the behavior patterns of individual children tend to be consistent throughout the years of their development, it becomes possible to plot curves on a graph in order to determine whether a given child is developing at a slower, faster, or average rate. Some studies show that there is some tendency for children to maintain the same relative position when compared with the same group of children on the same measures over a period of time. For example, Samuel R. Pinneau and Harold E. Jones (1959) found that nursery school children tended to show consistencies over a period of time in emotional, antisocial, and attention-getting behavior, although they also found little or no consistency in a number of other aspects of behavior they studied. The very complexity of human behavior and the internal and external forces that bear upon it make the identification and isolation of consistent patterns most difficult

The lack of consistency in individual patterns of development is also demonstrated by Figure 3-8, which shows the differences in reading development displayed by two girls of superior intelligence. Girl A and Girl B started at about the same point in reading ability, but Girl A showed more rapid progress for the first three years. Then Girl B improved very rapidly and caught up with Girl A within the space of eighteen months. It is interesting and useful to learn that Girl A had entered the prepuberal

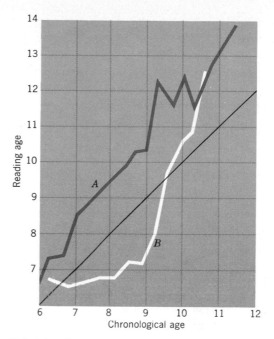

FIG. 3-8. Contrasted patterns of growth in reading age for two girls who reached similar status at age eleven (Olson, 1949).

stage of development when she was nine, that Girl A displayed more emotional and social maturity in nursery school than Girl B did, that Girl A's mother started to menstruate when she was fourteen, and that Girl B's mother did not start till she was seventeen.

But what about the fourth-grade teacher who had both Girl A and Girl B in her class? Both children were then nine years old. Girl A was some eighteen months advanced in reading, and Girl B was some eighteen months retarded. Who would have known, at that point, that both children would have a reading age of twelve when they were ten and a half?

What this comparison shows, among other things, are some of the risks teachers run in making predictions about children that are based on measurements made at any single point in time. Even a series of measurements can be misleading. Suppose that we had tried to predict the future reading development of Girls A and B on the basis of their growth in this ability through their eighth year. We would have been tempted to say that Girl A would continue to progress rapidly, but that Girl B, in spite of possessing above-average intelligence, would continue to lag. We would, of course, have been correct about our prediction for Girl A but wide of the mark for Girl B.

Some of the more conservative critics of education have deplored the fact that all adolescents, irrespective of their level of intelligence, attend common high schools in most American communities, whereas in England each child is classified by examination at age eleven and assigned to one of three levels of schools in accordance with his examination grade and the recommendation of his elementary school. Unfortunately, the British system creates problems for the late-maturing child whose best abilities may not appear until age fourteen or fifteen. Cases like Girl B are not unusual; it is quite common for high school students who have been indifferent students in elementary school and junior high to show a belated awakening of interest in school matters, an interest that is accompanied by a dramatic increase in marks.

The difficulties and problems that beset our attempts to predict the behavior of students indicate some of the pitfalls to be encountered when we fail to make allowances for individual variations. The school is an institution that is interested in fostering all aspects of maturity, especially intellectual maturity, but maturity is a quality that each individual attains in his own way and at his own pace.

Accelerated and Retarded Development

When an adolescent enters the puberal cycle earlier or later than his peers, however, some rather interesting patterns of behavior are likely to appear. A number of studies conducted by the Institute of Human Development at the University of California in Berkeley show that early-maturing adolescents tend to have an advantage over late-maturing adolescents. Early-maturing boys and girls were found by researchers to possess a better degree of psychological adjustment than late maturers, and early-maturing girls appeared to have more prestige in

junior high school than late maturers. Early maturers were also more likely to be student leaders and to show other evidences of popularity. Late-maturing boys tended to be more childish—animated, eager, and uninhibited—whereas early maturers were more relaxed and matter-of-fact. The researchers felt that these differences occurred because physically accelerated youths were more likely to be treated as more mature by adults and by other students, whereas late maturers were more likely to be treated as children and to behave accordingly (Jones et al., 1971).

It would be easy to overgeneralize on the basis of these findings and to assume that early and late maturers behave as they do solely because of the differences in their physical development, but such a conclusion would miss the point that both agemates and adults have different expectations for these more mature adolescents. Late and early maturers behave as they do partly in response to the attitudes of others, and these attitudes are in turn based to a large extent on the youngsters' physical appearance.

Although physical development can have a marked effect on the attitudes and expectations that others have for a given child, as we have shown previously, it sometimes happens that the way in which others behave toward a child also has an effect on the developmental skills, such as the ability to sit alone, crawl, and walk, which are usually associated with degrees of physical maturation. A partial substantiation for this statement may be found in a study by Wayne Dennis (1960) who observed the behavior of young children in three institutions for foundlings and orphans in Tehran, capital of Iran. One hospital, which we shall call Institution A, had a population of six hundred infants, three years and less in age, 90 percent of whom had been there since they were a few weeks old. The ratio of children to attendants was about eight to one. The children in this hospital received little or no handling or personal attention; furthermore, they had no toys and no visitors. Institution B was established a year before Dennis' research. Its population consisted of children from Institution A who showed the greatest degree of developmental retardation. However, children in Institution B received a great deal more attention than they did in Institution A. They were held while being fed and were supplied with toys. There was a plentiful supply of specially trained attendants, enough to assign one attendant to only three or four children. The results of this special attention are shown in Figure 3-9, which indicates that the children in Institution B were developmentally far advanced over those in Institution A.

Dennis reported that when children from Institution A went on to an institution for orphans aged three and older, they eventually developed normal behavior. He attributes the differences in development depicted in Figure 3-9 to lack of learning opportunities experienced by children in Institution A, but the work of other researchers suggests that the meager amount of personal attention may also have been a factor. In fact, Dennis' own more recent research, conducted with children in a foundling home in Beirut, Lebanon, bears this out. Dennis (1973) found that children placed in homes for

adoption showed increases in IQ that in some instances were dramatic, whereas the IQs of the children who stayed on in the orphanage remained at an extremely low level.

Still another study that shows a relationship between physical development and social stimulation was conducted a number of years ago by E. M. Widdowson (1951), who observed children in two German orphanages shortly after the end of World War II. Her findings suggested that the amount and kind of attention children receive may affect their physical growth and development as measured by gains in weight. The original intention of the study was to determine the effect of a more adequate diet on the gains made in weight over the period of a year. During the first six months of the study the children received only the meager rations of food that were generally available in postwar Germany. During the second six months, the children in one of the orphanages received supplemental rations of food. It was expected, of course, that the children receiving supplemental rations would show marked gains in weight.

The results did not turn out as anticipated, however. During the first six months when all children were on meager rations, the children at the first orphange gained only one third as much weight as the children at the second orphanage, where the gain was close to normal. During the second six months, the children at the second orphanage where the gain had been normal were given augmented rations, but much to the surprise of the group making the study, the children gained less than they had before receiving the extra food. At the first orphanage, in the meantime, the children started to gain rapidly, even though they were getting the same meager rations as before. Investigation indicated that the probable cause of the paradoxical results lay in the behavior of the matrons who were supervising the homes. The matron at the first home during the first six months (when the gain was subnormal) was a harsh, unpleasant, domineering woman, whereas the matron at the second home, where the children were gaining normally, was a bright, happy, motherly person. At the begin-

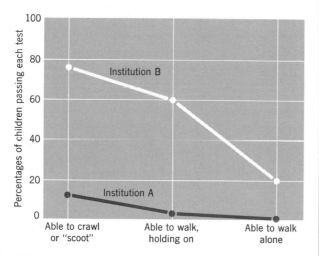

FIG. 3-9. Percentages of two-year-old children passing developmental tests in two Iranian institutions: Institution A, in which they received little personal attention and had little opportunity to play; and Institution B, in which they received considerably more personal attention and handling and also had much opportunity for play (after Dennis, 1960).

ning of the second six months, the pleasant matron of the second home left and was replaced by the harsh matron of the first home. The latter, in turn, was replaced by a third woman, who was a cheerful, motherly type of person. Hence the normal gains in weight occurred when the children were supervised by a cheerful, motherly type of matron, and the abnormally low gains occurred when they were supervised by a harsh, unpleasant, domineering matron. The implications of this study appear to be that when children's normal needs for love are thwarted over a period of time, their physical development may be retarded.

Providing for Individual Differences

When we discussed Maslow's hierarchy of needs in Chapter 2, we noted that the need for love and attention is fundamental to other social needs. It is a need that is most pronounced during the preschool years, when children are just learning to cope with the immediate social environment of the family. By the time children enter school, they are normally concerned with higher-level needs associated with group membership, belongingness, and status. From time to time, however, the need for love and attention comes to the fore, even for children with normal family experiences. This is especially true in times of stress. The need is never far beneath the surface, however, especially for young children, and many a teacher has found that a little personal attention works wonders in helping children cope with the demands of the learning situation.

Many children come from backgrounds in which love and attention are in scarce supply. Perhaps there is only one parent, or perhaps the attention that is available has to be shared among six or eight or more other children. When such children enter school they are likely to be either very demanding of attention or to have learned through chronic disappointment to play passive, noninvolved roles. It is a continuing and usually unresolved problem for teachers, especially in the primary grades, as to how far they should go in meeting children's needs for love and attention. With experience, teachers usually come to realize that limitations imposed on them by time, the competing and often simultaneous demands of two or three dozen children, and the requirements of their professional role make it impossible for them to make up for what a child misses at home. In the end, most teachers learn to do their best with the time and resources at their command. They are also reassured by the knowledge that most of these children eventually come to terms with their needs and the resources of their social environment and develop expectations that are appropriate for their age and stage of development. One feels that this process is more likely to take place, or takes place more rapidly, where teachers provide as much individual attention and support as they can and at the same time foster the development of attitudes of mutual warmth, acceptance, and fellowship within the classroom group.

Needs for love and attention are only part of the picture, of course. The role that the school must play in helping youngsters develop mature behavior varies with different aspects of maturity and with different individuals. Sometimes the school must stimulate and encourage, sometimes it must guide, sometimes it must enforce limits and controls, and sometimes it must stand aside and not interfere. The attitude of "hands off" is perhaps the hardest role for the teacher to play, yet there are times when youngsters must be permitted to make mistakes or when they must be given freedom to try out some newly discovered ability. Deciding when to control and guide and when to stand aside is a difficult task, but on such decisions good teaching depends. There is no rule of thumb to guide the teacher in making such decisions, that is, there is none that is very effective. The ability to make such decisions depends on the teacher's own emotional and social maturity, his love of teaching, and his understanding of children.

SUMMARY

Although the evidences of growth and development in children are all around us, it is difficult to maintain proper perspective and to be properly aware of the progressive changes that are continually taking place. One way of observing and evaluating these changes is to compare them with the amounts and levels of growth and development that are more or less typical of children of the same age. A child whose level of development is up to expectation may be considered reasonably mature for his age. Similarly, other children may be considered immature or advanced, depending on their behavior.

Development of children may be considered in terms of its cognitive (or intellectual), social, emotional (or affective), and physical aspects. In actuality, all these factors are interrelated and interact with each other. Schools traditionally have been preoccupied with cognitive development and have tended to ignore other aspects of development. There is, however, an increasing awareness that all aspects of development must be considered in constructing effective learning situations.

In recent years, the work of Jean Piaget, a Swiss psychologist, has attracted considerable attention on the part of American psychologists and educators. Piaget views cognitive development in terms of well-defined sequential stages in which a child's ability to succeed is determined partly by his biological readiness for that stage and partly by his experiences with activities and problems in previous stages. Piaget especially stresses the importance of sensory experience in learning, as contrasted with indirect experience through reading and being told. In this, his approach is similar to the approach of Maria Montessori, an Italian educator of the first quarter of this century. The theories of Piaget and Montessori are the basis of the innovative methods employed in the British infant schools and the "free schools" in the United States and Canada. Piaget and other European psychologists explain the appearance of cognitive skills in terms of the physiological and experiential development of the child, whereas most American educational psychologists are likely to conceive of such skills as resulting from learning and hence see the child's environment as the major factor. Each of these two points of view is supported by studies. It does appear that Piaget's idea that children go through cognitive stages sequentially is valid, although the age at which they enter and complete the sequence may vary from culture to culture. It also appears that the child's

environment is a crucial factor. For example, children in primitive cultures who receive no schooling may not proceed beyond the more rudimentary cognitive stages. A number of studies also shows that children who are exposed to environments in which they experience considerable verbal stimulation, and are given ample opportunity to learn cognitive skills, also make faster progress than do children in more deprived environments. Of the two large-scale attempts to provide enriched experiences for deprived children—Operation Head Start and the *Sesame Street* television program—*Sesame Street* has been the more successful. The amount of exposure seems to be the important factor. Only those children who attended Head Start programs over extended periods—not merely during the summer—were the ones who demonstrated cognitive gains, and the gains for children who saw *Sesame Street* were in direct proportion to the number of times per week they saw the program.

Although schools were initially concerned with merely the cognitive aspects of development, they have over the years broadened the scope of their activities to include social development as well. Social development moves in an outward direction during the childhood years, as is indicated by changes in the kinds of moral judgments made by children at different ages. Piaget's concepts of moral development have been elaborated by Kohlberg, who notes that children are initially preoccupied with avoiding punishment through obedience and then gradually become concerned about the needs, rights, and intentions of others. Moral development evidently depends on the availability of mature models whose behavior is imitated, a process termed "social learning."

Emotional development is probably basic to a child's ability to develop along cognitive and social lines. Important in this type of development is the ability of the child to exercise reasonable control over his impulses. Erik Erikson has analyzed the way in which stages of emotional development are correlated with stages of cognitive and social development. Perhaps physical development is the most basic of all aspects of development because it provides the bases and sets certain limits for all other types of development.

One of the difficult problems in studying the development of children and adolescents is the task of identifying the basic consistencies in motivational patterns. Recognizing such patterns is a necessary prerequisite to anticipating the developmental trends and problems that lie ahead for a given child, although the uniqueness of each child's pattern of development makes it difficult to make hard and fast predictions about future behavior and performance. There are some basic principles, however, that seem to apply. One is the need children have for love or attention. Another is the orderliness of stages of development. The systems of Kohlberg, Piaget, and Erikson are attempts to help us understand this orderliness.

Suggested Problems

1. Although the children in Miss Martinelli's first grade appear to be healthy and without noticeable defects, she has decided to postpone instruction in reading for about one-third of the class until the second semester. She will instead try to find other tasks for them to work at while she instructs the rest of the class in reading. Why has she made this decision?

2. When the police arrested Raymond for breaking into an elementary school one night and wrecking a classroom, the judge of the juvenile court referred him to the court psychologist for interviewing and testing. The report that the psychologist wrote contained a number of suggestions that the judge found helpful in deciding the action to be taken with Raymond. In his report, the psychologist referred to Raymond as "immature." Actually, Raymond was as tall and as heavy as other fifteen-year-olds, and the fuzz on his chin indicated that his beard was starting to grow. What did the psychologist mean by "immature"?

3. Look at Table 3-1, Erikson's eight developmental phases. What kind of problems might occur during early childhood if psychosocial crises during infancy were resolved in terms of mistrust, instead of trust? What kind of problems would occur during adolescence if crises during the school-age phase were resolved in terms of inferiority, rather than industry?

4. In what ways are Piaget's, Kohlberg's, and Erikson's classification systems similar? In what ways are they dissimilar?

5. Let us say that the school board of Township Manor is considering a proposal to institute concentrated training in cognitive skills in the nursery schools and kindergartens of the school system and decides to have a public hearing to sound out the public on this matter. What kinds of people would speak in favor of the proposal, and who would speak against it?

Suggested Readings

Bruner, J. S. et al. *Studies in cognitive growth.* New York: Wiley, 1966. Examines the growth of three systems for representing information in the developing child: action, imagery, and language. Takes into account the contributions of the culture, as well as the part played by maturational processes.

Cratty, B. J. *Perceptual and motor development in infants and children.* New York: Macmillan, 1970. (A paperback.) A simply written, well-illustrated manual.

Dinkmeyer, D. C. *Child development: The emerging self.* Englewood Cliffs, N.J.: Prentice-Hall, 1965. A general textbook in the area, emphasizing the development of the child's perceived world and his self-concept.

Erikson, E. H. *Childhood and society.* New York: Norton, 1950.

Flavell, J. H. *The developmental psychology of Jean Piaget.* Princeton, N.J.: Van Nostrand, 1963.

Ginsburg, H., and Opper, S. *Piaget's theory of intellectual development: An introduction.* Englewood Cliffs, N.J.: Prentice-Hall, 1969. (A paperback.) A brief introduction written for undergraduates. See particularly the "implications for education" section at the end of the book.

Gordon, I. J. *Studying the child in school.* New York: Wiley, 1966. (A paperback.) Makes a number of practical suggestions as to how teachers can develop a better understanding of the children in their classroom.

Kessen, W. (ed.). *The child.* New York: Wiley, 1965. A collection of papers written between 1693 and

THE GROWTH AND MATURATION
OF THE LEARNER

1942 by such diverse figures as Locke, Rousseau, Darwin, Gesell, John B. Watson, Freud, and Piaget.

Lindgren, H. C., and Lindgren, F. (eds.). *Current readings in educational psychology.* New York: Wiley, 1972. See Section 2, "Growth and development of the learner."

Mussen, P. H., Conger, J. J., and Kagan, J. *Child development and personality,* 4th ed. New York: Harper and Row, 1974.

Watson, R. I., and Lindgren, H. C. *The psychology of the child,* 3rd ed. New York: Wiley, 1973.

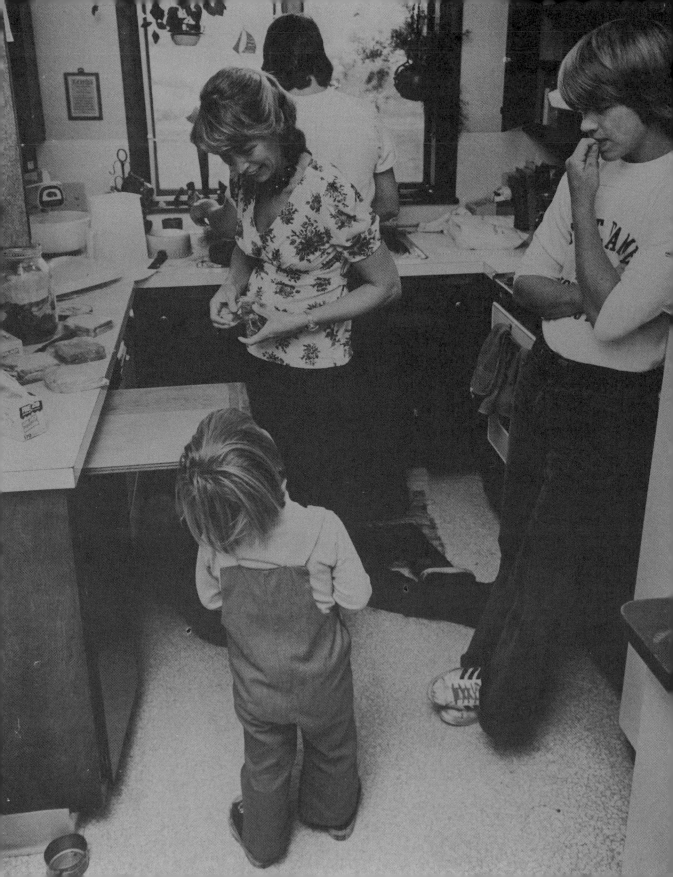

4

The Learner and His Family

The two preceding chapters have mainly been concerned with the learner's behavior as it is affected by "internal" forces, forces that are largely motivational in character. In order to fill out the picture of the learner, in this chapter and in the one that follows, we shall move the focus of our discussion out into the learner's social environment, beginning first with his family and then examining his relationships with his peers: his playmates, classmates, and friends.

It is quite obvious, when we stop to think about it,

that students do a great deal of learning outside the classroom. But sometimes we become so preoccupied with the task of teaching them social studies or reading or short division that we forget the larger learning situation in which they participate. We forget that they have accomplished a vast amount of nonacademic learning before they enter school and that they continue to learn from nonacademic sources while they are enrolled in school and after they graduate. This chapter and the one that follows will to a large extent be concerned with social learning—the nonacademic learning that occurs when children and adolescents interact with their social environment.

The Family as Teacher

The family, not the school, provides the first educational experiences of the child. These experiences begin in infancy with the first attempts to guide and direct the child—to "train" him, as we say. Some of these attempts take place at a conscious level, but most of the time parents are not aware that they are attempting to influence behavior at all. Probably most of the training that they undertake deliberately and consciously is not as effective as that which is undertaken unconsciously. This is most especially true of attempts to train infants. Infants *do* learn, but not necessarily what parents think they are teaching them.

> Mrs. Haskell started to toilet train her son Billy when he was six weeks old. Whenever she thought he was ready to urinate or defecate, she placed him on the toilet. Whenever he soiled his diapers, she scolded him; whenever he urinated or defecated in the toilet she praised him. This went on month after month. Gradually, Billy was soiling himself less frequently. His mother was pleased at his progress, although she wished that he would learn a little faster. Hence, she chided him more severely and occasionally spanked him when he soiled his diapers. Finally, when he was eighteen months old, he started using the toilet almost exclusively for bowel movements, but his bladder training was not complete until he was two years old. When this point was reached, Mrs. Haskell congratulated herself on having done so thorough a job of toilet training her son.

Actually, of course, Mrs. Haskell could have saved herself a great deal of trouble, inasmuch as children establish bowel control on the average at eighteen months and bladder control at twenty-four months, regardless of whether the training is started early or late. Maturation alone will not do the job of toilet training, of course, but starting toilet training before a child is, say, nine or ten months old has been shown to have little influence on the age at which control is established. Hence Billy was not

learning how to control his elimination during the first year of his "education." The progress that Mrs. Haskell thought Billy was making during this period was actually a reflection of her own learning, that is, she was learning to recognize his cycle of elimination and was putting him on the toilet at times that coincided with it. He was not adjusting his physical processes to her demands, but he was adjusting her demands to the timing of his physical processes.

Learning that Occurs Incidentally and Unintentionally

Although Billy did not learn to control his elimination during his first year, this does not necessarily mean that he learned nothing from his experience. Perhaps he learned that his mother was anxious about bowel and bladder functioning. Perhaps, because he was so often unable to meet her demands, he got the idea that his mother was disappointed in him. Or perhaps he got the idea that his mother would always be fluttering around him or hovering over him, anxiously looking, watching, waiting. Mrs. Haskell obviously was not aware that she was teaching Billy any of these things. On the conscious level, she thought she was teaching good habits of elimination, but below this level of awareness she was teaching Billy something about her attitudes toward elimination, dirtiness, and even toward life in general.

This kind of learning and teaching at different levels of awareness goes on all the time, in and out of school. Parents and teachers are always teaching simultaneously at different levels of awareness, and children are always learning simultaneously at different levels. Things taught or learned consciously may or may not be important and may or may not "stick." But what is taught and learned unconsciously is more likely to remain. You can test this by thinking back over your own school career. You probably have forgotten most of the facts you learned in high school (research indicates that most of what is learned formally is forgotten within a few months), but you are much more likely to remember the teachers you had and the kind of persons they were, particularly the attitudes you had toward them and they had toward you.

And so it is with learning that takes place in the family. Whatever it is that a child learns during the preschool years, he most definitely learns what feelings his parents have toward him and toward life in general. And these feelings are the basis for each child's concept of himself, the world, and his place in the world. A child who is despised learns to despise himself; a child who is accepted is likely to develop attitudes of self-acceptance.

Basic values are likely to be learned during these early years. These values enter into every phase of life experience and include attitudes toward success, competition, problem solving, self-expression, and many other areas of life, as well as the homely virtues of honesty, industry, cooperation, obedience, and the like, depending on what kinds of behaviors are reinforced by parents. A mother who always responds to her child's needs for affection but ignores (and, indeed, may be unaware of) his attempts at problem solving tends to reinforce affection-seeking behavior (emotional dependence) but not intellectual or cognitive striving. Albert Bandura and Aletha C. Huston (1961) found that nurturant behavior (behavior characterized by attentiveness and warmth) led children to copy the mannerisms of the adult who was teaching them to do a problem, but these children were not more successful in learning the task that she was teaching them than were children whose teacher was cool and detached: In other words, a loving relationship seems to lead to an emotional kind of identification, but it does not in and of itself stimulate cognitive development. Something more seems to be needed.

A child is typically quick to note what parents turn their attention to and he thus learns what their values are—what they believe is important. Inasmuch as parents are the models for behavior during the preschool years, it is hardly surprising that most children take on their values. We should remind ourselves here that we are referring to the values that are implicit in the parents' behavior, which may not be the ones that parents subscribe to publicly. Parents may be shocked to learn that their fourth-grade child is two years retarded in reading, yet in-

quiry will show that the parents' own reading is confined to newspaper headlines, comics, and the sports page, and that their recreation is limited to television, movies, radio and chatting with friends and neighbors. Where reading has little value for parents, it is likely to have little value for children.

Some of the relationships between children's behavior and parental values may be indicated by one of the many studies in this field of research. Anita Whiting (1970) interviewed parents of two groups of elementary school boys. One-half the boys were achieving successfully in school work; the other half were not. The mean IQ of both groups was "high average": 114 and 113, respectively. In every instance, the parents of the successful boys made it clear that they expected their children to master basic skills (dressing self, pouring milk, crossing a residential street) at earlier ages than did the parents of the unsuccessful boys. There were other differences between the two groups of parents as well, but one interpretation of Whiting's results is that the achieving boys somehow picked up the idea that their parents expected success, whereas the nonachieving boys had somehow sensed that their parents expected less of them.

We should not of course, overlook the fact that there are no hard-and-fast rules in child rearing. All children pick up values and behavior patterns through social learning, but some are more responsive than others. Nor do parents treat all children alike. The research that we reported earlier with respect to firstborns shows one major dimension of difference in child rearing; other factors are harder to pin down. How parents react to the behavior characteristic of a child appears to be of considerable importance in determining what the child becomes.

THE FAMILY SITUATION

Change and Instability

One of the most useful approaches to understanding the behavior of children is that of studying their family situation. The cumulative school records of students are full of answers to such questions as the following. How many children are in the family? Where does this child appear in the birth order—oldest, middle, youngest, or only? Has the family moved a great deal or has it lived at one address since the child began school? What is the father's occupation? Is the mother employed? How much schooling do the parents have? Do grandparents, other relatives, or boarders live in the home? Is this a home broken by divorce, death, or the prolonged or frequent absence of one or both parents?

School people ask such questions because they are looking for clues that will help them understand the student's general behavior and particularly his behavior as a learner. A student's ability to learn is likely to be affected by the presence or absence of marked changes in the home situation. Many children, particularly during their younger years, get tense, upset, and even behave in an immature fashion following the birth of a brother or sister. Sometimes the disturbance is the result of family moves. Americans move more frequently than any other national group: One family in five moves annually, and of those families who move, one-third cross county lines. The restless pace of constant change, which Alvin Toffler (1970) described in *Future Shock,* his classic analysis of today's culture, is hard enough on adults, but it makes life even more difficult for children.

What used to be called "the broken home," and today goes by the term "the single-parent family," is a course of additional stress for many children. U.S. Census reports for 1970 showed that one family in eight was headed by a single adult, and in nine single-adult families out of ten, the head of the family was a woman. Furthermore, the incomes, housing arrangements, and life styles of the majority of these single-parent families clearly reflect the economic disadvantages they suffer in comparison to other families (Taeuber, 1972). In recent years the number of single-parent homes headed by better-educated adults has increased, especially in urban and suburban areas.

It is difficult to discuss the problems of children from single-parent homes without becoming involved in a debate on such issues as the right of a parent to live without a spouse, the problems of the mother who lives on welfare, the responsibility of divorced or otherwise separated spouses to support their families, and so forth. Society has not found an adequate solution for these pressing problems, and the prevailing public mood seems to be that of defending the right of adults to choose their life style rather than that of concern about the difficulties that are created for children.

There seems to be little doubt that the welfare of children is likely to be affected. Every study that has been made in this area shows that the greater the instability of the family and its living arrangements, the greater the likelihood that children's emotional and behavioral problems will be aggravated. There is relatively little that the school can do about family difficulties, even though the child whose problems are being caused or aggravated by a troubled home situation is more likely to experience problems in learning or adapting to classroom programs.

Success in classroom learning depends to a considerable degree on children being willing to trust adults and to work at tasks that are often demanding, frustrating, and even tedious, in the expectation of future rewards. Although some school work is programmed in such a way that children get immediate results and reinforcement, a great deal of it depends on sustained effort over long periods of time—weeks, months, and even years. Children whose fathers are absent from homes by reason of divorce or desertion tend to have more difficulties in working under conditions of postponed rewards. This tendency has been demonstrated repeatedly by experiments in which children perform small tasks for a researcher and then are given the choice of a small reward immediately or a larger reward a week or so later. Studies conducted along these lines show that children from father-absent homes are much more inclined to choose immediate rather than delayed rewards, whereas children from intact homes are more willing to settle for delayed rewards (Mischel, 1958; Wohlford and Liberman, 1970). The implication of such findings seems to be that children from father-absent homes have less confidence in the future and are less able to trust adults.

What If the Mother Works?

Because children from single-parent homes are likely to have more problems, there is a general belief that the mother's employment is also detrimental to a child's welfare. Such homes may even appear "partially broken" because of the mother's absence during a good portion of the day. People also raise questions as to whether mothers who enjoy working "really love their children" and suggest that they are "shirking their duties and responsibilities." Inasmuch as about a half of the mothers of school children are employed outside the home either part or full time, this fact could constitute a major threat to children's emotional health and to their progress in school.

A review of a number of studies by Lois Wladis Hoffman (1974) indicates that the bad effects of maternal employment on children's behavior are probably exaggerated and that in many instances children are better off in their mother works. This is especially true in many single-parent families where maternal employment is an absolute necessity for survival. Working mothers are more likely to stress independence training, and daughters of working mothers tend to have higher IQs and to be more positively oriented toward achievement than are other girls. Hoffman could find no evidence that the children of working mothers are emotionally deprived. Although these women spend less time in the home than do nonworking mothers, they generally take special pains to give particular attention to their children by way of compensation for their absence, and this appears to make up for any deficit in attention due to their absence.

The studies of the effects of single-parent homes and employed mothers indicate, among other things, how dangerous it is to prejudge children on the basis of only one or two facts. Knowing that a child comes from a single-parent home or a family in which both parents are employed is only one item among the many factors that may influence his behavior. In many instances, such a fact may not in itself be very significant. For example, degree of happiness in a home has been found to be a key factor in determining whether adolescents will become delinquent, and unhappy homes in which both parents are present produce more delinquents than do single-parent homes in general (Nye, 1958).

The Emotional Climate of the Family

One aspect of the interaction between children and parents is what psychologists term the "emotional climate" of the family. Emotional climate may be thought of as the generalized attitudes and feelings that prevail in the family group.

> The members of the Case family are always bickering, yet underneath they feel a deep attachment for one another. During times of crisis, they work effectively together as a cooperative team.

> The morale in the Spencer family is chronically low. No one expects things to turn out right. Mr. Spencer cannot hold a job, Mrs. Spencer has been in the hospital twice for an obscure stomach ailment, and six-year-old Ruby is on the point of being sent to an institution for the mentally retarded. No one in this family bothers about carrying out or even making plans. The typical mode of conduct is to take what you can while you have the chance, regardless of who gets hurt. There is an underlying bitterness that colors the entire relationship among the members of the family.

> The members of the Kohl family spend most of their time doing hard farm work. They do not talk very much, except to evaluate what they have done and to plan the work that lies ahead. The need to work hard and keep the wolf from the door commands most of their attention and draws them close together. At the present time, they are beginning to find more leisure time than they had formerly and are spending it in church work. This helps keep them together because it enables them to share the same experiences and to maintain a feeling of closeness.

The attitudes, feelings, thoughts, and general behavior of the children from these three family units will reflect the emotional climate prevailing in their homes. If a child gets a sense of security from his home, such a feeling will enable him to cope more adequately with the tasks of classroom learning and other problems he encounters at school, but the more the home climate is characterized by such qualities as punitiveness, disorganization, or extreme rigidity, the more likely it is to produce problem behavior in children.

How Children's Behavior and Parental Attitudes Interact

Many of the studies of the relationships between parental attitudes and children's behavior have directly or indirectly made comparisons between homes where the prevailing atmosphere tends to be democratic or equalitarian (that is, where there is an emphasis on tolerance, understanding, and permissiveness) and those where the psychological climate is authoritarian or traditional (that is, where there is an emphasis on unquestioning obedience, conformity to parental wishes, and frequent punishment). Typical of such studies is one by Nancy Bayley (1964), who analyzed data gathered over a long period of time by the California Institute of Human Development (the Berkeley Growth Study) and found that seven-year-old boys were likely to be rated high on cooperativeness by teachers and psychologists if, during the first three years of life, their mothers respected their sons' rights to make their own decisions, evaluated them positively ("He's a good boy"), and expressed affection toward them. Conversely, seven-year-old boys were likely to be rated low on cooperativeness if their mothers were very strict during the first three years, used fear as a means of controlling behavior, and dealt with them in irritable ways. Jerome Kagan and Marion Freeman (1963) similarly found that when mothers dealt with children aged two to four in severely authoritarian ways, the IQs of the children were likely to decline subsequently during preschool and primary school years. In other words, child-rearing methods that are authoritarian appear to interfere with children's later social adjustment and to inhibit intellectual growth to some degree.

Other research indicates that the democratic-authoritarian dimension tells us only part of the story, that the relationships between parental attitudes and children's behavior are actually quite complex. Popular opinion tends to equate democratic child-rearing practices with absolute, unrestrained permissiveness, and this misconception was perpetuated in former years by researchers who classified parental behavior arbitrarily into "permissive" and "punitive" categories. Today investigators are more aware that parental control methods cannot be classified so simplistically, and that there are differences of both degree and kind. Total permissiveness has been found to create almost as many difficulties for a child as extreme punitivity. In the study we referred to earlier, Anita Whiting (1970) observed that the parents of underachieving boys were likely to be *either* highly permissive *or* authoritarian and restrictive. There are qualitative differences as well with respect to the amount of restrictiveness or permissiveness that parents exert.

Diana Baumrind (1967) for example, found a high degree of association between the personality patterns of children and the way in which their parents behaved toward them. She identified three major types of children in her sample of nursery schoolers: the self-reliant child, the immature child, and the anxious child. Self-reliant children were confident, were willing to accept blame when things went wrong, enjoyed the company of other children, followed rules, stood up well in stress situations, and helped other children deal with problems. Immature children cried easily, became childish or hostile when hurt, and were irritable, inconsiderate, boastful, obstructive, apprehensive, and impetuous. Anxious children shared all the traits of the immature children, except that they were not impetuous, and in addition did not enjoy themselves at nursery school, felt no guilt about wrongdoing, had poor relations with adults, and got other children into trouble. Baumrind rated behavior of parents in "structured" situations at the university clinic, as well as in naturalistic situations at home, according to four dimensions: *parental control* (willingness to use a variety of techniques, including firmness, incentives, and reinforcements), *parental maturity demands* (respecting children's decisions and encouraging independence), *parent-child communication* (use of reasoning to secure compliance, encouraging verbal give-and-take, and making it clear parents were the source of power), and *parental nurturance* (acting in supportive and loving ways). As Figure 4-1 indicates, parents of self-reliant children rated high on all four of these

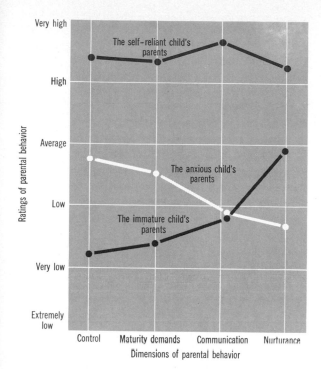

Very high

High

Average

Low

Very low

Extremely low

Ratings of parental behavior

The self-reliant child's parents

The anxious child's parents

The immature child's parents

Control   Maturity demands   Communication   Nurturance

Dimensions of parental behavior

FIG. 4-1. The relationship between personality patterns of nursery school children and the child-rearing practices of their parents (Baumrind, 1967).

dimensions; parents of anxious children tended to make few demands on them and were rated especially low in nurturance; and parents of immature children made even fewer demands, but were at least average in nurturance.

The kind of control parents exercise over their children is also related to their success in high school. In the nationwide survey we referred to previously, 24 percent of the students who were receiving failing grades reported that their parents were extremely strict, in contrast to 15 percent of those with excellent grades who made similar statements. On the other hand, 53 percent of the students making excellent grades, as opposed to 32 percent of the students who were getting failing grades, said that their parents were *moderately* strict (Erlick and Starry, 1970a).

We should note, in passing, that American parents by and large believe that children should be punished physically. A survey of California parents

of children aged three years and younger showed that more than one-half used physical punishment (Heinstein, 1965). This statistic is particularly interesting in view of the fact that, in contrast to parents in other countries, American parents also tend to be more permissive. One interpretation of this apparent contradiction is that within certain limits American parents permit and encourage a high degree of independence and self-determination, but when limits are violated, punishment tends to be severe, at least, as far as preschool children are concerned. We shall have more to say about the permissive attitudes of American parents later in this chapter.

FAMILIES AS AGENTS OF THE CULTURE

Teaching and Learning a "Life Style"

To some extent, the emotional climate of the family reflects the prevailing attitudes of the social culture of which the family is a part. Thus we would expect American family life to emphasize competition, independence, and self-assertion, whereas the family life of certain Southwest Indian tribes, such as the Hopi and Zuñi, would emphasize an approach to life that would be less individualistic and more group-centered. As American children grow into adolescence, it is expected that they will question some of the ideas held by their parents, whereas German children are expected to accept parental opinions at face value. This does not mean that American parents enjoy having their children disagree with them, or even that they encourage such differences with any deliberate or conscious intent. Yet when we compare family life in America and Germany, we are struck by the greater freedom for self-expression and self-assertion enjoyed by the American child. Hence we conclude that there is something about American family life that encourages children to express differences of opinion. Very likely American children behave in this way at least partly because their parents feel that freedom of speech is essential.

From an educational point of view, the family plays the key role in introducing or transmitting the values of the culture to the child. It is through their participation in the daily events of family life that children are expected to learn to value property, law, and order; to respect the rights and feelings of others; to avoid bad company; to be loyal to family and country. To be sure, the school is expected to continue such education, but it performs this function best when it can amplify and enlarge upon the education already begun in the family. And, of course, the family continues to bear the major responsibility for what we call moral education long after the child has started school.

Although there are some fairly basic similarities that characterize most American families, there are some important differences. Each family varies the basic pattern according to its individual needs and tastes, some more, some less. But between the individual variations and the basic pattern, there are some family patterns which are typical of certain groups—subcultures within the larger American culture. Inasmuch as the students in a typical classroom come from a variety of these subcultures, it is important to be aware of some of their characteristics.

Some of the most obvious variations on the basic pattern are the subcultures that develop among groups of people who still have strong ties to other lands—people who have not completely assimilated the American culture and who have not been assimilated by it. Such people are, psychologically speaking, in a marginal position. They are out on the margin of the culture that they left behind and on the margin of the American culture. They are, in effect, "between cultures." Although they may think of themselves essentially as, say, Greek, Italian, or Latin American, they actually think, feel, and act differently from those that they left behind. Their attitudes and behavior patterns may in some ways be quite American, but they differ markedly from those of native-born Americans. When their children "talk back," as so many American children do, they are far more enraged and upset than the typical American parent. Nor are these parents able to accept the higher status that children today enjoy in this country, as contrasted with other countries.

In an analysis of child-rearing practices over two thousand years, the late sociologist, J.H.S. Bossard (1954), pointed out that it has been only in this century, and almost exclusively in America, that children have been assigned status that is in any respect equal to that enjoyed by the adult members of the family. Bossard pointed out that even though we may be inclined to gloss over or obscure the status of children in former years, the plain fact is that they were often systematically and consistently exploited by their parents. During the Colonial Period in American history, children had no rights, except as they happened to fit the needs of their elders. Bossard continued:

("Dennis the Menace." © 1975 by Field Newspaper Syndicate T.M. ®)

"Listen, I may send YOU to bed!"

The democratic relationship that tends to be characteristic of child-parent relationships in America can at times have some rather annoying side effects.

Today the child is regarded as a human personality in a peculiarly vital stage of development. He is a coequal personality in the emerging democracy of the family. The guarding of this personality is the child's precious right, and the dangers that threaten it are recognized social problems; the development of this personality is his most precious opportunity, and the furtherance and guidance of that development are the concern of his elders.

Such attitudes are unfamiliar and disturbing to immigrant parents, coming as they do from cultures where child rearing is conducted along more authoritarian lines than it is in America. Children in other countries live in a great deal more awe of their parents than American children do. Harold and Gladys Anderson (1956) asked children in Finland, Germany, Mexico, and the United States to finish a story in which a boy who has been sent to the store to buy some wieners lost them through his carelessness. American children were much more inclined than were children in other countries to say that the boy should tell his mother the truth and admit his guilt. One interpretation of this difference is that American children are more likely to expect that their parents will treat them with acceptance and understanding in spite of their misdeeds, whereas children from other countries are less confident of such treatment.

Other cross-cultural surveys point up the tendency of American children to reject parental standards in favor of the standards of the peer culture. Urie Bronfenbrenner (1970) asked twelve-year-old children in the Soviet Union and the United States to indicate what they would do in ten hypothetical situations in which they were tempted to do something improper, such as make use of a copy of tomorrow's quiz which they and their friends had inadvertently found. The Russian children demonstrated a significant tendency to conform to adult standards in their replies, whereas American children showed only a slight tendency to do so and were more inclined to accept peer-oriented standards.

The tendency of American children to identify more with their age-mates' values and less with their parents' values is consistent with another pattern of behavior that has attracted the attention of observers: the close ties that bind the members of European, Latin American, and Oriental families, as contrasted with the looseness of American family ties. For instance, an American child is likely to select his playmates from children his own age and to spend his time in play groups composed of his age-mates, whereas a Mexican child is expected to play with his brothers and sisters (Maslow and Diaz-Guerrero, 1960).

Here is another difference between the American culture and the culture of the Old World. When American children grow to adulthood, they are expected to fend for themselves, to set up separate households, and to go into business or into careers of their own choosing, into fields that may be quite different from those of their parents. Families in the Old World and even in Latin America stay much closer together. Grown sons are expected to go into the family business; in many countries, a married son brings his wife to the family home and raises his children there. Family loyalty is a very important virtue in the Old World; the individual looks to his family to protect him against the hazards of life, whereas in America, the individual is expected either to cope for himself or to get help from agencies set up for that purpose. On the one hand the closeness of Old World families increases the emotional security of children, especially during preschool years, but on the other hand, it keeps children from learning to cope with a changing world.

Children's Problems and Culture Conflict

Children of foreign-born parents are subject to a greater number of psychological conflicts and pressures than are other children. Often there is a sense of insecurity, of not knowing what one should do. If the child tries to be the kind of person his parents expect him to be, he finds that this runs counter to what his playmates or his teachers expect him to do. Try as he may, he seems doomed to disappoint either his parents or his friends and teachers. It is hardly surprising, then, that second-generation American students report more than the usual number of problems. A survey taken by Paul Witherspoon (1960) in a San Antonio, Texas, junior high school found that students with Latin American parents encountered more difficulties in adjusting to school than their Anglo-American contemporaries did. As Table 4-1 indicates, they were more inclined to worry about receiving poor grades in school. They felt that they were not bright enough and were afraid to speak up in class. In general, they were more likely to feel inadequate and ineffective. This tendency to blame themselves for their difficulties was in marked contrast to the reactions of their Anglo peers, who were inclined to blame their teachers and the school for their problems.

Students whose parents are strict adherents to certain religious sects also experience special problems, especially if they are in the minority in the school and have been encouraged by their parents to develop a feeling of being quite different from the other children. Often such students are avoided by their classmates and considered to be a group apart. No one enjoys being excluded or rejected, and the usual result is unhappiness and feelings of insecurity and inferiority. Inevitably, tensions and conflicts that affect large groups of students create grave problems for the school. Nor do parents like to see their children excluded and humiliated. One common solution to this problem has been for parents to place their children in a parochial school, where they will not be subject to the prejudice and open hostility of other children. Another solution employed by Amish parents in Pennsylvania is to form school districts of their own, so that the majority of children in attendance will be Amish. Still another solution is that of providing some of the instruction, especially in primary grades, in the native language of the children's parents. Spanish is the language most frequently employed. The idea underlying this policy is that adjustment to school is facilitated for the Spanish-speaking child and that he achieves a higher degree of status because his cultural difference has been officially recognized by the school authorities.

TABLE 4-1. School Problems That Cause Concern, Showing at Least a 10 Percent Difference between Anglo-American and Latin-American Students Attending a Junior High School in the Working-Class District of San Antonio, Texas[a]

| | Percentage of Children Reporting Problem | | | |
Problem	Anglo Boys	Latin Boys	Anglo Girls	Latin Girls
Getting low grades in school	35	63	24	43
Afraid of failing in school work	30	46	35	47
Trouble with arithmetic	34	59		
Trouble with spelling or grammar	20	32		
Not spending enough time in study	20	36		
Can't keep my mind on my studies	28	42		
Trouble with oral reports	20	32		
Not interested in certain subjects	38	28		
School is too strict	25	15		
Teachers not practicing what they preach	25	10	35	9
Slow in reading	15	29		
Trouble with writing	10	20		
Not smart enough	11	36	11	41
Afraid to speak up in class	15	32	21	49
Worried about grades			29	47
Not interested in books			29	6
Too little freedom in class			24	10
Dull classes			21	11

[a] Witherspoon, 1960.

Social Class and Subcultural Differences

The subcultural patterns of behavior that are of the greatest potential interest to the teacher are the ones associated with the various levels of the social structure. Because of our democratic traditions, it is difficult for us to accept the fact that social classes exert an important influence in America. The research that has been undertaken in this field, however, indicate that there are not only well-defined patterns of behavior which are characteristic of people from different class backgrounds, but that individuals also can usually identify the social class to which they and their acquaintances belong. We are devoting several pages to the discussion of social class because it has a more pronounced effect on the behavior of children in and out of the classroom than any other variable in their social environment.

The pioneering study on social-class behavior patterns was conducted by W. Lloyd Warner in the 1930s. He and his research team studied a small New England town, which they called "Yankee City." They identified three major classes—upper, middle, and lower—which they further subdivided into upper-upper, lower-upper, upper-middle, lower-middle, upper-lower, and lower-lower. Figure 4-2

shows the percentage distribution of the classes as designed by Warner and his associate S. Lunt (1941). In the years intervening since Warner's study was done, there has probably been a shift in the proportions represented by the classes, with the middle classes increasing in size and the lower classes diminishing. One study of adults in Kansas City found that 32 percent of the respondents had moved up socially (Havighurst and Neugarten, 1957). However, because lower-class families tend to be large, it is likely that the majority of children in schools are from lower-class families.

Social-class Patterns of Behavior

As we read through the rather voluminous research on social class that has been published since Warner did his pioneering study, we find a number of recurring themes. In general, the higher the class, the greater the wealth. But surprisingly, wealth is not the most important factor in social status. Some of the members of the *lower*-upper class in Yankee City were wealthier than some of the members of the *upper*-upper class, and one individual in the lower-lower class owned property worth $20,000. The people with whom one associates on an intimate and friendly basis are the most important determiner of class. The social-status variable that is used in the majority of research studies, however, is the number of years of education completed, inasmuch as it can be measured with a fair amount of precision and has been found to be highly correlated with other social-class variables.

People in the upper classes live in the best houses in town. They are "the 400," the leaders of the "social set," and the "elite." Their support is sought for the promotion of civic enterprises, and their names appear at the heads of organizations such as the Community Chest, the Red Cross, the Civic Betterment League, and the Art League. Their children are more likely to be sent to private schools. Upper-class families are much more strongly knit than are families of other social classes, and there is greater concern for maintaining the family name and prestige. School people as

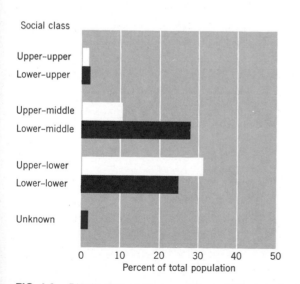

FIG. 4-2. Distribution of the population of "Yankee City" by social class (Warner and Lunt, 1941).

a rule have little contact with upper-class members of society. They constitute only a minute percentage of the population, their children are likely to attend elite private schools, and relatively little research has been done on their personality characteristics.

The middle class is numerically the largest of the three major classes in this country, and the values of its members are dominant in the American culture. Essentially, the middle class believes in hard work, self-reliance, initiative, independence, responsibility, economic security, success in business or profession, self-improvement through education, and fidelity in marriage. The need to achieve (n Ach) is well thought of and often takes precedence over affiliation needs (n Aff) and the need for power. Our educational system is closely geared to the needs of the middle class. Most school board members and teachers are members of this class. Middle-class families are relatively stable, although there is a marked tendency for married children to drift away from the family, in contradistinction to the close ties maintained by upper-class families. Middle-class people are sometimes called "the white-collar class." The great majority of professional men, businessmen, and government officials are middle class. Upper-middle-class people usually have completed college, whereas lower-middle-class people have usually completed high school, some having had a year or more at junior college.

The lower subclasses are sometimes referred to as "blue-collar" (in contrast to "white-colar") or simply as "working class." The upper-lower class consists of families headed by skilled and semi-skilled workers, who usually have completed high school. Many people in this class make a good income, build up substantial savings, move to better parts of town, and gradually become lower-middle class. Others make good money but seem to be unable to keep it; they spend it as fast as they earn it and are unable to put any aside for a "rainy day."

People in the lower-lower class are largely unskilled laborers and the chronically unemployed. Life for them is a continual struggle for survival, a struggle that many of them feel they cannot win without outside help. A.B. Hollingshead (1949) said that they "give the impression of being resigned to a life of frustration and defeat in a community that despises them for their disregard of morals, lack of 'success' goals, and dire poverty." This is particularly characteristic of people who live in rural and urban slums.

Middle-class and lower-lower class people differ sharply in their attitudes toward physical violence. Boys from lower-lower class families are often permitted or encouraged to settle their differences by fighting, sometimes with knives, clubs, and even guns. Middle-class children are expected to deny hostile feelings or to express them indirectly—through competition in the classroom and on the playground, for example. Settling difference of opinion by argument in an approved middle-class technique, but lower-lower class society favors direct physical aggression. Children growing up in slum cultures are less likely to develop the attitudes regarding property that are characteristic of middle-class people; hence stealing and destructive acts are more common. People from the lowest level of society are, therefore, more likely to come into conflict with the law than are the people from classes above them.

Aggression and Physical Punishment

The higher delinquency rate among lower-class individuals appears to be produced, at least in part, by antisocial and destructive patterns of behavior learned at home. One study of antisocially aggressive boys showed that, although their parents punished aggression directed against members of the family, at the same time they expressed approval of aggressive acts directed against persons outside the home. These attitudes thus had a generally reinforcing effect on the boys' aggressive behavior (Bandura and Walters, 1963). Severe punishment of children also seems to be related to tendencies to behave aggressively toward others. Elinor Waters and Vaughn J. Crandall (1964) found no difference between middle- and lower-class mothers in the amount of affection they displayed toward their children, but lower-class mothers were much more inclined to use severe physical punishment when their children misbehaved. When Robert D. Hess (1964) asked black mothers what they would do if they learned that their child had disturbed his class by some mild form of misbehavior, middle-class mothers were much more likely to give an answer along the lines of "I would try to find out why the child feels he must do these things," whereas lower-class mothers simply said: "I would just give him a good spanking."

Insight into the way in which children from lower-lower class homes experience aggression from parents and older siblings is provided by this account, based on visits to disadvantaged families of black and white preschool-aged children:

The method of punishment was fairly uniform among all families. Mothers kept switches or belts within arm's reach, and these tools were used to back up verbal warnings if unheeded for too long. Once an adult applied the belt or stick it was done with wholehearted vigor and vehemence.

Many adults adopted a teasing-testing method of play with their children. The adult seemed proud and amused at the small child's aggressiveness on the one hand, and yet on the other actually daring him to go beyond the limits. Many children innocently entered into the teasing activity only to be caught up in a spiraling frustration and anger which led them to exceed the limits for allowable behavior. This teasing routine always ended in physical punishment for the child until he became sophisticated enough to recognize the pattern (Bradshaw, 1968).

Cultural Values and Children's Attitudes

Another approach to the study of social-class differences is the comparison of parental values. What is it that middle-class and lower-class parents want for their children? Figure 4-3 suggests that lower-class parents are more concerned with the surface aspects of behavior. Lower-class fathers are more interested in having their children obey, be popular with other children, and be "good students," whereas middle-class fathers are more interested in

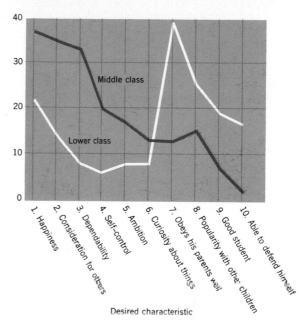

FIG. 4-3. Percentages of middle-class and lower-class fathers selecting certain characteristics as one of three "most desirable" for a ten- or eleven-year-old child (Kohn, 1959).

the qualities underlying good behavior: being considerate and dependable, and exercising self-control. These are qualities that facilitate classroom success, as is also true of other qualities preferred by middle-class fathers: being curious about things and being ambitious. Middle-class fathers are more likely to report that they want their children to be happy, whereas lower-class fathers say that they want their child to be able to defend himself (Kohn, 1959).

Norma Radin (1973) conducted an investigation in which middle-class and lower-class fathers were interviewed in the presence of their four-year-old sons. The interview took an hour, and it was assumed that the boy would get restless during that period. The investigator was especially interested in the means the fathers employed to deal with their sons' restlessness. In general, middle-class fathers paid more attention to their sons' complaints and expressed more understanding and sympathy, whereas lower-class fathers were less attentive, less supportive, and more restrictive. Similar social-class differences appeared when the father-son pairs were interviewed a year later. There were, of course, differences within each group of fathers, and these differences, interestingly, were significantly related to the boys' IQs. In general, boys whose fathers were supportive and concerned about their restlessness tended to have higher IQs, whereas boys whose fathers were more restrictive tended toward lower IQs. Those boys who had higher IQs also had fathers who engaged in educationally supportive activities—teaching them to count, to recognize letters, and to read.

There is much evidence that youngsters are likely to use their parents as models in making plans for the future. When high school students participating in a nationwide survey were asked about their educational aspirations, there was a marked relationship between their mother's educational level and the amount of education the students expected to receive. Figure 4-4 shows that students whose mothers had some college education were four times more likely to set their sights on postgraduate education than were those whose mothers had a

grade school education, whereas those whose mothers had a grade school education were four times more likely to limit their educational plans to high school graduation than were students whose mothers had gone to college.

The Middle-class Way of Life: Words, Words, and More Words

Most of the tasks that children must accomplish if they are to get through school successfully require a considerable degree of verbal ability. This requirement is, of course, most obvious in reading and writing assignments and in making oral reports. Even tasks that involve quantitative skills, however, require some verbal ability. Students have to read in order to do the problems in their math and science workbooks, and the kinds of group work that are carried on even in the most radical open-classroom arrangements require talking, listening, and understanding what others are saying—all verbal skills. The student who cannot translate experiences into words and words into experiences is severely

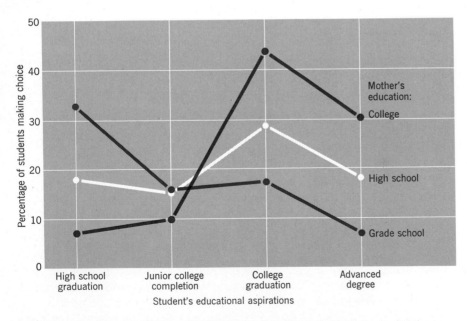

FIG. 4-4. Percentages of high school students choosing among various options when asked to indicate the greatest amount of education they expected to attain. Students are grouped according to mother's educational level (after Erlick and Starry, 1973).

handicapped in all kinds of educational settings— even on the playground and in crafts.

Although there is much variation within each of the social classes, there is a marked tendency for middle-class students to make greater use of verbal skills, especially reading, and to enjoy their use more. Figure 4-5 contrasts the amount of time high school students spend reading and watching television. As Figure 4-5 indicates, working-class students tend to do less reading but see more television than middle-class students do. Although television viewing does involve some verbal activity, its main impact is visual, and the preferences for this medium suggest that the working-class students are less interested in verbal experiences than middle-class students are.

Middle-class parents are inclined to orient their children toward verbal experiences at a very early age. In one study that demonstrates this tendency, Steven R. Tulkin and Jerome Kagan (1972) ob-

served the way in which middle- and working-class white mothers interacted with their ten-month-old daughters. The two groups of mothers spent about the same time with the infants, but the middle-class mothers talked to them a great deal more. They also were more inclined to encourage their daughters to vocalize and to imitate their vocalizations, and they praised their vocal efforts more. This study is only one of many that indicate that middle-class people prefer to deal with their environment in verbal ways.

Other investigations indicate that the highly verbal environment of the middle-class child has its effects at a very early age. In one experiment, two-year-old boys from middle-class or working-class white families were taught to find a small reward—a cookie—under one of five boxes. Each box had on it an object unfamiliar to the boys—a valve, a caster, and so forth. During the first experimental session, half the boys were told the names of the objects on the boxes, and half were told nothing;

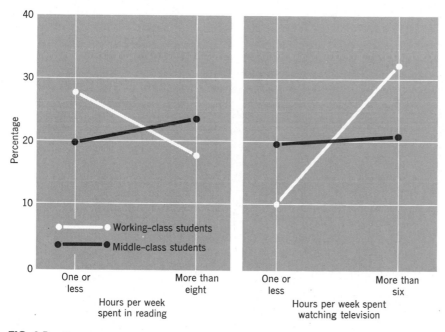

FIG. 4-5. Percentages of working-class and middle-class high school students who reported that they spent one hour or less, or more than eight hours per week, in reading (other than schoolwork) and percentages reporting that they spent one hour or less, or more than six hours per week, watching television (after Erlick and Starry, 1973).

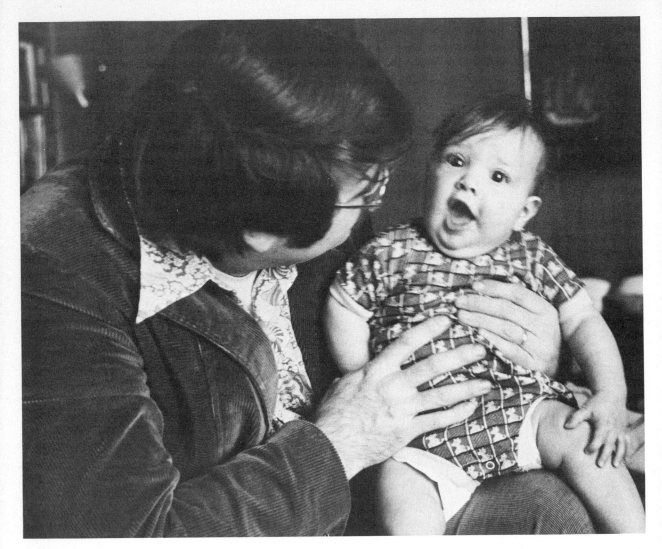

Middle-class parents spend a great deal of time in verbal interaction with their children, even encouraging preverbal vocalization in infants.

during the second experimental session, the conditions were reversed. Middle-class boys learned the task much more rapidly in the verbal condition when they were told the names of the object markers, whereas the working-class boys were only helped slightly by the information. In the nonverbal condition, when the boys were not given such information, there was essentially no difference between the groups (Golden, Bridger, and Montare, 1974).

By the time children are in kindergarten, the verbal supremacy of the average middle-class child is well established. In one study, white lower-class and middle-class kindergarteners were asked to describe colored slides, to describe pictures to another child, and to tell another child about an enjoyable experience. Middle-class children used half again as many words than lower-class children did, and their statements were half again longer. Lower-class children were also more hesitant, for they paused oftener and longer between statements (Jones and McMillan, 1973).

There are many factors that enter into the greater success that middle-class children have in school, but a major one is their greater verbal facility.

How an Understanding of Social Class Is Helpful

There are two principal reasons why we are giving so much attention to the subject of social class in this discussion. The first is that a knowledge of class background is very helpful in understanding the behavior of children, and the second is that the schools are not meeting the needs of children from lower classes very well.

Let us consider the first. We have said that the attitudes, values, beliefs, feelings, personality, and general behavior of a child are conditioned or influenced largely by the kind of experiences he has in early childhood, long before he enters school. Inasmuch as there are such sharply defined differences in the kinds of lives lived by people in middle-class and lower-class surroundings, as well as in their general behavior, it follows that children coming from these two different kinds of backgrounds will think and act differently. The teacher who encounters a variety of patterns of behavior in his classroom should have some understanding of social class because much of the behavior he encounters is the result of class differences. If we are to plan instructional methods and curricula in such a way as to make sense to students, their backgrounds must again be taken into account. A third-grade reader that describes a family whose father works in an office, whose children play with ponies and electric trains, and whose home is surrounded by wide, green lawns will have little real meaning for children who live in a crowded, down-at-the-heels section of a large city. The life that such a reader describes is just not a part of their personal experience; it deals with images that are foreign and largely unknown to them.

Furthermore, the attitudes of children toward education will be colored by the attitudes of their parents and their peer group. Middle-class students are expected to excel and generally expect themselves to excel. They are as a rule quite keenly aware that success in adult life depends on success in education. Lower-class students often see education as something that they are likely to fail at, something that is an unpleasant, frustrating, and dreary interlude in their lives. Sometimes a class of lower-class students will make wonderful progress for a teacher whom they really like, who understands their problems. But the next year when they go on to a new teacher, someone who does not understand them as well, their interest flags and they drop back into the old feeling of apathy and frustration. The educational effort of lower-class students is more likely to be on a personal basis; their attitudes and study behavior are largely colored by their relationship with their teacher and with the other students in the same classroom. Because they are less likely to see education as the means to progress and future success, the personal influence of the teacher means much to them. Middle-class students, on the other hand, are more likely to work hard even for the teachers they do not like, perhaps because they are anxious about nonsuccess. There are many individual exceptions to these generalizations, of course, and the patterns of behavior differ from school to school and community to community. The general trend, however, is for middle-class students to be more strongly motivated to work hard at the job of school learning in the expectation of future success, a kind of motivation that is often lacking with lower-class students.

A knowledge of social-class background is also important in understanding the social behavior of children at school. Lower-class students are rather commonly left out of the social activities of the school, particularly in the upper grades and in high school. The feeling of being excluded or not wanted naturally adds to their dislike of school. Perceptive teachers note that children from lower-class families often tend to have more problems in social adjustment than do middle-class students. In contrast to middle-class children, there seems to be a higher proportion of shy, psychologically withdrawn youngsters, especially among girls. Although disruptive, "acting-out" boys can be found at all social-class levels, a higher percentage of them appear to come from lower-class families. Both of these patterns are characteristic of individuals who have great difficulty in developing congenial, cooperative relationships with others. As a consequence, children of all social classes tend to rate middle-class children higher in such qualities as leadership, friendship, and attractiveness (Neugarten, 1946). This trend is not confined to American schools and appears to be universal. For instance, a study in Brazil showed that in elementary schools attended by both middle- and lower-class children, students tended to rate middle-class children higher on a measure of leadership (Lindgren and Guedes, 1963).

The trend continues in high school. Lower-class students are more likely to see themselves as socially unattractive to other students and are hence more anxious about being rejected. They are therefore less inclined to become involved in extracurricular activities and thus have fewer opportunities to learn the social skills that would enable them to fit in better with their peers. The findings of the nationwide survey of high school students we referred to

earlier confirm this. As Figure 4-6 indicates, about half of the lower-class students were involved in either one extracurricular activity or none at all, whereas half of the middle-class students were involved in three or four activities.

Meeting Needs of Learners from Lower-social-class Homes

The second reason that we listed for understanding the social-class background of children was the relatively poor success that results from attempts to educate those from lower-class backgrounds.

The school system as it exists today is geared to satisfy the needs and hopes of middle-class people. The people who serve on the school boards, manage the schools, and teach the children are inclined to see educational problems from a frame of reference composed of the values of their own class. When children and parents from other social classes come in contact with the middle-class values of the school, there is bound to be misunderstanding and confusion. Florence McGehee (1952) once described the plight of a teacher who tried to explain to a Mexican family of migrant farm workers

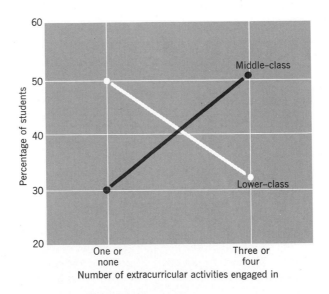

FIG. 4-6.   Differences in involvement in extracurricular activities, as reported by lower-class and middle-class high school students (after Erlick and Starry, 1973).

why they could not take their son, Jesus, out of school even though the tomato-picking season was at hand. The family naturally assumed that their needs took priority over the requirements of the school, and the middle-class, Anglo teacher had great difficulty not only in keeping Jesus in school but also in understanding why his family so naïvely expected that the school would let him go.

When members of a cultural group feel that their needs are not being met by a given group activity and that they are not really welcome, they are likely to drop out at the earliest opportunity. Hence it is not surprising that the school dropout rate is highest among the very poor. Horacio Ulibarri (1966) interviewed migrant and exmigrant workers of Mexican descent and reported that they expressed vague hopes that their children would become lawers, doctors, "or at least teachers," so they would not have to work so hard. When they were pressed, however, the parents doubted whether their children would even finish high school. The children were likewise pessimistic about completing high school, and neither parents nor their children were really very much concerned. The parents had completed about five grades on the average, and the children were leaving about three or four grades beyond the point at which their parents had dropped out.

In spite of the generally negative or apathetic feelings about school on the part of lower-class parents, quite a few children from these homes actually do become "success-oriented," sometimes because skillful teachers realize their potentialities, sometimes because of friendships with middle-class students, and sometimes because of a combination of favorable psychological and environmental factors. But such a student has to develop an unusually high degree of courage before he can break the ties that bind him to his culture. His older brother asks: "Why don't you drop out of school? You're old enough to quit. Why waste your time with that stuff?" And his father adds: "What's the matter with you? Do you think you're better than the rest of us? Afraid to get your hands dirty? Go out and get yourself a job—be a man! I didn't raise my son to be no pantywaist bookworm!"

Many of these children are not able to stand against the hostile and rejecting attitudes of their family and acquaintances and consequently lack the motivation to succeed in school. Whereas the middle-class child succeeds *because* of his parents and their values, the lower-class child who does succeed, succeeds *in spite of* them. Lower-class students sometimes do defy their family's attempts to discourage academic success. Such students tend to become more highly motivated to succeed than the average middle- or upper-class student. This is especially common with city children. Norman F. Washburne (1959) found that academic success in college was correlated more with the "urbanism" of students than with their socioeconomic status. In other words, students who came from city high schools made better grades than those who came from rural high schools, regardless of their social-class background. The problem, of course, is how to help the able lower-class child make the kinds of choices that will keep him in school until he is ready to enter college. Because of parental negativism or apathy, the teacher may be the only person in the lives of many children from lower-class homes who is able to encourage them to make progress in school. One possible solution might be that of persuading parents to be more encouraging of school success, but lower-class parents are "hard to reach" and are reluctant to visit schools or to confer with teachers.

We have shown earlier how lower-class parents reinforce hostile behavior and how the values they hold for their children are concerned with the more superficial aspects of social behavior, rather than with the development of positive attitudes toward others. This background helps explain some of the difficulties that lower-class children encounter in school. Their problems are further complicated by the fact that the kind of adult behavior that reinforces the responses of middle-class children does not serve as a reinforcer for them. Middle-class children come to school prepared to perform and produce in a system where reinforcers for learning (such as marks) are largely impersonal in nature, but lower-class children, as we have previously suggested, respond best to a highly personalized approach. These differences were brought out in a study showing that middle-class children's behavior could be reinforced if they were told merely that their answers were correct. Being told they were correct had little effect on lower-class children, but they did respond favorably to praise (Zigler and Kanzer, 1962).

The lower-class student's need for encouragement and praise is crucial in learning tasks that are demanding, frustrating, and tedious. Although the interest level of workbooks and other instructional materials is probably higher today than it was a generation ago, a great deal of learning activity can be tedious, especially for a youngster who is not very verbal. The importance of the teacher's understanding the special needs of lower-class students is underlined by an experiment conducted by Hermine H. Marshall (1969), who had white kindergarten children learn an interesting and an uninteresting game. Lower-class children learned the interesting game as readily as did the middle-class children, but their performance deteriorated when they tried the uninteresting game. The middle-class children, for their part, actually performed better on the low-interest than they did on the high-interest game. Whatever the reason for their greater success with the dull task, the fact that middle-class students work hard on uninteresting tasks without encouragement, and that lower-class students are more likely to be frustrated and to need support and reinforcement, suggests what teachers must do to meet the needs of these youngsters.

Although educational critics and researchers often disagree as to what should be done to change the schools, there is general agreement that there is a vast gulf between the actual accomplishments of the school and the unmet needs of one-third of the school population—the students from working-class and lower-class homes. This is not to say that the school should provide a separate curriculum for lower-class students or that it should abandon the idea of teaching middle-class values. The problem is rather one of understanding the values and self-concepts of students and parents who do not live in middle-class homes, of helping them to develop a greater feeling of membership in the school community and the community outside the school, and of making gradual adjustments in the curriculum of the school so that it meets the needs of all students, regardless of class origin.

Merely trying to understand children requires that we readjust our perspectives. If we continually compare all children with typical middle-class norms or patterns, we are likely to concern ourselves more with criticism than with understanding. This does not mean that we should abandon our middle-class principles but rather that we should be more "sympathetically aware" of other patterns of living and should try to understand other people in terms of their own value systems, rather than ours. Finally, carrying out such a program of reevaluation would mean that the school curriculum would be expanded, particularly at the secondary level, so that it might become more concerned with developing a wider range of students' abilities than most school systems do today.

We shall have more to say on how schools can help children from lower socioeconomic levels when we further consider the problems of socially disadvantaged learners in Chapter 16.

SUMMARY

The greater share of children's learning experiences occur outside the school. The most basic learnings—attitudes and ways of behaving toward oneself and others—take place in the home, particularly during the preschool years.

Many of the clues that help us understand the behavior of students can be found through studying their family backgrounds. The facts relating to the home situation can be quite useful—whether the family is headed by a single parent, whether the mother works, and so forth. Although the problems, as well as the rights, of single parents make what used to be called "a broken home" a touchy topic these days, evidence shows that children from such homes are more likely to have difficulties at school. On the other hand, there is little evidence that the fact that both parents are employed has a negative effect on children's adjustment. Irrespective of whether the family is headed by a single adult or whether both parents work, what is most important is the emotional climate that prevails in the home: what kinds of attitudes and feelings family members express toward one another, the quality of the relationship between parents and child, and so forth. Although research shows that too much control of children, especially punitive control, is detrimental, children do best when parents are willing to make demands and set limits on misbehavior.

The attitudes and values that parents express are to a large extent determined by the cultural group in which they hold membership. American children tend to have higher status in their families than do children in other cultures but at the same time are more inclined to challenge adult standards of behavior. Family ties are not as strong in the United States as they are in other countries. There are, however, many subcultural groups that vary to a greater or lesser degree from the dominant American culture, each with a value pattern of its own. Children whose parents are members of subcultural groups often encounter difficulties in school because of mutual misunderstanding and prejudice.

The most important of the subcultural groupings as far as schools are concerned is the one based on social class. Social-class differences are psychological, as well as economic, and a common measure of family social status is the amount of education completed by the parents. In contrasting lower-class or working-class parents with middle-class parents, the former are more inclined to be restrictive and to use physical punishment. They also express more concern about children's obedience and staying out of trouble, whereas middle-class parents are more likely to stress children's self-control and being considerate and dependable. Middle-class students tend to have higher educational aspirations than do lower-class students, to enjoy reading more, and to be more skilled in verbal activities. The middle-class child's exposure to and involvement in verbal activities begins in infancy, and his verbal skills are likely to be well-developed by the time he is a preschooler.

Schools are for the most part planned, directed, and staffed by middle-class people. As a consequence, the middle-class student is likely to be more successful in meeting teachers' expectations than the lower-class student is. Teachers, for their part, tend to have difficulty in understanding the problems of lower-class students. Lower-class students more frequently experience failure, find routine classroom tasks frustrating and unrewarding, and feel socially isolated. Their problems are further aggravated by the tendency of their parents to be uninterested in educational goals or to express negative attitudes about schools.

The school's responsibility toward students from lower-class homes is severalfold in nature. Teachers need to understand the values and attitudes that lie behind the behavior of these students, to eliminate or reduce the prejudices that isolate them from other students and from school life, and to revise the content of the curriculum in order that their educational needs may be met.

Suggested Problems

1. Select a person you know whose behavior indicates a rather consistent pattern of attitudes and values. From what you know of the person, how do you think these values or attitudes were influenced by his family and its background? You may use yourself as an example, if you wish.

2. Think back to your school days and see if you can remember any group of students who were set apart from the others because of their attitudes, values, and general behavior. How did the teachers regard these students? How did the other students regard them? What kinds of problems did the students create for the school? What kind of problems did the school create for the students? Do you have any idea of the way in which their families had shaped the values and attitudes of these students?

3. Discuss the family background of the popular and unpopular children in the schools you attended. To what extent do you think that their popularity (or lack of it) was related to their family background?

4. What specific changes do you think should be brought about in a school you attended (or

some other school known to you) in order to meet the needs and problems of students from lower socioeconomic levels of society?

Suggested Readings

Coopersmith, S. *The antecedents of self-esteem.* San Francisco: Freeman, 1967. A study of child-parent relationships that appear to be related to the development of favorable personality and character traits in children. Findings show that parents of emotionally healthier children are more accepting of their children but that they also set well-defined limits to their behavior.

Havighurst, R.J., et al. *Growing up in River City.* New York: Wiley, 1962. Longitudinal study of youth in a Midwestern city of 45,000 population, with special emphasis on social class and its effect on behavior and developmental trends.

Lindgren, H.C. *An introduction to social psychology,* 2nd ed. New York: Wiley, 1973. See Chapter 8, "Social status: Its effect on social motives and behavior."

Lindgren, H.C. and Lindgren, F. (eds.). *Current readings in educational psychology,* 2nd ed. New York: Wiley, 1972. See paper by Whiting in Section 2, as well as papers in Section 9.

Polansky, N.A., Borgman, R.D., and de Saix, C. *Roots of futility.* San Francisco: Jossey-Bass, 1972. An exploratory study of child neglect, focusing on the lives of 65 socially and psychologically depressed "poor-white" mothers living in the southern Appalachian Mountains.

Westley, W.A., and Epstein, N.B. *The silent majority: Families of emotionally healthy college students.* San Francisco: Jossey-Bass, 1969. Compares the family backgrounds of ten students judged the most "emotionally healthy" in their group and ten judged the most "clinically disturbed" according to psychiatric interviews and psychological tests. Findings show that the two kinds of families differ in a number of significant ways.

Yarrow, M.R., Campbell, J.D., and Burton, R.V. *Child rearing: An inquiry into research and methods.* San Francisco: Jossey-Bass, 1968. A critical study of research into methods of studying parent-child relations, with particular reference to variables such as dependency, aggression, and the development of conscience.

5

The Learner and the Peer Group

The Need to Relate to Others

Probably most of us have at times had the feeling of emptiness when we discovered that we were all alone at home with a long evening ahead, or when we were the stranger in a new group. This feeling of emptiness is one of the ways in which our need for others expresses itself. Being isolated or alone sometimes makes us feel insignificant or inadequate—as though, somehow, we were not complete. Just having one person to talk to makes a great deal of difference. Then the feeling of emptiness and incompleteness vanishes, and again we have the feeling of being "somebody."

This feeling of loneliness is actually a kind of anxiety—a fear of being cut off from others. Anxiety is what Rollo May (1950) terms "the fear of becoming nothing." The anxiety that we sense when we are alone is a reminder of how important other people are to our very existence as "somebody." Without others, we sense the anxiety and fear of being "nothing" or "nobody."

What this means is that there is a kind of "social hunger"—a need that can be demonstrated experimentally. In one study, first-grade boys were individually asked to do a simple and rather uninteresting task. Correct responses were either signaled by the appearance of a red light or were socially reinforced by the experimenter's saying "Good" or "Fine." Prior to the experimental trials, each subject was either "socially satiated" by the experimenter's chatting with him during the three-minute walk from the classroom to the room where the experiment was being conducted, or else "socially deprived" by the experimenter's refraining from any comment during the period in transit between rooms. Results showed that there was little difference in the performance of the boys who had been socially satiated, irrespective of whether reinforcement was given either socially or by the appearance of the light. Their performance, over eight trials, improved from an average of about 55 percent correct responses to about 65 percent. Boys who had been socially deprived and who were reinforced *nonsocially* performed about the same. However, boys who had been socially deprived and who were *socially* rewarded for correct performance improved from about 55 percent to about 85 percent correct (Dorwart et al., 1965). Evidently, the brief deprivation of social interaction led them to work harder for social approval.

In another study, institutionalized adolescents with chronic behavior problems were given a test specially designed to assess their attitudes toward themselves and others. Results showed that not only did they have a low level of self-esteem but also that they were more self-centered, less interested in developing interpersonal relationships, and less able to see themselves as members of groups, in contrast to normal adolescents (Long, Ziller, and Bankes, 1968). There is undoubtedly an interaction between cause and effect here. These young people probably had unsatisfactory interpersonal and group experiences during earlier periods in their development, which led them to reject others and to avoid contacts or involvement with them. Such behavior, in turn, led to their being avoided by others and isolated from groups. The main point is, however, that the need to associate with others is a "normal" one, and that an abnormally low level of this need is likely to be linked with psychologically and socially disturbed behavior. This is not universally true, but it is true often enough for social alienation and withdrawal from interpersonal contact to be a symptom that calls for professional attention and investigation.

As we indicated in Chapter 2, the roots of this need to "relate" to other people go back to earliest infancy. We see it in the behavior of the infant who is upset when his mother is upset. We see it in the early years of development, when the child develops his self-concept from the attitudes of others toward him; in effect, the child learns to know himself through the people around him. As he grows and develops through the stages of childhood, adolescence, and adulthood, he continues to depend upon the attitudes and feelings of others in order to develop his self-concept. As he becomes more mature, he is more selective and more critical of the appraisals others make of him. For example, during middle childhood and adolescence young people often come to depend more on the opinions of their peers and less on the opinions of their parents and other adults. We usually discover, however, that even our peers vary in their appraisals of us; hence we normally learn to check the opinions of others against our own perceptions and thus develop self-concepts that are arrived at more independently. The process of developing a self-concept that is based on a balanced appraisal of what others think of us and what we think of ourselves usually extends over the first thirty or forty years of our lives. Some people never achieve this level of emotional maturity and go through life completely dependent on the opinions of others.

There are practical, as well as psychological, reasons why others are important to us. There are the "survival" reasons: the very nature of our complex, urbanized society makes it necessary for us to depend on one another for food, clothing, shelter, and protection against danger and disaster. Generally speaking, however, such needs are met on a fairly impersonal level. We eat the bread baked by others and live in houses built by others, unconcerned with how the bakers and the builders might feel about us. But the personal factor—how people feel about us—is of paramount importance in satisfying basic needs other than those concerned with the maintenance and protection of the physical organism. Needs for attention and the need to belong, for instance, cannot be satisfied unless others have positive feelings toward us.

RELATIONS WITH OTHERS DURING CHILDHOOD AND ADOLESCENCE

The basic trend in growth and development from infancy to maturity is one of increasing independence. The infant is completely dependent on his parents for food, protection, and love. During the preschool years, the child is less dependent but only to a degree. During this period, he depends on his family to teach him the information and skills he needs to cope with the problems of his small but complex world. This learning, in turn, helps him to become less dependent on others.

Entering school is the first big step away from the family into the outside world. Many of the ties that hold the child to the family begin to loosen or start to dissolve at this point. Not only does the child begin to spend a large part of his time under the supervision of adults outside his immediate family, but he becomes a part of a "peer society"—a member of a group of individuals who are his approximate equals in size, age, and status. This group fills a great and growing need for him, for with them he learns to develop new feelings of adequacy and acceptance. For one thing, their standards are not the standards of adult conduct to which parents and teachers constantly compare him but are instead standards that are more readily attainable. Nine-year-olds expect nine-year-olds to behave like nine-

year-olds, and do things that nine-year-olds can accomplish. Hence they usually feel more comfortable in the company of other nine-year-olds than they do in the company of adults.

Who Children Like Best

When nine-year-olds prefer to work and play with other nine-year-olds, rather than with seven-year-olds or twelve-year-olds, they are responding to a drive that is expressed in the old saying, "Birds of a feather flock together." Psychological research has confirmed the validity of this observation, for studies show that the extent to which we are attracted to others depends largely on the degree to which their interests, values, and attitudes are similar to ours. By the time children have arrived at the middle elementary grades, they have a fair idea of how to judge the interests, values, and attitudes of their peers and have begun to form cliques, play groups, and gangs on that basis. It does happen, of course, that children with widely divergent interests form a group. If the group stays together, however, it is because the group members develop something in common with one another, that is, they share experiences and come to agree on matters that are important to their identity as a group. Often these shared experiences are not enough to weld the group into a cohesive force, and the members drift apart, seeking other, more congenial groups. Any group tends to exact some degree of conformity from its members, demanding that they develop ways of thinking and behaving that are "normal" for that group. These shared attitudes and behaviors are what are termed "group norms." The stronger the norms, the more closely the members identify with the group, and the longer the group will endure.

Children usually learn these facts of group life during the middle years of childhood. They also discover that group membership has a price: conformity to norms. There is a good deal of trial and error in this learning process. A child becomes associated with a group and then discovers that he will have to change his ways of thinking and behaving more than he wants to, so he will disengage himself and look for another group to join that is more congenial. Or he will try to form a new group by affiliating with one or two others who seem to have similar interests and values. By the time children arrive at puberty they have a fair idea of "who they are" and are less likely to make the mistake of attempting to join groups whose interests and behavior are incompatible to theirs. The general trend over the childhood years, therefore, is for more stability in friendships. One survey of friendship patterns showed that 62 percent of friendships in the fourth grade endured over a two-month period, in contrast to 64 percent for the sixth grade and 68 percent for the seventh and eighth grades (Busk, Ford, and Schulman, 1973).

The importance of similarity of values and interests in the formation of friendships is shown by a survey of students in eighteen high schools in New York State. Sex, age, and ethnicity were found to be the most significant variables underlying mutual attractiveness. In other words, if we picked any pair of friends at random in these schools, we would be fairly certain that they would be of the same sex, the same age, and the same ethnic group.[1] The probable reason for the prominence of these three variables is that attitudes, interests, and values are more likely to be shared by any two adolescents of the same sex, age, and ethnic group than by any two adolescents of differing sex, age, and ethnic group membership. What was especially interesting in this survey, however, is that the fourth most important variable was the use of marihuana. Students who used marihuana were more likely to have friends who also used it, whereas those who did not use it were more likely to have friends who also abstained (Kandel, 1973). Adolescents who use marihuana have values and attitudes that are quite different from those who do not use it, a matter we will

explore further when we discuss adolescent attitudes toward authority.

Early Stages in Peer-group Formation

The relationships that children develop with their peers normally follow a rather well-defined pattern, a pattern that can be most readily observed in play situations. In a study that has become a classic in developmental psychology, M.L. Parten (1932) observed the play of preschool children and classified their social participation into six forms or levels: unoccupied behavior, onlooker behavior, solitary independent play, parallel activity, associate play, and cooperative or "organized supplementary" play. The terms applied to the first three forms of activity are self-explanatory. Parallel activity describes situations in which a child plays beside other children but not with them. He does not openly influence them, nor do they try to influence him. In associative play, the child is more actively involved in the play of others. The children engage in activities that are identical or similar. They borrow toys and other materials and imitate one another. In cooperative play, the child is a member of a group that plays a game, or makes a product (such as mud pies), or engages in role playing (such as playing house or engineer and conductor).

Figure 5-1 shows the difference in the kinds of play preferred by older preschool children as compared to those preferred by younger ones. Children two years old are principally involved in solitary or parallel play, or in being onlookers. Four-year-olds still participate in parallel play, but they engage in far more interaction and cooperative play than do younger children.

Preschool children are likely to be individualistic. They are not very much concerned with developing group relationships. When they do play together cooperatively, it does not last very long. Preschool children will usually accept any child as a playmate, provided he wants to play what they are playing. Even adults are acceptable as playmates. There are exceptions to this, of course. Sometimes two or three preschoolers in a nursery school will choose

[1] Although the investigator did not solicit information on social-class membership, it seems quite likely that ethnic group differences in her sample reflected socioeconomic status because of the tendency for groups in a given school to be composed of a preponderance of individuals from the same social class.

PLAY PATTERNS OF PRESCHOOLERS
Play relationships develop in an outward direction, becoming more complex with each stage of maturity. The child learns the basic skills of play alone and as an onlooker, then plays in parallel situations, and eventually becomes involved in more complicated games and rituals that require cooperation.

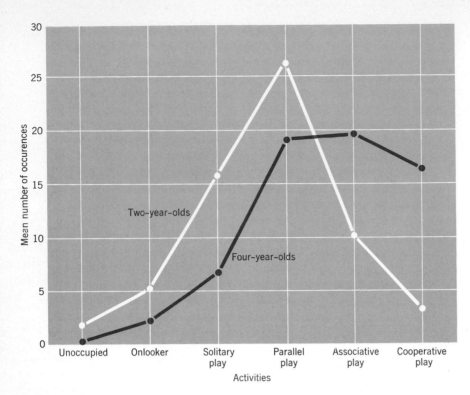

FIG. 5-1. Differences in two-year-old and four-year-old play patterns (data from Parten, 1932).

to play with one another and with no one else, and such an association may continue for months. More usually, however, their choice of playmates will change from day to day and week to week.

Because the group feeling of preschool children is not very strong, they do not develop their own standards of behavior. They have all they can do to conform to the standards that adults have set for them. Children of this age do not form close-knit, easily managed groups. When they are together, they are more "collections of individuals" than real groups.

The relationships that an individual maintains with others can be used as a rough index to the level of emotional and social maturity he has attained. The attitudes of the infant or the young child are self-centered; his concern about others is limited to the effect their attitudes and behavior have upon his sense of well-being. His relationship with his par-

ents is that of a small person who demands and receives attention, love, care, and protection. He is primarily a receiver rather than a giver. When he plays with other children, his self-centeredness expresses itself in the rule, "What's yours is mine, and what's mine is mine." With the help of his parents, his siblings, and older, more mature playmates, he learns to share his playthings and to take turns. Perhaps he learns this more socialized behavior as a compromise that helps avoid unpleasantness, perhaps this learning comes about as a way of avoiding the anxiety he experiences when his parents disapprove of his self-centered behavior, or perhaps he learns as a natural consequence of wanting to play with other children. Or it may be that all these factors and others operate simultaneously. For whatever reason, as he reaches the end of the preschool years, he becomes somewhat more concerned about the rights, feelings, and general welfare of parents and playmates. Usually this is on a minimal basis, for he is still more of a receiver than a giver. Nevertheless, this change represents a definite widening of the scope of his emotional and social life.

Relations with Peers During the Middle Years of Childhood

It is the school, of course, that is the great socializing agency during the middle years of childhood. Teachers consciously and deliberately encourage a wide variety of group behavior through such means as committee research, group play, study groups, and the like. American education differs quite sharply from education in Europe and elsewhere in the extent to which it encourages children to develop a group life of their own. This emphasis does not come about solely because school personnel think it desirable that children learn to function in groups. Actually, the ability to function adequately as a group member is a quality that is rated high in the American culture. If a child has difficulties in relating to his peers, his parents even more than his teachers are likely to be concerned with his "poor adjustment." A child is under considerable pressure to become the kind of person who makes friends easily, functions effectively in groups, is liked by others, and so forth.

The results of this early training show up most strongly in cross-cultural studies. One comparison with British children showed that American children were much more sociable and outgoing (Butcher, Ainsworth, and Nesbitt, 1963). The fact that American children are more peer-group oriented than European children is also shown by studies such as that of Britton, Britton, and Fisher (1969), who found that Finnish children aged nine to eleven were more likely to look to their parents as sources of praise and blame, whereas American children the same age were more likely to take cues for their behavior from other children their own age—their peers. The study by Bronfenbrenner (1970), which we mentioned in Chapter 4, also showed how strongly American children identify with the peer group.

It is probably more difficult for children to learn to orient themselves to their peers than toward adults; hence this process of turning outward toward peers requires a great deal of social skill and maturity. As a consequence, children make progress only by slow degrees. During the early years of elementary school, the typical arrangement is the "playmate" or "best-friend" relationship. Sometimes such relationships are formed even as early as the later nursery school years. This stage of social development occurs when children want to share their experiences with someone with whom they can communicate easily and readily.

They are no longer content to spend much time playing by themselves or watching over children, nor do they want to spend much time with adults. This is an age of exploration, of finding out things about the world outside the home, and it is more interesting if you can find out things in the company of a congenial playmate.

The group relationship is not very important at first. Children gradually become aware of the larger group, particularly when they begin to attend school. In school, the teacher talks to them as a group and directs them into group activities that require cooperation and collaboration. In such situations children begin to get a feeling for the interaction that takes place when a group of individuals come together and develop relationships with one another. But it is difficult for children in the five-to-eight-year stage of development to focus on the larger group relationship very long. They are more comfortable working and playing in small, closely knit groups of two or three. When two or three children this age are playing together and another child tries to enter, the original pair or trio often object. This is hard on the rejected child, of course, but he usually finds some other child who does not have a playmate. This is a normal and natural stage in social development, and it usually does not pay to force pairs of playmates to include another child as a member of their group. Children have a need to find out about other children at this age; it is a necessary prerequisite to their becoming functioning and effective members of larger groups later on.

Some of these "best friend" relationships are quite stable and last for months or years; others are temporary and vary according to whoever happens to be available or interested. But the urge to find a playmate is usually quite strong during this stage of development, and the child who cannot find anyone to play with generates some anxiety until he locates a partner or a small group that will accept him. During infancy and babyhood, the greatest source of anxiety for children is the feeling that their parents are rejecting them; during the later periods of development, they become anxious when they feel that their *peers* are rejecting them. Because of its ability to arouse anxiety, the peer group assumes more and more control over the attitudes and behavior of the child with each succeeding year of growth.

There are some important sex differences that we should note. One is that girls characteristically mature earlier than boys and are quicker to enter into relations with other children. Once boys begin to associate with others, however, they tend to form larger and more active groups than girls do. There is also some tendency for boys' groups to be somewhat more defiant of adult authority, and girls' groups to be more cooperative. This is especially true during the preadolescent and adolescent years.

As the child proceeds from the primary into the middle-elementary grades, the "best-friend" arrangement continues to be a dominant mode of social participation, particularly among girls. During the fifth and sixth grades, the social pattern of the classroom group becomes more complex, and small, close-knit groups appear, perhaps as a reflection of children's desire to move away from close dependence on adults. Being a member of a group, albeit a small one, gives a child a feeling of support and reassurance as he copes with and even challenges the world of adults.

A teacher who uses group methods with younger children should keep in mind that they have relatively little experience in groups that work toward common goals. Primary-grade children are fairly self-centered individuals, and most of them have some problems in learning the give-and-take that is necessary for successful group functioning. Their social immaturity is revealed in a study by Moses H. Goldberg and Eleanor E. Maccoby (1965), who con-

ducted an experiment with second-graders. The researchers formed groups of four children each and gave them the task of building towers out of blocks. During the course of the experiment, they changed the membership of some groups but not others. Those groups in which the membership was not changed were the more successful in completing the assigned tasks.

Conflicts Between Adult Demands and Peer-group Pressures

One problem that appears during the early and middle school years is the conflict between the need for affiliation (n Aff) and the need to achieve (n Ach). As we stated previously, American children receive much encouragement to orient themselves toward peer groups and to develop positive relations with them, and the foregoing discussion would suggest that this early training seems to be effective. But the American adults also stress the importance of personal achievement, a goal that often runs counter to the goals consistent with n Aff. Adults in middle-class society generally are able to work out some kind of a compromise between the conflicting demands posed by n Aff and n Ach, but the task of learning how to cope with this conflict is not an easy one for children. On the one hand, parents and teachers are saying, "Be socially successful; develop comfortable and easy relations with other children." On the other hand, they are also saying, "Achieve to the best of your ability, so that I can be proud of you, and you can be proud of yourself." The problem arises from the fact that it is difficult to achieve academically without comparing oneself or being compared to one's peers, and such comparisons are damaging to friendships. The student who through hard work and persistence has raised his C in spelling to a B finds his joy somewhat dimmed when he learns that his friend got an A with no trouble at all.

This conflict between needs for achievement and needs for affiliation also appears at a period when children are developing negative attitudes toward school. During the primary grades, children's attitudes tend to be generally positive; learning is an exciting adventure, as new skills are discovered and new vistas open up. But during the middle grades, something happens. Perhaps learning tasks are less novel and more repetitive, perhaps teachers are less supportive and permissive or perhaps children themselves develop goals and motives that are more in conflict with those of the school than they were during the primary grades. Another possibility is that the "peer culture," a by-product of the kind of socialization encouraged and fostered by teachers and parents, begins to set goals that compete with the ones of the school. At any rate, school becomes less interesting and attractive for children, a process that tends to continue through adolescence. James A. Dunn (1968) studied the responses of children in grades five, seven, and nine, and found that there was an increasing and a progressive tendency to express dislike for the academic and social aspects of school during the age span covered by his study. In elementary school, the girls in his study liked and valued academic activities more than boys, but these sex differences narrowed and disappeared in later years.

Although such findings are disturbing to teachers who want very much to have students enjoy school, they do not tell us the whole story. Even though students tend to become more resistive during the middle years of childhood, in most schools there is a considerable reservoir of good will. Once again, cross-cultural studies are reassuring. A survey comparing the attitudes of English and American children found that American children, irrespective of their social class or level of ability, were more inclined to give school personnel the benefit of the doubt and to view their school experiences positively (Berk, Rose, and Stewart, 1970). Perhaps American students do not enjoy school as much as their teachers would like them to, but at least they seem to enjoy it more than students in other countries.

Even adolescents feel more positively toward school personnel than is popularly believed. When high-school students were asked, in the course of a nationwide survey, how many of the faculty treat students as responsible individuals, 51 percent re-

plied "all" or "most," and only 18 percent replied "few" or "none" (Erlick and Starry, 1970b).

Relations with Peers During Adolescence

Both n Aff and n Ach involve a movement out of and away from the childhood home, in a psychological sense. During the earlier stages of adolescence, the young person is attracted to groups of his peers (n Aff), whereas n Ach leads him to think in terms of independence and self-sufficiency. As n Aff begins to become a strong source of motivation, children start to show a preference for peer-group standards of behavior, as contrasted with the standards set for them by adults. Thus the parent who has been able to set and enforce bedtime hours for his child suddenly finds that his twelve-year-old believes that 9 P.M. is an unreasonable hour because none of his friends have to go to bed so early.

The conflict between n Aff and n Ach that begins in elementary school becomes more acute in secondary school. Students who are college-bound, however, become aware quite early that their future chances of material and social success are dependent to a large extent on their school performance, and they begin to make an increasing proportion of decisions in favor of achievement goals. This implies an increase in adult orientation and a decrease in peer orientation. Thomas Ringness (1967) did a comparative study of the attitudes of bright eighth-grade boys (IQs 120 and above) whom he classified as High, Middle, and Low Achievers. He found that the Low Achievers tended to identify more with their peer group than did the High Achievers. He commented that inasmuch as the prevailing academic standard of the peer group was one of mediocrity, and that low achievers expressed less motivation for academic achievement, it follows that schools ought to find ways of fostering high achievement values in the peer group at large. The fact that a number of high achievers were not popular with the peer group obviously created difficulties. Ringness also found that the students did not regard teachers as fostering intellectual development and liveliness, but viewed them as being preoccupied with exacting conformance to regulations. Although schools were perceived by his subjects as places in which one prepared for future vocations, only a few saw them as places in which one could develop talents, pursue interests, and improve social skills.

The whole problem of the relations of adolescents with the school was studied by James S. Coleman (1961, 1965) who described the American high school as a compulsory, closed society that merely coexists with the world of adolescents outside the school. He reported that football, popularity, good looks, and having a good time were judged by students to be more significant than academic achievement. Athletics seemed to be especially important in the adolescent subculture because they provided an opportunity for achievement in a way that students could recognize and accept. In effect, the students rejected n Ach as an adult-imposed value and favored n Aff instead.

Coleman's image of an adolescent culture that is separate and estranged from the dominant adult culture has been accepted by some behavioral scientists but not by others. Orel D. Callahan and Stanley S. Robin (1969) put Coleman's ideas to the test by analyzing the kinds of leadership qualities preferred by high-school students, using a questionnaire approach different from that of Coleman. Their findings showed that students were likely to rate academic achievement, maturity, and good citizenship as more desirable for student leaders than popularity, good looks, and athletic achievement. In view of the fact that achievement, maturity, and citizenship are more adult-oriented, it would appear that high-school students are not as estranged from the values of adult society as had been feared.

There is no doubt, however, that many adolescents do openly express attitudes that run counter to adult norms. The question is: How seriously can we take them? Eldon E. Snyder (1969) conducted a longitudinal study of the 1962 graduating class in a midwestern town of 38,000 population. First, he asked high-school seniors how they would like to be remembered: as star athletes, popular leaders of activities, or academic achievers. His results supported Coleman's conclusions to some extent, in that the students expressed preferences for popularity, athletics, and social activities rather than academic achievement. As Table 5-1 shows, however, these values were transitory because the same individuals, when polled five years later, drastically altered their ideas of what high school should mean to students. The data also showed that there was no relationship between the values the students expressed and their later behavior. More than three-fourths of all the students went on to college, irrespective of the values that they had expressed, and those who wanted to be remembered as star athletes or activities leaders were actually more likely

TABLE 5-1. Values Expressed by the Same Individuals as High-School Graduates and Five Years Later[a]

Responses at High-School Graduation (Percentages)		Responses Five Years Later (Percentages)			
Would like to be remembered as:		Would like sons to be remembered as:		Would like daughters to be remembered as:	
MALE RESPONDENTS					
Brilliant student	28	Brilliant student	67	Brilliant student	54
Most popular	51	Most popular	7	Most popular	16
Star athlete	21	Star athlete	26	Leader in activities	30
FEMALE RESPONDENTS					
Brilliant student	21	Brilliant student	67	Brilliant student	46
Most popular	36	Most popular	13	Most popular	17
Leader in activities	43	Leader in activities	20	Leader in activities	37

[a] Snyder, 1969.

to receive their bachelor's degrees than were the others. Another interesting finding reported by Snyder was that the students who were socially more active in high school were more likely to graduate from college than those who were less active. The difference between the more active and the less active was particularly marked in the case of the students whose IQs were 110 or less. Thus it appears that social activity is a favorable, rather than an unfavorable sign, as far as future academic performance is concerned, and that the values expressed by students are misleading predictors of their later behavior.

Adolescent Relations with Authority

It is probably an understatement to say that adolescents' attitudes toward parents, teachers, and other authority figures tend to be mixed. Perhaps it is best described as a love-hate relationship, in which the "love" aspect generally is subordinated to the "hate" aspect. Although evidences of rebelliousness and stubbornness are easy to find, indications of positive feeling can be identified by any adult who is willing to be patient, sympathetic, and persistent.

Adolescence is, among other things, a period in which one finds out who one is, and one of the roads to self-discovery is that of challenging prevailing values and norms. Parents are in the difficult position of being both behavior models and objects of love and respect on the one hand, and authority figures who want to control and enforce limits on the other. Ideally, they should be able to help adolescents resolve some of their conflicts between the incompatible demands generated by n Aff and n Ach, but they themselves are emotionally involved in the outcome of the struggle and hence are often viewed by adolescents as being in league with the school in the enforcement of unnecessary controls that interfere with what young people regard as legitimate behavior. Often this leads to an estrangement between parent and adolescent. Hilda Taba (1955a) once observed that often parents do not seem like persons to their children: "Just givers, blockers, and not people who get irritated and tired

and have all the human feelings." And, further: "To some adolescents I have studied, parents are as incomprehensible as a foreign culture."

Since time immemorial adolescents have sought ways to proclaim their attainment of adult status and, simultaneously, their independence from their parents and other authority figures. Often this has taken the form of engaging in activities which are contrary to the rules and mores of society. Some of this behavior may be considered a form of experimentation, motivated by curiosity, and some of it is a smoke screen to cover up deep feelings of inadequacy and insecurity. In past generations, smoking, excessive drinking, and sexual promiscuity were the major ways of expressing these rebellious feelings; in the last decade or so, drug usage has been added to the list. As of the present moment of writing, the use of LSD, as well as the "heavier" drugs such as heroin, appears to have declined, after having peaked in the early 1970s, although the evidence for this is by no means clear. There seems to be little doubt, however, that marihuana usage is still a major ritual signalizing youthful nonconformity.

In the survey of the bases of friendship in New York state high schools we mentioned earlier, marihuana usage was found to be the most important variable, after sex identity, age, and ethnic membership. If high-school students can be roughly divided into three groups—those who never use marihuana, those who use it occasionally, and those who use it frequently—such groupings will reflect the attitudes toward adult authority that characterize each group: acceptance, ambivalence, and rejection. Although users of marihuana justify their conduct on the grounds that smoking marihuana is pleasurable and harmless, the fact that it enables them to defy adult authority and to affirm their membership in like-minded peer groups is an even more important motive from a psychological point of view.

Such insights do not make it any easier for the teacher or administrator who has to deal with marihuana smoking on school premises, but they do place the behavior pattern in some kind of perspective. Marihuana smoking, aside from legal and health considerations, thus appears as one of the several ways in which young people express non-conformity, just as its suppression by the authorities is one of the several ways in which society reacts to youthful defiance. In the unlikely event that marihuana smoking were to become as acceptable, say, as drinking coffee, youth would inevitably find some other way of signalizing its rebelliousness, and adult society would inevitably try to suppress it. The various controversies over the past few years about innovative forms of attire and the long hair of male students are other examples of the continuing tug-of-war between youth and authority.

Adolescents have often been heard in recent years to justify their rejection of and nonconformity to the conventions of society on the grounds that their parents and other adults act in ways that are manifestly false to the ideals and values they so piously proclaim. This is an accusation that strikes home and has made many an adult squirm with embarrassment and guilt. Valid as the charge may be, matters are not that simple. Kenneth Keniston (1968), who has through the years been one of the most sympathetic commentators and reporters on young people and their problems, has this rejoinder to make to this criticism:

. . . in no society do parents (or anyone else) ever fully live up to their own professed ideals. In every society, there is a gap between creedal values and actual practices; and everywhere this gap constitutes a powerful motor for social change.

He goes on to say that in most societies, especially when changes come slowly, there is a kind of "institutionalization of hypocrisy," and that children and adolescents learn routinely when it is "reasonable" to expect that the values expressed by adults will be implemented in their behavior and when they will not.

Another commentator on the perennial problem of youth-adult conflict is Lawrence Schiamberg (1969), who has noted that the transition between adolescence and adulthood is smoother in more primitive, nontechnological societies, where behav-ior norms and expectations are more clearly defined than in urbanized societies like our own. Part of the gap between adults and adolescents lies in the more extensive experience that adults have had with the complexity of modern life and their difficulty in communicating clear information as to its complicated nature. Schiamberg suggested that schools take some leadership in teaching students to accept the rapid change and uncertainty that are inescapable in today's world. He recommended further that the emphasis in schools shift from mere information-giving to the development of cognitive styles that permit a variety of combinations of information processing—problem-solving for instance. The school should also give more attention to young people's needs for self-actualization and be less concerned about the other drives—the so-called "deficit needs" in Maslow's scheme of basic psychological motives.

The Tyranny of the Peer Group

Abraham Gelfond (1952) once observed that adolescents find within the peer group a freedom they do not find in the adult world: freedom from control and freedom from (over)protection. These freedoms do not come without a price, however. Adolescent groups are inclined to exercise a dictatorship over the attitudes and behavior of their members that is more tyrannical than anything ever devised by the adult world. Nevertheless, a great many young people evidently have to go through the process of submitting to group domination before they are ready to stand on their own feet and to make their own decisions. It is hard for adults to understand the whys and the wherefores of adolescent behavior. When we see an adolescent engaging in actions that seem silly or illogical but which conform to the standards or norms of his group, we forget that he may not be psychologically free to behave differently. He is, in effect, a prisoner of the norm. The next stage in his becoming a mature adult consists of his freeing himself from the dead-level conformity to group norms that is so common of adolescent society. Unfortunately, a large number of young people never attain this freedom and become adults who are unable to do their own thinking and take responsibility for their own behavior. Because they have not progressed beyond the adolescent stage of psychological development, they may be considered to be adults who have not matured emotionally, socially, and intellectually.

Although we are often critical of adolescents' hunger to belong and be accepted, we should keep in mind that the underlying social need is a healthy one. In fact, the degree of acceptance that any individual receives from others is a valid index of psychological health and well-being. Social acceptance, as well as other indicators of emotional health, is positively related to school success. Raymond G. Kuhlen and E. Gordon Collister (1952) conducted a study that is as valid today as it was a generation ago. They asked sixth- and ninth-graders to rate follow students on a long list of characteristics and then followed up the students in later years to see what characteristics differentiated the graduates from the nongraduates. They found that sixth-grade boys who had been rated as "friendly," "popular with others," "cheerful and happy," and "good looking," and who enjoyed jokes, even jokes on themselves, were more likely to graduate six years later than those who had not received these favorable ratings. Ninth-grade boys who graduated were more likely than nongraduates to be rated as "friendly," "neat and clean," "popular with others," "cheerful and happy," and "good looking." And the only trait that distinguished potential graduates from nongraduates among ninth-grade girls with any consistency was that of being "popular with others."

MEASURING PEER ACCEPTANCE

Using Sociometry

In their attempts to measure the social acceptance of sixth- and ninth-graders, Kuhlen and Collister used what is known as a "sociometric technique," a way of measuring the "social distance" or of charting relationships among group members. Another way of studying the social structure of classroom groups is that of asking each student to list the three students he would most like to work with on a committee (or sit next to, or play with, or invite to a party, and so forth) and the three he would least like to do the same things with. The choices and rejections are then tallied and charted.

Figure 5-2 shows the kind of social structure one might find in a fifth grade. We note that Joe, Frances, and Barbara occupy central positions in "stars" of attraction, whereas Bill, Gordon, Emily, Lucy, and Karen are rejected—"isolates." In some ways they are like the nursery school children who are "onlookers." Some fifth-graders are unwilling and/or unable to develop the social skills necessary to proceed beyond the "onlooker" stage. To this extent, they are socially and emotionally immature. However, the classifying of such behavior as immature does not tell us very much about it. It does not say, for example, whether these childen are so painfully shy that they feel awkard in any social situation, nor does it tell us whether they are disliked by the other children or merely ignored. Usually there is an interaction of several factors: The child is diffident, shy and withdrawn, and the other children just do not want to bother with someone who is so ill at ease. Sometimes a child is not chosen because he belongs to an "outgroup"—perhaps he is a Negro child in a white group, or a Mexican child in an Anglo group, or even an upper-middle-class child in a group of children coming from working-class homes.

Figure 5-2 also depicts other stages of social development. George and Tom, Terry and Amy, Dolores and Sonya, and Debbie and Joanne represent the "best pal" or paired friendship pattern. There is a "chain of friendship" among the boys that includes Bernard, Nathan, Elton, David, Joe, Paul, Jason, and Mitchell. Generally speaking, friendship chains are characteristic of healthy group relationships because they help link a class together in friendly group spirit. The girls in this class are less friendly and more divided then the boys are. There is an exclusive clique composed of Jane, Frances, Loralee, and Barbara, with Mary apparently in-

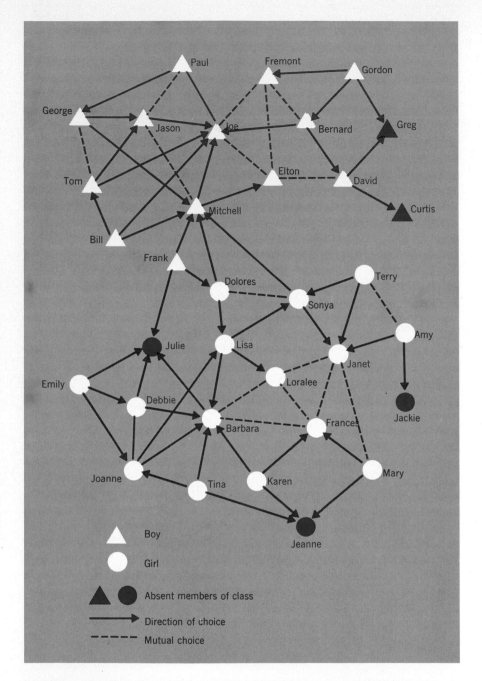

FIG. 5-2. Sociogram of a "typical fifth grade," based on responses to the question: "Which three children in this class would you like to invite to a party?" (from the files of the author).

cluded in the group part of the time. The chart also shows how boys and girls this age divide sharply along sex lines.[2] Only Frank expresses any liking for girls, and only two girls, Dolores and Sonya, indicate any preference for any of the boys. The boy in this case is Mitchell, who is also one of the most popular boys in his group. The fact that Dolores and Sonya like each other better than they are liked by any of the other girls in the class, plus the fact that they both like Mitchell, raises the possibility that they may be more physically mature than the other girls. It also raises the possibility that Mitchell may be more mature than the other boys. Very likely he is mature enough to be attractive to girls but not mature enough to be attracted in return. Frank likes girls but is not chosen by any of the boys, nor is he chosen in return by any girls. Very possibly his interests are more effeminate than those of the rest of the boys in his class.

Sociograms based on adolescent groups show these same basic patterns: "stars" of attraction, cliques, paired friendships, "chains" of friendship, and isolates. However, there is less division on the basis of sex; most of the small subgroups include both sexes, except for those who have not matured to the point of being interested in persons of the opposite sex. One phenomenon that appears during this period is the "crowd"—a group of boys and girls with more or less common interests and tastes who "hang around" together. One may see the crowd in a pizza parlor after school or working together to elect one of their members to a school office. The crowd is more loosely organized than a clique. It is less likely to be "a closed corporation" and consists of a larger number of members.

A particularly interesting study was conducted by Albert J. Lott and Bernice E. Lott (1970), who asked first-grade children not only to name the classmates whom they liked, disliked, or felt neutral about but to draw them as well. Such drawings are often used

[2] The tendency for friendship groups to divide along sex lines diminishes during adolescence but not entirely. The survey of New York state high-school students we mentioned earlier showed that in the great majority of instances, pairs of "best friends" were of the same sex (Kandel, 1973).

FIG. 5-3. Artist's copies of a first-grade boy's drawings of three classmates (Lott and Lott, 1970). Can you tell which classmate was liked, which was disliked, and which one evoked neutral feelings? (See end of chapter for answers.)

by clinical psychologists as measures of personality characteristics. Evidently they can also be used as sociometric devices to indicate interpersonal attitudes since, when a group of psychologists was asked to interpret the drawings in terms of the feelings each artist had for the child he was drawing, their estimates were quite close to the answers children gave on the sociometric questionnaires. Look at the drawings in Figure 5-3 and see whether you can determine what attitudes were being expressed.

Teachers' Estimates of Peer Acceptance

Teachers sometimes raise the question of whether sociograms are worth the time and effort because they feel that they can tell which students are accepted and which are rejected without the help of a special technique. A number of research studies, however, indicate that teachers generally do not know their students as well as they think they do. Alexander Tolor (1969) found that teachers were only 18 percent accurate in picking the most and least popular children among their fourth-, fifth-, and sixth- graders. Tolor's findings, as well as this author's observations, indicate that a study conducted some years ago by Norman E. Gronlund (1951) is still valid today. Gronlund noted that sixth-grade teachers typically overrated the peer acceptance of those children they themselves preferred and underestimated the status of children they least preferred. Evidently the reason why teachers fail to identify children who are accepted or rejected is that they are not fully aware of the bases that children use to make choices. In effect, their difficulty is one of low empathy—being unable to put themselves in the same frame of reference as children and to see things as children see them. One of Gronlund's findings is of more than passing interest. He found *no* relationship between the ability to judge a child's acceptance accurately and any of the following factors: the teacher's experience, age, years of college training, semester hours of education courses, size of class, marital status, and length of the time she had been in contact with the class. The only criterion that differentiated the best teacher-judges from the poorest was whether they had taken an in-service, child-development course set up for the purpose of helping teachers to understand the "whole child," with particular reference to his social adjustment. Teachers who had taken this course were significantly better judges than those who had not. However, as Gronlund pointed out, it would not be fair to say that taking such a course is the crucial factor, for it could be that those teachers who were interested enough to take such a course would also be the teachers best able to judge the social acceptance of children more accurately.

What Sociometric Data Tell Us About Children and Adolescents

Children and adolescents resemble adults in at least two ways that are of interest to both the psychologist and the teacher. For one thing, there is a tendency for individuals to be liked for their favorable traits of personality and not their unfavorable ones. For another, there is also a tendency for traits to "cluster" or go together. This means that students who have a key favorable trait are likely to have other favorable ones as well, and those who have a major unfavorable trait are likely to have other unfavorable ones.

This does not mean that students who have a lot of favorable traits do not have any unfavorable ones, nor does it mean that those who are troubled

with unfavorable traits do not have any favorable ones. That fact that children, like adults, tend to be consistent, does not mean that they are free of inconsistencies. It does mean, however, that children who start out with traits that are obviously favorable are likely to receive more advantages in terms of being accepted by other students and appreciated by their teachers, whereas those who start out with major psychological disadvantages are likely to have more than the usual amount of problems in terms of being accepted by other students and in getting positive attention from teachers. Although these are "facts of life," they are not immutable. One of the major tasks of the school is that of giving students an opportunity to become more competent and adequate in a number of different ways, and teachers can personally do much to help students with psychological deficiencies learn social as well as cognitive skills. For example, the teacher can use his insight into the problems of such students by planning learning situations (committee work, group projects, panel discussions, and the like) which enable children to work with others as equals and copartners.

The evidence that students respond positively to competence and adequacy in their peers is overwhelming. We will cite just two studies whose findings are typical of many. Merrill Roff and S.B. Sells (1965) asked each one of approximately 2800 fourth-graders in Minnesota and Texas schools to nominate four classmates they liked most and two they liked least. Students were then divided into four equal-sized groups according to their socioeconomic status and the one-sixth with the most favorable ratings in each status group were compared with the one-sixth having the poorest ratings in that group with respect to IQ. Their results, as presented in Figure 5-4, showed that children who were most often chosen by their classmates tended to have higher IQs than the children who were least chosen and that this difference held true irrespective of their socioeconomic class. The data also showed that the higher a child's socioeconomic status, the better chance he had of being chosen by his classmates. But notice that seldom-chosen children with high sociometric status tended to rate

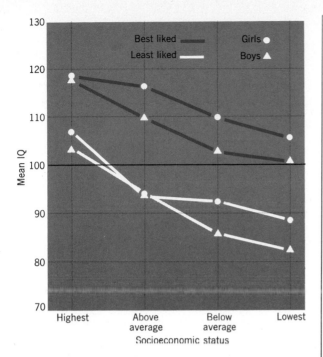

FIG. 5-4. The IQs of best-liked and least-liked fourth-graders, classified according to their socioeconomic level (Roff and Sells, 1965).

lower in IQ than oft-chosen children of moderate sociometric status.

A study that demonstrated a positive relationship between cognitive performance and personality traits was conducted by Gene M. Smith (1969), who asked members of high-school classes in Puerto Rico to rate one another on a long list of personality traits. The ratings were then correlated with each student's grade-point average. The results, as shown in Table 5-2, indicate that certain personality traits tend to go with high grades, whereas others are associated with low grades. In general, students who make high grades are perceived by others as being energetic and creative, and as behaving in socially positive ways, whereas students with low grades are seen as being either negative or apathetic.

SOCIAL FORCES INFLUENCING BEHAVIOR

Peer-group Norms

A few pages back we discussed the degree to which peer groups exercise an increasing amount of influence in the lives of young people as they go through the developmental stages of middle childhood, preadolescence, and adolescence. This influence is exercised through what psychologists

TABLE 5-2. Sociometrically Derived Personality Factors Correlated with Grade-Point Averages for 1022 Puerto Rican High-School Students[a]

More Characteristic of Students with High Grades	More Characteristic of Students with Low Grades
Considerate	Languid
Self-reliant	Quitting
Orderly	Happy-go-lucky
Original	Easily upset
Socially mature	Prone to daydream
Conscientious	Obstructive
Inquisitive	Crude
Responsible	
Fastidious	
Obedient	
Resourceful	
Frank	

[a] Smith, 1969.

call "social norms"—standards of conduct and behavior that grow out of the interaction of members of groups. Some norms are developed as a way of enabling members to differentiate between their group and other groups. A group of boys may wear a knitted wool cap, for instance, or a certain kind of fancy belt buckle as a way of expressing the feeling that they are somehow "different" from other groups. If the group has high status in the school, other boys may follow suit, and a fad is born. The ability to start a fad is an indirect measure of the status of a group. The wearing of knitted caps and other odd items of clothing is but one of the more obvious of the many different kinds of norms that function to direct or control the behavior of group members. Most norms are much less apparent but are nevertheless effective. For instance, take the norm that "no one tattles."

> When Miss Skelly left the room, she said she would be back in twenty minutes and she asked the class to read through the next chapter. Jerry read through the chapter in five minutes and looked about for something to occupy his attention. He got up and wandered about the room. Miss Skelly had left one of the top drawers of her desk partly open. It intrigued Jerry's curiosity and he pulled it open. There was nothing in it but papers and record books, so he closed it and opened another. There was nothing in that one but Miss Skelly's lunch. He was just opening a third drawer, when he heard Miss Skelly coming down the hallway. He shut the drawer, scurried to his seat, and buried his nose in the textbook.

What Jerry had just done is in violation of the code of behavior enforced by adults, which says, in effect, "You don't go through another person's desk." Even if twelve-year-olds are not bothered as much by such behavior, they nevertheless know what adults think of it. But when Miss Skelly returned to the room, no one mentioned what Jerry had been doing. If anyone even thought of telling on Jerry, he choked back the impulse. The norm is that you do not "tattle," and few children this age seriously consider doing it. Hence the norm operates in the class without anyone's giving it much thought. If Miss Skelly should suspect however, that someone had been tampering with her desk and

should ask the class who did it, then everyone would be conscious of the group code. And if they are like most sixth-graders, it would take much pressure to get them to tell. Even those who might want to tell would think twice for fear of running counter to the group norm.

The norms that develop in a school can have a very pervasive effect on the attitudes and values of students. Only 35 percent of the graduates of McCloud County High School go on to college, even though the mean family income in the county is higher than the national average. In some ways, this is not too surprising, inasmuch as graduates of rural high schools are less likely than are urban high-school graduates to think of entering college. But at Monroe County High School, also located in a rural area of comparable economic status, 90 percent of the graduates enter college. A norm has developed at Monroe High School that "everyone goes to college if he can." To be sure, this is a norm that must be endorsed and supported by the families who pay the bill, but equally important is the acceptance of college-oriented goals on the part of the high-school students who have taken their cues from a faculty that assumes, as a matter of course, that every Monroe graduate who has the ability will attend college.

The Teacher and the Peer Group: Collaborators or Antagonists?

Adults are often worried and concerned when young people develop strong peer-group loyalties. They are concerned because such ties may help reinforce youth's unwillingness to conform to behavior standards prescribed for it by parents and teachers. Furthermore, it appears easier to deal with one defiant young person than with a whole group.

There is some real basis for these concerns. It *is* true that young people who want to defy adult authority gain support and reassurance from the feeling that they are members of a group and that the group stands with them. It is not necessarily true, however, that it is easier to deal with classes that are merely loose collections of individual students than it is to deal with close-knit groups. There are some approaches that work very well with groups, just as there are some that work well with individuals away from the group setting. What sometimes happens is that teachers who have had some success with individual students try to use the same appeals and methods in working with the classroom group and meet with disappointment. Actually, the relationship between a group and a teacher is different from the relationship between a teacher and an individual student. Teachers forget, too, that classroom groups are not as a rule mere collections of individuals but have personalities of their own. People behave differently in groups than they do when alone. The boy who may be able to cooperate with the teacher when the two of them are alone may have a need to show off when he is with the class. The girl who may be able to talk sensibly when she is with the teacher may be tongue-tied with anxiety and fear when she faces the class.

Because teachers are inclined to think of the one to-one relationship of the teacher and the pupil, they are likely to overlook the fact that groups have a separate psychological existence and that certain aspects of group psychology may be used to the educational advantage of the student. The development of group relationships is an important phase in the social and emotional development of children; furthermore, it makes sense to use the natural drives that attract children to group life as a basis for classroom learning. In other words, teachers need to learn how to work *with* groups, rather than against them.

Some of the ways in which teachers can work with groups are presented in later chapters, but in order to give one example of what we mean, let us consider the matter of norms. One of the broader objectives of education is to help students think, examine their own behavior, reevaluate it, and improve it. Teachers can assist in the social development of students by giving them chances to explore and to discuss their own behavior. As we indicated earlier, groups often are not even aware that they have any norms. By helping students become aware of their own norms and able to examine them

critically, teachers can sometimes help them to develop more adequate behavior. In one high school, members of the student council expressed their embarrassment at seeing their campus littered with luncheon debris. The faculty sponsor gave sympathetic support to their comments and encouraged the council to take steps to deal with the problem. After trying out several proposals without much success, the council adopted a plan whereby the entire student body would have to stay after school the number of minutes it took the custodians to clean up the school yard. Although the plan was quite drastic, the student body voted for it, and it went into effect. As a result the campus was cleaner than it had been for years. Once students had recognized the problem and worked it through, they were able to modify their own behavior and develop new norms.

Cohesiveness

A classroom group that finds it has good communication with its teacher and among its members will enjoy being together. It will find working, learning, and playing together a rewarding and satisfying experience. This wanting to be together with the other members of the group is what we call "cohesiveness." Cohesiveness is also characterized by such feelings as loyalty, group pride, shared values and behavior patterns, and the "we" feeling. Cohesiveness facilitates communication among group members, whereas lack of cohesiveness impedes it. A group may lack cohesiveness because members are so interested in their personal goals, needs and feelings that they cannot become interested or involved in group goals. Groups of preschool children lack cohesiveness because they do not have the maturity needed to submerge some of their interests in deference to group goals. A lecture or theater audience tends to lack cohesiveness because there is little basis for developing any kind of group feeling. To the extent that a classroom group plays the part of an audience for the teacher and regards itself as an audience, it lacks cohesiveness. Classroom groups in European schools, where education is conducted on a formalized teacher-centered basis, are likely to be much less cohesive than are comparable groups in American schools.

Cohesiveness can also be impaired by sharp cleavages between subgroups within the larger group. The late Hilda Taba (1955a) once observed that when school populations contain groups from various social classes or cultures, there is a tendency for "we-they" relationships to develop. Under such circumstances, classroom discussion may be impeded because students have a tendency to attack one another instead of ideas, and any possibility of doing any thinking or planning as a group is blocked. Hence she argued for a greater understanding of the factors and forces that cause group cleavages and the ways in which they become obstacles to communication, to group participation, and to learning in general.

Morale

It can be assumed that groups that are operating effectively probably have good morale as well. This holds true whether the groups are army units, factory workers, or students. Most people are aware, too, that morale usually has something to do with happiness. It is because of this association that military commands provide entertainment for their troops and factory managements help workers organize bowling teams. There is no doubt that entertainment does help take people's minds away from the monotonous, tedious problems that are inevitably part of working and living with others, but morale is much more than being entertained.

The cultivation of morale, like any other dimension of mental health, cannot be based on a formula. Everyday observation however, will show that teachers who have the best morale in their classes are those who have a considerable degree of confidence that students will learn something in their classes. They are, in other words, optimistic about the possibility that learning will take place. Such teachers expect to commit themselves to the task of teaching and expect that students are going to commit themselves to the task of learning. They maintain this optimism in spite of occasional (or even frequent) setbacks and failures. They have a toughness of fiber that students respect. Under the

guidance of such teachers, classes get the feeling that success *is* possible and that the goals of learning *can* be attained. Sometimes the goal is a personal one, as it is with Tommy Flores, a fifth-grader who is struggling with fractions. Fractions are a confused jumble of numbers to Tommy, but he persists in his efforts because he knows from past experience with other school tasks that after a while they will make sense. He also knows that Mrs. Mark, his teacher, will help him with some of the difficult points. Furthermore, he knows that neither she nor any of his classmates will ridicule him for the mistakes he makes while learning.

Morale can also involve group goals. The military unit that is isolated on the front lines, cut off from the rest of the division, fights doggedly because of its loyalty to the cause and to the total military organization. If its members lacked faith in the cause or thought that the war was lost anyway or that further struggle would serve no useful purpose, they would not resist but would surrender. The boy who makes a sacrifice bunt at baseball is in a similar position. He knows that he will probably be "out at first," and that the thrill of coming in safe at home plate will not be his this inning, but the sacrifice will put his team in a more strategic position for scoring.

Good communication, cohesiveness, and morale are both causes and effects of satisfactory group activity. They are forces that work together to support the kinds of satisfactions that come from working and learning together. Conversely, a group that is discouraged or bored or apathetic will resist the efforts of a teacher to improve interpersonal relations within the group. It is not easy to build up the morale of a group whose attitudes are negative and resistive; yet it is an assignment that must be carried with some degree of success if any geniune learning is to take place.

The Psychological Climate of the Classroom

In Chapter 4 we discussed some of the ways in which the emotional or psychological climate of the home affects child behavior. Psychological climate, in fact, sets the conditions of behavior for any group. Follow a junior high school class as it goes from teacher to teacher in the course of a school day and note how differently the same class reacts and behaves as it enters the "climatic zone" of each teacher. With one teacher the class may be restless and fidgety; with another, noisy but enthusiastic and industrious; with still another, subdued and passive. In some classrooms the atmosphere is critical and negative. No one can do anything right. Every defect, every deviation from the prescribed pattern is noted and called to everyone's attention. In another classroom, everything is acceptance and agreeableness. No one ever makes a mistake, it seems, and the class meanders cheerfully, if somewhat hazily, through the prescribed curriculum. In still another class, the climate is one of high-pitched tension. The teacher is more like a ringmaster, putting students through their acts with military precision. One gets the impression that everything has been planned almost to the second.

The classic study of the effects of psychological climate on the behavior of children was conducted by Kurt Lewin, Ronald Lippitt, and Ralph K. White (1939) during the 1930s. In general, the investigators found that the behavior of children was markedly altered when a change in the adult leadership of their group was accompanied by a change in psychological climate. The three kinds of climate—autocratic (much control and direction), laissez faire (no control or direction), and democratic (cooperative relationship between leader and group, with the leader more of a collaborator than a director)—characterize three basic modes of group leadership. This study makes it clear that it is the teacher who is most responsible for the kind of climate which develops in the classroom, for it is he who can reward or punish, who can set and enforce limits rigidly, flexibly, or not at all. Furthermore, it is to the teacher that students look for cues that set the prevailing mood.

When we say that the teacher is the key figure in creating climate, however, this does not mean that he has unlimited freedom to develop the kind of climate that he thinks is appropriate or that suits his personality. There are other potent forces at work. For one thing, the administration of the school plays an important part in developing the psychological climate that prevails generally among the teachers and the students in the school. Hence a teacher will have great difficulty in developing an autocratic climate in a classroom when the prevailing climate in the school is democratic or laissez-faire, just as the teacher who tries to build a democratic climate will have difficulty if the prevailing climate in the school is autocratic or laissez-faire.

The Effects of a Competitive Climate

We have spent the last few pages discussing the forces, conditions, and factors that help to develop the kind of group attitudes and behavior that aid and support classroom learning. We should also be aware, however, of reasons why groups disintegrate or fail to develop "group feeling."

We have mentioned one factor already: the tendency of teachers to regard classroom groups as collections of individuals rather than as groups. Furthermore, some teachers deliberately prevent students from developing "group feeling." They use such methods as refusing to let friends work together on the same committees, forcing students to report one another's breaches of conduct, and pitting students against one another in intense competition. Indeed, the development of a tense, competitive atmosphere does much to break down good group relations in classrooms. Competition is very much a part of our national life, and we could not keep it out of the schools if we tried. Many children, particularly in the lower social classes, need to learn how to work within the framework of a competitive system without being continually defeated and discouraged by it. If competition is properly controlled, it can help make learning an interesting and stimulating experience, but if it is emphasized to the detriment of other goals, such as that of learning how to work together cooperatively,[3] it can break down group spirit and morale.

[3] The point should be made that "cooperation" as used in this book means "the ability to collaborate with others in working on a task, problem, or project that is of common interest to the persons involved." Cooperation implies a kind of partnership, a certain mutuality among the collaborators. Some teachers and parents think of cooperation as the same as "obedience," "compliance," or "following instructions," concepts that are quite different from the idea of equality and group sharing that is implied by our use of the word here.

"I beat! . . . I beat!"

One of the major tasks of the school is the task of helping students learn to work together cooperatively. Sometimes this means unlearning inappropriate patterns of competitive behavior.

One of the difficulties about the practice of encouraging unbridled competition in the classroom is the way in which it interferes with the learning of attitudes and skills that are basic to cooperation. As Alexander Mintz (1951) once put it, "Once the cooperative pattern of behavior is disturbed, cooperation ceases to be rewarding to the individuals; then a competitive situation is apt to develop which may lead to disaster."

Mintz based this conclusion on the results of an experiment that has become a classic in the field of social psychology. Subjects in his experiment were required to pull paper cones out of a jar by means of strings attached to the point of each cone. The mouth of the jar was just large enough to permit the passage of one cone at a time, and a degree of tension was introduced by the fact that the jar was being slowly filled with water through a tube that entered its base. When members of groups of subjects were each given a string and asked to cooperate with the others in removing the cones from the jar before the water reached them, they quickly learned how to take turns and were able to get the cones out in time. But when the subjects were told that the ones who got their cones out first would be rewarded and those who were slow would be fined, they were unable to work together successfully. The cones all jammed in the neck of the jar, and no one was able to extricate his cone. The point is that cooperation is made possible only by exercising a fairly complex group of skills that cannot be brought into play if competition has been introduced into the situation.

In another experiment, subjects were told either that their work would be rated as a group or that each member would be rated as an individual. Results indicated that the groups that were evaluated as a total group showed more group-oriented behavior and communicated more effectively than did the groups whose members were working for individual ratings (Grossack, 1954). In effect, group ratings promoted cooperative behavior, and individual ratings led to competition, which interfered with cooperation.

Much depends on the kind of task that is assigned. Some tasks, such as learning to spell, seem more individual-oriented, whereas others, such as learning how to function as the member of a committee, seem more obviously group-oriented. However, there are a great many skills that can be learned in a group setting and in which class members can assist one another. Even spelling can be studied through cooperative group interaction.

The way in which students regard learning tasks is also significant. Margaret M. Clifford and T. Anne Cleary (1970) found that fifth- and sixth-graders preferred to compete for rewards with students of their own ability and to avoid situations in which they had to compete with less able classmates. It would thus appear that cooperation would work best with heterogeneous groups, that is, groups containing individuals with differing levels of ability. A sex factor is also involved, in that boys, being generally more aggressive than girls, tend to enjoy competitive situations more. Students who rate high on n Ach also find competitive situations interesting. In most instances, they enjoy competing with themselves—bettering their own performance—as much as competing with others.

The problem of what to do about competition is an extremely complex one. The schools are often under a great deal of pressure to teach children to compete and to stress the competitive aspects of education because, as is so often pointed out, this is a competitive world. But people who put these pressures on the schools generally overlook the fact that the children usually have learned many of the techniques of competition before they enter school (they have learned to compete with their brothers and sisters, for example), and that many school practices (for instance, the giving of grades, honors, and other forms of recognition) already encourage a high degree of competition. Actually, there is no reason for the school to be *more* competitive than life outside the school, yet that is what

some critics demand. Another point to consider is that the skills of cooperation are far more crucial in today's world than are the skills of competition. Indeed, the survival of the civilized world will depend, in the final analysis, on our ability to learn to cooperate more effectively and to teach others how to do so.

Teachers sometimes defend an emphasis on competition on the grounds that it stimulates individual effort and thus produces greater gains in learning; however, some research by Lee Sechrest (1963) shows that such gains are likely to be limited to the student who is thus rewarded and that this advantage may be cancelled out by performance losses on the part of other students. His experiment showed that praising the performance of one member of a pair of children improved the performance of the praised member, but not that of the unpraised member. Incidentally, when one member of a pair was criticized in the experiment, his performance worsened, but his partner's performance improved.

In an intensely competitive classroom students are more likely to feel devalued than praised because no matter how well they do, the teacher implies or actually states that they could have done better. The student who is making average or even above-average progress is made to feel inadequate because he is not at the head of the class. Under intense competitive pressures, even students who are normally trustworthy may resort to such devices as copying term papers from encyclopedias, using the work of other students, cheating during examinations, and stealing or destroying one another's work.

HOSTILITY AMONG PEER GROUPS

Ethnic Prejudice

We discussed earlier the tensions that divide cultural subgroups and interfere with communication, cohesiveness, morale, and cooperation. These tensions often appear in the form of the prejudices that different cultural, ethnic, or religious groups express toward one another, and are based on the firm belief in the innate superiority of one's own group and the innate inferiority of certain other groups. These beliefs naturally lead to hostile and derogatory attitudes toward other groups, usually those groups that constitute minorities in a dominant culture or society. The tendency to make such discriminations and the hostility that often accompanies them are learned and are not biologically inherited, contrary to what many people believe. The first-grader who plays after school with a child of the "wrong" ethnic group or social class is reprimanded by his family: "Now I don't want to catch you playing with those children again. They're dirty (or they cheat, or they'll teach you the wrong kind of things)." Or the child learns how his family feels about other ethnic or religious groups by the offhand remarks made around the dinner table. In investigating some of the ways children learn to be prejudiced, Donald L. Mosher and Alvin Scodel (1960) measured the degree of ethnic prejudice expressed by sixth- and seventh-grade children in Ohio and found that it was significantly correlated with the degree of prejudice expressed by the children's mothers. They also found that mothers who were more rigid and punitive tended to be more prejudiced than mothers whose methods of dealing with their children were more sympathetic.

Some studies in which black and white children in nursery school and the early primary grades were asked to evaluate or choose black or white dolls suggest that children at that age have relatively little race prejudice (Cantor and Paternite, 1973; Katz and Zalk, 1974). Hostility toward other ethnic groups appears to have its major growth, however, during the preadolescent stage of development, a period marked by increases in antisocial behavior for many children. This is also a period in which group identity and group loyalties become intense, and differences between in-groups and out-groups are perceived as crucial by youngsters. Youngsters at this stage of development, as we noted earlier, are beginning to learn the techniques and advantages of forming groups. The strengths that they discover in these groups enable them to defy the

adult world more effectively, at a time when adults are increasing pressures to conform to adult expectations and norms, to take on new responsibilities, and to learn ways of applying the basic skills. Preadolescents express as much of their frustration and hostility as they dare toward adults, but there is much they cannot express, perhaps because of their fear of adults and their anxiety about jeopardizing major sources of love and security. Under such conditions it is perhaps natural for them to turn against other children in their attempt to find outlets for some of this unexpressed hostility. And it is particularly natural that they should direct their aggression against those children who are most vulnerable—children who are unwilling or unable to defend themselves.

The prejudice that we find in our classrooms thus comes from two main sources: first, the values and attitudes that students learn from others and, second, the tensions and frustrations experienced in coping with others. An individual's failure to cope with life stresses often leads him to develop attitudes of self rejection and self-depreciation. David Chabassol (1970) asked English-Canadian high-school students in one of the Maritime provinces their opinions of French Canadians, blacks, and Jews, and at the same time had them complete a personality test measuring self-acceptance. An analysis of the two sets of scores showed that there was a tendency for students with the most self-rejection to express the greatest amount of hostility toward minority groups.

Failures to cope in interpersonal situations, as well as with other kinds of frustrations, arouse hostile feelings; the means for expressing these hostile feelings are learned. Although children are notoriously cruel to one another, many of their negative attitudes are learned from adults.

Effects of Intergroup Hostility

Prejudice is a disruptive force. It arouses anxieties and tensions that interfere with the attainment of all positive social goals, including those of the school. As children who are the targets for prejudice learn how others feel toward them, they feel humiliated and inferior. They encounter unusual difficulties in their attempts to meet psychological needs for status and self-esteem. They tend to react to these frustrations in one of two ways: Either they become apathetic, submissive, and inept, working far below their real potentials, or they become aggressive, rebellious, hostile, and competitive. Neither orientation is conducive to mental health, cooperative group relations, or effective learning. Nor are children who generate prejudice immune from the effects of their prejudice. It is highly questionable whether a child can devote his best talents and energies to the task of achieving some of the broader goals of education—understanding of himself and others, learning to think for himself, learning to develop cooperative relationships with others, and developing a pattern of democratic values—if his attention and energy are directed into generating and expressing hostility toward children of other ethnic or religious groups, and if his concepts of life are so rigidly predetermined. Because of the many ways in which prejudice disrupts and disturbs effective learning, it is difficult to see how teachers can ignore this threat.

Most of the research on ethnic or race prejudice was conducted during the years before and after World War II. Although research interests of social psychologists today have shifted to other topics, the research findings of that era are unchallenged and are as relevant today as then. In one of the studies from that period, Marvin D. Solomon (1951) found that prejudice, rigidity in thinking, and the inability to use objective methods in solving problems were all closely interrelated. In other words, those individuals who were the most rigid in their thinking also tended to be the most prejudiced and the least able to solve complex problems. In reviewing his findings, Solomon concluded:

The rigid individuals seemed to show the inability to go beyond the mere factual information at hand in their attempt to solve a problem. They react on the basis of each individual fact separately. The rigid group [of students] does not indicate the ability to see a relationship of one piece of factual material information to others. The individuals of the rigid group may even refuse to consider some of the facts at their command.

The nonrigid individual, on the other hand, has the ability to see and to state the relationships existing and necessary for the correct solution of a problem. . . . [He] can take the individual facts under consideration and organize them into a single unified structure. The thought processes are broad and integrated and take all of the pertinent facts into consideration in arriving at a solution to the problems.

How Schools Can Deal with Intergroup Hostility and Aggression

The antidote for ethnic prejudice and the aggression it often generates lies in innovative ways of instruction. It is difficult to change students' attitudes if we depend on assigned readings, workbooks and study guides, and the like. On the contrary, dealing with prejudiced attitudes requires some form of open discussion and some flexibility in classroom management. This is not easy to do, and teachers have to work cautiously in arranging and conducting situations in which students can engage in an honest and productive interchange of ideas and feelings without aggravating hostility.

The fact that students in many classrooms come from diverse ethnic groups inevitably creates some tensions, but the presence of these tensions can be used as the basis for dialogue and understanding. We should also keep in mind that schools themselves provide a "socially cementing" influence by promoting interaction among students from different social and ethnic groups who ordinarily would have no opportunity to get to know one another. Psychologists who have studied the social composition of school populations report that the great majority of children choose friends from their own social class when they are away from school, but within the context of the school environment, most students choose some friends from outside their own social group.

Within the last decade or so, textbooks and other instructional materials have been criticized because they present a picture of a white, Anglo-Saxon, Protestant America and, hence, do not accurately reflect the contributions that have been made by Americans of other races and religions.[4] A number of publishers have produced a series of multiethnic readers and other materials in an attempt to correct this deficiency. John H. Litcher and David W. Johnson (1969) conducted a study of the use of multiethnic readers in an elementary school located in an all-white community. At the end of a four-month period, children in experimental groups showed marked positive gains in attitudes toward blacks, as contrasted with control groups of children who used conventional readers. The researchers explained the difference in terms of the fact that the multiethnic reader enabled children to associate positive types of behavior with blacks, instead of the conventional, largely negative, stereotypes.

The way in which children's attitudes toward others can be manipulated was demonstrated in an ingenious study by C. Joan Early (1968), who conducted a sociometric survey of fourth- and fifth-grade children in order to determine which children were the isolates—the least popular. All the children in the class then learned series of words in which the names of one-half the isolates (the experimental group) were paired with positive words, such as "friendly" and "happy," and the names of other isolates (the control group) were paired with neutral words. The subsequent observation of the behavior of the children in free play situations over the next few days showed that they were much more likely to approach the experimental than the

control isolates. Furthermore, a sociogram made subsequent to the experiment showed that the experimental isolates were rated more favorably than the control isolates. In other words, the experimental isolates were no longer isolates.

We are citing this study here not as a suggestion of how teachers should go about eliminating prejudice but, instead, as an indication of the way in which both favorable attitudes and prejudices are learned. Children learn prejudices by associating negative qualities with the individuals or groups concerned, and they develop positive and cooperative attitudes by learning to associate favorable qualities with individuals or groups.

The problems that produce prejudiced attitudes and the problems that result are very complex. If prejudice were a temporary phenomenon, occurring only in childhood and adolescence, it would be serious enough because it causes untold misery and discouragement. But the prejudicial patterns learned in childhood are usually retained in adulthood, blocking communication and causing dissension among large groups of our citizens, preventing cooperation, and aggravating crime and other forms of vicious behavior. The school that attempts, through intergroup education, to reduce or to eliminate prejudice (even assuming that community opinion is agreeable) has a difficult task, since prejudice is a way of life. Few individuals are completely free from prejudice, not even the people who are its chief targets. However, the methods that seem to work effectively in the reduction of prejudice are the same methods that have been developed by teachers in recent years as the best ways of meeting the emotional and social needs of children. In other words, if children in the classroom are free to communicate on a wide variety of subjects and issues, do not have to function in a fiercely competitive climate, if they are helped to work together cooperatively, work and play in a democratic atmosphere, and are given sufficient freedom and help to make their own decisions within the range of their capabilities, then we should be able to make real progress in reducing some of

[4] Somewhat similar criticisms have been made in recent years of the tendency of textbook authors and publishers to glorify the male role in society and to belittle the competence of females. Although women and girls constitute a numerical majority of the world's population, the fact that they occupy a relatively small percentage of the status positions indicates that they are the world's largest minority group.

the hostility and anxiety that makes prejudice so prevalent.

SUMMARY

The need to relate to others is basic to a great deal of human behavior. Without some kind of positive relationship to other people, we are "nobody." We can even experience a kind of "social hunger" if we are deprived of normal interpersonal contact. We are dependent on others not only for the development of our self-concept—"who we are"—but even for the satisfaction of our basic psychological needs. Children, like adults, are attracted to others to the extent that they perceive others to have attitudes and values similar to theirs. The tendency to be attracted to similar others increases during the childhood and adolescent years. A survey of high-school students shows that similarity in sex, age, and ethnic group membership was very important in making friends, but that use of or abstinence from marihuana smoking was also an important factor.

A child's relations with others his age pass through several fairly well-defined stages that may be observed in his patterns of play. Toddlers tend to be self-centered in their play and then gradually enter into associations with other children. Really strong attachments to others and to groups do not generally appear until the middle years of childhood. These attachments commonly take on the nature of a "best friend" arrangement and then blossom into larger friendship groups. Boys tend to form larger, more active, and less tractable groups than girls do. During preadolescent and adolescent years students are more or less troubled by conflicts between the need to achieve (n Ach) and the need to affiliate (n Aff) with the peer group. This conflict is especially strong during adolescence, when the power of the peer group is at a peak and often takes the form of rebelliousness toward adult authority. The picture is far from clear, however. Some experts maintain that adolescents develop a subculture of their own, with values that differ from those of adult society, whereas others hold that adolescent values are not much different from those of adults and that, in any event, the popular-

ity- and pleasure-oriented attitudes which young people express are no indication of their future behavior. There is no doubt, however, that many adolescents feel they must make gestures of defiance and nonconformity. The use of marihuana appears to have symbolic value to groups who take antiestablishment positions. Problems of communication and mutual understanding between adolescents and adults are aggravated by the strong hold that peer group norms have on adolescents, the increasingly early age at which puberty occurs, and an extension in the period of preparation adolescents must go through in order to participate adequately in a complex, urbanized society.

One of the most effective ways of studying the psychological forces at work in the classroom group is the sociogram—a way of charting the patterns of acceptance and rejection that students feel toward one another. Preferences expressed socio metrically have been found to be related to cognitive functioning, psychological health, and social status.

Groups commonly develop feelings of identification among their members by establishing norms for conduct. Sometimes these norms encourage or permit behavior that is contrary to adult standards. Whether or not high-school graduates will attend college is determined to a high degree by group norms. Hence it is understandable why teachers and parents might have misgivings about the desirability of students becoming involved in the activities of group life. Yet the psychological needs that attract children and adolescents to groups are natural and strong, and it is more sensible to work *with* these needs rather than *against* them. A group whose members can communicate effectively among themselves is more likely to develop cohesiveness and good morale. Cohesiveness and good morale cannot develop unless the psychological climate is favorable; teachers play key roles in determining the kind of climate that prevails in their classes. Although a little competition can make some learning tasks interesting and stimulating, an overstress on competition can be destructive to good group feeling. The skills and attitudes basic to cooperation can facilitate all kinds of learning and may be essential for society's survival.

Prejudice directed toward individuals or groups is

a disruptive, divisive force that can be used to justify intergroup hostility and aggression. It interferes with learning and may create and be created by mental health problems. Prejudiced attitudes are learned, usually from adults, but positive attitudes toward individuals and groups can be learned in their stead through intergroup education and the use of multi-ethnic materials.

In Figure 5-3, Boy A was disliked, Boy B was regarded neutrally, and Boy C was liked. Note that Boy A is depicted as being shorter than the other two; the drawing is less detailed, his facial expression is more "unbalanced," and there is some "fuzziness" about the way his head is drawn.

Suggested Problems

1. List some of the social groups in which you hold membership (that is, your family, the student body of your college, etc.). What are some of the ways in which these groups affect your behavior without you ordinarily being aware of it?

2. Observe a group of preschool children on a playground for a period of fifteen minutes. At the end of each minute, jot down the number of children falling into each of the categories listed by Parten in Figure 5-1. Do a similar observation of older children and compare the results with your observation of preschool children.

3. Construct a sociogram based on choices made by children in a small group with which you have contact: Scout troop, neighborhood playground group, Sunday school class, or the like. Discuss the implications of your findings. (*Note:* Be sure to keep your data confidential; you can avoid hurting the feelings of children by not discussing choices with the participants or their parents.)

4. What norms are prevalent among the friendship groups on your college campus? What psychological purposes do these norms serve?

5. Describe some of the social forces at work in a group that is well known to you. How cohesive is it? What is the level of its morale? What evidence do you have to support your conclusions?

6. What were the prevailing intergroup tensions and prejudices among the students of the high school you attended? If you were to undertake a program of intergroup education in your former high school, how would you go about starting the program? For instance, how would you get the program accepted by the teachers, the administration, the student body, the school board, and the community? How would you actually go about teaching intergroup education, assuming you received school and community support?

7. Why should the attitudes and skills basic to cooperation be more difficult to learn than those involved in competition?

Suggested Readings

Charters, W.W., and Gage, N. L. (eds.). *Readings in the social psychology of education.* Boston: Allyn and Bacon, 1963. Sections III and IV contain papers on school atmosphere and climate, adolescent values, sociometry, and the social structure of classroom groups.

Douvan, E., and Adelson, J. *The adolescent experience.* New York: Wiley, 1965. A survey of some 3000 American teenagers which raises questions about many commonly held ideas about adolescence.

Gronlund, N.E. *Sociometry in the classroom.* New York: Harper, 1959. Sociometric techniques and their application to educational problems.

Jennings, H.H. *Sociometry in group relations,* rev. ed. Washington: American Council on Education, 1959. A practical pamphlet on the methods of sociometry.

Jones, M.C., et al. *The course of human development.* Waltham, Mass.: Xerox, 1971. See research reports in Chapter 7, "Social development."

Lindgren, H.C. *An introduction to social psychology,* 2nd ed. New York: Wiley, 1973. Contains much material on topics covered in this chapter: group norms, morale, cohesiveness, climate, competition, and cooperation.

Lindgren, H.C., and Lindgren, F. (eds.). *Current readings in educational psychology,* 2nd ed. New

York: Wiley, 1972. See discussions of adolescent problems in Section 3.

McCandless, B.R. *Adolescents: Behavior and development*. New York: Dryden, 1970.

Watson, R.I., and Lindgren, H.C. *Psychology of the child*, 3rd ed. New York: Wiley, 1973. See Chapter 13, "Personality and peer relationships," and Chapter 16, "Peer influences and school relationships."

Problem Behavior in the Classroom

Teachers' Attitudes Toward Problem Behavior

Most teachers would probably agree with the definition of problem behavior as "behavior that interferes with teaching-learning processes." Many a teacher has had to bring class discussion or his explanation of the day's lesson to a halt so that he could direct his attention to one or more students whose disruptive behavior was making it impossible to continue.

Not all forms of problem behavior are disruptive of classroom procedures, however. A boy who is so shy that he cannot make a scheduled presentation to the class is likely to present a problem that calls for more-than-average attention on the part of the teacher. The girl who will not or cannot collaborate with others also may create difficulties in a class whose activities center around the cooperative interaction of students in small groups.

In its broadest sense, "problem behavior" is a term that applies to any kind of behavior that *creates difficulties* (interferes with the effective functioning of the student or the classroom group) or *reveals the presence of difficulties* (indicates that the student or the group is not functioning effectively). Hence such diverse symptoms as "chronic defiance of teachers and other persons in authority," "extreme shyness," "excessive daydreaming," "truancy," and "chronic unhappiness and depression" may all be considered to be varieties of problem behavior.

Some teachers take the position that they would rather not concern themselves with problem behavior, looking upon it as some extraneous factor that interferes with their teaching, something for which they should have no responsibility. Someone else, they feel, should handle the behavior problems that they encounter in their classrooms; hence they refer them to administrators, counselors, or parents for "straightening out." To be sure, referral of problems is often a good idea, particularly if it is done judiciously, after considering such factors as the probable effect on the child, the person or persons best able to deal with the problem and so forth. However, the eagerness to get rid of a problem by getting someone else to accept responsibility for it may actually keep the teacher from developing any understanding of what is involved and thus prevent his helping the student become a more effective learner. Even when problem students are referred to the school psychologist or some other authority outside the classroom, they usually remain in the classroom and must be dealt with there. Furthermore, a great many instances of problem behavior are produced or aggravated by school experiences or even by the behavior of teachers themselves. The opposite of this statement is also valid, of course: a great deal of problem behavior is prevented or allayed by school experiences and by appropriate attitudes and behavior on the part of teachers.

The point is that the teacher who is interested in fostering and promoting classroom learning cannot afford to ignore the psychological problems of his students and thus must have some understanding of the various symptoms of what we call "problem behavior." Not only should he know what kinds of behavior are likely to interfere with learning processes, but he also ought to know what problems should be referred to sources of help outside the classroom, what kinds he might deal with himself, and how he can understand and help students whose learning abilities are blocked or encumbered by emotional conflicts and tensions.

Most referrals of school-age children for psychological help are made or are suggested by teachers because it is in the classroom that problems are likely to appear. John P. Glavin and Herbert C. Quay (1969) note that the use of teacher judgment in referring psychologically disturbed children is generally justified, although teacher estimations alone are not a very valid index of psychological maladjustment. Most teachers are primarily concerned with the effect that a child's behavior has on their educational program and are often unaware of the psychological bases for the misbehavior.

If we intend to understand a problem, we must first develop some degree of objectivity. Objectivity does not come easily, especially when the child in question is engaging in a form of hostile or destructive behavior that we find personally obnoxious. Yet anyone who has observed a skilled teacher in action knows that it is possible to deal with hostile or destructive behavior without losing one's sense of objectivity. There is perhaps a natural tendency for us as teachers to be somewhat judgmental, tending to look upon misbehavior as something that should be suppressed—through punishment, if necessary—rather than as an indication that something is amiss with a student. This tendency of teachers to be judgmental has been the topic of a number of investigations going back to the 1920s. E. K. Wickman (1928) found that teachers tended to view problem behavior in ways that were quite different from those of psychologists and other mental hygienists. In many instances the two groups came to opposite conclusions. Table 6-1 lists some of the ratings that the groups assigned to various symptoms when they were asked to rank them from the most to the least serious.

TABLE 6-1. Changes in Attitudes Regarding Children's Behavior Problems, 1928 versus 1972, as Shown by a Sampling of Rankings[a] Made by Teachers and Psychologists in 1928 and 1972[b]

Behavior Problem	Teachers (1928)	Psychologists (1928)	Teachers (1972)	Psychologists (1972)
Heterosexual activity	1	26	32.5	36
Stealing	2	13.5	1	4
Masturbation	3	41	45	46.5
Obscene notes, pictures, talk	4	28.5	23	34
Untruthfulness (lying)	5	23	4	10.5
Truancy	6	23	5	17.5
Impertinence (defiance)	7	37.5	21.5	28.5
Destroying school materials	10	45	3	4
Disobedience	11	41	17	20
Unreliableness (irresponsible)	12	21	8	10.5
Profanity	15	49	34.5	46.5
Smoking	18	49	34.5	46.5
Unhappy, depressed	22.5	3	2	2
Easily discouraged	22.5	7	10	13
Unsocial, withdrawing	40.5	1	9	1

[a] Wickman's list consists of fifty behavior problems which were ranked from most serious (1) to least serious (50).
[b] Wickman, 1928; Rajpal, 1972.

More recent studies, however, show that although teachers and psychologists do not always see eye-to-eye, they are much more in agreement than they were a half-century ago, as Table 6-1 shows. Teachers today are no longer as concerned about sex matters, defiance, and profanity, and psychologists, for their part, have come to regard disobedience, destruction of school property, and irresponsibility as more serious than they considered them in the 1920s. An analysis of the rankings made by teachers and psychologists in 1972 showed that there was about a 70 percent agreement between the two groups on problems they considered to be most serious (Rajpal, 1972).

Another study compared the ratings given problem behavior symptoms by psychologists, experienced teachers, and inexperienced teachers. Experienced teachers were closer to psychologists in their views than they were to inexperienced teachers (Tolor, Scarpetti, and Lane, 1967). It appears that teachers are not only more sophisticated than they used to be, with respect to evaluating the behavior of students, but also that this sophistication is sharpened by classroom experience.

Even so, there is a tendency for teachers to rate the disruptive kinds of behavior as more serious and social withdrawal as less serious than psychologists do. The fact that passivity and other forms of withdrawal are more likely to escape attention of the teacher does not make them any the less serious. A number of studies show that tendencies to withdraw from social interaction are predictive of later psychological disturbance. In one study, high-school graduates who were later diagnosed as schizophrenic[1] and institutionalized were found, according to the summaries of their activities published in senior yearbooks, to have participated in significantly fewer activities than other students. (Barthell and Holmes, 1968).

Personal Difficulties and Learning Progress

The way in which personal difficulties and progress in learning may interact with each other is shown by a graphic analysis prepared by Loren A. Stringer

---

[1] Schizophrenia is a severe type of mental disorder that usually results in the patient's being hospitalized.

(1959), who used a variation of the Wetzel Grid (a growth progress chart used by pediatricians) to plot a child's *actual* progress against his *expected* progress, that is, the progress that is typical of the theoretically average child. Figure 6-1 presents the case of a boy who was referred for treatment to the School Mental Health Services of the St. Louis (Missouri) County Health Department. The boy had been doing well in the first grade until his mother died. He continued to make progress, but at a less-than-normal rate. He became greatly overweight, displaying aggressive and disruptive behavior. His 0.2 of a grade advantage at the end of the first grade became a 0.4 lag in the second grade and a 0.8 lag in the third grade. He continued to lose ground until his father remarried. The stepmother turned out to be a woman who was warmly concerned about helping the boy, sought out the boy's mental health counselor, and was able to develop a great deal of understanding of the boy's problem. This enabled

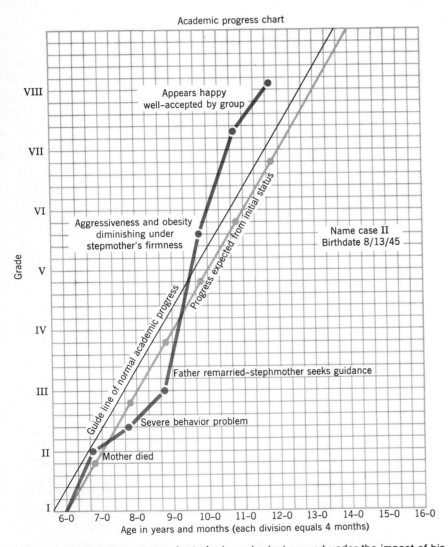

FIG. 6-1. Academic progress chart of a boy who lost ground under the impact of his mother's death but who made a good recovery through the help of his stepmother and a mental health counselor (Stringer, 1959).

her to establish a positive relationship with him, while at the same time she set firm limits to his aggressive and disruptive behavior. Within the next year he gained 2.6 grade levels in school achievement, actually surpassing grade expectancy; this gain was further increased the following year. In the meantime, his obesity and aggressiveness were well under control, and by the end of the sixth grade he was not only a well-accepted member of his class but was beginning to play leadership roles to some extent.

Everyday Types of Problems

Many psychologists who work with children classify the behavior problems they encounter into two major categories: *conduct problems* and *personality problems.* Conduct problems consist of behavior that is grossly disturbing to others and may in fact be directed against them, in that it is hostile, aggressive, destructive, and/or disobedient. It sometimes involves delinquency and psychopathology. Personality problems are more or less "neurotic" in character and often take the form of what may be called "withdrawal behavior," that is, behavior suggesting that the child is fearful of others, feels anxious, and is avoiding situations that might expose him to criticism, ridicule, or rejection. Children troubled by personality problems may also have some degree of hostility but, unless they are placed under an unusual degree of stress, they hold it back or direct it against themselves in the form of guilt or self-criticism and are usually unaware that they are hostile. Both conduct and personality problems may result from attempts to cope with much anxiety, although anxiety is generally more characteristic of

Most of the problem behavior that teachers report involves students' disruption of classroom activities.

children with personality problems. Conduct problems, on the other hand, are more likely to characterize the behavior of children who are relatively free of anxiety, that is, who do not have enough "normal anxiety" to feel any concern for the rights and feelings of others or for the consequences and implications of their behavior.

It is obvious that conduct problems are the type that are more likely to come to the attention of teachers. Not all classroom disturbances are caused by children with conduct problems, but these children are likely to cause or contribute to disturbance and to demand their full share (or more than their share) of the teacher's attention. The child with the personality problem, however, is likely to remain in the background and is thus not easily identified as someone needing help. He is usually compliant and obedient and consequently may escape notice altogether.

Herbert C. Quay and Lorene C. Quay (1965) have identified a third dimension of problem behavior that appears in early adolescence: immaturity. Table 6-2 lists the kinds of symptoms that were found to be associated with the three categories of behavior with seventh- and eighth-grade children. Note that there seems to be an overlap among the three

types: All three are, for example, characterized by distractibility, and students labeled as "psychopathic" (having conduct problems) and "immature" are both characterized as restless, hyperactive, and having a short attention span. There are two points here: One, that each list of symptoms must be considered as a whole in order to get the "flavor" of the kind of behavior problem it describes, and, two, making a decision as to whether a student belongs to one category or another has its pitfalls, even for an expert, because certain symptoms apply to more than one category.

Prevalence of Problem Behavior

A number of studies have attempted to assess the prevalence of problem behavior in the school population. The estimates in the more recent surveys vary from 22 percent designated as "moderately or seriously emotionally handicapped" in a school district in northern Minnesota (Stennett, 1966) to about 4 percent designated as "emotionally disturbed" in New York (McCaffrey and Cumming, 1967). Both studies were conducted in small towns or rural areas, but the first used a combination of teacher, peer, and self ratings, and the second used confi-

TABLE 6-2. Symptoms Characterizing Three Major Kinds of Behavior Problems in Early Adolescent Children[a]

Personality Problems (Neurotic)	Conduct Problems (Psychopathic)	Problems of Emotional and Social Immaturity
Unable to have fun	Restless	Restless
Self-conscious	Attention-seeking	Self-conscious
Feelings of inferiority	Disruptive	Feelings of inferiority
Preoccupied	Boisterous	Preoccupied
Shy	Short attention span	Short attention span
Withdrawal	Inattentive	Lacks confidence
Lacks confidence	Lack of interest	Easily flustered
Easily flustered	Laziness in school	Daydreams
Lacks interest	Irresponsible	Passive, suggestible
Irresponsible	Disobedient	Hyperactive
Daydreams	Uncooperative	Distractible
Aloof	Passive, suggestible	Impertinent
Distractible	Hyperactive	Nervous, jittery
Lethargy	Distractible	
Nervous, jittery	Impertinent	

[a] Quay and Quay, 1965.

dential interviews with teachers. The latter figure is consistent with the findings of Harlan H. Lewis (1951) a number of years ago, and it would average out to one or two children per classroom. The rather large variation among estimates may be accounted for the differences in standards used by researchers in classifying maladjustment. The figure of 4 percent probably represents children who ought to be referred to clinicians for special help, whereas the figure of 22 percent evidently includes candidates for psychotherapy as well as children who need special attention or encouragement from time to time.

One of the difficulties with surveys of the type we have cited is that they make distinctions between "normal" and "problem" children that may be somewhat artificial, and children who present problems in one situation may be problem-free in another. Ivan N. Mensh and his co-workers (1959) in the St. Louis (Missouri) County Health Department conducted a survey of problems reported by the

(The Wall Street Journal)

"He drives me crazy, too. But then you're getting paid for it and I'm not."

mothers of approximately eight hundred third-grade children and correlated them with indications of more severe maladjustment as noted by teachers and mental health workers. As Table 6-3 shows, less than one-third of the behavior problems reported by mothers had any significant association with emotional maladjustment as observed by teachers and mental health workers.

Attempts to classify children as "normal" and "problem children" is further complicated by the fact that everyone, children and adults alike, has some emotional problems. A longitudinal study of 116 boys and girls showed that one-third or more of them were reported to have problems with oversensitivity, tempers, jealousy, specific fears, and excessive reserve for the majority of the twelve years covered by the investigation. At eleven years of age, for example, more than a third of the children had difficulties with the problems mentioned, as well as with disturbing dreams, nail-biting, mood swings, and shyness (Macfarlane, Allen, and Honzik, 1971).

Some individuals have more problems or more symptoms than others, however, and they are the ones who usually cause greater difficulties for themselves and for others. Emotional adjustment, like all other human characteristics, is not only a matter of degree, but it also varies from one situation to another. A high-school junior may get along with his teachers and have many friends but may develop a bad case of "test nerves" every time he has to take an examination or quiz. A girl may be reasonably happy and well adjusted but may bite her fingernails down to the quick. Or a fourth-grader may be a model student but is also inclined to bully smaller children.

Psychologists who have conducted longitudinal investigations in which they have followed the same individuals from early childhood to adulthood have been surprised to find that childhood and adolescent problems are not very good predictors of adjustment during the adult years. Jean Walker McFarlane (1971), for example, surveyed the findings of the Berkeley Growth Study and noted that when the subjects in the study were children, the psychologists on the staff had been seriously con-

TABLE 6-3. Percentages of Mothers Reporting Various Kinds of Problem Behavior in Their Third-Grade Children, Classified in Terms of Their Relationship to Maladjustment Noted by Teachers and Mental Health Workers[a]

Related to Maladjustment in School Settings	Percentage of Mothers Reporting Problems
Nervousness	33
Daydreaming	21
Overactive	14
Speech disturbance	9
Difficulties in relations with other children	
Withdrawn behavior	7
Aggressive behavior	9
Destructiveness	7
Unrelated to Maladjustment in School Settings	
Eating problems	33
Temper tantrums	19
Unusual fears	18
Wets self	14
Lying	13
Crying	13
Thumb-sucking	9
Stomach-upset	8
Difficulties in relations with adults	
Withdrawn behavior	1
Aggressive behavior	6
Trouble with school	4
Sexual difficulty	2
Stealing	2

[a] Mensh et al., 1959.

cerned about many of them. These children displayed what appeared to be major personality handicaps and disorganizing problem behavior. The psychologists therefore predicted that this group of children, who constituted about half of the subjects in the study, would turn out to have "crippled and inadequate adult personalities." In actuality these children grew up to be well-adjusted adults, and one-fifth of the group had outstanding successes.

Another researcher studied a group of nursery school children and noted that not a single child was free of conflicts or developmental problems. A sizable number even required special help from teacher or parents and even psychotherapy. As adults, however, they turned out to be reasonably well-adjusted and normal (Murphy, 1956).

The lesson of both these studies seems to be that we should not jump to hasty conclusions and more overpessimistic predictions as to the future of any child, no matter how disturbed he seems to be. The human organism has remarkable recuperative powers.

Understanding the Meaning of Problem Behavior

From time immemorial, teachers have tried to deal with problem behavior by direct and sometimes drastic methods: physical punishment, banishment from the classroom, sarcasm, scolding, poor marks, detention, and the like. Sometimes such methods help a child who is wavering between conformity and antisocial behavior and who needs reassurance that the teacher means what he says. Very often, however, such punishment worsens the problem behavior instead of eliminating it. Direct and drastic treatment of problem behavior seldom gets at its source; it is unlikely to be based on any genuine attempt to understand the motivation and behavior of children.

Once school people have grasped the idea that it is necessary to go beyond the surface aspects of problem behavior in order to deal with it properly, they will be in a position to develop new and more effective methods of dealing with it. Katherine F. Tift (1968), speaking from her experience as a therapist in a center for disturbed children, suggests that teachers deal with the behavior of a disruptive child with understanding and sympathy but firmness. She feels that we should be honest with children: If behavior is genuinely disruptive, the teacher should not gloss over it and pretend that it is really satisfactory. Merely being honest is not enough; a teacher must also develop a number of strategies that help the child become involved in behavior that is more productive and less disturbing. The best strategies are those that enable a disturbed child to participate in constructive activities with more secure, task-oriented children. It is dangerous for the teacher to become too involved with a disturbing child because this leaves the rest of the class to its own devices. When distraction and similar strategies fail, she says, it may be that the child is deeply disturbed and needs more help than the teacher alone can give him. This help probably does not mean that the child will be taken out of the class, but that he will receive some special treatment, perhaps psychotherapy, perhaps remedial work with skill subjects, outside of class.

Any teacher who attempts to deal with a child's problem in class has a better chance for success if he understands its psychodynamics. Tift suggests that the teacher try to hypothesize why a child is refusing to do a task or is acting in a disruptive way.

The strategy the teacher employs thus becomes appropriate to the hypothesis. It is not to be expected that the teacher will succeed in every case: Perhaps the hypothesis is wrong or the strategy inappropriate. When this occurs, another hypothesis must be explored or another strategy attempted. In the meantime, the teacher uses whatever facilities are at his command to find out more about the child: He may discuss him with other teachers who have taught him, he may look for clues in his written work, or he may take note of the kinds of occasions in which he is attentive or involved in his work, and the like.

Understanding problem behavior is a difficult, but not impossible, task. One principle to keep in mind is that the symptom itself often tells relatively little about a child's motivation. "Why does John steal money from other children?" a teacher asks. Stealing is a hostile act, to be sure, but other than that, it tells us little about John's motivation. He may steal for any of an infinite number of reasons. Questioning him may help, but much depends on the kinds of questions asked and how the teacher listens to his answers. In such interviews, focusing on the behavior itself is usually of little value. Individuals who display disturbed behavior seldom are able to tell us directly why they act as they do. True, they may give explanations that sound very logical, but further psychological investigation inevitably discloses causes that are quite different, causes that the individual himself either is completely unaware of or is dimly aware of but cannot express.

EMOTIONAL PROBLEMS OF EVERYDAY LIVING

Anxiety as a Cause and Effect of Problem Behavior

According to the developmental scheme of behavior that we presented in Chapter 2, human behavior may be viewed in terms of attempts to meet basic needs or to cope with real or anticipated frustrations of these basic needs. When we feel apprehensive (perceive threat) about our ability to maintain satisfactory relations with others (n Aff), the feeling that ordinarily results is anxiety. Anxiety may appear

EMOTIONAL PROBLEMS
OF EVERYDAY LIVING

in other contexts, of course, but our relations with others are perhaps the commonest source. One group of researchers found that elementary school children who were least chosen by others on a sociometric test scored high on the Children's Manifest Anxiety Scale (had high anxiety), whereas the more popular ones scored low (McCandless, Castenada, and Palermo, 1956). In another study, the Children's Manifest Anxiety Scale, or CMAS, as it is commonly called, was used with nine-year-olds in the Rochester, New York, city schools to examine the relationship between anxiety and various sociometric, cognitive, and physical health variables. The investigators found that the higher the child's "manifest anxiety" score, the more likely he was to be referred to the school nurse's office, to be rated by his teacher as having negative behavior characteristics, and to be nominated by his classmates for a negative role in a mythical "class play." On the other hand, children with low anxiety scores were not only less likely to receive these negative evaluations, but were also more likely to get better grades and to score higher in reading comprehension (Cowen, et al., 1965).

Anxiety is a form of tension. When things are dull, we may risk a little anxiety in order to liven things up, but once we get involved in a difficult social situation, we may have more anxiety than we can handle for the moment and may make use of some more or less immature ways of coping with it without realizing that we are doing so.

Cathy Nadir is a rather plump, pleasant girl of fifteen. She is quite popular with her classmates and is always at the center of things. Hence no one was surprised when she was nominated for student-body vice president. The campaign lasted a week. It was a gala affair with posters, banners, and rallies. Cathy found it quite exciting. She neglected her school work and spent her afternoons and evenings with her friends at Hamburger Heaven, a place frequented by "the crowd." When all the votes were counted on the afternoon of election day, Cathy was pleased to find that she had won by a comfortable margin. However, when she went home that night, she found that two English papers were overdue, she had missed turning in her French assignments

for the whole week, and she had gained seven pounds!

Running for political office arouses anxiety. We wonder how we stand with the voters: Will they accept us or reject us? Cathy's way of handling or avoiding anxiety is to talk with her friends at Hamburger Heaven and to consume hamburgers. Although there is no *logical* relationship between the needs for status and acceptance and eating hamburgers, there is for Cathy an emotional or psychological relationship. Cathy kept saying that she did not care whether she won or not, but her behavior during the week tells us a different story. She did say that she worried "a little" about her homework and wondered once or twice why her dresses were getting tight. Hence she really had no great amount of insight into the causes of her anxiety.

Of course, there is nothing unusual or pathological about Cathy's behavior. It is the kind of thing that could happen to almost anyone. Our purpose in discussing it here is to show how the real significance of our behavior is hidden from us, and how we often do seemingly irrational things as a way of avoiding anxiety.

Mechanisms of Escape and Defense

Psychologists have given much attention to analyzing and classifying the various kinds of maneuvers that we use to avoid or reduce anxiety or tension. These habits and other forms of behavior are commonly called "escape mechanisms" or "defense mechanisms" because they enable us to escape from or defend ourselves against some tension-producing situation. Mechanisms of this sort range from perfectly normal-average gestures like drumming on the table with one's fingers, chewing gum, cracking knuckles, or calling up a friend for a chat, to more pathological ones like the inability to complete assignments or turn them in on time, extreme suspiciousness, tendencies to distort meanings, and complete social withdrawal. Most of the defense mechanisms that we resort to in everyday life lie at the normal-average end of the continuum, but because they play such an important part in problem behavior, we shall review some of the commoner types.

Rationalization

This type of defense mechanism is very familiar because we use it so commonly. Rationalizing consists of giving explanations for our behavior, explanations which often seem quite logical but which do not get at the real cause. For example, we might ask Cathy why she ate so many hamburgers during the campaign, and she might say that she was hungry. Or we might ask her why she spent so much time with her friends during that week, instead of studying, and she might reply that she wanted company. Or that she simply forgot about her assignments. All these explanations have a certain logical ring to them, but they evade the real issues. It is important to note that Cathy *believes* these explanations. We might point out to her that being hungry is no real explanation of her behavior—why she was hungrier than usual this week? If Cathy has any deep anxieties, she might even become angry at our questioning and accuse us of "picking" on her. No one likes to have his rationalizations dissected and analyzed and revealed as illogical. After all, their purpose is to *protect* us from our own anxiety; we are afraid that if the rationalization is taken away, we will have to face the anxiety.

Displaced Hostility

Cathy's chief opponent for vice president was Delores Burkhardt. Delores had been quite confident about winning and, when she lost, it came as quite a blow to her. She took it very well at first. She congratulated Cathy and insisted on buying a hamburger for her. However, when she arrived home, she got into a violent argument with her parents when they refused to buy her a cashmere sweater. Later in the evening, the boy with whom she had been going for four months called up and suggested that they go to the election dance together. It was a very informal affair, thought up by the elections committee at the last minute. Delores asked him whether he was deliberately trying to humiliate her, now that she had lost the election. One word led to another, both became angry—and that was the end of *that* friendship.

What Delores is doing, in a symbolic and not very subtle way, is taking out her anger, irritation, and disappointment on those around her. Perhaps she should really be angry with herself for not having been very realistic about the election. But Delores, like so many of us, is inclined to place the blame for her discomfiture anywhere except where it belongs. To take a good look at oneself and ask, "Where was I at fault?" arouses much anxiety. We do not like to take stock of ourselves because we are afraid of what we might find.

Self-punishment

Some people, of course, go to great lengths in blaming themselves when things go wrong. This is particularly common with individuals who grow up in families that are very strict, set excessively high standards of behavior, and are very critical. Such people find themselves unable to blame or criticize others, even when others actually are at fault. This is just as unrealistic as blaming others whenever things go wrong. What usually lies back of such behavior is the fear that "others won't like me if I criticize them." Such people often have an overpowering need to be liked and accepted. We all have needs to be accepted and liked, but we are being unrealistic and somewhat neurotic if such needs dominate our lives. What usually happens is that the self-punisher actually jeopardizes his chances for being accepted, inasmuch as his continual self-abasement and self-criticism make others feel uncomfortable.

Repression

One of the characteristics of defense mechanisms is that their true causes are concealed from the individual. The very anxiety that they arouse somehow distracts his attention from them and places them beyond the limits of awareness. Repression also helps us forget details in our lives that are painful. Sometimes this has an overall healthy effect, such as the forgetting of a humiliating and painful experience, but sometimes it causes us to forget something we should have remembered—like an appointment with the principal. There is every reason why we should have remembered an appointment with such an important person, but it really slipped our minds. Perhaps we were out shopping and got so involved in what we were doing that when we looked at our watch it was well past the appointed time. We feel terrible, of course, and cannot figure out why we should have done such a thing.

Probably most of us have some anxieties about meeting and talking to persons in authority, and occasionally this anxiety is enough to cause us to forget important engagements. It usually works the other way around, however. The anxiety that we would feel if we did *not* keep our appointment with the principal is greater than the anxiety we feel in keeping it.

Conformity

One of the commonest ways of avoiding anxiety is to conform to the expectations that others have for us. Because the principal expects us to be on time for the appointment, we may even arrive ten minutes or so ahead of time. Thinking and behaving differently from those around us (acting contrary to the norm) usually arouses anxiety because it brings up the possibility that others will reject us for being different. Hence we feel that it is much safer to conform, even when it may be in our best interest to do otherwise.

Conformity usually occurs as the result of "identification," that is, we pattern our behavior according to some person or group that we identify as the person or persons we would like to resemble. Thus a nine-year-old boy might identify himself with his father part of the time and at other times with a twelve-year-old boy who lives in the neighborhood and who has taken a brotherly interest in him. Sometimes the nine-year-old will wear the kind of cap his father wears golfing, but at other times he wants to wear the kind of clothes his friend wears.

Or a teenage girl may pattern her walk, speech, and mannerisms after those of a favorite singing star.

Identification and conformity are important aspects of the learning process. Children learn from their parents and teachers by identifying with them. By imitating adult behavior children work out patterns of conformity that enable them to get along with adults and help them to grow up to be like them. Unfortunately, identification is not a very selective process, for children are just as likely to copy the faults as well as the virtues. As someone has so aptly put it: "The trouble with the younger generation is that they are growing up to be no better than their parents."

Shyness

The inability to speak out in a group, to recite, or to perform before an audience is one of the commonest forms of avoidance behavior, although not a mental mechanism in the strict sense of the word. However, by begging off or refusing to speak, the shy student avoids exposure to value judgments on the part of others, an experience that would, in his opinion, be too painful to bear. The shy person often excuses his nonperformance by pleading inadequacy—"I really have nothing important to say," "Others can do it so much better," and the like. He may indeed feel inadequate at the time, although afterwards he often feels as though he had let himself down, and had also let down those, such as his teachers and his family, who would like to see him succeed. Then his guilt feelings may become as painful as his anxiety.

Some research by Allan Paivio (1964) suggests that there is a relationship between parental patterns of reward and punishment and audience sensitivity or shyness. Paivio collected compositions written by third- and fourth-grade children in Montreal schools on either one of these two topics: "Why I like to recite in class" or "Why I do not like to recite." A choice of the second topic was taken as an indicator of shyness. The parents of each child were then asked how they dealt with his social behavior and his achievements. Did they reward him for his achievements? Did they punish him for

TABLE 6-4. The Relationship Between Audience Sensitivity (Shyness) of Third- and Fourth-Grade Children and the Kind of Treatment They Received from Their Parents for Achievement or Nonachievement in Social Situations

Parents' Treatment of Child for Achievement or Nonachievement	Number of Compositions Written on Liking or Disliking Recitation			
	Boys		Girls	
	Like	Dislike	Like	Dislike
High reward, low punishment	13	1	9	5
Low reward, high punishment	1	13	10	6
High reward, high punishment	8	6	7	6
Low reward, low punishment	12	8	13	6

[a] Paivio, 1964.

nonachievement? Or did they do both? The results, as indicated in Table 6-4, show that the shyest boys were those who were not rewarded for achievements but punished for nonachievement. The opposite result was obtained for girls. Results also show that boys this age are shyer than girls. Another incidental finding was that when parents were active socially and made frequent appearances before audiences, their children tended to be less shy. These results tend to support the social-learning theory of personality development as proposed by Bandura and Walters (1963), in that children tend to use their parents as models for their social behavior.

Learning Defense Mechanisms

The chief function of defense mechanisms is that of helping us keep anxiety or tension to levels which are not painful for us. Mechanisms do not solve the problems that created the anxiety in the first place; their purpose is primarily that of enabling us to feel better, if only for the moment.

It is important to note that defense mechanisms, like most complex forms of behavior, are *learned*. Just as we learn when and where to be anxious, and what to be anxious about, so do we learn the behavioral tricks to use to keep anxiety within reasonable bounds. Knowing that mechanisms are learned is reassuring, in that we can assume that we can learn other ways of coping with anxiety. The student who reacts to an audience situation with

withdrawal can learn to face it more confidently. A student who regresses to a more childish pattern of behavior under stress can learn to deal with stress-producing situations in a more mature manner. This unlearning and relearning usually takes place gradually, over an extended period of time. Furthermore, as students develop and become more mature, they generally learn some of the more effective ways of coping with anxiety and drop some of the less effective ways.

Understanding defense mechanisms helps us identify some of the problems that commonly occur in everyday behavior, but there are other important aspects that deserve our attention. Why is George's anxiety more acute on some days than on others? Why does Jill show a great deal more anxiety than her brothers and sisters? In other words, what lies behind the anxiety that produces the defense mechanism?

BACKGROUND FACTORS IN PROBLEM BEHAVIOR

Emotional Conflict as a Basis for Problem Behavior

Very often what lies behind the anxiety is not just a simple frustration of basic needs—indeed, human problems are seldom simple but are infinitely complex and intricate. Usually there is some psychological conflict in the background. Fred's anxiety stems largely from the fact that he would like to be with other boys his age and enjoy their company. But his mother makes it plain to him that she feels he ought to spend more time at home because she "needs to have him around." On the one hand, he loves his mother and wants to please her, but on the other hand, he does not want to jeopardize his relationships with his friends. No matter what he does, he is bound to cut himself off from somebody. Most of the time his quandary is in the background but every so often something happens that brings it to the point of crisis, and then Fred's anxiety is acute. How he will handle his anxiety depends on many things, not the least of which is his habitual way of expressing himself. If he expresses his feelings easily, freely, and aggressively, he may take out his anxiety in the form of hostility—through displacement, projection, exhibitionism, chronic irritability, and the like. If he tends to withdraw and to suppress or repress his feelings, he may become moody or compulsive, or may bury himself in books.

One common conflict occurs when parental or family standards are at variance with the standards of the school. In Chapter 4 we described how personality and patterns of behavior are influenced by the attitudes and expectations of parents. It very often happens that children who come from homes where the cultural pattern is quite different from that of the teacher or the other students will have great difficulty in adjusting to the expectations and standards of the school.

It is commonly observed that there is a close relationship between the number of books in the home and the success of children at school. This does not mean that parents can boost their children's marks by filling their homes with books, but rather it is a reflection of the fact that families who have many books appreciate the ideas that come from books. Books are very much a part of their lives. People who own many books are, in general, people who believe in getting an education, developing responsibility, planning for the future, organizing one's work, and in similar middle-class values. These are also the values that help children make progress in school. People who have no books tend to live more for the immediate present, rather than the future. Their world is the world of things and of feelings, rather than of books and ideas. Therefore they see little value in carefully laid, long-range plans, developing responsibility for group goals, and organizing one's life so as to maximize future success. Their life values favor direct and immediate action, free expression of emotion, and impulsiveness. Thus their children often display behavior that is in direct conflict with the kind of "life style" that is favored by school personnel. What we often do not recognize is that if we succeed in getting children from lower-class surroundings to accept middle-class values and to conform to middle-class norms, we are helping them to erect a barrier between them and their families. Many children learn through their experiences at school to prefer a middle-class way of life, but they are understandably cautious about isolating themselves from their families. This is not to say that we should not teach middle-class values, but it does emphasize some of the problems we create for children thereby. The conflict between the middle-class values of the school and the lower-class values of the home is a common source of anxiety.

Problem Behavior and Students' Social Environment

Many instances of problem behavior that come to the attention of school authorities are acts that appear to be condoned by people living in rural and urban slums. Examples of such behavior are arguments accompanied by screaming and cursing, fighting with clubs and knives, destruction of property, and sexual aggression. Actually, it is not fair to say that such behavior is condoned, because children in lower-class surroundings are usually punished severely for these and other misdemeanors. On the other hand, however, when they see adults and sometimes even their own parents doing such things, they decide, perhaps somewhat cynically, that the punishment only means that behavior of this kind is reserved for adults, and that it is all right unless you happen to get caught.

Some researchers feel that the higher level of emotional disturbance commonly found in children from slum areas is partly due to lack of personal attention at home. Lower-class families are generally larger than middle-class families, and consequently parents are unable to devote much individualized attention to each child. Mary F. Waldrop and Richard Q. Bell (1964) observed the extent to which nursery school children tried to approach and make contact with their teacher and found that those children who were most persistent and most dependent tended to come from "high-density" families—families in which there were many children and a relatively low number of months between births. In such families, they pointed out, children would be more likely to feel deprived of their mother's love and attention and would be more likely to feel anxious. Their attempts to contact the nursery school teacher appeared to result from their anxiety and their need to satisfy their unmet needs for attention.

The problem behavior teachers will encounter in dealing with children from lower-class surroundings will vary with the community, the behavioral standards set by the parents themselves, and the attitudes of the school and the community toward the families. But the basic points of conflict that are potential sources of problem behavior with children from lower-class homes are the differences in behavioral expectations at home and at school, the hostility and suspicion that lower-class parents have for the school and the school has for the parents, and the inability or unwillingness of many schools to understand the needs of lower-class children and to make adjustments in curriculum and teaching methods in order to meet these needs.

It should not be assumed, however, that middle- and upper-class homes do not produce behavior difficulties in children. Studies of the incidence of *school phobia* indicate that it occurs most frequently among children from middle- and upper-class homes (Leton, 1962; Levison, 1962). School phobia is characterized in its earlier stages by habitual tardiness; in its later stages, even taking a child close to his school may bring on outbursts of crying, temper tantrums, nausea, vomiting, blind running, diarrhea, and loss of bladder control, as well as active resistance in the form of biting, kicking, holding breath, or fainting (Clarizio and McCoy,

(By Marty Links. EMMY LOU © 1966 United Feature Syndicate, Inc.)

"It certainly is a strange type of virus. . . . Always hits just before school starts on Monday morning!"

1970). An earlier study of school phobia in New York City showed that most of the children had average IQs or better, but were retarded in school achievement. The most constant factor was the personality of the parents. Mothers were overanxious, oversolicitous, domineering, immature, self-centered women; fathers were gentle, kindly men, dominated by their wives. Evidently, the phobia was to a large extent the result of the mothers' inability to relax their hold on the children and their jealousy or fear of the school's ability to attract the loyalty and attention of their children. The most effective treatment for school phobia involves a prompt return of the child to school, which not only restores the child to a growth-promoting environment, but also removes him from his involvement in a cycle of mutually reinforced and reinforcing anxieties in the home (Rodriguez, Rodriguez, and Eisenberg, 1959).

There are some indications that children from upper-middle-class and upper-class homes may be more troubled with problem behavior than is commonly supposed. A survey by Burchinal (1958) and others found that children of parents who had postgraduate college degrees also tended to have more problems of adjustment than did other middle-class children. The study by Mensh and others, also cited earlier, provides additional bases for believing that upper-class children have more than their share of problems. As Figure 6-2 shows, the percentage of upper-class children showing emotional disturbances was higher than that for middle-class or lower-class children. Further examination of the data provided by Mensh and his group (1959) indicates that the areas of greatest difficulty for upper-middle-class children, according to their mothers' reports, were: difficulties in relations with other children (both withdrawn and aggressive behavior), destructiveness, daydreaming, nervousness, and speech disturbance.

Hard data on school-related problems of upper-class children are difficult to obtain, because upper-class families constitute only a minute percentage of the population and rarely send their children to public schools. There is some indication, how-

ever, that the university students from upper-class families receive somewhat lower grades than students from middle-class and working-class homes, and are inclined to be less task-oriented (Rust, 1958).

The Hyperactive Child

In recent years, research with children who display severe learning disabilities has suggested that some types of problem behavior may have a neurological basis, that is, such behavior is not essentially the result of emotional conflict, anxiety, feelings of inadequacy, or other largely sociopsychological causes. The problem behavior of these children, instead, seems to stem from a tendency to respond and overrespond to stimuli that other children ignore or overlook. The environment in which we all exist is a veritable ocean of stimuli, and at any given moment an almost infinite number of stimuli are impinging on our sense organs. The resulting impulses are picked up by our sensory organs and transmitted by the relevant nerve trunks, but most of the data are screened or filtered out at some point or other in the central nervous system. This is the screening mechanism that enables us to concentrate on a given task and to give it all of our attention. The mechanism also permits us to be aware of significant stimuli that may have a higher priority than the ones involved in the task to which we are attending. We may be absorbed in an interesting book, ignoring the traffic noises outside the window or the fact that we are sitting in an uncomfortable chair, but should someone mention our name, we glance up to see what is wanted.

This ability to filter out the irrelevant and to focus on the relevant develops as part of the maturation process. When we say that small children have a limited attention span, what we mean, in part, is that they are less able to screen out distracting stimuli. As their neural apparatus matures and becomes better able to deal with distraction, and as they also learn habits of concentration, their attention span lengthens.

Screening out distracting stimuli requires some time and concentration, and younger children tend

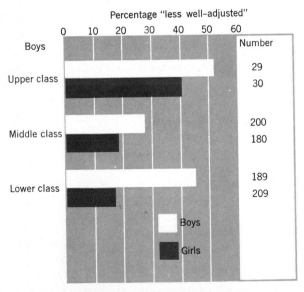

FIG. 6-2. Percentages according to social class and sex of third-grade children rated by teachers and mental hygienists as "less well-adjusted" (Mensh et al., 1959).

to be more impulsive than older ones. They are neurologically organized to react immediately to the first stimuli that present themselves, without waiting to see whether other stimuli change the nature of the situation and thus call for a different mode of action.

Some older children, however, seem to be unable to restrain impulsive behavior and to perform screening functions adequately, perhaps because of retardation in neural development or because of some other kind of neural malfunctioning. To use the concept we expressed diagrammatically in Figure 2-2 in Chapter 2, their transformation processes are swamped with input, and their output becomes highly erratic and unpredictable. Their feedback processes do not function adequately either, and they are less able to take the necessary steps to modify and correct their behavior. Such a child, in effect, tries to react to everything at once and cannot seem to sit still. He is, to use the proper technical terms, a hyperactive or hyperkinetic child. Because of the supposed relationship between chronic hyperactivity and impaired neural functioning, this condition is often referred to as minimal brain damage or MBD.

If a child's disturbance is truly a neurological one, it can be controlled by certain *amphetamine* or *amphetamine-like* drugs, commonly known as *dextro-amphetamine, Ritalin,* or *Deaner.* These drugs generally have an energizing or stimulating effect on normal individuals, and particularly on adults, but they have the opposite effect on hyperkinetic children. Other drugs used are the tranquilizers, such as *Raudixin,* and the *antidepressants,* such as *Tofranil* and *Aventyl.* None of these drugs can be secured without a physician's prescription, and the usual procedure is for parents, school authorities, and physicians to work together in deciding whether they are to be used and the conditions of their administration.

Reports of their use appear to be encouraging. Children who were so hyperkinetic as to be unable to concentrate on any learning task, and who were disruptive of classroom routines and often hostile and destructive, have been calmed down to the point where they have been able to make real gains

in learning and have become more socialized in their general behavior and relations to others.

The use of drugs with these children does, however, entail some serious risks, as Edward T. Ladd (1970) has pointed out. One is the possibility of serious side effects and the other is that of possible faulty diagnosis. Physicians generally believe that both of these risks are well under control at present. If, for example, a child really is not truly hyperkinetic, the administration of one of the amphetamine drugs will worsen his behavior and, thus, will serve as a signal that the disorder is not a neurological one. This approach has been questioned by other practitioners, who report that the indiscriminate use of drugs with children suspected of having minimal brain damage has raised the suspicion of some parents, especially those in some inner-city communities, that school authorities are proceeding along these lines because drugs are cheaper than providing an adequate learning environment (Wolff and Hurwitz, 1973).

Ladd maintained that the major problem is that physicians place too much confidence in teachers' appraisals of children and are inclined to take their recommendations at face value. There is also the danger that a teacher may overvalue quiet, orderly, and even passive behavior, and may base his ratings on such mild deviancies as interrupting others, stopping to talk to another student on the way back from sharpening a pencil, not getting down to work promptly, and the like. A great deal of behavior that is normal with preadolescent boys may be noted and reported by a teacher who overestimates what should be expected of the average child.

Ladd also noted that if education is of any help to children, it should enable them to find ways to control their impulses without the aid of drugs, and he wonders whether the child who depends on drugs to achieve an adequate emotional equilibrium is really learning self-control.

Still another problem is the possibility that the adults in the situation—parents, physicians, and school personnel—may be inadvertently contributing to what has been termed the "drug culture." The widespread use and misuse of both legal and illegal drugs today has been accompanied by and may actually be caused by a general increase in the willingness of adults to depend on drugs as a way of coping with the ordinary stresses of life.

Ladd concluded his review of the use of drugs with hyperkinetic children by giving a cautious endorsement to their use, provided that all the adults involved—parents, physicians, teachers, and school administrators—exercise greater care than they appear to be doing at present in determining which cases call for drug therapy.

Prevalence of Problem Behavior Among Boys

Anyone who has spent any time in schools knows that teachers have more difficulty with boys than with girls. Police report the same experience. The drug fad and its attendant problems have resulted in an increasing number of girls being arrested, but boys still are the major source of juvenile crimes, particularly those directed against persons and property. A glance at Figure 6-2 shows that even in the third grade, boys are having more emotional problems than girls are. The vast majority of children who are dyslexic (that is, who have severe reading problems) are boys. In one study, for example, 72 percent of children between the ages of eight and eleven, who were retarded at least two-and-one-half grades in reading ability, were boys (Spring, 1971). Boys also have more speech problems and are more likely to fail to be promoted to the next grade in elementary school.

Girls adapt to school more easily than do boys and receive better grades, on the average, an advantage they hold even in college and postgraduate training. This does not mean, however, that boys learn less than girls do. Sex differences in achievement, as measured by standardized tests, are so slight as to lack meaning in a practical sense. Hence the superior grades received by girls are based on something other than what they have learned in school.

Some of the explanation of their apparent superiority can be found in the fact that girls learn socially acceptable patterns of behavior more readily than boys do. Even as infants, girls tend to be attracted toward people and pictures of people, whereas boys tend to prefer objects, geometric forms, and patterns (Garai and Scheinfeld, 1968). The greater social interest of girls leads to or is facilitated by their greater aptness in picking up social skills. For example, they learn to speak several months earlier than boys do. Dorothea McCarthy (1953) once suggested that some of the difficulties in school encountered by boys stems from their slower acquisition of verbal skills. This would account for their high incidence of reading and speech problems, as well as difficulties in written expression.

There are some indications that differences in social and academic adjustment may be because of something other than differences in rate of maturity and socialization. Boys start life by being more physically active and also show greater aggressiveness than girls at an early age (Garai and Scheinfeld, 1968). Ellen A. Strommen (1973) conducted an experiment with kindergarten and primary grade children which featured their performance in the game "Simon Says." The game requires considerable maturity in that it places a premium on children's ability to restrain impulsive behavior and to think carefully about what they are doing. Hence the preschool children and the kindergarten children made far more errors than did the primary grade pupils, as Figure 6-3 shows. Figure 6-3 also indicates a higher error rate for boys, a result of their greater immaturity. Strommen also observed that girls in kindergarten and the first grade were able to improve their performance with practice, whereas boys were not.

The fact that boys and girls mature at different rates does not mean that adults are easier in their demands on boys. Ruth E. Hartley (1959) maintained that boys experience demands for "masculine" behavior before they are able to understand what the demands are and why they are being made. This situation is, she said, a perfect combination for inducing anxiety: "The demand that the child do something which is not clearly defined to him, based on reasons he cannot possibly appreciate, and enforced with threats, punishments, and anger by those who are close to him." As a consequence of this anxiety, a boy is likely to overreact against being caught doing anything feminine to the

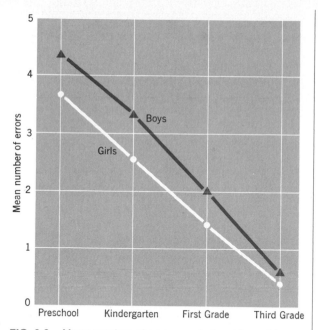

FIG. 6-3. Mean number of errors made by girls and by boys playing "Simon Says" (data from Strommen, 1973).

point where he even develops hostility toward females themselves. He rationalizes this hostility by deciding that women just do not like boys and actually prefer girls. Very likely this attitude is also based on reality. The world in which the elementary school boy lives is to a large degree a female-dominated world, since the people who are most concerned with his supervision are likely to be women.

There is some evidence that teachers do little to make boys' problems in adjusting to school demands any easier. One research team noted that kindergarten teachers are more likely to respond to boys' aggressive acts and to ignore the aggressive acts of girls. In contrast to girls' misbehavior, boys' misbehavior evoked louder reprimands as well. Furthermore, teachers gave girls increased attention when they were nearby but were less likely to give attention to boys who were in their vicinity. There were some mitigating circumstances, however. Those boys who did participate appropriately were more likely to receive teacher attention that was helpful and emotionally supportive than girls were (Serbin, O'Leary, and Kent, 1973).

The fact that girls are less likely to get into trouble with authorities than boys suggests that their standards of behavior may be higher. Richard L. Krebs (1968) found that sixth-grade teachers tended to rate the girls in their classes as being more trustworthy, more obedient, and as showing more respect for others' rights than the boys. In other words, they described their girl pupils as being more moral than the boys. Krebs than tested the children by administering a Moral Judgment Inventory developed from research findings of Piaget (1948) and Lawrence Kohlberg (1958). Results showed no superiority for girls, and actually indicated that middle-class boys in the group were significantly more moral than girls. Krebs then administered three tests that were so constructed that children were tempted to cheat and were led to believe that they would not be caught. In this instance, there was no difference between the sexes. Krebs concluded that girls, in spite of being viewed as morally superior, were actually no more moral than boys, but that their greater conformity to rules and authority made them appear so.

Even though the moral standards of boys and girls are similar, most adults take the view that it is how children actually behave that really counts, and everyday observation suggests that boys have more trouble with self-control than girls do. In one experiment, six-year-old children were trained not to turn around and look at a display of toys. They were then placed in another situation and asked not to turn around and look at what was to be a surprise (a hamster in a cage), while the experimenter was out of the room in search of a new game. Inasmuch as the experimenter was out of the room for ten minutes, it is not surprising that many of the children could not resist temptation and turned around to peek at the hamster. Boys, as might be expected, displayed less self-control than the girls and disobeyed instructions sooner (Kanfer and Zich, 1974).

The reason for the greater impulsivity and aggressiveness in boys and men is a subject for considerable controversy both in and out of the psychological profession. There is evidence that it is genetically predetermined by sex differences in neurological makeup, but there is also much evidence that the differential expectations that adults have for boys tend to reinforce patterns of behavior that may be inborn. Cross-cultural observations, such as those of Bronfenbrenner (1970), which we mentioned earlier, suggests that American culture, with its emphasis on independence in thought and action, may lead many adults to reinforce or at least condone boys' behavior that is nonconformist, uncooperative, aggressive, and irresponsible. These are the same adults, of course, who react swiftly and punitively when a misbehaving boy destroys their property, or steals their possessions, or interferes with their peace of mind in some way or other. This attitude of indulgence coupled with repressiveness creates many problems for boys and young men, for it encourages them to be socially immature and at the same time punishes them for their immaturity.

Whatever the causes of the large number of behavior disturbances displayed by boys, it is clear that the school, as well as the other agencies of our culture, is not meeting the boys' needs as well as it is meeting the needs of girls. This is a problem area that requires far more recognition and study than educators and behavioral scientists have given it in the past.

Discouragement as a Factor in Problem Behavior

The major factor that underlies most misbehavior, according to the late Rudolf Dreikurs (1957), is discouragement. Children whose morale is generally good are inclined to do the things that are expected of them provided, of course, that the expectations are reasonable. If a child's morale is good, he sees some point in trying to learn and to behave in socially acceptable ways. The child who is discouraged, however, may behave in disruptive ways in the classroom because he sees no point in being cooperative and agreeable. His misbehavior is what Dreikurs called an ''attention-getting mechanism'' because it serves the purpose of drawing attention to him. Discouragement may express itself in other ways as well: reading problems, withdrawing behavior, or even in attitudes of extreme dependence.

Some children who are extremely dependent are able to express their dependence in a charming and attractive way that serves to flatter the teacher's ego. To paraphrase Dreikurs' description of their behavior:

These children follow the teacher's orders exactly, tempting her to give them special attention and more than their share of help. Because they are so dependent, they have no initiative of their own, and few teachers bother to get them involved in projects that require them to behave independently. The underlying discouragement of these children is seldom apparent and may appear only when a teacher becomes impatient at the chronic passivity. Such children are actually more discouraged than those who use active-destructive methods to gain the attention of the teacher. The latter can be encouraged to channel their energy into constructive activities, but changing a passive child into an active one is difficult.

The task of encouraging students, either aggressive or passive, and of building up their sense of adequacy and optimism—morale—is not an easy one. It cannot be accomplished by giving them ''pep talks'' and telling them how able they really are. Often such approaches only increase the discouragement they feel. Some of the ways in which educators can help students develop more positive attitudes toward themselves and the tasks of learning are discussed in Chapter 12.

Unfortunately, the school itself often contributes to the child's sense of discouragement by setting perfectionistic standards and by making failure appear disgraceful. A certain amount of failure is normal in learning—only seldom do we achieve complete success the first time we attempt a new task or skill. Although it is difficult to get some teachers to relax their perfectionistic standards and to take a more constructive view of the place of failure in the learning process, the problem of getting parents to develop more supportive attitudes toward their children is even greater. Some parents display much anxiety when their child is not at the head of his class and become upset at any indication that his performance is anything less than "perfection."

School Policies and Conditions that Are Detrimental to Mental Health

Still another problem that is caused or aggravated by discouragement is cheating. Essentially, the student who cheats is one who has become discouraged about behaving in more constructive and acceptable ways. Perhaps he has become panicky about failure, or perhaps he has become cynical, deciding that if adults are more interested in grades than in intellectual growth or learning, it does not really matter how the grade is obtained.

There is a direct relationship between "academic pressure" and cheating. A survey of the relationship between grading practices of college faculty members and cheating by students turned up the fact that students were much more likely to cheat in courses taught by faculty who gave higher-than-average percentages of Ds and Fs and lower-than-average percentages of As and Bs (Lindgren, 1966). Another survey showed that students tended to feel that the more anxiety and hostility were aroused by the instructor and his testing methods, the more justified they would feel in cheating and in permitting others to copy their papers (Steininger, Johnson, and Kirts, 1964). As to the amount of cheating that goes on, the findings of Jev Shelton and John P. Hill (1968) are rather typical. The researchers administered a test of cognitive skill to a group of high-school students, scored them without making any marks on the sheets, and them returned them to the students the following day. This gave students an opportunity to "improve" their scores by adding more responses. Students were then asked to turn their papers in a second time. Subsequent examination of the papers showed that 53 percent of the students had cheated. The experimenters also manipulated the situation by telling some of the students what a "typical" performance would be for most students. This made it possible for some students to believe that they had failed the test, whereas others believed that they had been very successful. When the papers of students receiving this "information" were compared with those of students who had received no such report (the control group), it was found that 61 percent of the students who believed they had failed cheated, a proportion that was considerably higher than the 43 percent who cheated in the control group. Interestingly enough, 56 percent of those students who had been led to believe they had succeeded also cheated.

Shelton and Hill also measured the amount of anxiety the students experienced relative to taking tests and to other forms of achievement measures—what might be termed *achievement anxiety*. When they analyzed their data, they found that students who were less anxious were less likely to be affected by knowledge of the performance of their peers, but students with moderate to high amounts of achievement anxiety were much more likely to cheat when their performance was compared to their peers. They also found that students who made low scores on the test of cognitive skill were more likely to cheat, irrespective of the amount of anxiety they expressed. Translating these results to the classroom situation, it appears that, in any given situation, about one-half the students will cheat if they think that they can get away with it,[2] but that most of the cheating will occur among those students who characteristically make low scores or who are particularly anxious about academic success.

Although the high incidence of cheating has been blamed on the easy tolerance of dishonesty in today's society, studies like the above suggest that schools themselves create the kinds of conditions that make cheating prevalent. The more a school

[2] This figure is consistent with studies that have been conducted for many years. A nationwide survey of high-school students conducted in the 1950s reported that 50 percent of boys and 43 percent of girls admitted that they cheated "frequently" or "sometimes," in contrast to only 4 or 5 percent who said they never cheated (Horton and Remmers, 1953). These students are, of course, the parents of youngsters who are in school today.

attempts to increase the anxieties of students by undue emphasis on competition, grades, and superficial evidence of academic competence, the more likely students are to display various forms of problem behavior, including cheating. The really superior student is less likely to cheat, according to a study done by Ray R. Canning (1956). Evidently, such students are more likely to feel competent and adequate and are less likely to be discouraged. Canning also found that the introduction of an honor system reduced the amount of cheating, contrary to what might be popularly supposed. It is quite likely that students feel accepted and less threatened by the willingness of teachers to trust them.

There are other characteristics and practices of schools that produce or aggravate problem behavior. Many teachers and administrators appear to assume that adults are always right and children are always wrong. Any program that consistently places the comfort, convenience, and needs of adults above the needs of children is likely to produce problem behavior. This does not mean that the needs of adults should be ignored; rather, it is a question of emphasis. It is understandable how we might come to ignore the psychological needs of children without meaning to do so. There are all kinds of very human reasons why we should act on our own behalf and in accordance with our own needs and standards. Even when we *think* we are acting on behalf of children, we need to be careful that we do not interpret *our* psychological needs as theirs.

Ways in Which Schools Can Improve Mental Health

As far as the emotional health of most children is concerned, the positive contributions of the school outweigh the negative ones. For one thing, the school offers a variety of opportunities for children to learn satisfying ways of working and playing together. The aid it provides in helping children develop the necessary skills is what is called "group living" is of vital importance, inasmuch as the mental health of any person depends, in part, on his ability to develop sound relationships to and with other people. One of the most important skills children can learn at school, or anywhere for that matter, is how to express their feelings without injury to themselves and others. Some children express themselves through problem behavior because they have not learned more acceptable ways of self-expression.

The school also provides a reasonably stable environment in which children may develop and learn. Its hours are regular, its demands and expectations are well defined, and it is governed by rules and regulations. For many children, school provides the only stable, secure, and predictable experience in their lives. Someone once observed, with irony, that schools give a second chance to children who are unfortunate in the selection of their parents. It is important for children to have experiences with a well-organized, controlled, and stable environment, just as it is important for them to have experiences which permit freedom of thought, expression, and action.

The school is an institution that is dedicated to children. The adults who direct its activities and formulate its policies are for the most part sincere and conscientious individuals. Although school people, being human, generally find it easier to follow conventional and traditional ways of doing things, they have, through the years, gradually shifted their attitudes and practices in accordance with their growing understanding of children. Our best hope for eliminating or reducing problem behavior lies in our changing point of view toward children and toward educational methods.

Evidence that our point of view *is* changing is provided by the fact that schools are much pleasanter places than they used to be. Although physical punishment is still used in many schools, perhaps even in the majority, it is employed much less frequently than formerly. Just by way of contrast, look at the punishments prescribed for misbehavior by a school master more than a century ago (Table 6-5). Today, psychological and psychiatric services are becoming available for use by school personnel in an increasing number of communities. The fact that the demand for these services far exceeds their availability is evidence of the extent to which the

TABLE 6-5. List of Punishments Used in a North Carolina School in 1848[a]

No.	Rules of School	Lashes
1.	Boys & Girls Playing Together	4
2.	Quareling	4
3.	Fighting	5
4.	Fighting at School	5
5.	Quareling at School	3
6.	Gambling or Beting at School	4
7.	Playing at Cards at School	10
8.	Climbing for Every foot Over three feet up a tree	1
9.	Telling Lyes	7
10.	Telling Tales Out of School	8
11.	Nick Naming Each Other	4
12.	Giving Each Other Ill Names	3
13.	Fighting Each Other in Time of Books	2
14.	Swearing at School	8
15.	Blackgarding Each Other	6
16.	For Misbehaving to Girls	10
17.	For Leaving School without Leave of the Teacher	4
18.	Going Home with Each Other without Leave of the Teacher	4
19.	For Drinking Spirituous Liquors at School	8
20.	Making Swings & Swinging on Them	7
21.	For Misbehaving when a Stranger is in the House	6
22.	For Wearing Long Finger Nailes	2
23.	For Not Making a Bow when a Stranger Comes in or goes out	3
24.	Misbehaving to Persons on the Road	4
25.	For Not Making a Bow when you Meet a Person	4
26.	For Going to Girls' Play Places	3
27.	Girls Going to Boys' Play Places	2
28.	Coming to School with Dirty Face and Hands	2
29.	For Calling Each Other Liars	4
30.	For Playing Bandy	10
31.	For Bloting Your Copy Book	2
32.	For Not Making a bow when you go home and when you come away	4
33.	Wrestling at School	4
34.	Scuffling at School	4
35.	For not making Bow when Going out to go Home	2
36.	For Weting Each Other Washing at Play Time	2
37.	Girls Going to Boys' Play Places	2
38.	For Hollowing & Hooping Going Home	3
39.	For Delaying Time Going Home or Coming to School	4
40.	For Not Making a Bow when you come in or go Out	2
41.	For Throwing Anything Harder then your trab ball	4
42.	For every word you miss in your Heart Lesson without Good Excuse	1
43.	For not saying yes Sir & no Sir or yes marm or no marm	2
44.	For Troubling Each Others Writing affairs	2
45.	For Not Washing at Play time when going to Books	4
46.	For going and Playing about the Mill or Creek	6
47.	For Going about the Barn or doing Any Mischief about the place	7

November 10, 1848   Wm. A. Chaffin

[a] Coon, 1915.

educational profession is developing an understanding of the emotional causes of problem behavior and is seeing it as something that calls for treatment, rather than punishment. Attendance officers used to be called "hookey cops." Today, the trend is for them to function as social workers, because we have discovered that the problem of nonattendance is one that is primarily psychological and sociological, rather than legal.

More than a decade ago, William G. Hollister (1959), consultant to the National Institute of Mental Health, outlined the following trends in the programs that schools at that time were developing to deal with problem behavior. We repeat them here, supplementing with information regarding more recent trends.

1. *Use of consultation to strengthen classroom guidance of behavior.* This refers to the use of guidance workers, psychologists, social workers, and the like as consultants for teachers. Today, there is increased awareness that the teacher is the best person to deal with most of the problems that occur in the classroom.

2. *Employment of group methods of behavior guidance.* To extend their skills in dealing with behavior problems, teachers are encouraged to take in-service courses dealing with psychological factors of group behavior and are using devices such as sociometry, group discussion, and role playing.

3. *Emphasis on teacher-parent cooperation.* There is an increasing tendency for parents to become involved in school life, sometimes through parent-teacher associations, but also as paid paraprofessionals or as volunteer teaching aids, as chaperones on field trips, and the like. Many parents also expect that teachers will discuss children's behavior in psychological terms. It is still difficult to get parents of lower-class children to come to school, but progress is being made along these lines as well. Operation Head Start and Operation Follow Through, have, for example, done much to involve parents in the educational progress of their preschool and primary

grade children. In one experimental program, Oglala Sioux parents were invited to work with school administrators on common problems, such as chronic truancy. As a result of the collaboration, a closer bond was formed between the home and the school, and absences dropped from a daily average of sixty to two (Woodward, 1973).

4. *Concern about psychological factors in human behavior in teacher education.* This applies both to preprofessional, as well as to in-service educational experiences. A much wider range of curricular materials is available today in the form of films, pamphlets, and books dealing with the mental health of children.

5. *Interest in the use of measurement in evaluating mental health.* This trend has not continued. Evaluation today is, if anything, more concerned with school achievement than with mental health, as such. The classroom use of personality tests has diminished considerably and is actually banned in some states.

6. *Interest in introducing material on human relationships into the curriculum.* Mental health, human relations, family relationships, and other sociopsychological aspects of human behavior are dealt with more extensively today in curriculum guides and textbooks. There is also a greater interest in using material from a number of ethnic groups, such as Afro-Americans and American Indians. In addition to children's television programs, such as *Sesame Street,* and *The Electric Company,* which emphasize positive ways of interacting, as well as cognitive skills, a bilingual program (in Spanish and English) entitled *Villa Allegre* has been produced and distributed experimentally since 1973.

To the above trends, we can also add the use of behavior modification techniques (a topic we shall discuss in later chapters), the use of drug therapy with hyperkinetic children, and the increasing employment of specialists in various types of behavior problems and educational handicaps.

What these trends amount to, as far as the classroom teacher is concerned is that (1) more psychological understanding of children's behavior is being expected of him and (2) more consultants and resource people are being mobilized to help him. The problem behavior that occurs in the classroom of a particular teacher is today more likely to be perceived as the responsibility of the school as a whole, including its administrators and staff of psychological consultants, but there is also general agreement that the classroom teacher must be a major figure in whatever treatment is provided.

SUMMARY

Problem behavior is a matter of concern for teachers, not merely because some types may be disruptive, but also because all types, whether aggressive or passive, are likely to interfere with students' learning. Teachers should develop some understanding of problem behavior because the "problem child" usually remains in a classroom even if his problem is being treated elsewhere. Teachers and psychologists tend to view the problem behavior of pupils differently, although they are considerably more in agreement than they were a couple of generations ago. Understanding problem behavior means that teachers should become sensitive to the interaction between the forces and factors in the student's environment and his performance in the classroom. Although the pupils who display severe problems constitute only a small percentage of the total school population, they exert a disturbing force far beyond their numbers. The student with the "conduct problem" is more likely to come to the attention of the teacher because of his aggressive, disturbing behavior. Nevertheless, students whose problems are more in the nature of "neurotic" or "personality" maladjustments, as well as those who are emotionally and socially immature, may also be having difficulties with learning. Actually, all students are bothered with problems of emotional and social adjustment to some degree, although the problems are not usually severe or numerous enough to produce the kind of gross disturbances that underlie or accompany chronic problem behavior. The so-called "problem child" is one who has more than the usual amount of problems and is more severely troubled by them than most children.

Although adults who have to deal with children displaying problem behavior are easily tempted to treat it directly and drastically, such an approach often does not produce the desired results. Treatment of problem behavior has a better chance to succeed if it is based on understanding of what lies behind the disturbance. Understanding problem behavior is not an easy task, however, and it sometimes is necessary to call on psychological or psychiatric experts for special help.

One of the reasons why problem behavior is so difficult to understand is that it serves as an escape from or defense against anxiety. There are many different kinds of maneuvers that both children and adults use unconsciously as ways of coping with anxiety or tension. They are termed "defense mechanisms" or "escape mechanisms." These mechanisms have this in common: They are learned patterns of behavior, directed at reducing or eliminating anxiety, rather than solving problems that are the basic cause of the anxiety.

Problem behavior is often produced or aggravated by emotional conflicts. One of the commonest conflicts encountered by the teacher is that of the student from a lower-class home where values and acceptable forms of behavior are markedly different from the ones of the school. However, children from middle- and upper-class homes have their problems, too, school phobia being one example. Research has shown that some overactive and aggressive children are suffering from a malfunctioning of the central nervous system that can be corrected by the use of drugs. There is some controversy as to whether extensive use of drug therapy with these children is advisable and, in any event, the utmost caution seems to be in order.

Problem behavior is more common among boys than among girls. Boys mature less rapidly in social and linguistic skills and have poorer impulse control; hence they do not get along at school as well as girls do, although there is apparently little overall difference in their success, as measured by achievement tests. Boys' problems are often aggravated by the inconsistent ways in which they are often treated by parents and other adults: On the one hand their nonconforming, aggressive, and irresponsible behavior is encouraged, or at least condoned, but on the other hand it is punished. Boys are thus rewarded and punished for behaving in ways that the American culture considers "masculine.'' Such treatment increases their feelings of confusion and makes for more problems in school, as well as in the larger society.

Problem behavior is to a large degree caused or aggravated by the sense of failure and discouragement that many students develop as a result of their school experiences. On the other hand, there are other factors and forces in the school environment that foster good mental health and help to reduce or eliminate problem behavior. For example, students have opportunities in school to learn how to work and play together cooperatively and to express themselves in ways that are both satisfying and socially acceptable. Most students learn these skills to some degree; the problem child is one who is unwilling, or, more likely, unable to learn them. Schools also provide a climate of stability and predictability—qualities that help to foster emotional security. Today's teacher is expected to know more about the psychological aspects of problem behavior than was true in former years. Although an increasing number of specialists are available to help him with special problems, there is also recognition that the classroom teacher must play a key role in whatever programs are formulated and carried out.

Suggested Problems

1. When a teacher says, ''I have a couple of behavior problems in my class,'' what kind of behavior is he likely to be referring to? What kind of behavior problems are teachers more likely to overlook? Why?

2. Look over the list of problems reported by mothers in the study by Mensh and his associates (Table 6-3). Less than half the problems that they reported had any relationship to problems reported by teachers and mental health workers in the classroom. Suggest some hypotheses that might account for this discrepancy.

3. Life at Broderick Junior High has been disturbed this year by a small group of boys who have been extorting money from other students, threatening to beat them up unless they paid a certain amount a week. Their activities were brought to the attention of Mr. Eliades, the school principal, by outraged parents. The victims refused to identify their tormentors, however, not wanting to risk being beaten. The group was caught red-handed, however, by Mr. Ortiz, the vice principal, who overheard them making threats to a seventh-grader in the boys' toilet. Two of the three boys in the gang live with their mothers; one, whose father is a policeman, lives with both parents. When the parents were called together in Mr. Eliades' office, they said that they had all punished the boys for bullying other children previously, but that this was the most serious offense so far. They wanted to handle the boys their way, which was to give them sound thrashings and to confine them to the house every night and weekends for a month. Mr. Eliades wants to refer the boys to the Child Guidance Center, but Mr. Ortiz believes that the parents should handle the matter their way. Without any more information than you are given here, why do you think the parents want to deal with the problem themselves and not have the boys referred to the Child Guidance Center? What do you think would be the best course of treatment for these boys?

4. Psychologists maintain that we employ defense or escape mechanisms because they serve an important purpose or function. In view of the fact that such mechanisms often seem to be silly or useless or even deceitful, how can one justify saying that they have a function?

5. High-school students today are inclined to be more outspoken and to ''talk back'' to their teachers more than they did even a decade or so ago. In what way is this a healthy trend, and in what way is this unhealthy? If this trend continues, what effect do you think it will have on school practices and on the behavior of teachers?

Suggested Readings

Clarizio, H. F., and McCoy, G. F. *Behavior disorders in school-aged children.* Scranton, Pa.: Chandler, 1970.

Guerney, B. G., Jr. (ed.) *Psychotherapeutic roles for nonprofessionals, parents and teachers.* New York:

Holt, Rinehart, and Winston, 1969. See especially the paper by Ogden Lindsley on the use of teachers as classroom therapists.

Lindgren, H. C., and Lindgren, F. (eds.) *Current readings in educational psychology.* New York: Wiley, 1972. See Section 3 for articles on behavior problems.

Long, N. J., Morse, W. C., and Newman, R. G. (eds.). *Conflict in the classroom: The education of emotionally disturbed children.* Belmont, Calif.: Wadsworth, 1965. See especially Section 1, "How does it feel to be emotionally disturbed?" which contains 22 passages that are fascinating reading from Chekov, Dickens, Cather, and other writers. Section 2, "How can disturbed children be identified?" is also relevant to this chapter.

Newton, M. R., and Brown, R. D. "A preventive approach to developmental problems in school children." In W. G. Hollister and E. M. Bower (eds.). *Behavioral science frontiers in education.* New York: Wiley, 1967.

Tanner, L. N., and Lindgren, H. C. *Classroom teaching and learning: A mental health approach.* New York: Holt, Rinehart, and Winston, 1971. See Chapter 7, "Dealing constructively with behavior problems."

Weiner, I. B. *Psychological disturbance in adolescence.* New York: Wiley, 1970.

Woody, R. H. *Behavioral problem children in the schools.* New York: Appleton-Century-Crofts, 1969. Deals with recognition, diagnosis, and behavior modification.

English
Alden
Underline the
Mark the
treasure
elephant
mountain
stranger

Traditional / Conventional Views of Learning and Instruction

The Learning Process

Educational psychology, as we stated in the introductory chapter, is concerned with the learner, the learning process, and the learning situation. The five chapters that have preceded the present one have been largely concerned with understanding the learner, although in studying him, we have had to take into account both the learning process and the many different kinds of situations that serve as the background for his learning experiences. We cannot study the development of children and adolescents without considering the habits, attitudes, and character traits that they develop as a result of learning, or the situations that help determine habits, attitudes, and character traits.

In this chapter and the two that follow, we shift our focus to the learning process itself. In doing so, we have to keep both learner and learning situation well in mind because all three elements must be considered in relation to one another. It is important, too, to remember that all human behavior, including learning, occurs as an integrated whole, and that any attempt to isolate any single aspect even for the purpose of analysis and discussion in a sense violates this essential unity. The piston in a gasoline engine operates in relation to the other parts of the engine as well as to the intermittent explosion of vaporized gasoline. We may stop the engine, dismantle it, and pull out the piston in order to study it and thus gain a better understanding of it, but to understand its function in the fullest sense, we have to keep in mind its relation to the operation of the engine as a whole. Similarly, when we study the learning process, we must remember that it has no separate existence in and of itself. We emphasize this point because there is the danger—psychologists are sometimes guilty of this, too—that we may think of "learning" as something that can be filtered out of human behavior and experience and thus studied as a thing apart.

Everyone Has a Theory

Most of us take learning for granted. That is, we take it for granted until we encounter difficulties in learning or until we have to teach somebody something. On such occasions we are likely to fall back on one or more "tried-and-true" techniques, "tried and true" because they are a part of our cultural heritage. Indeed, such techniques are so much a part of "what everyone knows" that they may even be referred to as "common-sense principles of learning." What are these principles? Well, before we discuss them, and before you read any further in this chapter, read the following true-false questions, answering them in accordance with what you really believe:

T F 1. Whether students will do well in class depends on whether they are rewarded by their teachers for good work (through good marks, praise, honors, awards, and the like).

T F 2. Whether students will do well in class depends on whether they are punished for poor work (through low or failing marks, reprimands, and the like).

T F 3. In other words, whether a student learns at all will depend on the extent to which he is rewarded or punished by his teachers.

T F 4. Learning, particularly in subjects such as history, science, and social problems, is primarily a process of acquiring and absorbing facts.

T F 5. Once students *really learn,* as a result of having been *taught* properly, they will retain what they have learned.

T F 6. *Proper teaching* implies ample practice and drill. Things remembered best are the things that are reviewed frequently.

T F 7. One of the best ways to teach a child is to show him the difference between correct and incorrect ways of doing things.

T F 8. The best way to learn a new skill is to have the teacher present it one step at a time.

T F 9. In order to function adequately in a subject or a field, students must first be introduced to and have a thorough understanding of the key principles involved.

T F 10. The really important and significant things in life are not learned easily because they take a lot of hard, unpleasant work, whereas things that are learned easily and pleasantly are not likely to be of much value.

T F 11. Students cannot be forced to learn if they do not want to because "You can lead a horse to water, but you cannot make him drink." Therefore the best way to get students to learn is to make sure that "learning is fun."

The above statements, contradictory though some of them are, are more or less consistent with "what everyone knows about education." Many people would even term them "common sense." Everyone "knows," for example, that children learn primarily because they are rewarded or punished; that students who cannot spell, write grammatically correct English, or multiply fractions have not been taught properly; that learning consists of adding facts to one's "storehouse of knowledge"; and so forth. Perhaps it is going a little far to call these ideas "theories," but there is plenty of evidence that most of us, teachers and laymen alike, make use of these concepts in our own efforts at learning or in planning and directing the learning of others. The kind of "learning theory" that we subscribe to may be readily inferred from the way in which we deal with teaching/learning problems. Concepts like those embodied in the true-false questions above are, in effect, *"implicit* theories of learning"—implicit in the sense that the theory is *implied* by the way in which we go about the tasks of learning or teaching.

Let us say, for example, that you have to memorize a speech. If your approach is that of memorizing each sentence until you have the entire speech committed to memory, it can be inferred that you subscribe to a theory that learning is more successful if undertaken one step at a time. If the parents of four-year-old Tommy let him have dessert if he eats his food properly without complaint but withhold dessert if he balks or eats messily, it can be inferred that they are conforming to a theory that a child's success in learning depends on the application of reward and punishment. Here is an example of the way in which teachers reveal their beliefs or theories about learning:

The annual basketball game between the 9A and the 9B grades of the North Point Junior High School was usually marked by excitement and partisan enthusiasm, but this year the spectators were unusually noisy. With five minutes to go in the game, the score stood at 48 even. At this point, a 9B boy committed a foul, and a 9A boy got a free throw. As he stood, poised, concentrating on the throw, the 9B rooting section started to whistle and stamp. When the referee held up his hand to stop the noise, he was loudly booed. It was not until he threatened to stop the game that the group finally quieted down.

At a faculty meeting later that afternoon, several of the teachers expressed great concern about the unsportsmanlike behavior of the 9Bs. Although some teachers were not inclined to take a very serious view of the matter, the teachers who had 9B classes agreed that the incident would be used as a basis for class work the next week.

The next day Mrs. Del Carlo gave her 9B English class a lecture on good sportsmanship that included pointed reference to their behavior the previous day. She then assigned a five hundred-word theme on the topic: "Why good sportsmanship is important."

In a classroom a few doors away, Mr. Volker told his 9B class of the decision to use their behavior as a subject for classroom work. He then called for reactions. At first the students were somewhat resentful and belligerent, feeling that the assignment was an unwarranted imposition, but as the discussion continued, a number of them admitted that they had really been ashamed of the way the class had behaved. Mr. Volker then asked what the group wanted to do about the matter. As class members made proposals, he wrote them on the blackboard. There were a dozen suggestions in all. After further discussion and planning, a number of committees were formed to work on various assignments based on the proposals. One group was going to meet with the principal, the physical education teachers, and the student council to see what could be done to prevent the future occurrence of such incidents. Another group wanted to find out why good sportsmanship was important. Two other groups were going to debate the merits of having organized cheering sections as a way of keeping spectator behavior under control.

Let us go back over this anecdote to see how the behavior of the teachers indicates their beliefs or implicit theories about learning.

The decision of the teachers to use the conduct at the basketball game as a subject for classroom work was based on the assumption that an event in the immediate or recent experience of children is a good starting point for learning. They felt that the unsportsmanlike behavior of the 9Bs showed the need for correction and that the sooner it was begun, the more effective the learning of proper behavior would be.

Mrs. Del Carlo theorized that the 9Bs behaved as

they did because they had not learned proper modes of conduct. She therefore believed it was her responsibility to *tell* them what the proper modes of conduct were and wherein they had been violated. She then assigned the task of writing a theme as a kind of *drill* that would help students master the principles she had outlined for them. It is implicit in her behavior that she believes that learning results when a student is told something by a teacher and is required to repeat it back to the teacher.

Mr. Volker's conduct indicates that he believes that the enunciation of principles of proper conduct is more effective when it comes from the students rather than from the teacher. The fact that he does not lecture implies that he feels that telling students is a less effective way of promoting learning. Like Mrs. Del Carlo, he believes that students learn through some kind of activity, but he does not think that drill, as such, is very effective. He evidently feels that the learning activity that students engage in is more effective when undertaken more or less on their own initiative, rather than at the initiative of teachers. Therefore he had his students select the activities to be undertaken in this project. Mrs. Del Carlo believes that learning proceeds most effectively when it is initiated and directed by teachers; Mr. Volker believes that it proceeds more effectively when students take a hand in its initiation and direction.

The parents and the teachers whose approaches to learning we have just described hold a variety of beliefs or implicit theories about learning, some of them old, some of them new. It is our intention in this chapter to examine some of the older, more traditional beliefs because these are the beliefs that are basic to most of the attitudes and behavior of teachers and lay people alike regarding the processes of teaching and learning. These beliefs are so much a part of our everyday thinking that we regard them as *universal, natural truths*—as "common sense." To be sure, most of these theories possess some measure of truth and may even seem to be effective at times, but most of them are based on an inadequate understanding of learning processes and are hence to a large extent inefficient, if not ineffective. To use the term we employed in the introductory chapter, they are "prescientific."

We are devoting this entire chapter to the discussion of beliefs that are a part of "what everyone knows about learning" for the simple reason that "knowing" something that is not so, or is at best questionable, can prevent the development of any real understanding of the teaching-learning process. If we think that we already know how learning takes place, we are not likely to learn anything new about the process, particularly if the new concepts are contradictory to what we already "know." Therefore popular beliefs about learning have to be unlearned or set aside if we are to gain any new insights. Unfortunately, most of the teaching and educational planning that takes place throughout the world is based on outmoded and ineffective concepts of the teaching-learning process. The fact that students do learn is ordinarily taken as evidence that traditional/conventional theories about learning "really work," but evidence shows that they are highly questionable and that students often learn in spite of teachers' theories, rather than because of them.

The "Carrot-and-Stick" Approach

The basis for this theory is that people tend to do the kinds of things they find satisfying and avoid things that are painful. This is the theory that is followed by Tommy's parents when they give him dessert for eating his meals in a satisfactory manner and withhold it when his performance has been substandard. The idea is that proper behavior becomes associated with satisfactions and thus becomes habitual, whereas improper behavior becomes associated with penalties and is avoided.

There is both truth and fallacy in this theory, just as there is in most traditional and popular beliefs about learning. It *is* true that humans and lesser animals alike tend to repeat behavior that has satisfying or reinforcing consequences, and that they tend to avoid or to discontinue behavior that does not produce satisfactions or has obnoxious outcomes. These principles have been repeatedly demonstrated by experimental psychologists in their laboratories. In fact, it has become fashionable in educational circles to borrow the experimentalists' term "reinforcement" and to use it as roughly synonymous with reward.[1] But what adults consider to be rewards may not produce learning at all. This may occur when there is a long delay between the appearance of the kind of learner responses that the teacher wants and the appearance of the reward. An example of this is the writing of term papers that are not returned to students until the teacher has had a chance to read and grade them all, a process that may take weeks. And what a teacher believes is a reward may be perceived quite differently by students.

> Miss Chapman wanted to reward Timmy for having turned in the best social studies notebook; hence she suggested to the boys that Timmy be the lead-off batter when they played softball during morning recess. The boys agreed, although being lead-off was usually reserved for the more popular boys in the class. Timmy did not react to this honor as Miss Chapman expected. He was somewhat shy and awkward when it came to sports and would rather do almost anything than be lead-off in softball. On the way to the play yard he caught up with Ray, one of the leaders in the class, and asked him to bat first instead. When Ray agreed, Timmy felt much better.

Before continuing with our analysis of reward-based learning, we should consider its mirror image, punishment-based learning, because the two ideas are often used together, as when Tommy's parents offer him a choice of reward for good manners or punishment for poor manners.

In actual practice, teaching tends to be more punishment- than reward-oriented. When we are

teaching someone, we somehow become more responsive to his errors than his successes. "Doing things right" seems to be "normal" and not worthy of comment; "doing things wrong" calls for correction and criticism. It really does little good for us to say, as we often do, that such correction and criticism is uttered with the best of intentions, that we only want to help the learner, and that if he really wants to learn, he should take it in the spirit in which it was meant. It does little good to say this because most people, and children are no exception, develop negative feelings when they become the target for correction and criticism, that is, they become depressed, irritated, discouraged, anxious, or apathetic—whatever their habitual mode of response to psychological threat happens to be.

The opposite can also occur, that is, negative attention can be reinforcing under some circumstances. In one experiment, third- and fourth-grade children were either socially satiated or socially deprived before playing a simple game. The children in the first group were socially "satiated" by the experimenter who chatted with them in a friendly manner between the classroom and the room in which the experiment was being conducted. The other children were socially "deprived" by the silence of the experimenter during the walk to the room and, furthermore, sat alone in the experiment room for a ten-minute period while the experimenter went out "to make a phone call." Playing the game involved selecting and pressing one of two buttons. Correct responses were signaled by a light over the button pressed; incorrect responses by the light over the other button. The experimenter explained the game to each child and then took his place behind a panel that shielded him from view. During the playing of the game, whenever the child made an incorrect response, the experimenter opened a sliding panel, looked at the child, and said, "No, you're wrong." In other words, the only social contact between child and experimenter occurred in a "punishment" context. Each child was given the opportunity to make one hundred responses or trials.

Results showed that the performance of all children improved during the game, as they learned how to make correct responses. The improvement

[1] This does not mean that experimental psychologists use words such as "reward" and "punishment" in the same way that they are used outside the laboratory. B. F. Skinner (1963), for example, prefers the term "reinforcement" to "reward," because it is a neutral concept that he can use without making any assumptions about the organism's motivation or its subjective state. The term "reward" is a value-laden term that does have motivational implications. The same is true of "punishment." However, in this discussion we shall continue to use the terms "reward" and "punishment" in their usual sense because we are referring to conventional concepts of teaching and learning, rather than to laboratory experiments.

was much slower, however, with those children who had been socially deprived, and toward the end of the one hundred trials, their performance deteriorated and they began to show a preference for making incorrect responses (Gallimore, Tharp, and Kemp, 1969). For these children, the brief social deprivation they had experienced built up a need for social contact that was stronger than their need to succeed. Hence the appearance of the experimenter assumed a ''reward value'' that was more significant for the children than the ''punishment'' (''No, you're wrong.'') that he was administering.

The results of this experiment suggest an explanation for the behavior of children who are ''capable of better work'' but who continually perform poorly. The busy teacher, who does not have the time to praise (reward) each successful child, and who feels he has barely enough time for children who need help, unwittingly rewards failing behavior by limiting his contacts with children to criticizing their work and to admonishing them to do better. Such children continue to fail because the ''negative attention'' of the teacher assumes a higher psychological value for them than no attention at all. These findings also explain how disruptive behavior may persist or even escalate in a class in spite of warnings, threats, and scoldings on the part of the harassed teacher.

There is no doubt that the coupling of reward and punishment often ''gets results'' with students, but all too often the outcome is not in the direction of positive learning, that is, cognitive and affective development. What often results instead is a kind of blind obedience, an obedience that is conditional on the presence of the authority of the teacher. The repeated application of reward-and-punishment principles makes the teacher the central figure in the learning situation. If rewards and punishments are administered appropriately, learning will presumably take place. The teacher, in other words, takes on the burden of responsibility for seeing that learning takes place, and it is thus assumed that if he neither rewards nor punishes, he is not teaching and there will be no learning.

As a result of our commitment to reward-and-punishment principles in learning we have come to confuse *teaching* with *control*. If the chief objective

("Dennis the Menace" © 1975 by Field Newspaper Syndicate T.M. ®)

''I'll eat it. But I won't SWALLOW it!''

Traditional methods of dealing with children's behavior are often better at obtaining a superficial conformity than they are at obtaining the desired results.

of education were that of controlling students, there is no reason why teaching could not be simply a matter of administering rewards and punishments. However, if we are concerned with the *subsequent* behavior of students, particularly the behavior they will display when we are not on hand to direct them, then we may be in for some disappointments. The question is: Will they be able to solve problems successfully, undertake the tasks they are supposed to, and behave properly in other ways when teachers are not present to reward and punish them? Perhaps they will, but perhaps they will not; conformity to standards of proper behavior depends on many factors. The history of education is littered with the failures of those who believed that learning is the direct outcome of reward and punishment. Nor have employers, prison officials, military leaders, and others charged with the guidance, instruction, and control of persons placed under their supervision done any better using similar methods. Soldiers who are well-disciplined and neat under the watchful eye of the top sergeant sometimes behave in undisciplined and untidy ways when they are away on leave.

Individual differences in personality also complicate the effect of reward and punishment on learning. What classroom experiments often show is that praise facilitates the learning of some students, but that others perform better when they are criticized, whereas still others do best when they are merely given information as to their progress. Hani van de Riet (1964) found that praise resulted in slower learning among a group of very low achievers in grades 5 through 7 but in faster learning when used with a group of normal achievers from the same grades. These findings are consistent with those of another experiment which was conducted with mentally retarded children who practiced a card-sorting game for sixteen trials. Some of the children were given information, as well as praise and encouragement, as to their performance; others were given information alone. The results, as shown in Figure 7-1, indicate that information alone produced better results than did information and praise (Panda, 1971). What these two studies suggest is that under some conditions, slow learners may find encouraging comments distracting and actually do better if they are merely informed as to their progress.

The teacher who looks to research studies for help in determining whether he should praise, criticize, or merely inform will find few clues to guide him. What the studies do show is that the problem is not a simple one, and there are no standard answers. The question "Should I use praise or criticism?" must be answered with another question, "Praise or criticism for which student?" Answering the question, in other words, requires us to observe students and learn something about the way in which they characteristically react to feedback about their performance. The policy that many teachers have of using the same kind of incentive for everyone in the class seems questionable. Because students respond in different ways to rewards and punishments, it would appear that a standard treatment would produce variable results.

One difficulty which sometimes occurs when teachers use rewards and punishments in uncritical ways is in the reinforcing of the wrong kind of behavior. A ten-year-old boy who did well in all subjects except math was referred to a school psychologist. Analysis of his computation skills showed that he was having difficulty with all combinations involving the number "3." This difficulty was traced back to the first grade, where his teacher had become irritated with his slowness in learning to write a "3" and had whacked his hands with a ruler each time he produced a badly formed "3." Instead of the boy learning to produce a perfect "3," he learned to avoid "3s" and consequently was unable to use them in computation.

Another even commoner example of irrelevant learning occurring from the uncritical application of reward or punishment is that of the student who is praised for being the "best in the class," say, in reading. He continues to excel in reading in order to earn the teacher's praise again and again. But he makes little effort in math, in which he has average potential, because he cannot be "best in the class." He has learned that he can earn the teacher's praise through reading and sees no advantage in

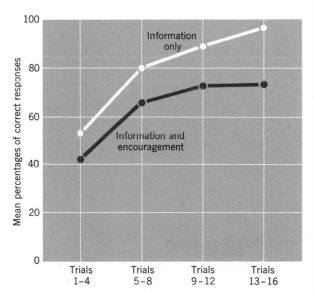

FIG. 7-1. Mean percentages of correct responses for mentally retarded children who practiced a card-sorting task for sixteen trials under conditions in which they were given either information as to their progress, or both information and encouragement (data from Panda, 1971).

TRADITIONAL/CONVENTIONAL VIEWS
OF LEARNING AND INSTRUCTION

putting any special effort into arithmetic. This is still another shortcoming of this approach to education. It focuses the attention of students and teachers on the teacher's power to reward and punish, instead of on the learning process and its inherent rewards. In other words, the emphasis is on *extrinsic* incentives, instead of on *intrinsic* incentives, where it should be.

Here is a "thumbnail case history" that shows the importance of intrinsic motivation in learning:

Rick did very poorly in ninth-grade algebra. He could not seem to get the hang of it at all. His mother tried to help him with his homework, but this only led to her losing her temper when Rick seemed to be unable to grasp even the simplest concept and kept making the same errors over and over again. Even though she frequently reminded him that his chances for getting into a university depended on his getting at least a B average, it seemed to her that he was not trying. For his part, Rick became tense and panicky whenever he worked on problems in algebra. With every failure, he became more and more convinced that he was stupid and inept. Yet he was doing well in all his other subjects. His mother finally gave up trying to help him and hired a tutor. Rick scraped through the course with a D.

A year later, during the summer after his sophomore year, Rick spent a month with his uncle, an architect. His uncle's workshop and office was located in his home, and he invited Rick to spend as much time as he wanted there, looking at architectural publications, catalogs of construction and decorative materials, and building plans. He also took Rick with him when he went out to supervise construction projects for his clients. These experiences opened up a completely new world for Rick. As his interest and curiosity grew, he asked many questions, which his uncle answered patiently and as fully as possible. By the end of the month, Rick was convinced that he, too, wanted to become an architect. But what to do about algebra? He talked the problem over with his uncle, who made a number of helpful suggestions. When Rick returned home, he startled his family by proposing that he take a "cram course" in algebra from the tutor who helped him during his freshman year. After their initial shock, his parents agreed, with the proviso that he pay for the lessons himself. To everyone's surprise, Rick agreed to the terms. He got a job as a newspaper delivery boy to pay

for the lessons and spent two hours a day on them during the month remaining in the vacation. When he entered school in the fall, he enrolled in second-year algebra and plane geometry. He continued to have a few problems with mathematics, but the old feeling of panic and inadequacy was gone, and he completed both courses with a grade of B.

If the idea that people learn only when they are rewarded or punished has so many flaws in it, why is it so popular? One reason is that it is a psychologically reassuring theory. All a teacher has to do is to reward or punish students appropriately and they will learn. The urge to find simple solutions to the complicated problems of life is universal. We do not want to face up to the fact that getting students to learn is a complex, difficult task, one that involves an understanding of psychological needs, personalities, and motivational patterns of students. Instead, we want to be reassured that teaching is simple—just a matter of applying the proper techniques.

Another reason why this belief is so popular is that it works—part of the time, at least. However, as we stated previously, a great deal of learning that seems to occur under reward-and-punishment conditions is what might be termed "superficial conformity" instead of real learning. When more permanent forms of learning do occur, they often take place in spite of the method used, rather than because of it.

Each teacher who is attracted to the idea that learning can be manipulated through application of rewards or punishment needs to ask himself if there are not more effective ways of teaching. One of the purposes of educational psychology is to lead teachers beyond the conventional and oversimplified ideas about learning that are based on popular belief and are part of everybody's cultural inheritance into ideas that are based on scientific investigation.

"The Mind Is a Storehouse"

This concept often appears in the form of the popular idea that "the mind is a storehouse for facts." Teaching is thus a process of filling the "storehouse" with facts, and learning is the process of acquiring or absorbing facts. The more facts, the more learning. People who have this concept about teaching and learning are likely to place great stress on memorization because the best way to learn facts, presumably, is to memorize them. Another popular formulation of this belief is that of referring to pupils as "empty pitchers waiting to be filled with knowledge." Learning is thus seen largely as a passive process: It is the learner's task to be receptive, and it is the teacher's task to see that the learner gets filled with learning.

Although this "additive theory of learning" has deep cultural roots and is popular with traditionalists in civilized and primitive cultures throughout the world, it is even more fallacious than the idea that learning results directly from the application of reward or punishment. It is true that people learn facts and information, but they do so by fitting them into what they have learned from previous experiences. In other words, facts and information are learned *in relation* to something—other facts, skills, needs, concepts—something that is already a part of the life and experience of the learner. Unless what we learn becomes a necessary or useful part of our functioning as individuals, we quickly forget it. We may remember an isolated bit of information for a short time in order to pass a test and thus escape the punishment of a failing grade or to avoid disappointing a teacher we like and respect, but once the grade has been assigned and the teacher is pleased, the useless material passes into the limbo of forgetfulness.

In partial defense of this theory, it is true that educated people generally have more facts at their command than do people of less education. But this does not mean that education is a process of amassing facts. Success in education involves the development of complex concepts and frames of reference which in turn, make it possible to learn broader and richer varieties of facts and information. These concepts and frames of reference help the individual to perceive how bits of information are related. Seeing interrelationships not only makes information more meaningful but more useful as well.

The conventional idea of education, as held by the lay public and a good many teachers, is unfortu-

nately that knowledge is something which has existed in its own right for many years, and that all the learner has to do is to reach out and acquire it. Presumably, if an entire class of children reaches out for the same knowledge, they will, of course, all know the same things. This notion has a great deal of influence on our thinking about the whole educational process, for it has molded curriculum design, school building plans, textbooks and workbooks, and, most important, our attitudes toward students.

The student who does not reach out and acquire the knowledge we offer is, of course, considered uncooperative and perverse. His negative attitude appears to us to be the only thing that stands between us and our success as teachers; hence we attempt to deal with it by coercing him. A whole structure of authoritarian coercion is set up by this mistaken line of reasoning.

What we actually do know is that differences in the amounts of what is learned depend on differences in readiness—that is, differences in what students already know, in experience, and in morale. Because of deficiencies in one or more of these factors, some students cannot learn what is expected of them. Perverseness or stubbornness has little to do with the student's inability to perform, although he may, when required to do what he cannot do, seem as though he is merely being stubborn.

"Didn't They Teach You *Anything* in Grade School?"

The expectation that things properly taught are retained indefinitely is more of an implicit theory than a belief, for most people would agree that some amount of forgetting is normal, no matter how good the teaching has been. Nevertheless, our attitudes and behavior toward learners and learning continually reveal our implicit and naïve faith in the long-range retention or the "permanence" of learning. We are, for example, surprised when a student has forgotten something we taught him last week or last month. And when he shows up in a college history class and confesses that he does not know the causes of the War of 1812, we say: "He obviously didn't learn (or wasn't taught) American history in high school," thus overlooking the possibility that he did learn but has forgotten.

Another situation that evokes this naïve theory is that of the student who enrolls in high-school English and does not seem to know the most rudimentary rules of grammar and punctuation. The teacher throws up his hands and asks: "Didn't they teach you *anything* in grade school?" Sometimes he may even ask the student if he had ever studied the parts of speech and the use of the comma. The student invariably looks blank and says that his teachers never taught him those things. Very likely, of course, they *were* taught, but he has forgotten. As far as he is presently concerned, it is as though he had never heard of them. And so the high-school teacher shrugs his shoulders resignedly and starts a review of basic principles of grammar. When the same student goes on to college or goes out into the world to get a job, he encounters an instructor or an employer who asks the same questions: "Why, don't you know the basic fundamentals of grammar? Didn't they teach you anything in high school?" And so a review of basic principles is undertaken once more, this time as preparation for a college course or for certain job operations.

What has happened, of course, is that the student has learned the basic principles and the rules of grammar not once but several times. He has also forgotten them several times. He learned them to pass tests or to satisfy teachers, but he never learned them for purposes of his own. Once the need to remember them had passed, it was just as though he had never learned them at all.

There is nothing abnormal or unusual about the forgetting that takes place after formal classroom learning. A number of studies conducted well over a generation ago shows that the amount of information retained by students several months after the end of a course is disappointingly small. For example, a study of the retention of American history revealed that, after a lapse of eighteen months, junior high students had forgotten one-third of the facts that they had learned (Brooks and Bassett, 1928). Another survey showed that students had forgotten two-thirds of the algebra that they had known a year earlier (Layton, 1932). Some research by Glenn W. Durflinger (1956) of sophomores and juniors at the University of California at Santa Barbara showed that although students retained reading skills very well, most of them were unable to function adequately in mathematics and an even larger percentage were unable to recognize parts of speech. Some of Durflinger's results are reported in Table 7-1.

TABLE 7-1. Percentages of University of California Sophomores and Juniors Making Errors in Elementary Mathematics and English Grammar[a]

Type of Error Mathematics	Percentage Making Error	Type of Error English Grammar	Percentage Making Error
Recognition and use of negative numbers	60	Vocabulary usage	22
Insurance and discount	46	Punctuating a quotation within a quotation	40
Multiplication of abstract numbers (algebraic terms)	38	Capitalizing names of persons and places	16
Subtraction of abstract numbers	32	Recognition of parts of sentences	26
Division of abstract numbers	31	Recognition of kinds of sentences	31
Multiplication of fractions and mixed numbers	25		

[a] After Durflinger, 1956.

One explanation of the results of these studies is obvious. The average student has little occasion to recall historical facts or to use mathematical skills. This does not account for the high error rate in English grammar because students do engage in a great deal of writing. The explanation here seems to be that one can write without recourse to the rules of formal grammar. In fact, studies that go back to the beginning of this century show that there is little relationship between knowledge of grammar and the ability to express oneself in writing (Hoyt, 1906; Asker, 1923; Miller, 1951). Hence it is hardly surprising that college students have forgotten much of the grammar they learned so painfully, not once, but several times over.

Even when a skill is practiced, it may deteriorate under certain conditions. Albert R. Kitzhaber (1963) conducted a survey of compositions and other papers written by Dartmouth College students and found that the number of errors in their writing declined during the freshman year, when they were taking courses in English composition, but increased during subsequent years. As Figure 7-2 demonstrates, seniors were making more errors than entering freshmen! What is involved here is not merely ignorance of the rules of grammar but an absence of supporting reinforcement from English teachers during the last three years of college. Because instructors in other fields apparently did not care whether students' papers were in good grammatical form, students naturally paid less and less attention to the formal aspects of their writing. What is needed to maintain a formerly attained level of adequacy is not, therefore, merely practice but some kind of assurance that what was learned has functional value.

"Practice Makes Perfect"

Whenever Abraham Lincoln read or wrote, he sounded each word, a habit he had learned in "blab school" as a child. The "blab schools" which prevailed in the early part of the nineteenth century were so called because the children committed the entire curriculum to memory and rehearsed everything aloud. Indeed, any child who was not working aloud was considered by the teacher to be loafing and was punished (Armstrong, 1974).

"Blab" methods of memorization are seldom encountered in modern schools, but the traditional nineteenth-century instructional method of teaching—drill, test, and drill again still lives on. Such methods are expressions of the idea that frequent repetition is the best way to get students to learn, and that those things learned best are the ones that get the most rehearsal. The research of Durflinger and Kitzhaber, however, raises questions about the permanence of any school learning, irrespective of how often it is taught. In instances where the material or skill has functional value, repetition may aid in its retention; in other instances, repetition may lead to apathy or boredom.

Psychologists became interested in memory, or *retention,* during the first few years of psychology's existence as a science. Early experiments by Hermann Ebbinghaus (1913), who set about the task of memorizing nonsense syllables, showed that the "forgetting curve" drops off sharply after a practice period and declines more slowly thereafter. The common-sense explanation for rapid fading away of material learned through drill is that it is not being used or repeated, but research with retention

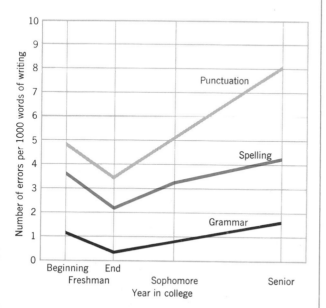

FIG. 7-2. Changes in proportion of errors in written English made by Dartmouth College students at various stages during their college careers (Kitzhaber, 1963).

shows that forgetting is more likely to occur as a result of the interference of other learned material. Our attempts to recall material we have memorized may be interfered with or inhibited by material we learned earlier (proactive inhibition) or by material learned subsequently (retroactive inhibition). Most forgetting takes place through proactive inhibition. We attempt to memorize a new telephone number but cannot recall it a day later. We can recall a good many other numbers that we have known for some time, however. It is as though our being able to remember the other numbers interferes with or inhibits the recall of the new number.

Retroactive and proactive inhibition are fairly technical and of interest primarily to experimental psychologists, but the main point here is that getting students to learn in a way that they remember what they have learned is not merely a matter of drill and repetition. The task is just not that easy because retention does not work that simply. If material can be presented in a way that enables students to associate it with what they already know, it will make more sense to them. It will make even more sense if they can make their own associations, with a minimum of help from the teacher. Such self-involvement enables the material to assume a degree of importance for them and thus enhances the possibility that it will be retained.

Perhaps this is the basis for learning that endures: It is perceived by the individual as somehow important for *him*. If he perceives a piece of information as being important, this fact will have more significance than his being made to repeat it a number of times as part of a drill. We have all had the experience of remembering information, concepts, and even skills that we acquired long ago and have no practical reason to remember. But we are able to recall them because somehow they are psychologically important to us. There may be some validity to the idea that things properly learned and practiced will be remembered, but this holds true only if they have acquired some kind of personal value for us.

"Teaching = Telling; Learning = Being Told"

A group of parents had just seen a film on juvenile delinquency, the highlight of which was a scene in which a small gang of adolescents smashed the windows of a warehouse—"just for fun." As the light came on and the discussion period opened, the group sat quietly for a while, thinking about the picture. Then one parent spoke up and asked: "Why do kids do things like that anyway'?"

Another answered: "My boy would never do a thing like that."

The first parent countered: "That's interesting; why not?"

"Why not? Simply because I have taken the time and the trouble to *tell him the difference between right and wrong.*"

The commonly held theory that people learn because someone *tells* them something is related, philosophically at least, to all three of the popular beliefs about learning we have discussed so far. It assumes that learning must start somewhere *outside* of the learner, that someone else must set the wheels in motion that finally result in learning. It also assumes that "what is learned" is the thing that is told, that this "thing" is somehow added to the store of knowledge already in the learner's head, just as you would add another brick to a pile of bricks already in a storeroom.

Like the other beliefs that we have described, this one is rich with tradition. It is basic to such educational practices as giving lectures and having students read textbooks. The idea is that learning is outside the student—in the lecture or in the textbook—and somehow he has to get it inside him. This was the theory held by Mrs. Del Carlo when she lectured the junior high English class on the subject of sportsmanship. She did not depend on this theory alone, however; note that she followed up her lecture with an assignment.

Sometimes we find evidence that students have gained much from hearing a lecture or reading a book, and this discovery appears to confirm this theory. However, such successes do not come merely because of what was said in the lecture or printed in the book. Any learning that occurs will depend on a variety of factors: the interest of the student, the extent to which he sees himself involved in the subject at hand, the way in which the material is presented, the student's opportunities to

TRADITIONAL/CONVENTIONAL VIEWS
OF LEARNING AND INSTRUCTION

discuss and think over what has been presented, and so forth.

Let us assume that the parent in the incident we presented above is correct when he says that his boy would not break windows in a warehouse. Very likely he *has* told his son the difference, or some of the differences, between right and wrong. But he really cannot say with any certainty that his son's good behavior was the result of being told this difference. It may have been due to other factors: examples set by parents, living in a law-abiding neighborhood, not going around with a group that would break windows, and so forth. In other words, even if his parent had *not* told his son the difference between right and wrong, these other influences would have been sufficient to keep him from breaking windows. We know this partly because the behavior of adolescent boys is likely to be influenced more strongly by what their friends do than what their parents say, but we also know that there is very little change in behavior when people are merely *told* something (Lewin, 1958).

Actually, *telling* is one of the more difficult means of conveying information that is to be remembered. In one investigation, psychologists were interested in finding out whether persons who had been counseled remembered the test scores that had been discussed with them. They found that counselees could remember the highest score but not the others (Froehlich and Moser, 1954). If students cannot remember anything as important to them personally as the scores they make on tests, how can we expect that they will remember information in which they are *less* involved?

How to Ride a Bicycle: "First You Master the Principles of Mass, Weight, and Motion, and then. . ."

The theory that underlies such curricular planning is that the best learning is that which results from deductive reasoning and that students should not have any direct experiences before they thoroughly understand the theoretical principles that underlie the skills or the body of knowledge they are expected to master. We can see the application of this theory in curricula that require students to under-

stand principles of French grammar before they attempt to speak, read, or write the language; they should learn how to add, subtract, multiply, and do fractions before they handle money; they should practice making circles and rhythmical strokes before they attempt to write; and they should understand botany and soil chemistry before they attempt to grow vegetables or flowers. The argument that theory should come before practice sounds very logical; hence it is not surprising to find it used almost universally as a basis for curriculum design in schools and colleges. In reality, however, it works out better for learners to have some kind of direct or personal experience with at least some aspects of the subject at hand before theoretical considerations are taken up. In other words, theoretical principles have more meaning for people who have had to cope with some of the problems to which theories are supposed to apply. Explaining how yeast plants turn sugar into carbon dioxide which in turn makes bread rise makes more sense to someone who has seen or participated in the making of bread than it does to someone who has not. People who have had direct experience with certain processes or materials see theoretical principles quite differently than do those who have not had such experiences. This is why students who sign up for teacher education are encouraged to participate in a variety of activities concerned with children: teaching Sunday school, camp counseling, recreation work, Scout leadership, and even baby-sitting. Without such direct and personal experiences, much of the potential value of discussions of principles and theory is lost on students.

The idea that learning should take place deductively, from the general to the particular, comes from the scholastic tradition that is part of our European cultural inheritance. In the older European tradition, scholars are men of ideas, not of action, and their particular contribution to education is that of providing the theories or generalizations that explain experience. Hence the teacher is traditionally a kind of "specialist in theory"—someone who stands apart from the experiences and daily events of the world. The American society, however, with its democratic tradition and demands for technological competence, has emphasized the practical aspects of education. Whereas in Europe a major purpose of education has been that of *qualifying* a person to fill a certain position in the social structure, American education has been more concerned with *developing competence*—vocational and civic competence, as well as competence in everyday living. For this reason, theory plays a secondary role in American life. American educators, however, have had to cope with the demands of a public concerned with competence in everyday life but at the same time have attempted to use an educational approach that was largely European, hence more concerned with theory and form than with practical outcomes. These differences are schematically shown in Figure 7-3. The "ideal" educational program is portrayed as one which draws upon experience and relates it to theory, which is then applied to a reevaluation of experience. The older European approach, which is characteristic of traditional education, is that of applying theory to experience.[2] This means that theory can be used to modify experience, but that experience can have no effect on theory. The "common-sense" approach favored by most Americans, on the other hand, has been only incidentally concerned with theory, which is modified in accord with experience.

The advantage of the "ideal" approach to learning is that theory and practical experience are used to supplement each other. Not only is experience used to modify theory, but also generalizations about experience are formulated which can then be applied to other and similar situations and problems. Indeed, one of the contributions of theory is that it helps the learner perceive similarities in other situations and problems and serves as a starting point or guidepost. This ability to apply what has been learned in one situation to another situation is what is called "transfer of learning."

Instructing students in the use of rules before

[2] To be absolutely fair, we should note that from the Renaissance era onward, European philosophers and educators, such as Locke, Rousseau, Pestalozzi, and Montessori, were critical of the scholastic tradition and the overreliance on the deductive method. Piaget's concepts of learning also challenge methods of instruction which emphasize the abstract and exclude or postpone direct experience.

they begin solving problems may also be termed the "expository method" because the role of the teacher is that of expounding or explaining. Both the expository and the discovery method were compared in a study involving more than four hundred pupils in sixteen fifth- and sixth-grade classes in Salt Lake City. Teachers were trained for twenty weeks in both methods of teaching arithmetical principles. Each teacher spent six weeks teaching two classes, one with the discovery method and the other with the expository method. Results showed that the expository method was superior as far as initial learning was concerned, but that the discovery method was superior in terms of what students retained over periods of five to eleven weeks after instruction. The discovery method produced superior results in terms of students' ability to use the principles that they had learned in other types of problems. An additional advantage of the discovery method was that it facilitated the development of what are termed *heuristics:* the ability to make intelligent guesses as to the probable solution when only a portion of the necessary data is provided.

The author of this study, Blaine R. Worthen (1968), concluded that if our aim as teachers is that of getting students to learn problem-solving methods that they will remember and be able to apply in a variety of situations, the discovery method is the one to use; but if we are primarily concerned about how students will do on a test immediately after they have been taught (which is the goal that all too many teachers have in mind), then the expository method is the one to choose.

A great many problems in life are solved heuristically, if they are solved at all, that is, we seldom have all the facts in hand when we encounter problem situations but must forge ahead and come to some decision. The continued experience with life problems teaches us how to improvise, estimate, and extrapolate in order to fill in the gaps in our data. We have been trying to reach an individual by phone. He is a busy man, seldom in his office. We, too, are busy and are difficult to reach by telephone. It is important that we talk to him. We resolve the problem by calling him at 6 P.M. because most people are home then and preparing for dinner. We

TRADITIONAL/CONVENTIONAL VIEWS
OF LEARNING AND INSTRUCTION

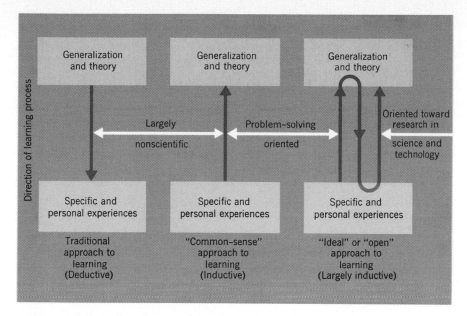

FIG. 7-3. Differences among various ways of introducing theory and direct experience into the learning process and their effect on the direction of learning.

do not *know* that he will be there, but we extrapolate from our experience with others in our culture and figure that the chance of our being able to reach him then is better than at any other time.

The problem situations we encounter in everyday life are full of data, many of which are irrelevant to the solution of the problem. We learn to deal heuristically with these situations by determining which data are relevant and by making intelligent guesses about data that are needed but that are unavailable for some reason or other. The problems students encounter in classroom learning situations are usually unrealistic: All the needed data are present and no irrelevant data are included. In recent years, more materials have been developed that develop heuristic processes, particularly the materials designed for use in programs intended to encourage creativity, but the conventional textbook author still trudges along the well-beaten path, and the conventional teacher strives to stifle speculation, improvisation, and other heuristic approaches by telling his students: "Be sure you're right before you go ahead," or "In this test, there is a penalty for guessing. When in doubt, don't guess!"

The chief problem faced by the teacher who wishes to get his students to use discovery or heuristic methods is that of motivation. Bert Y. Kersh (1958, 1962), who conducted some rather disappointing experiments in which college students were required to learn mathematical concepts, found that rote methods produced the best results, but that motivation was strongest among those students who had received no direction at all. Kersh noted, however, that "the motivating power does not appear in strength unless the student is required to learn almost completely without help and expends intensive effort over a period of fifteen minutes or more."

Experiments of this type show how difficult it is to manipulate a single variable in the teaching-learning process in the expectation of getting substantial results. Students who had a history of being taught by methods that encourage deductive thinking and which provide no experience in "learning through discovery" are likely to feel insecure and to flounder when placed in learning situations in which they receive little help or direction. Conversations this author has had with teachers indicate that a student's family backgound is also very significant. They report that they have the most success with the discovery method with students whose parents foster curiosity and independence of thought and encourage them to read, experiment, and explore. Children from homes in which parents are more traditional in their attitudes are likely to complain when they are required to dig out answers for themselves and often go to extreme lengths to avoid becoming involved in discovery learning and heuristic experiences. Lee J. Cronbach (1975) maintains that differences in children's ways of responding to expository and heuristic teaching methods follow social-class lines: "It begins to appear that the lower-class child responds better (on the average) to didactic teaching, with explicit requirements and close-coupled rewards. Problem-oriented, ego-motivated, supportive methods of teaching, which educational theorists have long been advocating, seem to benefit only a middle-class clientele."

"Geometry Is Good for You— It Teaches You How to Think"

Perhaps the most fundamental idea in education is the expectation or, rather, the hope that what is learned in the classroom will "transfer" to activities and problems outside the classroom. Unless students are changed by their educational experiences in such a way that their behavior is more intelligent and more effective, when contrasted with that of individuals who have not had the benefits of education, then the vast amounts of time, energy, and money that we invest in education have been wasted. The ability to understand the words in the fifth reader is a useless skill if students cannot use it to read newspapers and traffic signs, and the study of civics is a waste of time if students are not helped to become more effective citizens thereby.

Somehow, our assumption that classroom learning *ought* to transfer to life outside becomes transmuted into the assumption that it happens automatically. Often it does not. Here is an example:

A visitor to the fourth grade asked the children: "What do you do when you walk down the hall and you see a piece of paper lying on the floor?"

The children all knew the answer: "You pick it up and put it in the wastebasket."

A few minutes later, the recess bell sounded and the children hurried out to play down the hall that led to the play yard. The hall had been littered (by the visitor) with pieces of paper. A wastebasket stood nearby. No child stopped to pick up the paper.

The chief danger in the theory that all classroom learning will automatically transfer itself to everyday life lies in the false sense of security it gives us. As long as we can believe in automatic transfer, we do not feel the need to examine our course content and methods critically. Thus we keep courses in the curriculum that have long outlived their usefulness and teach otherwise valuable courses in such a way that whatever is gained in the way of learning is forgotten a few weeks or months after the final examination. The conventional approach to high-school mathematics is a good example. Although algebra and geometry can be related to events in the life of every student, they are usually taught as highly abstract, esoteric areas of knowledge. Teachers typically remind students at every turn how useful these two branches of mathematics are, but seldom make any attempt to demonstrate their usefulness.

The teaching of mathematics is commonly defended on the grounds that it "teaches students how to think." In other words, it is proposed that the logical processes learned in mathematics will be helpful in dealing with such problems as deciding which occupation we should enter, how to live within our income, and which political candidate deserves our vote. The point is that both the problems we encounter in mathematics and those we encounter in everday life call for logical analysis, and the logical analysis learned in mathematics should presumably be applicable to situations and problems encountered outside the classroom.

Such transfer *can* occur when the new situation resembles the learning situation. The missing link in this process is the student and his perceptions. The question is: Does he *see* the problems of geometry and political choice as having some points of similarity? Or, rather, does he see that the kind of logical analysis learned in geometry is useful in dealing with other problems of life?

Usually students do not develop this kind of perception, hence do not make this transition, partly because teachers are unaware that students need help in seeing relationships of this sort; partly because they are concerned with other matters, such as getting control of the class and seeing that students understand what is being taught; partly because of the natural resistance of students to a learning situation in which they do not feel emotionally involved; and partly because some of the transfer of learning we expect is rather far-fetched. Perhaps there is actually very little of what can be learned in geometry that can be applied to a situation involving the selection of a political candidate. However, human beings are very ingenious. If they are really involved and interested in a subject or a problem, they demonstrate a faculty of being able to pick up the most obscure clues in the most unlikely places and use them to advantage. It is quite likely that there are people who have been able to use the kind of logic that they have learned in geometry and can apply it to everyday problems successfully. But in view of the way in which geometry is usually taught and is usually learned by students, such instances must be rather rare.

"School Is Preparation for Life: Since Life Is Grim, School Should Be Grimmer"

The traditional methods of teach, drill, test, and drill again are expressions of the idea that repetition is the process itself. We insist, for instance, that the study of geography is in itself useless unless it leads to a better understanding of the world. However, there is an idea that was popular a generation ago, is still popular in Europe, and even finds considerable acceptance in America today: the idea that education is or should be some kind of a mental toughening process that has a value in and of itself. The assumption is that the mind is a kind of muscle that can be strengthened by vigorous exercise. People who hold this theory believe that the more difficult, frustrating, and unpleasant the subject, the greater its value to students.

Educators and psychologists have so far been unable to find any sound scientifc evidence for this theory. E. L. Thorndike (1924) found, over a generation ago, that high-school students who took mathematics *did* make slightly superior gains in reasoning ability, when their performance was contrasted with students who had taken dramatics, biology, and home economics, but that this slight difference could be explained by the fact that the students who enrolled in mathematics courses had higher IQs to begin with.

Like the other popular and traditional theories of learning, the idea that learning activities must be tedious or uninteresting to have any value has a very strong hold on people's minds. Joseph Mayer Rice (1897) encountered much opposition at the end of the nineteenth century when he conducted research into the relationship between the amount of time spent in spelling drill and competence in spelling. When he reported that the children who spent half an hour a day in spelling drill could spell no better than those who spent only ten minutes a day at this task, the educators and laymen of that day felt he had missed the main point: The chief purpose of spelling drill was to *discipline the mind,* not to teach spelling!

Today we are less likely to put much faith in this stress-and-strain theory of education. But sometimes we are disturbed when it appears that children are having too much fun in school. After all, education is supposed to be a rather serious business, and it is hard for us to accept the idea that learning might be enjoyable. This is one of the reasons why schools are frequently attacked for putting "frills" such as folk dancing, dramatics, and life-adjustment education into the curriculum. We wonder whether we are not being "too easy" with students these days, and whether they will learn "the hard facts of life," if learning becomes too pleasant.

These feelings are aggravated whenever we hear reports that the students in our community are deficient in arithmetic or science as compared with the students in an adjoining community or with Russian students. At such times, we set our jaw and say: "Students are just not having to work hard enough;

what they need is more discipline, more homework, and, above all, more drill in the fundamentals." Part of this feeling comes from wanting to punish our children for having let us down, but part of it comes from the feeling that learning should be, after all, a kind of drudgery.

"If Learning Isn't Fun, It Isn't Learning"

One of the intriguing facets of the study of human behavior is its apparent inconsistency. We seem to have an amazing ability to develop beliefs and take stands that are completely contradictory—even on the same subject. The same person who has criticized the local school administration for permitting a half-hour a week of folk dancing will, when meeting a child at the home of a friend, go through the same ritual of questioning that many of us employ in similar situations. The sequence of questions goes something like this: "What's your name? How old are you? What grade in school are you in? What school do you go to? *Do you like school"*

In America it is very important that children *like* school. In other countries it is much less important—it is even irrelevant. An American teacher reported, after a visit to France, that when he asked French school children whether they liked school, they were surprised at the question. Why should anyone be expected to like school? One went to school because all children go to school; one accepted this as a matter of course. And why should anyone, especially an adult, be concerned whether school was liked?

The people of America are proud of their educational system; even when they criticize it, they are proud of it. They are proud of it because they know that they have created it themselves. They see it as an institution that makes it possible for people to better themselves. They see education as providing the spark and the power that has made America a great nation. But most important is the feeling that the public school system is something that is created and directed by the people—it is *their* system. And it is something they have done for their children, not for themselves.

Because we feel so personally involved in our schools and because we have put so much time, money, and effort into them, we feel that children should *like* the schools we have provided for them, just as we want to have children appreciate and enjoy any other generous thing we might do for them. Yet we are not sure whether we have done as well as we could have done. We are not sure whether the system will do all that we hope. Hence we ask children for reassurance: "Do you like school?"

Very likely we are also asking whether they *appreciate* school, whether they see in school the great opportunity and challenge that we see. And very likely, too, we hope that children will like school because school is, or should be, a good thing.

The idea that learning should be fun is, in part, related to the assumption that educational experiences are good experiences, but it is also a reaction against the traditional idea that learning should be painful. The idea that learning can be fun is one that gets much of its support from teachers who like to see children happy or who themselves enjoy learning and, therefore, want to share their pleasure with others. No modern educator would have any quarrel with these points of view; indeed, we wish that all teachers enjoyed seeing children happy and were enthusiastic about learning. Two of the most basic qualities in good teachers are their interest in young people and their enthusiasm for learning.

Some of this common-sense idea that learning is enjoyable is endorsed by research and some is not. Research does not give very strong support to the idea that more successful learners, for example, like school better than less successful ones. Philip W. Jackson and Henriette M. Lahaderne (1967) found no relationship between scholastic success of sixth-graders and the attitudes they expressed toward school. There was a slight tendency for the more successful children to like school, in contrast to the less successful ones, but the relationship was not statistically significant.

There is, however, ample evidence from the research laboratory, as well as everyday experience, which indicates that individuals learn best when they are rewarded or reinforced, as we noted in our discussion of reward-and-punishment learning.

Nevertheless, there is a question as to whether *all* aspects of the learning process should be necessarily pleasurable and satisfying. There are times, for instance, during the learning of problem-solving strategies and techniques, when solutions are elusive, and the student tries first one approach and then another without success. Are we to expect that he would find these experiences enjoyable? Indeed, most of us would argue that frustrating experiences like these are a necessary phase of learning complex skills, and that they heighten the enjoyment of success when it is finally attained.

Those teachers who insist that *all* aspects of learning "should be fun" are likely to engage in all manner of interfering maneuvers that may actually interfere with normal cognitive development. Some teachers, like some parents, overprotect children by attempting to shield them from experiences that may have possible negative or disturbing overtones. Sometimes they plan their classwork in such a way that no child will fail (or discover that he has failed) in any task. To be sure, there is too much emphasis on failure in education, with the result that many a child becomes quickly discouraged, but the antidote in not the elimination of failure altogether. And we must distinguish between teacher-determined failure (any mark less than "perfect," for example), which may lead to cut-throat competition and public humiliation, and the failure that occurs on a small scale, privately as, for instance, when a student discovers that he has been using the wrong method in trying to solve a problem or cannot make sense out of a passage because it contains words he does not understand. Life for both young people and adults contains countless incidents of failure, and a major part of living is learning to cope with them. As Terence Moore (1969) says:

Without stress, life could never be. Tensions and relaxation form the natural rhythms of living.

Alma Bingham (1958) also wrote:

We must allow children failures. We quell many problem solving opportunities and give them limited experience by making sure they won't fail.

Keeping a child from experiencing failure is the result of mistaken ideas about the nature of the learning process. Every learner needs a chance to explore the problems that confront him, to test their boundaries or limits, and to try out various solutions. He cannot do this if he is never permitted to fail. One of the chief reasons we have difficulty in letting children fail is that our culture makes failure a kind of disgrace, and the very thought of it arouses our anxieties.

The initial stages of learning, too, are normally characterized by some degree of anxiety. The puzzlement and tension we experience when we are confronted by a problem that calls for the learning of a new skill or new information have the qualities of mild anxiety. Indeed, all really important learning is accompanied, or at least preceded, by some discomfort or anxiety. When learning really takes place, it means that there has been some change in the learner. We seldom welcome change. All that is childish and immature within us struggles against the necessity for change. It is much more comfortable to leave things the way they are and not to have to change. But when our environment is making demands on us, our old ways of behavior are no longer appropriate and we are made uncomfortable by the realization that we are out of step, that we cannot cope with the world as successfully as we would like to, that we need to make some adjustment. In effect, we realize that we are unable to meet our basic needs successfully, and we become anxious for fear that we might never be able to meet them. Perhaps we discover that we are nonreaders in a world of readers, or perhaps we realize that we can never cope with the world as skillfully as adults unless we learn to read. The normal anxiety that results from this realization acts as a spur that helps to urge children into the process of learning to read. Once they are successfully caught up in the process, learning becomes a satisfying experience, in the sense that they get the feeling of accomplishing something, of learning how to cope with the world and do what other people can do.

After reviewing research in six areas of mental development, Ralph W. Tyler (1948) came to the conclusion that mental development is actually facilitated by situations containing some element of conflict or frustration:

> In order that effective integration may take place in the child's mental development, conflicting drives, impulses, external demands, and ideas must be balanced, not eliminated.

The course of true learning—like that of true love—never does run smoothly. Even the successful reader experiences occasional frustrations in his attempts to extract meaning from the printed line. If he has a backlog of successes, he can meet each new frustration with confidence. He will be irritated when he encounters words he cannot understand, but he learns to persist and not to surrender to his irritation.

The teacher who bases his approach to learning entirely on reward-and-punishment principles knows that children learn in response to pressures, but he does not realize that these pressures should be internal, that is, they should be the result of the child's attempt to meet his own needs rather than an adult's idea of what is best for children. On the other hand, the teacher who insists that learning must be a completely pleasurable experience may be so successful at shielding children from uncomfortable realities like frustration and failure that little learning actually occurs. The first kind of teacher renders learning activities ineffective because he makes learning too painful or distasteful, whereas the second renders them ineffective by attempting to keep them entirely on a pleasurable plane.

The Pervasive Power of Traditional/Conventional Beliefs About Learning

Probably most people are not aware that their attitudes and behavior toward education are governed by the kinds of implicit theories we have described, or, for that matter, that they have any theories about learning at all. But the way in which people react when educational matters come up for discussion and decision provides unmistakable clues that these beliefs are very widely held.

Nor are educators exempt. The ideas covered in this chapter are very much a part of our tradition and cultural pattern, and, even, if we are professional educators who should know better, we continually find ourselves making decisions that are rather obviously based on the ideas that children have to be rewarded or punished in order to get them to learn, that teaching is telling, and that difficult subjects discipline the mind.

An example of this tendency is provided by an incident that occurred in a large city school system. A survey of basic skills showed the children to be slightly below national norms in arithmetic, although above the norms in other subjects. The immediate reaction of many of the teachers and principals was to recommend that more time be spent on arithmetic. Such a reaction is, of course, very understandable; it is an idea that would occur to almost anyone who has been given the task of trying to figure out what to do when children are below par in arithmetic. Educational research has showed us that answers to learning problems are seldom as simple as this. You just cannot improve learning in a certain subject merely by increasing the amount of time children spend studying it. Modern educators know this and have known it for some decades: it was one of the findings of J. M. Rice in his studies of spelling referred to a few pages back. But the belief that the cure for educational deficiencies is largely one of spending more time on the troublesome subject is rather firmly fixed in our cultural tradition, hence in our personal philosophies, and we have not been able to eradicate it by taking courses in education and finding out that learning does not occur this way. As we said a little earlier, learning produces changes in us, and we tend to resist being changed. This is true whether we are talking about learning in the fourth grade or learning how to teach.

Because these ideas about learning are so much a part of our outlook on life, it is difficult for us to accept evidence that they do not work. Hence when education based on these ideas fails to promote learning in students, it seldom if ever occurs to us to be critical of the theory that caused the trouble because we accept its "truth" as a matter of course. Instead, we criticize the students: They don't study enough, their parents don't set good examples and won't make them study hard enough. If we are parents, we find fault with the school. Teachers blame parents; parents blame teachers.

Further evidence of the importance placed by many people on these traditional and popular beliefs about learning is provided by the fears and anxieties that are aroused when educators try to develop curricula or use methodology based on newer ideas that have been found to be more effective. Traditional ideas have become so much a part of the thinking and behaving patterns of most people that any attempt to change educational methods for something better and more efficient is seen by them as a personal affront, as an attempt to attack the values they hold dear. Because the possibility of change, even for the better, arouses so much anxiety in people, educational reforms come slowly, if at all. Indeed, there is some evidence that the past decade or so has seen a return to the older, prescientific or nonscientific concepts of learning and teaching.

Earl C. Kelley (1954) once commented as follows with respect to the conflict between scientific approaches to problems of education and the traditional theories of learning we have been discussing.

With regard to the use of known facts, we are about where the medical profession was one hundred years ago. We would not think much of a doctor who gave us medicine simply because it had always been used. We expect him to be scientifically up-to-date. We demand the newest antibiotic. When George Washington became ill with pneumonia, the doctors, I am told, bled him because bleeding was held to be good for the sick. What he needed was more blood instead of less. So he died. If the doctors had not bled him, however, they might have been indicted for criminal negligence. Some of us who are teachers are "bleeding" our children on public demand.

The difference between the attitude of the public toward doctors and teachers shows that it matters a great deal which part of the [person] one ministers to. If you work on the physical, visible part of man, you are expected to use the latest scientific data. If you minister to the psychological, invisible, attitudinal, then superstition, tradition, and emotion are good enough.

SUMMARY

Each of us subscribes to several theories or ideas about learning, although we are not generally aware of doing so. The approaches we use in learning or in directing the learning behavior of others reveal the kind of learning principles we believe in. Most of these learning principles are part of our cultural inheritance and may seem like "common sense" to us, but they may also interfere with the effectiveness of our teaching or learning.

One of the commonest beliefs is the idea that learning occurs because the learner has been rewarded or punished. There is some scientific basis for this theory, but teachers forget that what may be a reward or a punishment in their eyes may not be perceived by a student in the same way. Furthermore, some students respond more favorably to rewards, whereas others respond more favorably to punishment, and there is always the danger that we may be reinforcing the wrong behavior through our uncritical application of reward and punishment.

Another popular idea about learning holds that learning is a process of accumulating facts and information. This theory overlooks the fact that everything that is learned is learned in relation to the student's previous experience, and that knowledge does not and cannot exist as something separate and outside the experience of the student.

The idea that a thing once learned properly is learned for all time is another theory that has many adherents. It is true that we are more likely to retain a skill or a concept that has value, purpose, and interest for us, but something that is of little value or purpose is quickly and easily forgotten, no matter how thoroughly it has been memorized. The same criticism applies to the belief that learning results from "being told."

The idea that learning should proceed deductively—from the application of theory to practice—is one that comes to us from our European origins. Opposed to it is the American idea that theory should grow out of practical experience. Perhaps an even more useful idea is the thought that experience should precede the development of theory, but that both theory and practice should be used to improve each other. Research with these concepts shows mixed results. Students taught by expository methods learn best if immediate recall is desired, but for long-range results, discovery or heuristic methods are better. Motivation tends to be higher if students use discovery methods, but a major problem teachers face is that of getting students who have been taught exclusively by expository methods to function independently and use heuristic approaches.

The idea that learning should be a toughening process—a kind of mental discipline—has fewer adherents than it formerly did, but it still appears in modified form. Sometimes we get disturbed when students appear to be enjoying themselves in the classroom, and we get the feeling that learning is serious business—it should not be "fun."

The mirror image of this theory is the idea that learning *should* be fun. It does not have the traditional background of the other theories, but it may interfere with effective teaching if it is interpreted to mean that learning must *always* be fun or that students should be protected against the frustration, failure, and normal anxiety that are a necessary part of most learning situations.

Although traditional beliefs have little scientific support, they are difficult to unlearn. Consequently teachers and administrators tend to use them as the basis for educational procedure, even though the fallacies of these beliefs have been pointed out to them in the course of their professional training. Traditional/conventional methods and points of view are attractive because they are psychologically comforting and reassuring, despite their ineffectiveness.

Suggested Problems

1. A "true" answer to each of the true-false questions listed near the beginning of this chapter is, of course, consistent with traditional and conventional beliefs about education and inconsistent with psychological and educational research finds. Try the same questions out on some of your acquaintances and see how much acceptance these theories have with the general public. Are they willing to agree that these theories are not very valid or effective? Comment on the degree of resistance you encounter in discussing these issues with them.

2. Researchers have shown again and again that the study of formal grammar is of little value when it comes to improving students' ability to express themselves in writing. Why do you suppose that English teachers continue to stress grammar? What methods of teaching English composition do you think would be more effective?

3. Drawing on your own experience, give some examples of a teacher whose methods indicated a belief that learning should be painful and some of a teacher whose methods indicated a belief that learning should be fun.

4. Select some institution outside the school that is engaged in the process of attempting to educate, such as the Army, mental hospitals, prisons, or business and industry. In what way are their methods characterized by popular theories of learning?

5. In this chapter we have given some examples of transfer of learning that do not succeed. Give some examples of classroom learning in which transfer is successful, and, using the psychological principles that have been presented so far in this book, explain why they succeed.

Suggested Readings

Bayles, E. E. *Democratic educational theory*. New York: Harper, 1960. Criticizes orthodox approaches to education.

Benjamin, H. *The sabre-tooth curriculum*. New York: McGraw-Hill, 1939. An entertaining and penetrating satire on the foibles of traditional curricula and methodology. His criticisms are, unfortunately, as relevant today as they were over a generation ago, when the book was written.

Dewey, J. *Education today*. New York: Putnam, 1940. See Chapter 2, "The primary-education fetish," and Chapter 3, "The people and the schools."

Highet, G. *The art of teaching*. New York: Knopf, 1950. An eloquent statement of the best that is in traditional education.

TRADITIONAL/CONVENTIONAL VIEWS
OF LEARNING AND INSTRUCTION

Holt, J. *How children fail.* New York: Dell, 1964. (A paperback.) A lively, impressionistic account of the way children avoid learning what they are expected to learn and, instead, learn to cope with the strategies of the teacher and the traditional system he represents to them.

Hudgins, B. B. *Problem solving in the classroom.* New York: Macmillan, 1966. (A paperback.) A how-to book that describes the teaching of problem-solving skills with a view to facilitating transfer of training.

Kelley, E. C. *Education for what is real.* New York: Harper, 1947. A stimulating discussion of education and reality from the standpoint of the learner's perceptual processes.

Phenix, P. H. (ed.) *Philosophies of education.* New York: Wiley, 1961. See particularly the statement by Arthur Bestor, "Education for intellectual discipline," a presentation of the traditionalist's position.

Psychological Concepts of the Teaching-Learning Process

Why Theory Is Necessary

One of the essential characteristics of man is his need to make sense out of the world around him. If he cannot fit his impressions of the universe into some sense-making framework, he becomes fearful and anxious. Very likely this need is related to his basic need to avoid danger and make his environment a safe place in which to live. Primitive man attributed the destruction of storms to the anger of the gods. By comparing the violence of storms to the violence of anger and by identifying or designating some superhuman source, he felt somewhat reassured. He might still be afraid of storms, but he felt as though he understood them better. Today we know that storms are caused by differences in the pressure, temperature, and humidity of air masses, and this knowledge is even more reassuring because we can now make reasonably accurate predictions of when storms will arrive, how intense they will be, and how long they will last. We are still afraid of them, but because we understand them better and can take precautions to defend ourselves against them, we feel more secure and less anxious.

Scientific research is a refined and highly developed outgrowth of man's need to explain and understand the world around him. His earliest attempts to understand his environment were based largely on surface phenomena—the way things appeared to him. Hence he explained the relationship of the earth and the sun by saying that the earth was a flat plain, warmed and lighted by a sun that rose in the east and set in the west. He ignored certain facts that did not fit into that theory, such as his inability to see beyond the horizon, because his theory explained as much as he wanted to know, and he was afraid that if anyone questioned it and proved it wrong, he might be left without any theory at all. So when skeptical people attempted to probe into the facts that did not fit the commonly accepted theories of the day, he killed them or tortured them in an attempt to force them to say that the facts did not contradict the prevailing beliefs after all.

The Development of Theoretical Concepts Based on Science

During the last few hundred years, however, we have become somewhat more tolerant of skeptical people who want to investigate facts that do not fit commonly accepted beliefs. We have now reached a point in the development of the human race where we allow a great deal of freedom to people who want to investigate the physical and natural world. For one thing, we now realize that certain practical advantages, such as the development of modern technology, have resulted from such research. We also permit people—the behavioral scientists—to investigate human behavior, but because such research strikes "closer to home" and raises questions about traditional theories and our most cherished prejudices, many of us have reservations about the freedom that we should allow for

this kind of research and the extent to which we should accept its findings. Indeed, many of the findings of behavioral scientists are contrary to our ideas of "common sense." What we are saying, of course, is that the physical or natural scientist enjoys much more freedom, acceptance, and support than does the behavioral scientist, particularly the psychologist or the educational research worker. In spite of this undercurrent resistance, the behavioral scientist has made much progress in recent years both in conducting research and in breaking down the prejudice and suspicion arrayed against him. Getting people to *apply* the results of this research is much more of a problem, however.

Like their fellow scientists in the natural and physical fields, psychologists have had to learn to be skeptical. They have had to learn to be suspicious of simple, obvious explanations of human behavior, just as earth scientists have had to learn to be suspicious of such obvious and deceptively simple theories as the idea that the world is flat. One of the discoveries that psychologists are continually making is the frustrating but stubborn fact that there are seldom, if ever, any simple explanations for human behavior. It is always more complex than it seems at first glance.

Take learning, for instance. Take the question: "Why do children learn to read?" The simple and obvious answer is that they learn to read because someone teaches them to read. But when we study the question, we find that the answer is not so simple and obvious. There are other causal factors involved. Children do not learn merely because they are taught. They must *want* to learn. Therefore another reason why children learn to read is that they *want* to read. But even this additional explanation does not explain why some first-graders who want to read do not learn to do so, and it does not explain why three-year-old children generally cannot be taught to read, even though they might want to. Nor does it explain why it is easier to teach children to read in schools situated in middle-class, Midwestern suburbia than in the rural South. When psychologists probe into these differences and inconsistencies, they find more and more underlying complexities.

Thus, when psychologists tell us about the seemingly endless complexities which underlie problems that appear simple and obvious, we are inclined to be impatient and to express skepticism about their findings. In other words, when we are faced with a problem like that of trying to teach a fifth-grade nonreader to read, we would like to have a simple explanation of why he cannot read, so that we could apply a simple solution to the problem. Hence we are disappointed when the problem seems even more complex than it appeared before. But what the psychologist is telling us, among other things, is that there are no simple explanations to human problems, and that there probably are no simple solutions. To be sure, we *do* occasionally resolve a difficult problem through some simple act or gesture, but the reasons why we succeed are as complex as those underlying the problems we solve.

Putting Traditional/Conventional Theories to the Test

Skepticism leads psychologists to put to the test what seem to be the most self-evident truths. Hence they are often charged with spending a lot of valuable time proving the obvious. It is true that psychologists sometimes do find support for conclusions that everyone else has taken for granted, but very often they do not. In Chapter 7 we referred to the traditional idea that material learned in one situation automatically transfers itself to other situations. An example of this is the common belief that taking courses in Latin improves one's ability to read and write English. Psychologists felt that this, like other beliefs about learning, should be investigated. What they found was that studying Latin has no discernible effect on competence in English (Thorndike, 1923; Woodring, 1925). But this does not prove that the study of Latin has no value as regards the study of English. It has proved only that Latin as *usually taught* does not help the study of English as *usually taught*. It is quite possible that both Latin and English could be taught differently

so that students could transfer learning from one subject to the other.

One of the commonest fallacies underlying much traditional/conventional teaching-learning theory is the assumption that when two things occur together, one causes the other. There are many instances of this kind of fallacious thinking in everyday life. One is the common belief that children learn to be delinquent by reading comic books. This belief gains credence from the increase both in juvenile delinquency and in the sale and consumption of comic books. It is only natural that our distaste for the kind of reading material to be found in comic books would lead us to assume a cause-effect relationship. This assumed relationship has not stood up under investigation, however. Children who read many comic books are no more likely to be delinquent than those who read few or none, and W. Paul Blakely (1958) found no relationship among seventh-graders between the amount or type of comic books read and problem behavior or school progress. As a matter of fact, children who read more comic books also read more library books. An incidental finding that is of general interest was the fact that parents interviewed in the study were not very accurate when it came to reporting the amount of comic books or library books their children were reading.

An examination of popular beliefs about learning, such as we undertook in Chapter 7, shows that there is a pressing need for us as teachers to understand the learning process, not only because it is important for us to possess expert knowledge of this key process, but also because popular beliefs actually lead us to misjudge and misinterpret what goes on in our classrooms. Learning is a relatively simple process, when viewed through the lens of traditional/conventional teaching-learning theory, but this very simplicity is deceptive. What we need are facts and theories about learning that have more of a scientific basis, help us view learning more realistically, explain why teachers succeed or fail, and above all will enable us to teach more effectively.

REQUIREMENTS OF A USABLE TEACHING-LEARNING THEORY

What an Effective Teaching-Learning Theory Should Do

If a theory of learning is to aid us in becoming effective teachers, it must accomplish the following:

1. *It must help us understand all processes of human learning.* Many if not most of the changes in human behavior that we ordinarily encounter or are aware of are the result of learning. This holds true whether the behavior occurs in the classroom or out of it. It also applies to the entire range of skills, concepts, attitudes, habits, and personality traits that may be acquired by the human organism. A good learning theory should help us understand how all these characteristics are acquired. One difficulty with traditional and prescientific teaching-learning theories is that they are too limited and are concerned almost entirely with the kind of learning that results or is *supposed* to result from instruction. Furthermore, they ignore phenomena such as individual differences in learning rates, motivation, incidental learning, unlearning, and relearning.

2. *It must extend our understanding of the conditions or forces that stimulate, inhibit, or affect learning in any way.* Traditional and prescientific teaching-learning theories about learning are concerned, to be sure, with the effect that the teacher has on the learner, but they ignore or deprecate important variables such as the learner's attitudes toward himself, his view of the world and life in general, the kind of strategies he uses in dealing with problems, and the level of his anxiety. Behind these personal elements is a whole array of background factors, such as parental attitudes, social class, and the emotional climate of the school and classroom, which have no place in traditional/conventional doctrines of learning. In order for a theory to be effective, in other words, it must take into account the *social* psychology of the teaching-learning process.

3. *It must enable us to make reasonably accurate predictions about the outcomes of learning activity.* As far as teachers are concerned, a teaching-learning theory is useful and valid only to the extent that it enables them to make better predictions about learning than they would make without it. The difficulty with traditional/conventional theories is that they lead us to view teaching-learning tasks in simplistic ways that take little account of factors that may predetermine failure. A good theory of learning should lead us to be open and sensitive to all kinds of data and to examine our assumptions, methods, and criteria critically. In short, it should result in more intelligent planning of teaching-learning procedures.

4. *It must be a source of hypotheses, clues, and concepts that we can use to become more effective teachers.* Traditional and prescientific theories about teaching-learning processes provide little in the way of new ideas and suggestions for teachers who have failed to bring about gains in learning on the part of their students. The traditional teacher has little choice but to repeat the same procedures over and over again in the hope that some progress will eventually occur. If this approach fails, the teacher then tends to blame students, rather than his methods. An adequate teaching-learning theory, on the other hand, should be a dependable wellspring of insights and ideas that suggest a number of different approaches to the solution of teaching-learning problems.

5. *It must be a source of hypotheses or informed hunches about learning that can be tested in the classroom as well as through experimentation and research, thus extending our understanding of teaching-learning processes.* No profession can be considered to be effective if it stands still, if it fails to expand its understanding of the processes and materials with which it deals. The infinite number of variations and complexities of human behavior mean that our understanding of learning is never complete. Continued research

PSYCHOLOGICAL CONCEPTS OF
THE TEACHING-LEARNING PROCESS

makes our understanding of learning more effective, but it also reveals problem areas that call for further research and study. On the one hand, the realization that our understanding is always incomplete is baffling and frustrating, but, on the other, the opportunity to grow in the profession and to develop new insights can be stimulating and challenging. Classroom experimentation and other kinds of research offer the means whereby ideas about learning and new techniques can be tested as to their validity and practicality.

Assumptions Underlying an Effective Teaching-Learning Theory

Any theory of teaching and learning must be based on some assumptions regarding human behavior. The theory that "teaching results from being told," for example, assumes that the learners will be attentive, will understand and accept whatever is told them, will modify their behavior accordingly, and will apply whatever is being taught appropriately. These assumptions may be valid under certain limited conditions, but they do not hold true in a great many situations. To base many teaching strategies on such assumptions will certainly lead to disappointing results over a period of time. Assumptions must be more firmly supported on what can reasonably be expected of students. The broader the base of a theory and the more human behavior it explains, the greater its validity. A teaching-learning theory that enables us to understand a broader range of behavior and permits us to make more and better predictions is superior to a theory that explains only a narrow range of behavior and that permits only a few narrowly specified and qualified predictions.

Let us then consider four basic assumptions about learning that have the advantages of being broad and also consistent with scientific knowledge about human behavior.

1. *Each human being has a continuing drive to become more competent and effective.* This mo-

tive, as we pointed out in Chapter 2, is basic to behavior that goes beyond the satisfaction of survival needs.

2. *Human competence and effectance are principally the result of learning.* Except for basic biological processes, our behavior may be regarded as a complex interrelated constellation of *learned* behaviors. Even basic physiological reflexes can be modified by learning (Miller, 1969). To a very significant degree, we *learn* what we are and who we are.

3. *The development of competence depends on learning processes that are set in motion when the individual perceives events in his internal or external environment that are new and different from the ones previously experienced.* Such learning consists of the individual's attempts to cope with changes, that is, changes within himself or elsewhere, or changes in the way in which the learner *perceives* his environment or himself. He may cope with these changes by using strategies or other behavioral sequences that have worked in the past, or he may try out new approaches. His attempts to cope with change may be successful or unsuccessful. If unsuccessful, he may try new approaches or change his perceptions. In any event, learning is a response to change of some sort and results in changes within the human organism: changes in the form of new responses and/or new percepts.

4. *Learning to be competent and effective is a continuous, lifelong process.* The individual's external and internal environment is continually changing, and these changes stimulate learning in the form of adaptation and adjustment. Our drive to be competent and effective leads, under normal conditions, to the development of greater effectiveness in dealing with ourself and our environment, but if we feel inadequate, or troubled by a superabundance of anxiety or fear of anxiety, we may build defenses that keep us from perceiving the changes that are taking place within us and our external environment. Such defenses lead to the rigid patterning of behavior,

the use of behavior inappropriate to the solving of problems, and other forms of immature, neurotic, or inadequate behavior. Under such conditions, we may learn self-deprecating attitudes or may learn behavior that causes us to ignore or misperceive our changing environment and thus avoid the problems that face us. A child who cannot cope with the teacher's expectation of a certain degree of competence in reading might find ways of denying that such competence actually is expected of him, might decide that he is incompetent or stupid, might distract the teacher through misbehavior, or might compensate for his inadequacies by attaining successes in other fields. Each of these is a *learned* pattern of behavior and is in turn likely to be based on the previous employment of such behavior patterns in stress situations.

Even though a behavior pattern is a familiar one that is being used in a new situation, learning takes place. The learner finds, for example, that the familiar behavior is appropriate or inappropriate. Learning includes such processes as unlearning, relearning, or confirming familiar patterns of behavior. It may take place on several levels simultaneously. The student who learns how to use a lathe in shop not only learns a new skill, but he also learns something about the kind of person his teacher is, the teacher's attitude toward him, and his own ability to learn.

One fact that is implicit in these assumptions is that learning is not a process that is limited to the interaction between teacher and student and the specific matter with which they are mutually concerned. Nor is it limited to the classroom. Furthermore, it may aid the intellectual or emotional growth of the individual, it may inhibit it, or it may cause him to regress to a less mature form of behavior. Admittedly, this concept makes learning a much more complex phenomenon than it is usually conceived as, but at the same time, it is much more realistic. The observer who watches a heavy-handed, hostile teacher try to bludgeon a class into learning the multiplication of fractions should realize that the children are not only failing to learn the techniques

of this rather intricate process but are also learning to be afraid of teachers and to be anxious about arithmetic.

Of course, we as teachers may focus our concern on a certain skill or body of facts that we want our students to learn. A focusing of this kind is often necessary in classroom teaching. When we do this, however, we should not lose sight of the fact that learning brings about changes, and changes in one part of the organism alter the relationship of that part to the whole. Whatever skill or information a student learns is acquired in relationship to whatever he has learned up until that point in his life. It may, depending on how relevant it seems to him, affect his concept of himself or his environment. Even the more basic biological processes may be involved in learning. An upset stomach can interfere with classroom learning, and difficulties that occur in the classroom can upset stomachs. Trying to hold the attention of children toward the end of a rainy day is difficult because they have not had their usual opportunities to run around and engage in other forms of large-muscle activity. These are but two of the many ways in which intellectual, emotional, and physical aspects of the human organism interact. Intellectual, emotional, and physical behavior are merely different aspects of the same human organism.

Students' Motives and Teachers' Theories

One of the shortcomings of traditional/conventional teaching-learning theories is the fact that they either do not take motivation into account or else reduce it to oversimplified dimensions. An example of the first is the belief that students learn when they are told and what they are told. An example of the second is the belief that learning results only when the teacher rewards or punishes. When motivation is mentioned by traditionally oriented teachers, it sounds like something that can be turned on or off. "How do you motivate a class that hates math?" a teacher asks.

The four basic assumptions we have made about the learning aspects of human behavior take the position that learning to be competent and effective is

PSYCHOLOGICAL CONCEPTS OF
THE TEACHING-LEARNING PROCESS

a natural, normal process, and that it is in the nature of being human to engage in such activity. The need is obviously stronger at some times than at others. Walcott Beatty and Rodney Clark (1972) suggest that the individual is motivated to learn when he realizes that an imbalance or a discrepancy exists between what he is or can do and what he should be or should do. According to this formulation, the motivation to learn is based on the drive to become more adequate and thus to eliminate the discrepancies between the self that is perceived and the self as it should be.

It is also useful for a teacher to have an understanding of the particular kinds of motivational patterns that are likely to affect the behavior of students in the classroom. Miss Kanzler is obviously going to have some trouble teaching the third declension in Latin this week because most of the boys in her class are involved in organizing a new secret fraternity. The fact that such fraternities are against the school rules only makes the project more exciting. Because of their involvement in this project, they are giving only superficial attention to their studies. In a week or two things will return to normal, and their academic performance will do likewise. Until then, Miss Kanzler's rather conventional and routine efforts to promote learning in Latin will have little success.

CONDITIONING OR REINFORCEMENT THEORIES

Classical Conditioning

Although the motivation to learn is universal, there are obvious differences in learning rates and in the kinds of performance displayed by learners. As we suggested in the preceding paragraphs, some of these differences are due to variations in the motivation of learners, but such variations obviously do not account for all the differences that occur. Some, probably the vast majority, are a function of the kinds of situations in which learners find themselves. These situations can be viewed as complex arrangements of stimuli that affect the learner and subsequent behavior in certain recognizable ways.

Since the early part of this century, psychologists have been investigating the interaction between living organisms and their environment in order to find out just how learning occurs. As a result of much painstaking research, they have found that when a certain stimulus produces a certain response in an organism, and when a second and irrelevant stimulus is introduced more or less simultaneously with the first stimulus, the response in question can eventually be evoked by the second stimulus, without the aid or presence of the first one. For example, if a light is directed into the eye of an individual, the pupil of his eye will contract. If a bell is sounded each time the eye is exposed to the light, after a while the sounding of the bell alone will cause the pupil to contract. The subject of the experiment has, as we say, become "conditioned" to the sound of the bell. This conditioning will disappear and become extinguished if he repeatedly hears the bell without being exposed to the light, but it can be reinstated with a few more trials in which the bell and the light are used together.

The process we have described is what is termed "classical conditioning," so called because the studies conducted more than seventy years ago by I. P. Pavlov, the Russian physiologist, are considered the first and therefore the "classical" examples of countless conditioning experiments that have since been conducted in physiological laboratories, particularly in Russia. There has been a fair amount of classical conditioning research in American laboratories as well, but it has, for the most part, been concerned with phenomena such as the eyelid reflex and psychogalvanic response (changes in electrical conductivity and potential of the skin) and thus has been of little direct or practical application to classroom learning.

In recent years there has been an attempt on the part of researchers outside the field of physiological psychology to engage in classical conditioning experiments. The study of Joan C. Early (1968) that we mentioned in Chapter 5 is one example. Classical conditioning leads the learner to substitute a new response in place of the one normally made to a given stimulus or set of stimuli. In Early's study, children learned pairs of positive or neutral adjectives that had been paired with the names of certain pupils who were social isolates in the classroom group. During the ensuing weeks, the children tended to approach the experimental isolates (those whose names had been paired with the positive adjectives) but not the control isolates (those whose names had been paired with neutral adjectives). Children also evaluated the experimental isolates more highly in a subsequent sociometric test. In other words, the children's previous response to the experimental isolates—one of avoidance—had been replaced by a new response: approach.

Operant Conditioning

Most of the research in learning conducted by psychologists in the United States and Canada has been concerned with an approach that is quite different from the approach of classical conditioning —an approach that is termed "operant conditioning" or "instrumental conditioning." Research with operant conditioning makes use of the simple observation that living organisms tend to repeat behavior that is satisfying and to avoid behavior that is not. The experimenter can thus manipulate and "shape" the behavior of experimental subjects by presenting stimuli that have satisfying effects whenever the subjects show any response that is of the type he is seeking. The presentation of such stimuli is said to "reinforce" the behavior in question. Corn is used to reinforce the behavior of pigeons, and both candy and praise have been used to reinforce the behavior of children in operant conditioning experiments. Complex organisms, such as pigeons and people, have a large range of responses they can make to any situation. Some responses are likely to have a higher priority than others in a given situation, but over given periods of time the subject of an experiment is likely to display several kinds of behavior. The experimenter's task is to reinforce certain responses and to ignore others, thus causing certain kinds of behavior that ordinarily would have a low priority to move up to a position of higher priority.

B. F. Skinner (1953), the leading exponent of research based on principles of operant or instrumen-

tal conditioning, has found that it is not necessary to reinforce every satisfactory response in order to get results. Both pigeons and people seem to work harder (make more responses) if they are reinforced only part of the time according to an irregular and (for them) unpredictable schedule. For instance, Thomas J. Ryan (1968) had first-graders play a simple game consisting of pressing a lever to obtain marbles. One-half the children were reinforced for every response; one-half were reinforced for 50 percent of the responses. This partial reinforcement led to more rapid responding than did the total reinforcement.

One of the reasons for the growth in interest in this type of conditioning is that it permits a much larger scope of operations for the researcher. Whereas the experimenter in classical conditioning is limited to preexisting linkups of stimulus and response, the operant conditioning researcher can, by presenting or withholding certain stimuli, get the organism to display a wide range of behaviors. Skinner has, for example, taught pigeons to play table tennis and to serve as the directional systems for guided missiles.

Reinforcements may be negative, as well as positive. A positive reinforcer, according to Skinner, is a stimulus that strengthens the probability of a response when it is *added* to a situation, whereas a negative reinforcer is one that strengthens response probability when it is *removed* from the situation. Stopping a loud, sustained noise, or turning off a painfully bright light, is an example of a negative reinforcer.

Whereas reinforcement, positive or negative, has the effect of increasing the probability of a response, punishment is intended to decrease response probability. The effects of punishment, however, are not easily specified. Although common sense would dictate that punishment is the opposite of reward, it does not have opposite effects. An organism can be induced to learn a new form of behavior through being rewarded, but it is not likely to learn the new behavior merely because other alternatives are punished. The effects of punishment are complex and are to a large extent unpredictable, and Skinner (1961) recommends that it be abandoned as a means of social control. In fact, his approach to programmed learning, which we shall discuss shortly, consists of eliminating anything that resembles punishment, including failure.

Operant Conditioning in the Classroom

"The most potent reward for classroom learning is the teacher's acceptance of what the pupil does and the way he does it . . ." (Symonds, 1955). Much classroom learning seems to be explicable in operant conditioning terms. Teachers reinforce the kind of behavior they prefer to see in students by comments of approval, marks, smiles, and the like. But teachers cannot respond to every pupil on every appropriate occasion, and students learn to be their own reinforcers through the discovery, for example, that their answers to problems are correct. In the normal classroom situation, a student is not reinforced for every response he makes. Rewards appear only occasionally, yet students put forth a great deal of work. This is consistent with Skinner's concept of intermittent reinforcement that we mentioned previously.

Often the expression of teacher interest has reinforcing value in and of itself. Ellis Batten Page (1958) conducted an interesting piece of research that demonstrates this principle. He asked seventy-four secondary school teachers to perform the following experiment. After they had administered, scored, and graded whatever objective test they happened to be using at the moment in their classes, they randomly divided the tests into three piles. The "no comment" pile received no marks other than those used for scoring and grading. On the test papers in the "free comment" pile they wrote whatever thoughts they felt were appropriate for the particular students and their performance on the tests. The "specified comment" pile received certain uniform comments which Page had prepared beforehand for all similar letter grades and which were considered to be "generally encouraging." The effect of this treatment, as revealed in the very next tests the students took, was consistent with operant learning theory. Students whose papers had been in the "free comment" and the "specified comment" piles showed improvement in their scores, with the "free comment" group showing the greater improvement. There was no improvement on the part of the "no comment" group. Incidentally, Page had asked the teachers to predict the effect the comments would have on student performance, and most of them said that the better students would be more responsive than the poorer ones. The results showed, however, that good and poor students alike responded favorably to the comments.

The Rise and Fall of the Teaching Machine

The administration and grading of tests is only a minor fraction of the teacher's classroom activity. How can he reinforce students' responses at other times? His problem here is confounded by numbers. A great deal of the time he must treat the class as a group and thus may have difficulty in being selective in applying or withholding reinforcement. Three students in a class of forty may be engaging in the kind of problem solving that a certain teacher is trying to encourage, seventeen may be paying attention only marginally, and the remaining twenty may be woolgathering, passing notes, whispering, doodling, or engaging in other behavior contrary to his goals. Schedules of reinforcement work best on a person-to-person basis, and the complexities posed by mass education make their use difficult, if not impossible, much of the time.

Skinner's answer to this problem is programmed learning, in the form of what has popularly been called the "teaching machine." The first experiments with automated teaching were conducted by Sidney L. Pressey (1926), who designed machines in which students were presented with series of questions, one at a time. Each question was followed by several possible answers (usually four), and the student pressed a button to indicate the choice that he thought was correct. Such machines did not attract much attention until Skinner, some thirty years later, developed models and programs that incorporated operant learning principles.

Figure 8-1 contains some excerpts from a program in high-school physics designed for use in one of Skinner's machines. The machine presents the student with incomplete statements, one at a time. As the student reads each statement, he writes in the word or phrase that completes it. He then operates a device that exposes the correct answer, he compares it with his repsonse, and he moves a lever that brings up the next question. In the material shown in Figure 8-1, the answer to the first question is quite obvious. The student's discovery that he has produced the right answer presumably reinforces the learning that is taking place, and he is thus motivated to try the next question. Because the second item builds on the first, the answer to this one is also obvious, and success again reinforces the student. The third item builds on the second, and so forth. If a program has been properly constructed according to Skinner's specifications, the student should be able to complete it without error. Proper "programming" is essential; if vital information has been omitted from any step, the student will fail, will not be reinforced, and learning will not take place efficiently. Item 28 in Figure 8-1 shows how difficult an item can be, when important intervening concepts are omitted.

Programmed learning is designed to help teachers to break the group situation of the classroom into individual learning situations in which the student does his own reinforcing by having successful

Sentences to Be Completed	Word to Be Supplied
1. The important parts of a flashlight are the battery and the bulb. When we "turn on" a flashlight, we close a switch which connects the battery with the _____.	bulb
2. When we turn on a flashlight, an electric current flows through the fine wire in the _____ and causes it to grow hot.	bulb
3. When the hot wire glows brightly, we say that it gives off or sends out heat and _____.	light
4. The fine wire in the bulb is called a filament. The bulb "lights up" when the filament is heated by the passage of a(n) _____ current.	electric
5. When a weak battery produces little current, the fine wire, or _____ does not get very hot.	filament
6. A filament which is less hot sends out or gives off _____ light.	less
7. "Emit" means "send out." The amount of light sent out, or "emitted," by a filament depends on how _____ the filament is.	hot
8. The higher the temperature of the filament, the _____ the light emitted by it.	brighter, stronger
9. If a flashlight battery is weak, the _____ in the bulb may still glow, but with only a dull red color.	filament
10. The light from a very hot filament is colored yellow or white. The light from a filament which is not very hot is colored _____.	red
(seventeen items intervene here)	
28. The light from a candle flame comes from the _____ released by the chemical changes as the candle burns.	energy

FIG. 8-1. Excerpts from a program in high-school physics designed for use in a Skinner type of teaching machine. The machine presents each item one at a time. The student completes the item by writing his answer in the blank and then uncovering the correct answer at the right (Skinner, 1958).

experiences with a teaching machine. This resolves the difficulty of how to provide reinforcement for individual students, but there are other problems. For one thing, there are not enough programs available to provide a satisfactory coverage of school curricula. Even if there were, few schools are set up to provide programmed instruction for all their students on any kind of a consistent basis.

Another and less costly development is the programmed textbook, which requires the student to answer questions and look on a certain page for the answers. If he has answered satisfactorily, he may go on to still another page of questions; otherwise the text refers him to pages containing simplified review material.

During the early years of programmed learning, many claims were made of its superiority to conventional classroom instruction. Research since then has shown that the claims were exaggerated. One investigator, for example, found that students who were capable of functioning independently did poorly with conventional programs (Lublin, 1965), and a pair of researchers found that students using a programmed text in a college course did no better than those who had spent much less time reading the chapter summaries of the textbook (Roderick and Anderson, 1968).

Today, some twenty years after the introduction of the teaching machine in schools, it appears that the simple "linear" type of programs developed by Skinner are seldom used. The programs that are being employed are of the more complex "branching" type which can be used by fast and slow learners alike but which are better suited to be used in computers. We shall have more to say about computer-assisted instruction or CAI in Chapter 12. Although the use of the Skinnerian type of teaching machine has declined considerably, the specially designed textbook is very popular, and "packages" of programmed materials can be found in many classrooms, especially in elementary schools. One can argue that these programs present no visible advances beyond the conventional instructional methods, but they do have the advantage of making a variety of learning materials available that are appropriate for students at different levels of sophistication and learning ability.

We should also take note of another application of learning theory: the use of reinforcement in controlling disruptive behavior in the classroom and encouraging cooperative and task-oriented behavior. We shall discuss this approach, termed *behavior modification,* in Chapter 11, "Discipline and the Learning Situation."

Learning Theory and Teaching Experience: An Unbridged Gap

Except for programmed learning and behavior modification, most of the experimental work on learning theory, as it has developed in the psychological laboratory, still remains somewhat remote from the classroom experiences of teachers and students. The situation still remains what it was more than twenty years ago, when Ernest R. Hilgard (1956) expressed doubts about the advisability of attempting to translate and apply laboratory findings to classroom practice. Even when human subjects are employed, learning research experiments are conducted under tightly controlled conditions and, as a consequence, take on an air of artificiality. Experimenters also tend to be interested in aspects of learning that are of little interest to teachers, and they are generally unconcerned about factors that have a significant effect on the classroom behavior of students, such as differences in social class, self-esteem, and need for achievement.

The proposition that people learn because their responses are conditioned or reinforced is one that is acceptable to teachers, psychologists, and laymen alike. It is an idea that helps explain the learning that takes place in a classroom—but only up to a point. It helps explain why Jean learned her multiplication tables faster than anyone else in the class, namely, because her performance was reinforced by the teacher's encouragement. But it does not explain why Sara, who could have learned the tables as fast as Jean, never learned them at all. We can say, of course, that the teacher's words of encouragement had a reinforcing effect on Jean's behavior but not on Sara's, but such an explanation leaves us at loose ends. *Why* did the teacher's attempts to encourage not reinforce Sara's behavior? Another shortcoming is that reinforcement theory does not give us any clues as to what we should do in order to reinforce learners.

One of the dangers that is implicit in a preoccupation with a conditioning or a reinforcement approach to learning is that we might become overly concerned with techniques. It thus becomes all too easy to believe that we can promote learning by the proper technique or combination of techniques. It is this belief in a mechanical approach to learning that leads us to ask the "experts": "How can I get my Sunday school class to learn the books of the Bible?" or "How can I get my child to stop sucking her thumb?" or "How can I teach students the importance of good manners?"

In a paper analyzing problems in the field of educational psychology, Ernest A. Haggard (1954) commented as follows on the reasons why experimental psychologists have had little influence on educational practices:

> *Most learning theorists still seem to think of their subjects as physicalistic machines which should display an invariant relation between input (stimulus) and output (response) variables. In such schemes learning tends to be thought of as a function of what the experimenter does, rather than what the subject already knows, or is interested in, or thinks and feels about the learning experience or the material to be learned. Consequently, learning has usually been defined as the modification of the relations between rather discrete stimuli and responses, or as the modification of response systems resulting from after-the-fact events (rewards or punishments) which presumably determine such modifications.*

Richard C. Atkinson (1968) took both experimentalists and educators to task:

> *For too long, psychologists studying learning have shown little interest in instructional problems, whereas educators have made only primitive and superficial applications of learning theory. Both fields would have advanced more rapidly if an appropriate interchange of ideas and problems had existed.*

Robert M. Gagné and William D. Rohwer, Jr. (1969), in a review of research related to techniques of instruction, observed that studies of human learning appearing in the most prestigious psychological journals often are of little value to teachers because the conditions under which experiments are conducted are unrepresentative of the conditions under which most human learning occurs, and tasks set for the learner (memorization of nonsense syllables and the like) are inappropriate in that they "range from the merely peculiar to the downright esoteric."

For the most part, theories of learning developed in psychological laboratories are attempts to explain learning processes in terms of simple and basic elements. These explanations are most useful when we are dealing with animals, infants, and young children but are of little practical value to the classroom teacher. In fact, in keeping with the trends in the "pure-science cult," the researcher may even maintain, as Hilgard and Bower (1966) put it, that "something is valuable precisely because it is remote from application; so long as it is precise, it does not matter how trivial it is." Hilgard and Bower criticize this position, however, on the grounds it is an attempt on the part of the researcher to escape responsibility for the relevance of his work and is a sign of weakness, rather than strength.

In recent years there has been a more concerted effort on the part of experimental psychologists to work in interdisciplinary settings and to develop research designs that include more variables and are more relevant to real-life learning situations. The development of computer-assisted instruction is one example of this type of work, as is the introduction of behavior modification techniques into the classroom.

To summarize, if we put theories based on conditioning and reinforcement to the test of "an adequate theory of learning," as outlined a few pages back, it appears that they undoubtedly extend and sharpen our understanding of *some* learning processes but not *all* learning processes. They extend our understanding of a limited number of the conditions and forces that affect learning, and within the confines of the laboratory situation they permit reasonably accurate predictions about the behavior of learners. They are most deficient when it comes to clues to improving teaching methods and generating hypotheses that can enable us to investigate the teaching-learning process as it occurs in real-life situations.

THEORIES WHICH EMPHASIZE THE WHOLENESS OF EXPERIENCE

Gestaltist Approaches

About the time Pavlov was conducting his classical studies of conditioning, a number of psychologists—Wolfgang Köhler, Kurt Koffka, and G. W. Hartmann,—were developing theories concerned with experience and perception. Both experience and perception are larger aspects of behavior than are the specific responses that form the bases of the research conducted in the learning laboratory. The inclusion of experience in a concept of learning means that the learner approaches the learning situation with a complex of attitudes and skills drawn from previous learning. He has some expectations of himself and learning situations in general. He is in a position to initiate, terminate, and direct his own learning, within the limits imposed by his ability and experience. Instead of responding to the learning situation in terms of specific, isolated stimuli, he perceives it as a whole and responds to the elements that seem significant to him. In effect, the learner organizes the stimuli that go to make up the learning situation into some kind of pattern or whole that has some meaning for him. What the learner

(Vahan Shirvanian, *Look Magazine*)

"That shows how high the water was. The same thing happens in our bathtub."

Learning that takes place through discovering similarities and relationships between two apparently unrelated events is based on insight.

perceives is for him a "Gestalt," the German word for "form" or "configuration."

According to the Gestalt psychologists, learning takes place through insight. A child trying to divine the meaning of an unfamiliar word will puzzle over it, perhaps sound it out phonetically, think of what familiar words it resembles, and try to see its relationship to the rest of the sentence. In other words, he uses his experience to test out several possibilities and tries to relate what he perceives to the larger idea embodied in the sentence. For a few minutes he makes no progress at all and is finally about to give up and ask the teacher what the word is, when all of a sudden, he recognizes it. This is the "aha!" phenomenon, the flash of insight, that we have all experienced at such times. This is no gradual process whereby we move closer and closer to the meaning of the unknown word. Instead, there is a preliminary stage where all is confusion, and then suddenly everything makes sense. Learning is thus seen as a process whereby problems are solved through a series of discoveries, discoveries facilitated by previous experience. By such organizing and reorganizing of experience, we learn to make sense out of the world around us.

The approach of the Gestalt psychologists is potentially more useful to the teacher than that of psychologists whose concepts of learning are limited to classical or operant conditioning. Gestalt theories take into account aspects of behavior, such as insight, which are useful in explaining problem solving and which have little place in popular and traditional concepts of learning. They do not go far enough, however; they do not attempt to explain why learners develop the particular perceptions they do develop, nor do they explain why some learning situations are perceived as problems to be solved, and others are not. For this extension of Gestalt psychology, we must turn to field theorists.

Field Theory

Concepts from physics were introduced into psychology by Kurt Lewin (1935, 1938, 1951). Of particular interest here is the idea that every object exists in a "field of forces" that move it, change it,

define it, or give it a degree of stability and substance. According to Lewin, the behavior of any individual at a given moment is the net effect of forces operating simultaneously in his psychological field. The attitudes, expectation, feelings, and needs of an individual constitute internal forces that interact with external forces and help determine his responses to them. Changes in these forces are, therfore, likely to produce changes in behavior. The psychological field consists of the enviroment as perceived by the individual.[1] It is important to note this qualification since teachers sometimes make the mistake of assuming that because the psychological field has changed as far as *they* are concerned, it has also changed for the students they are attempting to teach.

> Mrs. Hillegas had given Larry, a nonreader in her third grade, a book on locomotives, with many pictures and short words and sentences, in the hope that his interest would be captured enough for him to make an effort. A few minutes later she walked by his seat. The book was closed, and Larry was staring out the window.
> "Did you like the book, Larry?" she asked. "It's all about trains. Your Daddy works for the railroad, doesn't he?"
> Larry turned and looked at her without expression.
> "You forgot I can't read," he said.

Mrs. Hillegas assumed that giving Larry a book on a new subject would change the field for Larry, that he would perceive this book as different from the other books he had handled. But for Larry, who at the age of nine has a long history of failure and humiliation, all centered around books, a book is still a book.

In order to gain any understanding of a child's psychological field, adults have to develop a high level of empathy or sensitivity for the feelings and attitudes of children. If adults are concerned only with their own feelings and not with those of children, they will continue to misunderstand why children behave and react as they do.

Although the amount of experimentation under-

[1] See discussion of the phenomenal or perceived field in Chapter 2.

taken by field theorists has in no way equaled the quantity produced by the conditioning and reinforcement psychologists, much of it, particularly that performed with human subjects, has been of great value to the educational profession. One of the classic experiments in this area of psychology concerned the concept of "social climate" and was conducted by Kurt Lewin, Ronald Lippitt, and Ralph K. White (1939).[2] Four small groups of eleven-year-old boys were organized for the ostensible purpose of engaging in activities of a recreational nature. Each club was supervised by an adult leader for seven weeks, whereupon a different leader took over. Over a period of twenty-one weeks, each club was supervised by three different leaders. Leaders had been coached by the experimenters to play a different kind of role and thus create a different kind of social climate with each club they supervised. With one club they were supposed to be autocratic, with another they were to be democratic, and with the third they were to be laissez-faire (no control at all). The experiment was organized in such a way that each club had the experience of being directed by each of the three kinds of leadership. The theory that changes in the psychological field will produce changes in behavior appears to have been borne out by the experiment, inasmuch as the groups demonstrated a different kind of behavior with each of the three kinds of leaders. When the psychological field was influenced by leaders playing democratic roles, groups were characterized by greater interest and personal involvement in club matters. They took the responsibility for initiating and completing tasks. When club leadership was of a laissez-faire nature, the behavior of the members was characterized by frustration, discontent, and poor morale. Under autocratic leaders, boys were either apathetic or actively hostile.

Although this study is often cited as a demonstration of the superiority of democratic group leadership, we have described it here principally to show how a change in the psychological field produces changes in behavior. It is reasonably certain, too, that quite different kinds of learning would take

[2] See discussion of emotional climate in Chapter 5.

place in classrooms with each of the three different kinds of psychological climates we have described.

The work of the field theorists extends some of the ideas of the Gestalt pyschologists in that it is concerned with "whole" aspects of behavior and the "structure" of what is perceived by the individual. Such emphases are of interest to the teacher, who also deals with "behavior as a whole" and who tries to "structure" the teaching-learning situation in ways that will stimulate learning. Indeed, one of the main contributions of field theory is the idea that teachers can structure and restructure situations to produce different kinds of emotional or social climates, which in turn, have different effects on the learning of students.

Learning as Problem Solving:
A Cognitive Approach

A few years before Pavlov and the Gestaltists were starting down their separate paths in the study of learning, a New England-born philosopher named John Dewey took up the task of analyzing and understanding learning from a totally different point of view. One special difference in Dewey's approach was his concern with the kind of learning that goes on in classrooms, whereas the conditioning and reinforcement psychologists, as well as the Gestaltists, were primarily concerned with laboratory experimentation. Dewey produced no formal research; instead, he analyzed, probed, and theorized. He did not try out his theories in the laboratory, although he did test them out in the classroom in practical ways.

It is perhaps because Dewey was concerned with practical rather than research problems that psychologists, even educational psychologists, have ignored his work, even though he was one of the first presidents of the American Psychological Association. The audience for Dewey's writings, however, consisted of the educational, rather than the psychological, profession, because he communicated directly to the people who taught in the classrooms and administered the schools. The educational psychologists of Dewey's day were more likely to take their cues from E. L. Thorndike, who not only developed theories of learning along conditioning lines but also produced prodigious quantities of research data. Furthermore, the theories of Dewey were constructed on a large scale. They were concerned with the *whole* child in a *total* situation, rather than with the precise analysis of minute fractions of the learning process. His theories were therefore difficult to test, using the research methods that were available to the psychologists of that day. It is only in recent years that research workers have developed the methods and perhaps the inclination to put Dewey's theories to the test. For example, a growing percentage of research articles in educational psychology journals are concerned

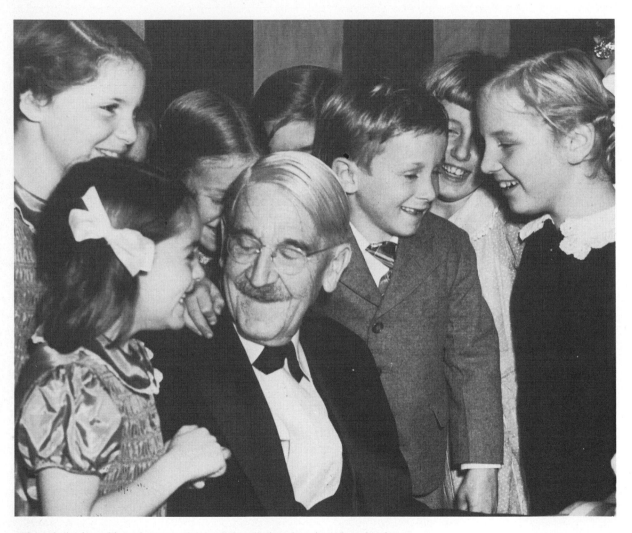

Although the breadth and scope of John Dewey's theories about learning have made it difficult to test them experimentally, the research that has been done with them tends to support his conclusions. The photograph shows him surrounded by children on the occasion of his ninetieth birthday, which he celebrated in 1949. He died in 1952.

with the motivation of the learner, the child's view of his social world, and the social dynamics of the classroom. Of particular interest are the studies that attempt to test Dewey's idea that democratic methods are, after all, the best means to help students learn how to function in a democratic society.

Although educators have traditionally thought of education as something done *to* the child (a view that is consistent with the environmental emphasis of the more experimentally minded educational psychologists), Dewey's position is much closer to that of Piaget in that both emphasize the importance of the child's *experience*. Dewey's statement regarding the development of the power of judgment in children reveals his point of view on this matter.

The child cannot get power of judgement excepting as he is continually exercised in forming and testing judgement. He must have an opportunity to select for himself, and then to attempt to put his own selections into execution that he may submit them to the only final test, that of action. Only thus can he learn to discriminate that which promises success from that which promises failure; only thus can he form the habit of relating his otherwise isolated ideas to the conditions which determine their value (Dewey, 1903).

And, again:

The only true education comes through the stimulation of the child's powers by the demands of the social situations in which he finds himself (Dewey, 1940).

In recent years the concepts and theories developed by Dewey have had an increasing effect upon the content and focus of educational psychology. Today we are more concerned with studying the child in relation to his social environment, as Dewey urged, than we were a generation ago, when we seemed preoccupied with measuring his various abilities and traits. The research of Lewin, Lippitt, and White and others into the social forces governing the behavior of children has lent support to the acceptance of Dewey's theories, as has the increasing interest in problems of mental health in the classroom. Indeed, there are few if any of Dewey's statements that would not be acceptable to mental health specialists today. Somehow, they do not seem as radical and as revolutionary as they appeared to be when they were first uttered, at the turn of the century. Classroom practice still lags far behind, of course, but it has made much progress since Dewey first uttered his challenging words. People who espouse the traditional position in education characterize Dewey as a kind of impractical visionary who somehow led educators astray. What these critics overlook, however, is that Dewey's criticism of traditional education was based on the most practical kinds of considerations. He felt that the education that does not develop the thinking processes of children and that does not improve their ability to solve problems outside the classroom as well as in it is largely a waste of time. And he was skeptical regarding the unfounded assumptions that traditionalists in education make all too readily—the assumption, for instance, that students automatically transfer the abstract concepts learned in the traditional classroom to the problems of everyday life.

A more recent exponent of problem solving in education is Jerome S. Bruner, an experimental psychologist who has become interested in the practical problems involved in teaching mathematical skills to children. Bruner (1961) has made use of such Gestalt concepts as "feedback," a process whereby the learner makes corrections and adjustments in his problem-solving strategy as a result of the errors he perceives. Discovery is an important part of effective problem solving, according to Bruner. He says:

Knowledge of results . . . should come at that point in a problem-solving episode when the person is comparing the results of his try-out with some criterion of what he seeks to achieve. Knowledge of results given before this point ei-

Jerome S. Bruner.

Trained as an experimental psychologist, Jerome S. Bruner became interested in children's cognitive development. He played a large part in bringing the work of Piaget to the attention of American psychologists.

ther cannot be understood or must be carried as extra freight in immediate memory. (1964b)[3]

Like Dewey, Bruner is pragmatic and practical. He points out that if the learner is to use information effectively, it must be translated into his terms. This means that the teacher must empathize with the learner, see the problem as the learner sees it, and

provide information that is consistent with the learner's perspective. Bruner also sees the goal of the teaching-learning process as that of producing an independent learner:

Instruction is a provisional state that has as its object to make the learner or problem-solver self-sufficient. Any regimen of correction carries the danger that the learner may become permanently dependent on the tutor's correction. The tutor must correct the learner in a fashion that eventually makes it possible for the learner to take over the corrective function himself. Otherwise the result of instruction is to create a form of mastery that is contingent on the perpetual presence of a teacher (1964b).

Another recent theorist is David P. Ausubel (1969), whose cognitive theory of school learning emphasizes meaningful as contrasted with rote learning (sheer memorization). Ausubel also takes a Gestaltist position when he maintains that the learner's existing structure of knowledge defines the conditions, determinants, and outcomes involved in the acquisition of new knowledge. The difficulty with so much instruction is that teachers or other authorities rather arbitrarily decide what material should be learned and how it should be presented, without any concern for what it will mean for the learner. As a result, learners either refuse to learn or use rote learning methods. Rote learning is inefficient because it takes more time and energy than meaningful learning and also results in a low rate of retention.

Phenomenological Concepts of Learning

Like the Gestaltist and the cognitive theorists, proponents of the phenomenological approach to learning place great stress on perception—the way in which the learner views the situation in which he finds himself. The phenomenologists who have had the most to say about education are Arthur W. Combs and Donald Snygg, whose theories we discussed in Chapter 2 when we were emphasizing the point that each of us behaves in accordance with

[3] Although there is a common tendency to believe that feedback is most effective when given immediately after a response has been made, research shows that a delay may be more productive of learning, the amount of delay depending, of course, on the maturity and experience of the learner. Arthur J. More (1969) had eighth-graders read articles containing information on natural and social science, whereupon they were tested. Some of the subjects were given immediate feedback as to their performance; others were given feedback at intervals of 2½ hours, one day, or four days. Retests conducted later showed that delays in feedback of 2½ hours or one day produced the most learning.

Arthur W. Combs (*left*) and the late Donald Snygg (*below*) have been influential in the development of curriculum and teaching methods that emphasize phenomenology, a highly individualized, perceptual approach to learning.

the way in which we view ourselves and the world around us. Each individual, we said, experiences a private world that constitutes "reality" for him. We also cited Combs and Snygg to the effect that changes in behavior are the result of changes in the way we perceive ourselves and our environment.

According to Snygg and Combs (1949, 1959), learning is a natural and normal process for children: It is an important dimension of normal growth and development. They were therefore much concerned with the enormous amount of energy that teachers invest in *making* children learn. They said on this point: "The task of our schools . . . is not to make people grow. By their very nature they are bound to grow and the task of the schools is only to help them grow in socially desirable directions."

Snygg and Combs' views on learning were in many respects consistent with those of Dewey, Bruner, and Ausubel. They maintained, for example, that many of the difficulties teachers encounter stem from their persistence in trying to teach facts and information that have no relevance to students' lives:

> One of the primary reasons for the ineffectiveness of our formal methods of teaching is that facts exist in the phenomenal field of an individual only if they have personal meaning for him. Facts that have no relation to him or his life task do not emerge into awareness, or they cease to exist in his field as their irrelevance has been discovered.

This comment is suggestive of some of the research of Hermann Ebbinghaus (1913), a pioneer psychologist, who experimented with the learning of various kinds of material, some of which had meaning and some of which did not. He found that it took approximately ten times more effort to learn nonsense material than meaningful material and that he forgot it more readily. To relate these findings to the theories proposed by Combs and Snygg and by Ausubel (1969), we can say that when students are assigned material to learn that has no meaning for them, they learn it only with great difficulty because this material is, as far as they are concerned, mere nonsense. In actuality, material that is arbitrarily assigned does take on a kind of meaning for students, but it is not the kind of meaning that leads to much retention.

Another related point brought out by Combs and Snygg is their observation that children are not able to solve problems they do not have, that is, questions or assignments that they do not perceive or experience as problems—because such problems have no relation to their everyday life or experience.

These points of view find support in a variety of studies of classroom learning. G. M. Haselrud and Shirley Meyers (1959), for example, had students work on two sets of problems. The subjects were given principles which helped them solve the problems in the first set but had to derive the principles themselves in order to work the second set. When they were tested a week later, they were able to do better in solving the kinds of problems for which they had had to derive principles than they were in solving problems for which principles had been given them. The point is that something we have learned "on our own" has more meaning and usefulness for us than something that is merely assigned or given to us because it is more personalized, has more meaning for us, and is thus more likely to be remembered.

Snygg and Combs made three recommendations for schools that want to facilitate learning by making use of the experience children bring to school with them.

First, they said, schools must provide opportunities for students to think of themselves as responsible and contributing members of society. A student must be given broad opportunities to identify with and be accepted by the socially desirable individuals and groups he admires. The student who identifies himself *with* society will not attack it as a delinquent.

Snygg and Combs maintained that such an approach implies a democratic classroom, a classroom where students are helped to develop a sense of personal worth, are encouraged to participate freely in group activities, and are permitted to express opinions and feelings as freely and as openly as any adult.

Second, students must have opportunities for success and appreciation based on positive and productive achievement. Students should feel safe enough from humiliation to face their deficiencies and inadequacies and to deal with them objectively.

Third, schools must take advantage of the drive that is universal in all human beings, adults and children alike, to achieve their best potentialities and to develop efficiently and adequately. If schools could achieve the goals that are the natural objectives of this drive, they would not have to rely on the artificial stimulation of competition and traditional marking systems.

Teaching for Mastery

Although Benjamin S. Bloom (1971) is not in the mainstream of the tradition that includes Dewey, Bruner, and Snygg and Combs, he is concerned about the attitudes that students develop as a result of their experiences in school and especially with the effect that failure has on their concepts of themselves. Bloom's approach to teaching emphasizes mastery by each student of the material in the curriculum. Bloom maintains that most teachers expect that only one-third of their students will demonstrate adequate learning, that another one-third will fail or just "get by," with the remaining one-third falling somewhere in between. He maintains that more than 90 percent of students can master the material in the curriculum. The majority fail to do so partly because of imperfect methods and curriculum design and partly because their teachers do not expect mastery of them. Bloom maintains that the difference between students lies not in their ability to master material but in their *rates* of learning.

According to Bloom, 90 percent of students can master a subject if there is a proper design of materials combined with frequent evaluation tests that give feedback to students as to their progress, and if both teachers and students understand what is expected of them. His method also makes considerable use of students' working together with each other and, occasionally, in small tutorial groups. Teachers who have used Bloom's methods generally report encouraging results.

A major outcome of learning for mastery, according to Bloom, is the effect it has on the student's self-concept:

Each person searches for positive recognition of his worth and he comes to view himself as adequate in those areas where he received assurance of his competence or success. Mastery and its public recognition provide the necessary reassurance and reinforcement to help the student view himself as adequate.

He goes on to say that frequent and objective reports regarding one's progress are a positive aid to mental health, and that many of the more neurotic forms of behavior displayed by high-school and college students are the indirect result of painful and frustrating experiences in school learning. Frequent indications of failure and learning inadequacy, he says, cause students to doubt their ability to cope and lead them to seek reassurance and adequacy in experiences outside the school. Today, the complexity of modern society requires continual learning not merely in school but also throughout the life span. There is a danger, says Bloom, that if schools do not give students a larger share of successful experiences in the classroom, they end up by rejecting learning altogether—both in and out of school. On the other hand, learning for mastery can give zest to school learning and can help students develop a life-long interest in learning of all kinds.

THE GREAT HUMANIST-BEHAVIORIST CONTROVERSY

Skinnerians Versus Rogerians

We should not close this discussion of psychological theories about teaching and learning without commenting on the controversy that has been carried on during the past two decades between the "behaviorists"—the more experimentally oriented psychologists, such as B. F. Skinner—and the "humanists"—the more experientially oriented psychologists, such as Carl Rogers.

There are many points of difference between these two groups. Behaviorists are more inclined to

Carl R. Rogers (*left*) is the best-known exponent of the humanistic movement in education today, whereas B. F. Skinner (*right*) is the acknowledged leader of the behavioristic approach.

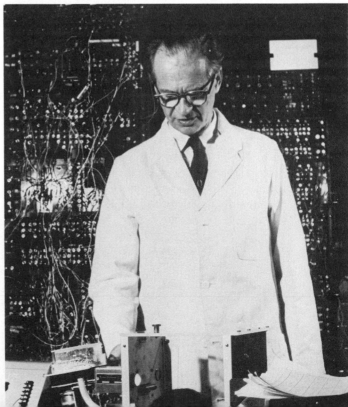

explain differences in human behavior in environmental terms and to be interested primarily in finding ways to manipulate the environment in order to bring about changes in behavior. They view the teacher's role as that of using combinations of rewards and penalties in order to produce the classroom enviroment that stimulates the most learning. Humanists think of learning as the way in which the individual develops his unique way of controlling his environment and attaining his best potential. The behaviorists view learning as something that is evoked from the student by his environment; the humanists view it as a process that is inevitable and unique for every individual. In this chapter, classical and operant conditioning explanations of learning are essentially behavioristic, whereas Gestalt, field theory, cognitive, and phenomenological theories are more or less humanistic.

Skinner and Rogers represent fairly extreme positions in the behaviorist-humanist continuum. Like many reformers, they tend to state their propositions in absolute terms. Eugene E. Swaim (1972), who has analyzed the positions of the two men, observes that the basic difference between the two lies in their explanations of "what man is" and "what man ought to be." Skinner looks upon the individual in mechanical terms, as incapable of making rational decisions and capable only of reacting to the stimuli in his environment. Rogers maintains that the individual can distinguish between himself and his environment and is inherently capable of making responsible decisions, without outside help, that lead to harmonious social behavior. Skinner is therefore concerned about external control, whereas Rogers looks for ways to eliminate external controls.

The two positions are irreconcilable and contradictory, according to Swaim. As far as education is concerned, Skinner's ideal school environment is one which provides precise control and predictable outcomes; Rogers desires an educational environment that allows maximum personal choice for the learner. Swaim observes that both Skinner and Rogers have something valuable to offer teachers, but that their theories should be used selectively and eclectically. Skinner's approach, for example, can be used in teaching specific skills, and Rogers' ideas can be employed to help learners who are having problems of adjustment.

A great many trends in education today derive their energy and direction from one or the other of these theories. The demand that educators be held accountable and show evidence that they have been able to teach learners appropriate skills and information is based on behavioristic assumptions. The idea that educational problems can be resolved by curriculum change, better methods of evaluation, or improved techniques of instruction is also behavioristic. Humanistic concepts, for their part, underlie such educational reforms as open schools, ungraded classes and "free" schools. Teachers with behavioristic leanings are likely to be concerned about reinforcement and performance, whereas those with humanistic leanings are likely to be concerned about "opportunities for creativity."

What Is Lacking: A Social View of Learning

The merits and demerits of the behavioristic and humanistic approaches to education have been debated for decades and will continue to attract enthusiastic and loyal partisans for decades to come. There is a difficulty, however, in attempting to plan for teaching-learning experiences if decisions are to be made solely on the basis of these two points of view. Each of these theories tacitly assumes a single learner, a learner who either responds to the environment that has been prepared for him by his teacher or else makes choices in terms of his unique needs. Skinnerians and Rogerians both overlook the fact that the learner is never really alone: He is always in the midst of a social situation that he is a part of and that is a part of him. Much of what the learner does or does not do is in response to social norms and the expectations of others. Whether he deviates or conforms, it is always with respect to these norms and expectations. Even when the learner is physically alone, say, in the library or the laboratory, he carries with him an awareness of how others—his peers, his teachers, his family, his friends—regard him and his behavior.

This means that the Skinnerian teacher who wishes to manipulate the learner's environment does not have as much power as he thinks he does. The "contingencies of reinforcement" that he arranges for a learner may be negated or otherwise modified by the demands of the learner's social environment. To be sure, the social enviroment can be manipulated, but that is a vastly more complicated task than selecting the kinds of reinforcements that are appropriate to a given learner. And the writings of Skinnerians indicate that they are as uninterested in understanding the learner's social environment as they are in understanding his motivation.

For their part, Rogerians who wish to free the learner to pursue his own needs seem to be unaware that some of the learner's needs were implanted by his social environment. A disruptive, aggressive boy may be reacting to a sense of discouragement and alienation, but he may be responding simultaneously to the norms of his immediate peer group. As long as he holds membership in that group, he will use their views as a point of reference for his behavior. Although everyone's needs can be considered as unique, it is also possible to make some fairly valid generalizations about the ways in which groups perceive their environment and in which individual learners respond to group forces. Rogerians are inclined to view the individual's responses to his need for group acceptance as something that interferes with his natural development, a position that makes if difficult for teachers to deal with learners and their problems realistically.

In sum, then, both points of view have value for the teacher who has to cope with the demands of society, the needs of the learner, his own expectations, and the structure of the teaching-learning situation in which he finds himself, but he can do his job more adequately if his theories of learning also take into account the fact that the learner responds to social forces both in and out of the classroom. The teacher who is effective deals not only with individual learners but also with the class as a group. It appears that in addition to being a part-time educational psychologist, the effective teacher must also be a part-time social psychologist.

SUMMARY

The need to develop theories to explain and make sense out of what goes on in our environment is as old as the human race. Scientific research and theory construction are but refinements of our attempts to satisfy this need. The climate of opinion has not always been favorable to scientific research, inasmuch as people have tended to prefer their traditional, though inaccurate, beliefs. In recent years we have become more willing to accept scientific research, particularly when it deals with physical phenomena. We still have difficulty in accepting and applying research findings in psychological and sociological fields.

One of the chief contributions of scientists is their skepticism about those popular beliefs that are seemingly self-evident. Sometimes they find that popular belief is fallacious, such as the assumption that material learned in one course of study automatically transfers itself to learning in another course. The idea that children learn to be delinquent by reading comic books appears to be equally fallacious.

In order for a teaching-learning theory to be adequate for teachers, it should expand their understanding of all learning processes, extend their understanding of the forces or factors that affect learning, enable them to make reasonably accurate predictions about the outcomes of learning activity, serve as a source of ideas that can increase teaching effectiveness, and encourage innovation and experimentation with teaching-learning techniques. The assumptions that underlie an adequate teaching-learning theory are four: man has a continuing drive to become competent and effective; competence and effectance are principally the result of learning; the development of competence depends on learning stimulated by perceived changes in the environment; and learning to be competent and effective is a continuous, lifelong process.

Traditional and popular teaching-learning theories are not very helpful to teachers, not only because they do not measure up to the above specifications but also because they are relatively unconcerned with motivation.

Much of the research in learning done by experimental psychologists is concerned with conditioning or reinforcement. B. F. Skinner developed a teaching machine which made use of operant learning principles. Skinner's teaching machine did not live up to its early promise, but it did stimulate the development of programmed learning, which is the basis of programmed texts and computer-assisted instruction or CAI. Although research has not demonstrated any superiority of programmed instruction over conventional methods, programmed materials do make it possible for students of different abilities in the same classroom to work simultaneously at assignments that are suited to their needs. Learning theory has also been applied in the form of behavior modification—attempts to control misbehavior and promote positive behavior in the classroom. Conditioning and reinforcement theories of learning are of considerable value to psychologists conducting laboratory experiments because they are the source of hypotheses that can be tested under highly controlled conditions. Although a number of experimental psychologists have recently been working in interdisciplinary situations to apply learning theory to practical problems, it is safe to say that the practical value to teachers of conditioning and reinforcement theories is still fairly limited.

There is another group of theories that treat learning in a much broader and more comprehensive way. These are the theories that are variously characterized as Gestalt, field theory, cognitive, and phenomenological learning. Such approaches take into account the way in which the learner perceives the learning situation and the various strategies he must undertake to solve problems. The problem-solving approach to learning developed by John Dewey has had great appeal to educators because it is based on an analysis of the whole child in a total situation. It has had less appeal to psychologists because it was not easily tested in a laboratory situation. In recent years, however, psychologists have developed methods which enable them to check some of Dewey's hypotheses, particularly those re-lated to democratic learning situations. More recent writers who espouse cognitive theories are Bruner, who is interested in teaching problem-solving strategies, and Ausubel, who emphasizes the importance of meaningfulness in learning.

The phenomenological concepts of Snygg and Combs also fit into this group of theories. Snygg and Combs viewed learning as a natural and normal human activity, one that does not have to be stimulated artificially by teachers. Actually, adults interfere with much childhood learning by attempting to substitute *their* goals for the ones already possessed by children. Therefore, children are forced to learn material that lacks meaning and importance for them. This material is learned with difficulty and is easily forgotten. Snygg and Combs maintained that if the schools are to help children learn, they must help them to identify with society, give them opportunities for positive achievement, and use the drive for learning that children already possess.

The major controversy in educational philosophy is between the behaviorists, as represented by the Skinnerians, and the humanists, as represented by the Rogerians. Behaviorists view teaching as an attempt to manipulate the learner's environment to produce measurable outcomes, whereas humanists want to free the learner so he can satisfy his unique developmental and psychological needs. The two points of view are irreconcilable, and the teacher must be selective in incorporating behavioristic and humanistic concepts in his instructional plan. He should be aware, however, that both points of view ignore the effect of the learner's social environment on his behavior.

Suggested Problems

1. Mrs. Rossi overheard David Schell, a kindergartener, say to another child: "It is very important for us to help each other." Because this is a very mature statement for a kindergartener to utter, she asked him: "Where did you learn that, David?" David answered: "From my father." David's father has been in this country for six years and speaks with a heavy German accent, but David's English has not the slightest trace of an accent. Using the various psychological theories discussed in this chapter, explain how Da-

vid happened to learn his father's attitude toward helpfulness but not his father's German accent.

2. How do the various learning theories discussed in this chapter explain successful learning in such skills as skating, bicycle riding, and swimming? Select some skill you have learned and analyze the procedure you went through, using the concepts of learning discussed in this chapter.

3. The parents of Jerry Wilson, age 4, like to amaze their friends by having Jerry recite the captials of the fifty states. Comment on the potential value that learning the names of these states has for Jerry.

4. When the United Food Corporation decided to launch a new breakfast food on the market, they called in Dr. Berman, an industrial psychologist, as a consultant to help them plan their advertising campaign. As Dr. Berman sat down with the vice president in charge of sales, he said: "The first thing we have to keep in mind is that getting the public to accept a new breakfast food is essentially a problem in learning." What did Dr. Berman mean by such a statement? Which of the various learning theories we have discussed will be most useful to him and why?

5. Mr. Meyer asked his fourth-graders to fill out a short questionnaire on leisure-time activities. When he divided the class into two groups, those that were above average in their reading ability, and those that were below, he found that the below-average readers had spent more time looking at television than the above-average readers. How might one account for this difference by operant learning principles? How might phenomenological theory account for the difference?

6. Two interesting contrasts in educational philosophies will be found in B. F. Skinner, *Walden II* (New York: Macmillan, 1948), and A. S. Neill, *A radical approach to child rearing* (New York: Hart, 1960). Read enough of the two books to get the "flavor" of their approaches and then compare and contrast the kind of teaching that might go on in two schools, one operated according to Skinnerian principles and one operated according to Neill's recommendations.

Suggested Readings

Andreas, B. G. *Psychological science and the educational enterprise.* New York: Wiley, 1968. Argues that laboratory-derived learning theory has more relevance for classroom teachers than is commonly believed.

Bigge, M. L. *Learning theories for teachers.* New York: Harper and Row, 1964. (A paperback.) A brief survey of the major theories of learning, with a fairly complete treatment of cognitive-field theory approaches.

Bruner, J. S. *The process of education.* Cambridge: Harvard University Press, 1960. A penetrating analysis of classroom learning by a leading exponent of cognitive theory and based on ideas developed in a conference called by the National Academy of Science.

Combs, A. S. and Snygg, D. *Individual behavior,* rev. ed. New York: Harper, 1959. The most complete statement of the phenomenological approach to classroom learning.

Dewey, J. *How we think.* Boston: Heath, 1910. Contains some of Dewey's best contributions to the concept of learning as problem solving.

Gale, R. F. *Developmental behavior: A humanistic approach.* New York: Macmillan, 1969. See particularly Chapter 11, "The learning self."

Hilgard, E. R. (ed.) *Theories of learning and instruction,* 63rd Yearbook of the National Society for the Study of Education, Part 1. Chicago: University of Chicago Press, 1964. A series of papers, some presenting a review of learning theories and some suggesting how theories might be applied to classroom teaching.

Kuethe, J. L. *The teaching-learning process.* Glenview, Ill.: Scott Foresman, 1968. (A paperback.) Another attempt to bridge the gap between laboratory research and classroom practice.

Lindgren, H. C., and Byrne, D. *Psychology: An introduction to a behavioral science,* 4th ed. New York: Wiley, 1975. Chapters 4 and 5 deal with learning theory and its applications.

Lindgren, H. C. and Lindgren, F. (eds.) *Current readings in educational psychology,* 2nd ed. New York: Wiley, 1972. See Section 4 for papers dealing with topics such as learning through discovery, phenomenological approaches to learning, and the application of learning theory to elementary school instruction.

Skinner, B. F. *The technology of teaching.* New York: Meredith, 1968. The most recent statement by the leading figure in operant conditioning.

Two pamphlets published by the Association for Supervision and Curriculum Development of the National Education Association are also relevant to this chapter: *Criteria for theories of instruction,* and *Learning more about learning.*

Cognitive and Affective Factors in Learning

In Chapter 2, when we discussed the "inside" and the "outside" forces in behavior, we made the point that it was ordinarily quite difficult to separate them, partly because every action is in some way the product of both kinds of forces and partly because it is often hard to draw the line between the two. Nevertheless, we said, it was worthwhile making the distinction for purposes of analysis and description, in order to gain a better understanding of why we behave as we do.

The same kind of distinction could be made with respect to "cognitive" and "affective" factors.

"Cognitive" ordinarily refers to behavior in which there is search for information and some degree of awareness. Thinking and problem solving are examples of cognitive behavior. "Affective" applies to aspects of behavior that involve feelings and emotions and that are more likely to lie outside the scope of awareness. Attitudes and values are often included in this category, not so much because we are unaware of them (actually, we may be very much aware) but because we often are unaware of the way in which they affect our actions. The interview that we presented in Chapter 2 between Miss

Roth and Dick Hansen, the prematurely tall sixth-grader, provides some examples of this. Dick is very much aware of his feelings. If he completed a personality questionnaire, he would very likely say deprecating things about himself and would express considerable hostility toward the world. Nevertheless, he does not see a relationship between his feelings of inferiority and the way he acts toward others.

Classroom learning is ordinarily thought of as a cognitive process. It involves information seeking, concentration, thinking—all cognitive activities. However, the amount of energy that we are willing to invest in order to carry out these activities is likely to be determined by how we *feel* about the goals and conditions of learning. To be sure, we can put our feelings aside and philosophically buckle down to the task of reading three chapters for tomorrow's quiz, but even this willingness to disregard our negative attitudes toward this task depends on other feelings and values, for instance, our atttitudes toward ourselves, our instructor, our future, and even life itself.

A great deal of learning takes place below the level of active awareness. Many behavior patterns, as well as attitudes and values, are shaped by the way in which others subtly reinforce some of our responses but not others. We are also unaware of learning that occurs incidentally, as a by-product of some seemingly unrelated activity. In one experiment, small groups of sixth-grade children played a series of games in which some children were active players and others watched. Some of the players won; others did not. Evidently losing or winning affected the attitudes of the group members because those who were in groups in which the players won felt more positively toward one another than did those in the losing groups. When children were subsequently asked questions about the color of the markers and the design of the cards used in the game, the children who had been in groups where players won remembered more than those in the other groups (Lott, Lott, and Matthews, 1969). This is a good example of incidental learning because the children had no way of knowing that they would be asked for this information later. The results of this experiment also suggest that students are more likely to be open and receptive to new experiences either when they are being rewarded or when they are in the company of others who are being rewarded. Nonreward, however, appears to lead to lower levels of learning, even when someone else other than the student fails to be rewarded.

Social learning also tends to be facilitated by positive feelings.

> Joelle Bransom admires Miss Klock, her physical education teacher. She likes everything about her—her skill, her poise, the efficient way in which she organizes chattering groups of ninth-grade girls into basketball and hockey teams. Joelle never had much interest in athletics, but now she does. She reads books on how to improve one's style in basketball, she volunteers for team sports, she practices after school, and in many ways indicates her interest in becoming expert in sports. In all this, she hopes, of course, that Miss Klock will notice and approve. This does not occur very often, but Joelle does have the satisfaction of knowing that she is developing greater skill in sports and in that way is becoming more like Miss Klock.

What we are describing here is "learning through imitation," a way in which we model our behavior after that of some admired person, usually without being aware why we are doing so.

The basic needs that we described in Chapter 2 can be said to function at a noncognitive level insofar as they affect learning. Here is an example of how the need for affiliation affects social learning. If we enter a new school, we begin to look around for people who might become friends. In doing so, we will learn that there are certain places where people socialize, that certain groups who meet there seem to be self-contained and apparently not looking for new members, and so forth. We are conscious of a feeling of being on the outside and a little lonely and may even be aware that we are actively looking for friends, although we are not so likely to be aware that we are actually learning how one contacts and makes friends in this new school. And so it is with other needs in the hierarchy.

The Need for Attention

The need for attention deserves special attention in this discussion because it is not ordinarily considered in relation to the more cognitive aspects of learning. According to popular belief, students learn because they are interested, because they want to get ahead, because they are expected to learn, and so forth. Most people would agree that there is a need for attention, but few are aware of the way in which it figures in learning.

In Chapter 8 we discussed a study by Ellis Batten Page (1958), which showed how giving attention in the way of written comments led both good and poor students to improve their performance on a subsequent paper. Another study showing how attention can stimulate favorable attitudes toward learning was conducted by Donald L. Thistlethwaite (1959), who compared two groups of high-school graduates who had been finalists in the National Merit Scholarship competition. One group consisted of a sample drawn from graduates who had received a certificate of merit and whose names had been published in a booklet distributed to colleges and universities throughout the country. In addition, the members of this group were acclaimed at high-school assemblies and were the subject of newspaper stories. The second group was drawn from a larger group of merit finalists who had received somewhat less recognition in the press. In fact, a count of press clippings showed that members in the first group received approximately two and one-half times more publicity than did the members of the second group. The two samples were matched according to college aptitude, father's occupational level, sex, and geographical region.

Six months after students had graduated from high school, Thistlethwaite had them fill out a questionnaire dealing with their attitudes toward intellectual activities and their vocational and educational plans. He found that the students who had received the greater recognition were more likely to have favorable attitudes toward intellectual activities, were more inclined to plan a career of college teaching or scientific research, were more stimulated to seek Ph.D. or M.D. degrees, and were more likely to seek scholarship assistance in college. These differences were most marked for graduates whose fathers were not employed in professional or semi-professional work. Because students from nonprofessional homes are usually less likely to plan on entering academic or research careers than are students from professional homes, the added recognition they received evidently had a pronounced effect on their attitudes and plans.

Recognition had an even greater effect on the plans of girls. Approximately 50 percent more girls in the group receiving special recognition, as contrasted with girls in the less recognized group, planned to seek Ph.D. or M.D. degrees and to become college teachers or research workers.

The relevance of these studies to our present discussion is this: If human beings did not have such well-developed needs for attention and recognition, writing comments on students' test papers or giving publicity to National Merit finalists would have little effect on their behavior. It is quite likely that people respond favorably to attention because it has what psychologists term an "arousal effect," that is, it is stimulating. In Chapter 2, we observed that the need for stimulation appears to be a basic one for animals, as well as for humans, and that it has a facilitating effect on learning and cognitive development, even leading to increased thickness in the cerebral cortex—the "thinking part" of the brain (Krech, 1969).

Some research on class size may be relevant here. Ernest D. McDaniel and John F. Feldhusen (1970) did a study of factors that related to students' ratings of the courses they were taking. They found that class size was the factor that was most consistently correlated with students' ratings of various aspects of the course. In every instance, however, the correlation was negative, which means that the smaller the size of the class, the greater the satisfaction expressed by the students, and the larger the class size, the less the satisfaction. The authors explained this relationship in terms of the instructor's ability to develop comfortable, mutually trusting relationships with students and to get some insight into student needs. But a more fundamental explanation may be found in the fact that smaller classes permit more interpersonal interaction and thus enable each student to receive more attention, either from the instructor or from the class as a whole.

The effect of attention is also implicit in a study of the effect of adult-child conferences on the independent reading of elementary school children. Children at various levels of reading competence in an elementary school in Madison, Wisconsin, participated in a program in which they discussed their out-of-class reading with their teacher or a teaching aide. A control group had no conferences. The adults were coached to serve as models for the children (as indicated by their own expressed enthusiasm for reading), as reinforcers (through smiles and praise), as goal setters (helping children move on to more difficult books), and as sources of feedback (such as telling children how many books they had read). In contrast to the control group, children who had conferences read more books and tended to show greater gains in reading achievement, as measured by standardized tests. The researchers concluded that the gains at least in part resulted from the fact that the children in the experimental groups received more attention than those in the control groups (Schwenn, Sorenson, and Bavary, 1970).

In the studies we have cited, learners appear to have been responding along both affective and cognitive lines. Such dualism in responses seems to be characteristic of complicated forms of learning. Evidently we respond to complex situations by attempting to arrive at some kind of a satisfactory balance or adjustment between our psychological needs and the demands made on us by our environment. Making a successful adjustment that solves a problem with which we are faced may in itself provide the kind of reward required to produce learning, but if this reward can somehow be doubly reinforced by the satisfaction of another need, the chances of learning taking place are enhanced. We naturally tend to select behavioral patterns that result in satisfactions to the greatest number of needs. This tendency can be observed at all levels of human development.

After much trial and error, a baby learns to carry a spoonful of food from his plate to his mouth without spilling too much. The accomplishment of this complex task indicates that he has learned to organize and control his hitherto random and erratic behavior. The accomplishment also signalizes success in meeting psychological needs at several levels. For one thing, he has learned a new and more effective way of getting food, a skill related to the meeting of needs at a very primitive and physiological level. His need for food is not the most important need satisfied by his new ability, however. After all, he *could* eat with his fingers. But, like all of us, he has a strong need to belong to the world of people around him, and one of the ways in which he can belong to that world is to eat the way others eat. Learning to eat with a spoon is one way of participating in a society where everyone eats with the aid of cutlery. Then there is the praise and recognition that he receives the first few times he demonstrates his ability to accomplish this difficult task. His tentative efforts at eating with a spoon called forth comment and encouragement—a foretaste of the reward he would receive if he accomplished this feat of learning successfully. And there is the pride of accomplishment at being able to tackle and master something on his own. In this he is rewarded by his own feelings of being adequate and competent.

Learning to write is similar in many ways to learning to eat with a spoon, except, of course, that it is a much more complex skill. It is not as obviously related to human survival needs, but, like eating with a spoon, it is a way of participating in a world composed of other people. Being able to write is an essential part of being a person in a civilized culture. In a culture in which everyone can write, the child who is unable to write feels left out. Not only does learning to write earn praise and acceptance from significant adults, but it also gives one a sense of adequacy and accomplishment. We do not have to work very hard at the task of convincing most children of the importance of learning to write, just as we do not have to convince most of them of the desirability of learning to eat with a spoon. There are children who are exceptions, of course, children who have needs or anxieties that for them have a higher priority than learning to write, and these children need special help and understanding. And when we say that all children feel the need to learn to write, we do not mean that the need is equally strong or that it occurs at the same age for all children. The main point is that the need to learn to write is, generally speaking, one that does not have to be artificially implanted or developed in children.

Intrinsic and Extrinsic Rewards

Although various kinds of responses can be reinforced by recognition, attention, encouragement, and similar kinds of "extrinsic" or "external" rewards, the strongest and most dependable motivation for learning comes from the basic and dominant need to be adequate and competent. Jerome S. Bruner (1961) described this need as follows:

The degree to which competence or mastery motives come to control behavior, to that degree the role of reinforcement or "extrinsic pleasure"

(The Wall Street Journal)

"Maybe they can force me to learn—but as soon as I'm old enough, I'm going to forget everything!"

wanes in shaping behavior. The child comes to manipulate his environment more actively and achieves his gratification from coping with problems. Symbolic modes of representing and transforming the environment arise and the importance of stimulus-response-reward sequences declines.

In our eagerness to get students to do their assigned tasks we often overlook the fact that motivation to learn springs from the needs of the learner, not from those of the teacher. As a consequence, we sometimes think of motivation as something we do *to* the student—a kind of winding him up before pressing the button that starts him off on a learning experience.

Often students will work with greater vigor at a learning task once they see its rationale. In one experiment, second-graders were given sets of easy arithmetic problems. As they completed each set, the experimenter said nothing; praised the child ("You are doing very well," "Good job," and so forth); or gave the child a series of reasons for learning arithmetic, such as "It's important to learn arithmetic so that you will know how much change you should get back when you buy something at the store." After the child had completed the sets of problems, the experimenter gave the child a booklet of problems of increasing difficulty with directions to call him when the child finished working. An analysis of the children's performance showed that those who had been praised—extrinsically motivated—did, as one might expect, complete more problems correctly than those who had received the "silent treatment." What is of particular interest, however, is that those who had been given reasons for learning arithmetic—intrinsically motivated—did an even larger number of the problems correctly and also worked longer at this relatively unrewarding task (Taffel, O'Leary, and Armel, 1974).

The results of this experiment are somewhat more supportive of the humanistic than of the behavioristic view of learning, in that reinforcement in the form of praise was not as successful a device as were comments that gave the task more meaning and relevance.

Factors Which Interfere with Learning

Although some of the material that students work on is clearly related to their needs to be competent and effective, the relevance of much of it is less obvious. Many of the experiences that make up the standard school curriculum would not be included if we used students' statements of their needs as our guide. These other experiences are put into the curriculum because adults think they are important. We teach the skills of arithmetic not so much because students feel the immediate need of these skills, but because we think they will have a use for them later on. We teach history not so much because students have an avid interest in finding out what went on in previous centuries, but because we feel that understanding something about the people who came before us and the significant events of our past as a nation are an important part of being a citizen. Few people would object to the principle that the coming generation of adults should be familiar with the thoughts and actions of past generations or with the skills of arithmetic. The great problem is how to help students develop this familiarity without losing sight of their psychological needs and without violating any of the principles of learning. When we attempt to introduce this important material into the curriculum without considering the points of view and psychological needs of students, our efforts are largely ineffective, as Snygg and Combs (1959) have pointed out (see Chapter 8).

There are, however, other sources of difficulty. Education must go on five days a week, forty weeks a year, regardless of whether students are eager to learn. Unfortunately, their learning readiness, as well as their learning ability, varies from time to time. No one learns at an even, steady rate. Any individual's curve of learning progress inevitably shows hills, valleys, and plateaus like the ones in Figure 9-1. In view of the fact that these variations in learning are universal, it is virtually impossible, given conditions of mass learning, to adjust curriculum and presentation to each student's learning progress. We should, of course, develop systems and practices that are as flexible as possible, but we should also recognize our limitations in this respect. In spite of the fact that mass education is by its nature inelastic to some degree, it is nevertheless the most efficient mode of meeting the learning needs of the largest number of children in any modern society.

At any time in any classroom group, some students will be marking time or even losing ground. Such "pauses in learning" are not necessarily time lost. Although there are various theories as to why they occur even under the most favorable learning conditions, there is some agreement that they may

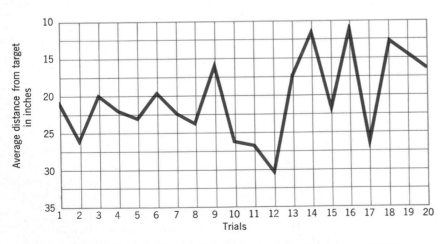

FIG. 9-1. Learning through practice: improvement in tossing ten pennies at a mark from a distance of fifteen feet (from the files of the author).

represent attempts to assimilate the information that has been acquired before forging ahead toward higher goals. Pauses may also occur when students are distracted by other needs. A return to the task later may also be accompanied by higher levels of motivation. Even periods without practicing a skill may produce learning. As William James once pointed out, we learn to ice skate in summer and swim in winter—that is, even when we are not actively practicing these skills.

THE CURRICULUM AND ITS PRESENTATION

Systems of Classifying Levels of Learning

Two frequently used systems of classifying what students are expected to learn are the ones developed by Robert M. Gagné (1970) and by Benjamin S. Bloom (1956). The systems are similar in that the initial levels are simple and rudimentary, and the final levels are complex and abstract. They differ, however, in that Gagné's system is concerned with learning processes, whereas Bloom's taxonomy is a classification of educational tasks. Table 9-1 lists them in such a way that learning processes are matched with appropriate goals.

The first three stages of Gagne's conditions of learning involve very simple responses, ones that can be performed by animals trained for the stage or in laboratories. Each successive form of learning is essentially a more complex form of earlier forms. Although Gagne's stages are sometimes cited by educational psychologists as a model for classroom learning, they are primarily useful for the design of experimental studies.

Bloom's taxonomy was produced by a team of educational specialists and hence is more closely related to the classroom than are Gagné's conditions of learning. Each of the tasks in Bloom's list, like the conditions in Gagné's hierarchy, build on the skills or competencies that go before it. Comprehension, for example, requires knowledge. The

TABLE 9-1. Gagné's Conditions of Learning and Bloom's Taxonomy of Educational Objectives[a]

Gagné	Bloom
1. *Signal learning:* Classical conditioning; involves involuntary responses	1. *Knowledge:* simple recall of information
2. *Stimulus-response (S-R) learning:* operant conditioning	
3. *Chaining:* combinations of sequential S-R responses	
4. *Verbal association:* like chaining, but the links are verbal units	
5. *Discrimination learning:* recognition of similarities and differences among stimuli	2. *Comprehension:* the lowest level of understanding
6. *Concept learning:* responding to abstract characteristics in classifying stimuli	
7. *Rule learning:* combinations of concepts	3. *Application:* using abstractions and principles in specific situations
	4. *Analysis:* distinguishing and comprehending interrelationships
	5. *Synthesis:* rearranging ideas into new wholes, creating new structures
8. *Problem solving:* using rules to achieve end goals in a variety of situations	6. *Evaluation:* making judgments based on internal evidence or external criteria

[a] Gagné, 1970; Bloom et al., 1956.

outline we have presented in Table 9-1 is only the framework of the taxonomy, which was designed for the use of curriculum planning and is spelled out in considerable detail in the manual produced by Bloom and his associates.

Although the two lists have considerable value, one for the researcher and the other for the curriculum planner, they are of limited use for the teacher who is interested in understanding the psychological implications of the kinds of tasks or goals that students are expected to accomplish. We shall therefore make use of a much simpler and less abstract hierarchy: (1) *skills and information,* (2) *concepts,* and (3) *attitudes and values.* The first two are cognitive; the third level is affective.

The Learning of Skills and Information

Skills and information are learned in an interactive manner, for it is impossible to learn one without the other. It is through skills, such as reading and listening, that we acquire information. The need for information about the world is a challenge that we can meet only by acquiring and using skills, and it is impossible to learn a skill without acquiring and using information. The information we possess is a guide as to what further information we need and how it may be secured.

The behavioristically oriented psychologist is inclined to emphasize the skill aspect of learning because he sees learning as a series of responses which are reinforced by the organism's interacting with its environment. He is relatively unconcerned about why the organism interacts at all and what it understands or comprehends as a result of its interaction. The more humanistically oriented psychologists and educators view learning in more global terms and see it as cause, process, and result—all integrated into a whole. The result or accomplishment of a single learning venture becomes the basis for the next venture, and the process of learning itself can be viewed as an outcome. For example, the child's attempt to build a tower of unequal-sized blocks leads him to experiment on a trial-and-error basis with the loose blocks that are available to him. In the process, he learns that it is more effective to put larger, flatter blocks at the base of the tower and reserve the smaller, chunkier ones for the top. This insight is an outcome of his having experimented with various sizes of blocks, but in the process of experimentation he also learns block-stacking techniques. It is difficult to draw the line between pure skill and pure information in actual learning experiences.

Education has traditionally differentiated between skill and information. This has come about partly because of evaluation demands. The school board asks the superintendent who asks the principal who asks the teacher how well the students read. Then the teacher is asked what the students know. He is seldom asked for a single reading-knowing package of information. The artificiality of such demands is shown by the fact that the two reports are almost always quite similar. For instance, students who are one grade advanced in reading are also likely to be a grade advanced in information about, say, geography or social studies. To be sure, measures of arithmetical skills sometimes tell a different story. Reading is something that children are likely to do outside of school either for pleasure or in connection with everyday problem solving. Unless a child is quantitatively minded and enjoys mathematical games or mechanical construction, he is unlikely to get much practice outside of school in anything beyond the most rudimentary arithmetical skills. Hence it often happens that children display sizable differences between verbal-competence areas (reading, vocabulary, social studies) and mathematical areas (computation, mathematical concepts). There are also students who are better in mathematical skills than they are in mathematical concepts, and vice versa, although the general tendency is for competence in the two to be related.

In life situations, skill and information are likely to be complementary, and, in the most effective learning situations, they are taught in an interrelated, global way. The fact that competence in the two can be measured and reported separately for administrative reasons has led to their being taught separately in some instances. Curriculum makers and teachers also are inclined to break a subject up into skill components and information components, arguing that it is easier to present them in this way. Unfortunately, the logic of instruction is not necessarily the logic of life.

The Learning of Concepts

Skills and information are best learned and best retained when they are organized into conceptual systems. In the primary grades, these systems are usually directly related to children's immediate experiences: a trip to the zoo or the collaborative painting of a mural. In later years there is an exploration of more complex and abstract areas of the environment: a visit to the city hall, an enactment of a historical event, or scientific demonstrations and experiments. Such experiences can involve a great range of cognitive skills and lead to the accumulation of much information. The experiences themselves serve as bases for organizing the information

into concepts. What the experiences do, essentially, is to give the information meaning and relevance.

Traditional instructional approaches attempt to organize the curriculum conceptually in the sense that the student is expected to learn, say, history, government, and biology. The basic idea is that the information and skills within these areas are interrelated. Such approaches usually leave two problems unresolved, however. One is that of relevance—embedding skills and information in the personal experiences of the learner—and the other is that the boundaries of traditional subject matter fields are largely artificial. Snygg and Combs (1959) viewed these problems as major ones and maintained that the education process has failed if they are not adequately resolved. Figure 9-2 depicts their concerns in schematic terms. The diagram represents the entire phenomenological field or pri-

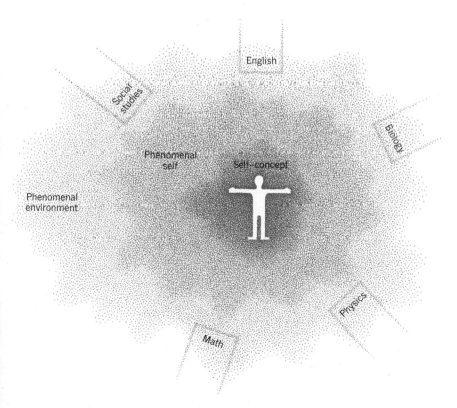

FIG. 9-2. The student's phenomenal field and the traditional school curriculum.

vate world of the learner, with the learning situation located out in his phenomenal environment. The school has blocked out certain subject matter areas which it sees as distinct and unrelated to one another.

Snygg and Combs recommended that teachers overcome the artificiality of this segmentation by empathizing with and coming to understand students' perceptions of their environment. Curriculum and instruction should be based on these insights, and not on academic convenience. They argued that unless education has affected the way in which the student sees himself and his world, no really significant learning has taken place. To be sure, some teachers and curriculum makers have attempted to reorganize traditional school subjects into core courses and other interdisciplinary instructional units, but Snygg and Combs would say that they should take the next step of finding ways to make the material relevant to the students' experiences.

The Learning of Attitudes

In October of 1957, the Soviets launched "Sputnik," the first space capsule. The reaction of many American educators, especially those in the fields of science and mathematics, was one of dismay.

The general conclusion was that the Russians were able to be "first in space" because of the superiority of their educational system. American instruction in mathematical skills, which are basic to all aspects of technology and research, was pointed to as especially weak. The difficulty with math instruction, the reasoning went, is that the traditional mathematical curriculum in the elementary schools was a hodgepodge of concepts and skills that gave students no real understanding of the logic of quantity and served as a very poor foundation for algebra and higher mathematics. Accordingly, a number of groups of mathematicians and teachers of mathematics developed instructional materials for what has been called the "new math."

Morris Kline (1973), in his book *Why Johnny Can't Add,* attributes the failure of the new math to its overemphasis on verbalization and precision, as well as on the fact that curriculum reform took precedence over the reform of teaching methods. Kline's criticisms seem valid, but anyone who has talked to elementary school teachers and to students can also attest that a major stumbling block to the learning of mathematical concepts is the anxiety that many of them express about dealing with quantitative concepts. Lewis R. Aiken (1970), in a survey of research dealing with attitudes toward mathematics, found that a sizable proportion of teachers and

(Drawing by T.S.; © 1971 The New Yorker Magazine, Inc.)

prospective teachers had negative feelings toward math, and that the attitudes of teachers were likely to be reflected both in the attitudes of students and their achievement.

In essence, what the new math experience shows is that no amount of tinkering with the conceptual aspects of the curriculum is likely to have much effect on learning unless there are some fundamental changes in the attitudes of teachers and students. If any curricular reform is to succeed, there must be some kind of energizing force that integrates or bonds the skills, information, and concepts which are to be acquired into the student's phenomenal field, so that they have meaning and relevance for him. This bonding process can occur only if teachers recognize that students must be involved through their feelings and emotions, as well as intellectually. Without affective change, there is no cognitive change.

Bruner (1960) once said that students must learn certain general attitudes toward science and literature that can serve as bases for developing an understanding of problem solving and the interrelationship of concepts. There are other kinds of attitudes that are equally important if learning experiences are to be successful—attitudes toward teachers, as well as toward the school, other students, and oneself. Teachers should recognize that all successful learning is accompanied by changes in attitudes. By ''changes'' we do not necessarily mean changes in the *direction* of attitudes. Children ordinarily have an interest in and an excitement about learning. In this instance, the change is concerned with helping children develop and integrate these attitudes in such a way that they will willingly become involved in more complex learning tasks. The attitudes of a first-grader are of tremendous importance when it comes to teaching him to read, and his positive attitudes toward himself, the teacher, the school, and the world in general will change in the sense that they will develop and will be strengthened as a result of his having learned to read. Favorable attitudes are likewise a prerequisite for successful learning experiences in high-school chemistry, and such experiences will in turn lead to the development of new attitudes toward science, oneself, and the world in general.

The learning of attitudes is basic to what Walcott Beatty and Rodney Clark (1972) have termed *significant* learning, which they distinguish from *instrumental* learning. Instrumental learning, as described by them, is mainly concerned with the acquisition of information, skills, and concepts. Although such learning occurs in response to the learner's needs, it has relatively little effect on his self-concept and his outlook on life. Significant learning, according to Beatty and Clark, involves changes in attitudes toward oneself or the self-concept itself. When significant learning has occurred, the individual is led to engage in a great deal of instrumental learning, in order to find ways of expressing the redefined concept of himself. The music student who belatedly discovers that he does not have enough talent takes a fresh look at his learning opportunities and sets out to try out other skills and to seek information about other fields. Instrumental learning, however, does not necessarily result in significant learning. The college-bound high-school student who takes a year of algebra and follows it by a year of plane geometry is usually little changed by the experience.

Some kinds of everyday learning experiences can, of course, have a cumulative effect. The child who is continually reprimanded for failures in spelling may learn to spell more accurately, or he may learn to be anxious about spelling and to think of himself as a chronic failure. When we train animals, rewards (and punishments as well) become attached to the behavior that is being reinforced, but when we educate human beings, the person, as well as the behavior, is himself rewarded or punished (Symonds, 1955). Thus any action of a teacher toward a student is likely to be perceived by the latter as saying something about him as a person.

The learning of attitudes generally occurs as an incidental effect of everyday classroom activity. John E. Anderson (1942) once observed that ''every form of learning develops a substantial series of attitudes, and that this by-product is often more sig-

AFFECTIVE FACTORS IN LEARNING

Although we are inclined to think of learning primarily as a cognitive process, the affective aspects of everyday living—values, beliefs, attitudes, and especially feelings—influence not only what is learned, but how well it is learned.

nificant for adjustment than the primary skill being taught the individual." An example of what Anderson referred to is that of the boy who transfers from another school a month or so after school has started. In order to bring him up to date, the teacher stays after school to give him a brief digest of the main topics the class has covered and to make some special reading assignments. This special attention may help the boy gain some understanding of what the class has been doing, but he may also learn something else that is even more significant, namely, that the teacher thinks he is important enough to merit this special attention. Such an experience may, furthermore, help him to develop positive attitudes toward adults in general.

Before we leave this section, we should take note of a continuing problem that plagues teachers and students alike: the deterioration in the affective cli-mate that takes place in the later elementary school years and in high school. This negative shift was pinpointed in a survey of 121 classes in 69 schools in Illinois, grades 6 to 12. Students were asked to rate on a four-point scale the amount of emphasis that prevailed in their classes with respect to a number of goals and activities taken from Bloom's (1956) *Taxonomy* and from a list of attitudes. The mean ratings of some of the classroom characteristics are shown in Figure 9-3. In general, the investigators found that activities that got students to participate, to use their imagination, and to engage in problem solving declined during the elementary school years and in high school as well. There was a corresponding drop in attitudes indicating positive involvement, such as excitement about learning and initiative, as well as an increase in anxiety about grades. The only positive note in an otherwise

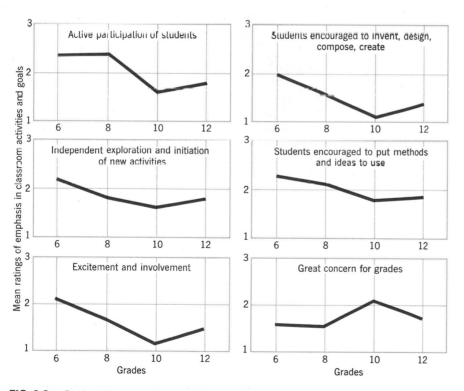

FIG. 9-3. Students' perceptions, as expressed in mean ratings, of what their teachers emphasized in their classes, grades 6 to 12 (data from Walberg, House, and Steele, 1973).

gloomy picture was a movement toward a more positive approach in the senior year of high school (Walberg, House, and Steele, 1973).

There are many reasons, of course, for this unhappy situation. One is the restive nonconformity and rebelliousness that some students, especially boys, display during the adolescent years. The natural tendency of teachers is to react repressively when their authority is challenged, to make assignments more specific and more detailed, and to set hard-and-fast rules about deadlines, length of reports, and the like. The accomplishment of learning tasks becomes more a measure of obedience and conformity than a source of personal satisfaction.

A somewhat related cause is the complexity and abstraction of subject matter with each succeeding year of school. When students are positively motivated, complexity and abstraction are less likely to cause block learning, but when teachers become more concerned about whether students have learned what they were supposed to have learned and less concerned about their motivation, the classroom situation takes on a coercive tone, and apathy or rebellion results.

Attitudinal Patterns and Classroom Learning

It is a common observation that boys usually have fewer difficulties than girls do with courses that emphasize problem solving, such as physics, chemistry, and higher mathematics. This advantage in such courses is traditionally thought to be the result of inborn differences in male and female mentality. There is some research evidence for this view. For example, studies of infants show that boys are more inclined to fix their gaze on geometric displays of stimuli, whereas girls are more inclined to look at faces (Garai and Scheinfeld, 1968). This trend apparently continues during the preschool years, for boys are more attracted to mechanical toys, and girls seem to be more interested in dolls (Maccoby, 1975). Even mentally retarded preschoolers show these differences, for boys show a preference for drawing vehicles, and girls prefer to draw humans (Israel and Heal, 1971). The debate as to the relative importance of heredity and environment on sex differences in behavior waxes furious among behavioral scientists these days, but irrespective of how the questions are eventually resolved, if at all, there is no doubt that most boys enter school with fairly definite predilections for activities dealing with the physical world, whereas girls this age generally are oriented to the social world.

It is one of the tasks of the school to broaden these interests and perspectives for each of the sexes, but teachers should nevertheless be aware that these differences in motivational patterns are a reality that they must work with. Sex differences in reading are a case in point. Girls begin to speak earlier than boys and are linguistically more capable at an early age. The fact that language competence facilitates social interaction may be a factor. In school, girls learn to read and write more readily than boys do; in fact, the great majority of the problem readers are boys. This does not necessarily mean that boys are mentally inferior, for some evidence suggests that the difference may be at least in part motivational. One study of fifth-graders, for example, showed that boys read as well as girls on material that they find interesting but were markedly poorer in material that does not interest them (Asher and Markell, 1974). (See Figure 9-4.) Another study indicated that willingness to attend to classroom tasks is highly correlated with the reading ability of first-graders. Not only were the girls more competent in reading, but they also spent a higher percentage of time attending to their work (Samuels and Turnure, 1974).

The tendency of girls to have more difficulty than boys with problem-solving tasks may also be a matter of motivation. The investigator in one experiment gave college men and women a questionnaire dealing with attitudes toward problem solving, as well as a series of problems to solve. As might be expected, men displayed more favorable attitudes toward problem solving than women did and also did better in solving the problems. The next phase of the experiment consisted of group discussions in which an attempt was made to build up the confidence of the subjects in solving problems and to develop favorable attitudes toward problem solving. The third phase of the experiment consisted of an

COGNITIVE AND AFFECTIVE
FACTORS IN LEARNING

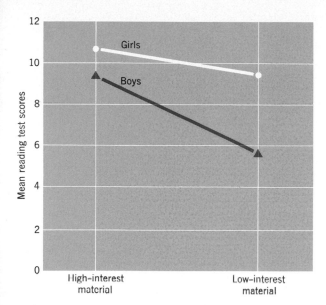

FIG. 9-4. Sex differences among fifth-graders in mean reading scores on high-interest and low-interest material (data from Asher and Markell, 1974).

administration of a second questionnaire measuring attitudes toward problem solving and an additional set of problems. Women improved their attitudes toward problem solving significantly and also increased their scores on the problem-solving test, whereas men did not. The results of the experiment indicated that the difficulties women have with problem solving are probably due to culturally determined attitudes and not to any lack of ability (Carey, 1958).

If a teacher attempts to teach attitudes directly, there is, unfortunately, no assurance that students will develop them. Let us suppose that a social studies teacher would like to see the students in his class develop attitudes that come under the heading of "respect for the worth of each individual." He may be able to point out that the Declaration of Independence and the Constitutional Bill of Rights are partially based on this attitude or principle. If he stops here, efforts may amount merely to an attempt to manipulate the external environment of his students without really affecting them personally. But if he can help the students in his class to experience

a deep respect and appreciation of the importance of the Declaration of Independence and the Bill of Rights in their daily lives, such a realization may aid the development of a genuine attitude of respect for people as individuals. It may be that the children in his class will need a great deal of help and guidance in developing the desired attitudes. Perhaps they have given the matter little thought in the past; perhaps they have not "lived enough." Hence the teaching of respect for individuals must rest on a broader base of experience. For example, the teacher himself can, in his relations with the class, show a respect and a tolerance for the feelings and opinions of students that adults demonstrate all too seldom; or he can arrange for certain kinds of learning experiences—panel discussions, group projects, or discussions moderated by students—which help to demonstrate his belief in this principle. Or there may be other methods more appropriate to the maturity of his class and the kind of relationship he has with them. But basic to any technique that he will use to help students change their attitudes in the direction of socially desirable behavior will be his ability to demonstrate his own belief in this kind of behavior.

Wholes and Parts

Common sense and tradition, as we stated earlier, often are misleading when it comes to developing effective teaching-learning strategies. There seems to be a natural tendency, when teaching or learning a skill or a complex area of subject matter, to take up each component one at a time, until the whole has been covered. In learning to play the piano, this would mean doing finger exercises and scales before attempting to play actual compositions. Compositions would be learned a few bars at a time, and each hand's part would be learned separately. This method was very much in vogue among piano teachers a generation ago, but many if not most teachers today prefer a form of the whole method. Piano students today learn to play entire compositions appropriate to their level of competence, and there is much emphasis on sight-reading, whereby students are encouraged to play unfamiliar pieces from start to finish, using both hands. In painting, the part method would require that individuals master the various strokes of the brush, highlighting, and techniques appropriate to various kinds of scenes before attempting to paint a picture.

Teaching via the part method has gradually declined partly because teachers have found it to be less efficient and partly because the interest and enthusiasm of learners tend to wane unless they can see some tangible or visible results. A piano student takes up the study of music because he wants to play compositions, not practice scales and finger exercises. Unless some whole experiences are introduced into the instructional sequence rather early, learners tend to lose interest and become apathetic. If no one were allowed to play tennis until he had mastered all the basic strokes, there would be very few tennis players. Incidentally, this example illustrates one of the fallacies often overlooked by the supporters of the part approach, namely, that mastery of all the basic strokes in tennis would not in itself mean that one could play tennis. The ability to play tennis may depend to a large degree on the mastery of strokes, but mastery of strokes does not constitute the ability to play tennis. There is an important integrating element that is usually omitted when the part approach is used exclusively.

The part approach to learning tends to ignore the learners' need to develop some kind of a frame of reference that will help them relate one aspect of what is to be learned to its other aspects and that will also help them relate their present learning experiences to previous learning. Hence it is not surprising that studies generally show that learning proceeds more efficiently if students are given material that is not too fractionated into segments and parts. Most of the research dealing with the relative value of part and whole methods goes back forty years or more, and the most recent review was done by Symonds (1957), who concluded that the results justified a complete endorsement of the whole-learning approach.

We pointed out in an early chapter that one of the prime objectives of education was that of facilitating transfer of learning. It is expected, for example, that the principles which students learn in classrooms will be transferred by them to situations and problems that they encounter outside the classroom. One of the advantages of the whole method is its facilitation of integration, that is, the learner is encouraged to look for interrelationships among the various elements of the problems and learning situations that confront him. In other words, the whole method encourages students to look for interrelationships and similar elements in the various problems and learning situations they encounter.

Problems Encountered in Using the Whole Method of Learning

Although the use of the whole method in learning has obvious advantages, it also presents some problems. One of the questions that the teacher must ask himself is this: How large should the whole be? Another problem has to do with interpretation: Just what *is* a whole anyway? What makes a whole a whole and a part a part?

The answer to such questions depends in part on the learner and in part on the material to be learned. The wholes for students who are intellectually less mature will be less inclusive and less complex than the wholes that can be comprehended by more mature students. Thus what is a whole for the less mature student would be considered a part for a more mature student. The basic problem is one of perception. In other words, is the learner able to see or perceive relationships among the parts of what is to be presented? If not, and if the material seems too complex or too ambiguous to him, it evidently needs to be broken down into smaller segments. If material seems significant to the learner, if he can see its importance and its relationship to his experience and to his self-concept, and if he perceives it as something that he can and should learn, it will probably have a "whole quality" for him.

"Whole" learning is generally better than "part" learning because the material to be learned "makes sense," because its various parts can be seen *by the learner* as interrelated, and because he sees a relationship between the central idea of the material to be learned and himself. An individual who has tried to play a game of tennis, however badly and amateurishly, will perceive the importance of developing a good backhand swing. The individual who has not had this experience does not see the relationship of the backhand swing to competence in tennis, nor does he see it as anything that he might be interested in mastering. In short, it has little meaning for him. It is not a part of a whole.

Another consideration is the student's educational set. Children who are set to perceive wholes turn out to be better readers than those who are preoccupied with details. This tendency is very strong and very consistent. Louise B. Ames and Richard N. Walker (1964), of the Gesell Institute of Child Development in New Haven, found that the tendency of kindergarteners to respond to Rorschach test blots as "wholes" was almost as good a predictor of their reading skill in the fifth grade as were their IQs. Evidently, the ability to perceive and understand larger concepts helps children to progress more rapidly in learning to read. Slow readers, on the other hand, concentrate on one detail at a time and tend to get bogged down if too many details are presented at once. One answer to this problem is that of changing the child's set in such a way that he begins to respond to wholes, rather than parts. This approach, however, does run the risk of pushing the slower learner faster than he may be able to go.

PERSONALITY FACTORS AND STUDENT PERFORMANCE

Personality Factors as Predictors

Pauline S. Sears and Ernest R. Hilgard (1964) have noted that problems of motivation in the classroom are intertwined with problems of personality. That motivation is related to the student's willingness or unwillingness to involve himself in the learning process is obvious; it is less obvious that school performance is related to personality. Yet the research data on this topic are substantial. In one study, measures of self-concept and ratings of ego-strength (self-sufficiency) administered to children entering kindergarten were better than intelligence tests

when it came to predicting their reading achievement two and a half years later (Wattenberg and Clifford, 1962).

The reason for the high relationship between personality factors and school performance may be found in the basic consistency that runs through human behavior. Kindergarteners who are confident and self-sufficient are likely to approach learning tasks optimistically and are less likely to be discouraged by initial mistakes. Ego-strength is a general, "omnibus" type of factor that is positively related to success of all kinds, in the classroom, as well as elsewhere. Other personality factors are specific in terms of the kind of school performance to which they are related.

Carl J. Cooper (1964) did a correlational study of factors related to success in German and found that a test in English grammar and a special test designed to predict success in foreign languages gave the best correlations. However, success on a "paired-associates" memory task also correlated highly and significantly with German grades. The paired-associates task requires students to memorize sixteen pairs of nonsense syllables during the course of twenty-four sets of trials, each set consisting of two trials in which the student was given the nonsense syllables and one trial in which he was asked to recall them. This task took an hour and a quarter and required a great deal of close concentration. Actual performance in such a task is a behavior sample of how an individual responds to a task that is difficult, boring, and offers few, if any, immediate rewards. Cooper suggested that students who are able to maintain enough interest and drive to complete such tasks are probably the same kinds of students who do well in foreign-language learning.

Some of the more significant research with noncognitive factors and school success has been done by Harrison G. Gough (1964) of the Institute of Personality Assessment and Research on the Berkeley campus of the University of California. Gough has used the California Psychological Inventory (CPI) to isolate eighteen personality factors. His research shows a high degree of correlation between at least eight of the traits measured by the

CPI and scholastic success in high school. As the data in Table 9-2 suggest, scholastic success is strongly influenced by such basic personality traits as energy, ambition, and social maturity. Although these findings are consistent with common sense, they do make the point that noncognitive factors play a significant role in academic achievement.

Readiness to Learn

Ideas about when a child is "ready" for certain kinds of learning experiences have undergone a change in recent years. Conclusions drawn from earlier studies of child development tended to be rather restrictive about what teachers could do with children. Teachers felt, for example, that reading could not be started before a certain age and that certain arithmetical concepts could not be introduced until the third or fourth grade. Children today, however, come to school exposed to a great deal more intellectual and quasi-intellectual stimuli than was true of children a generation ago. Today's children not only spend one or more hours a day

watching television but have spent more time being read to or actually looking at books. The greater availability of cheap paperback children's books in the local supermarket may have a great deal to do with this.

Some experts on learning question whether there is actually any such thing as readiness. Bruner (1960) maintains that "any subject can be taught effectively in some intellectually honest form to any child at any stage of development." Although Bruner accepts the validity of Piaget's sequential steps of cognitive development, he says that "instruction in scientific ideas, even at the elementary level, need not follow slavishly the natural course of cognitive development in the child." The child's intellectual development, Bruner states, can be stimulated by presenting him with problems that "tempt him into the next stages of development." He quotes an expert in mathematics education as saying that "young children can learn almost anything faster than adults do if it can be given to them in terms they understand."

This optimism is not shared by most other educa-

TABLE 9-2. Correlations Between Personality Traits Measured by Some of the Scales of the California Psychological Inventory (CPI) and High-School Grades[a]

Name of Scale and What It Measures	Correlation with Grades
Dominance: leadership ability, persistence, and social influence	.29
Capacity for status: the personal qualities that underlie and lead to status (not the individual's actual or achieved status)	.33
Responsibility: conscientiousness, dependability	.44
Socialization[b]: social maturity, integrity, seriousness	.34
Tolerance: possession of permissive, accepting, and nonjudgmental social beliefs and attitudes	.35
Achievement via conformity: interests and motives that facilitate achievement in situations demanding some degree of conformity	.38
Achievement via independence: interests and motives that facilitate achievement in situations demanding some degree of autonomy and independence	.36
Intellectual efficiency: degree to which the individual is seen as efficient, clear-thinking, capable, intelligent, progressive, planful, thorough, and resourceful	.41

[a] Gough, 1964.
[b] Not the same as sociability, which is measured by another CPI scale that correlated only .25 with grades.

tors and psychologists. David P. Ausubel (1962) grants that children can learn far more in the way of mathematics than they are currently being taught and that the learning of adolescents and adults is often impeded by the fact that they must *unlearn* certain concepts before they can assimilate new ones. But he points out that adolescents and adults have, generally speaking, a considerable advantage over children when it comes to learning complex material because they are more used to operating on a high level of abstraction than children are.

Irrespective of whether Bruner is overly optimistic or Ausubel overly cautious, the fact is significant that they do agree that children can learn more than current concepts of readiness would lead us to believe they can be taught. It seems likely that the attitudes of teachers, rather than learners, are the limiting factor here. As we noted earlier, students are very responsive to teachers' attitudes. If teachers do not believe that students are capable of learning certain concepts and skills, students are quick to pick up this negative feeling and develop expectations accordingly. The expectations that students have about their potentialities for learning play a large part in their readiness to learn.

In Chapter 2 we mentioned the effect that a child's locus of control (LOC) has on his behavior. Essentially, the child who sees himself as responsible for his own behavior (internal locus of control) is more likely to enjoy successes in school and among his peers than one who believes that he has little to say about the events in his life (external locus of control). Brenda K. Bryant (1974) studied the attitudes of sixth-grade boys and their teachers and noted that external LOC boys had attitudes that were considerably more negative than those of the internal LOC boys. The external LOC boys were more likely to feel that their teachers misunderstood them, got on their nerves, let them down, blamed them, confused them, and created difficulties for them. In contrast to the internal LOC boys, external LOC boys were also inclined to be very critical of themselves. The teachers, for their part, also admitted that external LOC boys gave them more trouble than the internal LOC boys.

Another study suggests that some of the prob-

lems of external LOC students are caused by their approach to their work. A computer analysis of the strategies used in working on a verbal-ability test indicated that internal LOC students used their time in a way that was systematically related to the difficulty of the items, whereas external LOCs spent as much time on easy items as they did on hard ones (Gozali, et al., 1973).

The work on locus of control is consistent with the observations we made in Chapter 6 about the crucial role that feelings of discouragement play in problem behavior. The external LOC individual not only is discouraged about himself and his relations with others, he also approaches his work with the expectation of failure. Consequently, he does not try to answer questions or uses random methods that are bound to fail.

The Influence of Anxiety on Learning

Although there are a number of theories regarding the nature of anxiety, psychologists generally agree that arousal and tension play an important part. Moderate levels of anxiety seem to facilitate general effectiveness. After all, we are better able to attend to problems when we are aroused and alert than when we are drowsy or apathetic. At high levels of anxiety, arousal and tension are at such a peak that we are more likely to be concerned about our own state of disturbance than we are about dealing with tasks or problems.

The use of the term "anxiety" is often confusing because, as Charles D. Spiegelberger (1966) has pointed out, the same term is used to refer to both a trait of personality and a state. Psychologists are using the term in its trait sense when they refer to "high-anxiety" or "low-anxiety" individuals. A high-anxiety individual is one who is consistently keyed up, who tends to be in a relatively high state of tension and arousal. A low-anxiety individual, conversely, is one who is characteristically slow to react, is very relaxed, and is not easily aroused. Most of us, of course, would fall into the middle between these two extremes.

Anxiety is also used to refer to responses to a specific event. Some situations generate considerable anxiety because they are more threatening or merely because they are more complex or confusing. Situations that are reassuring or are simple and unconfused produce little anxiety. In situations that characteristically are anxiety arousing, individuals in the high-anxiety category may find themselves so upset that they are less effective than usual, whereas low-anxiety individuals in the same situation may find the higher level of arousal beneficial.

In one experiment, subjects were asked to fill out a brief, four-item questionnaire describing "how you feel right now" at four points during the experimental session: at the very beginning; after they had finished a difficult, complex task; after they had finished an easy task; and at the end of the session, after a three-minute period in which they did nothing. The results indicated that the highest levels of anxiety were reached during the complex-task period and that the lowest levels were attained during the easy-task period (O'Neil, Spiegelberger, and Hansen, 1969).

Anxiety may furthermore be explained in terms of the energy-system model of behavior we mentioned earlier in this chapter, as well as in Chapters 2 and 6. Input leads to arousal; the more input, the higher the arousal. If the system becomes overloaded with input and has more than it can handle, transformation processes cannot function normally and efficiently, and responses tend to become less effective. A high-anxiety person is one who is more sensitive to the stimuli in his environment. He is in a relatively high state of arousal because there is more input, more transformation, and more response. A low-anxiety person tends to disregard potentially relevant stimuli. There is less input, less transformation activity, and less response.

Let us examine a number of everyday situations in the light of these general principles.

A student who rates high on trait anxiety is likely to feel powerless when teachers make demands on him. Such demands raise his input level and he functions less efficiently. Consequently, he sets up defense against the demands. He may, for example, say that there is no point in trying because he is going to fail anyway. He may even engage in activities that are sure to produce failure in order to prove that he was right. These "self-fulfilling prophecies" have the effect of preserving the individual's psychological defense and of reducing his level of involvement. Students who are characteristically low-anxiety individuals may also have defenses. They may enjoy nonstressful activities and will resist teachers' attempts to get them involved.

Students with very high- or very low-anxiety levels are sources of problems for teachers because anxiety and learning are intimately associated. Attention is basic to all forms of problem solving and learning, as B. R. Bugelski (1956) has pointed out. Attention may result from any number of motives—desire for reward, desire to escape punishment, curiosity, or whatever. Basic to attention is anxiety. The task of the teacher, Bugelski maintained, is that of creating the proper level of anxiety. The problem of deciding how much anxiety is a difficult one because too much anxiety will create a need to avoid the learning situation and too little anxiety will result in a lack of attention. One way of creating the desired level of anxiety, Bugelski (1964) suggests, is by arousing the student's curiosity—because curiosity is a disguised form of anxiety. Children tend to be curious about forms of endeavor in which they have had some initial successes. Therefore, says Bugelski, make certain that the student's first experience in a new area is a successful one.

As we indicated in an earlier discussion, a great deal of learning takes place because individuals seek to avoid or reduce anxiety. This is particularly true of the learning that occurs within the context of social situations. Children learn to modify and control their behavior in order not to offend and disappoint parents, playmates, and other people who are important to them. Even those skills classified as "intellectual" are learned, at least in part, as a means of reducing or avoiding anxiety. In other words, many children learn to read partly because all their friends are learning to read, and they do not want to experience the anxiety of feeling different or left out of the group. Furthermore, their parents and teachers expect them to read, and they do not want to disappoint these powerful adults whose good will is so important to their well-being.

On Being Normally Anxious

The term "normal anxiety" is sometimes applied to anxiety at moderate levels, particularly anxiety that promotes the acquisition of social skills and helps to smooth out interpersonal relationships. Individuals who characteristically function at a very low level of anxiety tend to be careless of the rights and feelings of others and to ignore the long-range implications of their behavior. They are likely to be self-centered, to have poor control of their impulses, and to be preoccupied with obtaining immediate satisfactions. With regard to these individuals it may be said: "They want what they want when they want it." Most children learn to develop some degree of normal anxiety that has a socializing effect on them and that promotes self-control and self-restraint, as well as the willingness to engage in activities that have long-range outcomes, but some do not.

However, all children who display selfish and shortsighted behavior are not necessarily devoid of anxiety. Many are victims of too much anxiety—"neurotic anxiety." Children who are troubled by an overabundance of anxiety have difficulty in making progress in learning tasks that are important or necessary if they are to meet their basic needs adequately and are to grow toward emotional, social, and intellectual maturity. Such anxiety, as we have noted previously, leads us to develop patterns of behavior that are not in our best interests. For example, the student who takes an examination in a state of heightened anxiety is likely to misinterpret or misread test questions, forget important facts, and produce a test paper that does not reflect his true level of competence or ability.

What seems to stimulate the most effective learning is anxiety in the middle ranges. F. N. Cox (1960) administered tests of anxiety to fifth-grade boys in Melbourne, Australia, and divided them into three groups representing high, middle, and low anxiety. The middle-anxiety group's academic performance was significantly better than that of the other two groups. The poorest performance was that of the high-anxiety group.

Other research in this field brings out some interesting if somewhat puzzling relationships between anxiety and learning. Apparently, a high level of anxiety aids the learning of simple material but interferes with the learning of complex material. Evan W. Pickrel (1958) found that persons scoring high on a test of "manifest anxiety" were able to solve problems with only a few alternative solutions faster than a group scoring low on the same test. However, when the performance of the two groups was compared on a series of more complex tasks that involved a great number of alternatives, the "low-anxiety" subjects did better than the "high-anxiety" group. Evidence that high-anxiety individuals have more difficulty with complex material is also provided by research conducted by Sheldon J. Korchin and Seymour Levine (1957), who found that high-anxiety and low-anxiety subjects did equally well in learning simple word associations, but that low-anxiety subjects did better in learning a series of "false equations," a more complex kind of task. The difference in learning rate between the two groups is presented in Figure 9-5.

What the research on the effects of anxiety on learning means for the teacher is not easy to say. There does seem to be little doubt that if students are to learn, some minimal level of anxiety is desirable, but the teacher who continually finds it necessary to raise the anxiety level of his class may be creating more problems than he solves.

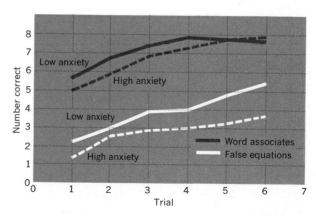

FIG. 9-5. Learning curves of high-anxiety (HA) and low-anxiety (LA) subjects on easy tasks (word associations) and difficult tasks (false equations) (Korchin and Levine, 1957).

Although a minimum of anxiety appears to be desirable as a spur to learning, most teaching problems stem from a superabundance of anxiety rather than a lack of it. There are many conditions in modern living that aggravate and intensify anxiety: the emphasis on competition, the importance of increasing one's social status, the separation of families, and the general inability that many people experience in trying to live according to their own ideals and standards. As parents and teachers develop increased feelings of anxiety as a result of these everyday pressures, they communicate these feelings to children. Some students are psychologically strong enough to resist the effects of an atmosphere that is laden with anxiety; others are not. The role of the teacher in dealing with the anxiety of the students in his classroom is a difficult one for a variety of reasons, not the least of which are his own problems of living in an age of anxiety. This is one reason why teaching makes such demands in the way of sensitivity to the needs and problems of students. The effective teacher is one who is able to sense the level of anxiety in his classroom and take steps to reduce it, make allowances for it, channel it into positive behavior, or perhaps even raise it somewhat, according to the needs of the moment. Anxiety is, however, a relatively unstable element, and its course of development, once initiated, is rather unpredictable. Like a fire in the woods, it is easier to start than to control.

SUMMARY

"Cognitive" refers to behavior in which there is some degree of awareness, as in thinking and problem solving. "Affective" refers to behavior that involves feelings, emotions, and attitudes. Both cognitive and affective factors enter into school learning, and it is often difficult to distinguish between them because much learning, particularly incidental learning, takes place beyond the limits of ordinary awareness. School progress is apparently facilitated when a teacher or other authority figure gives learners special attention; the fact that they respond favorably to this treatment suggests that the need for attention may be an important one. Recognition, attention, and encouragement as usually applied by teachers are forms of extrinsic rewards, which are not as effective as intrinsic rewards. One of the factors that interfere with our ability to help students find more intrinsic rewards in the learning situation is the necessity to provide education on a mass basis.

Two of the systems frequently used to classify what students are expected to learn are Gagné's *Conditions of Learning* and Bloom's *Taxonomy of Educational Objectives*. Both of these systems proceed from the very simple to the complex. Gagné's system begins with classical conditioning and ends with problem solving, whereas Bloom's taxonomy begins with knowledge and information and culminates with evaluation. Gagné's system is more useful in the learning laboratory, whereas Bloom's taxonomy is applicable to curriculum building. The discussion in this text is based on a three-fold system: (1) skills and information, (2) concepts, and (3) attitudes and values. Skills and information are learned in an interactive fashion: Need for information stimulates the development of skills, and the exercise of skills yields information. The distinction traditionally made between skills and information is artificial. Although they can be measured separately for administrative purposes, we use and develop them in integrated form, especially in conceptual systems. Although the subjects in the conventional school curriculum have some conceptual unity, they are nevertheless artificial segments of material that are usually organized and presented without reference to students' needs or experiences. The attitudes and values that students learn may provide some meaning to the material they learn. Teacher behavior has a significant effect on students' attitudes. Unfortunately, the attitudinal or psychological climate of the classroom tends to deteriorate in the later elementary school years and in secondary school.

Sex differences in attitudes, either inborn or learned, lead boys to have more difficulty with reading and girls to have more difficulty with complex problem-solving. Some studies suggest that these differences may be largely attitudinal. Again, students tend to view their teachers as models for the kinds of attitudes they develop.

In general, learning proceeds more effectively if material is presented in meaningful wholes instead of in segmented parts. It is not always easy to determine what a "meaningful whole" is because what is "meaningful" and "whole" for a teacher may not be "meaningful" and "whole" for students. Meaningfulness can be best introduced by relating material to everyday experiences.

Personality factors have a significant effect on learning at all levels. Research shows that personality traits and patterns are related to varying degrees of success in different subject-matter fields. There are also a number of traits that are positively correlated with school success in general. Although the question of whether there is such a thing as "readiness to learn" is somewhat controversial, there seems to be little doubt that students' attitudes toward themselves and their environment have a significant effect on their willingness to engage in learning activities. Students whose locus of control is external have more difficulties in their school work and with their teacher than do those whose locus of control is internal.

Apparently some degree of anxiety is needed for learning to take place. Although some research indicates that anxiety acts as a spur or drive that stimulates learning, other studies show that it has a highly variable effect and may even interfere if too high. Most teaching problems result from too much anxiety rather than from too little. Because anxiety is so much a part of everyday living, it is an ever-present factor in the classroom. Dealing with anxiety makes great demands on the professional skill of the teacher.

Suggested Problems

1. When Scott came home from school, he was almost bursting with wonderful news. Although he was only a first-grader, some of the second-grade boys had let him play marbles with them and had taken some time and trouble to teach him the rules of the game. In what way is Scott's learning related to his basic needs? In what way might it also be the result of normal anxiety?

2. The statement endorsed by Bruner (1960) that children can learn any concept that adults can learn and also learn it more efficiently seems somewhat outrageous. It is easier to refute such a statement than support it. Nevertheless, there must be some basis for making this claim. What evidence can you find, based on your own experience and/or research data, which suggests that Bruner's contention may have some degree of validity?

3. In reading over the curriculum for the fifth grade, Miss Hartwick notes that she is expected to develop a unit on the voyages of Columbus sometime around Columbus Day, October 12. What are some of the things she can do to see that children develop desirable concepts and attitudes from this experience?

4. Alfredo is supposed to start his first year of Latin, now that he is a high-school sophomore. You as the Latin teacher know, however, that there is no point in his starting it if he is not "ready." How might you go about determining his readiness for Latin?

5. Sue is planning on going to Mexico next summer, so she has decided to learn to speak and read Spanish. She has copied a list of "Five Hundred Commonly Used Spanish Words" out of a grammar and is attempting to commit them to memory. What assumptions is she making about the nature of learning? What principles of learning is she observing or violating?

6. Carlos makes the same mistake over and over in multiplying two or more digits, in spite of the fact that you have spent much time showing him how to do it correctly. He seems intelligent enough—he reads as well as the other children in the class. Without making any guesses for the moment as to his home background, what hypotheses might you develop about his learning problem?

7. Bill has trouble when he comes to bat at baseball. When he is off by himself, he can make nice clean wide swings, but when he comes to bat, he grasps the bat too close to the middle and makes a short, choppy swing that usually misses when it does not pop-up the ball into the pitcher's waiting glove. How do you account for his inability to transfer his learning from the practice situation to the actual playing situation?

Suggested Readings

Beatty, W. H., and Clark, R. A self-concept theory of learning: A learning theory for teachers. In H. C. Lindgen and F. Lindgren (eds.), *Readings in educational psychology,* 2nd ed. New York: Wiley, 1972.

Bloom, B. S. (ed.), *Taxonomy of educational objectives. Handbook I: Cognitive domain.* New York: McKay, 1956. A classification and description of cognitive goals that might reasonably be expected in school.

Bruner, J. S. *The process of education.* Cambridge: Harvard University Press, 1960. See the chapter on "readiness for learning," which contains his highly controversial proposals.

Dewey, J. *Interest and effort in education.* Boston: Houghton Mifflin, 1913. A brief but penetrating treatment of the problem of motivation.

Kratwohl, D. R., Bloom, B. S., and Masia, B. B. *Taxonomy of educational objectives. Handbook II: Affective domain.* New York: McKay, 1964. Classification and description of affective goals, such as attention and attitudes, that might reasonably be expected in school.

Levitt, E. E. *The psychology of anxiety.* Indianapolis: Bobbs-Merrill, 1967. (A paperback.) A survey of current concepts. See particularly the chapter on anxiety and learning.

Mager, R. F. *Developing attitude toward learning.* Palo Alto, Calif.: Fearon, 1968. (A paperback.) This book "is about a universal objective of instruction—the intent to send students away from instruction with at least as favorable an attitude toward the subjects taught as they had when they first arrived. It is about the conditions that influence this attitude, about how to recognize it, and about how to evaluate it."

Rubin, L. J. (ed.). *Life skills in school and society.* Washington: Association for Supervision and Curriculum Development, National Education Association, 1969. Speculates about cognitive and affective skills and their implications for the school.

Here are two pamphlets published by the Association for Supervision and Curriculum Development of the National Education Association that are relevant to this chapter:

Freeing capacity to learn.

The unstudied curriculum: Its impact on children.

10

Managing Classroom Learning

In this chapter and in Chapter 11 we discuss the learning situation primarily in terms of things done by teachers to manage, direct, and control students; in Chapter 12 we take up procedures in which students have more autonomy and in which teacher direction and control are minimized. In making this distinction we are not trying to create a "black-and-white" contrast between the two approaches, for the differences are likely to be relative, rather than absolute. We shall be somewhat critical about teacher domination of the learning situation, partly because teachers are inclined to provide more direction and control than students need, and partly because certain important kinds of learning can be accomplished more effectively when students have a greater degree of autonomy. At the same time, it is important to recognize that teachers play a vital role in creating situations that initiate and facilitate learning. It is also important to be aware of what they do that is helpful and what they do that is unnecessary or even harmful.

Are Teachers Necessary?

Some ten years ago, James S. Coleman and his associates (1966) conducted a monumental nationwide survey—the so-called Coleman Report—and reported that they could find little relationship between the achievement of students and the quality of their school, as measured, say, by the preparation of teachers. This finding has been challenged by a number of experts, largely because the variables underlying student achievement are highly complex and are not easily controlled for research purposes. The Coleman Report's findings have led to some speculation, however, that perhaps the characteristics or the behavior of teachers have little effect on students' learning. This possibility was explored by Donald J. Veldman and Jere E. Brophy (1974), who noted that the Coleman research teams employed entire schools as their unit of analysis and did not therefore concern themselves with the classroom performance of individual teachers or their students' learning gains. In order to determine what effect, if any, teachers have on student achievement, Veldman and Brophy analyzed the test scores of students of one hundred fifteen second- and third-grade teachers over a period of four consecutive years. Their results showed that individual teachers tended to perform in consistent ways. In other words, a teacher whose students made better-than-average gains in a given year was likely to elicit better-than-average gains from her students in other years, and a teacher whose students made poorer-than-average gains in a given year was likely to produce similar results in other years with other classes. These measures of teacher consistency also held up when schools in poverty areas were examined separately from other schools.

The findings of the Veldman-Brophy study are consistent with the common-sense view that teachers *do* have an effect on students' accomplishment, and that teachers differ in their ability to get results. To say that teachers are able to produce learning in students does not, however, negate the observations we have made elsewhere in this book, namely, that learning in the classroom may occur in spite of the teacher rather than because of him, that much of what students learn is acquired outside of school, and that teachers cannot force unwilling students to learn. These observations were made to

support the view that students should be the central concern of the educational process, but this does not mean that the teacher is not important or that student learning would be unaffected if teachers were replaced, say, by caretakers or uninvolved observers.

TEACHERS AS MANAGERS

The Teacher as a Model

Because the teacher is an essential ingredient in the educational process, there are some reasons for focusing on his role. One of the chief reasons for the existence of the schools is our general concern that the knowledge and values of our civilization be transmitted to the younger generation. The teacher becomes a key figure in this concern: He is, in effect, the representative of society who has been charged with the transmittal of this knowledge and these values. In his role as representative of adult society, he serves as a model for the learning of a wide range of behaviors and attitudes. Some of this modeling may be done consciously, but most of it occurs outside the ordinary limits of awareness because it is usually incidental to what the teacher considers to be the main business at hand.

The behavior of a model can have reassuring or discouraging effects. In one experiment, college girls who were afraid of snakes watched another girl's behavior toward a snake. In one-half the trials the behavioral model showed fear; in the other one-half she showed no hesitation in approaching and touching the snake. After she had observed the model, each subject was asked to approach the snake to the point where she felt uncomfortable. Results showed that students who had observed the unafraid model came much closer to the snake, and some even touched it (Geer and Turteltaub, 1967). Everyday classroom situations are not likely to involve snakes, of course, but the principle is still the same. The teacher's willingness to approach and to cope with difficult problems encourages some students, who then serve as models for the more reluctant ones. Conversely, if the teacher holds back and exhibits repugnance and distaste, few students will become involved in the task at hand.

The Teacher as a Psychological Weathermaker

Teachers also play important roles in determining the kind of social climate that will prevail in their classrooms. In Chapter 8, we cited the classic study by Lewin, Lippitt, and White (1939), who demonstrated how the behavior of children can be modified in very consistent ways by the kind of leadership displayed by the adult in charge. A study that confirms their findings is one by Herbert J. Wahlberg and Gary J. Anderson (1968), who administered achievement tests in physics to more than two thousand high-school students throughout the United States and asked them to describe the climate and the interpersonal relations in their classes. Tests given early and late in the term showed that those students who grew the most in science understanding were more likely to report that their physics classes were organized and operated democratically, with little friction among fellow students. The climate prevailing in the classrooms appeared to have a considerable effect on students' enjoyment of laboratory work in physics and their willingness to recognize its value. Students who engaged in the greatest amount of physics activities reported also that they had close, friendly relations with class members and were not strictly controlled by their teachers.

The teacher's personal qualities have a great deal to do with the kind of climate he creates. Morris L. Cogan (1954) surveyed junior high school students in thirty-three different classrooms and found a significant and positive relationship between the warmth and friendliness of the teacher and the amount of work, both self-initiated and required, done by students. Cogan considered the amount of self-initiated work performed by a student as an index to the degree of similarity between his values and those of the teacher. When students undertake self-initiated work, they are in effect adopting the teacher's values as their own. The importance of getting students to do this is demonstrated by a study by Haron J. Battle (1958), who compared the personal values of six high-school teachers and their forty-eight students. He found that students with the highest achievement had attitudes and values more like those of their teachers, whereas students with low achievement had attitudes and values that differed.

The Teacher as a Question-poser

The questions that teachers pose may also have a significant effect on student learning. In one study, researchers recorded on tape five consecutive classroom sessions of twelve high-IQ classes. Analyses of the recorded interaction showed that teachers were able to stimulate creative thinking in students by asking questions that encouraged speculation, guessing, exploration of ideas, and other heuristic behaviors, that is, questions that could not be answered by specific information or "what the book says" (Gallagher and Aschner, 1963). Unfortunately, most of the questions that teachers ask tend to focus on "what the book says."

Ned A. Flanders (1970) notes that more than two-thirds of all teacher questions are concerned with narrow specifics and have only one possible answer. When a team of six researchers observed two fourth-grade teachers ninety minutes a day over a two-week period, they found that the teachers showed a decided preference for "narrow factual questions, emphasizing recall: what, where, when?" over "broad, open questions which clearly permit choice in ways of answering." In spite of the fact that the students were above average in their acceptance of both teachers and schoolwork, one teacher posed one hundred three narrow, specific questions, in contrast to only thirteen broad, open ones, and the score for the other was seventy-nine to thirteen.

The kinds of questions teachers ask not only serve as stimuli for learning responses, but they also indicate to students what is important. Specific questions suggest that only isolated facts are significant, whereas broad questions suggest that knowledge is both broad and complex, and that facts are interrelated. It can be argued, of course, that teachers who prefer narrow, specific questions are protecting students from failure by making it easy for them to succeed. But, a strategy of this kind succeeds only at the risk of discouraging heuristics, originality, and self-directed learning.

Closed and Open Systems

Although there is ample evidence that the teacher is an essential ingredient in the educational process, we should resist the temptation to magnify his importance and to minimize the importance of the learner. A teacher-centered approach to teaching-learning leads the teacher to become preoccupied with what he does or is going to do and to be only minimally concerned with students' learning problems or how their behavior could be modified to encourage more effective learning. Traditionalists tend to be preoccupied with *teaching* rather than with *learning.* This makes for a *closed* system based on the assumption that as long as a properly educated teacher is in charge, the problem of providing adequate education for youth has been solved and no further questions need be raised. The approach of the educational psychologist is that of keeping the question of education *open* for further investigation. The educational psychologist, being concerned primarily with learning, is continually raising questions as to the kind and amount of learning that is taking place and even whether *any* learning is taking place.

The modern teacher or educational administrator, taking his cue from the psychologist, is continually raising questions about learning: whether it is taking place, how much and what kind is taking place, whether it can be improved and facilitated by different teaching methods, and so forth. Continual inquiry of this sort requires an open situation—one that can be explored and investigated at any time. It is this concern about learning that leads the psychologist and the educator of today to center their concern on the learner. Teachers and teaching are a matter of concern only to the extent that they affect learning. There is, furthermore, a considerable body of research that indicates that learning proceeds more effectively if the learner takes a major

share of the responsibility for his own learning and participates actively in the making of decisions about his own learning. We shall be reviewing some of this research in this and subsequent chapters. This approach is quite different from the educational arrangement preferred by the traditionalists, in which the responsibility for learning and for making decisions about learning is entirely in the hands of the teacher.

None of this shift in emphasis means that the teacher is in danger of becoming an unimportant figure in the modern educational scene. As we have tried to show, he is a very powerful figure because he has the ability to stimulate or prevent learning. The problem is not that of finding ways to restrict, harass, or eliminate the teacher but that of finding ways whereby he can become more effective.

TEACHERS' EXPECTATIONS AND STUDENTS' BEHAVIOR

The "Pygmalion Effect": An Elusive Phenomenon

We have indicated that teachers' attitudes have a pervasive effect, for they can influence the psychological climate of the classroom, as well as students' attitudes toward the material that is assigned. It would seem logical to assume that teachers' attitudes toward specific students would also have some influence. It is also obvious that a student is likely to be handicapped if his teacher does not like him, or that he has a better chance to succeed if his teacher is friendly, but how much influence *does* a teacher have? Can teachers get a student to overachieve by raising their expectations of what he can do, and can they cause him to underachieve by lowering them? Just how responsive *are* students to teachers' beliefs about them?

These intriguing questions were explored by Robert Rosenthal and Lenore Jacobson (1968) in a study that has become famous in and out of the education profession. The book reporting their results, *Pygmalion in the Classroom,* has become a bestseller. The researchers set the stage for their experiment by telling the teachers in an elementary school that certain of their pupils had been identified by a special test as "late bloomers," who possessed the potential for making an "academic spurt" in the near future. Unbeknownst to the teachers and the pupils, however, the selection of the "late bloomers" had been made randomly. Testing done at the end of the school year showed that the "late bloomers" had made gains in IQ that were considerably greater than chance would lead one to expect. The difference was especially marked in the first and second grades, where about half the "late bloomers" gained twenty or more IQ points, in contrast to only about a fifth of their fellow classmates who made similar gains. The researchers explained gains as resulting from the behavior of the teachers, who somehow communicated their expectations to the "late bloomers." These expectations, in turn, were alleged to have had an encouraging effect on the "late bloomers" who came to expect more of themselves and "blossomed" accordingly.

The study attracted a great deal of attention, partly because it seemed a clear-cut demonstration of "teacher expectancy," otherwise known as the "Pygmalion effect," after the character in Greek mythology whose ardent longings caused a statue of a beautiful young woman to come to life. The experiment has been of special interest to educators who work with disadvantaged children, for, if the results are valid, the poor academic performance of these children could well be a reverse "Pygmalion effect"—the result of the pessimistic attitudes of their teachers. If these teachers could be led to expect more positive results from their students, the Rosenthal-Jacobson study seems to say, the children would perform accordingly.

Subsequent research has, unfortunately, indicated that the Pygmalion effect is very elusive and, if it exists at all, is probably more complex than Rosenthal and Jacobson's explanation of it.[1] Most re-

---

[1] Lee J. Cronbach (1975) has stated that he has no doubt that there are teacher expectancy effects in classrooms, but that the Rosenthal-Jacobson study does not provide believable evidence for the phenomenon because it "merits no consideration as research." Like other critics, Cronbach considers the study to have been done in a grossly unscientific manner.

searchers have simply been unable to duplicate the effect, one of the problems being that many teachers these days apparently pay little heed to children's intelligence test scores (Grosswald, 1970). Rosenthal himself attempted to replicate the study by telling teachers of grades 1 to 6 in a predominantly black inner-city school that certain of their pupils had unusual potential for creativity. Evaluations of children's drawings made eight months later indicated that the "late bloomers" in only one of the grades had spurted ahead of their peers in creativity, a gain that was also accompanied by a significant increase in IQ (Rosenthal, Baratz, and Hall, 1974). The results are made all the more puzzling by the researchers' findings that teachers had treated the "late bloomers" more negatively than the other children.

In spite of these confusing and contradictory results, the principle that students tend to respond as their teachers expect them to seems to be psychologically sound. Jere E. Brophy and Thomas L. Good (1972) reviewed the original Pygmalion study and its replications, including an experiment of their own, and concluded that teachers' perceptions of students' ability can affect students' performance. In their 1970 study, they asked first-grade teachers to rank the children in their classes according to their views of each child's potential. The teachers were then observed to see how they treated the children at the top of their list (the highs) and those at the bottom (the lows). An analysis of the observations indicated that the teachers unwittingly reinforced more of the correct answers of the highs than those of the lows, did more rephrasing of questions for the highs, and also gave the highs more hints. Brophy and Good concluded that each teacher was, in effect, enacting a "self-fulfilling prophecy," for she reinforced the children in accordance with her expectations for them, and the children in turn responded in ways that confirmed the expectations that the teacher had communicated by her mode of reinforcement. As a result, the performance of children perceived by teachers as having promise was enhanced, wheras the performance of children perceived as lacking promise was depressed.

It is hard to say how much of a student's performance is affected by his teacher's expectations. Undoubtedly, the amount varies from student to student and from teacher to teacher. The fact that expectations are often communicated by subtle nuances in behavior that are difficult to measure makes the Pygmalion effect difficult to identify in an ongoing classroom situation. We should also take into account the extent to which a child influences his teacher's expectations by his own attitudes and behavior. As a consequence, it is easy for a teacher to be pessimistic about a child who is discouraged and who expects only failure for himself, and to be optimistic about a child who is self-confident and has an internal locus of control.

Student Norms Versus Teacher Expectations

Students' self-perceptions are only one of the many elements that enter into our attempts to arrange the learning situation in ways we believe will be of the most benefit to students. Even when we believe that we are adapting curricula and developing teaching methods in consideration of the needs of children and youth, we are prone to overlook the possibility that our concepts of their needs may be quite different from the needs that they perceive, for we tend to confuse *psychological* with *normative* needs (see Chapter 2). In other words, without being aware of it, we are interpreting our observations of the behavior of children and youth to mean that they should have the kind of educational expriences we think are necessary. Thus a specialist in foreign languages might decide that the inability of America's representatives abroad to converse in any other language than English means that children "need" to begin the study of foreign languages earlier than they ordinarily do. Or a county grand jury studying the increase in juvenile delinquency may conclude that what some high-school students "need" more than anything else is to attend a special class for disciplinary cases. In both situations, adults have come to their conclusions with honesty and sincerity, but instead of reporting children's needs *as experienced by children,* they have instead given us an *adult interpretation* of children's needs. To be

sure, any interpretation that an adult makes of children's needs is going to be colored by some kind of bias, even if the adult is a child psychologist, and the task of keeping this bias at a minimum is always with us. However, it *is* possible to test the validity of our findings by discussing them with trained and experienced observers and by testing them through research.

The problem of resistance to classroom learning takes on certain aspects of group phenomenon from the upper elementary grades onward through college. David Riesman speaks of the way in which students defend themselves against teachers' demands by setting norms or standards that determine how much a student can learn or the extent to which he can cooperate with teachers without being considered a "teacher's pet," a "ratebuster," or a "square." He points out that many students are on guard constantly against being "sold" by a teacher on the value of a concept or a subject. Such students see a danger in liking a teacher too much or becoming close to him in any way because such a relationship makes it difficult to resist the demands and expectations for learning that teachers are likely to make. The better the teacher, the more apprehensive students are, says Riesman, because an effective teacher is likely to make more demands on students and thus make it difficult for them to resist learning (Riesman, Jacob, and Sanford, 1959). Some research by Ned A. Flanders and Sulo Havumaki (1960) supports the idea that teachers can be influential by using the "divide-and-conquer" technique, but such an approach runs the risk of building up greater resistance. In many classrooms a kind of vicious circle of interaction develops, in which a dominant, friendly, and successfully influential teacher focuses on a few individual students, achieves some successes, and feels rewarded. But when resistance starts to build up in the class, the teacher is likely to become somewhat less friendly and assert his authority. This, in turn, increases the resistance of the class.

Although resistance to learning is an immature form of behavior, in the sense that it operates to inhibit students' intellectual growth and development, it is nevertheless a very real factor in the relationship between teacher and student, particularly from preadolescence onward. Ordinarily, when teachers encounter the negative attitudes that characterize resistance, they are likely to take them personally, not recognizing that they are a natural outgrowth of the kind of relationship that has developed between adults and adolescents in our society. Such attitudes constitute a problem that must be understood and dealt with objectively as a way of facilitating the learning process, just like any other problem that is characteristic of the stage of development the learner is going through.

What Teachers' Anxiety Does to Their Perceptions

We have said much about the effect that anxiety has on learners and learning but little about its effect on teachers and teaching. Teaching is a highly exposed affair; every teacher operates under the direct scrutiny of the students in his classroom, as well as the indirect observation of administrators, community, and parents. Few professional workers are "on stage" as much as teachers are. One inevitable consequence of this exposure is anxiety. The most effective teachers keep this anxiety well under control and actually use it as a stimulus to promote their best efforts. The least effective teachers are those who are either untouched by anxiety or are completely disorganized by it. The best that can be said for anxiety is that it makes teaching stimulating and interesting; the worst that can be said is that it induces teacher fatigue and leads teachers to behave in ways that are defensive or even somewhat neurotic.

An example of what this exposure does to less-experienced teachers is provided by an interesting experiment conducted by Linda Beckman (1970). She arranged a situation in which women student teachers were led to believe that they were teaching mathematical concepts to children who were observing them through a one-way mirror. Each teacher did four presentations of five minutes each. After each presentation, the "children" did a set of problems. The "children's" responses were rigged in such a way that performance (1) started out as

excellent and then deteriorated; (2) started out as poor and then improved; (3) started out as excellent and remained excellent; or (4) started out as poor and remained poor. When the teachers were asked to explain the children's performance, they tended to credit the improvement in some children to their teaching and to blame the deterioration in performance of others on the conditions (the artificiality of the one-way screen, not being able to see the students, and so forth) under which the experimenter required them to teach. Even when the teachers tended to blame their teaching for the deteriorating performance, they were inclined to say something like "Yes, my teaching was responsible, but these conditions made it impossible for me to teach effectively." In other words, under stress of anxiety, teachers were inclined to take personal credit for student successes and to blame the situation for student failures.

Another source of teacher anxiety is the fear that students will not learn what we are supposed to be teaching them. The posing of questions that have simple, specific answers is one reaction to this anxiety. Instead of creating situations that will permit and encourage learners to find answers for themselves and to become self-directive, we are likely to arrange highly artificial situations that enable us to direct and control student behavior in such a way that we get the responses we want. We become anxiously preoccupied with the responsibility centered in us as teachers and, hence, are not inclined to share any of it with students, forgetting that we cannot learn *for* them. If a student learns anything, it is because he has taken some initiative and responsibility and has learned it for himself.

Learning is a very personal experience. We cannot, therefore, "give" this experience to a student. The realization of this basic principle led Carl Rogers (1961) to deliver a provocative paper in which he questioned whether, in the final analysis, we can actually *teach* anyone anything of importance. He said:

I have come to feel that the only learning which significantly influences behavior is self-discovered, self-appropriated learning.

In a more recent statement, Rogers (1970) expressed the wish that every teacher forget that he is a teacher and instead take on the attitudes and skills of a facilitator of learning. Rogers' position is far removed from traditional or even prevailing classroom practices, although it is supported by those who favor student-centered learning. Nathaniel Cantor (1946) once said, "All genuine learning, in the final analysis, is self-education."

DIRECTING AND CONTROLLING LEARNING

Is It Guidance? Is It Manipulation? Does It Get Results?

Irrespective of *why* classrooms are more or less teacher-centered and teacher-dominated, the fact that they tend to be so oriented raises the question of what effect this has on learning. Is it desirable to have all learning activities directed and controlled—*guided,* that is—by the teacher?

After reviewing relevant research, B. R. Bugelski (1956) came to the conclusion that learning cannot occur by guidance alone. Guidance, it appears, may help if given early and in small doses but generally not in the initial phase of learning. If guidance is given when learning is well underway, it may even be harmful. The chief difficulty with guidance is that it prevents the learner from making errors. The making of errors is a very important part of the learning process because it is through making errors that the learner learns how to avoid making them. In teaching a child to skate or to ride a bicycle, Bugelski says, it is important that the child be allowed to fall. He should be protected from injury, of course, but the process of falling should occur, at least to some degree. It is only by experiencing the process of falling that the child can discover what leads to falling and how falling can be avoided.

Another term for guidance or direction of learning processes is "manipulation." The teacher who is taking full charge of a learning situation will manipulate the learner and the situation in an attempt to produce the desired learning. Manipulation implies maneuvering, direction, and control and is contrasted with methods that allow the learner the

maximum in freedom and self-direction. It may be argued that some manipulation is necessary to arrange the learning situation and to bring the learner face to face with stimulating problems. The difficulty appears to be, therefore, in the amount and kind of manipulation that is exercised.

The teacher's philosophy with respect to the desirability of guidance or direction is indicated by the extent to which he dominates classroom activities. In a teacher-centered classroom, the teacher does most of the talking because what he has to say is considered more vital than anything the students might say. In such a classroom, it is the students' duty to listen to what the teacher has to say, commit it to memory, and repeat it on command during recitation periods or in examination papers. Skills are taught by the teacher's telling, describing, demonstrating, and explaining the desired technique in a step-by-step fashion, whereupon he directs students in their attempts to master the techniques by drill, practice, and recitation. To be sure, today's practice materials are more ingenious, more interesting, and more readable than they were a generation ago, but the principle remains much the same.

In all fairness, the conditions under which most teaching takes place tend to foster teacher domination, manipulation, and intervention, rather than the development of a genuine helping relationship. Teachers not only operate in a climate of community opinion that expects them to dominate the classroom, but they also are required to dispense learning on a mass basis to classes of twenty-five, thirty-five, and even forty-five students or more. Class size is undoubtedly a factor in producing behavior that calls for frequent intervention on the part of the teacher. Jacob S. Kounin (1970) posted observers in forty-nine elementary classes ranging in size from twenty-one to thirty-nine each. Kounin found that the larger the class, the less children were involved in their work and the greater the likelihood of their engaging in "deviancy"—his term for inattentive or disruptive behavior. These findings suggest that in larger classes the teacher has less "impact" on individual students and is less able to affect their behavior.

In spite of these problems, it is possible—although not easy—to get teachers to talk less. Walter R. Borg (1972) described an investigation in which experienced teachers were trained to talk less and encourage student participation in discussion. The training was carried out by microteaching, a process whereby a trainee practices specific instructional skills in teaching a brief lesson to a small group of students. His performance is videotaped for later study and evaluation. During the training sessions, teachers were taught such techniques as redirecting the same question to several pupils, framing questions that call for longer pupil replies and that require higher cognitive processes (thinking), and seeking further clarification on the part of students. At the same time, teachers were encouraged not to repeat their own questions, answer their own questions, or repeat pupil answers.

Previous research in other classrooms had shown that teachers tend to talk about 70 percent of the time. This group of teachers was better than average. Even before special training they typically talked only 53 percent of the time. Immediately after the special training, however, their talk time was reduced even further to 33 percent. When they were followed up four months later, they seemed to be using what they had learned, for they were talking only 34 percent of the class period. But a follow-up three years later showed that they had started to slip back to their former norms, for they were now spending about 45 percent of the time in talking. In other respects, their performance in the third year was as good as or better than it was immediately after the special training. For example, they were redirecting more questions, were encouraging more thoughtful pupil answers, and were refraining from repeating their own questions, repeating pupil answers, and answering their own questions.

This study shows that teachers can be trained to dominate less and get students to participate more, but it also shows that without some kind of refresher training, teachers tend to drift back to some of their former habits. One of the "rewards" of teaching is that of being able to expound to a rapt and attentive audience, and the temptation to enjoy this reward is often irresistible.

"But Mom, I Have to Do My Homework . . ."

The problem of homework has been a source of dissension between home and school for decades, perhaps for centuries. European schools typically make heavy assignments, especially at the secondary level, and parents are expected to spend much time working with their children as tutors. The child's performance at school, as well as the work he turns in, are taken as evidence of the extent to which his family is interested in his academic progress and is willing to encourage it. Although European parents often complain about the heavy assignments schools make, they also recognize that homework gives them an opportunity to act in supportive ways toward their children.

Some American parents, especially those who have high ambitions for their children, expect teachers to assign homework and are upset if it is not assigned. Other parents are concerned about their children's having too much free time and look to homework assignments as a way of giving them something constructive to do. In neither of these instances are parents particularly motivated to be-

(Ford Button, *Phi Delta Kappan*, April 1973)

"How can I do my homework when the electric pencil sharpener conked out?"

come co-participants in doing homework assignments, however. In contrast to parents in more traditional cultures, American parents are inclined to think that it is better if a child deals with assigned problems himself. This attitude is defended on the grounds that parental assistance would weaken a child's independence.

A large number of parents, however, have attitudes that range from indifferent to negative about their children's homework. If the children complain too much about their assignments, such parents may ask teachers to scale down their demands. Their common complaint to the teacher is, "Why are you giving my child work he doesn't understand?" Some teachers, too, are reluctant to make assignments because it means that they will have to spend much out-of-class time in correcting them and recording grades.

Some school districts have developed formulas that specify how many hours of homework shall be assigned for children at various grade levels as an attempt to deal with the dilemmas posed by the conflicting demands of parents, teachers, and children.

Is homework worthwhile? The evidence is not clear. One of the characteristics of students who are vitally interested in a school subject is their willingness to spend a great deal of time outside of school exploring and studying related material.[2] Some of their most successful learning experiences will thus occur outside of class when they are pursuing their studies on their own. Because doing work outside of class is one of the earmarks of the highly motivated, eager student, however, this does not mean that we can get the same kind of results by *requiring* students to do homework. On the other hand, the student who does not study outside of

---

[2] According to parents' reports, school children who are at the top of their class spend about one hour per school day doing homework, in contrast to a half-hour per day spent by children in the bottom half of their class. It is interesting to note that students at the top of their class also spend about an hour a school day in recreational reading and an hour and a half watching television. Students in the bottom half of their class average less than a half-hour a day in recreational reading and about two and one-half hours a day watching television (Gallup, 1974).

class is probably doing very little real learning in the classroom. The dilemma here is how to get students to undertake out-of-class activities that will support classroom learning and still not arouse rebelliousness or stifle any interest they may have in learning.

The research data on the value of compulsory homework suggest that much of it is of negligible educational value. The classic study was done well over a generation ago by P. J. DiNapoli (1937). DiNapoli compared the performance of approximately six hundred children in the fifth and seventh grades of New York City schools who completed conventional homework assignments with the performance of an equal number who were given only voluntary homework based on topics agreed on by children and teacher. The conventional assignments were graded; the voluntary were not. The fifth-graders doing conventional assignments did slightly better on subsequent achievement tests than the experimental group, but the opposite was true for the seventh-graders. Other research also showed no consistent or significant relationship between the amount of homework and school achievement (Schunert, 1951; Strang, 1937). These early studies seemed to have resolved most of the issues because there has been little recent research on the topic.

Evaluation, Feedback, and Anxiety

Without evaluation of some sort, there can be little learning of any importance. In order for the learner to have any sense of accomplishment and to determine what steps he should take next, he must have some kind of information—feedback, to use the psychological term—about his performance. When evaluation requires some expertise, the teacher is probably the best person to provide the necessary feedback. Whether the teacher should also evaluate performance in instances in which the learner can find out for himself how well he has done is a somewhat controversial question. On the one hand, self-evaluation arouses less anxiety and is more productive in problem-solving situations, but on the other hand, there is the question of whether some learners would do any evaluation if left to their own de-

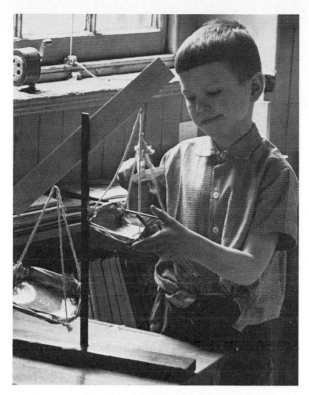

Any learning that is of any consequence is likely to involve some frustration or failure. Such experiences are most valuable when the learner discovers his own mistakes and thus attains insight that will enable him to avoid them in the future.

vices. Furthermore, the teacher who has planned and carried out the instruction in the subject is eager to find out how students performed so that he can monitor his own performance. Even though student self-evaluation has advantages, most teachers decide that it is just simpler all around if *they* do the evaluation.

A major difficulty occurs when we use tests and other forms of evaluation not only as aids to learning, but also as a means of ranking students and of making decisions with regard to success and failure. Thus many a student comes to look upon a test not as a means of finding out what progress he has made but as an instrument that may cause him to fail. Very likely much of the anxiety that students feel with regard to examinations is related to this fear of failure and feelings of inadequacy. As the

student realizes that he is being judged by the results of the test and that decisions may be made on his performance, the test may take on undue importance. But the test's importance stems from its ability to produce fear and anxiety, not from its usefulness as a learning instrument.

Like all forms of interaction between teacher and student, tests and examinations are a form of communication. Some degree of normal anxiety is perhaps needed to get the attention of the learner, but a common procedure is to inflate test-oriented anxiety out of all proportion, with the result that communication and thought processes become impaired. Thus the marks that students receive on tests are to a large degree a function of their ability to withstand stress and anxiety, whereas they ought to be an index to progress in learning. Examinations cause anxiety, too, because a great deal of education is mistake-centered. A great deal of the time and energy of the teacher is spent in preventing or correcting mistakes, and tests play a large part in his self-perceived function as a corrector of mistakes. Perhaps part of the preoccupation of teachers with mistakes comes about because teachers as a group tend to be very critical of themselves. Furthermore, they are in a profession that is exposed more than any other to public scrutiny and criticism. It is therefore understandable why they might be inclined to pass on some of the burden of this criticism to the students in their classes.

The greater the stress placed by teachers on tests and examinations and the greater the disgrace attached to mistakes, the greater the fear and anxiety that students are likely to develop. A natural consequence of this fear and anxiety is a lowering of moral standards. In Chapter 6 we mentioned research with college students showing that the courses in which the highest proportion of failing grades and the lowest proportion of superior grades occurred were also the ones in which most cheating occurred. When William J. Lodge (1951) conducted a survey of educational practices, he found excessive cheating to be the norm in classrooms where teachers were coldly formal and autocratic, whereas friendly, democratic classrooms were characterized by less cheating. He concluded that cheating was symptomatic of poor morale, caused at least in part by practices characteristic of teacher-centered, teacher-oriented classrooms.

Teacher-centered Versus Group-centered Methods

The real test of any form of educational methodology is its ability to produce results in the form of behavior changes in students. Thomas F. Stovall (1958) reviewed twenty-seven different studies that compared the results obtained with the lecture method (teacher-centered) with those obtained by the group-discussion method (group-centered). In general, the studies seemed to indicate a slight advantage for the lecture method when it came to mastery of factual material, but discussion was superior as a means of stimulating critical thinking and of aiding students in the attainment of a deeper understanding of subject matter, as reflected in the ability to make applications of newly acquired knowledge, to interpret, and to draw inferences. Furthermore, discussion had a greater effect on students' attitudes and values, as well as on their subsequent behavior.

The superiority of the discussion method in bringing about actual changes in subsequent behavior has been demonstrated in a number of studies reported by Kurt Lewin (1958) and concerned with such problems as getting housewives to use cheaper cuts of meat (during the shortages of World War II), to give their children more milk, and to give their babies orange juice and cod liver oil. Mothers who participated in group discussions were far more likely to carry out the suggested changes in diet than were mothers who listened to lectures given by experts. In one study, mothers who received twenty-five minutes of *individual personal instruction* in the use of cod liver oil for their babies were less likely to follow the suggestions of the expert than were mothers who participated in a twenty-five-minute group discussion of the problem. Betty Wells Bond (1956) also compared the value of lectures and group discussions in bringing about long-term changes in health practices relating to early detection of cancer. A follow-up thirteen months later showed that the group-discussion method was the more effective of the two approaches.

Jack A. Chambers (1973) conducted an interesting study that shows the long-range effect of teaching methods. Chambers asked a number of psychologists and chemists who had become well-known because of their creative work to name the teachers who had done the most to facilitate or to inhibit their development as scientists. When asked to describe the teachers who were facilitators, the scientists said that these teachers had strongly encouraged student participation in class discussions and had been greatly concerned about getting students to learn on their own and to do independent study. Those teachers who had had inhibiting effects, however, discouraged class discussions, did not tolerate disagreement, emphasized the memorization of materials, and deemphasized independent study.

Overdwelling and Other Dominating Habits

The teacher is just starting a reading group at the reading circle while the rest of the children were engaged in seatwork with workbooks. She sat in front of the reading group and asked, "All right, who can tell me the name of our next chapter?" Before a child was called on to answer, she looked toward the children at seatwork, saying: "Let's wait until the people in Group Two are settled and working." (Actually, most are writing in their workbooks.) She then looked at John who was in the seatwork group, naggingly asking, "Did you find your pencil?" John answered something inaudible. The teacher got up from her seat, saying, "I'd like to know what you did with it." Pause for about two seconds. "Did you eat it?" Another pause, "What happened to it? What color was it? You can't do your work without it." The teacher then went to her desk to get a pencil to give to John, saying, "I'll get you a pencil. Make sure the pencil is here tomorrow morning. And don't tell me you lost that one too. And make it a new one, and see that it's sharpened." The teacher then returned to the reading circle. This pencil transaction lasted 1.4 minutes."[3]

[3] Reprinted by permission

Jacob S. Kounin (1970) cites the above incident as an example of *overdwelling,* that is, the tendency of some teachers to dominate the clasroom in ways that not only waste time but that also increase students' apathy and passivity. In classrooms in which teacher behavior of this type prevails, there is a tendency for students to lose interest in really significant learning and to do only what is required of them. Teacher demands become viewed not as a road to intellectual growth but as something that must be yielded to in order to aviod adult disapproval. Under conditions of excessive teacher domination, most students do learn how to conform, obey, and follow directions, but they are less likely to learn heuristic methods of problem solving or concepts and skills that can be applied to situations outside the classroom.

There is some research evidence on the effect of overdwelling and related behavioral traits. Beverly I. Fagot (1973) observed teachers and preschool children during free-play periods. The classrooms in which children spent the most time doing something constructive, rather than wandering aimlessly around, following the teacher, or sitting and doing nothing, were the ones in which the teachers gave children fewer directions, criticized them less, and praised them more.

Why do teachers talk more than is necessary? One of the reasons seems to be insecurity. One study of kindergarten-primary teachers showed that the proportion of time they spent talking was negatively correlated with their morale, their enjoyment of teaching, and their satisfaction with the community support of the schools. In other words, the more the teachers talked, the poorer their morale was likely to be and the more dissatisfied they were with their work (Greenwood and Soar, 1973). Talking thus appears to have been a defense mechanism that unhappy and dissatisfied teachers used to cope with some of the tensions arising from job-related problems.

Teachers who are preoccupied with the need to dominate are also inclined to develop certain preferences with respect to the personality of students. Norma D. Feshbach (1969) asked two hundred forty student teachers to evaluate sixteen story situations that represented four different personality types. She found that they tended to prefer students who are conforming, rigid, passive, and dependent instead of those who are flexible, independent, and assertive. In interpreting her findings, Feshbach took note of research showing that teacher-training experiences tend to be stressful. As such, they are likely to be anxiety-arousing and to lead to a preoccupation with problems of classroom management and control, as well as to preferences for docility in children.

Other data that bear on this topic come from a nationwide survey of high-school students. Approximately 40 percent said that high schools are like impersonal factories; approximately 30 percent said that the atmosphere of high schools was repressive. But students were likely to take these positions when they also perceived the faculty as rejecting individuals who did not treat students as responsible individuals, did not attempt to understand them, listen to their opinions, use their suggestions, and encourage them to do their best. When faculty members were perceived as individuals who provided emotional and psychological support and attempted to deal with students without dominating them, students were much more inclined to agree with such statements as "Freedom is conditional upon the mastery of intellectual tools," a position that typically reflects the educational values of most teachers (Erlick and Starry, 1970b). These findings strongly suggest that teacher domination leads students to view the school with attitudes characterized by apathy and/or cynicism.

Getting It All Together Through Structure and Organization

As we pointed out in Chapter 9, traditional educational methods tend to interfere with transfer of learning and retention because they are based on a fractionated curriculum, a curriculum consisting of skills and blocks of information more or less isolated from one another. The teacher can readily perceive a relationship between knowing the sequence of the presidents of the United States and an understanding of the facts of United States history. For him, the presidents' names and dates serve as a handy guide or timetable. The War of 1812 is related to the presidencies of Jefferson and Madison, the building of the Panama Canal to the term of Theodore Roosevelt, and so forth. But the student who is required to commit the names and dates of the presidents to memory does not perceive these relationships. As far as he is concerned, the assignment is a relatively meaningless task that must be performed to secure the approval, or to avoid the disapproval, of adults. With reference to the research on sense and nonsense syllables that we discussed in Chapter 8, we can predict that most students who learn the names of presidents out of any context of meaning will forget them. The validity of this prediction can be checked rather easily by asking adults who were required to learn this sequence as children whether they still remember the names. If they do happen to remember any presidents' names or dates, such a memory will be the result of later associations and experiences rather than of the earlier experience of having learned the whole sequence as a memory feat. The same principle applies to any kind of material that students are required to learn out of any real context of meaning: rules of grammar, capitals of states and foreign countries, Revolutionary War generals, and so forth. Material that is learned out of any context of meaning is in effect nonsense, and the principles that apply to the learning of nonsense are applicable.

Some teachers object to learner-centered or student-participation methods of instruction because, as they point out, such classroom learning experiences may lack the organization and structure provided by the teacher in more traditional classrooms. This criticism may have some validity. It may be that in developing and experimenting with learning-centered approaches to education, teachers have been more concerned about giving students the freedom to think for themselves than they have been in organizing and structuring the experiences of the classroom, however.

In spite of these presumed shortcomings, the available research indicates that the educational results produced by student-participation methods are in all respects either equal to or better than the results of traditional methods. Just to cite one of the many studies contrasting student participation with more traditional methods, Donald R. Green (1954) compared scores made on a cancer-knowledge test by students in twenty-eight schools of medicine. He classified the students with respect to the number of hours they spent on the following: (1) listening to instructors talk about cancer (lecture), (2) talking with others about cancer (discussion), (3) working with tumors in laboratories, (4) watching others work with patients (observation), and (5) actually working with patients. Green found that the second method (discussion) was most frequently utilized by the schools whose students had the best scores; in fact, this method accounted for the major portion of the differences found. Actual practice with patients was also a valuable method, but it was not as helpful as discussion, as far as the results of the test were concerned. The schools making the poorest showing tended to use observation without discussion and actual practice, but observation combined with discussion and actual practice was used by the best schools. Green pointed out that the superiority of schools using discussion plus actual practice and the inferiority of schools using discussion plus actual practice and the inferiority of schools relying largely on lecture were not due to the superiority or inferiority of methods alone. "Instead, the fact that a school used these methods extensively was an indication that the faculty was sufficiently interested in teaching and in their students to put in the time and effort necessary to work closely with students individually and in small groups. Such an attitude should result in superior performances."

It may be that when teachers object to lack of integration in the newer methods, they are referring to integration from the standpoint of the teacher, overlooking the fact that, in the final analysis, integration must be supplied by the student. It is the *student's* frame of reference that really counts in learning, not the teacher's. It is quite possible that the discussions of cancer in the study cited above would have seemed poorly integrated from the standpoint of a well-organized lecturer, yet they proved to be a more effective way of conducting medical training than the better-organized lectures.

The Teacher as an Autocrat

Whenever individuals become preoccupied with control and domination, they tend to use strategies that are autocratic or authoritarian. Authoritarian modes of dealing with others are characterized by attempts to dominate, direct, and set limitations to the behavior of others; they may be contrasted to modes of behavior that are democratic or egalitarian and that attempt to initiate and to maintain forms of behavior that are permissive, accepting, and supportive. There is a tendency for the interaction between persons of unequal status and power to be characterized by authoritarianism, whereas equality in status tends to produce democratic modes of behavior. The fact that the status and power of a teacher are higher than that of his students makes it easy for him to slip into authoritarian patterns of behavior. What we have been urging is a retreat from authoritarianism and a movement toward more democratic, student-centered approaches. Such a movement can occur only when teachers recognize the rights of students to have needs and motives that must be met within the educational setting. This implies that teachers consider students more as partners in the teaching-learning process and less as pawns. The fact that the teacher is generally more expert than students and is held responsible for their learning by the administration should not be overlooked, but this does not prevent a teacher from behaving democratically and reducing some of the differences in status and power that separate him from students. The extent to which a teacher is able to do this depends on many factors: the kind of person he is, what students expect of him, the psychological climate of the community, and the amount of freedom he believes he has to adapt curriculum and design his own teaching strategies.

The teaching-learning relationship cannot be described as authoritarian or democratic in absolute terms. Like other human situations, it changes from moment to moment. It is possible, however, to describe teachers' behavior in *relative* terms. In any given school, some teachers tend to behave relatively more democratically than other teachers, whereas some teachers behave in ways that are relatively more authoritarian. Furthermore, although democratic modes of teaching are more productive of heuristic learning, creativeness, and self-directed learning, we should also recognize that there are some fairly authoritarian teachers who are quite effective, viewing their work in general terms, and some fairly democratic teachers who are quite ineffective.

There are also differences in students, with respect to the way in which they respond to differences in teaching. Bruce W. Tuckman (1969) studied the interaction of teaching styles and student personality in high-school courses. Teachers included in the study were classified as being either high or low on a scale of directiveness, that is, the extent to which they used formal planning and organization, placed a premium on factual knowledge, used absolute forms of punishment, gave students little opportunity to learn from mistakes, maintained formal classrooms, and kept their relations with students on a formal basis. In other words, the directive teacher could well be characterized as authoritarian or autocratic and the nondirective teacher as democratic or egalitarian. Students in their classes similarly were classified as "concrete-dependent" (individuals who process inputs in categorical, simple, and relatively fixed ways, relying heavily on authorities and group norms to avoid confusion and ambiguity) or 'abstract-independent" (individuals who process inputs in the most flexible manner, perceiving the maximum number of alternatives in information received, and are less affected by what others think of one's approaches). Tuckman found that abstract-independent students valued nondirective teachers higher and got high grades from them. One would think that concrete-dependent students would do better with directive teachers than with nondirective, but Tuckman found no difference. In other words, nondirective teaching styles had no adverse effect on the progress of concrete-dependent students but did facilitate the learning of abstract-independent students.

Communication and Intercommunication

Alice V. Keliher (1936) once made the following comment on a finding that a three-year-old child used more than 11,000 running words per day and a four-year-old used 15,000:

> Think how the formal teacher of five- and six-year-old children stems this flood by raising her hand against speech! I marvel that young children are actually able to inhibit speech as they do for four or five hours a day; but I marvel more at the continuing stupidity of schools which thus cut off the very life-blood of the intellectual development of children.

Keliher was referring to the fact that speech—oral communication—is a tool for learning. Students who cannot communicate cannot learn. And one of the chief difficulties with teacher-oriented methods is that they block and interfere with communication. Education, as any other social process, depends on communication for its effectiveness. Unless members of a group can communicate with their leader and he with them, attempts at collaboration will lack effectiveness.

The problem is not that the teacher does not recognize the value and importance of communication. Even the most autocratic teachers are concerned about getting students to understand them. The difficulty lies in the fact that teachers are inclined to think of communication primarily as a process whereby they transmit information to students. The need for students to communicate with teachers and with one another tends to be subordinated, overlooked, or dismissed as unimportant. Teachers forget that communication, if it is to be effective, should be a two-way or at best a three-way process.

Figure 10–1 depicts various patterns of classroom interaction. Type 1 is the most traditional and is characteristic of situations in which the teacher lectures or gives orders without seeking any immediate response. Type 2 is an improvement because the teacher seeks feedback in order to determine whether what he has said has been understood. This gives him an opportunity to correct errors on his part or misunderstandings on the part of students. In Type 3, communication is improved even further because students are permitted to learn from one another, and in Type 4, even more channels for communication are opened up.

It is, of course, easy to diagram ideal communication networks for class participation but not so easy to implement them. The study by Borg (1972) that we cited earlier shows that even teachers who are well-intentioned, when it comes to talking less and involving students more, are inclined to drift back into more domineering patterns of behavior. Perhaps the answer is one of gradual reform. In every learning situation, there are channels available for two-way communication. Even in the most formal and traditional situations there are assigments, quizzes, and term papers. The problem is that neither teachers nor students recognize the channels that exist and use them effectively. The initiative is, of course, up to the teacher; it is he who has the power to let students know that they have a right to communicate, that what they have to say will be listened to, and that their queries will be answered. How teachers do this and how rapidly they move to greater student participation depends on each teacher's instructional style and the kind of situation in which he finds himself.

Arthur W. Combs (1965) described his role as a communicator and an authority figure in the following terms:

> I have often observed in my classes that communication between me and my students increases in direct proportion to the degree of "earned" authority I hold in their eyes. . . . By "earned" authority, I mean the authority my students invest in me as a consequence of their personal dis-

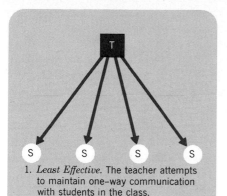

1. *Least Effective.* The teacher attempts to maintain one-way communication with students in the class.

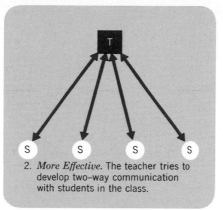

2. *More Effective.* The teacher tries to develop two-way communication with students in the class.

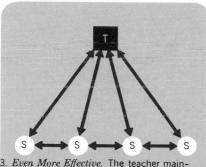

3. *Even More Effective.* The teacher maintains two-way communication with students and also permits some communication among students on a rather formal basis.

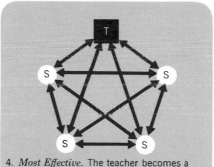

4. *Most Effective.* The teacher becomes a co-participant in the group and encourages two-way communication among all members of the group, including himself.

FIG. 10-1. Various types of communicative relationships between teachers and students, in order of their effectiveness.

---

covery of who I am, what I believe, and whether what I have to say is important. I do not have this earned authority when I meet these students for the first time. All I have is my "unearned" authority: my degrees, my reputation, and the catalog designation that I am the boss of this course. So long as these unearned authorities are in ascendance in our relationship, students hardly hear what I say. Accordingly they dutifully write things down because if they did not, they would forget them. Later, when they know me better, and if I have earned my place as teacher in their eyes, they do not bother to write much down. We do not forget what important people have to say to us.

Communication as an Essential Skill

In one sense, the basic purpose of education is the improvement of communication. The illiterate is, in effect, one who is unable to communicate adequately with his fellow-men. He cannot read; hence the past cannot communicate with him through books. Because he cannot deal with figures, he cannot communicate with others through arithmetical concepts. He has difficulty in discussing the affairs of the world and community because he has not developed a background against which to carry on such discussions. He breaks laws and rules because he is unable to understand them or, more likely, because he cannot express himself in socially acceptable ways and therefore must fall back on asocial or antisocial means. He is unable to comprehend the broad and pervasive relationships that unite him with other people; therefore he may act in ways that are self-centered and uncooperative, or in other ways contrary to the welfare of others. Because he does not understand the complexities of civilized society, he very often cannot take steps to act in his own behalf. He does not vote because he fails to see the importance of this communcative act.

Therefore, one of the most essential tasks of the school is to help future citizens to learn how to communicate. Communication includes not only the specific techniques commonly identified with communication—reading, writing, and speaking—but also learning things that are worth communicating, learning to recognize the desirability of effective communication, and learning that better communication is something worth working for. Good communication is not just a matter of learning techniques or opening up channels; it also involves the development of a generalized attitude of acceptance toward others. In a situation where good communication exists, individuals are not only concerned with finding more adequate ways in which to express themselves, but they are also willing to listen to others with sympathetic interest and attention. They recognize that communication is really a difficult task, a task that demands much, a task that must be worked at continually if better understanding is to take place. Many of the ills of the world are the result of inadequate understanding, which in turn results from poor communication, and the failure of many teachers to help students learn is the result of students not understanding teachers and teachers not understanding students.

The task of improving communication in the classroom is to a much greater extent the responsibility of the teacher than of the student. In the first place, the teacher as an educated and mature person has the greater communicative skill; in the second place, his position as the person in charge enables his to create the kind of emotional climate that will facilitate or frustrate communication. Traditional methods of education reverse the relationship to some degree, making it the responsibility of the student to understand the teacher, rather than the other way around. The teacher tells the students what is what, and it is up to them to figure out what the teacher is trying to communicate. This attitude not only leads to oversimplified ideas about the communicative process but also leads teachers to absolve themselves of any responsibility for improving their ability to communicate.

Within the last generation or so, a number of reforms have been instituted to improve classroom communication and thus make education more effective. The vocabularies of spelling lists and readers have been extensively revised to adapt their scope and content to the words actually used by children. There has also been considerable discussion of the advisability of teaching primary grades in Chinese, "black English," or Spanish, depending on the cultural background of students. Some educators believe that programs of this kind go too far, for if we limit ourselves to teaching children what they already know, how will we be able to extend and broaden their experience? The counterarguments are that we could "reach" children more effectively if we "start where they are." Information and skills learned in the primary grades are difficult enough without having to complicate them with the need to learn a new language. Furthermore, go the arguments, belonging to a deprived group is a humiliating experience, and meeting a child halfway by using his own language in communicating with him would go a long way toward building up his self-esteem.

Classroom language is also criticized on the ground that the vocabulary appropriate for the "average" child is too difficult for slow learners and too simple for the gifted. This puts us in the position of simultaneously frustrating slow learners and encouraging mediocrity in the gifted.

There are no easy answers to these dilemmas; they are problems that must be examined, resolved, and re-resolved at frequent intervals. And the perplexities of educators are not made any easier by the fact that whatever decisions are made are likely to affect relations between the school and the community and, hence, to have political implications.

The Increasing Complexity of Teaching-learning Problems

One of the lessons demonstrated here is that when we undertake the twin tasks of understanding students better and redesigning educational experience accordingly, we find that problems are not simplified but are made more complex. Hence many teachers become discouraged. Understanding students does not solve any problems, they say; it just creates new ones. Teaching is a job that is hard enough, they say, without trying to make it any harder. Therefore we should perhaps not be too critical if teachers elect to adhere to a teacher-centered, teacher-dominated approach to learning. If they do, they will have the support of most of the citizens in the community, who find it easier to understand schools that are adult-centered rather than child-centered. A number of schools, such as the Boston Latin Grammar School and some other outstanding preparatory schools, have had apparent success with teacher-centered curricula and methodology. What is usually overlooked is that such schools cater to a select minority of the population. Furthermore, it would be difficult to determine the extent to which the superior educational attainment of their graduates is due to the kind of formal education they received in school or to the informal education they received outside the classroom.

In some respects, education is where the natural sciences were a hundred years or so ago. Scientific knowledge was much simpler then, and people could, because of their ignorance, be more positive about things than we can be now. The more we learn about the world and the people who live in it, the more our certainties and easy generalizations are undermined. It is understandable how both educator and layman may often long for former days when problems were simpler and remedies more direct and drastic, but the increasing scope of our knowledge forces us to recognize that what seem to be simple problems are only the surface manifestations of complex conditions, and that direct and drastic remedies are often both inappropriate and dangerous.

Because the behavioral sciences, including psychology, deal with organisms whose behavior is infinitely more complex than the subject matter of the natural sciences, they must progress more slowly and tentatively. Nevertheless, the need for improved methods in education and other fields of applied science is so great that we cannot wait for final results, any more than physicians can afford to wait until they know all there is to know about physiological processes and virus infections. Physicians, educators, and other applied scientists need to apply the knowledge we have in order to press on to better understanding and better solutions of the problems that face us.

We as educators cannot make this kind of progress if we insist that it is neither necessary nor important to understand the children and adolescents we teach, their motivation, and the functioning of the learning processes. Nor can we make progress if we choose to ignore the fact that the attitudes and feelings of the teacher, as well as the relationship that develops between teacher and class, have an important effect on the success or failure of the educational program. And as long as we continue to make the teacher the central and dominant figure in the learning situation, we will be acting as though the understanding of the learner and his needs is unimportant, or at best, distinctly secondary to the needs of the teacher to communicate information.

SUMMARY

Although some research comparing different schools has raised a question as to whether differences in teacher's backgrounds make a difference in students' learning, studies analyzing the relationship between teacher performance and student achievement show that students do respond differentially to teachers. The teacher has an effect on students' behavior because he is a representative of society, serves as a model for behavior, creates social climates, and has a stimulating or inhibiting effect on thinking. These factors all operate to make classrooms teacher-centered, rather than learner-centered. The main problem is not to displace the teacher but to make him more effective.

Although studies of "teacher expectancy," or "Pygmalion effect," are vague and contradictory in some respects, there seems to be little doubt that teachers' expectations for individual students do have an influence on the students' cognitive development. There is a natural tendency for us to confuse pupils' needs with our own wishes. Even though such an attitude runs the risk of creating resistances to learning, teachers' anxieties about maintaining control and getting pupils to learn tend to make teachers more manipulative and less student-centered. There is some evidence that teachers can be trained to talk less and encourage more student participation, but there is also a tendency for them to drift back to their old habits after a few years. Nevertheless, such training seems to have a residual effect that is all to the good.

Although European parents accept the task of working with their children on their homework as one of their responsibilities, American parents are divided on the subject of how much homework should be assigned but tend to agree that children should do their homework without much parental help. Children who are most successful in school tend to do more homework than the less successful ones, but this does not mean that school success can be enhanced by requiring more homework. Teacher domination of the classroom is facilitated by the fact that teachers are charged with the task of evaluation and testing, a function that increases students' anxieties about learning. There is no doubt that evaluative feedback enhances learning, but evaluation as usually practiced also increases the possibility that the student will fail.

Research comparing teacher-centered with learner-centered methods indicates that the latter are more effective, particularly with respect to bringing about desired changes in behavior. Discussion methods, for example, appear to promote more effective integration of subject matter than do lecture and recitation. They can be used most effectively if teachers move from authoritarian modes of behavior to modes that are more democratic. Some learning problems may be traced to the fact that communication among students and between students and teacher is impeded. One of the reasons why some teachers talk more than they should and inhibit student participation is that they feel insecure and unfulfilled in their work. Because the need for improved methods in education is great, we should develop a better understanding of the complexities of learning and classroom behavior, but such understanding cannot make headway as long as classrooms are teacher-centered, and as long as we feel that the understanding of learners is not as important as the understanding of subject matter.

Suggested Problems

1. Think back over your own experiences in schools. Describe the classroom behavior of the teacher who you think was the most teacher-centered (or subject-matter centered) and the one who was the most student-centered.

2. What are some of the ways in which teachers can make examinations less anxiety-provoking and more helpful as learning devices?

3. Art educators have observed that children in kindergarten and primary grades are "natural artists," but that they tend to lose spontaneity and originality by the time they get to junior high. What are some of the forces and factors that very likely contribute to this change?

4. Let us say that you are about to take over a Scout troop. What are some of the things you can do to develop good communicative relationships among the members of the troop and between you and the troop?

5. Arthur W. Combs once said that good and poor teachers both know what the characteristics of a "helping relationship" are, but good teachers are able to be genuinely helpful, whereas poor teachers are not. He also said that the differences between these teachers lie in their feelings and attitudes toward themselves and others. How do you think these feelings and attitudes might differ?

6. In this chapter, Combs also described how communication in his classes improves when students perceive him as having "earned" his authority. What are some of the things you might do to "earn" your authority with students in your classes?

Suggested Readings

Dinkmeyer, D., and Dreikurs, R. *Encouraging children to learn: The encouragement process.* Englewood Cliffs, N.J.: Prentice-Hall, 1963. Suggests an approach whereby teachers can develop helping relationships with students.

Henry, N. B. (ed.). *Social forces influencing American education,* 60th Yearbook, Part II, National Society for the Study of Education. Chicago: University of Chicago Press, 1961. See particularly the chapter by Merle L. Borrowman, "Traditional values and the shaping of American education."

Holt, J. *How children fail.* New York: Dell, 1964. (A paperback.) Describes the ingenious ways that children consciously and unconsciously avoid learning demands in teacher-centered classrooms.

Kounin, J. S. *Discipline and group management in classrooms.* New York: Holt, Rinehart, and Winston, 1970. The latter part of the book deals with ways in which teachers succeed or fail to carry out their tasks in conventional classroom learning situations. Penetrating, down-to-earth, and practical.

Rogers, C. R. *Freedom to learn.* Columbus, Ohio: Merrill, 1969. (A paperback.) Rogers draws from a number of sources in presenting provocative ideas and suggestions with respect to creating educational situations that are learner-centered.

11

Discipline and the Learning Situation

Public opinion polls have found Americans in remarkable agreement year after year on what they consider to be the major educational problem: lack of discipline in the schools. Discipline is therefore felt to be more serious a problem than integration and segregation, school finances, use of drugs by students, difficulty of getting good teachers, and deficiencies in the curriculum (Gallup, 1974). In one poll, slightly more than one-half the respondents thought that discipline in the schools was not strict enough. Less than one-third thought it was "about right," and only 2 percent thought it "too strict." Approximately two-thirds felt that teachers or school authorities should be permitted to administer physical punishment to school children. Somewhat less than 40 percent of adults thought that high-school students should have more to say about school rules, a figure that contrasts with almost 80 percent of high-school juniors and seniors who felt they should have more to say about rules (Gallup, 1970).

It is important to keep this background of opinion in mind as we consider the problem of school discipline. Teachers are members of the larger society as well as professional practitioners. And they are likely to carry society's values into their work. Much of our discussion should be evaluated in relationship to that basic fact.

The Meaning of Discipline

There are three meanings that are commonly ascribed to "discipline"; hence it is not always clear what we mean when we use the word. For example, what does a teacher mean when he says: "What that boy needs is discipline"?

One common meaning is that of "punishment." In the sentence cited above, the teacher may be saying that he thinks the boy ought to be punished.

A second common meaning is that of "control by enforcing obedience or orderly conduct." If the teacher is thinking of the word in this way, he is saying that the boy should have someone direct, control, and limit his behavior, the implication being that the boy is unable or unwilling to direct, control, or limit his own behavior.

A third common meaning is that of "training that corrects and strengthens." The implication here is that the objective is *self*-discipline, that the purpose of the training is to enable the individual to do his own directing and controlling. Hence the teacher means, if he is using the word in this sense, that the boy should have experiences that will improve his self-control and make him a more self-directing individual.

The chances are, however, that the teacher does not sharply differentiate among the several meanings of the word and has all three meanings in mind. Very likely, he is thinking that if the boy is punished, and if he gets a great deal of direction and control, he will develop self-discipline. The teacher may very probably think in these terms because these are the kinds of ideas that people commonly have about discipline and its merits. Like so many popular ideas about human behavior, however, everyday concepts of discipline are based partly on sound principles and partly on wishful thinking. For example, it is true that children need control and direction, but it is improbable that they can learn self-control and self-direction if they are controlled and directed all the time and at every turn. The difficulty is that it seems to be easier for us to *enforce* controls than to help children do their *own* controlling.

Because enforcing controls is easier, we also find it easy to conclude that children can learn to control themselves through a regimen of enforced control.

Although teachers may disagree on the question of how much control and direction children should have, they are generally agreed that children should learn how to discipline themselves and thus grow up to become adults who are responsible, law-abiding, considerate of the welfare of others, and able to carry on the important responsibilities of life in the face of frustration, tempting distractions, and other difficulties. The question is: How can we help children develop these qualities?

One answer is that schools should help children develop self-discipline by teaching them such values and traditions as fair play, respect for the opinions of others, freedom to search for truth, and the right of weaker and subordinate individuals to be heard. Clarence W. Hunnicutt (1949) had reference to the teaching of such values when he made the following statement in delivering the J. Richard Street Lecture at Syracuse University a number of years ago:

> Not all our teachers have had this vision. There have been those who insist on dogmatic learning. They feel they should know all the answers and are afraid to let children explore into areas where the teacher cannot feel secure. These are likely to be the teachers who have not clearly differentiated between obedience and responsibility. They realize that their pupils are not accepting enough personal responsibility for their actions, yet at the same time they are preventing them from doing so by insisting on too strict obedience.
>
> Obedience and responsibility are contradictory. A child kept in a state of obedience to authority where he must accept the dictates of others without opportunity to test out his own ideas cannot become responsible. Only as he has liberty to make plans, to carry them out semi-independently and to see their results can he become a responsible citizen. The period from the kindergarten on through the secondary school should be a steady movement along the scale away from immature dependence upon external

control toward mature dependence upon individual responsibility. Teacher discipline gradually becomes self-discipline essential to a free democracy.

Self-discipline cannot thrive in an atmosphere of fear and rigid control. Where motivation for correct behavior is the effort to avoid displeasing some authority, children remain dependent personalities. When children have an opportunity to plan their own activities, when they help make their own decisions about the way in which they spend their time, when they learn voluntarily to subordinate some of their special self-interests to the total welfare of the group, then they are able to assume their rightful place in our culture. As a minor symptom of this growing maturity, the teacher can leave the room without the chalk beginning to fly. It is ironical that in many school systems the obvious chronology development is reversed. Children in the kindergarten, who have little maturity, characteristically have much freedom to choose their moment-to-moment activities. Yet high-school seniors with many added years of experience and presumed maturity are likely to have little voice in choosing what shall be done during a class period. They are given little chance to grow up educationally.

Self-discipline, as Hunnicutt is describing it, is one aspect of social maturity, a topic we have touched on in previous chapters when we discussed children's moral development, the shift from impulsive to reflective modes of behavior, and the change from an external locus of control to one that is internal. Hunnicutt's complaint is, essentially, that teachers become preoccupied with obedience and control and do not recognize how they can help students move in the direction of greater social maturity.

STYLES OF DISCIPLINE

Teacher-imposed Discipline

We have said that teacher-imposed control is necessary to some degree. It will certainly be needed more at some periods of life than at others. Pre-

school children playing together in a well-equipped and well-planned nursery school need very little discipline. There is little that they can destroy, and only the occasional child needs to be protected from his fellows. Elementary school children need much more control and direction because they do not know how to work and play in large groups. They are incapable, without considerable help, of creating the kind of group structure that is necessary for organized activities. By working and playing in what psychologists call a "structured situation," they learn some of the techniques and attitudes that are necessary to maintain the social or interpersonal "structure." They also learn to enjoy some of the security and stability that develops when the "structure" is largely created and maintained by the teacher. Gradually, as they learn to work and think as a group, to listen to each other and not to talk when others are speaking, and to assume some of the responsibilities of leadership, they become able to carry an increasing share of the direction and control and to create "structure" of their own.

As children become more mature, they not only develop the skills necessary for self-control and self-direction, but they also develop attitudes of preferring to work with self-disciplined groups and of wanting to develop standards of self-discipline of their own. But even when children are ready to be largely self-directing, as they are during the adolescent stage of development, there is a need for an adult to be in the background, to be used for consultation or emotional support or to be available in case of an emergency. Furthermore, the development of self-discipline and stability is not a constant, gradual growth curve, nor do children always welcome the help of adults, even when they have a pressing need for it. During the preadolescent period, for example, children often go through a "negative," rebellious stage, when they seem to delight in frustrating and annoying the adults in charge. Very often such behavior is a kind of psychological smoke screen for feelings of helplessness and uncertainty, that is, by adopting an antagonistic attitude, preadolescents try to avoid admitting to themselves that they have any need for either the control or the approval of teachers and parents.

One of the perplexing characteristics of young people, particularly during the adolescent period, is their need, on the one hand, to have someone set limits for their behavior and, on the other, to test or challenge the very limits that have been set. We often find ourselves drawn into a kind of trap because of these ambiguous and often contradictory motives. Some adults, when confronted by complaints of youngsters that limitations on their behavior are too severe, react by doing away with all or most limits. Thereupon they are appalled when young people respond to this greater freedom by actually worsening their behavior and blaming the adult in charge for what has gone wrong. On the other hand, adults who attempt to deal with this ambiguous situation by being severe, restrictive, and punitive cannot understand why some young people are so apathetic and why the behavior of others actually becomes worse.

Such experiences show that the behavior of children and adolescents cannot be handled on an "all-or-none" basis. The effective teacher is one who can allow children freedom to develop naturally and spontaneously but who can also set limits to their behavior at appropriate times. The better the morale of the group and the better the learning situation, the less need there should be to invoke limits.

The problem of the teacher with respect to discipline may be seen in terms of a problem in leadership, to which some of the findings that psychologists have made in this field may be applied. One approach to the study of leadership identifies two dimensions: *initiation of structure* and *consideration*. Leadership activities concerned with the initiation of structure include direction, control, punishing, setting limits, rewarding, manipulating, organizing, scheduling, maintaining standards, and the like. Consideration includes such behavior as extending sympathy and understanding, compromising, helping, inviting and using suggestions of group members, and being supportive. Questionnaires measuring these two dimensions of leadership have been developed and used under the direction of the Personnel Research Board of Ohio State University (Stogdill and Coons, 1957; Stogdill, 1969). Most leadership roles call for both structure

initiation and consideration, and it is generally undesirable to stress one dimension to the exclusion of the other. The relative proportions of structure initiation and consideration that should be incorporated into a given teacher's behavior will be a function of the maturity of the class, the kinds of activity undertaken by the class, the psychological climate of the school, the expectations of both teacher and students, and the personality of the teacher. Although there is no hard-and-fast rule that can be used to determine the proper proportion of these two dimensions, it is safe to say that most teachers tend to err in the direction of providing more than enough structure initiation and not enough consideration. Few teachers err in the direction of providing too much consideration. Perhaps the worst learning situations result when teachers provide *neither* structure *nor* consideration.

One of the perplexing problems in determining whether to emphasize structure initiation or consideration occurs when teachers encounter a student whose problems seem different from others in the group. Perhaps the teacher has been firmly "laying down the law" about late assignments, whereupon some student shows up with a late assignment and what appears to be a valid excuse. Furthermore, the student is a sensitive child who "overreacts" to criticism. Should the teacher emphasize the structure initiation or the consideration aspects of his role as classroom leader? Introducing structure initiation might seem harsh, but an attitude of consideration might seem weak and soft. Furthermore, is it not "democratic" to treat all students alike? If we modify our treatment of students in accordance with their apparent motivation, their background, and the kind of problems they present, are we not "making exceptions"? The comments made some years ago by Harold A. Delp (1949) are still relevant when it comes to teachers' problems today. Delp pointed out that the fear of making exceptions is in effect a form of the punitive theory of discipline. The belief that it is "democratic" to treat all cases of, say, truancy or stealing alike very likely covers up some of our more psychologically obscure reasons for wanting to punish, reasons that we would like to overlook or ignore. The more mature way of handling the problem behavior of children is to base treatment on an understanding of their problems and psychological needs and not according to some rigid, formulistic pattern. Specifically, Delp had this to say about the problem:

A child is an individual. As such, he should be treated like an individual. Regardless of his age, each child has certain attitudes of how he thinks life should go. A great absurdity in our culture is the common parental belief that when a mother calls a youngster to do some household task the youngster should immediately stop whatever activity he is doing and respond to the parent's wishes. There is no consideration of the child's own feelings, or even of his belief that his activity is much more important than that which his parent desired accomplished. Among adults it is accepted that when a request is made it be weighed in terms of the present situation and that this request be satisfied in a reasonable manner and span of time. For the child most adults deny him the privilege of this same consideration. When parents and teachers expect action it should be on a reasonable basis considering the child's point of view as well as the adult point of view. Included in any consideration of independence for both the home and school is the wise use of group pressure and group ideals. These factors can be indirectly modified and controlled in many ways to produce a healthier attitude toward independence on the part of the child.

A further comment on the controlling behavior of teachers is in order. Most teachers find it necessary to exercise controlling functions at some time or other. Aggressive and destructive behavior often has a contagious effect. As students see others violating rules, it becomes harder for them to resist the temptation to join in. Under these conditions, more aggressive students serve as models for the behavior of others, and a kind of antisocial social learning can occur, unless teachers intervene. How much intervention or control and at what point should it be administered are questions that each teacher must answer for himself. Jacob S. Kounin (1970) found, in studying what he calls "desist techniques," that no one technique was more effective than any other. Ideally, teachers should develop relationships with their classes that preclude the need to use firm desist measures. Kounin described one teacher who walked over to the light switch and flicked the lights on and off a couple of times. The children all stopped talking or working and sat in an attentive posture facing the teacher. Another teacher of the same grade tried the same technique and was ignored. It is obvious that the teacher-class relationships were different in the two classrooms.

The choice of what measures to use and when to use them will naturally depend on the psychological climate that prevails in the classroom and in the school as a whole, the degree of respect that the teacher has for students and that they in turn have for him, and the amount of disorder the teacher and class can tolerate and still make progress in the tasks of teaching and learning. Not all these variables can necessarily be influenced by the teacher. In some schools, for example, the level of hostility and disrespect for authority runs so high that more than half the teacher's time is spent in maintaining order. This is not, however, the usual situation. But there are many teachers who are unnecessarily preoccupied with control, that is, they err in the direction of providing more control than students need in order to function as effective learners.

Some research conducted with elementary teachers in Salt Lake City and suburban schools showed that teachers' insistence on control and order in their classes occurred at the sacrifice of qualities of personal warmth. Observers sat in on the class of one hundred eighteen teachers and wrote down the first utterance teachers made at the start of each minute of a twenty-five-minute period. There were four observation periods, and a total of one hundred statements was collected for each teacher. These statements were then rated by other researchers in terms of whether they indicated a concern with achievement, affiliation, control, or management. The ratings were in turn correlated with other measures of teacher behavior, including the general impression teachers made on observers. The results, some of which are shown in Table 11-1, show that teachers who were perceived as cold and controlling tended to behave toward students in ways that were perceived as punitive and rigid. Their classes were monotonous, and there appeared to be little concern with the students' academic achievement. This does not mean that a concern with control is necessarily a negative factor: Note that teachers who involve their students in much academic activity also exercise control and are systematic. The question appears to be: Control for what? The first type of teacher maintains order for its own sake, or because he finds disorder highly upsetting, whereas the second type uses control in support of a systematic program of classroom learning. Note that the insecure and anxious teacher exercises little direct control, punishes often, and is disorganized, whereas the vigorous and dynamic teacher needs to have relatively little concern with problems of control and discipline.

Punishment

Many teachers think of discipline as being synonymous with punishment, perhaps not necessarily physical punishment but punishment that is largely psychological or social in its impact: detention (keeping students after school or keeping them in the classroom during play periods), extra homework assignments, isolation (sending pupils out of the room or to the principal's office), suspension from school, humiliation (sarcasm, scolding in public), the assignment of failing marks in subject matter or in "citizenship," or giving students a "talking to" in private.

One might logically assume that punishment would operate the opposite of reward in learning situations, but this does not seem to be the case. Reward tends to reinforce a behavior, that is, increase the probability of its occurring again. Punishment may lead to the suppression of a behavior,

TABLE 11-1. Varieties of Teacher Behavior Tending to Occur Together or to Be Interrelated, Classified According to Teacher Types, as Determined by Objective Observers[a]

Type of Teacher			
Cold and Controlling (as Contrasted with Warm and Permissive)	Vigorous and Dynamic (as Contrasted with Dull and Quiet)	Insecure and Anxious (as Contrasted with Confident)	Much Academic Activity (as Contrasted with Little Academic Emphasis)
Type of Classroom Behavior			
Activities very orderly	Stimulating	Uncertain	Systematic
Much direct control	Excitable	Disorganized	Much direct control
Delegates little authority to students	Gives support	Much evidence of emotional frustration	Emphasizes learning
Low affiliation motivation	Vigorous	Dull	Functions often as a source of knowledge
Frequently punishes	Functions often as a source of knowledge	Excitable	High achievement motivation
Aloof	Very verbal	Frequently punishes	
Harsh		Negativistic	
Inflexible			
Hostile			
Dull			
Much evidence of emotional frustration			
Negativistic			
Neuroticism			

[a] After Wallen, Travers, Reid, and Wodtke, 1963.

but this is most likely to occur when punishment is a "natural" part of the situation, for instance, when a child who is burned learns to avoid a hot stove. When punishment is administered by another person, its outcomes are less predictable. A student who is punished for disrupting class activities may cease his interruptions, but he may also try to escape from the punitive situation, that is, he may become a truant or may turn to daydreaming. Or, as we have previously indicated, punishment may actually assume rewarding dimensions for students who are hungry for attention.

The chief arguments against punishment are that it is inhumane, deplorable, unethical, nonprofessional, or unnecessary. Furthermore, it may not work. The counterarguments are that it can facilitate children's learning, and that it may, in fact, be the only kind of treatment that will produce positive behavior in some instances (Gardner, 1969). The problem is, however, that most discussions treat punishment as a general topic and do not differentiate between physical and psychological forms of punishment, nor between degrees of punishment. Hence it is usually unclear whether an author who criticizes punishment is referring only to physical punishment and public humiliation, or whether he includes mild reproof, corrective feedback, and such devices as asking a child to stay after school so that his classroom behavior can be discussed with him. Nevertheless, two things seem rather clear. First, there is a negative relationship between teacher effectiveness and punitivity. In other words, teachers who are most effective in stimulating learning are the ones who use punishment least, and those who use it the most are the teachers who by all standards are ineffective teachers. Second, most writers deplore the use of *physical* punishment.

In spite of the criticism directed against the use of physical punishment, it is frequently employed in schools. It seems likely that the situation has not changed very much since Carol J. Henning (1949) surveyed Midwestern secondary school principals more than twenty-five years ago. About half of the

(Ford Button, *Phi Delta Kappan*, May 1974)

TABLE 11-2. Percentages of Teachers Favoring Judicious Use of Corporal Punishment with Elementary School Children. Results of Two National Surveys (1960 and 1969) and One Survey in Norfolk, Virginia (1974)[a]

	1960		1969		1974
	Men	Women	Men	Women	Both Sexes
Favoring corporal punishment	78	69	74	62	64
Against corporal punishment	15	24	18	28	27
Don't know	7	6	8	11	9

[a] National Education Association, 1970a; Patterson, 1974.

principals admitted they were using physical punishment, although they said they were using it infrequently, preferring to use social-psychological methods of the kind mentioned above. Nevertheless, only two principals out of more than two hundred surveyed indicated that they had anything but punishment in mind when students misbehaved. One of these said that the school should try to find out what was troubling the student, and give him something to do that he could excel in, and the other said that he made an attempt to understand the offending student's background and the basis for his misbehavior, following it up with conferences with the student and his parents, if indicated.

Approximately twenty years later, the National Education Association conducted a survey of teachers to determine their views on physical punishment. About two-thirds said that it was all right to punish elementary children physically, but when it came to secondary school students, about 55 percent of secondary teachers were in favor of this form of punishment, in contrast to 38 percent of elementary teachers. Male teachers were also more willing than female teachers to use physical punishment.[1] When the researchers compared these reports with those obtained in a similiar survey nine years earlier, there was a slight decline in the willingness to use corporal punishment, as Table 11-2 shows (National Education Association, 1970a). A

[1] These results are consistent with the results of a study by Lindgren and Patton (1958) who found secondary teachers to be more punitive than elementary teachers and male teachers to be more punitive than female teachers.

survey conducted in Norfolk, Virginia, in 1974 suggests that the percentage of teachers rejecting corporal punishment continues to increase, as Table 11-2 also shows (Patterson, 1974).

It appears that American teachers are not much different from the public at large. One survey shows that 84 percent of Americans admit that they have spanked a child, although only 61 percent admitted to having been spanked as children (Stark and McEvoy, 1970). But not all experts agree that punitive tendencies are diminishing. David P. Ausubel (1961) said that the trend toward permissiveness in the classroom has been reversed, and he endorsed what he considered to be the growing firmness in the attitude of teachers. He rejected the idea that rewarding honesty and good manners was a satisfactory way of getting students to suppress dishonest and rude behavior. He also maintained that the belief that "it is repressive and authoritarian to request pupils to apologize for discourteous behavior and offensive language" is a distortion of democratic discipline because such behavior on the part of students implies a disrespect for teachers, who are just as entitled to respect as students are. "There is good reason to believe," he wrote, "that acknowledgement of wrong-doing and acceptance of punishment are part and parcel of learning moral accountability and developing sound conscience. Few if any children are quite so fragile that they cannot take deserved reproof and punishment in stride."

Ausubel felt that there was little danger of the climate in American classrooms becoming as authoritarian and punitive as that of British schools. A teacher in British schools, he said, often begins the new term by showing his class a cane and announcing that he plans to use it on the first one who steps out of line. American teachers, on the other hand, treat discipline in an incidental way, expecting that it will be a natural by-product of interesting class sessions and wholesome teacher-pupil relations, and that the vast majority of students will respond positively if they receive fair and kindly treatment. The American teacher expects that he will be respected for his expertness, superior knowledge, and his position and is not inclined to depend on such props to his status as being "Sir" or "Ma'am" or the fear of the strap. Thus he treats adolescents as maturing young adults, rather than as unruly children, expecting them to respond in kind—which they usually do.

Tom Gnagey (1970) has come to conclusions that are similar to those of Ausubel. He says that it is very important for students to know what limits of behavior will be tolerated in a given situation and to expect that whenever they overstep the boundaries, they will be guided back within the limits. A second fundamental point is that the behavior and attitudes of students can be changed only if the teacher recognizes that there are wide individual differences in the way they perceive and respond to the events in their lives. A third point is that individuals do not continue in any pattern of behavior unless it is rewarding in some way to them. In other words, discipline is necessary, but it must be individualized if it is to be effective. Indeed, there is some evidence to show that when teachers are trained to respond to students individually, instead of as a total class group, their behavior becomes more learning oriented. In one such experimental program, in which teachers were trained to focus on individual children, rather than the total class, they tended to express less disapproval and punished less than did teachers in conventional programs. In the control programs, teachers expressed the highest rates of disapproval in the first grade, when children have their first contact with the school (Rosenthal, Underwood, and Martin, 1969).

Differences in the attitudes of elementary school children whose teachers had been characterized as "most punitive" or "least punitive" by assistant principals were studied by Jacob S. Kounin and Paul V. Gump (1961). Highly punitive teachers were characterized as follows: threaten children with consequences that really hurt; make threats that imply sharp dislike and real willingness to harm the child; and ever-readiness to punish. A typical less-punitive teacher was more likely to be described as one who neither punishes nor threatens. The researchers then asked children from classrooms of the two types of teachers to say what they thought was the "worst thing to do in school" and to indicate why it was so bad. Judging by the replies, it appeared that pupils of the more punitive teachers displayed a great deal more hostility and aggressiveness, were unsettled and confused about behavior standards, and were less concerned with learning and other positive types of school activities. They tended to show little understanding of the basis of school discipline. For instance, when they were asked why running in the halls is bad, they were inclined to say, "Because the teacher says so," and not give reasons such as "It disturbs others." Kounin and Gump also concluded that children who have punitive teachers are more likely to mistrust the school than are children who have nonpunitive teachers. Children whose teachers are nonpunitive are thus better able to identify themselves with the school, to accept its values, and to adopt them as their own.

Gump and Kounin (1957) also studied the reactions of kindergarten children who were looking on when teachers corrected other children for misbehavior. The behavior of the teacher was classified in one of three categories: *clarity* (the use of such statements as "Don't hit others," "We don't do that in kindergarten," and "Fold your hands and look at me"); *firmness* (actions indicating "I mean it," such as approaching, touching, or guiding the child, or being emphatic in speech or gesture); or *roughness* (angry words or looks, overfirm handling of child). The observers noticed that teachers' behavior characterized by *clarity* helped to reduce misbehavior on the part of onlooking children, but that *firmness* was less helpful. When correction was characterized by *roughness,* however, it tended to encourage *an increase in misbehavior* on the part of the observing children. This research is particularly significant because the results run counter to what would be ordinarily expected, that is, most teachers would expect that the more severe the reprimand, the greater the impression on the onlooking children. It is quite possible that roughness on the part of teachers had a disturbing effect on children and upset them to the point at which they were unable to exercise ordinary controls over their behavior, or perhaps children tended to identify with the offending child. Thus the study also provides a strong argument for the administration of reprimands in private.

Still another caution to be observed with regard to punishment was uttered by Percival M. Symonds (1956) in a review of psychological research and theory relating to the use of punishment in education. Symonds warned against using punishment with children who have already been damaged, psychologically speaking, by too much punishment on the part of teachers and other adults. Damaged children, he pointed out, are likely to evoke impatience, exasperation, and hostility on the part of teachers. The first reaction of the teacher, when challenged by such a child, is to want to punish the child further, thus adding to the damage. Damaged children, he maintained, need more than the average amount of forbearance, patience, and attention.

Here is an example of how a child can be damaged by teachers' preoccupations with punitive methods:

> John was nine years old and in the third grade when he came to the attention of the psychiatric service. His teacher was complaining about the fact that he did not do his written assignments and usually drew pictures on work that was to be turned in. However, his work at the blackboard indicated that he had an adequate understanding of the material that was being covered by the class.
>   An investigation of John's background showed that he was the first-born son and the first grandson on both sides of the family, and as a consequence was the focus of a great deal of adult attention. His brother was born when John was four, and he naturally had to share some of the attention he had monopolized up to that point.

John tried to regain some of the attention he had lost by making very slow progress and then only when his mother coaxed, reminded, and helped him. His experiences in the first grade were quite positive, for he learned to read and write, thanks to a sympathetic teacher who encouraged him and gave him help when he requested it. His second-grade teacher, however, decided that he must be made to work and do things for himself. When this approach failed, she forced him to wear a sign on his chest: "I am dumb and slow." John reacted by becoming even more passive and refused to make any effort at all. In the third grade, the teacher maintained the kind of pressure that the second-grade teacher had applied, but without results.

When John went into psychological treatment, his mother was advised not to follow the teacher's recommendations of sitting down with John and helping him with his school assignments. Instead, she was told to buy some interesting and informative books written at John's level, leave them lying around the house, but decline to read them to him. John picked them up and began to read them, even though he had never previously read a book. He also started playing anagrams with his mother and got so he spelled very well. His academic work began to improve.

Unfortunately, this improvement did not appear until the end of the third grade. At this point, the teacher recommended that he be kept back another year, saying that he was not ready to do fourth-grade work. The school superintendent concurred. The psychiatrist tried to explain to them that there was nothing wrong with John's competence, since his blackboard work showed that he had learned the material, and that making him repeat the third grade would merely intensify the attitudes and behavior that had annoyed the teacher in the first place. However, the school was adamant, and John was kept back (Dreikurs, 1951).

This anecdote illustrates a number of things about punishment. It shows how a child's negative reaction to criticism and humiliation is related to previous experiences. The second- and third-grade teachers' punitive treatment of John's learning problem merely engaged them in a power struggle with him, a struggle that they were bound to lose because he held the trump cards—his refusal to cooperate. Eventually, the school became more interested in punishing John than in teaching him.

This is shown by the teacher's refusal to promote him to the fourth grade, preferring to keep him back in the third grade, where he could be subjected to another year of punishment and humiliation. In this instance, it seems quite clear that the teacher was using punishment to meet her own psychological needs, rather than those of the child. This danger is, of course, always present when teachers find themselves challenged by a child or perplexed by his behavior.

It is, as we have said, difficult to conduct a balanced discussion of punishment. Macmillan, Forness, and Trumbull (1973) conducted one of the more judicious and realistic reviews of the topic. They point out that those who take a stand that is "totally against" punishment overlook an important fact, namely, that aversive consequences—events which have punishing effects—occur in every classroom, irrespective of how much consideration and understanding a teacher is trying to display. In the course of any given hour, some child is likely to be upset, hurt, made jealous, feel reprimanded, or whatever by something the teacher does or says. In most instances the teacher, who is trying to conduct the class session and at the same time monitor the behavior of two dozen or more children, is unaware that he has acted in an aversive way. Hence it is impossible and probably undesirable to eliminate aversiveness from children's daily experiences. The important thing is for teachers to be more aware of the aversive effects of their behavior and to use punishment more systematically and judiciously.

As a result of their review of research and theory on punishment, Macmillan and his co-authors came to these conclusions:

1. Punishment is more effective if the teacher already has a positive relationship with the pupil.

2. Punishment, if it must be used, should come early in a sequence of misbehavior and should be systematically applied.

3. Greater firmness at the onset of misbehavior may be more effective than the practice of gradually escalating the intensity. At the same time, teachers should guard against "punishment overkill."

4. The child should understand clearly what it is he is being punished for.

5. Punishment is more effective if a child has the choice of engaging in an activity that is an acceptable alternative to the misbehavior, especially an alternative that holds the promise of being reinforced by the teacher or, better still, is intrinsically rewarding.

6. The same aversive treatment should not be used repeatedly. For example, the wording of a reprimand should be changed.

7. It is generally better if reprimands can be delivered privately, rather than publicly, to the pupil concerned.

Group-imposed Discipline

In his task of helping students develop greater self-control, task-oriented behavior, and other indications of social maturity, the teacher does well if he can enlist the peer group as an ally. From the very beginning of school, the peer group plays an important role in socializing the child. As a child gradually frees himself from the need to depend on adults for control and direction, he simultaneously begins to look to his age-mates and peers for cues as to how he should behave and what he should think and believe. Although the full force of group opinion and group pressure usually does not make itself felt until preadolescence, the first indications of the development of norms and standards appear rather early.

Shauna, a second-grader, asked her father how to make a "b" in "real writing." The "b" she had been making looked more like a "g" than anything else, so he showed her what she was doing wrong and how he made a "b" in "real writing."
She objected: "Joanne says that *this* is how you make a 'b,'" indicating the "g"-like letter.
Her father's immediate reaction, which he did not voice, was: "If you were already satisfied with the 'b' that Joanne taught you to make, why did you ask *me* to show you how?"
Then he realized that Shauna felt there *was* something wrong with Joanne's "b's," but when an adult criticized them, she felt called upon to

stand up for her friend and to think, for the moment, that perhaps Joanne was right, after all.

So he said just that—"Perhaps Joanne is right"—and turned away.

A few minutes later he noticed that she was making her "b's" in the proper way.

The point is that even in the second grade the peer group is beginning to exercise a strong pull, and children are beginning to think: "Maybe I should do what other children do and not what adults want me to do."

Any kind of activity in a group setting is likely to prove frustrating at some time or other. Others are usually speaking when one wishes to speak, and one's personal needs must be subordinated to whatever the group is doing at the moment. A feeling of irritation is a natural reaction to this frustration. In a well-managed group, members put aside those feelings and go along with the group in order not to jeopardize their relations with other group members. When the program of group activities depends entirely on a single adult, however, the structure of the group is loosely knit, and there are few group-induced sanctions against deviating from the program.

With respect to the formation of children's and adolescents' groups, adults are inclined to take one of two courses: either to *ignore* young people's tendencies to develop their own standards of behavior and to enforce their own discipline, or to *prevent* the formation of groups on the grounds that they often defy and resist adult authority and control. It would make much better sense, both theoretically and practically, however, if we recognized the group needs of children as normal and natural aspects of their development and instead included them in our educational program. Thus, instead of struggling against the course of these natural tendencies, we would be employing them to the advantage of all concerned.

Self-imposed Discipline

The important thing to keep in mind is that the ultimate goal is *self*-discipline. When children have learned to respond to adult direction, they have successfully passed through one stage of social and emotional maturity; when they respond to the direction of their own groups, they are in a more advanced stage of development. In any event, if they are to grow to be responsible and thoughtful citizens, they must learn how to contribute to and develop group standards as well as respond to them. Sometimes the standards that groups set for their members are unwise. The individual who has not learned how to think through the meaning of his own behavior has no choice but to conform to the demands of the group, whereas the person who has been able to evaluate both his own standards as well as those of the group is in a position to contribute to the development of new and better group standards. The ability to contribute to the thinking of the group is a goal that ranks rather high on the scale of social maturity; it is one that many adults have not attained, yet it is one that the school must develop in students if it is to fulfill its obligation to future generations.

Task-imposed Discipline

We have discussed three kinds of discipline: teacher-imposed, group-imposed, and self-imposed. There is another kind of discipline that plays an important part in the learning process. It is *task-imposed* discipline.

"Philip," called Mrs. Bentley, "it's seven o'clock. If you want to see 'Space Mission' you had better come."

"Space Mission" was Philip's favorite television program. He always dropped what he was doing and came running so as not to miss a second of the program, not even the commercial. But tonight there was no Philip and no reply—at least, not for a few seconds. Then came his answer: "I'll be along in a minute or two, soon's I get this stuff fixed."

This wasn't like Philip. It was so unlike him that Mrs. Bentley walked down the hall to his room and peeked in. Philip was seated at his work table, sorting stamps from a large pile into a score of smaller piles. He looked up as his mother entered the room.

"Hi, Mom," he said. "I was just getting these stamps ready for the gang. We all chipped in a quarter and I sent for them. I want to get them sorted out by countries before they come tomorrow morning."

"Don't you want to see 'Space Mission'?" Mrs. Bentley asked.

"Sure," answered Philip. "But I want to get these stamps sorted out first. I'll be out in time for the real exciting part. You can tell me the part I miss." And he turned back to his stamps.

We are all familiar with the task that grips and holds our attention, that demands more of our time than we expected to give. Once we have started, it is difficult for us to put it down, even for activities that are normally very attractive. This is the Zeigarnik effect that has been found to figure in the need for achievement.

George is an eleven-year-old boy who is active and noisy. He likes to talk and show off. His parents think he is lazy because they can't get him out of bed before nine or ten o'clock on weekends, and he goes out of his way to avoid everyday chores like cleaning up his room or mowing the lawn.

But this is Saturday, and George has been up since 5:30 A.M. He packed a lunch for himself and even made his bed. He left the house at 6:15 to join a group of Scouts who were going to hike through nearby hills to observe birds and animals in their natural surroundings. George was out on this hike all day. During this time he neither talked excessively nor showed off. He sat quietly without moving for what seemed hours while the group was observing various kinds of wildlife.

Going out with this group of Scouts was a special privilege for George. He was not a Scout as yet, but suddenly, this week, it seemed that becoming a Scout was the most important goal in life. So he had gone to Mr. Ricci, the vice principal, who was also a scoutmaster. Mr. Ricci had said that he wasn't sure whether George was ready for the Scouts. When George insisted that he was, Mr. Ricci decided to let him come on the Saturday hike as a kind of trial. But he would have to be on his best behavior because the boys who were making the hike were two and three years older than George, and they would not like to have their day spoiled by a boy who talked too much and who was overactive. George promised to behave. And when the excursion was all over, Mr. Ricci had to admit that George was far more mature than he had thought.

Each kind of task has a discipline of its own, whether it is sorting stamps, going on a nature hike, learning to do short division, working on a committee, or whatever. The greater the individual's maturity, the better he can discipline himself and the easier it is for him to conform to the demands of the task he has set for himself. Less mature individuals cannot accept the demands made on them by the task; hence they become frustrated and discouraged and give up easily. There are varying levels of maturity among the members of any classroom group; some students will be able to practice more self-discipline than others and will thus be more able to shape their behavior according to the demands of the tasks they wish to accomplish. In a well-organized, activity-oriented classroom, these more mature students often help to develop mature behavior in other students by acting as pacesetters and models for the whole group.

Task-imposed discipline is based on positive motivation. Individuals must somehow see the task as important to their self-concept—as a part of their perceived selves. For some students, it is enough that the teacher thinks it is important. But for most students, particularly during preadolescence and adolescence, the endorsement of the group is even more essential. Even though an adolescent might have a personal interest in a task, he feels the need for the support of the group and looks to it for approval first. Hence one of the main responsibilities of teachers of middle and upper grades and in secondary school is to be sure that the group is positively motivated toward the learning tasks at hand.

METHODS AND TECHNIQUES OF DISCIPLINE

Class Management Through "Stage Setting"

Basically, there are three things that teachers can do to help classroom groups develop the motivation and the emotional maturity necessary for self-direction and self-discipline: "stage setting," reducing anxiety, and increasing anxiety.

Most teachers recognize that classroom management involves some "stage setting," but they are often unaware of the psychological implications of

VARIETIES OF DISCIPLINE
Most of us think of discipline in its teacher-imposed form, but group-imposed and task-imposed versions have effects that are more positive in the long run.

this method of control. Andrew I. Schwebel and Dennis L. Cherlin (1972) investigated the basis whereby teachers assigned pupils to seats. They found that teachers' main concerns were that of minimizing classroom disruption, for they attempted to keep potentially disruptive pupils apart and assigned them to seats where they would be less disturbing: at the ends of rows, between two "good" pupils, in the back of the classroom, or near the teacher's desk, where they could keep an eye on them. Other than this, teachers were unable to indicate any other basis for seat assignments. Observations by the researchers, however, showed that where children sat made an important difference, as far as their attentiveness was concerned. When children were reassigned on a random basis by the investigators to new seats, pupils seated in the front rows were the most attentive in the class, much more so than those in back rows. Students who had been moved forward in the reassignment tended to find more favor with teachers; those who had been moved back found less favor. Children in the classroom, for their part, reported that they thought the pupils who had been seated in the front of the room were more attentive and better liked by the teacher than those at the middle and back, but at the same time they felt that the front-of-the-room children were shyer. What the experiment showed was that children's behavior was affected by where they sat in the room, and that where children sat also influenced the way in which their teachers and peers perceived them. The experiment also suggests that teachers usually are aware that stage setting in the form of seating arrangements can have an effect on pupils' behavior, but that most teachers are unaware of ways in which such arrangements influence the attitudes of both students and teachers.

The instructional plans which teachers develop are also a means of behavior control through stage setting. With a lesson plan in mind, the teacher knows what concepts or subjects the group should be helped to focus on, what materials to have on hand, and what can be said to the members of the group to prepare them for each new activity during the day. Because the teacher has thought through these matters, he knows what is coming up next and is prepared to deal with the kind of problems that might occur. This feeling of knowing what is likely to happen next is reassuring; it helps the teacher's morale and feeling of security. The class, in turn, is likely to take its cue from the self-confidence of the teacher, and a class that is self-confident, that feels secure and self-assured, is less likely to disintegrate or become chaotic.

Stage setting is a way of "initiating structure," or "structuring," a term used in recognition of the fact that any ongoing situation has a certain "structure"—certain characteristics and cues that people use as a basis for action. Panel discussions, spelling bees, and the assignment of seat work are all different ways of structuring learning situations. Each of these situations is characterized by certain roles that are played by students and the teacher. Some situations, such as quizzes and lectures, are more highly structured than others. A discussion in which class members are free to bring up any subject and to interact with one another is an example of a situation that is loosely structured. In determining the amount of structure, teachers should, of course, be guided by the needs and interests of the learners and the amount of direction and control that will produce the best results in terms of learning. Routines, for example, may be helpful in giving structure to regular classroom activity, particularly in the lower grades. When properly used, they can have a stabilizing effect and can focus attention on the learning problems at hand, but if overused they produce boredom and restlessness, the forerunners of more serious misbehavior.

The Teacher's Role as an Anxiety Reducer

One of the important functions of the teacher, or of any leader for that matter, is that of reducing anxiety. Some minimum of anxiety is essential for most learning, but too much anxiety has a disturbing effect on a group. It may arouse hostility and provoke aggressive behavior, or it may cause a class to draw into its collective shell and refuse to participate in *any* positive learning experience. Over-anxiety also has a distorting effect. It prevents individuals from seeing the facts as they really are and interferes with effective communication.

One of the outstanding characteristics of experienced, effective teachers is their ability to sense the "anxiety level" of the classroom group. They are aware that little learning will take place if the group is more concerned about its anxiety than it is about learning. As we have indicated previously, individuals who are very anxious are preoccupied with their anxiety. The thing that they want most is to do something about their anxiety, and they are relatively unconcerned about participating in the experiences their teacher may have prepared for them.

When Genevieve entered the second-grade classroom the first morning of the new school year, she got a pleasant surprise. Miss Peters, the first-grade teacher she loved so much, was to be her teacher in the second grade! After school, she ran all the way home because she couldn't wait to tell her mother the good news. She had been a little afraid of going into the second grade; some of the second-graders she knew last year had told her it was much harder than the first grade. But now that she had Miss Peters again, she felt confident and happy.

But her happiness was short-lived. On the morning of the third day of school, Mrs. O'Hara, the principal, came into the room with a sheet of paper in her hand. She read off the names of eight children and asked them to collect their things and come to her office. Genevieve was one of them. As she picked up her pencil and ruler and collected her lunch and coat, she had the feeling that something terrible was going to happen. It seemed as though a big lump was pressing down on her stomach.

When the children gathered in Mrs. O'Hara's office she told them that Miss Peters' class was so large that it had been necessary to transfer some of them to Miss Durand's class. Mrs. O'Hara also said that she understood how it might be difficult to move to a new class when you had just started making friends and had got to know the teacher, but that she knew they would find Miss Durand and her class very pleasant. Whereupon she walked down the hall with them to the new classroom and introduced them to Miss Durand.

Miss Durand smiled at them all and said how glad she was to have them in her class and, after the children had put their things away and had settled in their seats, she said:

"We have been talking about the pets we have at home and some of the things they do. I have a canary that sings all the time, unless you put a cover over his cage. Betty has a puppy that chews her father's slippers. David has two turtles that sun themselves on a rock."

And she pointed to the blackboard, where she had written what the pets did. She went on: "Does anyone else have a pet?"

One of the new children said: "In Miss Peters' class, Genevieve told us about her pet rabbit."

Miss Durand saw this as an opportunity to help the new children to become integrated into the class, so she asked, in her most pleasant manner: "Would you like to tell us about your rabbit, Genevieve?"

But Genevieve couldn't say a word. She could only look at Miss Durand and wish she were back in Miss Peters' class. She wanted to get up and run out of the room. But here she was in Miss Durand's class, and she knew that she could never go back. She knew that she ought to reply to Miss Durand's question, but the only thing she could do was to put her head down on her desk and sob as though her heart would break.

Genevieve's anxiety is so acute that she is unable to participate in the class routine. But after she and Miss Durand have had a chance to talk by themselves a bit, she will feel less anxious. And because she is basically a happy child, she will find that she can enjoy Miss Durand's class as well as she did Miss Peters'.

Anxiety often starts with one individual and spreads through the class. When Genevieve broke down and cried, the anxiety level of the class was raised to the point where it was not possible, for a few minutes, to go on with the discussion of pets that Miss Durand had planned as part of the reading lesson. So instead of continuing, she sent Genevieve off to the washroom with another girl and helped the rest of the children talk about how it felt to come into a new class where you didn't know the teacher or any of the children. By the time Genevieve returned, the class was busily engaged in the "activity period."

Effective teachers generally move to help students reduce anxiety when it rises to a level that threatens to interfere with positive learning. Students who are troubled by anxiety are concerned only about avoiding or reducing their anxiety and have no interest in the learning task before them. Thus they are not able to develop the task-imposed discipline which is conducive to good learning and are less responsive to the pressures of group-imposed discipline. By helping students reduce the level of their anxiety, teachers are making it possible for them to become involved in the tasks of learning and are facilitating the development of more mature standards of behavior.

There is a wide variety of methods that can be used in helping students reduce their anxiety. Here are two of them. Sometimes the reduction may be accomplished through the medium of a "gripe session" whereby the group "gets its troubles off its chest," and sometimes it can be reduced through a change of scene or a restructuring of the learning situation.

> Mr. Hoskins wanted his social problems class to discuss the film they had just seen dealing with the pros and cons of the development of nuclear power by the federal government, but no one seemed to have anything to say. Mr. Hoskins felt sure that this was not really so because the film had brought out some rather provocative issues. He assumed the students were somewhat anxious about initiating discussion. As he looked about the group, it seemed to him that some of them would like to participate but were shy about speaking up. So he broke the class up into groups of six students each and had them discuss the issues for six minutes. Then he brought them together again. The discussion went much better then because the students discovered that they *did* have something to say about the film, and they were less anxious about expressing their opinions openly.

Anxiety is often difficult to identify because it appears in so many guises.[2] It may appear in a generalized feeling of resentment toward the teacher, merely because he happens to be an adult and a person in authority. It may appear in a kind of restlessness that seems to prevent the class from con-

centrating on anything for more than a few minutes. Or the class may be worried about some new area of subject matter that they think will be too difficult for them. Inasmuch as learning involves change, and inasmuch as change means abandoning old patterns of behavior for new ones, it is evident that some anxiety will be aroused if learning is to take place. One of the tasks of the teacher is to see that anxiety is at a high enough level to stimulate learning, but that it does not grow out of bounds and become disturbing or demoralizing.

How Much Anxiety Is "Enough?"

The responsibilities of the teacher in developing normal anxiety are often overlooked, partly because our understanding of anxiety is at best incomplete and partly because we are inclined to gloss over those aspects of education that appear somewhat negative. Furthermore, we are so much aware of the difficulties resulting from an overabundance of anxiety that we fail to realize that too little anxiety can also create learning problems.

As we indicated in Chapter 9, the individual who has no anxiety lacks concern for the rights and feelings of others. He is primarily interested in gratifying his immediate needs. It is the "good citizen," child or adult, who feels anxious when tempted to do something that will injure or embarrass others. It is the individual who does not possess this normal anxiety who is a threat to the welfare of the group and who must be helped to develop the anxiety that is basic to self-discipline.

What we have been calling "normal anxiety" is a quality that appears in what is commonly called "conscience," or to use a psychological term, "superego." The superego forces in an individual's personality may become so strong that they inhibit him at every turn and prevent his making the kind of positive moves that are basic to the development of full psychological maturity. But if superego forces are too weak, the individual is unable to function adequately as a socially mature human being. The basic psychological groundwork for superego development is, of course, laid down in preschool years. Even when children start going to school,

---

[2] See discussion of defense mechanisms in Chapter 6.

their teachers generally feel that the home should continue to bear the major or even the exclusive responsibility for the development of conscience. Some research into this matter shows, however, that school experiences contribute a great deal to superego development in children aged 7 to 13 and may even exert a more powerful influence than that of parents. Whether school personnel are aware of it or not, "they appear to be more successful than parents," the researchers reported, "in instilling attitudes toward misconduct that are more realistic and more in tune with general cultural values" (Kounin, Gump, and Biddle, 1957).

The task of maintaining the right degree of normal anxiety and aiding in the development of adequate superego structures is one that must be carried out on both an individual and a group level. Children who are otherwise considerate and sympathetic may do things that are quite heartless when they are together in groups. For example, they might tease or humiliate a child who is a member of a minority group or who is physically handicapped. Such negative behavior occurs when anxiety is too low or too high. Sometimes the normal anxiety of a group will be reduced when the proximity of an important event overstimulates and excites them; sometimes normal anxiety vanishes when one member misbehaves and initiates a kind of chain reaction of misbehavior that sweeps through the group.

The list of things that teachers can do to arouse normal anxiety would be endless. Sometimes it takes only a nod; sometimes it is just a matter of laying a hand on the shoulder of the student who is misbehaving. At other times a few words to remind students of their responsibilities are enough. The techniques themselves are of less importance than the way in which they are applied and under what circumstances. It is not always easy to gauge the situation and determine how much anxiety should be aroused. This raises the problem of where to stop. We want to arouse anxiety to the point where students have a reasonable concern about their responsibilities to themselves and to others but not to the point where it interferes with the learning process.

It is easy for teachers to give more help than is actually needed. As we indicated earlier, we are more comfortable when we are in the driver's seat. It is difficult to permit groups to manage themselves and learn by making mistakes on their own. Furthermore, there is much that we do not know about the best ways of helping groups manage themselves, for this is one of the newer fields in psychology and education.

Control of Misbehavior Through Behavior Modification

In recent years psychologists interested in the control of misbehavior have borrowed an operant conditioning technique from the learning laboratory, an approach that depends not so much on negative or aversive treatment, such as the arousal of anxiety, but, instead, on positive methods, such as rewards. We have stated elsewhere that teachers' reactions to misbehavior—scolding, nagging, and other forms of punishment—can actually have a reinforcing effect on misbehavior, particularly when it satisfies a need for attention or arousal. The rationale of what is termed *behavior modification* (or "behavior mod," for short) operates on the reverse of this tendency: Instead of the student receiving attention (and hence reinforcement) for misbehaving, he receives it only when he behaves in ways that are socially or cognitively effective. It is obvious that such a practice is contrary to common sense, which holds that the ignoring of misbehavior has the effect of encouraging it.

Actual use of behavior modification in classrooms, however, shows that the learning theorists are right and common sense is wrong, in this instance. In one classroom experiment, an experienced teacher was placed in charge of five hyperaggressive four-year-old boys and told to do her best in dealing with them. The results were chaos. The teacher tried the roles of disciplinarian, arbitrator, counselor, and peacemaker, all to no avail. By the end of the eighth day, each child was engaged in one hundred fifty aggressive acts per school day, as Figure 11-1 shows. Many of these acts were directed against the teacher and, in spite of her attempts to maintain role-appropriate behavior, she found herself "descending to their level," "trading a kick for a kick, and spit in the face for a spit in the face." On the twelfth day, the conditions were changed. The teacher was instructed literally to turn her back on all aggression and to reinforce co-operative behaviors with tokens exchangeable for special privileges. To make certain that she maintained the proper schedule, the experimenters gave her occasional reminders over a wireless communication system. This monitoring was used not only to keep the teacher "on target," but it also provided her with feedback that had a reinforcing effect. (Even the behavior of *teachers* can be modified through reinforcement!) As a result of this experimental treatment, aggressiveness dropped dramatically, and cooperation increased. After four days of this regimen, the teacher was instructed to punish

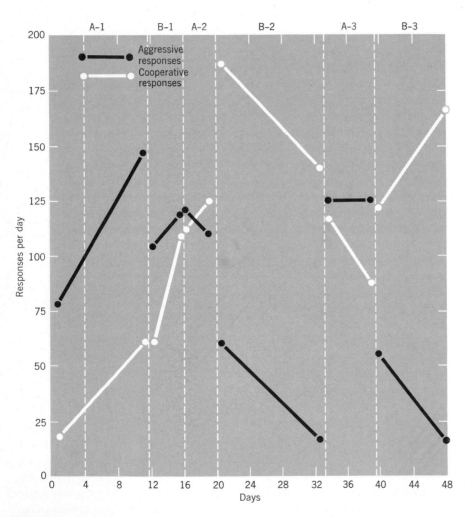

FIG. 11-1. Frequency of aggressive and cooperative acts by five four-year-old hyperaggressive boys during a 48-day period. In sequences A1, A2, and A3, the teacher attempted to punish misbehavior and only weakly reinforced cooperative behavior. In sequences B1, B2, and B3 she ignored aggressive behavior and used tokens to reinforce cooperative behavior (data from Hamblin, et al., 1969).

aggressive behavior by exacting a fine to be paid in tokens. Although aggression dropped at first, it quickly recovered, as the boys realized that aggression was again receiving attention and hence was being reinforced. After four days of this, the teacher was told to go back to ignoring misbehavior. As a result, aggression dropped and cooperation increased (see B2 in Figure 11-1). After twelve days of this treatment, conditions were again reversed. Boys were given tokens at the beginning of the day, and the teacher was told to do the best that she could without instructions. As we can see from A3 in Figure 11-1, aggression once again increased and cooperation decreased. Finally, in period B3, the experimental regimen was instituted once more. Aggression dropped to seven actions a day, whereas cooperation rose to one hundred eighty-one actions. Not only was the change remarkable, but the levels of aggresssion and cooperation eventually attained were much superior to that of normal boys in conventional nursery schools, who average about fifteen aggressive and sixty cooperative responses a day (Hamblin et al., 1969).

A natural question at this point is: Will the technique work with older children in an ordinary classroom setting? A number of studies show that it does. In one elementary school in which the students were 95 percent black and the majority were economically and socially "deprived," teachers were given training in "shaping" the behavior of certain "target students," whose conduct was particularly disruptive or otherwise undesirable. The method had to be tailored for each age level and classroom situation but was basically the same as the method described above. In general, teachers told children what kinds of behavior were expected of them and used positive attention (praise, smiles, head pats, and so forth) as reinforcers. Some teachers encountered more difficult problems than others, but results were generally positive. The most dramatic success was achieved with one teacher who was instructed to ignore disruptive behavior and to reinforce desired behavior for an entire class. As a result, the noise level of the class dropped considerably, and the behavior of two aggressive boys, who had been selected by the ex-

perimenters as "barometers" of possible changes in the class, became decidedly more positive (Becker et al., 1967).

In another classroom experiment, Gilbert W. Schmidt and Roger E. Ulrich (1969) used an ingenious method to reduce the noise level during study periods in a noisy fourth grade. A timer was set for ten minutes, with the understanding that if the sound level exceeded a certain number of decibels, as indicated by a sound-level meter, the experimenter would blow a whistle and set the timer back to ten minutes. If the ten-minute period passed without violation of the sound-level limit, the class would be awarded two extra minutes for their gym period and a two-minute break to ask questions, sharpen pencils, or whatever, before the next ten-minute study period. A room without students registers between 36 and 37 decibels of background noise, and the acceptable sound level was set for 42 decibels. The "baseline performance" of the class before the experiment had ranged between 47 and 57 decibels. During the first experimental phase, the noise level dropped to 38 to 41 decibels. When reinforcement was removed, the noise level increased to 45 to 50 decibels, and when reinforcement was again instituted, it dropped to 37 to 39 decibels.

Although we have discussed behavior modification in terms of its use in controlling classroom disturbance, it has many other applications as well. It has been used successfully to help children having reading problems (Egeland, 1970), to reduce anxiety in reading aloud before a group (Muller and Madsen, 1970), to reduce test anxiety (Cohen, 1969), and to improve the performance of mentally retarded children (Kreitman, Corbin, and Bell, 1969). The techniques of behavior modification are relatively easy to apply, provided that the reinforcing individual understands how it works and can dispense reinforcement that is sufficiently attractive to the learner. Parents have been trained to control problem behavior in children (Allen and Harris, 1966), and even fifth-graders have been trained to serve as "behavioral engineers" in shaping positive study behavior in first-graders (Surratt, Ulrich, and Hawkins, 1969).

METHODS AND TECHNIQUES
OF DISCIPLINE

Behavior modification, at least in the classic form proposed by B. F. Skinner, is all positive and not aversive. Indeed, Skinner (1973) says that "It is now clear that many of the disciplinary problems faced by teachers (truancy, vandalism, and apathy) are the by-products of a long history of aversive control, which has not yet come to an end." Some critics of behavior modification feel that this attempt to accentuate the positive and eliminate the negative is completely unrealistic. There are some instances, they say, in which ignoring misbehavior can actually be dangerous, and ask, "If one child goes after another with a sharpened pencil, should the teacher ignore it? When a child teeters precariously on the back legs of his chair, should the teacher look the other way?" These are fairly extreme, although not unusual, instances, and behavior modification specialists would probably say that emergencies of this sort should be dealt with sensibly and promptly.

But the critics of behavior modification have other misgivings. Let us say that the teacher notices that his attention appears to be reinforcing out-of-seat behavior, so he decides to ignore it. The critics wonder whether the children who have been staying in their seats up until now might not use the behavior of the out-of-seat children as a model. These children may perhaps say to themselves, "Well, he must not mind our getting out of our seats because he never does or says anything to Larry when he gets out of his seat" (MacMillan, Forness, and Trumbull, 1973). Behavior modification specialists would probably say that such concerns can be handled by, say, telling the children that Larry has a special problem that is being treated by the teacher. This could have the effect of removing from Larry his power to evoke modeling behavior. But such criticisms do indicate that behavior modification is a far-from-simple technique.

Behavior modification approaches have also been criticized as being somewhat mechanical, as not permitting teachers to use their professional expertise in dealing with children. The techniques we described, however, call for a considerable degree of skill, understanding, and self-discipline on the part of the teacher. Someone has to have enough understanding of the students involved to identify reinforcements that are really effective, and there must be some kind of observation and control in order to ensure that the reinforcement schedule is being followed. In the two examples involving parents and fifth-graders mentioned above, reinforcement schedules were designed by psychologists and modified from time to time during the course of the experiments.

The problems encountered by teachers who want to use behavior modification techniques are somewhat complex. If they have sufficient understanding of their students' motivation to find acceptable reinforcers, there is still the problem of fitting reinforcement schedules into classroom schedules. A teacher has to operate on a kind of bifocal level, attending to the material he is trying to present and at the same time attending to the behavior he is supposed to be reinforcing. Still another problem is that of getting feedback. Unless an observer is present who can note deviations from reinforcement schedules, who can suggest points at which more reinforcement can be given, and make suggestions about improving the program, success is likely to be elusive. On the other hand, the teacher who understands how and when to ignore or to reinforce is well on his way to attaining a classroom climate that can be productive of real learning. Much of this skill is already a part of the behavior repertory of effective teachers. Without having any particular training in behavior modification, teachers who are genuinely supportive of heuristic approaches, self-directed learning, and creativeness are already, consciously or otherwise, reinforcing desirable behavior and ignoring that which is counterproductive.

Teachers' Anxieties About Discipline

Most beginning teachers have not had enough experience to develop an effective behavior repertory, and they find that problems relating to discipline are a major source of anxiety. When a director of teacher education asked approximately three thousand prospective teachers, "What gives you the greatest concern or worry as you plan for your first teaching position?" 80 percent answered: "Discipline." One of the major differences between new teachers and experienced teachers, however, is that the latter are less concerned about problems of discipline and are more concerned about ways of improving their general effectiveness as teachers. And so we say to beginning teachers: "Discipline is a problem that will worry you less when you get to be an experienced teacher."

This is probably not a very reassuring statement, as far as the beginning teacher is concerned, because he wants to know the answers to such questions as the following, contributed by one class of prospective teachers:

If children are continuously noisy in their seats while the teacher is busy at the board or with other groups, what is the best thing to say to them?

What do you do to keep the group quiet while one child is reading or speaking?

How do you train children to keep their hands to themselves?

What can you do to keep children from answering out of turn or all at once?

How do you handle the sassy child, the child who pays no attention to the standards set up by the class in regard to courtesy and behavior rules?

How does one cope with the child whose mind is far off from school work and who does not want to join with the group? This child is always the last to come up for reading and numbers and keeps the group waiting in other distracting ways.

What do you do with the "tattle tale"?

What do you do with the "cry baby"?

What is the best method of maintaining discipline and silence while escorting your class through the school building?

How would you answer the child who retorts with the answer, "I don't want to," when he is called upon to do something?

The beginning teacher wants specific suggestions—techniques, if you like—that will enable him to handle such problems. It is difficult for him to grasp the point that discipline is partly a point of view, partly a feeling of self-confidence, partly a kind of relationship between the teacher and his class, but mostly a feeling that the class develops about its own behavior. These are the kinds of concepts that defy verbal description. They are the approaches teachers must learn through actual experience. Moreover, they are things that cannot be learned unless teachers have an open mind, a willingness to try to understand students and learn from them.

New teachers have anxieties about discipline because they feel anxious and insecure about their work. They have not had the experience of success and consequently have no assurance that they will succeed. Instead of seeing students as providing the opportunities for teaching success, they see them as potential threats. It is thus understandable how some might turn to rigid discipline as a way of coping with their anxieties. Robert H. Snow (1963) described what happens when teachers' inadequacies lead them to overstress discipline:

In the face of many uncertainties, the teacher may feel a desperate need for exercising rigid control within the classroom to insure that at least the outward appearance of constructive effort is maintained. When students seem orderly and attentive, it is easier for the teacher to feel assured that he is teaching successfully. Deviations from accepted behavior patterns must be sternly suppressed, because they destroy this sense of confidence. Furthermore, evidences of sloth or recalcitrance are interpreted as personal provocations, because they suggest that the teacher's services are not appreciated.

Some teachers appear to live in dread of insurrection, obsessively concerned with preserving order in the classroom at all costs. Coercive measures predominate; reproaches fill the air. Inordinate amounts of time are spent in enforcing minor regulations. The examination becomes a punitive device, chiefly intended to place students on the defensive rather than to measure achievement. The student regards the teacher not as one who guides and assists but as one who threatens and invokes penalties. A gulf widens between students and teacher. The classroom becomes an arena for opposing forces, rather than a laboratory for learning.

In some ways, telling beginning teachers how to face and deal with problems of discipline is like advising people on how to be happily married. In all conscience, we cannot say, "If you follow these rules carefully, you will have a successful marriage." But we can say: "If you can maintain an open mind, if you can love, trust, and respect each other, you will have the *basis* for developing a successful marriage." Generally speaking, if teachers like children, respect them as individuals, and are willing to take the time and trouble to understand them, they will have the basis for a good teaching relationship, and the problem of discipline will very likely take care of itself. There are exceptions, of course. There are schools where students are more rebellious or more apathetic than elsewhere, and there are schools where the atmosphere is not favorable to the development of sound relations between teachers and students. Helping boys and girls in such schools to become self-disciplining may demand more skill and understanding than most teachers possess. But the basic principles that are helpful in other schools are also the ones that will work in "problem schools" when the atmosphere again becomes favorable. If students are to learn to become self-disciplining, if they are to learn the discipline that is task-oriented and group-oriented—that is, *if* the problem of discipline is to be solved—relationships between them and the teacher must be based on understanding and mutual respect.

We began this chapter by mentioning some Gallup polls that showed school discipline to be the number one educational problem. In conducting one of the polls, Gallup's (1973) canvassers asked respondents this question: "When we talk about

'discipline' in the schools, just what does this mean to you?" We list some of the replies as a fitting end to this chapter:

Discipline is respect for the teacher on the part of the child; and respect for the child on the part of the teacher.

Discipline is self-control and a proper respect for other students, for those in authority.

Learning taking place without confusion.

Keeping children so interested in what they are learning that obeying rules is almost automatic.

Without discipline neither school nor society can exist. The world would be bedlam.

Proper discipline makes children happier. When they run wild, they are undone by the confusion they create.

SUMMARY

The majority of Americans are very much concerned about problems of pupil discipline and believe that schools are not strict enough. "Discipline" has three basic meanings: "punishment," "control by enforcing obedience or orderly conduct," and "training that corrects and strengthens." Although teachers commonly agree that students should learn how to discipline and control themselves, many of them are inclined to enforce discipline rather than to help students develop it themselves.

Children need some control and direction to help them become self-disciplining; the amount will vary with the situation and with their level of maturity. They cannot always be depended upon to set the amount of control and direction that they will require. At times, particularly during the preadolescent period of development, they will have mutually contradictory needs to have limits set for their behavior and to challenge these same limits.

Discipline, like other aspects of the leadership role, calls for a judicious balance of "structure initiation" and "consideration," to use two terms that have grown out of research in the psychology of leadership. One example of structure initiation is the stand commonly taken by many adults to the effect that it is somehow "democratic" to treat all instances of misbehavior in the same way, without consideration of circumstances or causes. A preoccupation with orderliness and control is apparently characteristic of teachers who are perceived as cold and hostile and who are not very interested in encouraging the academic achievement of students. An understanding of causal factors is basic to the proper handling of misbehavior, but many school people are inclined to think in terms of but one kind of treatment—punishment. Although there is much less physical punishment in the schools than there was a couple of generations ago, American teachers, like the general public, tend to favor its judicious use. The percentage favoring this mode of treating problem behavior has declined over the years, and American teachers are by and large not as punitive as their British counterparts. Students whose teachers are punitive seem to have difficulty in focusing on the more positive aspects of social control that can be learned in school contexts and are thus less able to trust the school and its teachers. Some research with kindergarten children shows that punitive attitudes on the part of teachers tend to increase the incidence of misbehavior. Some children react to punitive treatment by refusing to learn. This evokes further punitiveness on the part of teachers, accompanied by more steadfast refusal on the part of students, and an impasse is thus reached. Punishment is a difficult topic to discuss, partly because discussants do not always make it clear whether they are including all kinds of aversive treatment or merely the grosser forms, such as humiliation and corporal punishment. Some critics point out that it is impossible to eliminate all forms of aversive treatment from the classroom because a teacher will behave in aversive ways toward some students without being aware that he is doing so. The critics say that rather than try to eliminate all trace of aversiveness from the classroom, teachers should use punishment more systematically and judiciously.

Peer group norms play an important part in the young person's development of self-control, as well as in other aspects of social maturity, but teachers tend not to use the peer group to any great extent in helping students learn how to control and direct themselves. Another source of discipline is the learning task itself. The very process of becoming involved in a task or a problem has the effect of disciplining or setting limits to the individual's conduct. The greater the maturity of the individual, the easier it is for him to conform to the requirements of the task at hand. It is, of course, necessary for students to be motivated toward accomplishing the task under consideration before they are willing to accept the discipline it imposes.

Teachers can help students develop the emotional maturity and the motivation required for self-direction and self-discipline by "stage setting," reducing anxiety, and increasing anxiety. "Stage setting" involves planning and arranging the learning situation. Because the teacher has an idea of what is coming next, he feels secure and confident and is thus able to communicate some of this confidence to the group. Routines also have a limited usefulness in providing stability.

Although some minimum of anxiety is essential for most kinds of learning, it has a disturbing or negative effect when it is too strong. Individuals whose anxiety is at a high level are understandably preoccupied with reducing their anxiety and not with the learning tasks at hand. Hence one of the tasks of the effective teacher is to help students reduce the level of their anxiety so that they are able to direct their attention to the problems that are important for their welfare.

Helping students develop patterns of self-discipline and self-direction also involves raising the level of anxiety when they are inconsiderate or when they become involved in the chain reactions of misbehavior that sometimes sweep through groups. It is relatively easy to arouse anxiety but hard to know where to stop. The problem is how to keep the anxiety level of the class in balance, at the point where students are concerned with appropriate responsibilities, but not to let it rise to the point where it interferes with learning.

Psychologists have recently had some success in applying operant behavior techniques to the reduction and elimination of classroom behavior problems. This approach, known as "behavior modification," can be used by anyone who has some understanding of student motivation and who has control of reinforcers, but it cannot be used successfully without the aid of psychologists to plan, supervise, and advise. Behavior modification has been criticized by some on the grounds that it requires the teacher to refrain from punishment and restraint and to ignore all forms of misbehavior. Critics see this policy not only as impractical and even dangerous but also as permitting rule-breakers to act as models whose behavior may be imitated by their peers. Behavior modification specialists have answers for these complaints, but such criticisms do show that carrying out behavior modification procedures is not a simple matter.

Discipline problems are a common source of anxiety with teachers, particularly with student teachers or with those who have little experience in the field. Such problems tend to diminish in importance as teachers become more experienced, but this fact may not be very reassuring to the beginning teacher. He would like to know what specific techniques should be used in dealing with this or that situation. However, discipline depends not so much on techniques as on the willingness of teachers to respect learners as individuals and to take the time and trouble to understand them.

Suggested Problems

1. Ask four or five adults of your acquaintance what they mean by "discipline" with respect to the behavior of children. Are there any similarities or common patterns in the various points of view they express?

2. What advantages would group-imposed discipline have over teacher-imposed discipline? What advantages would task-imposed discipline have that group-imposed discipline might not have?

3. How can "stage setting" or "structuring" be used to cope with problems of discipline? Under what conditions would you be inclined to introduce more structure into the learning situation? Under what conditions would you be inclined to reduce the degree of structure?

4. What kinds of discipline problems are likely to result from too much anxiety? What kinds from too little anxiety?

5. Give an example of problem behavior and describe how it could be controlled through behavior modification. Indicate what reinforcement would be used and how it would be applied, and show how the behavior of the reinforcer would be monitored and feedback given to him.

6. Describe an experience in which a teacher used rigid forms of discipline on students in order to cope with his own feelings of inadequacy and insecurity. What indications are there that the teacher was inadequate? What was the outcome?

Suggested Readings

Fisk, L., and Lindgren, H. C. *A survival guide for teachers.* New York: Wiley, 1973. A brisk, anecdotal description of the major problems faced by the beginning elementary teacher and some ways to deal with them.

Guerney, B. G., Jr. (ed.). *Psychotherapeutic agents: New roles for nonprofessionals, parents, and teachers.* New York: Holt, Rinehart, and Winston, 1969. See Part 5 for a discussion of behavior modification as used by teachers.

Herndon, J. *The way it spozed to be.* New York: Simon and Schuster, 1968. (Paperback, Bantam Book, 1969.) The adventures of a white teacher in a black inner-city junior high school. Herndon has some unorthodox ways of maintaining discipline, but they work—usually.

Kounin, J. S. *Discipline and group management in classroom.* New York: Holt, Rinehart, and Winston, 1970. Has many suggestions for ways of structuring classroom situations to avoid inattention and disruptive behavior.

Lindgren, H. C., and Lindgren, F. *Current readings in educational psychology,* 2nd ed. New York: Wiley, 1972. See papers in Section 5 that deal with behavior modification and problems of classroom control.

Long, N. J., Morse, W. C., and Newman, R. G. (eds.).

Conflict in the classroom: The education of emotionally disturbed children. Belmont, Calif.: Wadsworth, 1965. Sections 5 and 6 deal with ways of managing and teaching emotionally disturbed children, with particular reference to discipline and punishment.

Yates, A. B. *Behavior therapy.* New York: Wiley, 1970. Although the author is concerned principally with the use of behavior modification techniques in treating psychopathology, Chapter 17 deals with the problems of "normal people," including those encountered in the classroom.

Good Listener
Responsible
Does home work
every night.
Studies Spelling
Punctual

12

The Learner-centered Classroom

IN THIS CHAPTER WE SHALL DISCUSS

- What is good (and bad) about traditional/conventional methods
- Education as a managed experience
- Characteristics of open or learner-centered methods: a rating scale
- The trends in modern schools that suggest a drift toward learner-centeredness
- Individualized approaches to instruction, including some that are subject-matter-centered, like IGE
- Individualized instruction in a (modified) open-schools program
- Computer-assisted instruction, or CAI
- Innovations in the classroom environment: the core course and team teaching
- Ways of getting students involved: contracting and token economies
- Students learning from students
- Group techniques: discussion, brainstorming, buzz groups, committees
- What happened to the free school movement
- How free schools' ideas have been adopted by public school systems
- Resistance to open schools and other learner-centered approaches
- How elementary and secondary school teachers view learner-centeredness differently
- What the future holds for learner-centered methods

Deficiencies and Strengths
of Traditional/Conventional Approaches
to Education

Traditional or conventional approaches to education, as we have pointed out in the preceding chapters, are characterized by an emphasis on "structure initiation"—a high degree of direction and control on the part of the teacher. We have said that some direction and control are necessary, the amount needed depending on such factors as the maturity of the class, the emotional climate of the school, and the emotional security of the teacher. We have also pointed out that teachers are inclined to direct, control, and apply disciplinary measures more than is necessary, and that such an orientation tends to interfere with cognitive development and particularly with the formation of favorable attitudes toward learning.

In all fairness to traditional/conventional schools, however, it should be pointed out that they do meet some psychological needs of students. All schools, modern and traditional alike, offer children and adolescents an opportunity to come together and interact with one another. This is an important contribution because it provides a kind of stimulation that is vitally necessary to the social and intellectual development of young people. The traditional, as well as the modern, school also brings children and adolescents into contact with the adult world outside the home, another very important source of social and intellectual stimulation. Furthermore, the ambitious student who can accept the adult-centered goals of the traditional/conventional school (which sometimes means that he must turn his back on his peers and age-mates) finds much that is well worth learning. To be sure, the adult values that the traditional school presents are often distorted or exaggerated. The regimentation found in many traditional schools has few counterparts in adult life, unless it is in military service or in custodial institutions; many traditional schools encourage a competitiveness that is more severe than that found in most employment situations; and much of the curricular content has been selected with more regard for its suitability to existing instructional plans than for its general usefulness and its contribution to human welfare and understanding.

Nevertheless, the traditional/conventional school often provides an atmosphere that is reassuring to the child who is looking for the kind of security that may be obtained from a tightly organized and highly predictable situation, one that will not make heavy demands on him in the way of self-direction, initiative, spontaneity, and creativity. There are many such students, and we would be less than realistic if we said that the kind of school that deviates from traditional patterns does not arouse their anxieties. The student who has especially strong needs to be emotionally and intellectually dependent on others thus feels more at home in traditional schools.

Most teachers are neither wholly traditional nor wholly innovative. Nat Hentoff (1970) of the School of Education at New York University visited an elementary school in Central Harlem and found himself "appalled in a fifth-grade room by the stern, seemingly authoritarian, no-nonsense zeal of *that* teacher to make sure that everybody left his class much more confident in basic skills than when he started." The approach of the teacher was so traditional that he appeared "anachronistic." As Hentoff continued to observe in the classroom, however, he found that the children were eager to learn, not because they were being "force-fed" but because of the teacher's belief that they *could* learn and his insistence that they *do* learn. One day the teacher brought an analog computer to class. All the children were anxious to make it work. The teacher told them to help themselves—the instructions were there. In time, a class that was composed of "slow readers" figured out the instructions and made the machine run. Such "learning by doing" had not been deterred by the teacher's stern concern with the "fundamentals" but was the direct result of his unshakable confidence in the children's ability to learn.

MODERN APPROACHES TO EDUCATION

The Managerial Approach

There seem to be two major trends in educational reform today. One is what might be termed the "management" approach to education. This approach is expressed in the emphasis on "accountability," which we have mentioned earlier and which we shall discuss in greater detail in Chapter 13. The management approach is a sophisticated development of traditional/conventional education in that it views the schools as governmental agencies, which are intended to provide certain services, just as the post office and the social security system do, for instance. When a management emphasis prevails, the objectives of the schools are spelled out by the representatives of the taxpaying public—the managers—who are only incidentally concerned with the psychological needs of students and teachers. What these managers are primarily interested in is getting the maximum results at the least cost.

The other trend, which is the one we have tended to favor in this book, is that of the learner-centered or "open school." Learner-centeredness, like the traditional/conventional approach, actually covers a wide range of views, from those of individuals who would like to eliminate schools, such as Ivan Illich, to those curriculum specialists, such as Benjamin Bloom, who plan highly structured learning sequences that virtually all students can master and thus avoid the disgrace of failure.

Characteristics of Learner-centered or "Open" Methods

At the heart of any educational philosophy are assumptions about learning. The traditional/conventional view, for instance, is characterized by the assumption that children learn best by copying the reality that is presented to them (Elkind, Hetzel, and Coe, 1974). Learner-centered or "open" views are more likely to focus on the learner's motivation: his drives and needs. To determine your own position on learner-centeredness, read over the following assumptions about learning and indicate your agreement with them, say, on the five-point scale (5 = strongly agree; 1 = strongly disagree):

1. Children are innately curious and will explore their environment without adult intervention.

2. Children's exploratory behavior is self-perpetuating.

3. Children will display natural exploratory behavior if they are not psychologically threatened.

4. Confidence in self is highly related to capacity for learning and for making important choices affecting one's learning.

5. Active exploration in a rich environment, offering a wide array of manipulative materials, will facilitate children's learning.

6. Play is not distinguished from work as the predominant mode of learning in early childhood.

7. Children have both the competence and the right to make significant decisions concerning their learning.

8. Children will be likely to learn if they are given considerable choice in the selection of the materials they wish to work with and in the choice of the questions they wish to pursue with respect to those materials.

9. Given the opportunity, children will choose to engage in activities which will be of highest interest to them.

10. If children are fully involved in and are having fun with an activity, learning is taking place (Barth, 1971).[1]

If your score on the above is more than 40, your position is strongly in favor of learner-centered approaches to education. Scores in the low 20s and below indicate a preference for more traditional methods.

Since John Dewey wrote his seminal books at the beginning of the century, the trend in education has been swinging slowly in favor of more learner-centered approaches, although the trend has been somewhat counterbalanced by managerial preoccupations with accountability. In spite of this drift toward learner-centered classrooms, the schools today fall far short of what Dewey would have considered to be ideal or even satisfactory. Theory has

[1] Reprinted by permission. For further discussion of these assumptions, see Roland S. Barth, *Open education and the American school,* New York: Schocken Books, 1974.

outstripped practice, of course, for teachers, when queried on their views, characteristically take a far more learner-centered position than one would think they would, judging from what goes on in their classrooms. In this they are no different from anyone else; in almost every walk of life we find that most people set standards that are higher than their actual practice. This is, however, the nature of progress: We stake out our goals and then move slowly, very slowly, in their direction.

As far as the schools are concerned, it is necessary to examine a span of years to determine whether there has been any movement in the direction of learner-centeredness. Such an examination will show the major trends:

1. *Teacher-student relations.* Although most classroom activities today are still essentially teacher-initiated, there has been a concerted effort on the part of many teachers to involve students to a greater degree in decision-making and planning. In some classrooms, student involvement is extensive; in others, it is minimal. Even when students are not consistently involved in decision-making, teachers today are generally aware that student motivation follows involvement and hence are on the lookout for ways to involve them.

2. *Individualization of instruction.* Whereas much of traditional education was built around a single textbook, teachers today are more likely to provide a variety of books as supplementary resources. In the better financed elementary schools, different readers and different math books are available for learners at different levels of competence. Books on a variety of subjects are available for free reading, and there is greater encouragement of children who want to read for pleasure. In secondary schools, supplemental materials are also available as interest builders or for students who wish to go beyond the ordinary limits of the curriculum. Teachers today, particularly in the elementary schools, are urged to break their classes up into small study groups, usually based on differences in skills

and competencies. Individualization has also been facilitated somewhat by a moderate but steady decline over the years in class size, accompanied by an increase in the number of nonteaching support personnel, both in and out of the classroom.

3. *Varied instructional techniques.* Recitations and written work based on reading and lectures were virtually the only methods of learning early in the century. Although these methods are still used a great deal today, they are ordinarily supplemented by workbooks, audiovisual aids, programmed instruction, group methods, field trips, and the like. In this there is a great variation from school to school and classroom to classroom, but the typical pupil in today's school is exposed to and involved in a much wider variety of learning experiences. The educational level of today's teachers is also higher; they tend to lead richer intellectual and social lives and, as a consequence, are more aware of educational resources.

4. *Openness of structure.* There is today a great deal of variation in the way that learning situations are organized, that is, more experimentation with ungraded schools, open schools, and other "fluid" arrangements. Some of this has come about because of a more concerted effort to individualize instruction. In an increasing number of classes, children are working alone or in small groups on projects and activities that are attuned to their special interests and needs. Such classrooms do not have structure, but it is one that may change from one hour to the next as children move on to other activities and join other groups.

5. *Relatedness to everyday life.* At the turn of the century, people were much more preoccupied with their daily work than they are today. There were more hours in the working day, more hours in the working week, less vacation time, and fewer years in school before joining the work force. Today there is not only more leisure for the average person, but there has also been a proliferation of various kinds of media of varying instruc-

tional value. Today's pupils are much more likely to have heard, seen, or read information about concepts presented in the classroom. Conversely, teachers and curriculum builders are also better able to find ways of relating school experiences to life outside the school. Energy crisis problems become related to science units, and the free reading list is likely to include some books devoted to the extraction and refining of fossil fuels. News stories and reports about the ecology also provide topics for natural science, social science, and language instruction.

These newer approaches to teaching and learning have made education more interesting and more relevant for students (and more complicated for teachers, incidentally), but they have also created problems and disappointments. When innovations are introduced, they often fail to bring about as much gain as had been expected. The worst that can be said for most experimental methods is that student performance, as measured by achievement tests, is no worse than with the older methods. The best that can be said is that the attitudes of both students and teachers involved in the newer programs become more positive, and some innovations do produce superior gains in skill and knowledge. Usually, however, the results are mixed. A common outcome is for the older method to produce a larger short-range gain, and for the newer method to produce better retention when students are tested some months later.

Individualized Approaches to Instruction

A number of innovative developments in education cannot be easily placed in the learner-centered or in the traditional subject-matter-centered camp. Individually Guided Education (IGE), as developed by the Wisconsin Research and Development Center for Cognitive Learning, is one of them. In a classroom operated along IGE lines, children are tested to determine where they are with respect to whatever skills and information are included in the curriculum. Instructional objectives and learning activities are then specified for each student, based on

the findings of this initial assessment, which may also include data regarding his motivational pattern and his general abilities. Out of a hundred or more pupils aged 9 to 11, one would expect to find that enough of them shared similar objectives and required similar learning materials, say, in mathematics, so that groups ranging in size from eight to twenty could be formed. Every four weeks or so, the composition of the groups is reexamined and students are shifted around from group to group, in accordance with the amount of progress they have made (Klausmeier, Morrow, and Walter, 1968). The general idea is somewhat similar to that used in Bloom's (1974) learning-for-mastery strategy we mentioned earlier.

IGE stresses subject-matter and skill competence, and hence seems more traditional in its focus, but the fact that it can be tailored to individual student objectives means that it is more adaptable to learner-centered classrooms than are most conventional approaches. At least one school has discovered that IGE can be integrated into a modified open-classroom arrangement. The school served about five hundred children aged 5 to 12 who were enrolled in a nongraded program. The building was constructed to permit the walls of twenty-four classrooms to be opened up to make six large areas, with three thousand square feet of space. The staff of the school strongly endorsed views of children's learning consistent with the ten assumptions we listed a few pages back and hence could be said to have subscribed to a learner-centered philosophy. The teachers were attracted to IGE because it permitted the setting of short-term instructional objectives for each child, provided curriculum materials that were suited to accommodate varying learning styles, and permitted "good reconciliation of the values of autonomy and accountability, small-group responsibility, and intergroup coordination." The children were required to complete minimum assignments daily in reading, writing, and math. The basic instructional unit was the small group, although there was a great deal of work done on an individual basis with teachers and teacher aides. The IGE units, as employed in this ungraded school, constituted, of course, only one of a range of experiences available to children. Children had their choice of a wide variety of interest or learning centers at which they could work at math, reading, creative writing, calligraphy, science, art appreciation, arts and crafts, and social science. Much use was made of some fifty parent volunteers, who worked in the school media center, as well as tutors and teacher aides in the classroom (Proctor and Smith, 1974).

Surveys of teachers' reactions to IGE in Nebraska schools indicate that they found it gave them more satisfaction than conventional methods because it enabled them to emphasize cognitive development and to deemphasize control for the sake of control. Teachers in schools that made the most use of IGE, in contrast to those in schools that made little use of it, were more likely to describe the psychological climate of their schools in favorable terms. Investigators found that the high IGE-use schools apparently had more intellectual activity, had a higher degree of teacher commitment and achievement, and were more friendly and democratic. Teachers in the high IGE schools also felt that the organizational environment in which they worked was freer (Kelley, 1974).

Computer-assisted Instruction (CAI)

Teaching machines and programmed instruction, innovations we described in Chapter 8, have been recommended by some experts, especially B. F. Skinner, as a way of tailoring curriculum to individual differences among learners. Although the individual differences referred to are primarily differences in competence and rate of learning, rather than differences in interests and attitudes, programmed instruction can bridge some of the gap between what school authorities specify are the skills and areas of information that constitute the curriculum and the ability of the individual student to cope with school demands.

We noted in Chapter 8 that the teaching machine is disappearing from the educational scene, and that it is being supplanted by the more sophisticated programs available through computerized methods. Computer-assisted instruction, or CAI,

may make use of a number of different aids, including teletypewriters, television screens, and an infinite variety of programmed materials. It is even possible to employ CAI to teach complex skills such as heuristic approaches to problem solving (Sutter and Reid, 1969). CAI is not merely an extension of programmed instruction. It goes beyond the teaching machines we described in Chapter 8 and "makes possible unprogrammed or student-controlled learning by utilizing teaching strategies which differ completely from the basic tutorial logic of most programmed instruction," according to D. Alpert and D. L. Bitzer (1970). Alpert and Bitzer maintain that CAI has proved to be more effective than standard educational procedures in teaching-learning situations calling for the exercise of judgment, the interpretation of complex problems, and the evaluation by the student of the validity of his own guesses and conjectures. A computer system may also be designed so that as many as two hundred to three hundred students can use it simultaneously.

In earlier CAI instruction, the computer was a bookkeeper, scorekeeper, and a guide to selected textual material, but the newer systems are much more flexible in that they aid the student to acquire information, to fit it into broader contexts, and to gain new perspectives.

Some of the educational gains that could be achieved by a large-scale CAI system include:

1. The gradual elimination of narrowly specific curricula in formal education, thus enabling students to learn at a rate determined by their own capacity and motivation.

2. The provision for remedial and tutorial instruction during regularly scheduled class hours for students who have insufficient preparation or who have special problems in learning.

3. Special instruction at home for physically handicapped students.

4. The development of competence in skill subjects without the interference of anxiety resulting from the exposed and often competitive atmosphere of the typical classroom.

William W. Cooley and Robert Glaser (1969) argue persuasively that CAI permits a greater individualization of instruction than is possible in the conventional classroom. They propose this general instructional model, presented as a sequence of operations:

1. The instructor specifies, in terms of the actual behavioral responses of the student, what goals might be reasonably expected for him to attain.
2. As the learner begins the instructional sequence, his capabilities, with respect to the goal criteria, are measured.
3. The student selects or is assigned to the type and/or level of instruction that is suitable to his capabilities.
4. As the student interacts with the CAI system, his performance is monitored and continuously assessed, and he receives continuous feedback as to his progress.
5. Instruction proceeds at a pace and a level that reflect the relationships among his success with the material, the available instructional alternatives, and the desired criteria of competence.
6. The student's interaction with the CAI system generates data that enables the teacher to check on his progress and to improve the instructional system.

Still another advantage to CAI is the possibility of combining flexibility with control of instructional method. This makes it possible to try out various teaching-learning theories through well-designed strategies unaffected by sources of unwanted variance, such as teacher personality or bias.

A factor that has deterred the wider use of CAI is its expense. For most school systems, the initial cost of installing CAI places it outside the realm of immediate possibility, even though the long-range savings in terms of pupil gain are tremendous. CAI systems presently in operation are operated on a demonstration or experimental basis and are funded by money grants from outside agencies instead of by school systems themselves.

Innovations in Curriculum and Instruction

Although the more elaborate forms of technical aids, such as CAI, are used to only a limited extent in schools, attempts at curricular reform have had a wider degree of acceptance. The core curriculum of the 1940s and 1950s and its more recent versions, the monodisciplinary and interdisciplinary curricula, are examples. Some of these curricular mergers have been accomplished merely by combining two related subjects, usually English and social studies. Others have been the result of long and careful planning that is aimed at bringing together "broad cultural clusters of knowledge" (Austin, 1969). In some of the integrated or merged courses, little is changed, except that the same teacher teaches both parts of a double course and attempts to relate the subject matter of each more closely than it is ordinarily. Another approach is to decide what kinds of "common learnings" each student should have as the result of his school experiences. The courses are then organized around these common learnings. From what we know about the learning process, it would appear that even a teacher-centered, integrated core course would constitute an improvement over the traditional secondary curriculum, in which little attempt is made to relate various subject-matter areas. After all, learning takes place more efficiently when the learner can see relationships among the various facts and concepts that he is expected to learn. When the subject matter "makes sense" to us, we are able to learn more effectively.

Those integrated courses which are organized around the interests, experiences, and needs of the students, however, would seem to have the best chance for success, inasmuch as they not only "make better sense" but are more likely to be perceived by students as worthwhile, interesting, and valuable. Theoretically, at least, such courses should succeed not only because they make better sense but also because students would be more highly motivated to participate in the learning process.

One of the many studies evaluating integrated courses was undertaken by Bernard Schwartz

(1959), who conducted a survey of 168 graduating high-school seniors in Yardley, Pennsylvania. Eighty of the seniors had taken core courses in the seventh and eighth grades; the others had not. Those who had participated in the core courses scored higher than the other students in understanding of natural science, ability to solve mathematical problems, vocabulary, reading ability, overall scholastic average, number of extracurricular activities in the tenth and eleventh grades, and ratings for the following character traits: responsibility, influence, seriousness of purpose, creativeness, adjustability, industry, and initiative.

Approximately a fourth of American schools make use of team teaching, an arrangement whereby two or more teachers work together in teaching the same group of students. Such teams might be interdisciplinary, as when a teacher of American history, a teacher of American literature, and a teacher who is familiar with music and art forms collaborate to teach various phases of American culture. These arrangements permit cooperative planning and coordination, as well as integration of subject matter and methodology. On the negative side, critics observe that members of teaching teams must spend a lot of time planning and integrating their offerings. There is, furthermore, a tendency for team teachers to become more specialized in their approach. An American literature teacher with a good background in history might decide to refrain from comments on the historical context of the writing that he is discussing, feeling that he would be infringing on the specialty of his colleague in American history.

Like other experimental approaches, neither curriculum merges nor team teaching can be considered a panacea, although the rationale of these two approaches appears sound from the standpoint of phenomenological principles of learning. One evaluation of team teaching yielded the usual set of findings: (1) Measured achievement in the experimental group (the classes being taught by teaching teams) was no different from that of the control group (the classes being taught by conventional methods), and (2) students' abilities in the experimental group were noticeably better than those in the control group. With respect to the latter finding,

teachers reported that students in the experimental group showed a remarkable improvement in self-discipline and in favorable attitudes toward the school (Zweibelson, Bahnmuller, and Lyman, 1965). Thus the chief contribution of experimental programs is not so much higher academic achievement as it is the development of desirable attitudes—the affective aspect of education that is largely neglected by conventional programs.

Getting the Student Involved

Although there are still many teachers, and educational researchers as well, who believe that instructional method is the key to promoting effective learning, the trend, as we have noted earlier, is toward concern about students' motivation. Without some individualization, it is difficult to get all members of a class to attend to the task at hand. An incidental finding of research with teaching machines illustrates how classroom learning can improve when the attention of students can be captured. In the study in question, the performance of fifth-graders learning Spanish with the aid of teaching machines was compared with that of a group in regular classes and another group that made use of a programmed textbook. The teaching machines were an early model that kept breaking down. The more highly trained teachers, who had been more thoroughly briefed on the machines, put them aside, sent for a repairman, and substituted other activities. Teachers with less training told the students to repair the machines and proceeded with the programmed instruction. In some classes, as much as 25 percent of the time was spent in repairing machines. The results of the study showed that students in classes where they were asked to repair the machines showed a higher degree of achievement than did students in any of the other groups. These differences showed up at every IQ level. The researchers explained the unexpected results in terms of the fact that students who repaired broken machines evidently became involved in the educational program to a much greater extent than did students in other groups. "They became proud of their ability to keep the machine going. It was their machine and they wanted it to do well." Because they had more responsibility, they were more highly motivated to learn (Schramm and Oberholtzer, 1964).

Gunars Reimanis (1970) has conducted research with preschool children that tells us something about the relationship between teacher behavior and children's self-involvement in learning tasks. Reimanis was interested in *internal* reinforcement control: the ability of a learner to serve as his own reinforcer. Children who are their own reinforcers have been shown in other research to be high achievers in school. Traditional teachers, however, are inclined to encourage dependent behavior on the part of students and to discourage them from "going off on their own," that is, thinking and acting independently. Often teachers do not do this intentionally, but their tendencies to retain control of the contingencies of reinforcement keep children from developing internal reinforcement control. One of the teachers in Reimanis' study was supportive of children's efforts to function independently; another was very affectionate but encouraged dependency, and was not very interested in children's achievement efforts. Both teachers were quite positive and accepting in their approaches to children. However, children in the first classroom engaged in half again more achievement-oriented behavior than did children in the second room.

Ways in which teachers can encourage or discourage achievement are suggested by some research by Jacob S. Kounin (1970b). Preschool children were likely to show considerable involvement in learning tasks when they were engaged in activities in which the next step in whatever was being done was signaled by their own behavior (for example, construction), when teachers and children were handling or investigating things together (for example, a lesson on "magnets"), or when teacher or record player was emitting a continuous signal (for example, storytelling). Children were least involved when teachers were attempting to get them to deal with cognitive issues (for example, learning of numbers), or when teachers and children were focusing on group activities (for example, singing or dancing). Although the same results might not hold

for older children, they do suggest that the more individual-centered the activity required by a task, the greater the involvement of the learner.

Even the teacher of past generations was aware of the need to "get students involved" and asked certain children to be "monitors"—to pass out papers, clean blackboard erasers, carry notes to other teachers, and so forth. This practice gave a limited number of children a feeling of importance, of participating in the teaching as well as in the learning process. Science teachers, too, discovered that laboratory experiences were usually more effective than lectures, textbooks, and recitations, when it came to securing student interest, attention, and involvement.

During the first quarter of this century, a number of educational plans were developed that had the partial intent of involving students more actively in the learning process. Among these were the Dalton Plan, the Winnetka Plan, and the "contract" plan. The Dalton Plan transformed traditional classrooms into subject-matter laboratories, where students worked at various tasks, individually or in groups. The Winnetka Plan abandoned lectures and recitations in favor of self-instructive practice exercises and diagnostic tests. The contract plan borrowed some of the features of the Dalton and Winnetka Plans. It allowed for individual differences by permitting and encouraging students to undertake tasks appropriate to their abilities and experiences.

Although these experimental methods attracted much attention in their day and seemed to produce superior results, none of them became very popular. With the renewed interest in individualized instruction today, however, contracting has been "rediscovered." Contracting is an important feature in IGE and other innovative programs, such as Individually Prescribed Instruction or IPI (Cooley and Glaser, 1969). Contracting has been integrated into CAI programs, as well as into programs that feature behavior modification. Daniel W. Myerson (1970) reported on an arrangement whereby sixth-grade students were asked to propose rewards that could be exchanged for tokens. They suggested more than two hundred rewards that could be given without expenditure of funds or disruption of normal school activities, such as "passing out papers" and "reading to the kindergarten." Students then decided on a graduated schedule that set forth the value in tokens of each reward. Tokens then became the reinforcers in an experimental program aimed at reducing absenteeism, increasing the number of daily assignments completed, improving scores on spelling and arithmetic tests, and increasing the number of students who contribute to class discussions, bring in news articles, and make original responses.

During the initial stages of the experiment the teacher awarded tokens liberally and then tapered off to an irregular and unpredictable schedule of reinforcement. Students were permitted to deposit excess tokens in a "bank," where they drew interest if not used immediately. Myerson reported that the changes in student performance were instantaneous and dramatic. Absentee rates dropped, arithmetic and spelling test scores increased as much as 400 percent, discipline problems became nonexistent, and involvement in discussion and other learning tasks became much more widespread.

Although much credit is due the teacher for initiating and conducting such an ingenious experiment, it should be noted that its success was to a large extent the result of the way in which students were involved in determining what the rewards would be and what their value should be in terms of tokens.

Helping Students Learn from One Another

We have observed that the group situation in which education must be dispensed makes it difficult to individualize instruction and leads teachers to become preoccupied with problems of discipline and control. There are, however, some built-in advantages to group situations as far as the facilitating of learning is concerned. As learners, it is not necessary for teachers to do all the reinforcing, since we respond to reinforcement from almost any source. Students can reinforce one another's responses very effectively. The problem here is a dual one: that of getting them to behave in ways that are potentially reinforcing, and at the same time getting them to reinforce the proper responses.

Children also use their teachers' behavior as a model in their interaction with one another.

Alice Bingham (1958), in her book on improving children's facility in problem solving, told of Brad, who was working on an assignment which required him to find the answers to questions in a textbook. One question asked the season of the year in which the story took place. Brad reported that he had finished the entire story but had found nothing to indicate the time of year.

Another student, Marianna, overheard Brad's complaint and asked the teacher if she could tell him the answer. The teacher replied that it would be best if Brad found the answer himself. So Marianna suggested:

"You have to look for clues."

Brad expressed puzzlement. "What kind of clues?"

"Like what kind of things happen at certain times of the year," Marianna replied.

When Brad expressed further confusion, Marianna asked him, "What happens a lot in winter?"

"Snow. Ice. We go sledding," Brad ventured. "But there is no snow or sledding in the story. Oh I get it. At least I think I do," he exclaimed as he opened the book and began to reread the story.

After some ten minutes of reading, he rushed excitedly up to the teacher's desk and said, "It's spring."

When the teacher asked him how he had decided, he said that there was mention of leaves coming out on the trees and of birds flying back from the south. Brad was proud of himself because he was able to deduce the answer to the question.

There are some things that students can learn more easily from one another than they can from adults or from books. For one thing, many students can accept correction from other children more readily than they can from adults. Being corrected by the teacher, particularly in front of other children, can be a humiliating experience, even when the correction is deserved. Although the teacher may attempt to make the correction in a gentle and considerate manner, many students are so defensive or so easily hurt that they are likely to be concerned solely with their hurt feelings and consequently are unable to learn from the correction. When the correction is done by a classmate, there is likely to be less defensiveness because the classmate is not an authority figure.

Donald D. Durrell (1961) developed a program of pupil-team teaching that was installed in forty-seven intermediate-grade classrooms of the Dedham, Massachusetts, schools. Students were organized into teams of two or more members who worked on study guides prepared for use in the regular elementary school subjects. Each team had a scribe, who recorded responses made by other team members. Teachers set the learning tasks, decided on the make-up of the teams, analyzed and evaluated achievement, and decided how much time to spend each day on team teaching and on all-class activities. The teacher also disciplined when nonworking noises appeared in a group, usually by separating pupils and having them work alone on the team task. Although some teachers resisted at first, most of them came to develop positive feelings toward the program. On an anonymous evaluation questionnaire, they rated the spelling, arithmetic, and reading programs as "superior" and the social studies and language arts programs as "good." Anonymous returns from parents were definitely favorable, with 95 percent reporting themselves "very pleased" or "satisfied." Attitudes of students toward school subjects showed favorable changes in the fifth grade, although there were no changes in the fourth and sixth grades. An evaluation of the quality of teaching by outside raters showed a marked improvement during the period of the experiment. Students in the experiment in general made significant gains in achievement, as contrasted with students in classrooms that were taught along more conventional lines.

Considerable interest has developed in recent years in having students tutor one another. This method of instruction has been used as far back as the eighteenth century, when it was called "the monitorial system." In those days student tutoring was employed as a way of reducing the cost of education, but today the aim is more psychological. One investigator found that fifth- and sixth-graders were as effective in teaching reading to second-graders as were college students who were taking a reading methods course. The college students seemed intent on coaxing their pupils to like them, to enjoy the materials, and to practice the reading skills. The child tutors, however, used a more direct, businesslike approach. They accepted the fact that the second-graders had learning problems and that the purpose of the tutoring sessions was that of teaching the assigned materials; hence they did not go off on tangents and discuss matters outside the lesson (Thomas, 1970).

Arthur Elliott (1973), in a review of research on student tutoring, concluded that it has a number of advantages over conventional modes of instruction:

1. It increases the amount of teaching that is actually done in the classroom.

2. The learner gets a great deal more feedback on his performance, and he receives it immediately.

3. It reduces the amount of teacher talk and increases the amount of student talk.

4. The student who serves as tutor experiences an enhanced sense of personal worth.

5. The student tutor has a chance to see the teaching-learning situation from the teacher's point of view. This insight helps to convert the classroom climate from one of suppression to one of cooperation in the pursuit of learning.

6. Student tutors may be able to identify learning problems, as well as adjustment problems, that may have escaped the teacher's notice.

An additional outcome is that students who have learning deficiencies may be helped by tutoring children whose competence is less than their own. In one experiment, tenth- and eleventh-grade students who were reading at a rate two years below their age norms were paid to tutor fourth- and fifth-graders who were also having reading difficulties. Over a five-month period, the children who were tutored gained six months in reading ability, as compared to an untutored group who gained three and one-half months. The tutors, however, gained almost three and one-half *years* in reading competence (Cloward, 1967).

Students who tutor often make greater gains than the ones they tutor.

LEARNERS IN GROUP SETTINGS

Promoting the Major Objectives of Education

One of the "frontier" areas of education that psychologists and educators are exploring is the use of the classroom group in promoting some of the major objectives of education. By major objectives we mean some of the broader objectives that are basic not only to the developmental tasks faced by children and youth but also the acquisition of specific skills and information. Examples of such basic objectives are the ability to think critically and constructively, the development of self-discipline, the ability to work with others cooperatively and effectively, and the willingness to accept responsibility for oneself and others. These are objectives that appear as by-products or as the incidental outcomes of subject-matter competence in many educational curricula. In some schools they are even taught in a formal manner, like any other academic subject.

As twentieth-century educators became concerned about the relative inability of teacher-centered methods to motivate students in the direction of the attainment of these broader objectives, they devised experimental programs of instruction. Although many of these programs made use of large and small groups, their chief focus was on the individual student. It is only within recent years that attention has been directed to the deliberate use of the psychological forces within the group in the attainment of educational goals. The research that psychologists have conducted in the field of group processes during the last two decades has helped bring about this change of emphasis.

What educational psychologists are discovering is that motivation for learning is based on attitudes, and that attitudes are to a large extent shaped by psychological processes within the group. If the classroom group develops attitudes that are consistent with what the teacher or the school is attempting to accomplish, the chances are that its members will perceive the problems presented by the curriculum as interesting or valuable and will therefore attempt the solution of such problems. If the prevailing norm is one of hostility, cynicism, or apathy, however, most students will be inclined to resist any attempts to promote positive learning. Any progress that a class makes in the direction of the major or subsidiary goals of education will thus depend in large measure on the extent to which group norms permit and encourage members to become involved in the educational process.

As we noted in our discussion of the behaviorism-humanism controversy at the end of Chapter 8, teachers must become part-time social psychologists as well as educational psychologists. In other words, effective teaching requires a good working understanding of the effects that classroom groups have on individual learners. Indeed, most of the teacher's daily activities involve transactions with groups, rather than with single individuals. The two types of transactions require different kinds of information and skills.

Group Relations in the Classroom

The teacher who wishes to help the classroom group develops norms and standards that are favorable to learning does not have an easy task. For one thing, the traditional philosophy of education that appears to have a kind of normative power over the teaching profession makes it difficult for individual teachers to "break the pattern" and try some of the newer techniques. Furthermore, each teacher needs to experiment with a variety of group methods before he finds the ones that are personally "comfortable" for him and are appropriate to the kind of goals that he is attempting to attain in his classes. Actually, this is not a disadvantage, for evidence shows that continued experimentation with educational methods is one of the best safeguards against slipping back into older, more rigid patterns of teaching.

Although group methods had been used in a number of experimental programs during the 1920s and 1930s, they did not gain any real acceptance until the period after World War II. It was during those years that Jean D. Grambs (1952) outlined basic assumptions about group activities that are still valid for today's schools:

1. The relationships of children to each other, the feelings of acceptance or rejection, materially affect the kind of learning they do, the attitudes toward learning that they develop.

2. A good learning situation is one in which these feelings of children are taken into account in organizing work and study groups, play groups, and individual work.

3. The pattern of interaction, the ways in which one child moves into leadership one day and is a follower the next; the growth of antipathies toward seemingly normal youngsters; the group code that governs what is done or not done—these are part of the teacher's concern in working with students in a classroom.

4. There are ways of finding out about the structure of the child society which the teacher needs in order to gain access to this hidden world [that is, sociometric methods].

5. No class becomes a genuine group except for short periods of time when it has successfully accomplished a class goal through the efforts of the subgroups in it.

6. Every class is made up of many small natural units built from mutual need, propinquity, interests, and the "X" factor that makes one person like another.

7. The teacher creates unity of effort and orderly learning situations by working with the subgroups much as a symphony director works with the instrumental groups in the orchestra; each is different, each is composed of different numbers of persons, and they play different instruments;

together they complement, supplement, and harmonize.

8. Group skills develop in individuals as they are helped to see themselves objectively in their group relations. Discussions of leadership roles, member roles, things that help the group move forward, things that interfere, and the process of problem solving are essential.

9. The relationship between classroom group living and out-of-school group membership must be made explicit. Different types of group belonging and group identification must be spelled out with the children many times, in many different situations, and at each grade and age level.

The assumptions proposed by Grambs not only are basic to the techniques and methods we are presenting but also constitute a redefining of the traditional role of the teacher in the light of recent research in the field of group processes.

The last point in Grambs' list deserves special emphasis, however, because the way in which these basic principles should be applied by teachers will vary in accordance with the level of maturity of the class. In general, group work with younger children requires a great deal more teacher participation than does group work with adolescents. For one thing, younger children have a shorter attention span and are more interested in expressing their own ideas and feelings than in listening to others. Although there are great variations among groups of older children with respect to their ability to function effectively in groups, they need much less control and direction than young children do.

Group Discussion

The most basic form of group participation method is the class discussion, a technique that may range from the teacher-directed (and often teacher-centered) "Socratic method" that attempts to get students to explore problems and issues through questioning, to the highly permissive, unstructured, and uninhibited "brainstorming." Socratic questioning is usually (but not necessarily) used to lead students to discover certain information or con-

cepts known to the teacher. These methods, like most teaching-learning techniques in formal situations, are termed "convergent" because they converge on a single "right answer." Brainstorming is one of a number of teaching-learning techniques in which a problem is posed, and students are encouraged to find as many different solutions or answers as possible. Such approaches are termed "divergent" because the student uses the problem as a starting point and seeks many different solutions, instead of the "right one." Divergent methods are best suited to the teaching of heuristics because they encourage inventiveness, creativity, and the transfer of learning.

The inventor of brainstorming, Alex F. Osborn (1957), claimed that groups who brainstormed could produce problem solutions that were superior to the solutions that would have been obtained if each of their members had worked alone. Experiments testing this proposition have produced contradictory results. E. Paul Torrance (1970a,b) found that two-person brainstorming groups were more creative than individuals working alone, but Dunnette, Campbell, and Jaastad (1963) got better results when subjects worked alone than when they brainstormed in a group. Group brainstorming appeared to produce some positive results, however, because those subjects who worked alone *after* they had brainstormed were more productive than those who worked alone *before* they brainstormed. The freewheeling interaction of group brainstorming evidently had some kind of warm-up effect. Lindgren and Lindgren (1965a,b) found that college students working on a verbal task were more productive after they had brainstormed in small groups than they were before. Women students working on nonverbal tasks (sketching and designing) were also more creative after group brainstorming (Lindgren, 1967).

Brainstorming also seems to work with larger groups. In one experiment, entire classes of fourth-graders brainstormed unusual uses for ordinary objects (a part of Torrance's [1965] Test of Imagination). Then they worked alone, making lists of unusual uses for another object. In contrast to pupils in control classes, who worked alone throughout the two phases of the experiment, the children in the experimental classes produced more responses during the second phase of the experiment. Furthermore, their responses were judged more creative (Buchanan and Lindgren, 1973).

It is not difficult to see why group brainstorming facilitates creativity and learning. Verbal interchanges among group members arouse interest, and what may seem initially to be a trivial task becomes more interesting. Even students who are normally apathetic find it difficult to reject an assigned task when others in the group are working on it enthusiastically. The patterns of behavior that develop within a group become *social norms* that have a powerful effect on the behavior of group members, an effect that remains even after they have left the group (Sherif, 1936). Furthermore, members of problem-solving groups learn from one another by imitating the techniques and strategies that they observe others using.

As we noted in Chapter 2, we all have needs to belong, to achieve status in a group setting. Small groups, whether informal brainstorming sessions or more formally structured committees, enable students to satisfy this basic need. They also provide the teacher with an opportunity to open up new channels of communication and to find new ways of reinforcing learning behavior.

It is evident, then, that the most effective kinds of class discussion are the ones that involve the members in an interchange of ideas with one another instead of solely with the teacher. The most elementary form of discussion is one in which the teacher directs questions to students and then discusses their answers. This is really a variant of the traditional lecture-recitation method. A somewhat more effective plan is for students to direct questions to the teacher. This still means that the students talk a little and the teacher talks a lot. Many, if not most, discussions do not get beyond this stage, partly because teachers have so much to say and feel more comfortable when *they* are talking, partly because students have been educated by traditional methods in traditional classrooms and have learned to prefer to have the teacher take the initiative and responsibility, and partly because teachers do not use

any techniques to help students move on to a more effective pattern of discussion.

One of the ways of breaking out of the second stage of discussion is for the teacher *not* to answer a student's question but to throw it to the group, saying, for example: "Would anyone like to try to answer Bill's question?" Or, "I could comment on this, but I would rather hear what some of the rest of you think," or, "There are a number of points of view that people hold on this problem. Does anyone know what some of them are?"

Often the teacher can keep from being the target for every question by partially withdrawing from his position as discussion leader. One way he can do this is to assign himself the task of writing down important points on the blackboard as group members bring them up. This has the added effect of giving students the feeling that their contributions have been accepted. The teacher may also assign the position of discussion leader to one of the students and sit off in one corner of the room.

The success of classroom discussions can be enhanced if participants are seated in a circle or a hollow square so that everyone can see everyone else. Talking to the back of someone's head, or listening to someone whose face cannot be seen, seems to have a dampening effect on participation.

The leading of discussions is a difficult art but one well worth developing. Teachers have to experiment a while, sometimes for a number of years, before they develop techniques that are both effective and comfortable. Experimenting is also necessary because certain methods will work with some groups but not with others, even though the students may be of similar age and background. And the methods used with younger children are, of course, quite different from those used with older ones. For one thing, very young children are more concerned with self-expression than they are with listening to the contributions of others. This does not mean that discussion should not be used in the lower grades but rather that discussion should be used in a different way. Learning to listen to others is an important aspect of developing social maturity.

There is no lack of problems to discuss. Robert H. Bauernfeind (1951) asked three hundred chil-

WAYS OF GETTING STUDENTS INVOLVED
Although personal attention is probably the most powerful approach the teacher can use, group activities, such as student government and field trips, facilitate the development of interest, morale, and cohesiveness.

301

LEARNERS IN
GROUP SETTINGS

dren in the fourth, fifth, and sixth grades to write essays on the question, "What Are Your Problems—the Things That Bother You—the Things You Worry About?" Here are two of their essays that are strongly suggestive of leads for fruitful classroom discussions:

> One of my problems is trying not to fight. I hope I don't like to fight too much. I fight with my sisters but not my friends. Also I fight with 3rd, 4th, and 5th graders. Another one of my problems is blowing my money. I make about $4.00 a week. I put all my money away. But when I want something I get my money. At the end of the week I haven't any money left. Then I wish I hadn't spent it. Yet each week I keep spending. Also I get into a crabby mood and get my friends, family and others mad at me. I have tried everything to stop me. When I get crabby I get very mad at people. I sure wish I could get these off my mind.
> . . .
> I worry about tests in school, mostly geography tests. I lay awake nights thinking about my health and the condishion of my teeth. I worry mostly about my school studies. I worry about things that I was suppose to have done and didn't do. I also worry about things I've done wrong and haven't told anybody about.

Bauernfeind also asked the children to check a problem inventory. The three items most commonly checked were: "It is hard for me to pay attention in class," "I'm afraid of making mistakes," and "I wish I could be more calm when I recite in class."

In other words, the school situation was the chief source of problems for these children. Bauernfeind suggested that problem-solving experiences be included in the curriculum by having the teacher ask the class several times a week: "What problems do some of you have that you would like to tell about?" Discussions might then center around possible solutions for the problems that children have raised.

Most of the problems that students will bring up in this way have sufficient common appeal to serve as the basis for stimulating and rewarding discussions. They will be problems relating to the school, parents, brothers and sisters, and getting along with others. However, there are also advantages in going outside the personal experiences of the members of the class and bringing in new ideas, impressions, and concepts. Audiovisual methods are particularly valuable in providing *common experiences* that can serve as a basis for discussion. If all children in a class have been on the same field trip, visited the same museum, heard the same recording, or seen the same film, they can pool and compare their impressions and perceptions. Following up an audiovisual experience with a discussion helps to deepen and enrich the learning that results. Discussions help review important aspects of the experience, correct misapprehensions and misunderstandings, and provide a broader and more complete picture of the entire event.

It could be argued, indeed, that films and other audiovisual aids should always be followed up by discussion, in view of the fact that discussion contributes much to enhance the learning stimulated by the audiovisual aid. L. L. Mitnick and Elliott McGinnies (1958) used an antiprejudice film, *The High Wall*, with twelve groups of high-school students. Half of the groups saw the film and participated in a discussion about it, and the other half saw the film and had no discussion. Although the ethnic prejudice of all groups was reduced by the experience, as indicated by tests given a month later, the groups that had participated in the discussion were more significantly affected by the experience. Furthermore, those who had actively participated in the discussion learned more than those who had not.

Because there is a natural tendency for teachers to be dominant and directive in classroom situations, we have gone to some pains to show how they can make discussions more student-centered. With older children and adolescents, small-group discussions may even work better when there is no teacher involvement. In general, however, group methods need some kind of overall structure or direction. A group of high-school science students may feel more like discussing last night's basketball game or the virtues and deficiencies of popular musicians. A skilled discussion leader will allow some straying from the subject but will eventually bring them back to the matter at hand.

The Use of "Buzz Groups"

Although free discussion in large groups has its merits, there is a tendency for a few students to dominate and for the other members of the class to participate only occasionally, or not at all. The teacher can get a wider degree of participation by calling on nonparticipants, but tactics of this kind tend to make discussions teacher-centered and less free. The problem of how to get more students involved in discussion and still maintain a permissive atmosphere is not easily resolved. Some teachers present the issue to the class and request their help: "How can we make it possible for more of us to participate in our discussions?" Others use a "panel-discussion" method, with a complete change of personnel on each occasion.

One of the most effective methods of spreading participation is the "buzz session."

The energy crisis came up for discussion in one social studies class. Mr. Farber, the teacher, noted that there was considerable tension, aggravated by a great deal of "blaming." Some students blamed the greedy oil companies, others blamed the bumbling government, some blamed the wasteful consumers, and so on. Everybody wanted to talk at once. Mr. Farber decided that the moment was ripe to break the class into buzz sessions. He asked for quiet, and then summarized the main points at issue and said that the real problem that faced people was not that of assessing blame but of finding solutions. He then broke the topic down into specific questions: "What can the Congress do?" "What can the consumer organizations do?", and so forth. Each question was assigned to a buzz group of four to six students. Mr. Farber issued the following instructions to the groups before they began to discuss their questions:

1. Appoint a recorder to take notes and to report conclusions back to the entire class after the buzz period was over.
2. Discuss the possible answers to the question for ten minutes, and try to agree on two or three conclusions.

To the casual observer, it might appear that Mr. Farber assigned students to the groups in a random manner, but he actually balanced their membership in a number of ways. Each group consisted of members of both sexes, at least one very talkative student, and at least one very quiet one. He was careful to break up cliques and to see that the seven black students in the class did not all end up in one or two groups.

When the buzz period was over, the recorders made their reports, and Mr. Farber wrote brief summaries of their recommendations on the blackboard. The discussion that followed was much calmer. As the hour ended, Mr. Farber summarized the major points briefly and complimented the class on their thoughtful approach to a complex and difficult problem. As the class was leaving the room, two of the students came up to their teacher and volunteered to write up the conclusions of their buzz session in the form of a letter to the editor of the local newspaper.

Buzz groups are also helpful as "warm-up" devices. Some classes have difficulty in getting started in their discussions, perhaps because they are afraid to say something that might be wrong. Buzz sessions also help a classroom group to become involved in a new subject. Perhaps the group thinks it has no interest in, say, highway safety. But if they have a chance to break into small groups to discuss the subject "What can we do to make our highways safer?" latent interests will be developed that will carry over into the larger-group discussion.

Committees

Committee work can also make major contributions to the major goals of education. Like the buzz sessions, committees enable a larger number of students to participate than do large-group discussion methods. Furthermore, they may aid in the development of a wider variety of skills and activities. Committee work projects can also be developed through teacher-pupil planning. As teacher and students discuss the project they have decided to undertake, they break it down into tasks or groups of tasks that can be assigned to committees. When the committees are organized (preferably on a volunteer basis), they may break down their assignment into further subdivisions of tasks that can be undertaken by the individuals who comprise the group.

The amount of guidance that students will need in committee work will differ widely from class to class and from one age group to another. Like the other group methods that we have discussed, the supervision of committee work makes many demands on the teacher. He must give each committee enough help so that they will not become too discouraged but not so much that the project becomes the work of the teacher rather than of the children. Knowing where to draw the line between these two is not easy. The teacher who uses group methods must expect some failures, but if he and the group can learn through these failures, as well as through their successes, the experience will have been worthwhile.

Committee projects can also be used to change the social structure in a classroom. The typical class in the middle and upper grades usually contains some rather tightly knit, exclusive cliques, as well as some children who are ignored or rejected by other members of the class. This kind of social structure prevents the classroom group from being cohesive which, in turn, affects the ability of its members to communicate and to develop good morale. Teachers can deal with this problem by setting up committees to work on projects in such a way that students who have been ignored or rejected are given some measure of responsibility. Manipulation of this sort has to be done carefully, of course, in order not to interfere too drastically with preexisting interpersonal relationships. When committees are carefully structured, the social isolates are likely to become more visible and better liked, and the general cohesiveness of the class improves accordingly.

Getting the Most out of Group Methods

We end this section by summarizing some of the suggestions made by Hilda Taba (1951), who was one of the most insightful and influential leaders in getting teachers to think along social psychological lines:

1. Working in groups requires new skills, and neither teachers nor children will learn these skills all at once. Therefore working with groups requires experimentation and is never smooth at the start.

2. Useful work with groups needs to be planned both in the light of the content to be used and the processes to be employed. We must remember that it is important to teach useful ideas while carrying on group processes. Without such content, group processes are empty tricks.

3. Productivity of groups depends both on the feelings group members have about each other and on the skills they have to carry their jobs forward.

4. Group skills are learned by experiencing them and analyzing them. They cannot be learned merely by talking about them.

5. All jobs in the classroom are not group jobs. Many things need to be done by individuals separately, or by the whole class as a collection of individuals, but at the same time.

Taba's points are applicable to a wide variety of classroom group activities, but they are particularly relevant for educational experiences designed to make students more aware of motivational factors in interpersonal behavior and to help them develop more effective ways of living and working with others.

CURRENT STATUS OF LEARNER-CENTERED METHODS

Whatever Happened to Free Schools?

A phenomenon that has attracted a great deal of attention on the part of educators, as well as the lay public, has been what has been termed the "Free School Movement." This movement, which owes a great deal of its direction and impetus to the Progressive Education movement of the 1920s and 1930s (but also goes back to Jean-Jacques Rousseau in the eighteenth century), began in the early 1960s to stir the imaginations of Americans interested in social experimentation. The hero of the free school movement was not Rousseau or even John Dewey, but A. S. Neill (1883–1973) whose books expounding radical views on education and describing his experimental school, Summerhill, excited or outraged readers all over the world.

Summerhill is one of a very few British schools which were established in the first quarter of this century and operated along unconventional lines. Although there were teachers and classes at Summerhill, attendance on the part of students was voluntary, and the major stress was on social and emotional adjustment and self-expression. This policy reflected Neill's views of formal learning. Since school subjects bored him, he was certain that they bored children as well (Skidelsky, 1969). The school was self-governing. Pupils met weekly in the main hall to discuss rules and to enforce their regulations against offenders. Everyone over eight years of age, including Neill himself, had one vote; the chairman and the other officers were selected in rotation, every pupil over eleven being eligible. Everyone was encouraged to participate in the discussions, which usually concerned bedtime rules, smoking, conduct in the nearby village, and aggressive behavior, such as bullying. Rule-breaking was usually punished by money fines. The philosophy underlying the self-government was that children would be more likely to observe the rules if they had made them themselves. Neill felt that transferring discipline from the teacher to the group removed a major barrier between adults and children, thus enabling them to be friends.

Neill's view of human development drew heavily on those of Wilhelm Reich, who was first a disciple of Sigmund Freud, but who later broke with him and developed theories that integrated Freudian thinking into social philosophy. In Reich's view, social order was created by a small, despotic ruling class who suppressed and deformed the individual's normal developmental drives. Neill, in following this line of reasoning, felt that his role as a schoolmaster was that of saving children from being mishandled and suppressed by their parents, by giving them as much freedom to develop as was feasible.

Neill's book, *Summerhill: A radical approach to education,* became a best-seller in America and started many young people to dreaming about founding their own Summerhills, a dream that led to the development of the Free School Movement. By 1970, the leaders of the Movement claimed that two thousand free schools, enrolling sixty thousand children, were providing a "major alternative" to parents who wanted to liberate their children from the lockstep of the public schools, and they predicted that in five years the Movement would be educating as many as a million and a half children. Robert D. Barr (1973), who has analyzed the history of the Movement, notes that reports were vastly exaggerated and that, instead of expanding and growing in strength, the Movement began to fade rapidly thenceforth. Part of the problem was that the founders of the schools lacked "staying power," for few of the schools lasted longer than eighteen months and most of them folded within a year of being opened.

Another difficulty has been that the spokesmen for the Free School Movement attacked the traditional/conventional modes of teaching with a no-holds-barred hostility that was bound to alienate teachers and many laymen who had moderate free school leanings. Albert Shanker (1971), head of the New York City teachers union, said that it was the arrogance of these more radical critics of the schools that led most teachers to reject them. Hence a great deal of potential support for the Movement was lost by the militancy of its leaders.

The Movement was also weakened by dissension from within. Jonathan Kozol (1972), whose criticism of traditional/conventional schooling gave him a large following in the Movement, savagely criticized middle- and upper-class "hippies" who went off to the Vermont forests to teach handicrafts such as weaving, basket making, and the construction of birchbark canoes that Indians themselves no longer wanted. Kozol felt that free school people should invest themselves in inner-city education, where the need for reform was the greatest, in his opinion. One should note, parenthetically, that inner-city parents are the *least* receptive to free school ideas. When they demand "quality education" for their children, they usually have in mind something on the traditional/conventional model. They can be persuaded otherwise, as we shall see, but the greatest support for the Free School Movement is found,

CURRENT STATUS OF
LEARNER-CENTERED METHODS

when it occurs at all, in the more affluent suburbs of the great cities.

Barr took note of the fact that many public school systems are providing alternative forms of education that incorporate some of the features of the schools founded by the Movement to a greater or lesser degree. He doubted, however, that these innovations have come from within the Movement, but rather from the efforts of many educational leaders "within the system" who were working for school reform long before there was a Free School Movement. The development of these "alternative programs," he said, "has been slow and steady work, for success has demanded the reeducation of many boards of education, parents, and administrators."

One of these alternative schools is an open-education program in Hartford, Connecticut, which started with fifty children in 1968 and was enrolling ten thousand four years later. The program, as described by Joseph D. Randazzo and Joanne M. Arnold (1972) would be located somewhat to the "right of center" on a continuum that ranges from Ivan Illich and Summerhill on the far left to Montessori, with its highly structured skill-oriented approach, on the far right. The program has special features to involve inner-city children, especially those who would ordinarily be labeled as "low-normal" or "hyperactive."

The development of the open-education program in Hartford went through the following stages:

1. Teachers and administrators asked themselves, "Where are we going?" and "Are we teaching children to adapt, cope fully, and think creatively?"

2. In their attempt to answer these questions, the school staffs explored the ways in which children learn and studied the environments that seemed to be best for learning. In this, they examined the writings of Montessori, Bruner, Pestalozzi, and Piaget.

3. The school people agreed that whatever program they developed would not be based on commercially prepared "teaching-learning packages." Teachers were to be permitted to use such materials selectively, if and when they judged them appropriate.

4. Teachers participated in a three-week training program whereby they acquired "the techniques and philosophy of openness by experiencing it themselves." Over a six-year period, some one thousand teachers and paraprofessionals went through a "mind-opening process designed to recapture the passion of teaching."

5. A concerted effort was made to involve parents and leaders at all levels of the community. The major aspect of this effort was the hiring of three hundred paraprofessionals, many of them from the inner city.

6. A Teacher Renewal Resource Center, centrally located and open all day, was set up as a place where teachers could get advice, attend seminars, develop teaching materials, or meet informally with other teachers.

7. The curriculum has gone through a continuous process of change, as teachers experiment with their own innovations, as well as with commercially prepared materials.

Although elementary schools generally provide a more sympathetic environment for open-classroom reform than do secondary schools, some high schools also have had success with the newer methods. Some four hundred to six hundred high schools in the United States operate or have operated "free" or "alternative" schools. One of these is Herricks High School in New Hyde Park, New York, which operates an alternative "free school," called a Community School, within its walls. The eighty students the Community School serves consult with teachers and decide what topics should be included and what books should be read. Classes, which are not compulsory, seldom have more than ten students, and extensive use is made of outside consultants who have volunteered to help. There are no grades, but each student keeps a file summarizing what he learned from a given course or from working on an outside job. The file also includes the teacher's or work supervisor's evalu-

Influential figures in the free school
movement.
The writings of A. S. Neill (*left*), the
headmaster of the innovative British school,
Summerhill, were very influential in the
development of the free school movement in
America. Much of Neill's philosophy can be
traced back to Jean-Jacques Rousseau
(*below*), the eighteenth century French-Swiss
social philosopher.

ation of the student's performance. Students monitor one another's progress and may recommend that a student who is not working be given a warning or denied credit. One or two students each year fail to gain full credit or are prevented from graduating on time. Most of the students at Herricks High prefer the conventional curriculum, and the small group who do participate in the "free school" must apply for admission and also secure their parents' permission (Ricklefs, 1974).

Resistance to Open Schools and Other Learner-Centered Methods

It would be unrealistic for us to say or even imply that the introduction of open classroom and similar learner-centered methods has made much more than a start in solving the problems that schools face in involving students more deeply in the educational process. Indeed even the minimal introduction of learner-centered methods creates some rather acute and difficult problems. For one thing, they call for the development of new and unfamiliar skills on the part of the teacher. More traditional approaches to education require principally that the teacher know his subject matter thoroughly and maintain control of the class. Today's teacher must not only know his subject matter but must also understand the motivational aspects of the individual and group behavior of children. Furthermore, he must be able to adjust a variety of methods to the needs of the class. As if this were not enough, he must practice these new skills and maintain this flexibility surrounded by a climate of community opinion that is often unfriendly to newer methods of education.

Because open classrooms permit greater freedom, traditionalists claim that "children are permitted to run wild" and that "children decide what they will learn and whether they will learn." Such charges are given credence by situations in which teachers have abdicated control and responsibility to children, excusing themselves on the ground that they were conducting "open classrooms." What this shows is that there are inadequate teachers among the more "progressive" members of the profession, just as there are inadequate teachers among the traditionalists. If children run wild in a classroom, this is evidence that teachers and administrators either do not understand children or are unable to translate their understanding into practice.

What traditionalists object to, essentially, is the greater freedom that students have in many modern classrooms. Teacher-centered education requires an attentive student, a student who speaks only when spoken to, who leaves his seat only when given permission. Traditionalists feel that without these conditions the result would be chaos. On the other hand, teachers using "open" methods believe that there is a world of difference between the chaotic classroom and the group which is busily, if some-

(Drawing by Saxon; © 1975 The New Yorker Magazine, Inc.)

"What did you learn in school today?"

what noisily, engaged in working on projects. There is a difference, they say, between "busy noise" and "noisy noise"—noise for the sake of noise.

The public appears generally to believe that most instruction in the public schools today is characterized by "open-classroom" methods. The facts are, however, that the open classroom is neither as widespread nor as accepted as is popularly believed. Although a few schools have embraced the philosophy and point of view of the open method wholeheartedly, most have either rejected it or adopted it only in part. The programs in Hartford and in the Herricks High School, which we mentioned, are examples of *modified* open-classroom plans. An even more common situation is for a school or a school system to introduce a few learner-centered activities into its classrooms without making any essential changes in its traditional subject-matter-centered and teacher-directed approach to education.

The greatest use of the open approach is, of course, made by kindergarten and nursery school teachers. Probably most of the instruction in the first three grades is more or less characterized by such methods in most American schools, but it is very likely that not more than half of the teachers in the intermediate grades make very much use of open methods. The higher the grade, the more for-

mal the learning situation tends to be. Education in primary and preschool years tends to be informal and characterized by learner-centered methods, whereas high-school and college instruction is more likely to be highly formalized and subject-matter-centered.

A study by the present author and Gladys May Patton (1958) supplies some clues to the greater willingness of elementary teachers to use learner-centered approaches. When both high-school and elementary teachers completed a questionnaire of attitudes toward educational practices and child behavior, high-school teachers were found to have attitudes that are more characteristically traditional and teacher-centered. The items that discriminated most sharply between the two groups of teachers are listed in Table 12-1.

If elementary teachers are more inclined to be interested in children's psychological needs, it follows that they will also be more likely to develop learner-centered programs. In defense of secondary schools, it should be noted that the instruction in the elementary schools, where children spend the entire school day or most of it with one teacher, is more conducive to the kind of flexibility that the activity program requires. Another difficulty is that the subject matter of the secondary schools is more abstract: It is relatively easy to translate the funda-

TABLE 12-1. Statements About Educational Practices and Child Behavior, Together with Responses Which Tend to Be More Characteristic of Elementary Teachers than of High-School Teachers[a]

Statement
1. How a student feels about what he learns is as important as what he learns. (Agree)
2. The classroom experiences that are the most helpful to boys and girls are the ones wherein they can express themselves creatively. (Agree)
3. It is more important for students to learn to work together cooperatively than it is for them to learn how to compete. (Agree)
4. Some pupils are just naturally stubborn. (Disagree)
5. It is better for a girl to be shy and timid than "boy crazy." (Disagree)
6. The first signs of delinquency in a pupil should be received by tightening of discipline and more restrictions. (Disagree)
7. A teacher should lower grades for misconduct in class. (Disagree)
8. A great deal of problem behavior results from fear and guilt. (Agree)
9. Most pupils need some of the natural meanness taken out of them. (Disagree)

[a] Lindgren and Patton, 1958.

mentals of arithmetic into projects growing out of the interests of children; it is relatively more difficult to do the same with history or geometry.

Prospects for Learner-centered Methods

Whether experimental, learner-centered programs are introduced in a school depends, in the final analysis, on the climate of public opinion. It is the public who, through its elected representatives and its votes on school bond issues, determines the direction of education. Parents and taxpayers are inclined to be skeptical and even suspicious when it comes to the introduction of learner-centered curricula and methods. This raises the question of whether the teaching profession has been sufficiently active in educating citizens as to the need for progress and experimentation. Before teachers set about convincing the public that there is a need for reform, they themselves must be convinced that reform is necessary. When educators do suggest innovations, the changes involved tend to be more concerned with administrative procedures than with classroom practices. One list of innovations, subtitled "Summaries of 628 best school practices adopted by 323 good school systems, 1957–1964," consisted principally of ways in which existing teacher-centered or subject-matter-centered programs could be made more efficient (Fallon, 1966). Not more than 20 percent could be considered to be innovations aimed at making instructional practices and curricula more learner-centered.

Teachers tend to be rather conservative and inflexible in their perceptions of what can and cannot be done to improve teaching-learning processes. Some studies conducted by William C. Morse (1961, 1962) and by Dunn and others (1964) show that teachers generally believe that it is impossible to achieve both cognitive and attitudinal goals and at the same time give due attention to the group processes within the classroom. They also believe that it is impossible to develop good intergroup relations in the classroom and also at the same time give adequate attention both to the mental health of individual students and to cognitive learning. Students in their classes, however, do not see these three

goals as mutually incompatible. Students reported that progress toward any one of these goals tends to be accompanied by progress toward the others; in other words, where there is good achievement in classroom learning, there also tends to be adequate attention given both to mental-health needs of individual students and to group processes. Students' perceptions of what makes for sound educational practices were thus consistent with those of educational psychologists, but teachers seemed to think that an emphasis on one of these goals made it impossible to achieve the others. In fact, this belief is in line with the objections often expressed by teachers who are resisting the introduction of new or experimental methods: "Yes, I could give more attention to the mental-health needs of children, but their reading would suffer," or "It would be nice to have a more relaxed group atmosphere in the classroom, but you can't get as much work done, and besides, if I start working with the group, individual students will lose out." What Morse's research shows is that such arguments are unfounded and probably serve as excuses for not changing methods that teachers have grown accustomed to using.

The question of teacher morale is, however, an important one and should not be treated lightly. Moves to bring in new or experimental methods must be discussed at length with teachers before they are actually introduced. Precipitous decisions on the part of administrators inevitably arouse anxieties, feelings of inadequacy, and resistance. There are many teachers who achieve fairly good results within the setting of the traditional classroom. We would be hesitant about disturbing anyone who is doing an adequate job of teaching, even though we might feel he would be even more effective if he adopted the aims and methods of the new education and even though we are quite sure that many other, less able teachers are using traditional methods as a support or mask for their inadequacies.

In deciding whether to introduce learner-centered practices into the classroom, we should keep two things in mind. First, the research evidence for the superiority of learner-centered methods is not strong. The usual finding is that there is little difference in academic achievement between groups taught by experimental and by conventional methods, but that there are significant attitudinal and motivational differences favoring the experimental group. Second, it is a good idea for teachers to change their methods every few years, if only to increase their own interest, enthusiasm, and feeling of involvement. As Stephen S. Willoughby (1969) said in a review of research in the field of mathematics instruction:

> Whether experimentation gives reliable results is probably not of as much importance as the fact that the experimentation is being carried on.

SUMMARY

Traditional forms of education fall somewhat short of meeting the psychological needs of students because they more or less deliberately frustrate students' attempts to socialize and to seek outlets for self-expression. On the other hand, traditionally oriented schools do make positive contributions to the psychological development of students by providing a stable, predictable environment in which to work and by bringing students into contact with the adult world outside the home.

The two major trends in educational reform are the "management" approach to education, which is a sophisticated expression of traditional/conventional philosophy, and the learner-centered or "open" school. Learner-centered views focus on the learner's motivational drives and needs. The trend today is toward learner-centered views, although the movement is slow, and theory outpaces classroom practice. Newer methods of education are characterized by more extensive and intensive student involvement, individualization of instruction, a greater variety of instructional techniques, openness of classroom structure, and relevance to everyday life. Some methods, such as Individually Guided Education (IGE), seem to be largely traditional/conventional because they are skill- or subject-matter-centered, but they can also be used in modified open-classroom situations that focus on the needs of the individual learner. Computer-assisted instruction (CAI) also can be employed in programs that are learner-centered. Other innovations include the merging or integrating of courses into core, monodisciplinary, or interdisciplinary curricula, which can be taught by single teachers or by teaching teams. Such experiments work best when students are allowed or encouraged to become more deeply involved in learning processes and to be their own reinforcers.

The contract plan of instruction that was developed fifty years ago has reappeared in the classroom in recent years as a way of individualizing instruction. Behavior modification methods are also used to improve student motivation. Students can often learn from one another as effectively as they do from specially trained adults. The monitorial system of the eighteenth century has reappeared in the form of student tutors, who not only are quite effective in some instances but also learn to play responsible roles in the classroom and gain a better perspective of the teacher's problems as well.

Group interaction is an important dimension in the learner-centered or open classroom. Group methods not only have stimulating effects on cognitive processes, but also help improve communication, group morale, and cohesiveness. Teachers can be more effective in group discussions if they play less-directive roles and help group members interact with one another. Topics for group discussion can be based on the problems that students encounter in everyday life or can be drawn from some common experience, such as field trip they have taken or a film they have seen.

One of the shortcomings of large-group discussions is that some students tend to monopolize and dominate, and others participate only occasionally or not at all. Participation can be spread by the use of small-group discussions or "buzz sessions." Buzz sessions can also be helpful in opening up a new subject or in getting the classroom group involved in a topic that they had not previously considered to be important.

Committee work is also a useful way of spreading participation. It is a way of giving students opportunities to learn how to work cooperatively and to think for themselves.

The Free School Movement in America was initiated by young people who were stimulated by A. S. Neill's book describing Summerhill, an English school which was run largely by its students and whose curriculum deemphasized formal educational subjects in favor of self-directed emotional and social experiences. Disciples of Neill founded a large number of small, private "free schools" during the late 1960s and early 1970s and at one time claimed that they had started a reform that would provide educational alternatives for a million or more children. This prediction has not been realized, and the movement has faded somewhat in recent years. The philosophy and some of the free-school methods have been incorporated to a greater or lesser degree in a large number of open-school or open-classroom programs in the public schools.

Although open-classroom or learner-centered methods have attracted a great deal of attention on the part of the education profession and the public at large, their acceptance has been rather minimal. Both the public, who must in the end approve of innovative programs, and the teachers, who must staff them, have been reluctant to support them because of a concern that too much freedom may be given students. Where learner-centered programs have been instituted, they have usually been in modified form. Elementary teachers tend, for a number of reasons, to be more receptive of learner-centered methods, and secondary school teachers are prone to be more resistive. In general, teachers tend to be cautious about instituting changes, particularly those that are concerned with improving group relations in the classroom and working toward mental-health goals. Making too many changes too fast would probably be unwise, however, partly because many traditionally oriented teachers are doing a reasonably effective job. Still, it would be a good thing if every teacher did some experimentation, if only to stimulate his interest in his job.

Suggested Problems

1. Joe is an unhappy, frightened fourth-grader. His father is an alcoholic who works only occasionally and who beats his son and his wife whenever he engages in one of his drinking bouts. Joe's mother works all day long. Joe has just transferred to the George Washington Grammar School, which is a traditional, formal school in the older part of the small city in which he lives. Envision for yourself a formal educational situation and indicate some of the ways in which

going to such a school might be both helpful and rewarding for Joe.

2. Suppose that the George Washington Grammar School had an educational program that was learner-centered, instead of traditional. In what additional ways could Joe be helped? In other words, how could some of his needs be met better in a learner-centered school than in a traditional teacher-centered school?

3. Have you ever attended a movie or watched a television program that caused you to change your mind about something you had always believed? If so, perhaps you can describe how the process took place. Or have you ever had your mind changed as a result of participating in a group discussion? Perhaps you can recall some of the factors that led to the change.

4. Compare two learning experiences you have had, one where you sat passively and "absorbed" what was taught, and another when you "learned by doing." Which was the more personally satisfying? Which was the more successful?

5. The available research comparing lecturing with discussion methods indicates that students learn approximately the same amount of subject matter with each method, but that they prefer the discussion and find it more interesting. Yet far more teachers, particularly in colleges and universities, prefer the lecture method. What are the probable reasons for their unwillingness to change?

Suggested Readings

Ashton-Warner, S. *Teacher*. New York: Simon and Schuster, 1963. (A paperback.) Vivid description of a creative, learner-centered program in a primary class for Maori and white New Zealanders.

Association for Supervision and Curriculum Development. *Individualizing instruction*. Washington: National Education Association, 1964. Surveys the ways in which education can be made more learner-centered.

Esbensen, T. *Working with individualized instruction: The Duluth experience*. Palo Alto, Calif.: Fearon, 1968. (A paperback.) An administrator describes the operation of experimental learner-centered programs in considerable detail.

Fisk, L. and Lindgren, H. C. *Learning centers.* Glen Ridge, N.J.: Exceptional Press, 1974. A manual describing the use and construction of learning or interest centers for elementary classrooms.

Glasser, W. *Schools without failure.* New York: Harper and Row, 1969. A psychiatrist examines school programs in the Los Angeles area, including Watts, and concludes that the main cause of learner failure is that conventional schools are designed to produce failure. Glasser recommends classes become teacher-led counseling groups.

Good, T. L., and Brophy, J. E. *Looking in classrooms.* New York: Harper and Row, 1973. Although intended as a manual for teachers who want to become more aware of their behavior, the book has many suggestions about ways in which instruction at all levels can be individualized and made more meaningful to students.

Horowitz, M. M. *The teacher utilizes group forces,* in *Learning and the teacher,* 1959 Yearbook of the Association for Supervision and Curriculum Development. Washington: National Education Association, 1959.

Leonard, G. B. *Education and ecstasy.* New York: Dell, 1968. (A paperback.) One of the more extreme criticisms of conventional school programs and their methods.

Postman, N., and Weingartner, C. *Teaching as a subversive activity.* New York: Delacorte, 1969. Lively and interesting discussion of many of the types of methods mentioned in this chapter.

Skidelsky, R. *English progressive schools.* Baltimore: Penguin, 1969. (A paperback.) Recounts the history and describes the current status of these interesting experimental programs, including the more radical Summerhill, as well as the more conservative Abbotsholme School.

Taba, H. *With perspective on human relations.* Washington: American Council on Education, 1955. A study of peer-group dynamics in an eighth grade.

Thelen, H. A. *Dynamics of groups at work.* Chicago: University of Chicago Press, 1954. A handbook dealing with the application of principles of group processes to a variety of tasks. See particularly Chapter 2, "Educating children through need-meeting activity." Available as a paperback Phoenix book.

United States Office of Education. *Educational research and development in the United States.* Washington: Government Printing Office, 1969. See particularly the chapters relating to a historical review of educational research, description of experimental programs, and outcomes of programs.

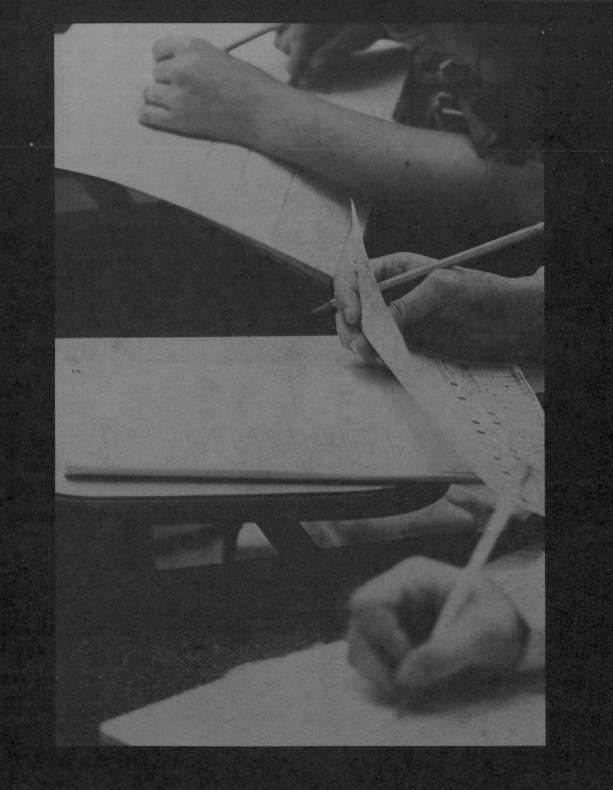

13

The Evaluation of Learning

No aspect of education is more charged with anxiety than is evaluation. This is true for teachers as well as for students, for the level of attainment reached by the student is perceived, rightly or wrongly, as an indication of how well he has been taught.

Because of the anxiety that is generated by evaluation, some people feel that it should be eliminated from the classroom. Yet if classrooms are to be segments of the real world, and not isolated and alienated from it, evaluation is inevitable. In actuality, evaluation cannot be eliminated from any human encounter. When two individuals interact, each evaluates the other's behavior, usually subconsciously. This evaluation serves as the basis for such decisions as: "Should I continue the conversation, or move to terminate it?" "Should I change the subject?" "Can I take him literally, or is he joking or exaggerating?" Each individual evaluates his own performance as well, in terms of how well his statements express what he wants to say, what kind of impression he is making on the other, and so on.

Evaluation, therefore, is as inevitable as life itself. As we shall show, it has special relevance for teachers and learners. The main problem is not how we can get rid of it, but how we can understand it and do it better.

The Teacher's Role as an Evaluator

Evaluation is the result of the teacher's concern with the goals of education. In his role as an evaluator the teacher asks himself such questions as the following: "Are students making any progress in the direction of the goals appropriate to this learning situation? What evidence indicates whether or not they are progressing? How much progress, if any, are they making? To what extent can their success (or failure) be attributed to the experiences that they have had in the classroom?"

The teacher's role as an evaluator of learning may appear to be somewhat at odds with his roles as a stimulator and promoter of learning. Many a teacher has worked with a class for a number of weeks, trying to build group morale, cohesiveness, and group feeling, only to see the class freeze up and suddenly become uncommunicative when he announces an examination. At such times he might wish that final marks in his course were limited to "pass-fail," thus relieving him of the responsibility of grading the performance of individual group members. These problems are aggravated when the teacher has become immersed in the group process and has come to think of himself as a fully functioning member of the classroom group.

It may help to resolve some of the confusion if we think of teachers as having two basic roles: that of the participant and that of the observer. In his role as the participant, he plans educational programs, develops methods and uses materials in order to carry out the programs, and participates in the social interaction of the classroom, while performing his specialized functions as a teacher. In his role as an observer, he is more detached: He analyzes students' backgrounds, notes how students are reacting to his methods and materials, and comes to cer-

tain conclusions regarding the progress made by individual students, as well as by the class in general. There is a tendency for teachers to subordinate one of these roles to the other. Some teachers become immersed in the daily give-and-take of the teaching-learning process, whereas others play detached, judgmental roles, never fully committing themselves to active participation. In the final chapter we shall discuss at greater length the various roles that teachers play, but for the present let us keep in mind that the teacher is responsible to the community, the administration, his profession, and to himself, as well as to the students in his class. The community, the administrators, and very likely the teacher himself will want to have some indication as to whether the educational program is succeeding with students. A teacher may not enjoy making the kinds of observations and providing the sort of information that will enable others to judge the progress of his students, as well as his own work, but he should recognize their right to make such judgments. Furthermore, if he does not supply them with the data they want, they will find ways of collecting their own data. The teacher has little to gain and much to lose by refusing to participate in the evaluative process; it is only by participating that he can have anything to say about the bases on which teaching-learning is to be judged and the kinds of judgments that are to be made.

It is not easy to coordinate the warm and human roles of the participant in teaching-learning with those of the cool, detached, and objective roles of the observer, but this is a problem that every teacher must face and resolve. It would seem that he can preserve the greatest amount of professional freedom if he resolves the issues himself, rather than have them resolved by external authorities. If he is to create some kind of a balance between participant and observer roles, he should be as familiar with evaluational techniques as he is with teaching techniques. "Evaluation," as Herbert J. Thelen (1969) says, "plays a part in all strategies of instruction." If the teacher does a bad job of evaluation, he not only has inferior data to communicate to authorities and to his students, but he may develop misconceptions about the effect that his teaching is having on students. The best justification for evaluation is our desire to improve teaching and learning, and if we want this evaluation to have any real meaning, we should do it as objectively and as carefully for ourselves and our students as we otherwise do it on behalf of others.

OBSERVING AND MEASURING PROGRESS TOWARD GOALS

Specifying Goals in Behavioral Terms

All education takes place with respect to goals or objectives. Usually the goals are implicit: We include courses in mathematics in the high-school curriculum because we believe that high-school graduates should have some understanding of and skill in the use of mathematics. Understanding and skill in mathematics thus are implicit goals—they are *implied* by our inclusion of mathematics courses in the curriculum.

One of the first steps the teacher-evaluator should take is that of making the goals explicit—determining what his goals actually are. It is important that goals be thought of in terms of the behavior that should occur as a result of the student's having gone through the educational program under consideration. If the teacher thinks of educational goals in terms of his *own* behavior, he may find himself unable to do any objective evaluation. To take a simple example, it makes a great deal of difference whether the goal of a course unit is stated as "As a result of this unit, pupils should have a better understanding and appreciation of Inca civilization," or whether it is stated as "My objective in this course is to teach the facts about the Inca civilization that children of this age level ought to know."

The first kind of statement requires the teacher to look for evidence indicating the extent to which students have or have not gained an understanding and appreciation of Inca civilization. This is not easy; it is a difficult problem that has no final answers or solutions. Hence it is understandable that the teacher might be tempted to avoid some of the issues and challenges it poses. The second kind of

statement does not present such a problem, for the teacher can say: "I achieved the objectives of the curriculum because I taught the facts about the Inca civilization." In the first instance, the criterion for success lies in the *changes* that have taken place in the behavior of the students; in the second instance, the criterion depends on the teacher's reaction to his own behavior—if he approves of what he has done he has succeeded, regardless of whether or not his students have demonstrated any intellectual growth. The second kind of objective is more characteristic of traditional, teacher-centered education because this approach assumes that the teacher is right: If anyone fails, it is the student who fails—because he did not apply himself or had insufficient background. The teacher who states his goals in terms of student behavior, however, expresses a more scientific attitude, for he is continually putting the entire teaching-learning situation to the test: If the goals were not attained, he must examine the adequacy of the teaching, the background of the students, or the validity of the goals themselves. The teacher who uses behaviorally oriented goals is continually looking for evidence indicating whether or not his objectives have been attained. The easy way out is, of course, for the teacher to assume that his objectives were attained if he taught the course to his own satisfaction.

In traditional programs of education there is generally a heavy emphasis on evaluation, although there seems to be an unspoken assumption that it is learning and not teaching that is being evaluated. Because traditional teaching practices stress tests and examinations so heavily, some teachers who have introduced innovative, group-centered methods in their classroom have overreacted and have abandoned evaluation, claiming that it interferes with group processes. It is true that much evaluation is done in a way that is punitive, but this is not likely to occur in programs that are truly learner-centered. The assumption that evaluation is "bad" is not only unnecessary but may actually interfere with learning. Evaluation, in the form of feedback, is as essential to learning as it is to teaching. Without evaluation, both teaching and learning are likely to become haphazard activities. The problem is not that of eliminating evaluation, but of including it in such a way that it is not punitive, does not lead to invidious comparisons, and is genuinely supportive of positive growth.

In its best sense, evaluation is concerned not only with how well teachers and learners are doing but also serves to focus their attention on:

1. Helping teachers and learners, as well as other interested groups and individuals, to clarify educational goals.

2. Gathering information that indicates the extent to which goals are being realized.

3. Helping teachers and learners to determine whether the teaching-learning activities actually being used facilitate progress toward the desired goals.

4. Gathering information that provides clues as to how goals might be attained more readily or how the goals themselves should be modified.

These tasks are stated in general terms. As we undertake them, we might break them down into the following more specific steps:

1. Formulating and classifying the objectives or goals that are appropriate to the educational program and that learners might reasonably be expected to attain.

2. Stating objectives or goals in terms of the actual behavior of learners. Two questions are relevant here: (a) What are the important things that learners will do when they have attained the objective(s)? (b) How will their behavior differ from that of individuals who have not attained the objective(s)?

3. Identifying situations that give learners opportunities to show progress toward objectives.

4. Selecting or designing tests, critical situations, or other media that will yield feedback data.

5. Using Numbers 3 and 4 to gather data relative to Numbers 1 and 2.

6. Organizing and analyzing data.

7. Arranging for a review of objectives and methods to determine whether they should be revised.

The step that usually gives the most difficulty to evaluators is Number 2, stating objectives in behavioral terms. There is a natural tendency for curriculum planners to write objectives along these lines: "Students will know the causes of the Revolutionary War," "Students will *really* understand the Constitution," "Students will *fully* appreciate nineteenth century romantic poets," or "Students will grasp the significance of the Gettysburg Address." Such terms as "know," "understand," and "appreciate" are, however, vague and open to many interpretations. Evaluation is likely to be more effective if terms such as these are used instead: "write," "identify," "differentiate," "solve," "construct," and "compare" (Mager, 1962).

Here is an example of an objective used as a basis for writing test items to be included in the vocabulary section of the California State Reading Tests for grades 2 through 12:

Given a phrase or a sentence with a missing word and a list of 3–5 choices, the student will select the choice that correctly completes the meaning using the semantic (that is, meaningful) content of the phrase or sentence (Law, 1974).

Note that this objective is highly specific and that it leaves little room for doubt as to what it means. Hence its accomplishment can be measured with some precision.

Measurement, Evaluation, and the Use of Tests

The terms "evaluation" and "measurement" represent concepts that are sometimes confused or misused by educational workers. Some teachers apparently feel that they are "evaluating" when they give tests to students and record the scores without attempting to interpret them or to relate them to what is going on in the classroom or to any other aspect of student behavior. Others evidently feel that they are doing an adequate job of evaluation when they make judgments (in the form of grades) regarding student progress which are unsupported by any kind of objective data.

In order for a program of evaluation to be effective, it should be based, at least in part, on measurement of some sort, that is, it should involve the gathering of data that are descriptive and that can be related to some appropriate standard or norm. But evaluation consists of much more than the collection and recording of data. As Robert L. Thorndike and Elizabeth Hagen (1969) point out, evaluation is more inclusive than measurement. Evaluation includes informal and intuitive judgments about pupil progress, as well as the act of "valuing"—saying what kind of behavior is desirable and good. However, "good measurement techniques provide the solid foundation for sound evaluation, whether of a single pupil or of a total curriculum."

Although most educators would agree that evaluation should always be concerned with results, and that these results should be considered in the light of the goals or objectives of the curriculum, there is no general agreement on the best way to conduct a program of evaluation. Some experts in the field believe that evaluation should depend largely on the results of objective, standardized tests, that is, tests that have been carefully prepared and refined statistically in order to make them more precise and valid. Others object to depending on tests of this sort, pointing out that objective tests do not tell you how an individual thinks because they may measure only isolated bits of knowledge and information and may thus by-pass the major objectives of the curriculum. Some educators prefer tests of the essay variety because they show how students can deal with a problem and develop it to its logical conclusions. On the other hand, those who favor the standardized test feel that the essay examination lacks sufficient objectivity. Still others object to any approach to evaluation that depends solely on testing because they feel that progress toward the major objectives of the curriculum really cannot be measured adequately, at least by the kinds of tests commonly used in the classroom. Another criticism of evaluation that is based solely on the results of tests is that it is concerned only with "paper-and-pencil behavior"—behavior that may bear no relationship to the everyday life of the pupil. It is possible, for instance, for a student to get a very good score on a geography test and still not be able to make sense out of an ordinary city map. Or he might get good grades in English tests and still not be able to write an adequate letter of application for a job. These educators therefore argue in favor of an additional and broader base of evaluation—one that is based on the teacher's observations and impressions of the behavior of individual students, as well as that of entire classes. As Thorndike and Hagen (1969) point out, "The more elegant procedures of formal test and measurement must be supplemented by the cruder methods of informal observation, anecdotal description, and rating if we are to obtain a description of the individual that is usefully complete and comprehensive."

Although these data cannot be easily quantified and can become more or less biased by the teacher's attitudes and feelings, they can nevertheless serve as sources of valuable information that cannot be obtained in any other way, information that most teachers actually find essential. For example, a teacher can learn to sense the degree of interest, apathy, receptivity, or resistance that his class expresses when he presents new material or works with them on a learning task. Most experienced teachers use this kind of appraisal as a basis for deciding whether they should modify their approach, capitalize on a sudden surge of interest, make a bid for closer attention, or review briefly—whatever their analysis of the situation suggests. Over a period of time, these brief "clinical appraisals" begin to shape into a general impression of a student or a class, and the teacher is able to make evaluative statements such as the following: "A rewarding group to work with, but so eager to learn that sometimes they fall over themselves"; "I feel we have got nowhere this term and I must find out what is blocking our progress"; or "The general atmosphere of the class is cautious and even resistive, but there are three or four students who are eager to learn and who help get things moving."

Much of what we call "teaching ability" consists of the ability to make valid and objective judgments about the progress made by learners. Learning to teach means, in part, learning what to notice and what to ignore in the way of behavior, and what interpretations and conclusions to draw. It is difficult, however, to tell potential teachers in so many words exactly how such appraisal and evaluation should be accomplished, partly because it is impossible to predict what kinds of potentially useful data will be encountered in a given class, and partly because the individual style of each teacher will determine what data he will consider are important and how he will use them.

Nevertheless, an example of how teachers' observations could be employed as part of an overall program of evaluation might be helpful at this point, if only to suggest the kinds of things that teachers look for. Let us take an objective that is difficult to measure, yet is basic to progress in learning—the objective of student interest. A teacher whose class is studying Peru might state this objective as follows: "The student becomes interested in the history and culture of Peru." Success in attaining this objective may be reflected by the extent to which students ask relevant questions, the eagerness with which they participate in discussion, the frequency with which they linger after class to ask questions and continue discussion, and the like. Willingness to carry out independent activity is another indication of interest. For example, a boy might become fascinated by the Inca civilization and hence aks the teacher what books he might read. The fact that he refers to the books in subsequent discussion is an indication that he has in fact read them. Or perhaps he makes a collection of stamps from Peru that show the influence of Inca art and culture. These are but a few examples of the kinds of behavior that would reveal the extent to which students have developed an interest in Peru.

Evaluational Feedback and Learning

We have mentioned feedback a number of times in various contexts. To recapitulate, the total learning situation, including what the teacher and the rest of the classroom group is doing, is a source of input for the learner. This input is transformed (the learning process) and results in output in the form of learner responses. Evaluation takes place whenever these responses are recognized, identified, and classified in terms of a goal or objective. This may be done by the learner or the teacher or both. When evaluation is undertaken by the learner, it generates feedback data that can be incorporated with other input from the learning situation and can be used as a way of monitoring progress toward the goal. The learner may initiate the feedback process, or his attention may be drawn to his responses by the teacher or by other learners. The teacher also may use the responses of learners as feedback as to the effectiveness of his own behavior as a facilitator of learning.

The principle that learning is facilitated by feedback is well established. In Chapter 8 we discussed the study by Page (1958) in which students who received teachers' comments on their quiz papers showed more improvement on the next quiz than did students whose papers were only graded. Another study showed that students retained (remembered) material covered in quizzes best when they received feedback in terms of the instructor's discussing the correct answers with them. This method was more effective than having students look up the answers in the book or having them check their replies against a list of answers written on the blackboard. All three of these methods were, of course, better than no feedback at all (Sassenrath and Garverick, 1965).

There may be two other reasons why feedback aids learning: (1) It focuses the learner's attention on certain important aspects of the learning task, and (2) it raises the learner's level of interest. Research is lacking on these two points, but they seem to follow logically from studies that have been conducted. One problem, as we noted in the chapters on the learning process, is that of maintaining a sufficient degree of normal anxiety. Learning proceeds best when the amount of tension or anxiety is at a moderate level, and feedback of data regarding learning progress should help maintain a moderate degree of tension. We have also mentioned the fact that teachers have to compete with many distracting stimuli in the world outside the classroom, and anything they can do to attract the attention and interest of students should facilitate success in classroom learning.

What works for students also seems to work for teachers. When sixth-grade teachers received reports of anonymous pupil evaluations of their behavior, they tended to change their methods in a learner-centered direction. This was borne out by subsequent anonymous evaluations by students (Gage, Runkel, and Chatterjee, 1960).

Feedback, like any other step in the teaching-learning process, can be overemphasized. There should be enough to keep the learner's interest level high but not so much that he is continually distracted from the main task. Frequency of feedback is more desirable during early stages of learning new skills; it is less useful with respect to broader, more pervasive objectives such as the learning of attitudes and concepts. The most effective types of learning tasks are those that have some kind of built-in feedback that obviates the necessity of frequent teacher intervention. In other words, it makes for better learning progress when the learner can monitor his performance in order to see how he is progressing and to determine what he should do next. Learning cannot occur in the absence of reinforcement of some kind, but if our aim is to encourage independence and self-instruction, then we should strive to create learning situations that have self-reinforcing potentialities.

One advantage to self-evaluation is that it removes a major source of anxiety. Anxiety is a natural consequence of having one's work appraised by others. As we indicated earlier, education without evaluation would be unreal. The task of the teacher is not to eliminate evaluation but to defuse it of some of its anxiety-producing potential. Tests or quizzes that are for informational purposes and that do not count toward course grades are one method. Open-book tests are another way of reducing anxiety.

A major problem with respect to feedback is the problem of getting both learners and teachers to recognize it as an essential step in the teaching-learning process. It is much easier to plod unthinkingly through the rituals of teaching and learning than it is to raise what may be awkward questions that may lead to changes in methods or goals. It is also easy for a teacher to criticize learners for not taking enough initiative in monitoring their performance. What teachers generally overlook is that the need to evaluate applies to them as well. The teacher who seeks feedback as to his *own* effectiveness and who enlists the help of learners in the process will have much less difficulty in persuading learners to do likewise.

Attitudes Toward Evaluation

The anxieties that teachers and learners have about feedback stem from the attitudes that students, teachers, and parents alike have toward measuring and judging academic performance. Because of these attitudes, the whole task of evaluation becomes charged with the utmost anxiety. Parents whose child receives a lower mark or test score than they expected often act as though the evaluation of their child's performance is a reflection on their ability to rear an intellectually competent child. When confronted with this attitude, the teacher reacts defensively by saying that if the child had tried harder, he would have done better. After all, it was not the teacher's fault that the child did not try hard enough. This puts the responsibility back on the parents, who then suggest that if the teaching had been better, the child would have tried harder. And so it goes.

Without trying to oversimplify what is admittedly a most complex problem, it may be suggested that tense interchanges like these could be avoided if teachers and parents realized that test scores, marks, and other indices of academic performance are *relative* measures, which at best are only approximate. Both grades and the scores made on tests somehow become charged with some kind of magic power that reifies them, that gives them a certain finality, a certain aura that causes us to regard them as the end product in learning, if not as learning itself. What we keep forgetting is that test scores, as well as the grades that are based on them, are only one index to the amount of learning progress that has taken place. Although research does indicate that persons who get superior grades

OBSERVING AND MEASURING
PROGRESS TOWARD GOALS

tend to have a better-than-average chance for success after graduation, the biographies of the great and near-great often mention academic failure. Furthermore, children *do* change over time, and our evaluations as teachers are wrong often enough for us to be more tentative than we generally are in interpreting the results of the tests we give and the grades we assign.

What is needed is a little "enlightened skepticism" toward measurements. We should realize that educational measurements are not "yardsticks," as measurements are in the physical world. A pound of flour remains a pound of flour under an infinite number of situations and conditions, but George, who scores "82" on his spelling paper and who is average for his third-grade class, would score near the bottom of a group of fifth-graders in spelling, or at the top of a group of second-graders. He may rate "above average" in spelling if compared to a group of children who attend a one-room school in the mountains, but "below average" if compared to children in an upper-middle-class suburban school. George's score of "82" may be typical of the kind of work he does when he is interested and not overstimulated, but when he is bored or hyperactive he may score "50" or "60." On a different kind of test, he may score, "10," "30," or even "113." The point is that there is nothing as permanent or definitive about a test score as there is about the measurements that are made in the physical world. Educational results, like physical measurements, are always relative to other higher and lower results, but unlike physical measurements, there is no real "zero," although test scores sometimes come out as "zero." A "zero" on a test does not mean that no learning has taken place, but rather that the test is unable to measure whatever learning may have taken place. Physical increments come in fairly equal units, such as pounds and inches, but educational increments are never equal even though they look the same on paper. Sam scored "41" on the same test on which George scored "82." Does this mean that George spells twice as well as Sam? Or that George can spell twice as many words as Sam? It is most unlikely.

We also need to develop some sophistication about the meaning of scores. A score of 50 means one thing if there are 55 items in a test but something else if there are 155 items. A score of 50 means one thing if the "middle student" in the class received a score of 25 and something else if the middle student received a score of 75. In other words, a student's score takes on meaning in terms of the possible range of scores and particularly in terms of the scores made by other students. The first step in developing sophistication about scores is that of keeping in mind that scores refer to individuals and their competencies on a certain test, rather than to arbitrary increments of subject matter.

In spite of the ambiguous qualities of educational measurements, they are very useful tools, and we could not do without them. We should be skeptical about their ability to reflect learning status or progress in any kind of exact way, but we should also be realistic enough to recognize that we must have some kind of data on which to base judgments about the success of the educational program or the progress of individual students.

Contract Plans with Built-in Evaluation

In recent years, educational technologists have developed a number of teaching- learning approaches that combine goal-setting, instruction, measurement, feedback, and evaluation. Some approaches begin with teacher and learner determining what a reasonable goal would be with respect to the acquisition of some skill, say, in mathematics. The student then is introduced to a program that is suitable for his level and ability. He receives feedback as he proceeds and finishes by obtaining mastery of the skill or material.

In Chapter 12 we mentioned two examples of "packaged" instructional programs that meet these specifications: Individually Prescribed Instruction, or IPI, and Individually Guided Education, or IGE. Another packaged program that features contract planning with built-in evaluation is Project PLAN, developed by the American Institutes for Research in collaboration with a number of school systems and the Westinghouse Learning Corporation. PLAN makes use of a structured curriculum that includes sequences of objectives, evaluation instruments, procedures for planning individualized programs, learning materials, and supervision procedures. Each cooperating school has a computer terminal that is connected to a master computer. As each student proceeds with his work, data generated by his performance are stored in the master computer to be used in monitoring his progress and as feedback. At the start of a school year, a student, as well as his teacher, obtains a printout of his past performance, together with other relevant information. These data then serve as the basis for decisions regarding the work he is to undertake during the school year and the units with which he is to begin. Computer printouts also aid in selecting the immediate objectives toward which the student will work and the learning exercises he will undertake to attain the objectives. When it seems probable that he has mastered the first set of objectives, his achievement is measured, and the results are used in determining what he should do next. Although PLAN involves highly structured curricula, it does make individualized student teaching-learning experiences possible and permits considerable opportunity for student choice in determining goals (Lindvall and Cox, 1969). Because of the usefulness of the "instructional package," many school districts have developed their own "packages" in response to local needs and objectives.

TEACHER-MADE TESTS

Some of the data on which teachers' judgments are commonly based consist of scores made on tests or examinations. The emphasis placed on tests and examinations will vary with the age of the student, the subject, the objectives of the curriculum, and the educational philosophy of the teacher and the school, but they will figure to some extent in the evaluation program of almost every teacher. For the sake of our discussion we will divide tests into two categories: those devised by teachers—teacher-made tests—and those prepared by test publishers, commonly called "standardized tests."[1] Teacher-made tests are the quizzes and examinations that teachers construct and give at various times during the school year in order to stimulate learning through review and to determine status and progress in learning. There are a number of similarities between teacher-made and standardized tests, but we are postponing discussion of the latter to the next section, where they may be considered in terms of their special characteristics.

Oral Examinations

A century ago, most tests and examinations were conducted orally.[2] The teacher (or a committee of school visitors) put questions to each student in turn and marked him on his ability to reproduce what had been taught him. This method relied very heavily on the student's ability to memorize material word for word and repeat it orally before his classmates and his teacher. The student who could learn essential facts and concepts but who was unable or unwilling to memorize details or who was unable to maintain his composure before a group was at a distinct disadvantage. One of the chief flaws in this method, however, was its inefficiency. Because it took so much time to question an entire class, one student might get a chance to answer only one or two questions during the examining period. A student might have a fairly good grasp of the subject matter, but the one or two questions directed at him might fall within an area less familiar to him. Or he might have a rather poor grasp of the subject matter and be asked questions he knew rather well. In oth-

[1] Teachers occasionally develop their own standardized tests by the same statistical methods used by test publishers. However, because most teachers do not have the training, the time, or the inclination for this task, most standardized tests used in the schools are tests supplied by publishers.
[2] In many countries oral tests are still considered to be more valid and more significant than written tests, although it is common practice to give both kinds of tests.

er words, the oral method did not permit a fair sampling of what students had learned.

Essay Examinations

The method which was proposed by Horace Mann, among others, to supplant this inefficient method of evaluation was the written examination—what we now commonly call the "essay examination." The written examination permits a much wider sampling of subject matter, and the student does not have the feeling of being under the scrutiny of his classmates and teacher while he searches for ideas and words to convey his knowledge. Writing gives him an opportunity to express himself in relative privacy. Furthermore, students can be given questions to be answered in the form of short essays, thus making it possible to test their ability to develop a subject logically.

Although written tests provide some distinct advantages over oral examinations, they have their shortcomings. The chief disadvantage lies in the difficulty in obtaining objectivity in scoring. The Educational Testing Service (1961), a nationwide, nonprofit organization concerned with preparing, administering, scoring, and interpreting educational tests, conducted a research study into the methods used in grading the compositions written in college English classes. A panel of fifty-three judges read three hundred essays written by freshmen at Cornell, Middlebury, and the University of Pennsylvania, and graded them on a scale ranging from 1 to 9. One-third of the essays received grades that ranged the full scale from 1 to 9; 60 percent received seven or eight out of the nine possible grades; and no essay received fewer than five different grades. In another study, seventy history teachers gave a paper in American history marks ranging from 43 to 90 (on a scale ranging from 0 to 100). The question naturally arose whether the same variability would occur in mathematics, which presumably lends itself to more precise and objective measurement than the humanities or the social sciences. After all, said the mathematics teachers, the answer to a problem in mathematics is either right or wrong. But the results obtained from a similar study with a geometry paper

were most disillusioning: The grades ranged from 28 to 92 (Starch, 1927).

Another and more recent study was conducted among teachers scoring examinations in Lebanon. Nine teachers graded two packets of essay examinations in philosophy. As Figure 13-1 shows, the average grades they assigned to each packet showed wide variations. Teacher B was obviously an easy grader: He gave an average mark of 100 to the first packet and 87 to the second. However, Teacher D gave the first packet an average grade of 60 and the second packet a 73. Teacher H was quite consistent: He gave both packets an average grade of 69 (Valin, 1961). S. A. Akeju (1972) reported similar findings when he analyzed the scores assigned by seven trained examiners who graded the written compositions of ninety-six candidates for the West African General Certificate of Education in Ghana.

Not only do grading standards vary from teacher to teacher, but a given teacher will vary from time to time. A teacher may, for instance, assign a paper one kind of mark if he grades it near the start of his work period and a different mark if he reads it after looking at examinations for four or five hours.

What these studies show is that a great deal of the variability of the marks that students receive on examinations is a reflection of the variability of persons doing the marking. In other words, four examinations graded A, B, C, and D by different teachers could conceivably be on about the same level of quality. Many a college student has received an A on an essay, has retyped it, and handed it in to another instructor the following semester, only to have the second teacher grade it a C or less! Most teachers are, unfortunately, unaware of the great variability in their marking standards. It is difficult for a teacher to determine when he grades a paper in, say, history, how much he has been influenced by the student's ability to express himself in a clear and interesting way. He may think that he is grading the student's understanding of history, but he is actually grading his ability to express himself.

Some recent research shows that much intergrader variation can be reduced by the use of computers. But the question still remains as to whether using essay tests adds anything to the teacher's ability to evaluate student performance. The Educational Testing Service (ETS) has been conducting extensive research in this field. College teachers of English have expressed great dissatisfaction with objective, computer-scored tests of English usage administered to college applicants, saying, in effect: "What we need to have is evidence that the applicant can *write,* not just guess the right answers on a multiple-choice test." In response to such requests, the College Board section of the ETS developed an experiment test consisting of five essays, two taking forty minutes each to write and three twenty minutes each. The tests were then read by five scorers, who worked closely together in order to avoid the kind of variations that we have observed in Figure 13-1. When the scores on the essays were compared with scores on an objective test of English usage, which students had also taken, the ETS researchers found that the scores on the two types of test correlated to a very high degree, almost to the point where one test could be substituted for the other. The study showed, among other things, that an objective, multiple-choice type of test could do a very respectable job of estimating

or predicting students' ability to write clearly and competently, and that there was no special advantage to using essay tests (Educational Testing Service, 1963).

There are many reasons for using essays and essay testing, other than for purposes of assigning grades. If the objective of an English course is that of preparing students to write effectively, such an objective can only be achieved if students write. In fact, the more they are encouraged to write, the better able they are to express themselves in writing. It is quite possible, too, that cognitive processes involved in answering essay questions are different from those used in answering objective-type questions. Any of these would serve as justifiable reasons for retaining essays as assigned work or as examinations. The important thing for teachers to keep in mind is the difficulty in maintaining objectivity and the consequent danger of misjudging student performance. The risk of misjudgment is possible with all types of evaluation but is probably higher with essay tests.

Paul S. Diedrich and Frances R. Link (1967) have described an innovative program of "cooperative

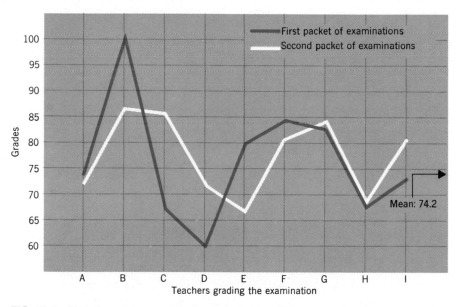

FIG. 13-1. Variations among teachers grading two groups of essay tests in philosophy. Notice (1) the extreme variations among graders and (2) the tendency of an evaluator to grade both groups in somewhat the same way (Valin, 1961).

evaluation" in which a number of the pitfalls inherent in grading essay materials were circumvented. They found they were able to obtain a high degree of objectivity by having papers evaluated by faculty committees who used rating forms that specified the number of points that could be given for different aspects of each student's paper. By "depersonalizing" evaluation in this way, greater objectivity was obtained. Greater objectivity also meant that more precise records could be kept on each student's progress over a period of several years. This material could be used in "departmental autopsies," in which it was examined and analyzed by faculty members in terms of the kind of progress students and teachers were making with respect to curricular goals. The scores also enabled teachers to identify weak points in the curriculum and to make suggestions to one another with respect to different methods of instruction.

When it came to examinations, however, the authors preferred objective questions. An essay question, they said, may mean that the teacher has merely put off until grading time the task of making up his mind about the kinds of responses he expects. At that time, "although the professed aim may have been to get at something lofty like creativity and imagination, it may turn out that none of the answers can be reasonably regarded as either creative or imaginative" (Link and Diedrich, 1967).

Choice-type or "Objective" Tests

One of the ways in which educators have tried to deal with the lack of objectivity in scoring examinations is by devising test items that restrict the possible variability in the answers that may be given, thus simultaneously reducing the variability in scoring. Such tests are called "objective tests," in contrast to written tests or "essay tests." Robert L. Ebel (1951) suggested that essay-type items be called "supply-type items" because the student is required to *supply* the proper answer. Most types of objective-test items he would call "choice-type" items because the student is required to *make a choice* among the alternatives that are supplied as possible answers.

Although we shall occasionally follow the common procedure of referring to choice-type tests as "objective tests," the term "objective" is actually misleading to some extent, inasmuch as the "objectivity" of these tests refers entirely to their scoring—the degree to which different scorers will get the same results. Decisions such as when to give a test, what material to include, the kind of items to use, the language of the items, and what grades to assign to various scores all involve considerations that are more or less subjective. Objectivity in scoring is a considerable advantage, but we should not overestimate the objectivity of an "objective test."

The most common examples of choice-type test items are those that involve two choices (such as true-false items) and those that involve a number of choices, usually four or five, termed "multiple-choice" items (see Figure 13-2).

The main advantage of tests composed of such items is that error and bias on the part of the grader are eliminated. Scoring consists merely of laying a key alongside the answers marked by the student and counting the number of correct responses. The small percentage of error that sometimes creeps into hand scoring can be reduced, particularly for students beyond the primary grades, by having them record their answers on an answer card or sheet which can then be scored by machine.

The ease with which the so-called objective tests may be scored makes them very attractive to teachers. It takes much longer to construct an objective test than a test composed of supply items, but once it is constructed, its items can be used again and again. Furthermore, it is possible to do a much more extensive sampling of a given area of subject matter, inasmuch as an hour's test might consist of, say, fifty multiple-choice or a hundred true-false items, as compared to the half dozen or so items that might be included in an essay test.

Tests composed of choice-type items are often criticized on the grounds that they seem to penalize the more able students and reward those who are able to memorize isolated facts or those who are merely "test-wise." Some critics claim, for example, that multiple-choice tests punish students who are first-rate, deep, subtle, creative, strong-minded,

Examples of choice-type items.

nonconforming, unusual, probing, profound, and truly important and reward students who are second-rate, superficial, merely clever, nimble-witted, and cynically test-wise (Hoffmann, 1962). Many students share these views. One study conducted in a university setting showed that students who were test-wise and able to detect ambiguity were able to get better scores on multiple-choice items in English composition than those who were not. But students who were creative, independent, and able to deal with complex concepts also did well on the same test. To a considerable extent, the creative-independent-complex students were the same ones who were test-wise and able to detect ambiguity (Alker, Carlson, and Hermann, 1969).

Many of the complaints made by students about multiple-choice tests turn out to be the result of carelessly written test items that are concerned with trivial details. But the kind of multiple-choice questions given as samples in Figure 13-2 show that it is

(*Peanuts* © 1966 United Feature Syndicate, Inc.)

Students often share adult misconceptions about essay and objective tests.

possible to design items that measure understanding and the ability to think, as well as memory. Choice-type items are also criticized on the grounds that they do not indicate whether students can *recall* or *reproduce* the right answer without being prompted. Essay items do not, of course, generally provide such clues. Nevertheless, the second ETS study that we cited showed that it is possible to construct choice-type tests whose results correlate very highly with those of essay tests. Thus it is very likely that the two kinds of tests measure the same kinds of competencies for most students. In fact, students making high grades in an English course in which marks were based on compositions and essays also made high scores in multiple-choice tests measuring general ability and competence in English composition (Alker, Carlson, and Hermann, 1969).

Another charge often directed against choice-type tests is that they fail to measure the ability of students to analyze and think through problems, to organize their ideas, and to present logical and coherent points of view. There are two counterarguments to this criticism. One is that choice-type items can be designed to measure much more than the ability to recognize correct or incorrect information; they can be designed to measure critical thinking or any other higher-level process the test maker wants to test. The only limitations are the imagination and the skill of the test maker. The other argument is that essays or papers assigned during the course of the school term are better instruments for measuring the student's ability to think on paper and to analyze and develop a subject than are essay questions posed in a midterm or final examination. The stresses and anxieties of the all-too-brief examination period make it difficult for the student to present any kind of a fair sample of his ability to think on paper.

The argument against choice-type tests does gain some validity, however, when we realize that the tests a teacher gives are an important way of communicating his educational objectives. Research has shown that students tend to use different methods in preparing for an examination, according to whether they are studying for a choice-type test or an essay test. Because choice-type tests are so often used to measure limited, informational-type goals, the instructor who uses them exclusively may be giving his students the idea that his educational objectives are concerned solely with isolated bits of information.

There are other forms of so-called objective testing that are also rather widely used. The *completion test* attempts to combine some of the features of the choice-type and supply-type items. We already encountered that type of item in our discussion in Chapter 8, when we described the teaching machines developed by B. F. Skinner. Whereas true-false and multiple-choice items require students to discriminate between correct and incorrect information, the completion test (see Figure 13-3) requires him to recall it. It is thus basically a supply-type test item but is included among the "objective tests" because the number of possible answers is restricted, thus reducing variability and increasing objectivity in scoring. On the other hand, its scoring is not as objective as that of other choice-type

Directions: Complete each of the following sentences by writing the one word that makes the best sense in the blank at the right.

1. If we shine a bright light on an earthworm that is in the dark it will . . . (_____)
2. Slipper shells, limpets, and abalones are all . . . . (_____)
3. Moths and butterflies have a long, coiled tongue that really consists of extensions of two . . . . (_____)
4. Fermentation is produced by microscopic plants called . . . . (_____)

FIG. 13-3. Completion test in life science.

items. For instance, the desired response in the first item in Figure 13-3 is "recoil." Probably most teachers would give full credit as well for "withdraw." But how would one score "try to hide"? It contains some elements of the desired answer, but consists of more than one word. And what should be done about the student who misspells an answer or writes part of an answer?

The *matching test* is really a complex multiple-choice test that attempts to measure the student's ability to recall relationships between pairs of items. It is often used in history courses as a way of measuring the ability to relate names to events, although it may be used in other subjects as well (see Figure 13-4).

One variation also used in history courses is that of having students place events in chronological order. Still another is that of having students match numbered parts on a diagram or a map with a list of terms, events, cities, or other appropriate terminology. The number of varieties of choice-type test items is limited only by the ingenuity of test makers.

Directions: In the blank preceding the names of each of the psychologists in the left-hand column, write the letter indicating the area of research with which he is identified.

Psychologists	Research Areas
_____ 1. Lewin	a. Laws of learning
_____ 2. Gagné	b. Taxonomy
_____ 3. Piaget	c. Heuristics
_____ 4. Bloom	d. Einstellung
_____ 5. Skinner	e. Self-concept
_____ 6. Kounin	f. Classroom management
_____ 7. Maslow	g. Social climate
_____ 8. Combs	h. Basic needs
	i. Conditions of learning
	j. Teaching machines
	k. Cognitive development
	l. Late-maturing adolescents

FIG. 13-4. Matching tests in educational psychology.
Key: 1. g; 2. i; 3. k; 4. b; 5. j; 6. f; 7. h; 8. e.

Reliability and Validity

One of the outstanding advantages of choice-type tests is that they lend themselves to statistical refinement much more readily than do supply-type or essay tests. For instance, it is relatively easy to gather data regarding the *reliability* of a choice-type test, that is, to measure its consistency, its stability, the extent to which it would give the same results under repeated usage.

An example of an unreliable test would be one consisting of ten true-false items of medium difficulty. The theoretical "chance score" on such a test— the score to be obtained by sheer guesswork— would be 5, inasmuch as the chances are one out of two that any single item would be guessed correctly. This means that there is a span of only 5 points, from 6 to 10, to reflect any knowledge of subject matter. Furthermore, experience will show that some scores in the 6-to-10 range might also be obtained by chance or guessing. If this test were to be given to the same group on two separate occasions, there would probably be much variability between the scores, some persons who scored high on the first administration scoring low the second time, and vice versa, because only a few points separate "high" scores from "low" ones. If the true-false items in question measure only narrow aspects of educational experience, it would also be possible for some good students to get low scores on such a test and for some poor students to get high scores. Such a characteristic would bear a relationship to the factor of validity, which we discuss below, but it is also related to the reliability or consistency of the test.

The reliability of a true-false test (or any kind of test) can be increased by making it longer, assuming, of course, that the items are readable, straightforward and not "tricky," and are within the scope of what students can be reasonably expected to know. This does not mean that ten-item true-false tests should not be used. Actually, if several such tests are given during the school term, and the scores averaged or cumulated, the results would be about as reliable as a single true-false test consisting of the total number of items involved. In other words, five ten-item true-false tests would be approximately as reliable as one fifty-item true-false test.

Tests can also be checked for *validity*—the extent to which they measure what they are expected to measure. An example of a choice-type of objective test for which validity has been demonstrated statistically is the Scholastic Aptitude Test (SAT) that has been developed by the ETS for use in conjunction with the College Board examinations. The SAT is a general ability test (or, more accurately, an academic aptitude test) whose scores are used by many colleges and universities as a basis for predicting the academic success of applicants for admission. The validity of the SAT is shown by the fact that individuals who score high on the test tend to get superior grades, whereas individuals scoring low tend to get inferior grades. In other words, there is a fairly close relationship between the scores received on the SAT and the grades received subsequently in college work. Therefore we can say that the SAT is a fairly valid measure of academic aptitude or potential. Incidentally, the SAT is also a highly reliable test. Its several forms give consistent results when compared with one another, and there is a high degree of relationship between the scores made on two different administrations of the same form of the same test.

A test of mechanical ability, however, would be an *invalid* test of academic aptitude because scores made thereon bear no relationship to grades made in academic subjects. Tests of competence in individual high-school subjects, such as biology and foreign languages, would, of course, be much more valid than mechanical aptitude tests as predictors of success in college, but they would not be as valid as the SAT. We make this point because one might logically assume that a test that measures what one has learned in specific high-school subjects would be a better predictor of college success than the SAT, which measures only vocabulary and reading ability.

The validity of a teacher-made test will depend on what the test is supposed to measure. Inasmuch as most tests, even essay examinations, measure

rather narrow areas of educational experience, teachers should not assume that a test measures more than it actually does. If one of the objectives of a high-school science course is the development of an appreciation of the science method, we should not assume that a student who does well at answering informational questions or at solving chemical equations is necessarily appreciative or even aware of the value of the scientific method. It is not even safe to assume that a student who is able to write out a statement about the scientific method has actually developed an appreciation of it.

It is also possible to make unwarranted assumptions about the validity of printed, standardized tests. It is very easy for us to assume that because a test is called an "intelligence test," or a "test of foreign language aptitude," or whatever, it measures what the title says it measures. All too often the necessary research has not been undertaken, or the evidence supporting its validity is so slight that the user should have strong reservations about placing any confidence in the results.

The question of validity also arises when a test measures too narrow an aspect of ability or achievement, or when it measures a different dimension or quality of a skill or aptitude than the one the user had in mind. In other words, validity also depends, in part, on how tests are used and how they are interpreted. An intelligence test may be a valid measure of academic aptitude but may be a rather poor or relatively invalid measure of the ability to make certain kinds of decisions which also involve some aspect of intelligence, decisions that might have to be made by say, truck drivers, personnel managers, or real estate salesmen. The ability to make decisions of all kinds may be included in the test giver's *concept* of intelligence, and he may assume that, because the test he is giving purports to be a test of intelligence, it measures the qualities or abilities he has in mind. He might even say that as far as he is concerned a test that does not measure these qualities is not a test of intelligence. However, whether a certain test measures what the test giver thinks of as intelligence depends on the extent to which his idea of intelligence is consistent with the concept held by the author of the test. Many test users are not aware that there may be differences of opinion and accept test results without further thought. As a consequence, important decisions are sometimes based on invalid tests or, rather, on tests that are otherwise valid but have been used in ways that render their results invalid.

The answer to the problem of developing valid tests is twofold. The most important thing to be done is to educate teachers (or teachers-to-be) in the use of tests by helping them to develop tests of their own that are more effective and more efficient than the ones they have been using and by showing them how to select standardized tests that meet the educational needs of their students. The other important thing we can do is to improve the available standardized tests to make them more reliable and more valid.

STANDARDIZED TESTS

The reliability and validity of tests can be improved by standardizing the testing and scoring procedure and providing standards of norms against which results can be compared and interpreted. The tests that are supplied by reputable educational and psychological publishers are examples of tests that have been standardized by putting them through a number of different processes before they are published and distributed to the professional public.

Standardized tests exist on every conceivable variable that is of interest to teachers: intelligence, achievement in almost every subject of the curriculum, personality, vocational interest, special aptitudes, and so forth. The usual procedure followed in preparing a standardized test is to engage one or more experts in test construction to work with experts in the educational or psychological variable to be tested. Items are written and directions for administration are formulated for one or more experimental forms of the test. These tests are then administered to sample groups of individuals of the type for which the test is appropriate. In other words, if the test is designed to measure the competence of fourth-, fifth-, and sixth-graders in arithmetic, the test is administered to samples of stu-dents in grades 3 through 7 or 8 who represent a full range of ability. The test items and directions are then analyzed for flaws. Some flaws will show up in the practical problems that arise in administering or scoring the test; others will show up in the statistical analysis of responses to various items. The test may then go through a number of experimental forms until one or more final forms are produced that meet the specifications of the test makers. These final forms may then be administered to proportionate samples of fourth-, fifth-, and sixth-grade students (reflecting also regional, urban-rural, and social-class differences) in order to gather data on which to base "national norms." The mean or average score for the combined group of children in each grade constitutes the norm score for that grade. With some manipulation of statistics it is possible to produce norms for each month in the three grades covered by the test. A given child may be said, for example, to be at the 5.5 level on the test (fifth month of the fifth grade) or the 6.1 (first month of the sixth grade). Norms may also be extrapolated to grades above and below the population covered by the test. Thus a sixth-grader who makes a superior score on the test may be said to score at the eighth-grade level, and a fourth-grader with an inferior score may be said to score at the third-grade level. Such "grade placements" are theoretical, of course, because the test in question was not standardized on samples above the sixth grade or below the fourth.

The Growth of Standardized Testing

During the period after World War I, standardized tests began to be used in great quantities. One factor that contributed to their popularity was the growing concern about the unreliability of written examinations. Another factor, perhaps related, was the feeling that the time had come to "take some of the guesswork out of education" and put it on some kind of a scientific and businesslike basis. Administered on a mass basis, standardized tests provided data for hundreds of school surveys during the decades between the two World Wars. Still another factor was the increased number of children from all social levels who began attending school. This more extensive participation of children of all social levels in educational programs is reflected in the fact that whereas the American soldier in World War I had an average of approximately seven years of education, the average World War II selectee had completed between ten and eleven. The gains were most noticeable in the secondary schools, whose enrollments rose with the enactment of laws postponing school leaving until the teenage years. The schools were thus required to educate large numbers of various kinds of students they had not encountered before; in order to develop some understanding of the potentialities and deficiencies of these new kinds of students, they turned to the new standardized measuring instruments that were being placed at their disposal by the psychological profession.

Most of the standardized measures that have been developed for use in the schools are termed "norm-referenced tests" because scores are interpreted by referring them to the tests' norms. Some of the standardized tests that have been produced in recent years are termed "criterion-referenced tests" because scores are referred to the extent to which students have met specific criteria in the skills or concepts they are designed to measure. We will have more to say about criterion-referenced tests at the end of this chapter.

Teachers in most classrooms generally prefer to construct their own tests rather than use the standardized norm-referenced or criterion-referenced tests that are now available in great variety. The chief reason for this preference is that the curricular areas which are covered by standardized tests are those that are common to a large number of schools and school systems. Hence they are not very useful when it comes to measuring progress toward curricular goals peculiar to a given community, school, course, or teacher. New York City, for instance, found it necessary to develop and standardize special tests for its program in elementary school mathematics and science because the available standardized tests did not adequately measure the content and objectives of the local curriculum (Ebel, 1960).

Norm-referenced tests can nevertheless serve very useful purposes. They help answer the question: "How does the achievement of my students compare with that of students in other schools with regard to basic skills and information?" Such tests can provide a precise, though partial, answer to this question. We say "partial" because there are many factors that enter into the measurement of educational competence. Decimals and fractions are not introduced in the same grade in every school; a school that has decided to introduce them later rather than earlier may find that its students appear to be retarded when compared on a standardized test to those of other schools. Or a high-school English department may have developed a curriculum based on the writings of contemporary authors. A standardized achievement test in literature that has been developed on the assumption that high-school students are familiar with *Ivanhoe, Silas Marner,* and *Twelfth Night* would hardly provide a fair measure of the effectiveness of teachers or the competence of students in that high school.[3]

Standardized Achievement Test Batteries

The difficulty of finding norm-referenced tests that are suited to the curriculum is more aggravated in secondary schools than it is in elementary schools, partly because there is less agreement as to what should be learned during these years than during the first few years of school. Everyone agrees that children should learn to read, write, and cipher, and should acquire a fund of basic information about our national and cultural heritage and the world around us. But as we go up the educational ladder, there is less and less agreement about the skills, information, and concepts that should constitute the common core of learning. Furthermore, the talents, interests, and aptitudes of children become more varied with each year of development. What this means is that "batteries" of achievement tests are somewhat less useful in secondary schools than in elementary schools.

[3] Some test publishers provide local norms for their tests in an attempt to compensate for this deficiency.

Most school systems use some kind of an achievement battery as a check on the learning of basic skills learned in the elementary grades. Some of the batteries used most extensively are the Comprehensive Tests of Basic Skills and the California Achievement Tests (CTB/McGraw-Hill); the Iowa Tests of Basic Skills (Houghton Mifflin); the Metropolitan Achievement Tests and the Stanford Achievement Test (Harcourt, Brace, and Jovanovich); and the SRA Achievement Series (Science Research Associates). Batteries of achievement tests generally used on the secondary school level (subject to the limitations noted above) are the Iowa Tests of Educational Development or ITED (Science Research Associates) and the Essential High School Content Battery (Harcourt, Brace, and Jovanovich). The Tests of Academic Progress or TAP (Houghton Mifflin), the Comprehensive Tests of Basic Skills, the California Achievement Tests, and the Sequential Test of Educational Progress or STEP (Cooperative Test Division of the Educational Testing Service) all have forms for both elementary and secondary schools.

In addition to the batteries of achievement tests, there are many more or less specialized achievement tests for various school subjects. Some of them, for instance, the diagnostic tests of certain arithmetical processes, deal with highly specific skills or content; others deal with subjects outside the conventional curriculum, such as music appreciation, draftsmanship, and Russian.

Diagnostic tests can be useful tools in the hands of the teacher who is able to make the "leap in logic" between the content of the test and the content covered by his instruction. A diagnostic test of reading may, for example, report that certain students score low in "following directions." It is thus up to the teacher to determine what he must do in order to improve their ability to comprehend printed directions. The means for correcting the deficiency is seldom obvious from the test score itself.

One practical way of using achievement tests diagnostically is to study the papers or the computer-scored printouts of students scoring low in the test. Batteries of achievement tests are now given routinely by most schools, and the score sheets, together with the test manuals, have a wealth of information for the instructor who wishes to focus his teaching on the areas in which students need the most help.

In spite of the wide usage of achievement tests, teachers nevertheless express a number of anxieties about them. Some teachers, according to Robert L. Ebel (1968), feel that standardized tests fail "to get at" the real essentials of achievement in certain skill or foundation courses. Such a teacher may even assign a child a mark that is inconsistent with his performance on the standardized tests. Ebel confesses that he is unsatisfied by this "mystical devotion to a hidden reality of achievement which is more essential than overt ability to perform," and wants to know the evidence which indicates that this hidden reality really exists. A common example of this malpractice is the boy who scores at the 90th percentile on the English sections of an achievement battery, but who is getting Ds and Fs in English, or, conversely, the girl who scores well below grade level on the quantitative sections of the battery, but who is getting Bs in math. Further investigation usually shows that the boy has not been "cooperating" when it comes to assigned work, and the girl is very model of "cooperation." What the teacher means when he complains about the test in these instances is that he is looking for a kind of social behavior that is not measured by the test and is really not very concerned about mastery of subject matter.

Ebel also comments on teachers' overconcern with the possible anxiety and stress children might experience as a result of testing. He believes that it is better since a child should not be shielded from "the educational facts of life," and that it is better for his mental health to know how he is progressing.

Still another criticism relates to the uniqueness of a school's objectives. Ebel states that whatever constitutes a good education in Maine is not much different from what is considered to be a good education in California. A teacher should not expect standardized tests to reveal data on everything he has taught but only on those things that "all teachers ought to have taught."

Teachers often ask: "How can we decide which is the best test to use?" This is a difficult question to answer in any kind of definitive way. The *Mental Measurements Yearbooks,* edited by O. K. Buros (Gryphon Press, Highland Park, N. J.), provide useful information regarding the validity and reliability of every standardized test that has been published, but the interpretation of this information takes a considerable amount of sophistication in testing. Test manuals themselves are also useful sources of information. But the best advice that can be given the teacher in search of the ideal test for his situation is to consult an expert in testing. Most large-city school systems have bureaus of guidance or bureaus of educational research that have test experts on their staffs, and test experts are often attached to the staffs of county and state superintendents' offices.

Interpreting Test Results

Most of the norm-referenced tests used in elementary school provide scales whereby the results may be translated into grade placement. Such scales enable the teacher to see how his students compare with the average scores made by other students of their age and grade. For instance, Ann may be in the first month of the fifth grade, but her achievement test results show her to be performing at grade level or even better in most language skills but only at the third-grade level in arithmetic skills. Her computerized test-score report is depicted in Figure 13-5. The column RS (raw scores) indicates the number of items correct for each of the subtests in the battery; the GE column shows the grade in which typical students in the nation obtained the indicated raw score. Ann's spelling score of 27 was, for example, equal to the score obtained by typical students in the fourth month of the eighth grade. Ann has also taken a test of academic aptitude, and the score she received on that test is used to select a comparison group of students of similar sex, grade, age, and aptitude. The average grade-placements of this comparison group are listed in the column headed AAGE, and marked differences from this norm are in the "Difference" column. We can

see that she is doing about three grade levels better than we might expect in spelling but about a grade and one-half below expectations in arithmetic. Her other scores are not significantly different from those of the comparison group.

The lower one half of the report form provides an item-by-item report of her performance, organized by broad diagnostic categories. A teacher can locate the areas in which Ann is particularly weak, such as division, or he can go back to the test booklet and examine those items on which she failed or succeeded, in search of clues as to her learning problems.

The final column of the upper left-hand box is labeled "Nat'l %ile." It indicates the percentage of fifth-graders in the national sample who scored lower than Ann. These percentiles are related to the "National Percentile" box at the right. Inasmuch as any score is only an approximation of a student's achievement, Ann's scores are reported in terms of rows of X's that give the approximate range within which she is likely to be achieving.

Percentile rankings are *not* the same as the percentage grades that were popular in most schools a generation or more ago (100 was "perfect"; 60, 65, or 70 was "passing"). Instead of being a comparison with some presumably fixed standard of excellence, which was the concept underlying percentage grades, percentile rankings represent comparisons with the scores of other persons taking the test. The individual whose score is equal to the 70th percentile has a score higher than those attained by 70 percent of the individuals taking the test; and the individual who scores at the 32nd percentile has a score higher than 32 percent of the individuals taking the test. The relative position of an individual in his group can thus be stated with some precision. Although the use of percentile rankings has some statistical weakness, it is a very convenient way of reporting and comparing scores. This weakness amounts to a tendency to overstate the differences around the 50th percentile (the middle of the distribution) and to understate differences at the ends of the distribution.

This tendency of percentile scores to distort dif-

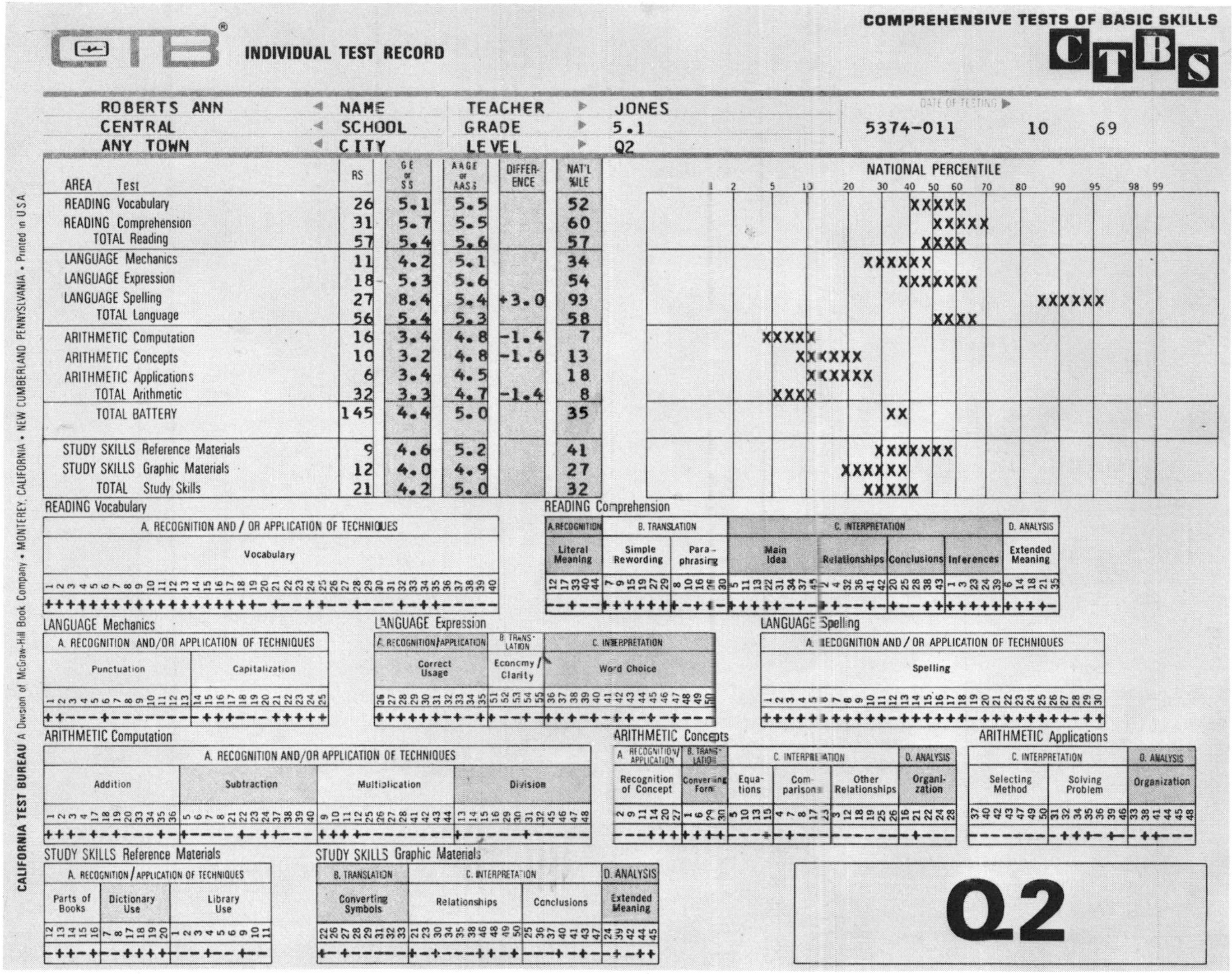

COMPREHENSIVE TESTS OF BASIC SKILLS

CTBS

INDIVIDUAL TEST RECORD

	NAME	TEACHER	JONES		5374-011	10	69
ROBERTS ANN	SCHOOL	GRADE	5.1		DATE OF TESTING		
CENTRAL	CITY	LEVEL	Q2				
ANY TOWN							

AREA Test	RS	GE or SS	AAGE or AASS	DIFFER-ENCE	NAT'L %ILE
READING Vocabulary	26	5.1	5.5		52
READING Comprehension	31	5.7	5.5		60
TOTAL Reading	57	5.4	5.6		57
LANGUAGE Mechanics	11	4.2	5.1		34
LANGUAGE Expression	18	5.3	5.6		54
LANGUAGE Spelling	27	8.4	5.4	+3.0	93
TOTAL Language	56	5.4	5.3		58
ARITHMETIC Computation	16	3.4	4.8	-1.4	7
ARITHMETIC Concepts	10	3.2	4.8	-1.6	13
ARITHMETIC Applications	6	3.4	4.5		18
TOTAL Arithmetic	32	3.3	4.7	-1.4	8
TOTAL BATTERY	145	4.4	5.0		35
STUDY SKILLS Reference Materials	9	4.6	5.2		41
STUDY SKILLS Graphic Materials	12	4.0	4.9		27
TOTAL Study Skills	21	4.2	5.0		32

NATIONAL PERCENTILE

Q2

FIG. 13-5. Scores made on the Comprehensive Tests of Basic Skills by a fifth-grade girl, © 1968, by CTB/McGraw-Hill and reproduced by permission.

ferences among pupils has led to an increased preference for a more accurate system of reporting scores. This system is based on the normal curve of probability, that is, the distribution of scores that tends to result when measures or scores on most variables (height, weight, intelligence, reading ability, or whatever) are ranked in order from highest to lowest. As Figure 13-6 shows, such a distribution assumes the form of a bell-shaped curve, with most of the scores clustered in the middle and with only a few scores at the high and low extremes. There are certain dividing points in the distribution, which can be expressed in terms of standard deviations, or differences from the midpoint or mean of the distribution. Note that about 34 percent of the scores fall between the mean and a point one standard deviation removed. About 48 percent of the cases fall between the mean and a point two standard deviations above or below. In other words, almost 96 percent of the scores will be expected to fall between a point two standard deviations below the mean and two standard deviations above.

A glance at the scale of percentile scores arrayed below the curve in Figure 13-6 shows how they distort student performance as measured by tests. The difference between students scoring at the 50th and the 60th percentiles is actually slight, but the difference between students scoring at the 90th and 99th percentile is considerable.

It is because percentile scores invite such distortions that test publishers are encouraging teachers to make use of "stanines" when using and interpreting test results. Stanines are so called because they are based on standard deviations from the mean and consist of nine divisions of the full normal range. The seven central divisions are equal in terms of the amount of the variable being measured, and the top and bottom stanine scores represent the ends of the distribution. The scale below percentile scores in Figure 13-6 shows the dividing points for stanines, as well as the percentage of cases that are included in each stanine score. There are other types of score-reporting systems that are based on the functions of the normal curve.

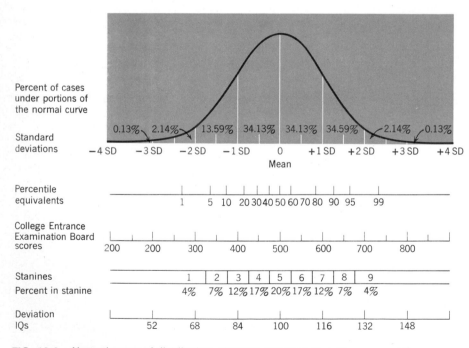

FIG. 13-6. Normal curve of distribution, showing standard deviations, percentile scores, stanine scores, and deviation IQs.

Interested readers are referred to the texts on measurement listed at the end of this chapter for description and explanation of these systems.

Accountability: The Search for Hard Evidence

Whenever we spend money, we are likely to be concerned about getting our money's worth. To put this in psychologist's terms, we want to be sure that input (what we are spending) is equal to output (what we receive). It is relatively easy to follow through on this when we are buying commodities and other goods, but it is somewhat more difficult to apply to the purchase of services, particularly the services in which the outcome or payoff will not be known for years. When the services are expected to yield long-range benefits for the community, for instance, those produced by improved mental health, public-welfare programs, the preservation of the ecology, or public education, it is very difficult to determine whether we, as taxpayers, are "getting our money's worth." In spite of this ambiguity about end results, the average American, through his taxes, spends more for education than anyone on earth and justifies it as an investment that will produce returns in the form of literate, enlightened, law-abiding, and productive future citizens. The average citizen has also more-or-less willingly paid for annual increases in school costs for many years, but now he is likely to question whether the eventual output will be worth the increased input. As a result, citizens groups, legislators, and government officials are increasingly demanding evidence that the expenditure of large sums of money is having some results.

The move to hold schools accountable received its greatest impetus during the 1960's, when they were asked to participate in the federal government's "War on Poverty." Legislators were willing to appropriate billions of dollars for experimental programs, such as Operation Head Start, but they insisted that they obtain some kind of feedback to indicate what results were being achieved. Unfortunately, the reports that were received from the schools were not very reassuring, partly because of the difficulties of hastily putting together an entirely new program, partly because short-term results do not tell the complete story for any innovative educational program, and partly because the complexity and breadth of educational results do not readily lend themselves to precise statistical reporting. A natural reaction to these reports was increased public skepticism about schools' ability to do anything. Educators complained that expecting them to raise the educational level of millions of children in a year or two was expecting too much, particularly when most of the causes of educational retardation were beyond the control of the school. The public, however, was in no mood to accept such explanations, and the psychological atmosphere was not improved by strikes of students and teachers and the rebellious and/or self-indulgent behavior of a small percentage of high-school and college students who seemed to be rejecting the values and the standards of behavior the schools presumably had been teaching them.

The New Look: The Management Assessment Model

One of the more significant social phenomena that have appeared in the twentieth century is what has been called "management science" or "operations research." The techniques and theories that characterize this speciality have enabled management experts to make bureaucratic systems in both business and government establishments operate more efficiently and productively. The changes wrought by these experts have even been referred to as a kind of "managerial revolution" (Burnham, 1960). The public has generally taken the view that the benefits of the revolution are greater than its costs, although this is a matter that is highly controversial and forms a ready topic for debate in dignified editorials, as well as in noisy barroom arguments. The power of management specialists and the scope of their activities have in recent years been greatly extended by the development of the computer, and a mutual interest in innovative methods of data processing has brought about a close working arrangement between management scientists and the behavioristic/experimental group of educational psychologists.

Public education today is being administered by a new breed of educational managers who resemble their colleagues in other government agencies in many respects, especially in the manner in which they attack problems. Educational operations, especially in the more populous states, are being forced by these administrators into a management assessment pattern—what is also called a "deficiency model." The steps in such a model are quite simple.

1. *Criteria setting.* The public, through its representatives, indicates in general terms what "educational product" they want. These expectations are then broken down into specific competencies, and some kind of a determination is made as to how well students at various grade levels should read, what their level of attainment should be in other skills, what concepts and information they should know, and so forth.

2. *Initial status.* Tests are administered to assess the deficiencies, that is, to find out what the differences are between students' actual accomplishments and the criteria specified in Number 1.

3. *Survey of resources.* Determination is made of what resources (personnel, equipment, buildings, special programs) are available and can be secured to enable the schools to bring the students to a point where they satisfy the criteria.

4. *Program planning.* Operations are planned that deploy available resources in programs aimed at bringing students' competencies up to criteria standards.

5. *Program implementation.* The programs planned in Number 4 are carried out.

6. *Product assessment.* At various stages in the program, students' performance is measured by tests similar to those used in Number 2, in order to determine how close they have come to meeting the criteria.

7. *Review.* After each assessment, the programs are reviewed and analyzed to determine whether any aspects should be changed: criteria, tests, resources employed, type of program, or whatever.

Legislators and educational administrators are increasingly taking the view that management assessment programs, as we have outlined them, are essential if public demands are going to be met. Management assessment procedures make it possible to extend responsibility for accountability throughout the school system to the point that the teacher and even the student become participants in the process. The trend toward management assessment is also both a cause and effect of deeper community involvement in the schools, for accountability gives organized groups of ethnic minorities, parents, and taxpayers an entry point whereby they can exert leverage on the schools. The greater the demands made by these groups with respect to the "educational product," the more specifications the educational engineers will build into the criteria that students are expected to attain and the more sophisticated the "instrumentation"—the testing programs—will become. There has already been an upswing in state-mandated testing programs.

Accountability and Teaching

One obvious outcome of the trend toward management assessment programs is that testing and evaluation services provided by administrators are becoming more detached from the teaching-learning process. Instead of testing being a process that enables students and teachers to receive feedback as to their performances, it becomes something that is done for the administrator, the school boards, and organizations outside the schools.

There are other criticisms as well. Robert F. Bundy (1974) characterizes accountability as a "classic example of myopic thinking and narrow vision." He sees it as a misapplication of industrial concepts to nonindustrial problems and says that "It is the misplaced response of frustrated consumers who have little place else to focus their anger." Hulda Grobman (1973) agrees that some accountability is necessary and desirable, but considering how much we do *not* know about the nature of learning and measuring outcomes, attempts to institute accountability measures do more harm than good. Jacob Landers (1973) observes that the real danger is that *"aims of education will be increasingly restricted to those which can be more easily measured, rather than those which are most important"* [italics in the original].

Arthur W. Combs (1973) points out that the behavioral objective approaches that are basic to accountability are essentially closed systems of thinking that do not take into account the multiplicity of environmental forces that bear on the student. He writes:

Students do not only go to school; they are affected by everything that happens to them. The attempt, therefore, to isolate the peculiar stimuli responsible for remote outcomes is thus a study in futility.

Combs' response to those who wish to force accountability on the schools is that the educator's emphasis should be on the creation and maintenance of the teaching-learning process—"to confront students with problems that constantly keep them stretching and to join and assist them in the discovery of appropriate answer." Teachers, he says, should be judged in terms of their success or failure in establishing these processes, not in terms of specific, behaviorally stated objectives that are the heart of management assessment programs.

W. James Popham (1973) strikes a note that is both realistic and somewhat reassuring. He says that although there has been a great deal of talk about accountability, no practical procedures for making it work have been devised. This may be small comfort for teachers who have to make major alterations in their classroom procedures in order to accommodate the "instrumentation" of the educational engineers, but it does suggest that the tight control of teaching and learning that is claimed by proponents of management assessment may be more theoretical or imagined than real.

"Never Mind the Details—Just Tell Me in Words of One Syllable. . ."

Although the shortcomings of accountability are obvious to most teachers and to many educational observers, especially those of a humanistic orientation, the public continues to have a great deal of faith in the large-scale achievement testing that makes accountability possible. Results of a nationwide poll suggest that three-fourths of the American people want children in their community to be given national tests in order to determine how their achievement compares with the achievement of children elsewhere. About two-thirds want teachers and administrators to be held accountable if children are below the norm, and one-half insist that teachers should be paid according to the quality of their work (Gallup, 1970).

The public's preoccupation with accountability has had some unfortunate side effects. Private concerns, claiming to be able to produce better results than existing school systems, have entered into contract with school districts whereby they would be paid for every student who exceeded the norm. These negotiations have not only shaken the public's confidence in schools even further, but they have led to rather unprofessional conduct on the part of some contractors. In one instance, students' "achievement" was enhanced by coaching them on items taken from the final evaluation test.

The idea of tying accountability to the results of nationwide and statewide testing programs is based on a general misunderstanding of educational processes and goals, as well as the meaning of test scores. It is questionable as to whether scores attained on a single test or series of tests can accurately reflect the quality of any educational program. There is a natural tendency to assume that there is poor teaching in any school or a class that scores low on achievement tests, whereas the more likely explanation for such scores is that students have come from poverty homes. Perhaps the students and teachers in question are doing their best in spite of handicaps, or perhaps not, but the test scores tell us nothing about the amount and kind of effort that has gone into the educational program. Sophisticated computer programs can take students' socioeconomic status into account, but the public tends to look with suspicion on reports that are complex and detailed and asks educational authorities to tell them "in words of one syllable" just what it is that students have learned.

Some data from a nationwide testing program show how difficult it is to determine what test reports mean. Figure 13-7 summarizes the results obtained when students in Louisiana public schools took reading tests administered by the National Assessment of Educational Progress in 1973–74. When compared to the median or midpoint performance of students either from the Southeastern states or from the United States taken as a whole, Louisiana students who are nine and thirteen years old appear less competent, for they score a few percentage points below the norms. Seventeen-year-old Louisiana students, however, score a few percentage points above the norms. There are several

possible explanations for the superior performance of Louisiana seventeen-year-olds. One is that the secondary schools of Louisiana are not only doing a better job with reading than local elementary schools but are even doing better than secondary schools throughout the United States. If so, this rather unusual situation suggests further investigation. Another possible interpretation, suggested by the local director of the National Assessment program, is that Louisiana students with reading problems are being assigned to remedial classes in the fourth grade, and that the impact of this special attention is being seen later, when they get into high school. It is possible that a similar procedure is followed in other states, however. A third explanation is that poor readers may be dropping out of school before they are seventeen years old, and that those who stay in school are superior readers (Worcester, 1974). It is the last explanation that seems to be the most valid because records show that Louisiana has a much poorer record than most states, as far as school dropouts are concerned.

In states that have a good record for keeping students in school and preventing dropouts, comparisons with nationwide norms present a picture which is the opposite to that shown in Figure 13-7. The achievement of students in California, which ranks among the top half-dozen states in "holding power," shows an apparent decline between grades 5 and 11 when compared to national norms because California schools are retaining students who are less competent and who would have dropped out in other states (California Superintendent of Public Instruction, 1965).

The point is that statistics which report the results of nationwide, statewide, or even community-wide testing require a great deal of careful interpretation when they are communicated to persons unfamiliar either with statistics or with the complex variables that lie behind them. When such interpretations are made to laymen, there is unfortunately a tendency for them to feel that school people are being overly defensive and are probably trying to "hide something" in their attempts to disprove what seems to the laymen to be simple and obvious.

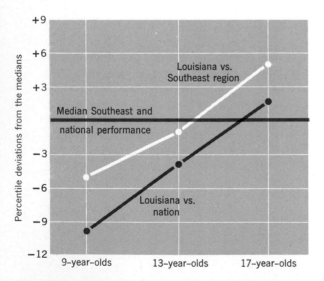

FIG. 13-7. Performance of Louisiana students on National Assessment reading tests, expressed in terms of percentile deviations from the median performances of students in the Southeastern region of the United States and in the entire nation (Worcester, 1974).

Criterion-referenced Testing

We have previously mentioned and described Bloom's mastery learning, a teaching-learning strategy that enables most of the students in a class to have the experience of 100 percent success, an experience that is satisfying and morale-building because it saves students from the trauma of failure, disappointment, and humiliation. The extent to which a student has succeeded in mastering the material in a mastery-learning unit is measured by a test that is criterion-referenced. In other words, the test that evaluates work on a mastery-learning unit is related to a criterion that specifies the skill or information that is to be mastered. If a mastery-learning unit, for instance, is supposed to teach the adding of two-place numbers, the attainment of criterion will be measured by a work sample or test involving the adding of two-place numbers. Hence the term "criterion-referenced testing."

The kinds of standardized achievement tests we have been describing, such as those prepared by test publishers or the National Assessment of Educational Progress, are norm-referenced tests because the performance of a single student, a class, a school, or any group of students is interpreted by comparing it to performance levels that are typical—normal—for the sample of students on which the test was standardized. A criterion-referenced test, however, gives us results that can be interpreted with respect to the performance of the student who completed the work unit, a unit that was presumably selected for him because it was appropriate to his level of competence and his educational needs. A score made by the same child on a norm-referenced test would tell us how his performance compared with that of the typical performance of the average child, but little about his work. On the face of it, then, criterion-referenced tests can be used in ways that are more individual-student-centered, whereas norm-referenced tests are more oriented to the expectations of teachers, of the school authorities, and of society as a whole.

Criterion-referenced test performance can also be used as a source of information that can be presented in the form of reports which enable a student to tell at a glance how far he has progressed in a given field and what lies ahead of him. The Mathematics Goal Record Card employed in the public schools of Winnetka, Illinois, is an example of such a report (see Figure 13-8). The fact that the goals of mastery learning can be stated in behavioral terms, as they are on this record card, also means that they are compatible with assessment programs de-

Recognizes number groups up to 5 . . . .

Recognizes patterns of objects to 10 . . . .

Can count objects to 100 . . . .

Recognizes number to 100 . . . .

Can read and write numerals to 50 . . . .

Recognizes addition and subtraction symbols . . . .

Understands meaning of the equality sign . . . .

Understands meaning of the inequality signs . . . .

Can count objects:
by 2's to 20 . . . .

by 5's to 100 . . . .

by 10's to 100 . . . .

Recognizes geometric figures:
triangle . . . .

circle . . . .

quadrilateral . . . .

Recognizes coins (1c, 5c, 10c, 25c) . . . .

Knows addition combinations 10 and under using objects . . . .

Knows subtraction combinations 10 and under using objects . . . .

Recognizes addition and subtraction vertically and horizontally . . . .

Shows understanding of numbers and number combinations
1. Using concrete objects . . . .

2. Beginning to visualize and abstract . . . .

3. Makes automatic responses without concrete objects . . . .

Can tell time
1. Hour . . . .

2. Half hour . . . .

3. Quarter hour . . . .

Addition combinations 10 and under (automatic response) . . . .

Substraction combinations 10 and under (automatic response) . . . .

Can count to 200 . . . .

Can understand zero as a number . . . .

Can understand place value to tens . . . .

Can read and write numerals to 200 . . . .

Can read and write number words to 20 . . . .

Use facts in 2-digit column addition (no carrying) . . . .

Roman numerals to XII . . . .

FIG. 13-8. A portion of the Mathematics Goal Record Card used in the public schools of Winnetka, Illinois (as cited by Airasian and Madaus, 1972).

signed by educational managers. In other words, mastery learning and criterion-referenced testing can easily be integrated into accountability programs. It is argued that this integration represents the best of all possible worlds because it provides for individualized learning, as well as for the gathering of information for the reports that administrators and public agencies require in order to determine what students are learning and how much progress they are making. The same process, of course, also makes it possible for administrators to control what students learn and to alter the rate with which it is learned. The general public, educational managers, and behaviorally oriented psychologists are inclined to approve of linking mastery learning, criterion-referenced testing, and accountability; humanistically oriented psychologists and educators see such attempts as educationally stifling and detrimental.

But even behaviorists and traditionalists are unlikely to find that criterion-referenced testing satisfies all their aims. William Coffman (1974) has pointed out that the kinds of learnings that are most important are the ones that involve complex skills and hence develop slowly over the years. Criterion-referenced tests and mastery learning units are, however, concerned only with information and skills that are taught and measured most easily, and these are likely to be of a simpler order. Coffman, who is a past president of the National Council on Measurement in Education, observed:

To the extent that measurement deals only with the simple learnings and ignores the more complex, it encourages the training of simple responses without emphasizing the fact that the way in which the simple learnings are developed may be crucial for the development of more complex ones. Thus, to specify, as some have, that the criterion of an acceptable item for a criterion-referenced test is that it be responsive to teaching (over the short pull), is to reinforce a superficial concept of what education is all about.

Reporting Pupil Progress

For many years there has been a chronic controversy regarding the reporting of students' educational status to their parents. In recent years, parents have been demanding more information and have thus given considerable support to the move to increase the use of standardized achievement tests. These demands present school people with a dilemma: There is no doubt that parents do have a right to have access to data relating to their children, but it is also true that few parents are qualified to interpret the data. Indeed, they often become confused or angry when teachers try to explain what test scores mean. It is, perhaps, for this reason that school marks continue to be used year after year, in spite of the fact that school people feel that they are inadequate measures of student performance. The conventional A-B-C-D-F system at least *looks* simple, and many parents insist that it be continued along with statewide testing. Letter grading or numerical grading is currently used in about three-fourths of all schools (National Education Association, 1970d).

What most educators prefer in lieu of letter grades, at least in elementary schools, is a report that summarizes the progress a student is making, what might reasonably be expected of him, and the kind of learning problems he is having. Conferences with parents are especially desirable in communicating this kind of information. Here are some suggestions made by Clarence Mahler and Harry Smallenburg (1963) that should be helpful:

1. Report to the parents in terms of the child's achievement in relation to his capacity—how he is developing in relation to his strengths and limitations.

2. Report on the child's attainments in any learning situation in relation to the others in his group.

3. Report also on the child's aptitudes and achievements in relation to the larger numbers of children beyond his particular school and community—by reference to published norms.

4. Make certain that parents and teachers share observations about the child. The teacher should listen rather than lecture.
5. Differences in points of view should be respected.
6. Avoid comparison of the student with individual classmates.
7. End conference on a constructive note of confidence in the child and his development. Consider all aspects of the child's growth—not just intellectual.

Like any other kind of school activity, the reporting of pupil progress should contribute to the increased effectiveness of learning. To be sure, teachers have traditionally used failing marks as a goad for lazy and less competent students, and have awarded high marks as a kind of prize to students whose achievement was especially pleasing. The efficacy of this approach, like that of other traditional approaches to learning, is rather questionable. Psychological research *does* show that learning is facilitated if students are informed of their

(The Wall Street Journal)

"It's not me, Dad. It's the system that failed."

progress, but it does not support the idea that a single grade really communicates very much information. Furthermore, the same criticisms can be made of the single course grade that we have made of the marking of essay tests: There tends to be considerable variation among teachers, as well as variation within the standards of a single teacher. In addition, there is variation among schools and subjects. It is common experience in colleges, for instance, for science and mathematics instructors to assign more Ds and Fs and fewer As and Bs, and for instructors in, say, music and art, to assign higher proportions of As and Bs and lower proportions of Ds and Fs than is typical of the college as a whole. There is some evidence to show that these differences are due to differences in the personality traits characteristic of the teachers in each of the fields, rather than to any intrinsic difficulty of the subject matter.

Although there is probably an overall relationship between grades and achievement, it is by no means a very close one. Girls characteristically receive higher marks than boys, as we have shown elsewhere, even though their levels of achievement, as measured by standardized norm-referenced tests are approximately the same. One study demonstrated, for instance, that teacher's marks were more closely correlated with the IQs of seventh-graders than with their standardized achievement test scores (McCandless, Roberts, and Starnes, 1972). Other data tend to show that students who are obedient, conforming, and industrious tend to receive higher grades than those who are rebellious, nonconforming, and lazy, even though the amount of learning according to objective measures may be the same. What such findings mean is that grades are influenced by some factor or factors other than progress in learning.

Although grades are subject to the variations we have noted, they do tend to have a certain overall consistency. The grade-point average of students tends to be rather consistent from one semester to another, and high-school grades are the most effective predictors of college success—better, even, than all the batteries of college entrance examinations. What this means is that college instructors are inclined to use much the same criteria that are used by high-school teachers in assigning marks. This rough consistency indicates that grades *do* measure something. What they measure is by no means certain, but it is likely that they are a kind of "index of scholastic adjustment,"that is, they show how a student has been able to adjust or adapt his behavior to the expectations of teachers. To the extent that (1) the behavior of a student is similar in various classes and (2) teachers have similar expectations of students, to the same extent will the student receive similar grades. The fact that a given student's grades tend to be consistent, therefore, reflects consistencies in both student behavior and teacher expectations. Sometimes, of course, a student's grades are inconsistent. He may, for example, get high marks in science and mathematics and low marks in history and English, or his overall grade average may suddenly decline. The fact, however, that grades are *generally* consistent for most students makes deviations of this kind all the more noticeable. They are, indeed, potentially useful signals as to the presence of psychological problems.

Grades also appear to be related to nonacademic performance. Calvin W. Taylor and Robert L. Ellison (1967), in a survey of the background of more than two thousand scientists, found that high-school and college standings were predictive to creativity in their chosen field. Marshall H. Brenner (1968) found that teachers' ratings were better predictors of job success than were the test scores applicants made on special aptitude tests. Chester J. Judy (1969) reported that the high-school performance of airmen was a better predictor of their success in technical training than was a composite score based on Air Force classification test results.

The main objective of anything we do in schools, and this includes testing and all aspects of evaluation, should be the stimulation and encouraging of learning. We should, however, take note of a second type of objective, one that is stressed particularly in traditional schools: selection. Many such schools, especially in Europe and Latin America, hold that one of their major functions is that of se-

lecting or screening students for higher education. In these schools, tests and examinations are viewed primarily as devices to "weed out the unfit," rather than as a part of the teaching-learning process. The use of tests in this way is best suited to societies in which the social structure is largely predetermined, and schools are assigned the task of sorting out and assigning graduates to their appropriate level in the hierarchy of positions that are available. In the United States and Canada, where positions are more freely accessible than they are in more traditionally oriented cultures, education is likely to be considered as a means for stimulating cognitive development and for encouraging students to develop their best potentialities, whatever they may be. This can best be done by systems of evaluation that are aimed at promoting and stimulating learning, rather than by systems that have the purpose of supplying a sufficient number of candidates—and no more—to fill the small number of positions available in a highly structured status system.

SUMMARY

Although evaluation evokes anxiety, it is an inevitable and usually unconscious accompaniment to all forms of human interaction. Since it cannot be eliminated from teaching-learning situations, the teacher's task is to see how it can be done better. Anything a teacher does to determine the extent to which the teaching-learning process is succeeding comes under the heading of evaluation. Evaluation must be considered with respect to goals, which can best be related to the evaluational process if they are stated in terms of the behavior a student can be expected to demonstrate when he has attained the goals. The teacher's role as an evaluator is that of being a participant-observer in the educational process. Even though he may prefer not to evaluate, he should recognize that learning of many types is facilitated if students get some feedback as to their progress, and that others in the school system, as well as in the community, have the right to obtain information regarding student progress. Indeed, if the teacher does not evaluate, others may do it for him. Evaluation focuses attention on clarifying educational goals, identifying situations in which progress can be observed toward goals, construction tests, and other measures, and gathering information that can be used to improve the educational program.

Although tests and examinations are probably the most frequently used educational technique, they actually measure only a small segment of learner behavior. Success in attaining some of the more significant educational objectives cannot be measured by tests but must be identified by other means, such as the observation of behavior in various situations. However, because of their obvious advantages, tests and examinations will always play an important role in evaluation.

Feedback of evaluational information to the learner enables him to correct or adjust his attempts at learning and also helps to maintain his interest in the material being learned. Anxieties about evaluation can be kept at a minimum if it is not overstressed to the detriment of other educational processes, and if teachers and students realize that marks and test scores are both approximate and relative. In recent years, individual student evaluation has been placed on a more scientific basis with the use of contract plans, some of which involve elaborate computer hookups to store and process data regarding the performance of the learner.

At one time, evaluation was based mainly on recitation and oral examination. This method was not only inefficient but produced results that were inaccurate. The written or essay examination began to replace oral methods during the nineteenth century. Although essay examinations are an improvement over oral examinations, they tend to be an unreliable measure of learning. Not only are there great variations in the way different teachers mark a given examination paper, but a teacher may also vary from time to time in the marks he assigns a given paper. Some of this unreliability can be reduced by committee grading of essay tests.

The development of choice-type items has enabled teachers to eliminate bias from the marking of examinations. The term "objective," which is commonly used to refer to tests made up of choice-type items, is actually a misnomer. Inasmuch as subjective factors enter into the writing of the test items and the selection of the dimension of learning on which the items are based, the only objective thing about them is their scoring. Some common forms of choice-type items are the true-false, multiple-choice, completion, and matching. Tests composed of choice-type items have sometimes been criticized because they measure the student's ability to recognize correct answers, rather than the ability to produce them himself. However, it is possible to develop choice-type items that can measure almost any kind of mental process the test maker wishes.

The reliability or consistency of objective tests can be checked by administering a test twice (or by administering two comparable forms) and comparing the results. If the scores of students change markedly from one testing to the other, the test probably lacks reliability. In general, longer tests are more reliable than shorter ones.

The extent to which a test measures what it is expected to measure is its validity. Validity may be checked by comparing the results of the test with some other objective criterion for example, the scores on a college-entrance examination can be checked against actual success in college. The validity of teacher-made examinations is more difficult to check. Teachers are on sounder ground if they assume that their tests measure only narrow areas of educational experiences rather than some of the broader and more basic objectives of the curriculum.

Whether a test is valid depends a great deal on how it is used and interpreted. A test may be valid in one situation but not in another. Or it may be valid in measuring what it was intended to measure but not in measuring what the test giver thinks it measures. The problem of validity can be approached and solved both by helping teachers to gain a better understanding of tests and by improving existing tests.

Educational performance can be measured by standardized tests which are more reliable than teacher-made tests and which provide norms based on large samples of students. Results of such tests are reported in terms of grade placement (particularly for elementary school subjects), percentile scores, and stanines.

Standardized tests are useful when teachers want to compare the achievement levels of their students with national norms, or when they are looking for diagnostic information regarding the learning problems of their students. Such tests report a student's educational status in terms of grade placement, that is, where he stands with respect to others in the same grade. Additional data may also be given, for instance, his status with respect to others of similar age, sex, aptitude, and grade in school. Data are also reported in terms of percentile scores and stanines.

Governmental agencies, legislators, parents, organized minority groups, and the public in general have been inclined, in recent years, to hold schools and school personnel accountable for failures of students to learn what is expected of them. Concerns about accountability have led educational administrators to adopt a "management assessment model," which they have taken over from large government agencies and from business. The model calls for administrators to determine the extent to which students fall short of what the public expects of them in the way of educational accomplishments, to plan and implement programs in order to remedy the deficiency, and to measure students' subsequent performance. Managerial assessment has the effect of divorcing testing from teaching and imposes sets of narrow criteria on classroom activities. It also forces teachers to be more concerned about behaviorally determined goals and outcomes and less concerned about the processes of teaching and learning. The public's demand for accountability has led to an increase in statewide and nationwide testing programs, but the results of such tests are not easily interpreted by the layman. Criterion-referenced testing is employed to measure students' progress with respect to specific skills and information. Although it is used to measure success in individualized learning mastery programs, it also can be integrated into assessment plans, a move that is favored by those who wish to control learners by manipulating their environment but decried by those who see learning as a process of growth and fulfillment.

The reporting of pupil progress is an area that is fraught with controversy and confusion. Teacher-parent conferences appear to be the most effective way of reporting evaluation of students' work. Progress reports should be used to promote learning, but many teachers use them as rewards or punishments. Letter grades tend to have a fair degree of reliability or consistency. Although they are supposed to measure what students have learned, they very likely measure other factors as well—for instance, the ability of students to adjust or adapt their behavior to the expectations of teachers.

Suggested Problems

1. Write up some of the objectives for a college course you are currently taking. Be sure that you state them in terms of changes that will presumably take place in student behavior as a result of the course. How would you go about evaluating a student's progress in the course in the light of the objectives you have drawn up?

2. What are some of the objectives of high school or elementary school education that do not figure in the kinds of tests and examinations that are commonly given?

3. Devise a series of test items based on this textbook, using the following types: essay, true-false, multiple-choice, completion, and matching. Try to devise items that will measure students' ability to apply what they have learned to the solution of realistic classroom problems.

4. What are the arguments for and against the use of "pass-fail" or "pass-no-report" grades in high school and college, as contrasted with the grading systems now being used?

5. Every spring the Educational Testing Service of Princeton, New Jersey, gives the National Teacher Examinations on behalf of school departments which are looking for new teachers. These examinations are to a large extent concerned with knowledge and application of educational principles. Let us assume that a superintendent of schools is trying to decide whether he should use these examinations in the selection of teachers. What would be the arguments for and against their use? How valid are these arguments? What would the superintendent probably want to know about these examinations before making a decision?

6. Many people maintain that a teacher's pay and tenure should be based on the extent to which his students have progressed academically during the previous school year. Examine this position from the standpoint of the taxpayer and/or parent, give the arguments pro and con that a school administrator might make, and indicate how you would vote if a measure providing for this policy were placed on the ballot at election time.

7. High-school and college grades have a low but positive correlation with overall measures of success after graduation. In what kinds of situations or positions is the correlation likely to be higher and in what kinds is it likely to approach zero or even to be negative?

Suggested Readings

DuBois, P. H. (ed.). *Toward a theory of achievement measurement: Proceedings of the 1969 Invitational Conference on Testing Problems.* Princeton: Educational Testing Service, 1970. (A paperback.) A series of statements, some of them controversial, on achievement testing and accountability.

Engelhart, M. D. *Improving classroom testing.* Washington: National Education Association, 1964. Pamphlet No. 31 in the series "What research says to the teacher," a joint production of the Department of Classroom Teachers and the American Educational Research Association, both departments of the NEA.

Gronlund, N. E. *Determining accountability for classroom instruction.* New York: Macmillan, 1974 (A pamphlet.) Relates accountability to norm- and criterion-referenced testing.

Gronlund, N. E. *Measurement and evaluation in teaching,* 2nd. ed. New York: Macmillan, 1971. A standard text in evaluation with a practical orientation.

Gronlund, N. E. *Stating behavioral objectives for classroom instruction.* New York: Macmillan, 1970. (A pamphlet.) A brief handbook explaining how curricular objectives can be stated in behavioral terms and related to an evaluational program.

Karmel, L. J. *Measurement and evaluation in the schools.* New York: Macmillan, 1970. A general text, aimed especially at teachers.

Lessinger, L. M., and Tyler, R. W. (eds.). *Accountability in education.* Worthington, O.: Jones, 1971. A brief paperback presenting several sides to this controversial topic.

Lindgren, H. C., and Lindgren, F. (eds.). *Current readings in educational psychology,* 2nd ed. New York: Wiley, 1972. See section on evaluation.

McLaughlin, K. F. (ed.). *Understanding testing: Purposes and interpretations for pupil development.* Washington: United States Office of Education, 1960. (Pamphlet OE-25003.) A very useful pamphlet available for 25 cents from the Government Printing Office.

McLaughlin, K. F. *Interpretation of test results.* Washington: United States Office of Education, 1964. A useful 30-cent pamphlet that explains the construction and selection of tests in simple language. Obtainable from Government Printing Office, Cat. No. FS5:2 25:25038.

Nelson, C. H. *Measurement and evaluation in the classroom.* New York: Macmillan, 1970. (A paperback.) A brief handbook covering techniques of test construction and interpretation of results.

Tanner, L. N., and Lindgren, H. C. *Classroom teaching and learning.* New York: Holt, Rinehart, and Winston, 1971. See Chapter 10, "Evaluation and mental health."

Thorndike, R. L., and Hagen, E. *Measurement and evaluation in psychology and education,* 3rd ed. New York: Wiley, 1969.

Tyler, R. W. (ed.) *Educational evaluation: New roles, new means,* 68th Yearbook, Part II. Chicago: National Society for the Study of Education, 1969.

Wilhelms, F. T. (ed.) *Evaluation as feedback and guide.* Washington: Association for Supervision and Curriculum Development, NEA, 1967. Useful for discussion of the "human side" of evaluation and for description of experimental programs combining evaluation with curriculum development.

The U. S. Public Health Service of the U. S. Department of Health, Education, and Welfare has prepared a number of pamphlets based on data from the National Health Survey conducted 1966–70. Some recent pamphlets that are relevant to achievement testing are: *School achievement of children 6–11 years,* June 1970 (Series 11, No. 1030), *School achievement of children by demographic and socioeconomic factors,* November 1971 (Series 11, No. 109); *Literacy among youths 12–17 years,* December 1973 (Series 11, No. 131); *Reading and arithmetic achievement among youths 12–17 years,* February 1974 (Series 11, No. 136). All pamphlets are available from the Superintendent of Documents, Government Printing Office, Washington D. C. 20402.

14

Individual Differences and Their Measurement

What Is "Different" About Individual Differences?

It is said that scientists first became aware of the importance of individual differences as the result of an incident that occurred in 1796 at the Royal Observatory at Greenwich. A laboratory assistant named Kinnebrook was dismissed from his post because of a consistent difference of eight-tenths of a second between his observations of the transit of stars and those of the Astronomer Royal. The differ-ence was, of course, assumed to be due to Kinnebrook's incompetence. Some twenty years later he was vindicated when an investigation showed that he was right and the Astronomer Royal was wrong. The results of the investigation showed that people tend to differ in reaction time, that they probably differ in other characteristics as well, and that such differences are quite normal and usual. The scientific world was greatly annoyed at this discovery because it raised questions about the accuracy of observations that scientists make during research. As time went on, however, physiologists and psychologists became interested in measuring these individual variations, and this interest led eventually to the development of the field of psychological measurement. The most important and most significant measuring device to appear during the early years of psychology was the intelligence test.

MEASURING COGNITIVE DIFFERENCES

The First Intelligence Tests

The pioneer intelligence tests were not the printed booklets of multiple-choice items that are so familiar today, but were schedules of tasks, scaled according to the maturity of the person being tested. In 1905, Alfred Binet of Paris developed the first widely used intelligence test: the Binet-Simon Scale. He was concerned with the problem of identifying children who were not benefiting from instruction because of low intellectual capacity. By using Binet's scale, examiners could find out whether a child had the capacity to perform the tasks that could be successfully completed by the average child of his age. To the degree that a child could *not* perform these tasks, he was considered intellectually retarded for his age, and to the degree that he could perform *more* than his quota of tasks, he was considered intellectually advanced. It was thus possible to think of a child's "mental age" as something apart from his chronological age. For example, a child of eight might be able to perform no tasks more complex than those performed by a child of six. His mental age would therefore be six years.

The Binet-Simon Scale came to the attention of Henry H. Goddard, who translated it into English and used it with American children in 1908. A revision was also translated by Frederick Kuhlmann in 1912. In 1916, Lewis Madison Terman of Stanford University published still another revision of the test, which he called the Stanford-Binet Scale, together with norms based on a fairly extensive sampling of American children. The Stanford-Binet received widespread acceptance, and even today is a

standard against which many intelligence tests are checked.

The results obtained by administering a Stanford-Binet to a child may be reported both as mental age (MA) and as intelligence quotient or IQ. With the earlier forms of the test, the IQ was obtained by dividing the mental age of a child by his chronological age (CA) and multiplying the result by 100 (to avoid the bother of decimals). This formula can be expressed algebraically as

$$100 \frac{M.A.}{C.A.} = IQ$$

In other words, the child of eight, already mentioned, who had a mental age of six, would be considered to have an IQ of 75. A child of ten with a mental age of twelve years and six months would have an IQ of 125. The IQ is a way of expressing a child's actual rate of mental growth as a ratio of the expected (that is, "average") rate of growth up to the age at which he is tested. Thus the child of eight with an IQ of 75 shows a slower-than-average rate of mental growth, whereas the child of ten with an IQ of 125 shows a faster-than-average rate of growth.

We have given the older formula for the IQ in order to illustrate the reasoning that lies behind the IQ as an expression of the relationship between chronological age and mental development. This formula is, however, no longer used because of statistical flaws that made for problems of interpretation when it came to comparing IQs that children made during preschool years with those they made during the middle years of childhood. The IQ that has been used with the Stanford-Binet since 1960 is based on the normal curve, with 100 representing the average or mean IQ for any age and 16 IQ points representing one standard deviation. This type of IQ is called the deviation IQ, and its relation to the normal curve of probability may be seen in Figure 13-6.

The Stanford-Binet, like its French predecessor, is an "individual" intelligence test. It can be administered to only one child at a time. Furthermore, it can be given only by a person who has had special training in the administration, scoring, and interpre-

PIONEERS IN THE DEVELOPMENT OF
INTELLIGENCE TESTS.
The Stanford-Binet scale, the most famous
intelligence test of all time, was developed by
Lewis Madison Terman *(left)* from a scale
produced by the French psychologist, Alfred
Binet *(below)*.

tation of the test. It is a relatively expensive test to use, inasmuch as a highly trained professional person must spend at least two hours preparing the testing situation, establishing good relations with the child, scoring the test, and interpreting and reporting the results. Although Stanford-Binet scores are expressed only in terms of mental age and IQ, a good clinician can use the test data to develop important clues to the intellectual, emotional, and social functioning of the child.

In the years since 1916, when the Stanford-Binet Scale was first published,[1] a number of other scales and tests have been developed for use as individual tests. David Wechsler, of Bellevue Hospital in New York City, first published his Wechsler-Bellevue Scale in 1939. The Wechsler Intelligence Scale for Children (WISC) became available in 1949, and the scale for adults was revised and issued under the title of Wechsler Adult Intelligence Scale (WAIS) in 1955. The Wechsler Pre-Primary Scale of Intelligence (WPPSI) was published in 1963. The Wechsler scales make use of the deviation IQ in somewhat the same manner as the Stanford-Binet.

The Stanford-Binet IQ is largely a measure of verbal ability, although many of the items used with younger children are of necessity nonverbal (see Figure 14-1). Wechsler scales report a verbal IQ, a performance (nonverbal) IQ, a total IQ, and part-scores on eleven different scales, or subtests, thus facilitating the collection and interpretation of more precise diagnostic information than is possible with the Stanford-Binet. On the other hand, Stanford-Binet IQs tend to be better predictors of school success.

Group Intelligence Tests: Their Promise and Disappointment

Intelligence tests were introduced into schools on a large scale during the 1920s. This move did not get its impetus so much from individual tests such as the Stanford-Binet as from the Army Alpha Test—the first group intelligence test to be administered on a mass basis. The rapid expansion of the Army during World War I created an enormous demand

for commissioned and noncommissioned officers. In order to improve the basis for selecting candidates for special training or promotion, the Army requested some of the outstanding psychologists of the day to construct some intelligence tests suitable for group administration. The Army Alpha and the Army Beta (nonlanguage) Tests were the results. The tests—particularly the Alpha—were so successful that within a few years a sizable number of group intelligence tests appeared on the market. These tests, as well as the ones that followed them, were variations and improvements of the original models—the Army Alpha and Beta.[2]

The use of standardized group intelligence tests became widespread during the 1920s. Business firms and governmental agencies used them in some form or other as a basis for selecting employees, a practice that continues today. Educators employed them essentially for two purposes: as a basis for ability grouping and as a way of understanding the individual learner. The idea underlying ability grouping was that of efficiency: Teachers believed they could teach more effectively if the pupils in their classes were of approximately the same level of intelligence. This practice, also termed homogeneous grouping, was also viewed as being in the best interest of the child, on the grounds that it would permit brighter students to move ahead at a rapid pace, unencumbered by having to do boring assignments that were too easy for them. Slower students, it was also argued, would avoid the embarrassment of being compared unfavorably to abler, more successful peers. Homogeneous grouping has never produced the advantages that were claimed for it, although many school districts still use it in some form or other. We shall examine the practice in more detail in Chapter 15.

[2] Some of the group intelligence tests that are used by schools today are the California Test of Mental Maturity (published by CTB/McGraw-Hill), Kuhlmann-Anderson Intelligence Tests (Personnel Press), Pintner General Ability Tests and Otis-Lennon Mental Ability Tests (Harcourt Brace Jovanovich), Cooperative School and College Ability Tests (SCAT) (Educational Testing Service), Lorge-Thorndike Intelligence Tests and Henmon-Nelson Tests of Mental Ability (Houghton Mifflin), and Tests of General Ability (TOGA) (Science Research Associates).

[1] The Stanford-Binet was revised and restandardized on new norms in 1937 and again in 1960.

Intelligence test results have also been rather a disappointment when it comes to helping teachers understand individual children. The IQ is a rough estimate of a child's mental ability at a given moment and can be used to predict future performance in school, but it can vary over time and means different things for different individuals. Even though it is a simple two- or three-digit figure, it represents a very complex concept that has to be interpreted in the light of a great deal of other data, much of which does not appear in a typical child's cumulative record. In any event, a teacher who has two or three dozen students to supervise seldom has the time or the inclination to dig into the ambiguities of what his students' IQs really mean.

Some researchers have demanded that intelli-

Unfinished man: 3 years   3½ years

4 years   5 years   6 years

FIG. 14-1. Tests for preschool children have to be largely nonverbal. The unfinished drawing of a rounded stick man at the left is presented to a child. The examiner says: "What is this? You finish him." What the child says about the man and the way in which he draws additional details gives us clues to his personality and intellectual maturity. Three-year-olds are likely to make meaningless doodles in the general area of the face and arms. Sometimes they add nothing or merely say: "That's not the way to make a man." By three and a half, most children try to put limbs in the right places. With each succeeding year, the average child adds more details and executes them with increasing skill and sense of proportion (courtesy Arnold Gesell and "Life Magazine," based on material drawn from A. Gesell et al., "The First Five Years of Life" and "Infant and Child in the Culture of Today," New York, Harper, 1940 and 1943).

gence tests be banned on the grounds that a teacher's knowledge of children's IQs may influence his expectations for them as learners—the "Pygmalion effect" we referred to in Chapter 10. Pressures have also come from organized ethnic minority groups, who have claimed that IQs are being used to shunt certain children into programs in which they receive substandard instruction. Schools have always been sensitive to community pressures, and it is hardly surprising that intelligence tests are no longer given on a mass basis in a large number of districts. New York City eliminated them in 1964,

and in 1974, their use in California was limited by court order. Leona E. Tyler (1972) observed that there has been a revolt against IQ-dominated technology that has prevailed for the last half century, and she questioned whether they serve any function at all in the schools.

In light of all this, education students are likely to wonder: Why give any attention to intelligence testing at all? If intelligence test scores are likely to be unavailable for individual students, why bother?

There are a number of answers to these questions. One is that intelligence tests, whatever defi-

Although intelligence tests have received a great deal of critical attention in recent years because of their limitations, they fill an important need in individual appraisal, as well as in educational research.

354

INDIVIDUAL DIFFERENCES
AND THEIR MEASUREMENTS

ciencies they may have for individual prediction and diagnosis, do tell us something about cognitive functioning in a general sense. A perusal of any professional journal dealing with educational research will show that intelligence testing is very much alive and functioning. The IQ is still the most commonly cited statistic in research reports, after such demographic measures as age, grade, and sex. One of the reasons for the universal use of the IQ as a measure is that it is important for the readers of research reports to know something about the cognitive level of the subjects of a study in order to interpret the results. Intelligence tests are not limited in their usage to theoretical or scholarly papers, for they are also used by investigators employed by school systems who wish to examine, analyze, or compare the effect of various instructional strategies or educational policies. We cannot generalize about the results of such investigations unless we have some understanding of the cognitive levels of the children involved.

A teacher can, of course, remain apart from these activities and concern himself strictly with what goes on in his classroom, but if he wishes to have some understanding of the investigations and decisions that are going on around him and in which he himself may be involved, he must have some grasp of intelligence and intelligence testing. The IQ has never been understood very well by teachers, much less by the lay public, and now that it is taking on political relevance, it is more important than ever to understand what it does and does not mean.

What Intelligence Tests Measure

One of the problems psychologists encounter in trying to understand the effect that genetic and environmental factors have on cognitive development is that intelligence tests measure something in addition to *intelligence* or *"mental ability,"* as defined as the ability to solve problems, to deal with abstractions, and to learn. The studies that we have cited in this chapter and elsewhere in this book show that intelligence tests also indirectly measure such affective factors as emotional adjustment, socioeconomic status, the amount of stimulation experienced, interest in problem solving, and

competitiveness. The question of whether intelligence is compounded of all these variables or whether it is what is left after all these variables have been controlled or eliminated, is a controversial one in psychology. Actually, psychologists are not agreed among themselves as to "what intelligence really is," let alone what intelligence tests measure, although this lack of clear definition has not seriously hampered the development and use of such tests. One way of determining what intelligence tests measure, however, is to find out what their scores correlate with. It is clear, for example, that the high correlations usually found between intelligence test scores and school marks show that the tests are measuring some quality or trait that probably should be labeled "scholastic aptitude."

The ability of intelligence tests to predict grades, however, seems to depend on the extent to which a group of test takers is attuned to middle-class values. In North America, the largest percentages of middle-class individuals are found among whites and orientals, and intelligence tests administered to members of these groups are indeed highly predictive of academic success. Sectors of the population who are black or who have Spanish surnames have much lower proportions of middle-class members, and intelligence tests administered to members of these groups have lower correlations with academic success (Green and Farquhar, 1965; Baldwin and Levin, 1970; Goldman and Richards, 1974).

Subject to these culturally defined limitations, intelligence test scores tend to be correlated with other kinds of success, although the correlations are not as high as those obtained with school marks. Gordon Liddle (1958) found that fourth- and sixth-graders who scored in the top 10 percent on intelligence tests were likely to be perceived as leaders by their classmates and to show more than the usual amount of artistic ability. They also tended to have better emotional adjustment. In another study, students with high IQs were found to score lower on test anxiety (Denny, Paterson, and Feldhusen, 1964). A survey of high-school boys who were outstanding in athletics, science, fine arts, leadership, or academic achievement showed that the only quality they had in common was their tendency to score high on intelligence tests (Clarke and Olson, 1965). One interesting study of the difference between high- and low-IQ children was conducted by Willavene Wolf and others (1965), who photographed the eye movements of fifth-grade children watching educational television. They found that children with higher IQs spent more time watching the areas of the screen that were pertinent to the general intent of the teaching unit, whereas children with lower IQs spent more time in watching distracting areas of the screen (for example, watching the instructor's face instead of his hands when he was demonstrating a technique). Low-IQ children also spent more time looking at the edge of the television screen or not watching the picture at all. Such differences suggest that children with higher IQs have a higher degree of interest in learning and are better able to focus their attention on material that is to be learned.

Whatever it is that intelligence tests measure, it seems to be positively correlated with success and good adjustment in a wide variety of fields. Perhaps "the tendency to behave competently and effectively" is a good rough-and-ready definition of "intelligence" as measured by such tests. This definition would actually not be far from the concept of intelligence as conceived by the layman.

The fact that intelligence tests are fairly good measures of what most people would recognize as intelligence does not mean that a single score, such as an IQ, can routinely be considered a definitive index to the competence of individual students. Although children who score high on such tests are more likely to possess skills, insights, and attitudes that are superior to those of other children, not every single child with a high IQ has all these characteristics, nor does every child with a low IQ lack them. There is many a boy who is highly competent at repairing motors (mechanical intelligence) or in organizing class parties (social intelligence) who scores in the average ranges on standard intelligence tests. And countless teachers have wondered why the boy who has the highest IQ in his class has barely average or failing marks. The point is that a single test score or an IQ does not tell us everything about a student. Whatever test scores tell us must be considered together with other kinds of data if we are to gain any understanding of students and their behavior.

Stability and Change in IQ

It is a characteristic of personal qualities or traits that they *tend* to be stable over time. A hyperactive boy of seven is likely to be hyperactive at nine, and a shy, withdrawn boy of eight is likely to be shy and withdrawn at eleven. This same stability that characterizes personality traits also applies to IQ, for within rough limits IQs are *relatively* stable. By "relatively stable," we mean that the IQs of, say, 60 percent of children will shift no more than 15 points between the ages of two and eighteen, and only about 9 or 10 percent will vary much as 30 points. A shift of 15 points is not much of a change if we are thinking in gross terms, but in practical terms, the difference between an IQ of 75 and one of 90 can make a difference in some schools as to whether a child is put in an average or a slow-learning group, and a difference between 115 and 130 IQ can make a difference as to whether a student is considered bright-average or gifted.

The longitudinal study that produced the above results also found that some of the IQ changes followed certain discernible patterns. For instance, there was a pronounced tendency for changes in mental-test scores to be in the direction of the family norm as indicated by the parents' education and socioeconomic status. In other words, children who initially had middle- and lower-range IQs tended to have higher IQs as they grew older if they lived in families with upper-middle-class status, headed by college-educated parents, whereas children who initially had middle- to high-range IQs tended to have lower IQs if they grew up in lower-class surroundings with parents who had grade school education. Children whose scores fluctuated the most also showed unusual swings between disturbing and stabilizing experiences in their lives (Honzik, Macfarlane, and Allen, 1971).

Other longitudinal research has shown similar results. Richard G. Stennett (1969), for example, compared the IQs of eight hundred London, Ontario,

INDIVIDUAL DIFFERENCES
AND THEIR MEASUREMENTS

boys and girls divided into equal groups on the basis of sex and socioeconomic status (SES). His data, as reported in Figure 14-2, shows a tendency for the IQs of children above average in SES to rise over time, whereas the IQs of children below average tend to decline. It should be noticed, in passing, that the SES differences were relative and not absolute. The mean IQ for the lower SES group in his study was approximately 106 in grade 9, a score that is suggestive of middle-class status.

Stennett's data show boys' IQs rising more than girls'. Similar findings were reported in a set of longitudinal studies conducted at the Fels Research Institute for the Study of Human Development, located at Antioch College, where researchers found that 62 percent of the children showed IQ changes of as much as 15 points between the ages of 3 and 10. Most of the increases observed were for boys, particularly during the school years, whereas most of the IQ declines were for girls. Increases in IQs were associated with such personality traits as independence, aggressiveness, self-initiative, interest in problem solving, and competitiveness (Sontag, Baker, and Nelson, 1958).

What these findings suggest is that certain kinds of personality trends may facilitate changes in IQ. The vigorous, problem-solving, and competitive child is likely to show gains in IQ because his mental ability develops at a faster rate than that of his peers. The apathetic, listless child is likely to show a decline, as is the child whose restless, destructive

behavior is a smoke screen for feelings of inferiority and discouragement.

Changes in children's environment may also shift IQs. The studies by Tizard and Rees (1974), Dennis (1973), and Garber and Heber (1973), which we mentioned in Chapter 3, show that in one way or another, exposing children to increased amounts of cognitive, affective, and social stimulation is likely to raise their IQs to higher levels. These are but a few of a considerable number of studies conducted in recent years which show that IQ improvement can be brought about by making *major* improvements in children's environments. We emphasize *major,* because research evidence showing *minor* alterations in environment tends to be rather shaky. By way of illustration, it makes a great deal of difference whether children go to school or not, as far as their intellectual development, as measured by IQ, is concerned, but it probably makes little difference— again, in terms of IQ—whether they are taught by computer-assisted instruction or by more conventional means. Of course, the failure of the IQ to respond to minor environmental changes may also reflect the relative insensitivity of the IQ.

The Environment-Heredity Controversy

Most psychologists believe that individual variations in IQ are the product of genetically inherited characteristics interacting with the environment. Just how much individual IQ variation is due to genetic factors and how much to environmental factors is a matter of controversy, although the majority of psychologists hold that any observed IQ differences between social *groups* (race, ethnic groups, social classes, or national populations) are explicable in terms of cultural—hence environmental—differences among the groups. Although some physical differences among groups (body build, skin color, and the like) can be linked to genetic differences, most psychologists maintain that evidence suggesting that group differences in cognitive functioning are also genetically determined is questionable. These majority views have been challenged by Arthur R. Jensen (1969), who claims that 80 percent of differences among the IQs of individuals can be at-

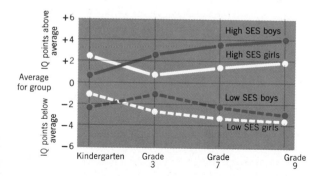

FIG. 14-2. Mean IQs of eight hundred boys and girls of high and low socioeconomic status (SES), expressed in terms of differences in IQ points from the group average (after Stennett, 1969).

tributed to differences in genetic factors. Further-more, the fact that American blacks get, on the av-erage, lower IQs than American whites or orientals is explained by Jensen in terms of differences in genetic makeup of the groups.

Jensen's position has been attacked by other psychologists on a number of grounds. Jerome S. Kagan (1969) says, for example, that the same data on which Jensen's conclusions are based can also be interpreted to show that environmental differ-ences are more significant than genetic ones, and Irving Gottesman (1968) writes:

My evaluation of the literature on race differ-ences has led me to conclude that the differ-ences between the mean IQs of Negro Ameri-cans and other Americans can be accounted for almost wholly by environmental disadvantages that start in the prenatal period and continue through a lifetime.

The importance that Jensen places on intelli-gence test scores as precise measures of cognitive functioning may also be misplaced. In the foregoing section, we have observed that individual IQs are highly variable. Kagan reports, furthermore, that low IQs reported for children from poverty homes may have been the results of poor rapport between test administrators and children, with many children fail-ing to understand directions and what their roles should be when tests are administered.

Research by Francis H. Palmer (1970) also sheds some light on the heredity-environment contro-versy. Jensen and other psychologists holding to a hereditarian (rather than an environmentalist) point of view maintain that differences in IQ among chil-dren from different socioeconomic backgrounds are because of genetic rather than environmental differences. If this were true, social class differ-ences should be evident at any age. Palmer, how-ever, found no IQ differences among groups of black male children three years old who had been born to families of different social status. Other re-search shows that IQ differences between black and white children rarely appear before the age of

twenty months (Schaeffer, 1969). These results sug-gest that differences appearing later are the result of environmental rather than genetic differences.

The views held by Jensen and his supporters[3] have been attacked on other grounds. Christopher Jencks (1972) says that Jensen's estimate of IQ heritability is much too high. Carter Dennison (1975), a medical geneticist, attempts to take a mod-erate view of Jensen's conclusions, recommending that social scientists consider them seriously, but he also notes a number of methodological flaws in Jensen's reasoning and admits that he himself does not find Jensen's case a compelling one. David Lay-zer (1974), after a detailed analysis of Jensen's rea-soning and mathematics, concluded that data do not exist on which to base a case demonstrating that IQ differences between races and social classes are genetically determined and that "re-search along present lines directed toward this end—whatever its ethical status—is scientifically worthless."

Jensen's manifesto has stimulated a great deal of research into the nature of intelligence and the con-ditions that affect it. Studies conducted by Jensen (1974) tend to confirm his contentions, although he admits encountering difficulties in securing enough black subjects at middle and upper economic levels to control this source of possible variance. Most other researchers report results that disconfirm Jensen's theories. An investigation by Sandra Scarr-Salapatek (1971), for example, strongly sug-gests that environmental limitations are the major cause of the low IQs commonly found among inner-city children. Scarr-Salapatek analyzed the verbal and nonverbal aptitude test scores of over fifteen hundred Philadelphia school children, both black and white, at three social-class levels. She rea-soned that if Jensen's theory that environmental factors have little effect were valid, the variation or range of test scores would be the same at each so-

[3] Those best known among Jensen's proponents are Richard Herrnstein, an experimental psychologist; H. J. Eysenck, a British measurement psychologist; and Wil-liam Shockley, a professor of electronics engineering and one of the inventors of the transistor.

cial-class level. If, on the other hand, environmental factors had a noticeable effect on cognitive functioning, the test scores of upper- and middle-class children would show much variation, whereas the test scores of children from the inner city would vary within a considerably narrower range. (The rationale for this hypothesis is that middle- and upper-class children grow up in environments that do not restrict their cognitive development, and their cognitive ability is hence free to vary in accordance with individual differences in their genetic make-up. The aptitude scores of inner-city children, however, would show little variance because their discouraging environment would have a generally depressing and suppressing effect on their cognitive development.)

The results of Scarr-Salapatek's study favored the environmentalist position, for the test scores of the slum children showed significantly less variation than those of children at higher social levels. There was no difference in variation between the two races, suggesting that the environmental factors were having similar effects at corresponding social-class levels of the two racial groups.

Are Intelligence Tests "Unfair" to Some Children?

If we are interested in predicting school success, intelligence test scores can be fairly useful in a general sense, provided we are dealing with *groups* of white or oriental Americans. They are somewhat less useful as predictors of *individual* performance, partly because of their instability over time, as we indicated earlier. They are even less useful as predictors for *groups* of black and Spanish-surnamed Americans, as we also pointed out, and are still more chancy when used with *individuals* from these groups. It is for this reason that Kenneth B. Clark (1972) wrote:

> *If a child scores low on an intelligence test because he cannot read and then is not taught to read because he has a low score, then such a child is imprisoned in an* iron circle *and becomes the victim of an educational self-fulfilling prophecy.*

It is said that intelligence tests that are available for general use are poor indicators of future success for some ethnic minority children because test items assess the knowledge of concepts that are middle-class artifacts and hence are outside the experiential scope of the disadvantaged poor. Such criticisms are not new. Allison Davis (1951), a black sociologist, pointed out many years ago that middle-class children were bound to do better than lower-class children in tests that expected students to understand words such as "symphony" and "sonata." He maintained that the usual twenty-point difference between the IQs of middle-class and lower-class children resulted from the "unfairness" of standardized tests, and that intelligence tests that were "culture-fair" would show no difference. Davis' hopes were, however, doomed to disappointment. He and Kenneth Eells constructed a test composed of problem situations presented pictorially. Each item was tested with inner-city children to establish its culture fairness. When a test composed of these culture-fair items (the Davis-Eells Games) was administered to black and white children in Detroit and Hamtramck, the results were much the same as if a conventional intelligence test had been employed; namely, middle-class children scored higher than children from poverty-stricken homes. In fact, lower-class boys actually did better on conventional intelligence tests than they did on the Davis-Eells Games (Fowler, 1957). Similar results have been found when other types of nonverbal, "culture-fair" or "culture-free" tests have been administered to children of various ethnic groups at all social-class levels. In general, lower-class children do poorer on the culture-fair tests than they do on conventional intelligence tests (Doppelt and Bennett, 1967).

Reasons for the poor showing made by children from poverty homes on the Davis-Eells Games and other "culture-fair" tests are not difficult to understand. Middle-class children are more likely than lower-class children to possess attitudes favorable to school and to the kind of cognitive tasks that are commonly assigned by teachers. Middle-class children are also more interested in getting involved in the kind of competition that leads both to academic success and to top scores on intelligence tests.

It may be, as Davis suggests, that middle- and lower-class children are not as far apart in their mental ability as their scores would lead one to believe, since changes in the way tests are administered may reduce differences in scores. When Mexican and Anglo-American adults took the Cattell Culture-Free Intelligence Test with and without the usual time limits, the Mexican-American subjects demonstrated proportionately more gain in the untimed condition (Knapp, 1960). In other words, the time limitation penalized the Mexican-Americans more than it did the Anglo-Americans.

Another study employed the Peabody Picture Vocabulary Test, another "culture-fair" instrument used extensively with disadvantaged children. In this experiment, the same psychometrist administered the test twice to lower- and middle-class preschool children. As might be expected, children in both groups tended to do better the second time around. The middle-class children made a mean gain of 3 IQ points, but the lower-class children gained an average of 10. Thirty-nine percent of the lower-class children made similar gains. In another phase of the study, the psychometrist played with some of the children for fifteen minutes before giving them the test. The lower-class children who had this warm-up experience scored almost 10 IQ points higher than those who were tested "cold," whereas middle-class children who had had the warm-up play actually scored about three IQ points lower than those who had been tested without it (Zigler, Abelson, and Seitz, 1973). These results supported the investigators' impressions that the low test scores made by economically disadvantaged children were not due entirely to cognitive deficiencies, but rather to their apprehensiveness about being tested and their fear of strange adults.

In sum, it appears that so-called culture-fair or culture-free tests provide no advantage to students from lower-class homes and that, if intelligence tests are to be used at all, conventional tests would probably give a better estimate of the cognitive level at which they are functioning. It is significant that those who criticize conventional intelligence tests have been unable to produce instruments that pos-

sess a reasonable degree of reliability and validity. The research also shows, however, that the usual conditions under which tests are given penalize lower-class children unduly. Unless these children are motivated to do well on tests and are helped to control or reduce their test anxiety, their test scores are likely to represent a gross underestimation of their ability. This may be the reason why standardized tests are poor predictors of academic success for some ethnic or culturally defined groups.

Underachievers: A Puzzling Problem

As we have noted, for most children in the schools, intelligence tests are fairly good predictors of academic success. Hence a high IQ leads us to predict that a child will do superior school work, whereas a low IQ leads us to predict poor work. Inasmuch as correlations between intelligence test scores and grades are not perfect, there is bound to be a minority for whom these predictions are false. Those children who achieve higher grades than their IQs would lead one to expect—the overachievers— pose no special problem. The test scores obviously were an underestimate. But the children whose academic performance is strikingly lower than one would expect from their IQs—the underachievers— are puzzlers and hence intrigue the researcher. Although a low IQ may be achieved inadvertently for any number of reasons, a high IQ is unlikely to be an accident. A high-IQ student is obviously *capable* of high performance: Why then does he not perform as expected?

The answer to this question seems to be motivation. Evelyn Morrison (1969) administered a personality test to a group of underachieving fifth-grade boys and found that they showed more hostility toward authority figures than did normally achieving boys and were rated by teachers as being more "passive aggressive" (stubborn and uncooperative). They also scored higher on achievement tests than one would expect from their marks, showing that they were actually learning but were unwilling or unable to provide the kind of achievement evidence teachers look for. Hugh V. Perkins (1965) compared bright fifth-grade achievers and underachievers in upper-middle-class suburban commu-

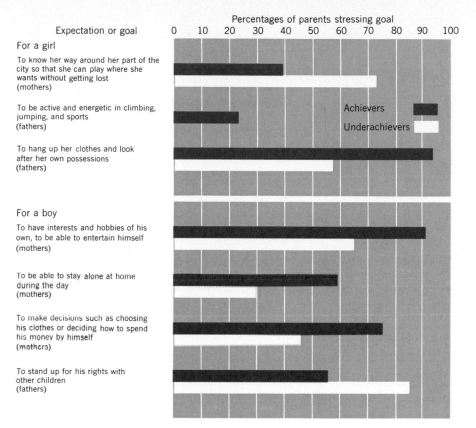

FIG. 14-3. Differences in expectations or goals emphasized by mothers and fathers of achieving or underachieving high-school students (Shaw, 1964).

nities and discovered that underachievers were shyer and also were more inclined to spend class time working on something unrelated to the topic of the moment, whereas achievers engaged in more work-oriented interaction with other students. In another study overachievers and underachievers worked on tasks that they had previously rated as liked or disliked. It made little difference to the overachievers whether they had liked or disliked the tasks; they did equally well on both types. The underachievers, however, did significantly poorer on tasks they disliked (Rychlak and Tobin, 1971).[4]

[4] This intriguing finding keeps coming up in studies of school achievement. Boys read as well as girls, as long as material is of interest to them, but do poorly on uninteresting material (Asher and Markell, 1974), and a number of studies indicate that interest value and relevance is of more importance to disadvantaged students than it is to more advantaged ones.

Taken altogether the research on underachievers suggests that they are students who have passive or negative attitudes toward doing work that is required and which has little relevance or interest for them.

Patterns of classroom performance and social behavior characteristic of underachievers seem to be related to parental attitudes. A study by Merville C. Shaw (1964) of the expectations held by parents of achieving or underachieving high-school students has turned up basic differences in the two patterns of achievement. As the data reported in Figure 14-3 suggest, parents of underachievers tend to stress goals that are unrelated to achievement and that do not promote social maturity and independent thinking. Parents of achievers are more likely to expect their children to be responsible, to have interests and hobbies so that they can amuse themselves, and to know how to make decisions. They also expect them to share adult interests at an earlier age. Parents of underachievers seem to have attitudes which resemble those of lower-class parents that we reported in Chapter 4.

Although the research with underachievers raises questions about the validity of intelligence tests, at least with certain students, it does suggest how such tests may be used to identify children who need special help. If one of the tasks of the school is that of helping children to learn to work up to their best potential, a comparison of IQs and grade averages would enable teachers and guidance workers to identify those who may not be achieving because of problems of adjustment, motivation, or lack of clarity of goals. Such use of intelligence-test scores would seem to be in the best interests of the child.

David A. Kolb (1965) described an interesting study in which the academic progress of twenty underachieving boys who had gone through an experimental summer program designed to teach them the characteristics of a high-achieving person was compared with thirty-seven other underachievers who had taken a regular academic summer course. A follow-up six months after the end of the program revealed no significant differences between the two groups, but a second follow-up eighteen months later showed that the grade-point average of those who had participated in the experimental course increased significantly. Unfortunately, most of the increase took place in the grades of underachievers having higher socioeconomic status. Those with low socioeconomic status did no better than those who had taken the regular academic course. Increases in grades tended to be accompanied by increases in measures of need for achievement (n Ach), a finding that serves to emphasize the importance of attitudes in school learning.

APTITUDE, INTEREST, AND PERSONALITY MEASUREMENT

Measuring Special Aptitudes

An intelligence test is sometimes referred to as an "aptitude test" because it is used to measure characteristics that can be used to predict future performance. Achievement tests presumably measure the amount of learning that has taken place. In effect, they look backward and ask the question: "What has been accomplished?" Aptitude tests look ahead and attempt to answer such questions as "What level of performance can we expect from this student?" or "What are the potentialities of this student that show promise for development?"

An intelligence test is ordinarily used as a measure of general ability or aptitude. The tests of verbal and quantitative thinking that are used in connection with college entrance tests are examples of attempts to divide general mental ability into two fairly specialized dimensions. Another test that is commonly used in secondary schools, the Differential Aptitude Test, or DAT, makes use of an even more specialized classification of abilities. In general, the verbal parts of these tests are the best overall predictors of academic grades, although the quantitative (mathematical) parts provide useful clues to probable future success in science and mathematics courses. There are, in addition, a wide variety of tests of various types, some measuring abilities and some measuring attitudes and feelings, that are also used to make predictions. Some of these, such as reading-readiness tests, are given at one point in the school program and are not repeated. Others, such as the interest and personality tests, are given chiefly for guidance purposes.

Tests of special aptitudes (for example, reading readiness, mechanical aptitude, and musical aptitude) are, like IQ tests, attempts to probe into the future and to make predictions about the probable success of the individual. Very often they serve as the basis for decisions with respect to the educational plan to be followed. Reading-readiness tests may be used to decide who should have the regular first-grade experiences, which include learning to read, and who should be given a different kind of experience. Mechanical-aptitude tests are sometimes useful in deciding such questions as who should be permitted to enter such specialized advanced courses as those in aviation or Diesel mechanics. These tests may also be useful in vocational counseling. Musical-aptitude tests, as well as art aptitude tests, are sometimes used to advise prospective students, but there is little evidence as to their validity as predictors of performance in these fields.

Some special-aptitude tests can be useful as guidance tools because they take much of the guesswork out of the appraisal of individual aptitudes. They should always be used with caution, however, and even then only by people with adequate training and experience in the use of tests.

Measuring Vocational Interests

Another type of instrument that is frequently used for guidance purposes is the vocational-interest test. Interest tests are more useful in secondary years. Children in elementary schools have not as a general rule developed the concepts and perspectives that enable them to make choices relating to the selection of an occupation. Furthermore, their interests, as measured by standardized interest tests, are not very stable or reliable.

Interest tests are often given at the beginning of the ninth grade, when decisions have to be made about which of several courses to follow—college preparatory, commercial, mechanical, agricultural, and so forth. They are also given during the twelfth year, when students are ready to make decisions about the kind of work they will actually attempt to enter. Probably a great many ninth-graders are really not ready to make decisions related to vocational choice, and it might be better, on psychological grounds, for each student to explore his special interests through elective courses, but the current system of college- and university-entrance requirements means that the student who is thinking of going on to higher education must make his decision when he enters high school, if not before.

Counselors who are faced with the problem of advising students who need to make vocational and educational decisions have found that the results of interest tests can be very helpful. An interest test, such as the Kuder Preference Record, the Occupational Interest Inventory, and the Cleeton Vocational Interest Inventory, to name three of those most commonly used, requires the student to make a series of choices, each from among two or three alternative activities. The results are then reported in

terms of interest areas. The interest profile of George Miller, who has taken the Occupational Interest Inventory, presented in Figure 14-4, shows that he is most interested in the fields of personal and social service and the arts, and that he is least interested in activities involving the outdoors, science, and computation. George says that he wants to be a doctor, which poses an interesting problem for the counselor. Because George has taken the interest test, however, the counselor has much more data at his command than he would if he had to rely on George's simple statement that he wants to be a doctor.

The cautions we have uttered with respect to other tests apply with equal strength to interest tests. They are useful when we look to them for trends, for rough and approximate indications of how a given student's interests compare with those of his peers. When we go so far as to make important decisions *for* students on the basis of interest tests, then we are on dangerous ground.

Celia wanted to take a home economics course, but the counselor was so impressed by her high score on the clerical scale of the Kuder test that he enrolled her in the commercial program over her protests, saying that she would like business courses once she got into them. As it turned out, she did not enjoy business training at all, although her marks were excellent. Each year at registration time she asked to be transferred to the home economics program, but each year the counselor refused, feeling that the test score was a much more valid indicator of her true interests than her own feelings. Unfortunately, such misuses of tests are all too common.

George Miller's counselor handled his problem much more judiciously. He talked to George about the discrepancy between his stated interest in medicine and the results of the test (see Figure 14-4) but he did not want George to accept the results of the test as an infallible guide. He merely raised a question with respect to the goal George had chosen. When George brushed aside the test results and insisted on taking the science curriculum, his counselor permitted him to do so, with the understanding that he was to reconsider the decision each year. George made average grades in science the first year and perhaps would have continued if his counselor had not pointed out that average grades were not good enough for college entrance and might

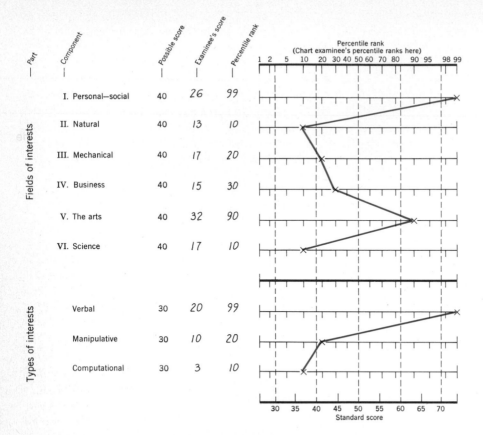

FIG. 14-4. Portions of the interest profile of George Miller, a high-school student who has taken the Occupational Interest Inventory (after Lee and Thorpe, 1956).

even keep him out of medical school. He suggested that George try some music and drama and keep one science course. George agreed and found, after a semester, that he liked drama much better than science, whereupon he changed his major to English.

Questionnaire Measures of Personal and Social Adjustment

In the years since World War II there has been a great surge of interest in personality testing on the part of the general public. The *Mental Measurements Yearbook,* for example, lists more personality tests than any other type. Originally designed for research purposes and for use in the treatment of psychopathology, personality tests are now widely used as selection instruments for potential employees and for a variety of purposes in schools and

colleges. Undoubtedly, this interest in personality tests reflects our increasing concern about mental health and emotional adjustment.

Most of the personality tests used with school children are questionnaires that elicit responses regarding attitudes, social behavior, interpersonal tensions, and anxieties. The more problems and anxieties a child reports, the poorer his adjustment score. One flaw in this method (and this is also a flaw in the methodology of the vocational-interest tests we mentioned) is that the individual is at liberty to "slant" his responses consciously or unconsciously—to answer any question the "right" way or the "wrong" way at will. Thus the overly conscientious but well-adjusted child may report a great many problems and receive a "poor" score, whereas the emotionally disturbed child who does not want teachers probing into his private life will admit to few problems and receive a "good" score. And the child who has many problems but is unable to admit, even to himself, that he has them will receive a "good" score because he has selected all the "right" answers. Such distortions of personality-tests results are not unusual. Furthermore, different children react to the same items in different ways, and children with roughly similar problems may get quite different scores on the same test.

Personality tests are, in a way, shortcuts to be used in place of personal, diagnostic interviews. A teacher cannot sit down with each student in his class and spend an hour or two looking for problems. A personality test is helpful, then, as a quick way of locating problems that might be bothering children and interfering with their learning. It might also indicate which children should receive special psychological help. Such data are useful in schools where school psychologists or counselors are available for referral or as consultants or where teachers have sufficient time, training, and supervision to give children some of the special help they need. When personality tests are administered by teachers who lack adequate training or supervision, there is always a danger that the results may be misused or not used at all. It is important to keep in mind that the questions posed by a personality test are concerned with personal and rather sensitive areas of life. Hence if teachers go so far as to arouse the anxieties of children by giving them a test of this type, it would seem that they are under an obligation to make use of the data in some kind of positive and helpful way.

The main types of personality tests are self-rating questionnaires, problem checklists, and projective tests. The Thorndike Dimensions of Temperament (TDOT) asks the test-taker to indicate whether descriptive statements such as the following are like him (L) or different from him (D):

Nothing seems to work out right for you.	L	D
You are always "on the go."	L	D
You tend to "blow up" in an emergency.	L	D
You usually plan things well in advance.	L	D

The TDOT is an attempt to portray the individual as he sees himself, as well as how others see him.

Norms are based on high-school and college students, and the scores show how the individual compares with others on these personality dimensions: sociable-solitary, ascendant-withdrawing, cheerful-gloomy, placid-irritable, accepting-critical, tough-minded-tenderminded, reflective-practical, impulsive-planful, active-lethargic, and responsible-casual (Thorndike, 1966).

The Mooney Problem Check List (Mooney and Gordon, 1950) includes such problems as the following:

Not interested in books (Junior High School Form)

Having dates (High School Form)

Too few dates (College Form)

Not finding a suitable life partner (Adult Form)

Assessing Personal and Social Adjustment with Projective Tests

Projective tests employ a totally different approach to the problem of investigating and appraising the emotional life of individuals. There are many types of projective tests, but they all involve presenting the individual with some kind of a stimulus (inkblots, incomplete sentences, pictures, and the like) in which there is some degree of vagueness or ambiguity. Inasmuch as the individual does not know what answer is expected of him, he is likely to respond in ways that are more or less revealing, rather than in accordance with what he thinks is the "right" answer. One of the chief difficulties with personality questionnaires, as we have indicated, is that students are aware which responses would be considered to be "good" or "poor," hence they may be led, consciously or unconsciously, to "fake" a "well-adjusted" or a "poorly adjusted" score.

Projective tests are generally used as part of a psychological interview designed to identify problems that may be troubling an individual who has been referred for psychotherapy. Generally speaking, they accomplish this task without upsetting him and thus without spoiling the relationship or "rapport" between him and the psychologist. Figure 14-5 consists of a picture included in the Picture Situ-

FIG. 14-5. A card from a projective test consisting of a series of pictures designed to investigate perceptions, feelings, and attitudes of boys and their mothers with respect to punishment (Morgan and Gaier, 1956).

ations Index, a projective test designed to obtain information about punishment at home, a sensitive area of life for many children. As the child is presented with each picture in the series, he is invited to tell what is happening in the picture, what the characters in it might say or do, and how they would feel (Morgan and Gaier, 1958). The use of such devices enables children to discuss their problems behind the facade of talking about the picture.

A test that is frequently used with children, and that resembles the Picture Situations Index, is the Symonds Picture Story Test (Bureau of Publications, Teachers College, Columbia University), a test that presents the child with a series of pictures, with the request that he tell a story about each one. The Rorschach or inkblot test (Psychological Corporation) requires the individual to say what he sees in a series of inkblots or what they remind him of. Some psychological workers like to use a "sentence-completion" type of test, whereby respondents are asked to finish sentences that start with such phrases as:

Other children
I think that my mother

Sometimes teachers
If my father

All of these methods can be useful techniques in the hands of skilled and trained psychological workers, but they are, generally speaking, inappropriate for use by teachers. For one thing, administration and interpretation of even one test may take many hours. Projective tests are primarily tools for the research worker or for the clinician, the person who is spending a great deal of time working with a few emotionally disturbed children who need intensive treatment.

Public Criticism of Personality Assessment

During the past few years, there has appeared a small but vocal group of laymen who are upset by attempts of school personnel to test for, identify, or record data regarding personal problems of students. This group is convinced that personality tests are an invasion of family privacy because such tests ask questions about child-parent relations, and that teachers and school psychologists are primarily interested in asking such questions because they have a busybody's curiosity about matters that do not concern them. There is also the natural fear on the part of some parents that they will be made to appear inferior or ridiculous when such data are recorded and discussed by school staff members. Their concern has been heightened, furthermore, by occasional instances when teachers have behaved in an unprofessional manner and have communicated confidential data to unauthorized persons.

The concern about personality tests has not been confined to those used in schools. Personnel specialists in industrial and governmental organizations have been criticized in the press for their use of tests, and a few best-selling books have made capital of the fears and anxieties people have about "brain watchers." In fact, a congressional hearing was held in 1965 to examine all sides of the question. Although the results of the hearing were inconclusive, the fact that they were held is an indication that many people are concerned about the problem.

As a result of these concerns, there has been a reduction in the amount of mass personality testing by both governmental and nongovernmental employers but especially in the schools. The legislature of the State of California passed a law forbidding the administration of any "test, questionnaire, survey, or examination containing any questions about the pupil's personal beliefs or practices in sex, family life, morality or religion, or any questions about his parents' or guardians' beliefs and practices in sex, family life, morality and religion . . . unless the parent or guardian of the pupil is notified in writing that such test, questionnaire, survey, or examination is to be administered and the parent or guardian of the pupil gives written permission. . . ."[5]

Although a number of personality tests, notably tests of the projective type, would technically be legal under this law, most school administrators in California interpret the law as forbidding personality testing of all kinds. Even school psychologists and

[5] State of California, Education Code, 1969, Vol. 1, Div. 9, Ch. 1. Article 9, "Tests."

counselors must secure written permission from parents before administering tests in connection with treatment of students having emotional problems.

Few states have laws as strict as California's, but a number of school administrators, after consultation with parents' groups and teachers, have taken it on themselves to ban the use of personality tests, except by school psychologists and counselors.

The trend is not altogether a bad thing. Personality tests and questionnaires rarely provide the kind of information that teachers need in order to work with students. This does not mean that teachers should remain unaware of the affective aspects of students' behavior. Actually, the whole area of feelings, attitudes, and values, as we have indicated previously, is closely related to learning progress. Many of the goals of the school are also of an affective nature.

Observational Appraisals of Pupil's Social Behavior

Teachers do not need questionnaires and projective tests in order to study the affective aspects of student behavior. One method of gathering needed information is sociometry, which we discussed in Chapter 5. Sociometric devices yield valuable data about the psychological forces at work in a classroom group and can tell teachers a great deal about the adjustment of individual members of the class who may need special help. Sociometric data are also very helpful to the teacher who is trying to create better interpersonal and intergroup feeling in his classroom.

Another useful approach is the anecdotal record, a kind of diary or log of incidents jotted down soon after they occur. A single, isolated impression of a student's behavior, noted in the midst of a busy day, does not tell us much about him, but if the teacher jots down something about that same student every day or so for several weeks, he will begin to see some general patterns of personality emerging.

For instance, Miss Kellogg may note that Gordon went over to George and patted him on the shoulder after he had hit a home run at softball. Her immediate reaction may be one of pleasure: "It's nice to have the children appreciate each other." Or she may decide that Gordon is a rather friendly boy. But when this incident becomes one of a series of short observations about Gordon, she may notice that he is nice only to George and virtually ignores the other children in the class. Then it becomes apparent that this friendly pat on the shoulder was part of a very special relationship that exists between himself and George. Miss Kellogg's reaction might now be: "I didn't know that Gordon and George were such close pals. No wonder they put up such a fuss when I assigned them to different committees."

The point is that a series of observations on one student may reveal a pattern in his behavior. Keeping anecdotal records can help the teacher develop a frame of reference that may be quite different from the one he has previously used in reacting to the student.

One of the problems in using this technique is that of being completely objective. There is the danger that the teacher will write down his *interpretation* of an incident, instead of what actually occurred.

For example, Miss Kellogg might write: "When Sandra asked Gordon to help her with the Junior Red Cross parcel, he was uncooperative and nasty."

Whereas she should have written something like this: "Sandra was wrapping up a parcel for the Junior Red Cross. She needed to have someone put a finger on the knot she was tying. Gordon was standing nearby, talking to George. Sandra asked him to help her, and he said: 'Aw, ask your boy friend!' and turned back to talk to George. Sandra said nothing in reply but called to Josette, who helped her finish wrapping the package."

The first anecdote contains value judgments regarding Gordon's behavior. In some ways, it tells us as much about the teacher as it does about Gordon. For instance, it tells us that Miss Kellogg disapproves of Gordon. The second anecdote has more detail and takes longer to write, but it presents a much more complete picture. Read in connection with other anecdotes that Miss Kellogg has jotted down regarding Gordon, it suggests the hypothesis that he acted as he did partly because he felt that

Sandra was interfering in his relationship with George.

Arthur W. Combs (1965) takes a somewhat different approach to anecdotal records. He asks his student teachers not to make detailed, factual records when observing children, but instead suggests that they

> Get the "feel" of what's going on, to see if they can get inside the skin of the person being observed, to understand how things look from his point of view. I ask them, "What do you suppose he is trying to do?" "How do you suppose he feels?" "How would you have to feel to behave like that?" "How does he see the other kids?" "What does he feel about the subject?"

Such recommendations are in keeping with Combs' contention that people behave in terms of how they perceive their environment and themselves. It is only when we understand these perceptions that we can understand their behavior.

There are other approaches, in addition to sociometry and anecdotal records, that perceptive teachers can use in developing an understanding of the emotional and motivational life of their pupils. Students often reveal helpful bits of information, wittingly or unwittingly, in their casual remarks to one another, in their written work, and in their conversations with teachers. There is no lack of vital psychological data in everyday classroom experiences. The problem is one of perceiving more sharply and objectively, and of organizing and understanding what we see and hear. Many schools employ specialists of various kinds who can be of considerable assistance in helping teachers acquire a better understanding of the psychological aspects of the behavior that they observe in the classroom. Some of the functions of these specialists are described in the chapters that follow.

APPRAISING AND FOSTERING CREATIVITY

Divergent and Convergent Thinking

Psychologists have, during the last decade, developed an intense interest in creativity as a topic for research. This interest has led to the development of theories about the nature of creativity, of questionnaires and other instruments to measure creativity, and of experimental techniques designed to encourage, foster, or stimulate creativity.

Much of this research has been initiated as a result of a paper published by J. P. Guilford (1959), in which he differentiated between convergent and divergent thinking processes. Most education, he pointed out, is concerned with promoting convergent thinking, the kind of thinking in which students are encouraged to find the "right answers" to problems. Such a process assumes that there is a single right answer and that it exists somewhere, usually in the textbook or in the course of study. Divergent thinking, as we noted in our discussion of brainstorming techniques in Chapter 12, is concerned with approaches such as speculation, imagination, heuristics, and invention, processes that are based on the assumption that there may be several good ways in which to solve a problem. Creativeness depends on an individual's ability to innovate and to perceive new relationships and therefore demands some divergent thinking.

Inasmuch as most class instruction, fact-oriented as it is, reinforces convergent thinking, students do not have to think divergently to get top grades. Divergent thinking is usually regarded by teachers as irrelevant, time-wasting, or merely "wrong," and consequently is likely to go unrewarded. Most standardized, objective tests, including tests of intelligence, measure convergent thinking, which may be one of the reasons that they are correlated so highly with teachers' marks. The routine admonition "don't guess" is indicative of the bias against divergent thinking. Convergent-type thinkers refrain from guessing and are not inclined to answer a question if they are not certain of the answer.

This state of affairs has led some psychologists and educators to criticize teaching methods and measures that penalize (or, at least, do not reward) creativeness and thus place the more creative student at a disadvantage. In one study, Jacob W. Getzels and Philip W. Jackson (1962) elicited teachers' reactions to students scoring high on tests of intelligence and creativity. Students who scored high on one measure tended to score high on the other, but there were some students who scored high on intelligence but not so high on creativeness (the "high-intelligence" group), and others who scored high on creativeness and not so high on intelligence (the "high-creative" group). Both of these groups did equally well on standardized tests of academic achievement, but teachers reported that they preferred to work with the high-intelligence rather than the high-creative group. Indeed, the latter group could qualify as "underachievers," using the criteria we discussed earlier.

Independence, Nonconformity, and Creativity

Some of the reasons why teachers favor intelligent, convergent thinkers over creative, divergent thinkers are suggested by research which shows that more-creative students are inclined to describe themselves as "bitter," "irritable," "gloomy," "sarcastic," and the like, whereas less-creative students are more likely to choose such adjectives as "peaceable," "contented," "conscientious," and "patient" in characterizing themselves (Lindgren and Lindgren, 1965a, b). It is hardly surprising that teachers prefer the less-creative student: They probably find him more agreeable and more cooperative.

A number of writers contend, however, that more-creative students should be encouraged and supported irrespective of whether they are rebellious, moody, or whatever. In the first place, they state, teachers should not favor a student merely because he is a conformist, and, in the second place, schools should be encouraging, not discouraging, creativeness and more-creative students. The complex problems posed by today's world call for *more*, not less, creative solutions, they say.

Part of the difficulty faced by teachers, of course, is that they are reacting to the negative and more-or-less uncooperative aspects of the behavior of many of the more-creative students, rather than to their creativeness. There are many nonconforming students in classrooms; some are highly creative, but an even greater number are not. It is difficult for teachers to cope with nonconforming behavior in overcrowded classrooms, and when matters threaten to get out of hand, they are more likely to

(S. Harris in *Phi Delta Kappan*)

"I don't care if he does have an I.Q. of 169—I still think he's faking."

Many teachers have difficulty in recognizing and identifying creativity when it appears in the work of their students.

settle for more conformity and less creativity. Not all nonconformity is the same, however, and the teacher who genuinely wishes to foster creativity should learn how to distinguish between behavior that is disruptive for the sake of disruption and that which represents a harmless deviation or is the expression of an innovative mind and spirit. Distinctions of this kind are not easily learned by teachers. In one large-scale study, teachers from North Carolina high schools were trained to observe and rate students in terms of adolescent characteristics that had been found to be predictive of adult scientific creativity. A follow-up survey showed, however, that teachers tended to confuse creativity indications with their own definition of what was desirable in student behavior. Ironically, the school marks the teachers gave students were more closely correlated with actual creativity indicators than were the special ratings they were attempting to use (James, Ellison, McDonald, and Taylor, 1968).

Although a number of writers make a point of the differences between creativeness and intelligence, a review of their research tends to show that they are referring to students with very superior IQs, say, from 120 upward. Up to that level creativeness and intelligence are highly correlated and may, in fact, be somewhat different dimensions of the same basic ability. One survey of three hundred eighth-graders, for instance, reported a very high correlation (.56) between standard intelligence test scores and creative thinking ability as measured by six of Guilford's tests (Seitz, 1964). Nathan Kogan and Ethel Pankove (1974) conducted a longitudinal study in which students' scores on various tests administered in the fifth and tenth grades were correlated with tallies made of their creative accomplishments in the tenth grade and at graduation. Contrary to what the investigators expected, intelligence tests predicted creative accomplishment rather well, but tests specially designed to measure creative potential did not.

In general, what students of creativity report is

that persons with high IQs show a great range of creativity, from high to low, whereas persons with low IQs generally show only low creativity scores. Thus a high IQ does not guarantee high creativity but appears to make it more possible.

Can Creativity Be Taught?

One solution to these problems, as well as the general problem of how to raise the level of creativity for all students, is that of providing more opportunities in the classroom for divergent thinking. In general, permissive methods such as free group discussion, which we described in Chapter 12, are also more likely to encourage divergent thinking than are more structured approaches to teaching.

Robert L. Spaulding (1963) studied twenty-one fourth- and sixth-grade classrooms in ten different schools, recording teacher-pupil interaction. He found that there were two styles of teaching which tended to diminish flexibility and originality (both aspects of divergent thinking and creativity) on the part of the pupil: (1) formalized, highly structured situations in which teachers maintained control by shame, ridicule, or admonition, and (2) tendencies of teachers to respond to social-emotional qualities of students, rather than to their cognitive performance. Note that the latter type of classroom is characterized by permissiveness, but also by a *lack* of concern for achievement and performance. The point is: Permissiveness is not enough. Teachers should also note that classmates of creative children may not be particularly tolerant of this divergent thinking. In fact, they may regard the creative child as "the one who has all the crazy ideas."

Sidney J. Parnes (1966) conducted an experiment in which groups of secondary school students were taught creative problem solving either directly by an instructor or by programmed instruction. The instructor-led students turned out a superior performance and found the course more interesting, but the students who completed the program did better than an untrained control group, showing that creativeness can be taught by programmed methods. In another experiment, the creativity of black fifth-graders from lower-class homes was facilitated by

giving each of them a reward of one cent for each idea they produced. The experimental procedure did not level out creativity differences among the children, as might be expected, since the creativity of each child tended to increase relative to his baseline performance, that is, relative to his performance before the experimental regimen was begun (Ward, Kogan, and Pankove, 1970).

The kinds of problems faced by teachers who wish to encourage creative thinking in their classes have been listed by Torrance (1964):

1. Students may propose unexpected problem solutions that may disconcert teachers who have been anticipating more prosaic ones.

2. Teachers may be strongly tempted to tell students solutions in order to "save time."

3. Students may see relationships and meanings that teachers and other experts in the subject-matter field might have overlooked.

4. Students may ask questions that teachers cannot answer.

5. Teachers may feel guilty about permitting or encouraging students to guess.

6. Time pressure and scheduling problems may sometimes make it difficult to allow or consider all the questions that students want to ask.

7. Quite realistically, teachers sometimes have to get students to conform in many ways in order to teach them how to "get along."

Another problem relates to the creativity of the teacher. It would appear that more creative teachers would be likely to foster creativity in their students to a greater extent than would less creative teachers. For one thing, if creativity is to be fostered in students more than is done at present, this calls for methods that are more ingenious, inventive, and experimental than those that are currently being used. Less creative teachers are not likely to develop such methods and may even resist using them. For another, a teacher's drive to be creative himself may lead him to encourage creativity in students. Torrance (1964) found a relationship between teacher creativity and student creativity. Students of teachers scoring above the median in a test of creative motivation or intellectual curiosity showed significant growth in creative writing ability over a three-month period, whereas students of teachers scoring below the median made no gains. Probably more teachers would be creative if they received encouragement and support from administrators. Unfortunately, such support is often lacking. One survey of school principals' ratings of teacher effectiveness showed that teachers who showed more ingenuity (one aspect of creativeness or divergent thinking) tended to get lower ratings (Jex, 1963). Everyone seems to be in favor of creativity but not of creative people.

SUMMARY

The first intelligence tests were developed by Binet and Simon in France and by Terman in American. The Binet-Simon Scale and the Stanford-Binet are "individual tests," that is, they are administered in the setting of a personal interview. Results are usually reported in terms of the intelligence quotient or IQ. The IQ indicates the extent to which a child is advanced or retarded intellectually as compared to other children his age. The Wechsler Intelligence Scales, which have both adult and children's forms, have also been widely used.

Group intelligence tests made their appearance on a large scale during World War I in the form of the Army Alpha and the Army Beta Tests. Most of the intelligence tests that are used today are, in effect, variations and improvements on these two models. School people adopted intelligence tests as a way of grouping pupils according to their intellectual level in order to make instruction more efficient. They also believed that what they learned from a child's IQ would enable them to understand him better and thus teach him more effectively. Unfortunately, intelligence tests have not produced the looked-for advantages and now are under some pressure because they are said to bias teachers against low-scoring children. Some states and cities now ban intelligence testing. Psychologists nevertheless find intelligence tests useful in research studies, and teachers who wish to understand the

research that is being done in the schools need to understand the rationale of the IQ.

The question "What do intelligence tests measure?" can be answered in part by determining what intelligence test scores correlate with. For ethnic groups that include a high proportion of middle-class members, intelligence tests correlate fairly well with academic success, but correlations are not as high for ethnic groups whose members are largely lower class. Subject to this limitation, intelligence test scores are also highly correlated with achievement in arts, science, and athletics.

Individual IQs tend to be relatively stable over time; about 60 percent shift less than 15 IQ points between infancy and adulthood. The IQs of active, independent children tend to increase, whereas those of passive or antisocial children tend to decline. Major improvement in the living conditions of children who would otherwise have low IQs also appear to produce increases in IQ. Some psychologists, notably Arthur Jensen, hold that most IQ variance is produced by genetic factors, and that racial and social-class differences in IQ are genetically determined. This position seems to be shaky on statistical grounds, and most researchers find little evidence to support it. Intelligence tests in common use have been criticized as unfair to some minority groups, but specially designed "culture-fair" tests provide no advantage. Much of the difficulty that disadvantaged individuals have with tests seems to be affective rather than cognitive because when they are not forced to observe time limits and have opportunities to reduce test anxiety, their scores improve markedly.

Motivational problems also underlie the poor school performance of "underachievers"—students with relatively high IQs and relatively low academic achievement. For one thing, they evidently are reluctant to work on tasks that do not interest them, whereas other students do not need to be so motivated. Underachievement also tends to be associated with high levels of hostility and low expectations for social maturity on the part of parents.

Aptitude tests, such as intelligence scales, look forward, in the sense that their scores are used to predict future performance, whereas achievement tests look backward, in the sense that they are used to appraise the learning that has taken place. Special aptitude tests, covering such varied fields as reading readiness, mechanical aptitude, and musical aptitude, are also commonly used as aids in vocational and educational counseling and in selecting students for various kinds of specialized courses. Vocational-interest tests are helpful when students are faced with the need of making plans for the future. Such tests should not be used to make plans on behalf of students but rather to *help* them gain a better understanding of themselves, preparatory to making decisions.

Attitudes, interpersonal tensions, and social behavior can be measured by personality questionnaires or by projective techniques. Specialized training and experience is needed to administer and to interpret these tests effectively, and they are not recommended for general use by teachers. Some parents object to their children being given personality tests, and a number of school systems have stopped using them. Most of the data yielded by personality tests is of relatively little value to the classroom teacher, but valuable information regarding classroom dynamics and the attainment of affective goals can be secured by observational methods: sociometric techniques and anecdotal records, to give two examples.

Divergent thinking, which includes the use of imagination, invention, heuristics, and guessing, is considered more characteristic of creativity than is convergent thinking, or the kind of thinking that involves the identification of right or correct answers. Convergent thinking is involved in the usual types of intelligence tests and in most classroom learning. Students who are more creative seem to be more nonconforming and hostile than less creative students; hence teachers tend to prefer the latter to the former. Creativity may, however, be merely one dimension of general intelligence. Some teaching methods have been found to stimulate creative and divergent thinking, but teachers themselves need to become interested in creativity in order to apply them.

Suggested Problems

1. Purchase, with the assistance of the instructor and the college bookstore, one or two specimen sets of some of the tests mentioned in this chapter as being appropriate for elementary or secondary schools. Administer them to yourself (and to another person, if possible), observing all time limits and directions contained in the manual. Score them and compute the norms as indicated. Evaluate your experience in terms of the following suggested points. To what extent does each test appear to meet the need for which it was intended? What evidence does the manual give regarding its reliability and validity? If you were giving the test to a classroom group, what problems would you anticipate and how do you think you would solve them? Discuss what seem to you to be the strengths and weaknesses of the test. What do the critics in O. K. Buros' *Mental Measurements Yearbook* say about the test?

2. It is said that when L. M. Terman was looking for gifted children to serve as candidates for his monumental *Genetic Study of Genius,* he found that he could not depend on the judgments of teachers, for very few of the students they nominated had IQs that were high enough. He found that the most efficient way of locating children with high IQs was to give his test to the youngest children in each class. Why do you suppose teachers did so poorly at selecting the most intelligent children in their classes? Why did Terman's method meet with better success?

3. Now that the use of intelligence tests is being discouraged in many communities, how will schools determine who should be placed in classes for the gifted or the mentally retarded?

4. What are the arguments for and against the use of intelligence tests in schools? What are the arguments for and against the use of personality tests?

5. What could be done to encourage creativity among students in the subject or grade level in which you plan to teach? What kind of problems would more creative students pose for you? How should teachers deal with such problems?

Suggested Readings

Anastasi, A. *Psychological testing,* 3rd ed. New York: Macmillan, 1968. See sections on intelligence and personality testing.

Buros, O. K. (ed.). *Sixth mental measurements yearbook.* Highland Park, N. J.: Gryphon Press, 1965. An enormous but invaluable compendium of reviews and other useful information on all available standardized tests.

Cronbach, L. J. *Essentials of psychological testing,* 3rd ed. New York: Harper, 1970. A comprehensive, readable text.

Cronbach, L. J. "Environment, heredity, and intelligence." Reprint series No. 2 *Harvard Educational Review,* 1969. (Paperback.) Contains papers dealing with the heredity-environment controversy touched off by Arthur R. Jensen's statements.

Hunt, J. McV. (ed.). *Human intelligence.* New Brunswick, N. J.: Transaction Books, 1972. A brief paperback containing provocative essays on intelligence and related themes that have appeared in *Transaction,* a semipopularized behavioral science monthly.

Lindgren, H. C., and Lindgren, F. (eds.). *Readings in educational psychology,* 2nd ed. New York: Wiley, 1972. See section on individual differences.

Lindgren, H. C., and Byrne, D. *Psychology: An introduction to a behavioral science,* 4th ed. New York: Wiley, 1975. See chapter on intelligence and creativity.

Thorndike, R. L., and Hagen, E. (eds.). *Measurement and evaluation in psychology and education,* 3rd ed. New York: Wiley, 1969. See chapters on intelligence or scholastic aptitude, special aptitudes, and self-appraisal questionnaires and inventories.

Torrance, E. P. *Creativity.* Washington: National Education Association, 1963. Pamphlet No. 28 from the series, "What research says to the teacher," issued jointly by the Department of Classroom Teachers and the American Educational Research Association, both departments of the NEA.

Tyler, L. *Individual differences.* Englewood Cliffs, N. J.: Prentice-Hall, 1974. A brief, simply written statement of how individual differences, especially intellectual ones, are measured, and what the measures mean in everyday life.

15

Exceptional Children: Learners Who Have Special Needs

Adapting Educational Practices to the Needs of Learners

The accepted policy in public education, until the years before World War II, could have been stated somewhat as follows: Schools are the molders of children; therefore it is the responsibility of children to adapt themselves to the school. Education was thought of as something fixed and well defined. There was a body of information and skills that had to be learned, and children were considered to be educated to the extent that they could learn it. In effect, if the child who was to be educated was unwilling or unable to adapt himself to the molding influence of the school, he was uneducable.

Probably most teachers at times wish for the days when students who were unwilling or unable to learn could be dropped from school without further consideration. Such feelings are likely to be aggravated when students show lack of appreciation for the time, trouble, and expense that has gone into the development of the educational program, or when the best efforts of teachers to help students meet with repeated failure and frustration. Yet although teachers may occasionally long to be delivered of this burden of responsibility, they know that such thoughts are unrealistic and perhaps unworthy; they are not in keeping with the philosophy of education that we have been developing along with our ideas of political democracy—the philosophy that everyone has a right to the benefits of free public education. We have come to believe that education is a necessity in a democracy, that the whole structure of our national culture rests on an educated population. The laws that require children and youth to attend school are but one expression of these concepts.

The people of many states and communities in the United States have reached a point in their thinking about education where they are saying that the schools must teach *all* children, not just those who are interested or able to benefit from the standard curriculum or who can be taught without special facilities. Together with the development of this philosophy has come the idea that all students cannot be expected to learn the same things in the same ways. This trend appears to be psychologically sound. Students *are* bound to learn different things and in different ways, even when they are in the same classroom and work under the direction of the same teacher. Because of the differences in their personalities, background, abilities, and needs, each will learn and retain what meets his needs and is best related to his experience. Just as both the lay public and teaching profession are coming to understand the *individuality* of education, so are they also beginning to accept education as a *process* through which each child is helped to develop his potentialities and abilities to the greatest

degree, with due regard both for his strengths and for his limitations.

There is, unfortunately, a large gap between good intentions and practice. Even though we know that patterns and rates of learning are highly individual, we still conduct much of the educational program as though students were standardized. Patrick Suppes (1964) maintains that the fact that students differ widely in rates of learning was the most *unaccepted* principle of learning in the day-to-day practice of classroom teaching. Even children who have been preselected on the basis of high IQ show great differences in learning rate. Figure 15-1 shows the difference in progress in arithmetic between the slowest and the fastest student in a class of forty gifted first-graders whose IQs ranged from 122 to 166 and whose mean IQ was 137. By the end of the seventh week, the class had learned the concepts usually taught in first-grade arithmetic and were well into second-grade work. The slowest student in the group had completed approximately 2200 problems, but the fastest student had completed approximately 3400, 50 percent more. In another experimental program, Suppes introduced a special reading program to thirty-eight unselected kindergarteners. The fastest child needed only 196 learning trials to complete the program, whereas the slowest child needed 2506. Suppes' conclusion after these and other studies is that "by far the greatest improvement in subject-matter learning will result from an almost single-minded concentration on individual differences."

Suppes' research and comments point up the need to individualize instruction for all children in the classroom, a need that cannot be met under present conditions, partly because we tend to overlook individual differences in learning, but also because the limitations in personnel, facilities, and funds commit us to a program of mass education, with all its shortcomings.

We have, however, made some progress in providing more highly individualized education to students who apparently need this type of attention the most, and particularly to those children who have for one reason or another been unable to participate in the regular school program.

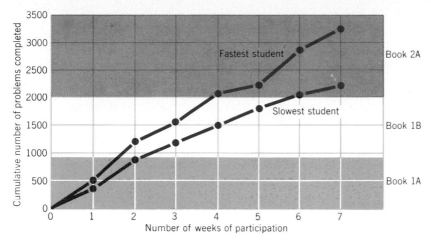

FIG. 15-1. Number of mathematical problems completed at the end of each of seven consecutive weeks by the fastest and slowest student in a gifted first-grade class of forty students (Suppes, 1964).

SPECIAL EDUCATION FOR EXCEPTIONAL CHILDREN

What Is Special About Special Education?

What we are referring to is a new sense of responsibility that has come to the schools and the communities that support them, a belief that certain children should not be excluded from participation in normal educational experiences merely because they are unable to learn without special help. Both educators and laymen are beginning to say that children are entitled to an education even though they learn more slowly or with greater difficulty and even though such special education takes more teaching personnel and is more costly.

Children who are in need of such specialized help are the "exceptional children"—youngsters who require special attention because they are physically or emotionally handicapped, mentally retarded, or intellectually gifted. Samuel Kirk (1972) gives this definition:

The exceptional child is the child who deviates from the normal or average child (1) in mental characteristics, (2) in sensory abilities, (3) in neuromuscular or physical characteristics, (4) in social or emotional behavior, (5) in communication abilities, or (6) in multiple handicaps to such an extent that he requires modification of school practices, or special education services, in order to develop to his maximum capacity.

It is difficult to determine how many exceptional children there are; even experts are not agreed on what the best criteria should be for determining who should have special help and who should be handled in the average classroom. Some schools may find, for example, that they can take care of the needs of a child who is subject to occasional epileptic seizures without undue readjustment of classroom routine, whereas other schools may feel that such a child needs special supervision or even special classes. One estimate made by the United States Office of Education (1964) placed the proportion of exceptional children at 12.8 percent of the school-age population, or about one child in eight. A breakdown by categories is given in Table 15-1, which also includes the number actually enrolled in special programs. The figures in Table 15-1 show a considerable degree of variation in the extent to which children who are technically and potentially candidates for special treatment actually receive it. More than one-half the total number of speech-impaired children are receiving special aid, but only 3

TABLE 15-1. Number and Percentage of Children Needing and Receiving Special Education in the United States, 1970 to 1971[a]

Categories	Percentage Overall[b]	Estimated Number[c]	Number in Programs
Speech impaired	3.5	1,820,000	1,237,000
Mentally retarded	2.3	1,196,000	830,000
Intellectually gifted	2.3	1,196,000	481,000
Crippled and special health problems	2.0	1,040,000	395,000
Emotionally disturbed and socially maladjusted	2.0	1,040,000	113,000
Deaf and hard of hearing	0.6	312,000	78,000
Visually handicapped	0.1	52,000	24,000
	12.8	6,656,000	3,158,000

[a] U.S. Office of Education, 1964, 1973.
[b] Based on a 1963 survey.
[c] Based on 1970 census estimates of 52 million children, aged 5 to 17.

percent of those designated as "emotionally disturbed and socially maladjusted." Table 15-2 provides another index to our perception of needs for special help. Programs for children designated as "culturally deprived" received the largest amount of dollar aid from the United States Office of Education during the years 1964 to 1968, and there was a 641 percent increase in aid during this period. (We shall discuss the special problems of this large group of children in Chapter 16.) Programs for foreign-language-speaking children and the physically handicapped also received large increases during the five-year period, but programs for emotionally disturbed children received the smallest increase. The percentage-of-increase figures are interesting because they indicate trends in the amount of concern expressed for the special needs of children in the various categories.

The amount and kind of attention given to children with special needs varies partly according to the severity of their problems and partly with respect to the kinds of modification that must be made in content, instructional methods, and learning environment. An analysis of the relationship between children's needs and the changes that schools should make is presented in Table 15-3. One tendency has been to care for children with *severe* physical handicaps—blind and partially seeing, deaf and hard-of-hearing, cerebral-palsied, and children with rheumatic fever—in residential schools where trained personnel can give them the special education and medical attention they need. However, a countertrend is to have children live at home, where they can receive the psychological benefits of living with their family group, in which event they attend special schools or special classes in their community. The latter solution is, of course,

TABLE 15-2.
United States Office of Education Financial Support for Special Programs in Schools, 1965 to 1968[a]

Categories	Dollars (Final 000 Omitted)	Percentage of increase 1964 to 1968
Culturally deprived	41,265	641
Physically handicapped	12,023	394
Intellectually handicapped	10,598	114
Emotionally disturbed	3,232	66
Foreign language speaking	3,150	405
Intellectually gifted	2,039	93

[a] United States Office of Education, 1969.

TABLE 15-3. Adapting the School to Meet the Needs of Exceptional Children (XX—Major change needed; X—Minor change needed)[a]

Categories	Aspects of Educational Program To Be Modified		
	Content (What Is Taught)	Methodology (How Content Is Taught)	Learning Environment (Where Content Is Taught)
Severe-Chronic (Required for entire school career)			
Moderate and severe mental retardation	XX	XX	XX
Deafness and severe hearing loss	XX	XX	XX
Blindness and severe visual impairment	X	XX	X
Schizophrenia and autism	XX	XX	XX
Orthopedically handicapped	–	X	XX
Severe communication problems (cleft palate, cerebral palsy)	–	XX	X
Transitional (Needs may be met by limited, intensive treatment)			
Educable mentally retarded	XX	XX	X
Hard of hearing	X	XX	X
Partially sighted	–	X	X
Articulation problems in speech	–	X	X
Emotionally disturbed	X	X	X
Specific learning disabilities (for example, reading handicaps)	XX	XX	X
Intellectually gifted	X	X	X

[a] After Gallagher, 1975.

feasible only if the disability is not so severe that it constitutes an undue burden on the family, and the success of the educational program for such a child depends on the existence of special schools and classes, as well as on the cooperation between the parents and the school.

Attitudes, Motives, and Treatment

The problem of what to teach in special schools and classes is a complex one. The first and obvious requirement is that the child be helped to function as independently and as normally as possible. This means that children with cerebral palsy must be helped to learn to dress themselves; blind children must be taught how to move about and work in the company of others without injuring themselves; and children who are deaf must be taught how to read lips. Helping children to function independently may not be easy. Some children who have handicaps find it difficult to stop being dependent; very often they have led lives that were far more sheltered than was necessary, and they have come to believe that they are incapable of doing things for themselves. In effect, they have come to "overaccept" and to exaggerate the severity of their disability. Other children resent their disability and are inclined to bear a grudge against the world. They express their hostility by resisting efforts to help or teach them. The attitude of adults often interferes with the education of children with handicaps. A common attitude toward the handicapped individual

LEARNERS WHO NEED SPECIAL ATTENTION
The mentally retarded. The visually handicapped. The gifted and creative. Children with communication disorders.

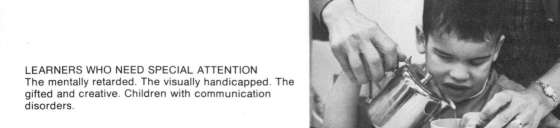

tends to be one of mixed pity and shame, of over-protection and rejection. It is hard for us to accept him as an individual when we are fascinated or repelled by his handicap. Indeed, one of the chief arguments in favor of including handicapped children in "normal" classrooms is that it is as necessary for "normal" children to learn to live with the handicapped child and accept him as one of them as it is for the handicapped child to learn to live with so-called "normals."

Some of the attitudes and problems that keep handicapped children dependent and that interfere with their learning are illustrated by this brief case history:

> Monty was a very pleasant and agreeable ten-year-old boy who had been crippled by polio at the age of three. He was confined to a wheelchair a great deal of the time because of residual leg weakness. In spite of this handicap, he was a charming, outgoing child who made friends easily, particularly with adults. However, he was evasive and stubborn when it came to carrying out any kind of responsibility, such as school work. He had been so protected and catered to because of his handicap that he had never been forced to make an effort on his own part to learn, to take exercises, and to follow regular routines at home, at school, and in the hospital. As a result, he became a problem to nurses and even to other patients in the hospital. On the one hand, he would bring out their interest in him by his charming, appealing ways, but on the other hand, when it was time for him to do his school work or when he was asked to conform to hospital routines and regulations, he resisted. During his frequent hospitalizations, he stayed up until late hours every night talking to any adult who was interested, watching television, and cruising about in his wheelchair. Any attempt to pin him down to a schedule, to get him to complete his school work, or to do his exercises, Monty met with stubborn resistance and resentment (Phillips, Wiener, and Haring, 1960).

Labeling and Classifying Children: More of a Hindrance than a Help

Sometimes children with special educational needs are called "atypical." However, the use of such a label implies that there are "typical" children. Actu-

ally, the "typical" child does not exist. Every child has his individual problems and needs. Indeed, every child is in some degree "handicapped" or "atypical," in the sense that there are some things that he cannot do well. Frances is one of the top students in her class. She is well liked by both adults and age-mates. But she must wear glasses because her right eye tests 20/60 on the Snellen Chart. Jim appears to be a perfect physical specimen; he is skillful on the playground and does better-than-average work in the classroom. Jim's great sorrow, however, is that he has no talent or ear for music. He comes from a musical family and feels "left out" of many of their activities.

Exceptional children have handicaps and problems, just as Frances and Jim do, but their handicaps or problems are of such a nature that they need specialized help with some of their learning activities. Frances and Jim need specialized help for various problems from time to time, too, but they need it less often and less consistently than do children who are candidates for "special education." Unless exceptional children get the help they need, they are likely to become discouraged and disheartened. What happens so often is that instead of getting the help they need, they are labeled and categorized:

> Jane appears on summary school records and state reports as "mentally retarded, educable." What the reports do not say is that Jane cannot read, is attractive and pleasant, and is in need of dental care.
>
> Bill appears on school records and state reports as "visually handicapped," which is correct, as far as it goes. What is not reported is that he is a diabetic, that his IQ is at least 160, and that he is an expert musician.
>
> John's status, according to summary school records and state reports, is "emotionally disturbed." The records do not say, however, that his father is an alcoholic who tyrannizes the family. Nor do they say that John makes movies of remarkable perceptiveness (Trotter, 1975).

> "You can't do much with Mike—he's hard of hearing."
> "Frank's a pretty good kid and I like him. But since he's taken to running with his brother's gang, there isn't much the school can do. We

can send the truant officer after him to drag him back, but he'll just play hookey the next day and the day after that.''

"Yes, Esther's quiet and she never bothers anyone. But she can't particpate in the committee work we do in this class because she can barely read. Her IQ is somewhere around 70. There doesn't seem to be much to do, just let her alone.''

Nicholas Hobbs (1974) says that such labeling, which is supposed to help exceptional children, is actually more of a hindrance. He and his coworkers warn that "categories and labels are powerful instruments for social regulation and control, and they are often employed for obscure, covert, or harmful purposes: to degrade people, to deny them access to opportunities, to exclude 'undesirables' whose presence in some way offends, disturbs familiar custom or demands extraordinary effort.'' There is the danger that labeling these children as "different" may cause them to be stigmatized for life, denied educational and job opportunities, or confined to institutions where, under the guise of being given treatment, they are forgotten and neglected or even abused.

The late Rudolf Dreikurs (1962b) also expressed outrage at the too-facile practice of using the disabilities of children as a basis for labeling them. His statement is remarkably consistent with the conclusions of Hobbs and his coresearchers:

Unfortunately, being different implies in our culture not merely a difference in individual characteristics, but also a difference in social status. In the competitive atmosphere of our times, the yardstick of superiority or inferiority is applied to any outstanding difference. Furthermore, any deviation from normalcy, particularly if it is based on a deficiency, evokes unfavorable reactions. For this reason any classification of children based on a comparison with others, is damaging. Whatever handicap the child may experience through his minus or plus deviation from others is accentuated by being placed in a special category.

Actually, the child has the right to be understood as he is and not to be compared with any other. Fundamentally, each is a human being and has to be respected in his own individuality, appreciated for what he is, and exposed to such treatment as he individually needs. Even the so-called normal children are by no means alike; they too require the same individual understanding and treatment. Classifying people and putting them into categories implies by necessity the setting up of a hierarchy, the use of a frame of reference which establishes superiority and inferiority, and in the end deprives each individual of his secure place in the group. For this reason, any classification must be considered artificial and damaging. The assumption, and even more the accentuation of inferiority and superiority, creates new difficulties and disturbs the social relationship of the child. Social living in a democracy presupposes a social equilibrium based on fundamental social human equality. Without feeling equal to others, the child cannot become part of the group. It is equally detrimental to the social adjustment of a child to feel inferior or superior to the others. Far from discouraging such comparative attitudes, the classification of being exceptional enhances such mistaken attitudes in the child.

Failure and Overprotection

One condition that aggravates the feeling of inferiority that is so common among children classified as "exceptional" is the theme of failure that appears to run through the lives of many of them. As we have pointed out previously, we should not overprotect children against the experience of failure because children need to have the experience of making some mistakes as a necessary part of the normal process of learning. Making mistakes is an inevitable part of everyday living; the important thing is to learn how to avoid them and how to correct them once they are made. Too much failure, however, can lead only to discouragement, and the handicapped student has more than enough opportunities to experience both failure and discouragement. Overfamiliarity with failure and discouragement inevitably leads to learning problems.

The problem of failure and discouragement is accentuated by the attitudes we tend to have toward handicapped children. We are inclined to be "underexpecting" and "overprotecting" with students who are crippled or who have visual disabilities, but we are also inclined to be "overexpecting" and even "rejecting" with slow learners, with students who have social or emotional maladjustments, and even, at times, with the hard of hearing.

Teachers and parents sometimes raise the question of how much of the regular school curriculum should be taught to the exceptional child. If intelligence or academic ability is within normal limits, the standard curriculum should not constitute any more of a problem than it does with any other student. This is particularly true of the lower grades, where a major degree of attention is paid to the learning of basic skills. Adjustments may have to be made with regard to physical education, field trips, or other activities that conflict with the limitations of the handicapped student, but they should not interfere with the normal progress of learning. At the same time we should recognize that handicapped children are inclined to have more than their share of emotional problems, which, in turn may interfere with learning.

Curricular problems tend to become more complex for exceptional children when they enter secondary school because decisions must be made as to whether a student should receive special vocational training to prepare him for immediate employment on graduation or whether he should take the standard college-preparatory curriculum. One might argue that what he needs most are the skills necessary for self-support, but to prevent his taking a college-preparatory course merely because of his handicap would be a form of discrimination. This is a problem that can become especially difficult when the student's IQ is marginal as far as the prediction of college success is concerned—say, in the 100 to 110 range.

PROBLEMS OF SLOW AND FAST LEARNERS

Concepts of Mental Retardation

When intelligence tests were first introduced, designating labels such as "idiot," "imbecile," and "mo-ron" were drawn from the medical terminology of the day and applied to individuals who scored at the bottom of the distribution of scores. There was a tendency at first to give these terms a degree of reality that went far beyond the simple fact that they were artifacts representing relative differences in performance in a standardized interview or on a questionnaire blank. The labels also had a "final" sound to them which was consistent with the widespread idea that there was no point in trying to educate or to train "such people," and that they would be better off if hidden away from the rest of society in an institution.

Today we are both more sophisticated and more optimistic in our attitudes toward individuals who score low on mental tests. First, "slow learners" or "mental retardates" are terms that more correctly refer to the behavior that is causing problems and that avoid the insulting connotation of "moron." Second, we have a better idea of the causes of mental retardation. Much of it is due to environmental conditions that discourage or do not reinforce cognitive growth. Edward Zigler (1967) maintained that 75 percent of children classified as retarded do not have neurological defects and are the products of social deprivation, such as is found in families living in urban and rural slums. Some children, particularly those that are more seriously retarded, do have neurological damage, but even in these instances a much higher percentage is born into families of the very poor, both black and white. The high incidence of brain-damaged children born to poverty families can be explained in terms of inadequate prenatal care, nutritional deficiencies, lack of adequate medical care, and an inability or reluctance to use medical services that are available (Amante, et al., 1970).

A third point is that we are much more willing today to work with slow learners and try to find ways of helping them realize their best potentials. The realization that some of the retardation may be the result of environmental deficiencies has led us to experiment with different environments at school and at work in an attempt to upgrade performance. Evaluations of mental retardation made during childhood are likely to underestimate developmental potential. Don C. Charles (1953) once did a study of twenty-four individuals who had been classified in 1935 as mentally deficient, with a mean IQ of 58. Fifteen years later, as adults, their mean IQ was 72. All of them made gains in IQ, except for one whose IQ was 68 on both testings.[1] Most of the group made an adequate or more-than-adequate adjustment to the demands of adult life, and only a few had been institutionalized.

The social stimulation resulting from the associations, demands, and give-and-take of everyday living probably accounts for the increases in competence shown by Charles' subjects. A number of studies show that increases in social stimulation promote mental growth in retardates. Guinevere S. Chambers and R. N. Zabarenko (1956) once conducted an experiment directed at trying to increase the IQs of institutionalized mentally deficient patients by the administration of glutamic acid. The drug turned out to have no effect, but patients who participated in the study either in experimental or control groups showed IQ gains, whereas nonparticipants did not. The increases were attributed by the researchers to the social stimulation patients received in connection with their having been subjects in a research project.

Helping Mentally Retarded Children

Although the general practice a generation ago was to place more severely retarded children in institutions, the trend nowadays is for them to remain at home and to receive special training in special classes at school. The educational program provided for mentally retarded children varies primarily with the severity of the retardation. At approximately 50 IQ downward, children are considered "trainable," and training is aimed at self-care, social adjustment at home and within the neighborhood, and preparation for economic usefulness in a sheltered workshop or working at home. Retardation at this level is likely to involve some physiological defect, such as brain damage. Approximately one-half become institutionalized after they leave school, a fact

---

[1] When these individuals were retested in the early 1960s, virtually all of them received higher IQs than they had in 1950. The mean gain was 6 IQ points (Baller, Charles, and Miller, 1967).

that reflects not so much the incompetence of the retardate as it does the failure of the community to provide proper employment opportunities, supervised recreation, and counseling. Children with IQs of about 25 or below are usually considered "custodial" and are placed in institutions.

An IQ of 50 is usually taken as the approximate minimum required for beginning reading. Children at this level and up to about IQ 70 are considered "educable." The milder the retardation, the more likely they are to be included in regular classes. These children, however, require more than the usual amount of attention on the part of the teacher, and their inability to keep up with other children tends to have discouraging effects. One solution seems to be the special class supervised by a special teacher, but this approach has the disadvantage of stigmatizing and drawing special attention to the child. As with other types of educational problems, there seems to be no "one best way" to help the educable retardate. Each school has to work out the problem in accordance with the facilities and personnel available, involving our community agencies and parents as much as possible.

Joe was a source of disturbance from the very beginning. He had a constant need to move around, and whistled, sang, or made nonsense sounds. He would strike at and hurt other children without apparent reason. His desk was always very orderly, and when he attempted work it was neat. Making an error upset him so much that he would destroy the paper rather than complete it. The teacher found that she could not give him the time and attention he needed and noted, furthermore, that his behavior disturbed the other students. However, when his parents took him to the family doctor, the only report they could get was that the boy was hyperactive.

When Joe entered the second grade, the school advised the family to refer him to a special diagnostic center, where his case was diagnosed as neurological impairment with suspected aphasia (speech difficulty due to brain damage). A child welfare agency then included Joe's mother in a counseling program with a group of mothers of brain-damaged children. This enabled the family to accept Joe's limitations and to learn new ways of managing him. The family doctor prescribed medication that helped in controlling impulsive behavior. As a result of the diagnosis of aphasia, the school put Joe in its special progam for speech and hearing handicapped children. The school custodian converted a regular desk into a "stand-up" desk in order to give Joe a place to work when he became restless from sitting. A tutor was secured to aid him in subject-matter areas in which he was retarded.

Things went much better in the third grade. Joe received a great deal more understanding and acceptance from adults than previously. The medication enabled him to remain in school for longer periods of time than had been possible, although he was frequently unable to remain for a full day. When he left school early, his mother now did not punish him as she had formerly, and instead she gave him something constructive to do. He began to have some successes in school, although areas of significant retardation remained. Hitting other children was almost eliminated. Having Joe in a regular classroom, however, still presented many problems for all concerned. Nor was it feasible to put him in a class for mentally retarded children, since the activities would have been too stimulating. The best arrangement was a small class with a teacher trained to work with brain-damaged and hyperactive children (Lovos and Norton, 1962).

As a result of the collaboration of school, social agencies, and parents, Joe was receiving a great deal more attention of a positive nature than he did formerly. This was beginning to have some positive effect on his behavior.

Nonpromotion of Slow Learners

There is an unfortunate tendency for many schools to try to treat the problems of slow learners administratively, without regard for their special needs. Requiring children to repeat a year's work is one type of administrative action that seldom has beneficial results. This practice is one that has considerable support, however, among traditionally oriented teachers and laymen, who conceive of the subject matter of a given grade as something self-contained and concrete, something that must be mastered before one goes on to the next grade. Research so far reveals no advantages in such a policy—only disadvantages. For example, W. H. Coffield and Paul

Blommers (1956) conducted a survey of 302 Iowa school systems in search of seventh-graders who had been failed at least once since the third grade. The 147 students they located were matched, on the basis of their third-grade achievement, with pupils who had been promoted. There turned out to be no difference between the two groups in their performance in the seventh grade; the promoted and the nonpromoted were functioning at the same level. Hence no useful purpose had been served in holding the children back an extra year. John I. Goodlad (1968) concluded, on the basis of his own studies, as well as those of other investigators, that the social adjustment of the promoted slow learner was superior to that of the nonpromoted, and that slow-learning children profit considerably more from promotion than from nonpromotion. Philip E. Kraus (1973) conducted a longitudinal study of nonpromoted children in the New York City schools and observed that "for these children, retention had a deleterious effect upon their progress in reading," and that "it is ironical that the very purposes which retention in grade was supposed to have served were so completely unrealized." In one highly successful experimental program, seventh-graders who were a year behind the grade for their age were given an opportunity to take two years in one and thus catch up. Two years later they were not only doing adequate work, but also a lower percentage had dropped out of school than is usually the case for students who have been held back (Chamberlin and Caterall, 1965).

The Problems of Gifted Children

During the late 1950s and early 1960s there was an awakening of interest in the educational fate of children from the opposite end of the intellectual spectrum—the fast learners, or so-called "gifted children." The attitude that had been prevalent, and one that still is very common, is that students with high IQs can "shift for themselves." After all, being intellectually gifted is an asset, rather than a liability, and it is hard to see why such children need any special help or attention. Yet if one of the prime objectives of our schools is to help children develop their potentialities and talents to the fullest, it is highly probable that we have failed to attain this objective for a large proportion of students with exceptionally high abilities.

One of the difficulties faced by intellectually gifted students is their very superiority in academic ability. Rudolf Dreikurs (1925b) once said:

> A high I.Q. does not guarantee success at all. In many cases, it is actually a handicap. The child is exposed to constant pressure because his parents and teachers expect extraordinary achievement from him. He becomes easily discouraged if he finds himself unable to live up to these expectations. An increasing number of children with a superior intelligence give up any effort toward achievement, to the extent that they fail even to learn writing and reading. But even if they manage to succeed to the point of excellence, their emotional and social equilibrium remains precarious. They cannot stand defeat without feeling crushed. The obligation to be superior is, therefore, as damaging as the label of inferiority.

Perhaps the problem will be clearer if we remember that it is equally as frustrating for the intellectually gifted child to slow down the pace of his learning to that of the "average" member of the class as it is for the mentally retarded child to attempt to meet standards that are continually beyond his reach. Gifted children react to such frustration in various ways. Some lose interest in their daily work and seek escape in excessive daydreaming. Others become hostile and express their frustrations through disruptive behavior. Still others become apathetic and lose interest in work that presents no real challenge to them. A very common problem with some bright children is their lack of persistence with difficult or complex tasks that are outside their general field of competence or interest. Success comes so easily for them in their areas of special interest that they are inclined to give up easily whenever they encounter problems. Occasionally this lack of persistence will extend to a wide area of school learning.

Identifying Gifted Students

Much of the pressure for special treatment of the gifted student comes from parents, particularly in middle-class urban and suburban areas, who quite understandably want their children to receive extra consideration. Many such parents lose interest, however, when they discover that the usual definition of a gifted child (using the standard employed by Terman in his study of the gifted) is one who obtains an IQ of 140 or higher on the Stanford-Binet. Some psychologists are willing to consider children with an IQ of 130 or higher as "gifted," but even this standard would include only about 3 percent of the children in the average school system. Some school systems, perhaps out of consideration for ambitious parents or perhaps to ensure having a sufficiently large group of children to justify the development of a special program, have lowered the limits of the "gifted" group to 120 IQ or even less, a range to which most psychologists would apply the label "bright" or "above-average bright," rather than "gifted."

(*Peanuts* © 1966 United Feature Syndicate, Inc.)

Some school systems have recognized that the intelligence test is a rather limited instrument for identifying students who have potentials that may deserve special attention. The San Francisco public schools, for example, have developed a list of behavioral criteria for the guidance of teachers who wish to nominate students for the school district's gifted student program. The list is especially interesting because of the wide range of behaviors it covers:

1. Is an avid reader.
2. Has received an award in science, art, literature.
3. Has avid interest in science or literature.
4. Very alert, rapid answers.
5. Is outstanding in math.
6. Has a wide range of interests.
7. Is very secure emotionally.
8. Is venturesome, anxious to do new things.
9. Tends to dominate peers or situations.
10. Readily makes money on various projects or activities—is an entrepreneur.
11. Individualistic—likes to work by self.
12. Is sensitive to feelings of others—or to situations.
13. Has confidence in self.
14. Needs little outside control—disciplines self.
15. Adept at visual art expression.
16. Resourceful—can solve problems by ingenious methods.
17. Creative in thoughts, new ideas, seeing associations, innovations, etc. (not artistically).
18. Body or facial gestures very expressive.
19. Impatient—quick to anger or anxious to complete a task.
20. Great desire to excel even to the point of cheating.
21. Colorful verbal expressions.
22. Tells very imaginative stories.
23. Frequently interrupts others when they are talking.
24. Frank in appraisal of adults.
25. Has mature sense of humor (puns, associations, etc.).
26. Is inquisitive.
27. Takes a close look at things.
28. Is eager to tell others about discoveries.
29. Can show relationships among apparently unrelated ideas.
30. Shows excitement in voice about discoveries.
31. Has tendency to lose awareness of time (Cummings, 1975).

Special Programs for the Gifted

Once a school determines which of its students to designate as "gifted," it may deal with them in three different ways: acceleration, enrichment, and assignment to special classes.

Acceleration has generally been in disfavor among educators. They point out that the eleven-year-old child who has been accelerated, say, to the seventh grade is out-of-step physically, emotionally, and socially with most seventh-graders and should be kept in the fifth grade with his age-mates. Their preferred solution to the problem of the gifted is *enrichment,* a solution that enables the gifted student to remain with students his own age and at the same time to partake of intellectual experiences that are more in keeping with his abilities and interests.

Unfortunately, enrichment is a subject that receives more attention in educational literature and at conferences of educators than it does in the classroom. Developing a program of enrichment is a task that takes a great deal of preparation, planning, and experimentation and cannot be done casually or haphazardly. Enriching the curriculum for one or two gifted children in a class is likely to become an extra burden for an overworked and harried teacher. Some teachers attempt to deal with the problem by grouping their class according to ability and assigning simpler tasks to those with lower aptitude and more complex ones to those with higher aptitude. One of the difficulties with this technique is that students are quick to sense that they are being treated differently from others and often object to being given assignments that are more difficult than those being given other students. The fear of being "different" is one that is fairly common among students in the preadolescent and adolescent years, and many students deliberately do mediocre work in order to avoid being thought superior.

When experimental programs for enrichment have actually been planned and carried out carefully, they have been received favorably by students, teachers, and parents. As we pointed out earlier, experimental programs usually can be counted on to produce conceptual learning and favorable attitude changes, even if no academic advantage is apparent. Research with enrichment programs produces results that are consistent with that statement. For instance, a follow-up by J. A. R. Wilson (1959) of students who had participated in an "ideal" enrichment program in a California junior high school showed no measurable advantage or disadvantage for those who had participated, although both students and teachers thought highly of the program.

Educational psychologists have today lost much of their earlier interest in special programs for the gifted. Edward C. Frierson (1969) commented:

Since 1965, research related to the gifted has indeed shifted dramatically from a concern for the gifted child to a concern for the creative process. So marked has been the trend away from studies concerning gifted children in favor of studies of creativity and cognitive factors that publications of associations for gifted children have experienced dwindling subscriptions and memberships.

Part of the problem has been that programs for gifted children have been based more on the guess of teachers and parents as to what should be appropriate, rather than on research findings. Frierson observed that "little innovation in curriculum has been based on knowledge of giftedness."

Does "Double Promotion" Help or Hinder Gifted Children?

Nonpromotion of slow learners appears to have negative effects, as we noted previously, but the same cannot be said for rapid promotion of fast learners. Virtually all the research evidence to date shows either that it has beneficial results or that it has no negative effect. Melita H. Oden (1968) conducted a follow-up survey of adults who had scored at 140 IQ or higher when they were children. She divided the men into "most successful" and "least successful" groups, using eminence, productivity, occupational status, personal and social adjustment, and income as criteria. As Figure 15-2 shows, 75 percent of the most successful group graduated from college at age 21 or younger, in contrast to

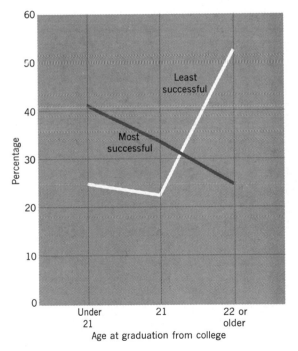

FIG. 15-2. A comparison of the most and the least successful men in a larger group of high IQ individuals in terms of the percentage graduating from college at different ages (Oden, 1968).

only 47½ percent of the least successful group. These findings are consistent with a survey conducted come years ago by Sidney L. Pressey (1946) who contrasted Amherst College graduates who attained national and international prominence with those who were failures and unemployed at the time of the survey. Of those who had graduated at 20 and under, 23 percent became eminent and 5 percent failed, whereas of those who graduated at age 24 or older, 3 percent became eminent and 25 percent failed. The Fund for the Advancement of Education (1957) conducted a survey of 1350 students who entered college about two years younger than the average freshman. Although practically none of these students had completed high school, they not only made academic records that were much better than those made by the average student in their college, but also did better than a group of students who were matched with them in aptitude but who entered college at the usual age. The accelerated students participated more extensively in extracurricular activities, were awarded more academic honors than would be ordinarily expected of students of similar levels of ability, and made a satisfactory social and emotional adjustment to college life.

The finding that accelerated students were well adjusted in spite of having to participate with students who were older is especially interesting, in view of the fears and misgivings that educators often express about the emotional and social adjustment of the accelerated student. Other research studies also fail to show that acceleration has any negative effects on the adjustment of bright students (Kraus, 1973). Vagharsh H. Bedoian (1953, 1954) reported, as the result of a sociometric study of 743 sixth-grade students from twenty-two classrooms, that children who had been accelerated actually tended to be *more* accepted than the average student. One the other hand, students who were "overage" in their classes (presumably because they had been "held back" for one or more years) constituted a large proportion of the children who were most rejected by their classmates. Not only do gifted children react favorably to acceleration, but it

may even be a disservice *not* to accelerate them. D. A. Worcester (1956) noted that gifted children who are held back with their age-mates are more likely to develop personality and behavior problems than those who are accelerated. Furthermore, gifted children often become frustrated and bored by educational tasks that are too easy and may thus develop work habits that are characterized by laziness and carelessness.

One of the principal objections teachers have to acceleration is that significant areas of learning may be skipped or slighted, thus putting the gifted student at a disadvantage in the group into which he is accelerated. Some research by Klausmeier, Goodwin, and Ronda (1968) suggests that these concerns are baseless. The researchers did a follow-up survey in the ninth grade of a group of bright children who had been accelerated from the second to the fourth grade after a five-week summer session and found that they were doing at least as well as the average bright ninth-grader, even though they were six months to a year younger. The research of Klausmeier's group shows that with proper instruction bright children should be able to cover in five weeks whatever is taught in the third grade and still maintain a superior level of academic performance.

It is the suggestion of James R. Hobson (1963) that schools grant early kindergarten admission to bright children, rather than disrupt their school career by having them skip grades. Hobson's conclusions are based on the experience of the public schools in Brookline, Massachusetts, which have had a policy of admitting children as young as four years (nine months below the statutory age) to kindergarten, provided their mental test scores, physical health, and mental health are sufficiently above average. Over the years, children who have started school under this early admission plan have done consistently better than those admitted at the usual time. They have, for example, won proportionately twice as many honors at high-school graduation as other students, their grades have been higher, they have participated and played leading roles in more extracurricular activities, and they have had a 60 percent better chance of being admitted to college.

Ability Grouping: The X, Y, Z of Homogeneity

A third method of dealing with the problems of the gifted student is that of creating special groups. In high school, special classes for the gifted are sometimes called "honors courses," as a way of suggesting a similarity with the kind of independent study arrangements that are found in British and some American universities. Although some high schools have bona fide honors programs, many who claim that they do actually do not, and instead of allowing so-called honors students to do independent study, they put them into classes in which assignments are heavier and grading more severe than in the usual classes (Hausdorff and Farr, 1965). Such classes are actually the top level of systems of "homogeneous grouping," in which pupils are sorted out into classes according to their IQs or their scores on tests of educational achievement.

One of the purposes of homogeneous grouping is that of improving the efficiency of education by providing for each intellectual level the kind of instruction and educational program that is most suitable. Ideally, the students in the top group participate in an enriched curriculum and make faster-than-average progress, whereas those in the lowest group deal with simpler material and proceed at slower-than-average rates. There are a number of practical difficulties that are not apparent at first glance, however. One difficulty is that groups can never be really homogeneous. There are so many ways in which children can differ from one another that any attempt to separate them into truly homogeneous groups is bound to fail. John I. Goodlad (1960) described a fifth-grade class from which children with IQs of over 120 and under 90 were removed, as might be done for the purpose of setting up a system of homogeneous groups. The reading ability of the children in the remaining group (which would be the middle group in a threefold ability grouping arrangement) ranged from the second-grade to the eleventh-grade level.

Let us take a look at a sixth grade that has been separated into X, Y, and Z sections on the basis of IQs. The X section consists of students with IQs over 110, the Y section contains those whose IQs are 95 to 110, and the Z section contains those with IQs of less than 95.

As we might expect, most of the students in the "X" section are making better-than-average progress in school, but Bob Crandall is in the "X" section too because of his IQ of 125, even though he did so badly in the fifth grade that he had to repeat it. He is still doing failing work in the sixth grade. Libby Friend is also in the "X" section. She gets excellent marks in social studies but failed arithmetic and spelling. Linda Hidalgo is only in the "Y" section, but would be anyone's choice as the most outstanding student in the sixth grade. Everyone likes her, and her essay on "What It Means to Be an American" won first prize in the American Legion contest last year. Most of the children in the "Z" section do not do very well in their classwork. They need a great deal of help with their reading and arithmetic. But many of them work harder and are better behaved than some of the children in the "X" and "Y" sections. In fact, this year's "Z" section is much quieter and more cooperative than either the "X" or the "Y" sections.

The chief reason why educators and psychologists object to homogeneous grouping is that it encourages students to make invidious comparisons. Even though the basis of the grouping is often concealed from the students, they eventually ferret it out. Students who are assigned to lower-level sections are likely to feel ashamed and discouraged. Children have a horror of being considered "stupid." Deborah Elkins (1958) once pointed out that ability grouping tends to isolate lower-class children even further from the chance of equal participation with middle-class children. Because being assigned to a "Y" or a "Z" section is a mark of inferiority that reflects on the parents, as well as on the child, many parents put pressure on their children to try harder in the hope of getting them placed in a higher group. Even the child who is fortunate enough to be placed in the "X" group is not immune. If he gets anything less than top grades, pressure is put on him by parents and teachers to "work up to capacity." And if there is some emotional reason why he is unable to "work up to capacity," putting more pressure on him will worsen rather than improve his ability to benefit from his classroom experience.

The attitudes children have toward homogeneous grouping is revealed by a survey conducted by Earl J. Ogletree (1970), who asked fifth- and sixth-graders from working-class and poverty homes (90 percent black) to tell him how they felt about being assigned to the group they were in. Table 15-4 shows some of their replies. It is evident that children in A group felt inordinately proud of their status, those in B group felt ambivalent, and C group children felt hostile and unhappy. When they were asked where they wanted to be placed, A group children were mostly divided between preferring to stay and preferring assignment to a heterogeneous (normal, nonability-grouped) class, and both B and C group children tended to prefer A group. Although work demands would presumably be lighter in C group, the only children who expressed a preference for it were a few in B group. About 20 percent of the children in B and C groups said they often thought of staying away from school, and teachers of these groups reported a greater amount of absenteeism. It seems clear that ability grouping has considerable psychological impact on children, most of it negative.

Homogeneous grouping is usually defended be-cause children presumably perform more ade-quately when educational programs are geared to their capabilities. What is, perhaps, the most extensive test of this proposition was conducted under the direction of Walter R. Borg (1964) of Utah State University. Borg and his co-workers compared two adjacent school districts, one of which was just introducing homogeneous grouping while the other was continuing to follow the standard practice of heterogeneous or random grouping, with enrichment for the more able students. Research data were collected over a four-year period, and the study included some four thousand students from grades 4, 6, 7, 8, and 9. Samples in each of the two districts were matched on the basis of IQ, subjects taken, and social class. During the first year of the study, there were some small differences in achievement that favored homogeneous grouping in the elementary school, but they disappeared during the succeeding years of the study and were counter-balanced by differences favoring random grouping. Comparisons between the two districts' junior high and high-school students showed no advantage for homogeneous grouping. Borg concluded that any decision to use either homogeneous or random grouping would have to be based on some other consideration than the expectation of superior achievement.

TABLE 15-4. Replies Made by Fifth- and Sixth-Graders from Working-class and Poverty Homes to Questions Regarding Their Assignment to Different Levels of Ability Groupings[a]

Group	How do you feel about being placed in this group?	Why were you placed in this group?
A	This is a smart group. I like it here. I don't like to be with stupid kids.	I'm smart, what else. I do good work. I'm not stupid.
B	Give me A group. I like this group. I'm glad I'm not in the dumb group.	Because I get my tests right. I'm half dumb and half smart. I'm not as dumb as the other group.
C	Please, put me in another class; I don't like it. This class is bad. I feel so good in another class.	I don't work hard enough. Because I hate school. I'm not good in books.

[a] Ogletree, 1970.

Borg and his staff also found that schools using homogeneous grouping did have a better distribution of overachievers and underachievers, thus supporting the contention that superior students are challenged more under this system. But they also found that students in homogeneous groups showed more emotional disturbance; this was particularly true of low-ability pupils. As part of his research, Borg reviewed some forty research studies on homogeneous grouping, conducted over a span of almost forty years, and found no basis for assuming that ability grouping had any advantage over random or heterogeneous grouping. Another study conducted by Goldberg, Passow, and Justman (1966) covering about three thousand fourth-graders in forty-five New York City schools found that ability grouping produced slight gains for some groups, which were cancelled out by negative results with other groups. The researchers observed that gains were made by slow learners in heterogeneous classes in which teacher overall expectations were likely to be high and concluded that poor performance in "slow-track" classes was because of the tendency of teachers to underestimate the capabilities of slow learners. When teachers expect less, students learn less, as we noted when we discussed the "Pygmalion effect" in Chapter 10.

Dominick Esposito (1973) reviewed the more recent research on homogeneous grouping and concluded that it aggravates social and economic differences among children and is of no demonstrable value in improving conditions for teaching and learning. Unfortunately, homogeneous grouping is one of the most frequently employed methods for classifying children at both the elementary and secondary levels, and its use appears to be increasing.[2]

The continued failure of research to find data supporting homogeneous grouping leads one to wonder why teachers remain firmly convinced that it will produce superior results. One possible explanation is that ability-grouped classes are easier to plan for and perhaps easier to control. Teachers

somehow have the idea that reducing the intellectual range of the class will cut down the number of different kinds of teaching-learning problems with which they are faced. If this is true, then teacher convenience, rather than student performance and achievement, may be the issue. However, a sounder way of reducing the number of teaching-learning problems might be that of reducing the number of students in the class.

Most elementary teachers do some informal ability grouping *within* their classes. Children may be organized into groups depending on how far they have progressed in reading, written expression, or arithmetic. A child may be in the fast group in arithmetic, in the middle group in reading, and in the slow group in written expression. Such groups are relatively flexible, and children may be moved from one to the other in accordance with their progress or lack of it. This practice does not have the shortcomings of a schoolwide or systemwide homogeneous grouping policy that we have described above.

Most of the questions that we have raised about the desirability of homogeneous grouping do not apply to special classes for *severely* retarded children, who need a specialized type of attention which they are not likely to obtain from the average teacher in the average-sized class. They can best be helped by teachers with specialized training, who can also work with their parents. Special classes for this type of child are more readily justified than the usual type of homogeneous grouping, providing that teachers are willing and able to adjust curriculum and methodology to the special needs of the group. Too often, mentally retarded children are taught the regular school curriculum but more slowly and more repetitiously, whereas a specially designed curriculum would be more suitable for their needs.

SOCIAL AND EMOTIONAL MALADJUSTMENTS

Almost every child who needs special education arrangements has a problem with respect to social and/or emotional adjustment. Sometimes the problem is that of helping him accept the limitations of

<hr>

[2] About two-thirds of the school districts in the United States make use of some form of homogeneous grouping (United States Office of Education, 1969).

his disability; sometimes it is one of helping him to realize the potentialities that have somehow become overshadowed by the disability; and sometimes it is a question of helping him to cope with the oversolicitous or rejecting attitudes of adults or other children. A disability usually carries with it the implication of deviation from the norm, and deviations usually arouse anxieties.

There are some disabilities, however, that not only give rise to emotional problems but are themselves caused by or are symptoms of emotional problems. Such disabilities are characteristic of children who have speech difficulties, are retarded readers, are delinquent, or are "just maladjusted."

Communication Disorders

We are likely to classify children with speech and reading difficulties separately from the other two categories that we mentioned because their difficulties seem, superficially at least, to be ones that should be amenable to retraining and reeducation. We tend to think of the child with a speech handicap as one who needs to learn better ways of speaking and the child who has a reading handicap as one who needs to be taught how to read. Such prejudgments often lead us to ignore the emotional problems which underlie these symptoms. Furthermore, reading disability, or *dyslexia*, is often associated with other types of communication disorders. In one study of children with "receptive language anomaly," or the inability to listen effectively to speech, all of the subjects were found to have reading difficulties (Friedlander and de Lara, 1973).

The fact that communication disorders are linked with emotional problems does not mean that retraining is futile. Actually, a great many children are able to improve speech and reading with the help of specialists. But it is doubtful whether they are helped merely because they have learned better *techniques* of speaking or reading. Very likely the emotional support received from having a speech teacher or a reading specialist show personal interest and attention is in itself an important factor. And, of course, many children do not learn to read or

speak properly, even though they get special tutoring and work very hard at trying to improve.

One hypothesis that suggests itself as an explanation for the failure of teachers and specialists is their inability to relieve a child's basic anxiety. This condition is usually the result of parental attitudes. Children are inclined to reflect the anxieties and expectations of their parents. If the parent is afraid that the child is never going to read or to speak properly, it is difficult for him to avoid communicating this anxiety (often unwittingly) to his child. The late Wendell Johnson (1946), who did a great deal of work with stutterers, believed that stuttering is caused by parents being hypercritical about children's early attempts to speak. It is quite normal, Johnson said, for small children to mumble and mispronounce words and to stumble a bit as they learn to talk. The overanxious and overcritical parent, hearing these mispronunciations, is quick to correct his child, fearing that the child may never learn how to say things correctly. The child senses the parent's anxiety about his speech and becomes embarrassed and self-conscious about it. The more self-conscious he becomes, the more likely he is to stutter. It may be added that parental anxieties seldom come singly. Parents who are overanxious and hypercritical about speech are likely to carry this attitude over into other areas of life, or, more likely, the overanxiety about speech may just be one aspect of their feeling about life in general or about their child. Hence stuttering is likely to be a symptom of an overanxious or hypercritical relationship between parent and child, rather than merely an overconcern about speech. Attitudes toward parents often "generalize" toward all persons in authority and persist through the adult years. In one study, stutterers aged 16 to 52, with an average age of 25, read passages aloud before two groups. One group was composed of individuals (the "authority listeners") who were introduced to subjects with the title "Doctor" and surname (for example, "Doctor Jones") and the other individuals (the "peer listeners") who were dressed more informally and were introduced by first name or nickname and surname (for example, "Tom Brown"). As expected, the subjects did more stuttering when reading to the "authority listeners" (Sheehan, Hadley, and Gould, 1967).

The relationship between reading problems and problems of emotional adjustment has been shown by a number of studies. One of the more recent ones compared the personality test scores of two groups of children matched in IQ, with one group reading at the second-grade level and the other reading above the norm for the sixth grade. As Figure 15-3 shows, the poor readers scored lower on every scale in the personality test. The two groups were also tested with one of the Thematic Apperception Test (TAT) pictures, which depicts a boy contemplating a violin resting on the table before him. The children were asked to say what is happening in the picture and to give it a title. Their stories give an indication of the differences in attitude between children who have gone far ahead of their class in reading and those who have lagged. One poor reader said:

He don't like to play his fiddle. He's sad. He would like to break it, tear it up, or something. His mother might make him play it. He wanted to play it but he found out he couldn't. He don't play it no more. Title: Sad Fiddle.

Another poor reader said: "He's wishing he couldn't play a violin." When asked why, he said he didn't know. His title: "Violin without a noise."

Some good readers' stories also expressed negative or hostile attitudes, but their general "feeling tone" or "flavor" was quite different:

A boy with a sad face looking at his violin. He was trying to sneak out when his mother told him to go practice his violin, and he didn't want to, so in his room he sat down and just looked at his violin. His mother will ask him why he isn't playing his violin, then he will start playing, but he will be thinking about playing baseball. I think a good title for it is: A Boy Can't Always Win

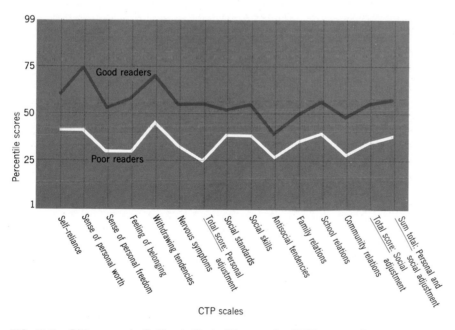

FIG. 15-3. Differences in California Test of Personality (CTP) percentile scores for a group of poor readers (reading grade placement = 2.2) and a group of good readers (reading grade placement = 6.6) matched in IQ (Zimmerman and Allebrand, 1965).

Most of the stories by good readers stressed achievement-oriented motives such as initiative and hard work, with a payoff in terms of future success. For example:

There once was a boy who wanted to play a violin but he didn't know how, and he felt awful about it. His friend knew how to play it, but he still didn't. He tried, tried, and tried again. Finally he did it, he can play it now. P.S. He's the best of them all. Title: Try, Try Again (Zimmerman and Allebrand, 1965).

Because communication disorders are likely to be caused by or, at least, involve emotional and social disturbances, a good many specialists today use an approach that combines tutoring and psychotherapy. In one study that compared different methods, this combination was found to produce better results in a group setting alone or psychotherapy alone (Roman, 1957). In another study, boys who had been reading below the expected grade level showed improvement when their mothers, who had expressed hostile and rejecting attitudes toward their sons, received group therapy. The attitudes of the mothers also improved during the study (Studholme, 1964).

Behavior modification methods may also work, probably because they generate a great deal of feedback and encouragement in a way that is quite different from ordinary classroom instruction. Byron Egelund (1970) conducted an ingenious experiment in which third-grade boys with reading problems were first reinforced (with candy) for every correct response. After six lessons, the reward was changed to poker chips that could be exchanged for toys, and the ratio became one reinforcement for every two correct responses. At the end of the school year, the boys in the experimental group showed more improvement than a comparison group that did not participate in the experimental program. The experimental program had more success with second- than with third-graders, probably because the older boys are more concerned about peer-group recognition than toys. Nevertheless, the

experiment shows how innovative methods can succeed where more conventional approaches fail.

One of the reasons why operant conditioning methods succeed may be found in the tendency of many poor readers to have poor impulse control (Lytton, 1968). What the experimenter does is to reinforce effective responses and to ignore the others, thus ensuring the recurrence of the former but not the latter. This is quite different from conventional methods of teaching and tutoring, in which the ineffective response gets more attention than the effective one.

There is still much that we do not know about the relationship between emotional problems and difficulties in speech and reading. Occasionally, of course, the difficulty is organic, that is, the child may have a cleft palate or may be unable to coordinate the movements of his eyes. Maturation, too, may be a factor. Both speech and reading are verbal abilities, and boys tend to develop more slowly than girls in respect to speech and reading difficulties. As we have noted previously, boys outnumber girls in most kinds of problem behavior. Perhaps these differences are due at least in part to boys' being forced to learn verbal skills before they have reached the proper point in their maturational development, as Dorothea McCarthy (1953) once suggested, or perhaps at all types of problem behavior, including speech and reading difficulties, are related to our inclination to expect problem behavior from boys. Very likely both factors are important and operate together.

The Delinquent

Probably no one in school gets more special attention than the delinquent, if we include in that category the child who misbehaves in school as well as the child who has a juvenile court record. In many respects, his problem is more severe than that of the child who has a physical handicap or the child who has difficulties in speech and in reading. We can be sympathetic toward the child with a physical handicap and even toward the child who needs help with speech or reading, but the delinquent child usually evokes more hostility than sympathy. When we hear of some delinquency, our first reaction is likely to be the hope that the guilty party will be caught and punished. Indeed, we often mistakenly assume that the guilty one is delinquent because he has not been punished enough, whereas the likelihood is greater that he may have been punished too often rather than too seldom.

Because the delinquent arouses our hostility and irritation, we are much less inclined to want to understand his problem. Thus the kind of attention we are likely to give him has the general effect of worsening his behavior rather than improving it. Fortunately, there is a growing trend to view delinquency as a sociopsychological problem and to treat it as objectively and as sympathetically as we do, say, the problems of blind or crippled children.

There are, roughly speaking, two main sources of delinquency. Some children engage in delinquency because antisocial behavior is very much a part of their background. Children who grow up in the slums or who come from families where there is little understanding or regard for law and order are likely to find adjustment to school and society more difficult than do children who come from more typically middle-class backgrounds. Inasmuch as we are inclined to prejudge children on the basis of their background, it should be emphasized that *not all or even most* children coming from slum homes will engage in delinquent behavior, but rather that a somewhat higher proportion of them will do so. Usually, what middle-class people think of as antisocial and delinquent behavior has quite a different meaning for children coming from a lower-class background. Allison Davis (1948) once made this comment in comparing middle-class values with the values of children from the slums:

Whereas the middle-class child learns a socially adaptive fear of receiving poor grades in school, of being aggressive toward the teacher, of fighting, of cursing, and of having early sex relations, the slum child learns to fear quite different acts. His gang teaches him to fear being taken in by the teacher, of being a softie to her. To study

homework seriously is literally a disgrace. Instead of boasting of good marks in school, one conceals them, if he ever receives any. The lower-class individual fears not to be thought a street fighter; it is a suspicious and dangerous social trait. He fears not to curse. If he cannot claim early sex relations, his virility is seriously questioned.

Although the description Davis has given us of slum values may not be generally applicable to all or even most children who come from lower-class backgrounds, it does help to make the point that such children operate in a different frame of reference than do children from middle-class surroundings. Hence when we attempt to change their behavior, we are, in effect, trying to modify an entire culture. This is not to say that we should not attempt to change their behavior, but rather that we should recognize the scope and kind of problem we are undertaking. In short, the problem is not one of reeducating a child here and a child there, but of helping a sizable segment of the community to develop new values and standards of behavior.

One advantage that the middle class has over the child from a poverty home is his ability to deal with frustrations in verbal ways. He can, for example, argue, discuss problems, and find out the reasons for incidents that are causing difficulty. The child from a slum culture has fewer verbal skills and is more likely to deal with frustrating situations directly, aggressively, and even destructively. Delinquency, then, may be caused or aggravated by the inability to verbalize, and part of the treatment of delinquents is to help them find more verbal and less destructive ways of expressing emotions. In one study, treated and untreated delinquents were asked to write stories in connection with the administration of projective tests. Over a ten-month period of psychotherapy, the treated delinquents showed an increase in verbalization and particularly with respect to control of hostility, whereas the untreated delinquents did not (Shore and Massimo, 1967).

A classic and oft-cited study of background factors in delinquency is a survey conducted a generation ago by Sheldon and Eleanor Glueck (1950). Their data showed that social class is not the only determining factor in delinquency. The Gluecks compared five hundred delinquent and five hundred nondelinquent boys from inner-city homes, matched as to background, residence, age, and intelligence. They found that the family relationships of boys in the two groups were quite different. The families of delinquent boys were less cohesive; the other members of the family were indifferent or frankly hostile toward them; their parents were inclined to use extremes of laxity and harshness in discipline, and were far more careless and neglectful in supervising them. Figure 15-4 indicates that delinquents were far more likely to get into trouble at school than were nondelinquents. Furthermore, they got into trouble earlier. The average age of the first school misconduct was nine and one-half for delinquents, or some three years less than the average age of the relatively few nondelinquents who had disciplinary problems at school. The Gluecks made the point that children who become chronic delinquents show certain characteristic signs at a very early age of the direction in which they are traveling. For example, almost one-half of them are under eight years of age when they commit their first delinquencies (Glueck and Glueck, 1950).

The Gluecks also translated their findings into a

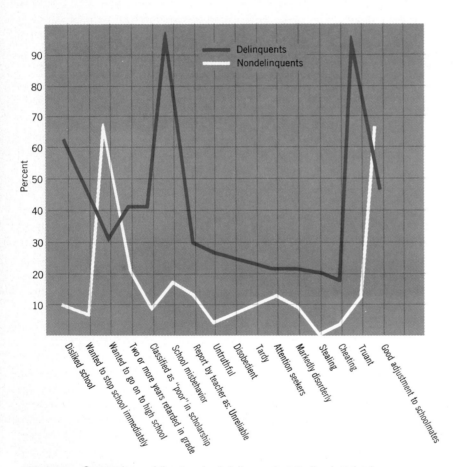

FIG. 15-4. Comparison of five hundred delinquents with five hundred nondelinquents, all from inner-city homes, with respect to attitudes and behavior toward school (Glueck, 1953).

scale which they claimed enabled the very early prediction of future delinquent behavior. The New York City Youth Board, for example, made predictions for a number of children between the ages of five and one-half and six and reported that the predictions proved accurate in 86.5 percent of the cases. A more careful examination of their statistics, however, showed that the percentage of cases of delinquency predicted correctly was closer to 35 percent. The danger of using index figures to predict the future delinquency of a child lies in the possibility of making a "self-fulfilling prophecy." The Council of the Society for the Psychological Study of Social Issues, who analyzed the Youth Board's figures, pointed out that "children who are identified and labelled as probable future delinquents are likely to be treated and isolated as 'bad' children by teachers and others who are now subject to the virtually hysterical climate of opinion concerning juvenile delinquency. Such treatment is likely to increase the child's sense of social alienation and, thereby, increase the probability of his becoming delinquent or of developing other forms of psychological maladjustment" (SPSSI, 1960). This is another instance of the dangers of labeling that Hobbs (1974) and Dreikurs (1952b) warned about, as we noted earlier.

A second group of juvenile delinquents are those who come from middle- and upper-class homes. Delinquency in these groups appears to be on the increase. Some of it can be blamed on parents who are overinvolved in activities outside the home, are too caught up in their own problems to be much concerned about their children, are literally afraid of their children and the problems they pose, or who openly or tacitly violate moral standards (Tobias, 1970).

In this respect, there is little difference between the delinquency of middle- and upper-class youth and that of lower-class youth: Families of delinquents of all social classes are characterized by more psychopathology than are families of nondelinquents. One should keep this basic fact in mind in evaluating the rather elaborate defenses that are often made of middle-class delinquency—the argument, for example, that young people have a right,

maybe even a duty, to rebel against adult society. Arguments of this kind are more usually made in defense of middle-class, rather than lower-class delinquency, and have been used to condone all kinds of minor and major delinquencies. There is nothing essentially new about these arguments; misbehaving upper- and middle-class adolescents have used them in one form or another for centuries. What is new is that some adults are now inclined to accept them at face value.

This accepting attitude has advantages and disadvantages. On the other hand, it permits a more understanding and sympathetic approach to adolescents and their problems that may, indeed, help clear the air and open up new channels of communication between the generations. On the other hand, there is the danger of overlooking the psychopathology inherent in the more serious and destructive forms of delinquency. As long as delinquency is perceived as virtuous or healthy, it cannot be dealt with successfully by psychotherapy, disciplinary measures, or any other form of treatment.

The attitude that more generally prevails in the adult world, however, is not that of condoning, defending, or even trying to understand delinquents and their behavior, but that of dealing with it severely. Public attitudes are typically unselective, impulsive, and repressive. This is particularly true after there has been an "incident"—a bombing or a school burning by unknown persons, or a police raid on a "sex orgy" or a "pot" party. At these times there is a tendency for public authorities—police, school administrators, and juvenile court judges—to "overreact" and to mete out severe punishments for minor misdemeanors and even for congregating on street corners and in other public places.

It is not easy to abandon traditional ideas and methods in favor of a more enlightened approach to delinquency. Unfortunately, it is more satisfying emotionally to punish a youthful delinquent than to spend a great deal of time, patience, and energy in understanding and working with him. The policy of patience and understanding does not go down well with citizens who want immediate action. Therefore schools and other public agencies that wish to deal intelligently with the problems of delinquency are often faced with the necessity of carrying on a continuing program of public education, if they wish to gain support for a more enlightened program of dealing with youthful delinquents.

Vulnerability to Delinquency

All children are at times subjected to pressures and temptations that pull or push them in the direction of delinquency. The children who yield to these pressures are the ones who are more vulnerable than the others or who have to cope with greater pressures. Children who spend the earlier years of their lives in family situations characterized by chronic anxiety, fear, hatred, and insecurity tend to be more vulnerable than other children. Because of the precarious conditions of life in deprived areas such as slums and migrant-worker camps, children from such environments are more vulnerable to the pressures and temptations of delinquency. Furthermore, because of the disturbances in family life during recent years, many middle-class and upper-class children have been rendered especially vulnerable; such conditions suggest themselves as a probable cause of the current increase in juvenile delinquency.

When children reach school age, the kind of community they live in begins to assume even greater importance. If the community is keenly interested in meeting the needs of youth through the development of effective schools, adequately supervised recreation, and well-equipped and staffed youth organizations, the pressures on youth to become delinquent will not be as strong.

On the other hand, communities in which citizens are apathetic or cynical and which shirk their responsibility toward the needs of youth unwittingly foster conditions that make it difficult for youth to resist pressures to engage in delinquent behavior.

The school has an important part to play in creating an atmosphere that strengthens the resistance of children to the pressures of delinquency. One of the ways in which it can play its part is to make school learning a vital and interesting experience. The youth who becomes bored, rebellious, or apathetic is the one who will maintain a record of poor attendance and who will drop out of school at the minimum age for leaving, if not before, if he can find a way. Once out of school, he is a relatively easy prey to delinquency.

The best school programs for combating delinquency are those that are developed for reasons that are psychologically and educationally sound. If these programs are administered by dedicated, sympathetic teachers who are genuinely interested in young people and their problems, who are supported by administrators and school boards, and who are "backed up" by counselors who are both available and helpful, then problems of delinquency are likely to diminish. On the other hand, programs that are developed in an atmosphere of fear and tension, and are supervised by adults who regard every adolescent as a potential delinquent, have little chance for success. Often it takes a crisis for a school system to examine its educational program critically, but reforms should be planned and adopted not to "keep delinquency under control" but to involve both teachers and students in programs that are worthwhile for their own sake.

The Severely Disturbed Child

Thus far in this chapter we have said little about the child who does not come under any of the headings that we have mentioned but who needs help, not because of some special reason such as delinquency or the inability to read, but simply because he is emotionally disturbed. A child who has severe emotional problems, however, is likely to display other symptoms, that is, he may stammer or be retarded in his reading or have difficulties in getting along with other children. Disturbance in one aspect of life usually leads to or is accompanied by disturbance in other areas of life. On the other hand, there are many children who have rather severe emotional problems but who somehow "get along." The teacher may not notice them because they are doing average or acceptable work for their age and grade and are not disturbing classroom routines. Sometimes these children are identified by the discrepancy between their IQs and their achievement; sometimes they say or write revealing things about their problems; sometimes the report comes to the teacher at second or third hand.

Emotionally disturbed children are likely to have educational as well as adjustment problems. Of a sample of 116 children referred to the Child Psychiatry Service of the State University of Iowa, almost 60 percent were below normal limits for their age in reading ability and 74 percent were below in arithmetic. Only 20 percent were above the norm in reading and 9 percent in arithmetic (Stone and Rowley, 1964). Sometimes the first clue a teacher has that a child is emotionally troubled is the fact that he is having difficulty in learning.

Teachers generally do a rather good job of identifying children who need special psychological help. A follow-up study done by Marian J. FitzSimons (1958) with students referred fifteen to eighteen years earlier by teachers in Grosse Pointe, Michigan, shows that teachers were able to identify with a high degree of accuracy those students who became delinquent and those who became seriously disturbed emotionally.

The teacher has the problem of deciding, when he encounters a student he thinks is emotionally disturbed, what he should do. He has to determine whether he has the time to follow through, whether proper facilities—child guidance services, school psychologists, or school social workers—will be available in the event the child must be referred for further help, and whether his attempt to help would be disturbing or even resented. Sometimes it is best not to interfere with a child's struggles to maintain a somewhat precarious emotional balance amid the conflicting forces and events in his life. As we have noted previously, even children who are badly mistreated by their parents tend to have a strong loyalty to them. We used to think that the best policy was to take children out of unsatisfactory homes, but now we are more inclined to keep families together and try to help create healthier relationships within them. Hence it is best for teachers to go slowly—to "feel their way," in effect—in attempting to help children with emotional problems. If a child is having trouble with his school work or in his adjustments at school, the teacher's role is somewhat clearer, for he has a "legitimate" reason for entering the picture, although it is best, under such circumstances, to proceed slowly and cautiously. But if there is no obvious difficulty at school, the teacher should decide on the extent to which he can include the roles of social worker or psychotherapist in his professional role as a teacher. It is usually helpful and desirable to discuss problems of this sort with psychologists, guidance workers, or administrators.

There are no easy ways to deal with the problems of disturbed children. Even highly skilled and sophisticated professionals have a high percentage of failures. This fact is brought out in a comparative study of four hundred boys from poverty homes—about equally divided as to black and white—who had been identified early in life as maladjusted. When the boys were in the seventh grade, they were divided into an experimental and a control group. The experimental group was enrolled in a Work-Study program—a program combining on-the-job employment and school work—with the expectation that its members would show improved social adjustment and earlier competence in adult social skills than the controls, who remained in the regular school program. Six years later, 55 percent of the youths in the experimental program still showed social and educational maladjustment. Those who had been identified as "work adaptive" and "school adaptive" had improved, but those who had been identified as "severely maladjusted," "marginal," and "erratic" had not. The failure of the program to aid more than one-half the subjects was explained by the authors in terms of a pathology-creating social environment, an environment that was characterized by a high incidence of "problem families." Their results led them to make five recommendations regarding the needs of maladjusted boys:

1. *Teachers with endless patience and determination.* Unfortunately, many teachers are unable or unwilling to develop the kind of flexibility basic to those qualities.

2. *More male teachers.* Nearly every one of the four hundred boys had no close relationship with an adult male who led an orderly, stable life.

3. *Employers who are friendly and helpful.* The boys who were able to profit from the work experience got as much from the man-boy relation-

ship with their employers as they did out of the work skills they learned.

4. *Counselors in the early grades.* Counselors in the secondary schools are generally brought in after the damage has been done. It would make better sense to provide help in the third or fourth grade before serious trouble sets in.

5. *More tolerance on the part of the school and society for delinquent behavior.* Many boys of this type "grow out" of their adolescent maladjustment when they become adults, marry, and settle down as employed citizens (Ahlstrom and Havighurst, 1971).

It is not always feasible to provide early treatment for children's problems. School psychologists, counselors, and social workers characteristically have more patients than they can handle, and many a teacher is left to cope with the problem as best he can. Nor is there any certainty that psychotherapy will give children the help they need. Carolyn Ashcraft (1970) compared the scholastic performance of emotionally disturbed children who were given psychological treatment with the performance of children who were not. The treated children tended to do better than the untreated children for about two years and then declined. At the end of five years, they were worse off than the untreated children. Ashcraft suggested that a psychological follow-up of the children after treatment had been terminated might have enabled them to sustain their initial improvement. She also raised questions as to whether the standard diagnostic procedures used by psychologists are appropriate. Like others who have written on the subject, she urged that teachers and parents learn to recognize significant indicators of emotional problems.

Irving N. Berlin (1965) has had many years of experience in consulting with teachers and other educational personnel on the problems of emotionally disturbed, neurologically handicapped, and other types of children with learning problems. What he has to say on this subject is relevant here:

Teachers must first become aware that these youngsters' problems are longstanding ones and will not be easily modified; thus, the teachers' self-expectations must be modest. Secondly, it is important that teachers recognize that the learning process itself provides therapeutic experiences for the child. A teacher's patient and persistent help to the child to take the next step in acquisition of skills and knowledge, despite the many obstacles, is vital to the child's feeling that someone cares and believes that he can be a more effective and successful human being. Third, the teacher needs help in understanding how each child's already acquired methods of dealing with adults in his environment can slowly be altered by new experiences, the teacher's behavior with the child. For example, the emotionally disturbed or neurologically handicapped child has often learned that his temper outbursts in the face of learning tasks usually result in the adult's vacillation and withdrawal of the task. Such a child desperately needs to experience an adult who can live through these temper outbursts with him and who can then firmly help him carry out the learning task. From such experiences, these children begin to develop a different image of themselves, the adults around them, and of their own capacities to learn.

Some research making use of analyses of video tape-recorded sessions of regular elementary classrooms, each containing one or more emotionally disturbed children, has shed some light on the way in which such children may be helped. Contrary to what most teachers believe, there appeared to be no particular techniques that "work" with such children. Instead, the level and kind of activity in which they were engaged reflected the general activity of the other members of the class. Teachers who were able to get *all* students interested and involved in the tasks of learning were the most successful in getting emotionally disturbed children involved as well. Likewise, teachers who had problems with the other class members also had problems with emotionally disturbed children. Teachers who showed the most awareness of what was going on in the classroom seemed to have the best success, both with the emotionally disturbed and with other pupils (Kounin, Friesen, and Norton, 1966).

Identifying "Exceptional Children"

Although we have, in the present chapter, taken up and discussed various factors that create special needs in students, it is to be hoped that discussing these factors will not encourage their being labeled or classified. Identifying a child as mentally retarded, delinquent, educationally handicapped, or emotionally disturbed often leads to "snap judgments" and stereotyped thinking. To quote Rudolf Dreikurs (1952b) once more on this subject:

> Despite our best efforts, exceptional children will remain so until society stops considering them as such, and treats them as human beings who are respected and needed. Then it will become apparent that it is less important what we have, than what we do with what we have. There is no human being—with the exception of the complete imbecile—who cannot be useful and contribute to the welfare of others. Usefulness and contribution are the real basis for social integration, in contrast to our prevalent assumption that superiority gives social status and inferiority deprives. The emphasis on each child's ability to be useful and to participate is the only means to bring the best out in him. Judgmental evaluation, comparison, criticism and humiliation may be effective with a very few, but are damaging to almost all. Success and failure become insignificant if we stop measuring and comparing, judging and condemning. Then alone can we stimulate children in their development and function, not toward becoming a success, but toward becoming a useful social being, who has a secure place in the group regardless of what he is and how much he can do.

SUMMARY

Although it has been traditional in education to feel that children should adapt themselves to the school, there is a growing belief that the school should meet the needs of the children—even the needs of children who require more than the usual amount of educational services. When schools successfully meet the needs of children who require special help, they have been able to do so only by individualizing instruction. Approximately 13 percent of students can be classified as "exceptional children," but less than half of these are enrolled in special programs. Speech-impaired and mentally retarded children comprise about two-thirds of those receiving special instruction. The more chronic and severe the child's problem, the longer he must receive specialized help and the more adjustments must be made in the curriculum, methods, and the learning environment. The attitudes that exceptional children have toward themselves, as well as the attitudes that others have toward them, often complicate efforts to help them learn. Labeling children as atypical or typical, according to their problems, seems to be more of a hindrance than a help. Exceptional children are more likely to experience failure; this leads to discouragement, an attitude that is aggravated when adults try to overprotect them.

Terms such as "idiot," "imbecile," and "moron" have been replaced by "slow learner" in the professional vocabulary, in an attempt to focus on their main problem in school. The various degrees of mental retardation are: 25 IQ and below, "custodial"; 25 to 50 IQ, "trainable"; and 50 to 70 IQ, "educable." The policy in most schools to deal with slow learners administratively, by nonpromotion, has no advantages, only disadvantages. Slow learners have better social adjustment and make more progress in reading if they are promoted along with their age-mates.

Intellectually gifted children have more educational problems than is commonly supposed. Our tendency to expect a very high level of academic performance of them may serve to complicate their problems. Schools that want to provide special treatment for these children may do one of three things: accelerate them, enrich the learning situation, or assign them to special classes in some kind of system in which students are grouped according to their scores on mental-ability tests. Acceleration produces the best consistent results but meets with the most disfavor from teachers and administrators, who feel that a child may miss something important if he skips grades or that he may be socially or psychologically immature. Instead they favor enrichment or ability grouping. The trend is to stress training for creativity, rather than special enrichment programs for the gifted, but ability grouping is still extensively used. Research thus far has failed to produce any evidence favoring homogeneous ability grouping but shows, instead, that it tends to increase anxieties and feelings of inadequacy among children who are put in the slower groups. Teachers' expectations also appear to influence the amount of learning that will take place. In spite of negative research findings, teachers continue to favor the use of ability grouping, perhaps because it seems to eliminate the necessity of varied preparations. Grouping can be defended when a teacher uses it in an informal and flexible way to deal with various learning levels in his classroom. Administratively, however, random or heterogeneous grouping is preferable in assigning students to classes.

Most children who have special education needs also have emotional problems of some sort. Communication disorders—such as speech and reading difficulties—are common. Very often speech and reading problems are an outgrowth of children's early, difficult relations with parents. Although communication disorders are often treated tutorially, they are likely to be the result of emotional causes and to require psychological treatment in connection with special instruction. Behavior modification methods also have been used successfully.

The problems faced by delinquent children are generally more difficult and complex than those of other "exceptional children" because of the hostility and resentment they must face from society. Because we have less sympathy with delinquent children, we are likely to worsen their situation by drastic treatment of some sort. According to Allison Davis, some delinquent behavior is not so much willful misbehavior as it is a normal behavior pattern of lower-class groups. But a study by Sheldon and Eleanor Glueck indicates that there are factors which predispose some children from underprivileged areas to delinquency. Delinquent behavior outside of school is usually accompanied by misbehavior in school, retardation, truancy, and a general distaste for school. Middle-class delinquency has been on the increase, perhaps because of family problems. Middle-class youth are more inclined to argue that their delinquencies are justified rebellions against adult society. This does not make their actions any the less pathological and does make treatment more difficult. The school, as well as the other agencies of the community, can help reduce delinquency by becoming a more psychologically attractive and interesting place for youth. Youth's

vulnerability to delinquency is increased if school is the kind of dreary, uninteresting place from which one must escape to find satisfaction and freedom.

Some children need special help, not so much because of abilities or disabilities, but because they are emotionally disturbed. When teachers discover these children, they must decide how much help they can give them or whether they should be referred to professional workers or agencies who specialize in helping children with emotional problems. There are no easy answers to the question of what to do with emotionally disturbed children. Even skilled specialists are often unsuccessful, and much depends on the teacher's skill, patience, and firmness.

Above all, teachers are urged not to label children as "exceptional" but to treat each child as an individual who deserves respect and is entitled to as much help as he needs—but no more—in his task of learning to become a mature and adequate person.

Suggested Problems

1. Visit the local office of the State Bureau of Vocational Rehabilitation or the Vocational Rehabilitation Office of the local Veterans Administration (having first written or telephoned for an appointment). What are some of the key problems they encounter in their work, particularly with regard to the attitudes of their clients and the general public?

2. What facilities are available in your community to help families who have children with special needs of the kind we have listed or described in this chapter? What kind of services do they offer—financial assistance, vocational counseling, casework, psychotherapy, placement? How extensive is the help they provide?

3. What psychological and social work services are available in your community for children who become delinquent? What work of a rehabilitational nature does the Juvenile Court do to help delinquents become emotionally healthy and socially mature? What is the Court or the community doing to prevent delinquency?

4. What would some of the chief arguments be for and against placing a severely disabled child—

blind, deaf, cerebral-palsied, or mentally deficient—in an institution as compared with keeping him at home and letting him attend special classes or schools in his community?

5. What are some of the important factors or conditions that make children "vulnerable" to delinquency?

6. It is common practice in many school systems to exempt from school the students who are considered too disturbed to profit from the school program. What are the arguments for and against this policy?

Suggested Readings

Borg, W. R. *An evaluation of ability grouping.* Logan: Utah State University, 1964. (Obtainable from the University Bookstore.) The most extensive study of ability grouping to date.

Donahue, G. T., and Nichtern, S. *Teaching the troubled child.* Glencoe, Ill.: Free Press, 1965. A study that takes issue with traditional methods that isolate emotionally disturbed children from their families, their peers, and the community. Suggests the use of "teacher-moms," who provide a meaningful one-to-one relationship.

Farber, B. *Mental retardation: Its social context and special consequences.* Boston: Houghton Mifflin, 1968.

Goldberg, M. L., Passow, A. H., and Justman, J. *The effects of ability grouping.* New York: Teachers College Press, 1966. A study of the effect various kinds of ability grouping had on the scholastic and psychological development of over two thousand elementary school children in New York City.

Hewitt, F. *The emotionally disturbed child in the classroom.* Boston: Allyn and Bacon, 1968.

Hobbs, N. *The futures of children.* San Francisco: Jossey-Bass, 1974. A compelling report conducted for the Department of Health, Education, and Welfare dealing with the effect that classification—labeling—has on exceptional children.

Kirk, S. A. *Educating exceptional children,* 2nd ed. Boston: Houghton Mifflin, 1972.

Lindgren, H. C., and Lindgren, F. (eds.). *Readings in educational psychology,* 2nd ed. New York: Wiley, 1972. Part 8 contains a number of selections dealing with the problems of students who need special attention.

Long, N. J., Morse, W. C., and Newman, R. G. (eds.). *Conflict in the classroom: The education of emotionally disturbed children.* Belmont, Calif.: Wadsworth, 1965. Contains many interesting selections dealing with the diagnosis and treatment of disturbed children in the classroom, as well as in the clinic.

Reynolds, M., and Davis, M. (eds.). *Exceptional children in regular classrooms.* Minneapolis: University of Minnesota Press, 1971.

Sarason, S. B., and Doris, S. *Psychological problems in mental deficiency,* 4th ed. New York: Harper and Row, 1969.

Witty, P. A. (ed.). *The educationally retarded and disadvantaged,* 66th Yearbook, Part I. Chicago: National Society for the Study of Education, 1967.

Woody, R. H. *Behavioral problem children in the schools.* New York: Appleton-Century-Crofts, 1969.

16

Problems of the Socially Disadvantaged Learner

Social Deprivation and Poverty

The continued presence of poverty in the world's richest land is a fact that has troubled many Americans and is a matter for deep concern and even guilt. Therefore when President Johnson declared a "War on Poverty" in 1964, most Americans readily agreed with him that there was a need to provide "every citizen with the opportunity to advance his welfare to the limit of his capabilities."

In America, it is virtually a national credo that public education should provide the means for developing capabilites and advancing one's welfare, and for this reason, among others, schools have been made free and open to all who can profit from them.

The presence of so many poor people is evidence, however, that the formula of personal success through free education has not worked for a good many. Inasmuch as virtually all children spend some time in the schools, one obvious explanation of continued poverty is that schools have failed in their responsibility to provide millions of children with the help they need to improve their economic situation.

In the early days of the "War on Poverty," much money and time was spent by various governmental agencies in investigating the cause of the schools' failure. One result of these investigations has been the publication of a monumental report of the work done by a task force of researchers headed by James S. Coleman (1966). The Coleman group administered achievement test and self-report questionnaires to approximately six hundred thousand children enrolled in grades 1, 3, 6, 9, and 12 in about four thousand schools that were largely representative of all levels, but that had some deliberate overrepresentation of minority group children. In general, the findings showed that the socioeconomic background of the children in a school was the most significant predictor of their performance. In other words, students in schools populated largely by middle-class children had much higher achievement test scores than did students in schools populated by children largely from homes "below the poverty line." Furthermore, minority-group children tended to do better when they were not in racially segregated schools. These findings are generally consistent with other research done before and since the Coleman report. Nancy H. St. John (1970) noted, in a review of such research, that following the desegregation of schools, students generally perform no worse and in most instances do better. She also observed that desegregation often brought educational changes (in Washington and Louisville, for example) that provided a psychological boost for teachers.

Students from poverty homes, whose progress (or lack of it) is a matter of deep concern to educators, are the ones who are variously described as "socially disadvantaged" or "culturally deprived." Both these terms have been criticized by social reformers, but no other term has been proposed that meets with general acceptance. Both terms are in common use by sociologists, psychologists, social workers, and educators, although there has been a trend toward preferring "socially disadvantaged" or simply "disadvantaged."

Socially disadvantaged children are those who grow up in various cultures or subcultures outside the middle-class culture. They make up a sizable proportion of the school population in most countries of the world. The common denominator that characterizes these children is poverty, and the majority of them live in urban and rural slums. In the United States, most disadvantaged children are white, but substantial numbers of them belong to minority groups, especially blacks, American Indians, Puerto Ricans, and Mexican-Americans, whose poverty is made all the more burdensome by racial or ethnic discrimination and prejudice.

Although the law in each state requires children to attend school, it cannot force them to learn. This does not create much of a problem for middle-class children. In the main, they learn more-or-less willingly and respond to teachers' demands and expectations with some eagerness. Socially disadvantaged children, however, often seem unable to respond to classroom instruction as readily as the children of middle-class families. Growing up poor, many of them seem unable to learn the skills and attitudes that are required if they are to escape from a poverty environment, and they thus find themselves doomed to lives of frustration and apathy. As Lee Rainwater (1970) has said, "The lower-class world is defined by two tough facts of life as it is experienced from day to day and from birth to death. These are the facts of deprivation and exclusion. . . ." And, further, "Lower-class subculture . . . can be regarded as the historical creation of persons who are disinherited by their society. . . ."

Our urbanized, industrialized culture grows more complex with each succeeding year. This complexity is to a significant degree a reflection of the fact that the needs and interests of our population are growing more diverse. This complexity also allows for a greater degree of individuality and self-expression, but only for those persons who have learned the kinds of skills and attitudes that are needed to function within such a culture. Those who do not learn these skills and attitudes find themselves to an increasing degree alienated from the rest of society. As they stand on the outside, looking in, they are unable to understand why it is that they do not enjoy the benefits and freedoms that others seem to have just for the asking. It does little good to explain to them that economic and social rewards in our culture must be earned; that the attainment of these rewards takes long-range personal planning, as well as work that is at times tedious, at times interesting, but always demanding; and that a reasonable degree of personal commitment and dedication is essential. They are unable or unwilling to accept such explanations and instead prefer their own oversimplified version, namely, that success is a matter of luck or chance. They maintain that inasmuch as they are the unlucky ones, they will never succeed by their own efforts, and it is therefore the responsibility of the successful (lucky) person to share his good fortune with them. Their usual reaction to their own status tends to be one of apathy and resignation, but the accumulation of resentment and frustration sometimes boils over in the form of urban riots or sporadic episodes of crime and violence.

Legislators and the general public are beginning to realize that because the attitudes and expectations of the socially disadvantaged and the school are so far apart, the educational system does not work very well for a large minority of the nation's children.[1] Some children from disadvantaged homes are able to respond to the demands of the system and to progress satisfactorily through the secondary schools and even in universities, but the majority never really become fully integrated. The

---

[1] Just how many children come from homes in which self-perpetuating poverty prevails is hard to say. The most conservative estimate is 15 percent, which breaks down, on a nationwide basis, into 20 million English-speaking Caucasians, 8 million blacks, 3 million Spanish-speaking, and one-half million American Indians (Havighurst, 1970). The proportion of children from poverty homes is much higher in metropolitan schools and may even run as high as 70 percent in some cities, but the poorest families of all, white or black, are found in the rural South.

many federal, state, and local programs, staffed by paid professionals and volunteers, are a visible indication of the growing public awareness that our schools, as presently constituted, are failing to reach large numbers of lower-class children, and, in effect, are perpetuating their alienation from middle-class society.

PSYCHOLOGICAL EFFECTS OF SOCIAL DEPRIVATION

The Inner-city Environment

It may be well, as we begin this discussion of social deprivation, to describe in more detail one kind of environment that is likely to be populated by socially disadvantaged children. The environment from which most of them come is not as confused, disintegrated, or turbulent as the one we are about to describe, but most inner-city settings possess some of its qualities.

This particular slum was created almost overnight, when the New York City government took over an old hotel and filled it with indigent families. The changes that took place in the neighborhood are described vividly by the late Samuel Tenenbaum (1963):

Hordes of children, like milling cattle, cluttered the once empty street; children of all ages, from one year to—well, they looked like eighteen and twenty. Boys and girls mixed in packs, and it was difficult to think of them as single, individual children. They shouted, they screamed, they pushed, they fought. In the midst of play, they would suddenly get into individual fights and collective fights. Violence, aggression, play, and friendliness seemed all mixed up. Every wall on the block was used, either to play ball on or to throw things on. The streets became cluttered with debris, especially broken glass. Where they got all this glass to break is beyond me. The area around this hotel became one vast accumulation of litter. Also, it was quite common for children to throw things at passersby. The parents apparently did not object, for I never saw a parent rep-

rimand a child for this. The children resembled an uncontrolled, undisciplined herd, doing what they wished, with neither mother nor father in sight to curb, admonish, or chastise. . . .

The parents of the children . . . acted strangely. In all states of undress, they hung out of windows, while below mixed adult groups, and groups including children congregated, drinking beer, joshing, pushing each other about and carrying on in a merry and boisterous way through all hours of the night. . . .

Tenenbaum lived in a respectable middle-class apartment house across the street from the old hotel. His neighbors were understandably consternated by the transformation that had taken place:

There was one type of behavior, however, that affected my neighbors beyond all others. I cannot say that they liked to see children smoking or engaged in open sex play; it violated their sense of morality. But they could somehow stand that. What they couldn't stand, what frightened them, was the violent, hostile way in which lower-class families found their amusement. An almost palpable atmosphere of aggression and violence hovered over the street. The children would attack an automobile—literally attack it as locusts attack a field—climb on top of it, get inside, and by combined co-operative effort shake and tug until they left it a wreck. The older men would strip the tires from a car and sell them. A three wheeled delivery bicycle from a local merchant provided a special holiday. The children gathered from nowhere and everywhere, piled on the delivery bicycle, and drove it up and down the street loaded with humanity. When they made no dent in the vehicle by this misuse, in disgust they poked at it and pushed it in an effort to make it come apart. I have never seen young people work so assiduously as they did riding, pushing, and shaking the cart. They didn't give up until it was completely destroyed. I have seen children, several of whom could not have been more than seven or eight years old, at this job of destruction past 10 P.M.; and they all appeared to be having

the merriest time. Even their innocent, friendly play was violent. Suddenly, strong, tall, gangling adolescent boys would dash pell-mell down the street, like stampeding cattle, shrieking and screaming, pushing, shoving, mauling each other.

Tenenbaum continued his analysis by speculating on the problems that such children would have in the typical school, organized as it is to teach and perpetuate middle-class values and behavior:

I could see how wrong, how incongruous and meaningless this school was for lower-class children; how their very being was an irritant to it, and to them; how ill-prepared they were for the demands of the school; how what they were and how they lived would elicit from their middle-class teachers scorn, resentment, rejection, hostility, and—worst of all—how these children would create in their teachers fear, a physical, sickening fear, as thirty or forty of them crowded together in one room hour after hour, day after day. This was the most demoralizing feature of all. For once fear sets in, you can no longer understand, appreciate, or help; what you want is distance, separation, safety; or if this is impossible, you want the backing of superior strength or a counter fear; and one cannot educate or help another human being through force or fear.

. . . Like my neighbors, teachers remain in a perpetual state of fear of these children, at their acting out, their defiance of discipline, their destructiveness and vandalism. "Look what they did!" a teacher will say, pointing to a desk ripped open or shattered panes of glass, speaking as if some holy altar had been violated. Looking at these lower-class children distantly, unapprovingly, and judgmentally, as my neighbors did, many teachers feel trapped, frightened, helpless. Like my neighbors, when a child gets into trouble with the law, they often take a smug satisfaction in the tragedy, as if their original judgment had been vindicated. "I knew he would come to a bad end." Middle-class virtue is written all over them.

Some conclusions of a research team headed by Salvador Minuchin (1967) are consistent with Tenenbaum's observations. The behavior of children from slum families, they noted, showed the effects of impermanence and unpredictability in home and family life. This showed up particularly in the socialization of children: Parents' responses to children's behavior seemed to be random and were concerned more with getting them to stop doing what they were doing instead of guiding them into desirable behavior patterns. This random inhibition of behavior and lack of guidance make it difficult for children to "internalize" the behavioral norms and values that are basic to successful group life. In such families, a communication system evolves in which people do not expect to be heard and disagreements are never resolved.

It is no surprise that the behavior of children from these families is characterized by inattention and impulsive, random responses to the social and physical environment. Such training as children get tends to focus their attention on the person who addresses them, rather than on the message itself. This obviously makes it difficult for children to participate in classroom teaching-learning processes, and creates disturbances in their cognitive learning style. Disadvantaged children also learn to attend primarily to the everchanging physical aspects of adult behavior and to be adept at making rapid maneuvers to cope with it. As a consequence, slum children have difficulty in maintaining the sustained attention necessary for conceptual problem solving, heuristic or otherwise.

The Socially Deprived Preschool Child

Some examples of what happens when socially deprived children enter the classroom have been contributed by Newton S. Metfessel and J. T. Foster (1965), who conducted a series of observations in a preschool setting. Here are their conclusions, together with examples of the kind of difficulties experienced by these children and their teachers:

1. *Disadvantaged children seem generally unaware of the "ground rules" for success in school settings.*

A child disrupted group activity by making silly noises and facial expressions. He was removed from the group, the problem was discussed with him, but he resumed his disturbing behavior when he was returned to the group.

One child came late to school, interrupted a group story by saying in a whining voice that there was sand in his shoes. The teacher told him that he could empty the shoes outside and went back to reading the story. A short time later she looked up to see him shaking sand out of his shoes onto the floor.

2. *Disadvantaged children are less able to learn from being told than are middle-class children.*

Although the teacher held repeated discussions with children with regard to the need to observe safety regulations and follow the "traffic-circle" protocol when using wheeled toys, one child persisted in going in the wrong direction and was surprised when his fire truck rammed an Irish Mail.

A child was asked to sit and talk with the teacher about crashing into another child's tricycle, but found many excuses for getting up and running off.

A policeman visited the school and talked to the children about the need to be careful in crossing the street. The next day when the teacher showed the children a picture of a policeman helping a child across the street, they insisted he was taking the child to jail. Although the teacher persisted in questioning the children, they were still unable to tell her that he was helping the child across the street.

3. *Disadvantaged children are often unable to make simple symbolic interpretations.*

When one child was shown a picture of an apple and was asked what he saw that was round and good to eat, he said "Chicken."

4. *Disadvantaged children tend to have short attention spans and consequently have difficulty in following directions.*

A child who had been working with a group decorating Christmas wrapping paper, wandered away when he was not helped with a succeeding step by the teacher, even though the work of other children at the table could have been used as examples of what to do next.

5. *Disadvantaged children have difficulty in using language in flexible ways.*

Although a child had been taught that there are a number of different kinds of animals, when the teacher introduced a picture of a cat with the words, "Now I'm going to show you a picture of an animal . . ." he interrupted by saying, "That's not an animal, that's a cat."

6. *Disadvantaged children tend to have little concept of relative size.*

A child was unable to select "the large piece of paper" while working on an art project, even though the teacher had shown the difference between paper sizes.

7. *Disadvantaged children are less likely to perceive adults as people to whom they can turn for help.*

A child who wanted to use a tricycle stood by and cried instead of asking a nearby teacher for the toy.

A child who was having difficulty in using a toy pounded at it in vain, although a teacher was standing nearby and would have helped him, if asked.

8. *Disadvantaged children seem to have a low level of curiosity about things.*

None of the children explored or investigated a barrel that had been placed out in the yard in a conspicuous place.

The teacher showed the children a box that jingled when shaken. When she asked them to guess what was in the box, none of the children responded.

9. *Disadvantaged children's experiences lie within a very narrow range.*

The teacher told the children a story and then asked them questions about it. It turned out that almost none of them had any idea of the animals mentioned in the story: cow, sheep, goat, duck, and bear.

Some of the children had never been to a park or a restaurant or cafe.

The Home of the Socially Disadvantaged Child

One middle-class value that has great importance both for child rearing and for school practice is that each person is an individual, with rights, privileges, freedoms, and responsibilities that help to define and maintain his individuality. This principle is less important or completely ignored in homes of socially disadvantaged children. Children there are less likely to be regarded as individuals with different personalities—they are just "young'uns." This comes about partly because there are likely to be many children spaced closely together, thus making it difficult for parents to give any single child much individual attention without neglecting the others. Furthermore, lower-class life is always precarious: There are many crises and crushing problems. Hence parental attention that might ordinarily be directed toward children is likely to be distracted by some situation that demands immediate attention, such as trying to talk the man from the loan agency out of repossessing the family car, looking for a job, or trying to salvage something out of the family dinner that fell on the floor when the rickety old table collapsed.

Obtaining nourishing food in proper quantities is always a problem in poverty homes. One survey of newborn children showed that infants of poor mothers were about 15 percent smaller than those of other mothers from the same neighborhoods and were more likely to have anatomical defects (Naeye, Diener, and Dellinger, 1969). These findings help to explain the greater number of mentally retarded children with neurological defects born into families of the poor. Malnutrition can also affect children's cognitive functioning. In one experiment, the behavior of malnourished infant monkeys was compared with the behavior of normal monkeys. The malnourished monkeys were observed to behave like socially deprived or stimulus-deprived monkeys in other experiments in that they showed more fear and avoidance responses when presented with novel objects. The researchers felt that their results could be generalized to malnourished human infants as well: "With a decrease in responses to new stimulation and the development of response patterns which withdraw the infant from the environment, the stage is set for the production of a retarded organism" (Zimmerman, Strobel, and McGuire, 1970). In other words, it is difficult to tell whether the difficulties poverty children have in classroom learning situations are because of the sociopsychological features of early experience or malnutrition. Undoubtedly, both factors often make a contribution.

The way in which mothers of different social classes interact with their children may also be related to differences in the way children later respond to adults, and particularly to teachers. Steven R. Tulkin and Jerome Kagan (1970) observed the behavior of white middle- and working-class[2] mothers, each of whom had a ten-month-old daughter. Middle-class mothers were much more likely to interact verbally with their daughters: They initiated more vocalization, followed infant vocalization with comment, imitated infant vocalization, and praised infants more. It is interesting that the two groups of infants *produced* the same amount of vocalization; the difference was in the behavior of the mothers. Middle-class mothers more often entertained their infants by showing them pictures and giving them playthings. They responded more often and more quickly to infants' frets and were also more likely to react verbally, whereas working-class mothers were more inclined to placate their daughters with a bottle or cookie. Working-class mothers were less likely to believe that their daughters possessed adultlike emotions or the ability to communicate, and one working-class mother who spoke to her

---

[2] Although the working class is above the "poverty level," its cultural norms are much closer to those of the poverty class and can be considered to be suggestive of the kind of differences in child-rearing patterns that may be found in middle-class and poverty homes.

daughter often lamented that her friends ridiculed her for "talking to the kid like she was three years old."

Tulkin and Kagan observed that some of the differences between the behavior of the two groups of mothers may result from the fact that working-class mothers have less time to play with or talk to their children, but they concluded that the main difference was probably due to different beliefs about child development and life in general. The working-class mother, for example, is more likely to feel powerless to change her own environment and hence is less likely to try to influence her child's development, tending to take a fatalistic attitude.

The main tasks of school learning, as we have stated earlier, make heavy demand on verbal skills, and one of the principal differences among children of different social classes is their ability to function verbally. Research like that of Tulkin and Kagan suggests that social-class differences in school performance have their roots in the way children are treated from infancy onward by their parents. Middle-class parents believe in listening to and responding to their child, in trying to communicate with him on his level, and in attempting to adjust some of the conditions of the home to his particular interests and needs. The lower-class parent is less likely to attend to his children on an individual basis, even though he may be genuinely fond of them. He is also much more likely to agree with the statement: "Too much love and attention will spoil a child."

Jules Henry (1963) has pointed out that middle-class homes contain a "hidden curriculum" that enables children to adjust to their first school experiences. By this statement, Henry refers not so much to the incidental information and the verbal skills that middle-class children pick up during preschool years, but to the orientation that they obtain to life in general and to themselves as individuals. But the most significant part of a middle-class child's early training, as far as school success is concerned, is the kind of reinforcement for behavior he receives and learns to expect.

The psychological advantages are not all on the side of the middle-class child, of course. In contrast

SOCIALLY DISADVANTAGED LEARNERS

Families of disadvantaged children are characterized by the common denominators of poverty, poor housing, low educational level, and a sense of being alienated from the mainstream of society. Although the majority are rural, English-speaking Caucasians, those who are black, Spanish-surnamed, American Indian, or Eskimo suffer a double handicap by being more visible and by having to cope with the demands and expectations of two different cultures.

to middle-class children, inner-city children are likely to be more direct and spontaneous and are often more anxious to please adults. Personal pride and family loyalties are often stronger among inner-city children, perhaps more so in some subcultures than in others. Observers have also commented on the generosity, friendliness, and warmth of inner-city children.

Rewards: Ego, Social, and Direct

In our earlier discussions of learning, we mentioned the operant theory of learning, a theory holding that we learn to repeat certain forms of behavior that have become reinforced because they have become associated with or rewarded by pleasurable or satisfying stimuli. One of the problems with applying such a theory to classroom learning has been the matter of determining what kind of stimuli will be reinforcing for students. Evidently, there are significant differences between what is rewarding and reinforcing for lower-class students and what performs the same function for middle-class students. An experiment conducted by Roger A. Johnson (1974) produced results that are consistent with this conclusion. In this experiment, children in grades 3 through 5 attending a rural school in Georgia were divided into advantaged and disadvantaged groups on the basis of whether they were qualified to receive free lunches at the school. The children were given a number of tasks from the Torrance Tests of Creative Thinking. Some were told that if they worked hard at the assignment they would receive a prize; others were told nothing. Results showed that the creativity scores of the disadvantaged children were significantly higher when they were promised a reward than under the no-reward conditions, whereas the scores of the more advantaged children were actually a little higher when no mention was made of a reward. In actuality, one can say that some reinforcement was available in the no-reward condition because some of the children found the creativity task intrinsically interesting and hence rewarding. This type of satisfaction is what is termed an "ego reward." It is symbolic and abstract in nature, whereas a prize is "real."

The outcome of this experiment is somewhat similar to one conducted by Zigler and his associates (1962), which we mentioned briefly in Chapter 4. In their experiment middle-class children performed better when they were reinforced with ego rewards in the form of praise or being told they were correct, whereas lower-class children did best when they were given prizes.

The children's performance in the two experiments is consistent with what can be observed in most classrooms. In other words, middle-class children apply themselves to learning tasks if reinforced by social rewards, such as the approval of the teacher, either expressed on the spot, so to speak, or communicated at the end of the term in the form of a grade. Middle-class children also respond positively to ego rewards, that is, they apply themselves because they get pleasure out of learning a skill or completing a task and knowing that it is done correctly. They are, in effect, *self*-reinforcing. This is a tremendous advantage for the teacher of some thirty or forty children because it means, for example, that when children are doing "seat work," he does not have to go around the class and say or do something encouraging to each child every few problems or so. The teaching machine developed along Skinner's principles which we discussed in Chapter 8 also depends on ego reinforcement. The student answers the problem and then checks to see whether he was correct. The knowledge that he was indeed correct is assumed to be sufficient reinforcement for him to go on to the next problem.

Lower-class children are much less likely to be reinforced by these more or less indirect methods. They prefer rewards that are concrete. School grades represent both social and ego rewards for middle-class students, and poor grades are likely to arouse both guilt and anxiety. James Olsen (1965) says:

For the middle-class child, how one does on a test determines one's mark and that determines promotion and the likelihood of future academic success. When a teacher threatens a middle-class child with a failing grade, he is really threatening the basis of that student's personal worth.

Children from socially disadvantaged homes, however, are less likely to be moved by grades. Nor do the other kinds of social reinforcers, either positive or negative, have much effect:

Unlike middle-class children, the lower-class child rarely responds to moral exhortations which are intended to evoke feelings of guilt or shame.

What Happens When Rewards Are Postponed

Another point relates to the time interval between completion of a step in a learning task and the reinforcement or reward. In general, learning is likely to be accelerated if reinforcement is applied promptly. This is not feasible in most school situations. In the seat work example given above, the teacher would find it impossible to reinforce the learning behavior of each student with each increment of progress. Instead, reinforcement is postponed until workbooks can be corrected and grades assigned. The experiences that middle-class children have had during early childhood have prepared them for such postponement of reward. From infancy on, they are told: "Eat your spinach and then you can have a chocolate sundae for dessert." "If you are a good boy this week, Grandad will take you to the rodeo Saturday."

Socially disadvantaged children are unable to have much confidence in a social system in which the payoff is largely in future reward. In Chapter 4, we described an experiment conducted by Walter Mischel (1958), who found that children from father-absent homes were inclined to accept small, immediate rewards in preference to large, future ones. Richard T. Walls and Tennie S. Smith (1970) used Mischel's approach with children in the second and third grades and found that disadvantaged children were less likely to accept a delayed reward. With some training, they were able to get the children to

accept longer delays, but they were unable to get them up to middle-class norms.

Socially disadvantaged children have difficulty in visualizing *any* future reward, and are inclined to regard the school as a fairly risky situation. Rewards for them have to be not only concrete, but immediate. In their world, promises mean nothing; what counts is what they get right now. This is another reason why school marks mean little to them. Not only are marks social or ego rewards that count for little in their world, but they also appear hours, days, weeks, and even months after the behavior to which they are appropriate has taken place. As a consequence, the child is unable to perceive any relationship between school marks and his performance in learning tasks. If he gives marks any meaning at all, it is in terms of whether the teacher likes him or not.

Some research and comments by Albert H. Yee (1968) are relevant here. He found that teacher attitudes of warmth and permissiveness were more important to lower-class than to middle-class children. Unfortunately, teachers tend to regard lower-class children more negatively than middle-class children, and the more teaching experience they have, the more negative their attitudes become.

n Aff Versus n Ach

Although the socially disadvantaged child is likely to feel isolated from the middle-class culture represented by the teacher and school, his need to belong is undiminished. Actually, his need for affiliation (n Aff) is likely to run higher than that of the middle-class child. Living as he does in a primarily hostile culture, family and group ties are very important to him. A lower-class family may be split by endless quarrels and feuds, but it will unite to defend a child or adolescent who has been threatened by an outsider: a gang, another family, or the police. It does not matter what the youngster has done or whether he was the instigator; the fact that he is under attack is enough to bring his family or his gang rallying around him.

Such group solidarity does, however, have its price. Culturally deprived people tend to be quite suspicious of the motives of anyone in their group who wishes to better himself. The slum resident who tries to become middle-class is regarded with jealousy and downright hostility: He is accused of being "uppity," "too good for his friends," or "trying to become one of *them.*" Lower-class people tend to believe that a person can improve his lot only at the expense of others. In factories where piecework systems prevail, lower-class workers will limit their production to what they believe is adequate and refuse to work harder and make more money because of the fear that the pay rate would be lowered, whereupon they would have to work still harder to make the same amount of money. Workers tend to feel that they are better off if they present a united front against the employers and thus remain free to make their own decisions as to how much they should produce. The few workers who produce more are regarded as traitors, harassed, made the targets for abuse, and called "rate busters." This attitude of intense loyalty to the group, accompanied by discouragement of individual effort and achievement, affects the performance of lower-class school children, as well as that of their parents. The need for achievement (n Ach) is not likely to be very strong when n Aff dominates students' motivation. If achieving means being successful in academic competition, such a student prefers not to achieve.

"Good Behavior" Versus Achievement

Although some lower-class parents maintain a defiantly hostile attitude toward school and school authorities, just as they do toward other governmental agencies that levy demands on them, most of them make at least a show of compliance. They are, after all, members of a national culture in which school is considered to be a "good thing." They may not understand the reasons *why* school is valued in our culture, but they understand enough to know that children should be sent to school, and that they should "behave themselves" while there.

Indeed, "good behavior" may be emphasized by them to the exclusion of other aspects of school life. A lower-class child is likely to be admonished by his mother to "Be good, do what the teacher tells you, and don't get into trouble." A middle-class child is exhorted to "See if you can't get *all* your arithmetic problems correct today," or "How about making an A in social studies instead of a B!" The lower-class parent glows with pride when the teacher says, "He's a good boy," but the middle-class parent is more concerned with the child's progress and wants to know, "Is she doing any better in spelling?"

SOCIAL DISADVANTAGE AND COGNITIVE DEVELOPMENT

Differences in Rates of Cognitive Development

In our chapter on intelligence and creativity, we suggested that the IQ is a useful and convenient index to human effectiveness and competency. Although the IQ is certainly not absolute or definitive, it can be used as a general measure of the cognitive functioning of people studied collectively. We would therefore expect that differences between socially deprived and enriched environments would be reflected in differences in IQ. Benjamin S. Bloom (1964) of the University of Chicago has done an intensive study of environmental effects on human characteristics and reports that a conservative estimate of the difference between a deprived and an enriched environment is 20 IQ points. In other words, persons who might get IQs of around 100 in an enriched environment would be expected to receive IQs of around 80 in an impoverished one. Twenty IQ points is, as Bloom points out, a considerable gap. It can make the difference between institutionalization and a reasonably productive life in society, or it can make the difference between a professional career and a semiskilled job.

Bloom also points out that the earlier children have the kinds of experience (social and intellectual stimulation) that are consistent with later success, the greater is the likelihood that they will develop the skills and attitudes relevant to success. Early environment is thus more significant for development than later environment. Figure 16-1 shows how this principle works. Notice that black students

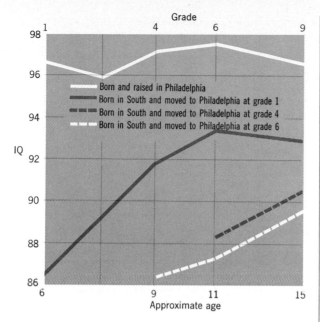

FIG. 16-1. Changes in IQ for black students born and raised in Philadelphia, as contrasted with those who came to Philadelphia when they were in the first, fourth, and sixth grades, respectively (Bloom, 1964, after data by Lee, 1951).

born and raised in Philadelphia maintained the same mean IQ (in the 96 to 97 range), whereas the IQ level reached by other black students depended on when they left the more rural environment of the Southern states for the more stimulating, urban environment of Philadelphia. Children who arrived when they were first-graders started with a mean IQ of 86 but had attained a mean IQ of 93 by the ninth grade. Those who did not arrive in Philadelphia until they were in the fourth or sixth grade showed some improvement but not as much as those who had arrived as first-graders or who were born in Philadelphia.

IQ and Social Deprivation

There are two important observations that we should make about lower-class IQs at this point. One is that they tend to decline with age during childhood, and the other is that they are not as good predictors of school success as they are for middle-class students. Let us consider these points in order.

During the early days of intelligence testing, Hugh Gordon (1923) did an intensive study of British canal boat and gypsy children. Both groups of children attended school only a few days a month and both showed declines in IQ. The fact that their IQs declined did not mean that children were becoming less intelligent with each succeeding year, but rather that they were growing mentally at a slower rate than other children. Hence they were dropping farther and farther behind with each succeeding year. Their *relative* position in their age group dropped each year; therefore their IQs showed a decline. The same thing happens to socially disadvantaged children in this country under usual conditions. A study by Robert L. Green and Louis J. Hofmann (1965) of black children in rural Virginia shows how their IQs drop with each succeeding age group. Although socially disadvantaged, these children had the benefit of some schooling. A second group that was unable to attend school because of a legal dispute over racial desegregation showed somewhat less overall decline in IQ, but the IQs were markedly lower (see Firgure 16-2).

Mental growth that lags behind the norm is accompanied by lags in school performance. In other words, the child whose IQ is declining year after year tends to fall further and further behind in his school work. Let us take reading as an example, for intelligence-test scores are highly correlated with reading-test scores. A child who has an IQ of 90 in the first grade has, shall we say, an IQ of 82 in the third grade. By now he is reading at the second-grade level. When he is in the sixth grade, he has an IQ of 74 and is reading at the third-grade level. In three years he has progressed one grade in reading ability. He has gone ahead but at only one-half the rate of the average school child. One of the goals of the "intervention" programs—the attempts to provide enriched educational experiences for disadvantaged children—is that of halting declines in IQ. We will comment on this phenomenon further when we discuss the Early Training Program conducted by the George Peabody College for Teachers.

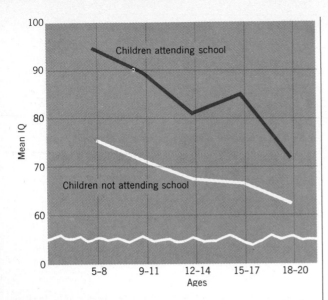

FIG. 16-2. Declines in IQ with age for two groups of socially disadvantaged black children and youth in Prince Edward County, Virginia. One group was educated elsewhere during a four-year period in which public schools did not operate, and the other group received no schooling (Green and Hofmann, 1965).

The second point, that intelligence-test scores are not as good predictors for disadvantaged children as they are for the more advantaged, is one we discussed in Chapter 14, where we mentioned the study by Robert Lee Green and William W. Farquhar (1965), who calculated correlations between verbal intelligence tests and grades for eleventh-graders in Detroit high schools. Correlations between the two variables were .62 and .21 for white boys and girls, respectively, in contrast to − .01 and .25 for black boys and girls. What is of particular interest is their finding that tests of academic achievement motivation correlated .37 and .55 for male and female black students, and .50 and .43 for male and female white students, thus indicating that the motivational measures were better than cognitive tests as predictors of school success for the black students.

Experiences of Black Children and Youth

One interpretation of these differences lies in the different experiences that middle-class white and inner-city black students have during childhood. The attitudes of black children toward themselves and toward school are, for example, more likely to be affected by their being targets of race prejudice. They also have other problems that harass them. A survey conducted by Deutsch and Brown (1964) turned up evidence showing that fathers of inner-city black children were more likely to be absent from the home than was true of white children in the same social-class grouping. Furthermore, decades and centuries of being thought inferior, and consequently thinking of oneself as inferior, are bound to have some effect on attitudes, work habits, achievement motivation, locus of control, and willingness to compete academically.

As we noted in Chapter 14, there is no sound evidence to show that there are any differences in mental functioning between races that cannot be explained in terms of environmental factors. For example, a study by Ira J. Semler and Ira Iscoe (1963) contains findings that are typical. They found differences between black and white children aged 5 in their ability to accomplish a learning task, but these differences could be accounted for in terms of the extent to which white children's environment had been enriched and the black children's environment had not. The white children, for example, had access to kindergartens, but the black children did not. At the age of nine, however, when both sets of children had participated in schools that were both comparable and adequate, the differences in learning ability had disappeared.

A great deal of attention has been paid in recent years to differences between standard American English and "black English." It has been demonstrated that the English spoken by inner-city and rural black people varies somewhat from standard English in grammatical structure, vocabulary, and pronunciation. The fact that the lower-class black child must learn to communicate in two languages, black and standard English, is seen by some educators and psychologists as a major handicap that keeps him from benefiting as much from the average classroom learning situation as nonblack children do.

The evidence on this question is of two types. First, studies have shown that teachers tend to be biased against black speech. For example, a sample of white teachers were asked to rate the oral replies of sixth- and ninth-grade boys to typical school questions such as "Why do we celebrate Thanksgiving?" and "What is the difference between a discovery and an invention?" What the teachers heard were tape recordings of middle-class white and lower-class black students speaking identically worded replies to the questions. Results showed that teachers tended to grade answers made with a standard English pronunciation higher than those replies that had black English characteristics (Crowl and MacGinitie, 1974).

The experience of the author, as well as that of others who have taught in the public schools of Hawaii, suggests that the same results would have been obtained if a similar experiment had been run in Hawaiian schools comparing teachers' ratings of identical answers made in standard English and in the Hawaiian "pidgin English" or "creole" that is spoken and understood by many of the children in that state. The point is that teachers tend to react negatively to nonstandard English whatever its form may be. It can be argued that teachers ought to respond to the *content* of children's answers and

not to the way in which they are delivered, but in this respect, teachers are probably like most people. Research by social psychologists indicates that our attitudes toward others is influenced more by the language they use than it is by their race, appearance, opinions, or social status (Triandis, Loh, and Levin, 1966). The fact that teachers have a special responsibility to be objective and supportive is all the more reason why they should be aware of this unconscious source of bias and thus attend more carefully to what children are saying, rather than how they are saying it.

The second kind of evidence concerns the ability of black students to cope with standard English. A number of investigations shows that standard English poses no special difficulties for them. In reviewing the research on this topic, Vernon C. Hall and Ralph R. Turner (1974) found no evidence indicating that the dialect of black children presents any unique problems in comprehending standard English. They noted that black children do not live in an isolated cultural environment, for they have much contact with standard English in television and radio programs and with nonblack people outside their home and neighborhood. They concluded that

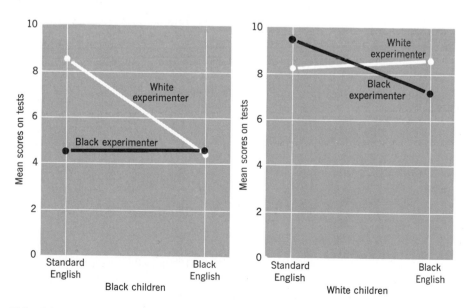

FIG. 16-3. Mean score differences on equivalent standard English and black English reading tests administered to black and white second-graders by black and white experimenters (data from Marwit and Neumann, 1974).

423

if the goal of the school is comprehension of standard English, it would serve no useful purpose to teach black primary students in black English. Findings typical of such studies were reported by Samuel Marwit and Gail Neumann (1974), who gave black and white second-graders one of two forms of the California Reading Test. One form was the regular version, as received from the test publishers; the other was identical, except that the textual material, as well as the instructions, had been translated into black English. A black experimenter administered the test to some of the children, whereas a white experimenter administered it to others. Results, as depicted in Figure 16-3, showed that both black and white children did better on the standard English version of the test. Furthermore, black children who had been given the standard English version by a white examiner did as well as the white children.

The findings of these and other investigators have led Jere E. Brophy (1974) to conclude that "the term 'black' is no more useful than the term 'white' for describing the student or indicating his educational needs." Blacks, he says, are as heterogeneous and varied as whites. This is also true of black English, which has rural and urban, as well as regional, variants. The major differences among students appear to be socioeconomic in origin and character and may be found in all ethnic groups. Disadvantaged children have more difficulties with school learning than do advantaged children, and this is as true of blacks as it is of oriental Americans, Anglo-Americans, American Indians, and Spanish-surnamed students.

To summarize then, the research does show that social-class differences, rather than ethnic differences, have the more significant effect on both the problems and the successes that children experience in school.

TASKS FOR REMEDIAL PROGRAMS

Preparation for Free Choices

It may be well at this point to review some of the things a remedial program of education must accomplish if it is to prepare socially disadvantaged children for the kinds of tasks they will face in school and in employment situations. In doing this we are not solely concerned with trying to mold children in order to fit them into a predetermined role in rigid and unyielding situations. For one thing, most schools and most employment situations today do permit a considerable degree of choice and freedom for self-determination. Most schools provide a variety of programs and a rich array of experiences; similarly, there is an infinite number of possibilities in employment. For another, preparing a child to be successful in school means giving him a chance to find himself. The difficulty with life in deprived circumstances is that the individual has few choices for self-expression and self-determination. The educated person has many more options as to what he can learn, what he can work at, or what he can do with his leisure time. Preparing a child to benefit from education means preparing him to learn how to be free, in the broadest sense of the word.

Building Ego Strength

In order to bring a lower-class child to the point where he can derive as much benefit from the schools as a middle-class child can, we must help him develop self-esteem, self-confidence, and ego strength. Ego strength is characteristic of a child who "seems to act on a fairly good estimate of reality, who exercises good self-control, who is able to stick with a task, and who can use spontaneous imagination" (Wattenberg and Clifford, 1964). The socially disadvantaged child rates low on these qualities. Growing up in a restricted environment, he is unaware of the social reality of the larger society outside the slum; he is likely to be highly distractible, hence he cannot "follow through" on frustrating and tedious tasks; and neither self-control nor imagination is a prized quality in his social environment. Lower-class children, particularly girls, are oppressed by strong feelings of inferiority that lead them to approach learning tasks with premonitions of failure.

These inferiority feelings are further aggravated by a feeling of being alienated from the mainstream of society. As we have noted in various contexts, the lower-class child feels like an outsider in school. Not only is he likely to be a slow learner and earn poorer grades, but he tends to be ignored by other students, who turn to middle-class children for their leadership.

We have also noted that the lower-class child's poor start in school is due in large measure to a home environment in which he receives less adult attention than the typical middle-class child, an environment that is more likely to be disorganized and unpredictable and in which the emphasis is on good behavior and keeping out of trouble, rather than on achievement and accomplishment.

Attitudes of Teachers in Remedial Programs

In order to help the socially disadvantaged child compensate for the shortcomings that we have listed, a remedial program must be staffed by warm, understanding, and accepting adults, and not by persons who are shocked, disgusted, or afraid of lower-class people and their behavior. They should also be aware that, being human, they are not immune to unconscious bias. The tendency to react negatively to nonstandard English is one source of unconscious prejudice, as we noted above.

Programs have their best chances for success if they begin during the child's early years, partly because the evidence is incontrovertible that preschool experience improves children's chances for school success, and partly because of the need to have lower-class children begin the first grade on a more equal footing with middle-class children. We have pointed out that many children who are behind in the first grade build up an increasing lag as they go through school.

Remedial programs should concentrate on children's attitudes, values, and interests, as well as on skills that are more obviously identified with school success. In other words, it is as important for deprived children to learn to become interested in achieving as it is for them to learn how to use crayons and pencils and how to handle books. These skills are important, of course, but attitudes are more basic. Middle-class teachers tend to think of

paper, crayons, and books as intrinsically interesting materials. They certainly are to middle-class children, who see in them opportunities for self-entertainment, but they may appear quite different to a child from deprived surroundings, who is more interested in finding an adult whom he can hug and who will hug him back.

One of the most significant contributions that adults who staff remedial programs can make to the culturally deprived child is that of treating him as an individual, showing an interest in *his* needs, *his* interests, and *his* accomplishments. The area of personal development is not only one in which homes in deprived conditions are most deficient, but it is also one in which a remedial program can make the most significant contribution. Without some individual attention, the child may lack the incentive or interest to develop the ego strength that he will need to undertake the more frustrating, trying, but nevertheless rewarding tasks of school learning.

THE EARLY TRAINING PROJECT AT GEORGE PEABODY COLLEGE

Background

Programs that introduce changes in the social environment of children in an attempt to help them make up the deficit resulting from social deprivation are termed "intervention programs" because the psychologist "intervenes" or comes into the child's environment in a hopefully significant way. What is probably the most successful of the preschool intervention experiments is the Early Training Program (ETP) developed and supervised by Susan W. Gray and Rupert A. Klaus (1965a, b; 1968, 1970) of the George Peabody College for Teachers in Nashville, Tennessee, under grants of funds from the National Institute of Mental Health and the National Institute of Child Health and Human Development. Its success is due in large measure to the fact that it satisfies all the criteria that we have listed in the foregoing paragraphs.

The ETP conducts experiments designed to determine whether certain procedures could offset the progressive retardation that many deprived children display during their school years, and is also a demonstration project for the purpose of developing techniques that can be used in other kinds of enrichment programs. The children who took part in one of the major longitudinal studies conducted by the ETP staff came from socially and economically disadvantaged black families living in a town of 25,000 population located in Tennessee. The mean number of children per family was five; fathers were absent in 40 percent of the homes; most of the fathers who were present held unskilled or semi-skilled jobs. Two experimental and two control groups were drawn from children born the same year and who showed the most extreme social deprivation. One experimental group received the special enrichment program beginning when they were four, and the other was started when they were five. The first control group did not, of course, participate in the enrichment program, although these children had a special recreation program the summer before they entered the first grade. The second control group was comparable to the other three groups but was located in a city sixty miles away.

Reinforcement of Learning Experiences

The first experimental group participated in three special summer school experiences of ten weeks each, supplemented by weekly home visits during the rest of the year. The second experimental group received the same treatment, except that it was started a year later. The program was deliberately designed along operant conditioning principles (see Chapter 8) to provide the kind of reinforcement that would reorient children's approach to learning and problem situations. The program of reinforcement was ordered as follows:

1. Each child was to receive more reinforcement than he would at home. Parents in deprived families tend to be preoccupied with household tasks and other problems and give their children little individual attention, unless their behavior is causing a problem. They are more concerned with *coping* with their children's behavior than with forming or shaping it.

2. The source of the reinforcement was to be an adult, where possible. Because socially deprived children have relatively little interaction with their parents, such reinforcement as they experience is likely to come from their siblings and peers, or from inanimate objects—playthings, for instance.

3. Much of the reinforcement was to be verbal, inasmuch as the socially deprived child is likely to receive little reinforcement of this type at home, and this type of reinforcement is important in his social development.

4. The reinforcement was to be directed at getting children to explore, experiment, and try things. Such reinforcement as he is likely to get at home is directed toward inhibition, that is, toward getting him to stay out of trouble and be quiet.

5. Reinforcement was to be focused on specific aspects of the child's performance, so that he would know what was expected of him. Such reinforcement as there is in deprived homes tends to be very general, such as, "You're a bad boy" or "You're a fine girl," which does not give the child any clues to what he should do or not do.

Each experimental group of twenty children had a head teacher, with one assistant for every five children. The staff was evenly divided according to sex and race. The high ratio of adults to children was necessary in view of the extensive and intensive reinforcement that the ETP called for. The reinforcement was direct, immediate, and physical at first, consisting of hugs, pats, being carried, candy, cookies, and gifts of plastic toys.

As the program continued, the staff shifted to rewards of a more symbolic nature, such as gold stars and having one's name posted on the blackboard. The reinforcement was specific at first, that is, it helped the child to focus on some particular aspect of his behavior that was correct or incorrect. Children also received more reinforcement at first because it was the task of the ETP staff to get them to interact with their environment, to take the initiative to try things.

As time went on, reinforcement became more selective and was focused on activities that were just within the range of a child's ability, and on the kinds of behavior that have a high rate of payoff in school, such as looking for and finding new relationships between objects and events, persisting with difficult tasks, or wanting to redo a task (a drawing, for example) that the child felt was not quite right. Although reinforcement was prompt and immediate at first, it became more and more delayed as time went on, inasmuch as delayed reinforcement is more the norm in the school situation. Rewards, too, were shifted from the direct and physical to the abstract and symbolic, and finally to "bookish" objects and activities, such as drawing paper, crayons, books themselves, and records. Gray and her co-workers have this to say about their policies:

> In general terms one should keep in mind that an interested reinforcing adult has tremendous impact on young children, particularly deprived children, who have received inadequate rewards from adults. This means that in general teachers and other workers with young children will have tremendous power in shaping a child's efforts and activities. Thus one can couple one's social approval of a physical sort with verbal social approval, and also later with more abstract and delayed rewards. As an example, one may find as the months go by that such token rewards as gold stars, little trinkets, or colored seals will come in the child's view to stand for a measure of the adult's approval of his activities.
>
> The next step from such "abstract" and symbolic rewards is that of the child's internalizing his own reward systems, of building up his own standards of performance. One can hardly hope to have preschool children do much internalizing. It can be helped, however, by encouraging the child to set his own standards, to evaluate his own performance, or by such simple techniques as trying to arouse a child's pride in his activities—"Aren't you proud that you painted such a good picture!" and the like.

Developing n Ach

In respect to the last point, one of the chief objectives of the ETP was that of developing the child's need for achievement (n Ach). Movement toward this goal had its pitfalls. When deprived children are given adult approval and affection, they tend to respond to it dramatically. Close relationships developed between the children and members of the staff, but it was necessary for the latter to keep in mind that these bonds had to be severed at the end of the summer and that children had to be helped to become independently self-reinforcing, to enable them to find satisfactions and reinforcements elsewhere. Games provided many opportunities for staff members to encourage children to better their performances away from the ETP. They could ask, for example, "Did you bounce the ball more times at home last night, Joe, than you did here at school?"

Achievement was encouraged at first whenever a child performed simple tasks adequately—for example, when he found his own towel and returned it to its proper hook after he had used it. Later, reinforcement was reserved for the successful completion of more complex tasks. The staff made deliberate attempts to indicate that they were interested in achievement. For example, the stories they read to the children were not only those in which children could identify with key characters, but they also involved the achievement of goals in spite of difficulties. Children were encouraged to work for several days over things, such as booklets, that could be taken home as tangible evidence of their success. There was also a booklet for each child that was used to record his progress. Such booklets became the focus for small-group discussions concerned with evaluation that dealt with questions such as, "What has Helen learned this week? What will she learn next week?"

Delay of Gratification and Reinforcement

The researchers were well aware that only those children who are willing and able to delay gratification can succeed in school. Deprived children are unable to respond favorably to situations in which gratification is delayed. Hence the staff addressed themselves to the problem of helping children develop the ability to work for a delayed reward. Their planning proceeded along these lines:

1. In order to be willing to work under delayed-reward conditions, children must be able to trust adults. Hence teachers never promised rewards they could not give.

2. Children were given many opportunities to choose between immediate and delayed rewards. At first, the delay was not great, perhaps an hour. At the end of the program, they were expected to accept a delay of several days.

3. Children observed the consequences of delayed rewards. In a situation in which children were given the choice between one stick of candy immediately or two sticks when they finished the task, those who elected the immediate reward got to see the child who had chosen to delay receive his two sticks of candy.

4. A child who elected to delay rewards was reinforced immediately by social approval, so that both he and the other children were made aware of the significance of his decision.

Learning to Persist

Another problem that troubles deprived children in school is their inability to persist with difficult, frustrating tasks. Persistence is not the same as perseveration—the repetition of behavior that has no particular aim in view. The staff began with simple physical tasks, such as throwing a ball into a wastebasket. Some children could succeed in this task even though they stood six feet away; others had to stand two feet away to be successful. After the staff member had determined what the child's normal performance was, he encouraged him to try to get the ball into the basket from a point just beyond the distance at which he was successful. He was kept at this task for a short period of time and received much adult approval for merely trying. Whenever he was successful, both the adult and the other chil-

dren roundly cheered. The comments of the authors are relevant here:

If one looks at the probable environment of young deprived children, one characteristic of it is surely that persistence has not paid off. That is, the environment is disorganized sufficiently both spatially and also from the standpoint of time schedules that the child has difficulty in learning sequences of events or consequences of his acts. One characteristic approach of persons in deprived homes, from children to elderly people, seems to be an apathy that grows in part out of a feeling, often realistic, that the individual can achieve very little by his own efforts. He sees himself as being shaped by the environment rather than by being able himself to make changes in that environment.

In practical terms, this means that when one wants to promote persistence toward a goal in young deprived children, one must think in terms of having a clear and orderly environment in that it is highly predictable, one in which the child can see the consequences of his acts, and one in which the situation is so arranged that persisting toward a goal is followed by attaining the goal often enough that the child learns that putting forth effort is likely to be rewarded.

The "hidden curriculum" in middle-class homes we have mentioned previously prepares children from such homes for successful participation in school activities. Socially deprived children, on the contrary, do not have experiences in using paper, looking at books, counting, and the like. In the early phases of the ETP, children were given crayons and told to mark on the paper. Then they were shown how to hold crayons for drawing. When staff members looked at picture books with a child, they encouraged him to turn the pages. Each child's progress book was also used to record his learning of school-related tasks. There were squares, for example, that children could color in each color he could name, and squares that could be checked for each number he could count in sequence.

Follow-up with Mothers

Another feature of the ETP was its program of follow-up work with parents. After all, the children spent only a few hours of each day and a few weeks of each year in school. Most of their growing lives were spent at home. This part of the ETP was carried out by a former preschool teacher who had training in sociology and social work. Her weekly contacts with parents throughout the year were aimed at three objectives: (1) providing some kind of a bridge for children between one summer session and the next (this involved bringing school materials to the mothers and showing them how to use them); (2) giving mothers information on how school success is related to occupational success; and (3) trying to promote greater feelings of personal worth in mothers, and, correspondingly, a greater regard for the personal worth of the children. Every month the visitor brought a copy of *Ebony* magazine to each of the homes and went through it with the mothers, pointing out articles and pictures related to the successful accomplishments of blacks, particularly those not involved with entertainment and sports. Some of the mothers were actually quite timid about reading stories to their children, and the visitor helped them overcome this emotional block by role playing, in which the visitor played the role of the mother and the mother played the role of the child. The visitor pointed out to mothers that they were, in effect, the first teachers of their children, and that they had at their command many things they could teach the child. Visits were also supplemented by monthly newsletters which carried news of the ETP's activities and always included a brief item for mothers to read to their children.

As the experimental program continued, the researchers stopped using professionally trained home visitors and began using "paraprofessionals": women from the community who were trained, coached, and supervised to carry out the home-visiting role. This change was made because researchers realized that local women would be more readily accepted by mothers. It was important to in-

volve mothers in the experimental program because the child's mother is the most significant teacher in his life. Unless she reinforces the kind of behaviors initiated at school, they will become readily extinguished, and the child will be no better off. As a result of the change of personnel, there were significant changes in the mothers' behavior toward their children: They became more specific, more positive, and less negative (Barbrack and Horton, 1970).

Results

A follow-up of the children who went through the early series of experimental programs has shown that changes in IQ and other indicators of cognitive functioning were not dramatic but were encouraging. Figure 16-4 reports data for the first two experimental groups and contrasts them with a control group (T4) located in a town sixty miles away. The top dotted line represents the theoretical growth in intelligence of an imaginary group of children whose IQ remains at 100 for six years. The lower dotted line represents the theoretical growth of children who begin with 89 IQ (the average for the experimental and control groups) and remain at that level for six years. (These theoretical performance norms are included for purposes of comparison.) The experimental groups show an immediate gain, which they held fairly well through the two-year program and afterward. During the same period, the control group lost ground. Both experimental and control groups showed a growth spurt when they were tested the summer of 1965 after they had completed the first grade. From that point onward they continued to show growth but at a slower rate. The schools they attended were populated almost entirely by other black children from poverty homes, a condition that generally leads to declining IQs and retardation in mental growth, as we noted previously in the study by Green and Hofmann (1965).[3] (See Figure 16-2.) The encouraging sign is that the

[3] A few ETP children who were able to attend racially integrated schools were by the end of the fourth grade achieving a full grade ahead of those who had been attending all-black schools.

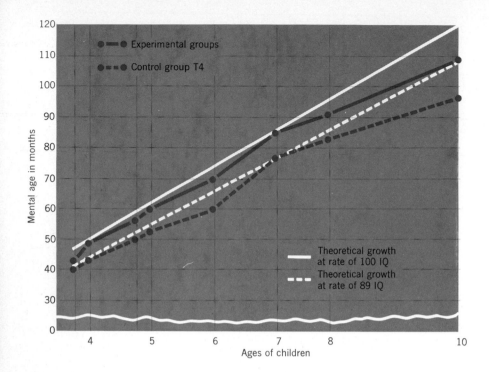

FIG. 16-4. Differences in intellectual growth, as measured by Stanford-Binet, between children who participated in preschool intervention programs (Experimental groups) and children who did not (Control group T4) (after Gray and Klaus, 1970).

ETP children were still holding their edge of superiority to the control group and not declining as much as would be expected.

When one considers that the ETP children spent less than 2 percent of their waking time from birth to six years in some kind of contact with ETP personnel, the results obtained have been remarkable. As Gray and Klaus (1970) point out, however, a relatively brief intervention program, such as theirs, cannot be expected to carry the entire burden of progressive mental retardation that is characteristic of poverty children. "Without massive changes in the life situation of the child," they wrote, "home circumstances will continue to have their adverse effect upon the child's performance." Well-conceived and well-executed intervention programs, they said, can make some relatively lasting changes

but cannot do the whole job. "They can provide only a basis for future progress in schools and homes that can build upon that early intervention."

In light of our earlier comments that ethnic identity has little to do with the cognitive development of children, but that social and economic deprivation is crucial, one would expect that intervention programs would help disadvantaged white children as well as black ones. Frank Kodman, Jr. (1970) has reported on an experimental program in which poor white children[4] living in rural Appalachia received preschool enrichment. Over three successive years, children in the enrichment groups gained an

[4] Although Kodman's report did not mention the race of the children, he has indicated in a personal communication that 90 percent of the forty children involved in the study were white.

average of 4, 16, and 10 IQ points, whereas control groups either lost IQ points or remained unchanged. Kodman's study was on a much smaller scale than the ETP, but it shows that even a moderate amount of enrichment during the crucial preschool years has considerable influence on children's cognitive development.

PLANNING AND OPERATING INTERVENTION AND ENRICHMENT PROGRAMS

The Need for Careful Planning

It takes more than enthusiasm and hard work to produce a successful educational intervention program for deprived children. The ETP was successful because it was carefully planned to take advantage of the motivational patterns that are part of each child's psychological makeup, and because it provided good supervision for carefully selected, trained personnel. Other programs, for instance, many of the programs undertaken under Operation Head Start, have not been so successful. Unfortunately, in the rush to get preschool enrichment programs started, many school districts were unable to plan or to supervise adequately, and teachers often had little idea of what they were supposed to do. In one intervention program instituted for socially disadvantaged Indian children in the Southwest, a teacher decided that she could control the children best by demonstrating skills and by having them participate in routines. When she tried to get the children to make piggy banks from plastic bottles and masks from paper bags, they stood around in bewilderment, and she had to end by doing the job for them. Very little learning took place in her classroom, as is indicated by the fact that at the end of six weeks, none of the children could recognize a picture of a flag, although they had started each day with the pledge to the flag.

Teachers who worked with other Indian children, however, were able to discover ingenious ways of attracting and involving their attention. One teacher found that children would not listen to stories, so she tried the approach of sitting at a table and cutting figures out of construction paper. The children gathered around to watch. As each figure emerged from the paper, it took its part in the story she was telling. Another teacher saw that the children were entranced by the paper cutter, so she gathered a scissors, a can opener, a razor blade, and a knife. She then started discussion by asking how these different objects were similar. Still another teacher found that her children were too shy to enter into planned activities, so she divided her class into "families" of six children each. Each family then picked a "mother" and a "father," who were inevitably the more mature, self-assured children. These "parents" then directed their "children" into activities that they previously had avoided (Zimmerman, 1965).

Verbal Facility and "Cute Little Boys"

The findings of H. Ellison Pusser and Boyd R. McCandless (1974), who conducted a longitudinal study of disadvantaged black and white children from kindergarten through the second grade, caution against making easy generalizations about the effect of preschool enrichment programs. Although a number of educators and psychologists, especially those who are strongly oriented to a Montessori approach, are inclined to stress manipulative-spatial experiences in preschool and primary years, Pusser and McCandless found that the most important factor predicting the children's school success was verbal facility, that is, verbal skills as rated by teachers, quality of speech, activity versus passivity in speech, and scores on verbal portions of intelligence tests. The relationship between verbal facility and school success was especially crucial for boys.

The investigators also turned up evidence which suggests that prekindergarten experiences facilitate later adjustment to elementary school for girls but may interfere with that of boys. They observed:

Four-year-old males are still treated as "boys will be boys, especially cute little boys." That is, they are allowed [by preschool teachers] to be aggressive and even encouraged to be creative, spontaneous, and curious. Creativity, spontaneity, and curiosity for young males are likely to take the form of physical aggression. When these children begin the traditional, passive-obedience-oriented first grade the following year, the females may be much better prepared than the males to adjust. Young males, especially young black males, from first grade on are no longer allowed to be cute, aggressive, little boys and, therefore, are not able to cope with their anxiety in any way that would not affect their verbal facility. The males may have been pushed by the system and their teachers back toward passivity and withdrawal as coping techniques. . . . It seems safe to say that males ran into something of a brick wall when they entered the public schools.

The Pusser-McCandless study suggests that some of the preconceptions that most of us have about the kinds of preschool experiences that are best for children must be rethought and restudied. The findings of their investigation, like those of most studies, do not indicate exactly how we should go about selecting the best procedures and policies to be followed in preschool enrichment, but they do suggest that the types of preschool programs that have been developed for advantaged children are not necessarily the best ones for disadvantaged ones, and that disadvantaged boys require special handling—perhaps judicious amounts of control and direction.

Programs for Adolescents

There have been a number of programs that have attempted to compensate for the cultural deprivation of students in the higher elementary grades and in secondary schools. The Mobilization for Youth's Homework Helper Program hires high-school sophomores and juniors from low-income families to tutor elementary students who are retarded in reading or arithmetic. Such a program aids in two ways: The elementary school children get special help with their studies, and the teenag-

ers not only earn money, but have the experience of helping others and being valued for their skills and maturity. The Higher Horizons Project in New York City was developed for the purpose of identifying and encouraging talented teenagers. Children from deprived homes are, as we have noted, easily discouraged, and the school drop-out rate is high even with bright children. The New York schools used a number of different approaches to counteract these effects. The number of counselors was increased from one per fifteen hundred students to one per two hundred fifty; counselors were directed to interview students who were succeeding, as well as those who were failing; students were encouraged to read more books by such devices as making attractive paperbacks readily available; homework study rooms were staffed by college student volunteers; students were taken to concerts and theaters in an effort to provide cultural enrichment. The success of the program is indicated by the fact that the mean increase in IQ was 13 points. Approximately 40 percent more students finished high school than had been the previous experience with comparable groups, and the number of graduates going on to college or some form of higher education increased by three and one-half times. (Schreiber, 1962, 1963).

Other programs report very good success with only a minimum investment of time. Myron Woolman (1964) developed an approach that he called the Accelerated Progressive Choice Reading Program, or APCR, a specially programed technique designed to permit students to progress at their own rate of speed, incorporating materials oriented to the interests and values of socially disadvantaged youth and using a step-by-step procedure. One of the advantages of the program was that it required little teacher participation. After only forty hours of instruction, disadvantaged youth participating in Washington (D. C.) Action for Youth groups showed a mean gain of 1.28 years in reading ability. In another Washington program, Edith H. Grotberg (1965) found that teachers using an intensive remedial approach were able to help disadvantaged ninth-grade boys fourteen to seventeen years old raise their reading level an average of 1.5 years with only thirty hours of instruction. Irwin Katz (1967) tells of some older children, retarded in reading, who were given the task of tutoring younger ones. Both groups of children showed gains, but the improvement in the older children was phenomenal. Playing the role of the tutor not only increases task involvement, but raises self-esteem, an essential factor in successful classroom learning.

One of the difficulties with intervention programs planned for adolescents is that it usually takes a great deal more time and effort to bring about minor changes at this age than it does during the preschool years. Attitudes and patterns of motivation are more likely to be set by this age, and the resistance to change is likely to be greater. On the other hand, the adolescent is also in a position to realize that his future is at stake, since if he can learn the skills that the program is trying to teach him, his chances for occupational success are immensely improved. In some programs this motivation is evidently sufficient to bring about the kinds of changes that are desired.

Another problem is that of evaluation. Few experimental programs are as well planned, supervised, or controlled as the Early Training Program (ETP). As a consequence, one often must take the subjective evaluations of those in charge of intervention programs on faith. Perhaps this point is not very important. Perhaps the important thing is that more and more ingenious and creative programs are being developed to help those children who have been so long ignored by our schools. But lessons learned from evaluation in other kinds of programs would suggest that learning will be more successful, and public support more easily obtained, if evidence can be systematically collected to show what kinds of differences enrichment programs make in the school progress of the children and youth who participate.

Learning to Work with Inner-city Adolescents

But what of the teacher who is not in an intervention program, who wants only to develop the kind of relationship with inner-city students that will make their work with him a rewarding and, hopefully, an enjoyable experience?

Herbert L. Foster (1974), who has had sixteen years of experience in teaching the disadvantaged in New York City high schools, says that most teachers go through a four-phase "rites of passage" in inner-city schools. The first stage is *friendship:* The new teacher does not want to commit the same racist acts he has seen other teachers do, he does not want to be a tough disciplinarian, and most of all he *does* want to be a friend to the students. The student, however, is not looking for a friend: He wants someone to teach and to discipline him. Hence when the teacher's efforts at friendship fail, which usually happens very quickly, the scenario moves on to stage two.

The second stage is *classroom chaos:* The students involve the teacher in abrasive, hostile games—"ribbin', jivin', and the dozens." The teacher not only loses control of his class, but he also feels humiliated and rejected. There is no one to turn to and he feels all alone. Some teachers leave the profession altogether at this point.

The third stage is *discipline.* In this stage the teacher reassumes his authority and enforces a tight control. "There's quiet in the room; there's calmness. It's a level where the teacher gives out worksheets all day. . . ."

Humanism is the fourth stage: At this stage the teacher relaxes some of the control and humanizes or individualizes the classroom. Foster says that only two or three out of ten teachers get to this stage.

In an interview for the educational professional journal, the *Phi Delta Kappan,* Foster said:

> My idea of the natural inner-city teacher has three or four aspects: great inner strength; high organization and self-discipline; outgoing qualities, tempered with introspection and self-understanding; a very good sense of humor; and an awareness and knowledge of what's going on in this country. The second aspect is the subject taught. The teacher has to love his or her sub-

ject, because that love or feeling for the subject being taught helps motivate the students. The teacher must understand all aspects of student culture—what TV channels and shows they watch. . . .

Foster also suggested that teachers dress conservatively and neatly, because students are very conscious of what adults wear. The idea that some teacher trainees have that "they could relate better to blacks by dressing in a slovenly way" is, in his opinion, "a very racist feeling." He continued:

The final necessary aspect of the natural inner-city teacher is disciplinary ability. No matter how we slice it, the natural teacher has to be in control of that class. Again I'm not suggesting that the child sit in straight rows with hands clasped, but the sense of control must be there (Cole, 1974).

As Rudolf Dreikurs (1952a) once said, what teachers need to express is both kindness and firmness—kindness out of respect for children and firmness out of respect for oneself.

Using Paraprofessionals in Inner-city Schools

One shortcoming of intervention programs, irrespective of whether they are introduced at the elementary or the secondary school level, is that they are more concerned with changing the child than they are with changing the school. The rationale for this approach goes somewhat like this: The reason why children from poverty homes cannot learn is that their background (attitudes, skills, or whatever) is inadequate; therefore they must be "fixed" in order to benefit from the school program. In other words, the child, not the school, must be changed. There is, however, another point of view that holds that *schools* must be changed in order to meet the needs of the child. Some intervention programs, such as the ETP, are highly innovative and make use of methods that are totally unlike the methods of traditional schools, but many school systems are highly resistive to change and thus force the inno-

vator to concentrate on the child and his environment.

Minority-group communities in urban poverty areas are today much more aware of their political power and are demanding the right to have a say in determining the character of services that are provided for them and their children, particularly health services, public welfare, and education. Their interest in having something to say about education came at a time when schools were introducing the teaching aide or paraprofessional into the classroom to help teachers with clerical duties, collecting milk and cafeteria money, correcting tests, tutoring slow pupils, and the like. It made a good deal of sense to hire people from neighborhoods in which schools are located to serve as aides because they could serve as a link between the school and the community and also give parents some voice in the way their children are being educated. According to Frank Riessman and Alan Gartner (1969), the introduction of aides into the classroom has led to improved pupil performance on achievement tests, very likely because teachers have been freed from a number of petty details, but particularly because children have received a great deal more personal attention.

Riessman and Gartner would like to have the paraprofessionals become a force for change within the schools. They say:

The most important danger is that the new careers movement may not become deeply linked with other developing movements of our time: decentralization, and reorganization of human services with accountability to the consumer. It may be deaf to new black demands, youth unrest, self-criticism of the profession, and the aspirations of paraprofessionals.

Teacher aides hired from the community can bring into the school system what the community wants in the way of education. Ideally, they will not be trained by the system; they will help to change it.

The new aides must be involved in a career pattern. They are not part-time volunteers; they are part of a powerful new consumer control. Of-

ten poor—not middle-class—housewives, they are becoming rehabilitated, learning themselves through helping others. This is not a movement merely to hire new manpower to patch up outmoded school systems. This new manpower, the indigenous paraprofessionals, must be involved in providing new patterns of instruction directed toward new education goals.[5]

SUMMARY

The fact that so many million families are below the "poverty level" in a rich country that makes opportunities for self-improvement through education so freely available is both puzzling and troubling. The problem has been investigated by surveys, and experimental programs have been funded to help children from poverty families benefit from schools. Surveys show that segregated schools populated by poverty children make the poorest scholastic progress. Such children are described as "culturally deprived" or "socially disadvantaged." Many of such children come from a slum environment, one that is characterized by social disorganization, unbridled hostility, destructiveness, passivity, and aimlessness. This type of environment produces a child who does not fit very well into a well-ordered, middle-class school. The lower-class child is less likely to be adequately nourished; his parents are likely to be too preoccupied with many pressing problems to give him much attention; and his interaction with adults is less likely to be of a verbal character. On the positive side, inner-city children have been described as being warmer and more spontaneous than middle-class children. Whereas the middle-class child responds to ego rewards and generally learns to be self-reinforcing in his approach to learning, the child from a deprived environment is more likely to respond to more tangible reinforcements. The need for affiliation (n Aff) is likely to be stronger than the need for achievement (n Ach) for a socially disadvantaged child. This means that he is less responsive to opportunities he encounters in the school that lead to self-improvement and progress. Lower-class parents are also likely to value a child's good behavior more highly than his achievement.

Benjamin S. Bloom says that the difference between a culturally deprived and an enriched environment is 20 IQ points. Environmental factors that affect IQ are likely to have their greatest impact during the preschool years. The mental growth of children who transfer from a disadvantaged to an enriched environment is ordinarily accelerated, but if this transfer takes place later in childhood, there is less likelihood that they will reach the norm for their age. The retarded mental growth of deprived children shows up in such phenomena as IQ decline and dropping further and further behind in achievement levels. IQ is not as highly correlated with teachers' marks for lower-class as for middle-class students. Interest in differences between black English and standard English has led to research as to its effects on students and teachers. Results show that teachers are somewhat biased against black English, but that use of black English in instruction provides no advantages to inner-city students. Research also shows that the major problems experienced by inner-city children stem primarily from being socially and economically deprived, rather than from their ethnic identity.

Programs designed to remedy deficiencies in the cultural and social environment of disadvantaged children can succeed only if they are able to build up children's ego strength and help them develop certain task-oriented attitudes. This can best be accomplished if adults who staff the program are warm, accepting people, who are able to give children the kind of attention that they have lacked at home and thus guide them into developing the attitudes, values, and interests that will stand them in good stead at school. Such programs have their best chance for success if they concentrate on the preschool years, in order to start disadvantaged children off on a level comparable to that of the middle-class children.

The Early Training Project (ETP) conducted under the direction of Susan W. Gray and Rupert A. Klaus of George Peabody College appears to satisfy

[5] Reprinted by permission.

all these criteria. Two experimental groups aged 4 and 5, respectively, participated in intensive summer programs in which they received a great deal of adult attention. Reinforcement was immediate and physical at first, but toward the end of the program children had learned to respond to reinforcement that was verbal, social, symbolic, and delayed. They learned to take pride in their work and to develop need for achievement. This involved their learning habits of persistence when faced by frustrating tasks or distractions. Records were kept of children's progress in a form that they themselves could interpret. A teacher-social worker visited the homes of the children weekly during the entire year, partly to create a "bridge" between the summer sessions, and partly to interest the parents in participating in their children's intellectual development. During later stages of the experiment paraprofessionals were employed as home visitors and were found to have more of an impact on mothers' behavior. During the preschool period and through the first year of school, IQs of children in the experimental program increased relative to the IQs of a control group. The IQs of both groups declined thereafter, with the control group showing the greater decline. Such decline is usual in schools populated entirely by children from poverty homes. The authors conclude that well-planned intervention programs can raise scholastic aptitude for the short run, but that gains will not hold unless they are supported by changes in children's social environment.

A number of early intervention programs have been tried, not all of them successfully. Few are as well planned and executed as the Gray-Klaus ETP, and the kind of evidence needed for adequate evaluation is often lacking. Research by Pusser and McCandless suggests that preschool enrichment programs for disadvantaged children should stress verbal development, and that the stress in such programs on self-initiated activity and spontaneity may aggravate tendencies toward aggressiveness and nonconformity in boys. They observed that these tendencies caused grave difficulties for the boys when they entered the more restrictive environment of elementary school. A number of innovative intervention programs have been created to help inner-city adolescents. Although such programs have inherent problems because the behavior patterns of students are likely to be more firmly set at this age, reports have been encouraging. Foster recommends that teachers in inner-city schools exercise firm control over themselves and their classes before they set about humanizing and individualizing their instruction. The employment in classrooms of teacher aides or paraprofessionals from poverty homes has facilitated the scholastic achievement of disadvantaged children and has provided a potentially influential link between slum community parents and the school.

Suggested Problems

1. What are some of the things teachers can do with disadvantaged children in the primary grades in order to help them develop the kinds of attitudes and skills that are needed for school success?

2. If you were a principal of a junior high school in the inner-city, what kinds of innovations would you introduce in order to help compensate for the disadvantages your students have?

3. Why should kindergartens and nursery schools in deprived areas have higher adult-child ratios (more adults to fewer children) than schools in middle-class areas?

4. Most kindergarten teachers like to have well-organized schedules for each day's activity. In what way might such programs interfere with the success of a program designed to compensate for social and cultural deprivation? In what way might they help?

5. Some staff members of compensatory programs complain that parents do not want to talk with them about their children. Why do you suppose this occurs?

6. Let us say that you are teaching English to an eighth grade located in an inner-city school. Although you know how important it is for children to learn to write, you cannot get your class to write more than a couple of sentences at a time. Most of them give up after they have spent

three minutes or so on the task. Why do they have this problem, and what can you do about it?

Suggested Readings

Beck, J. M., and Saxe, R. W. (eds.) *Teaching the culturally disadvantaged pupil.* Springfield, Ill.: Charles C Thomas, 1965. Analyzes problems of the socially disadvantaged learner, presents descriptions of teaching procedures, and discusses teacher preparation and roles for the community and for school principals.

Bloom, B. S., Davis, A., and Hess, R. *Compensatory education for cultural deprivation.* New York: Holt, Rinehart, and Winston, 1965. A paperback report of a conference on education and cultural deprivation.

Foster, H. L. *Ribbin', jivin', and playin' the dozens: The unrecognized dilemma of inner-city schools.* Cambridge, Mass.: Ballinger, 1974. A down-to-earth book, full of suggestions, based on years of experience in New York City's "600" schools—inner-city schools for disadvantaged and emotionally maladjusted children.

Gray S. W., Klaus, R., Miller, J. O., and Forrester, B. J. *The early training project: A handbook of aims and activities.* Nashville, Tenn.: George Peabody College for Teachers, 1965. A clearly written, readable manual describing the special project mentioned in this chapter, with descriptions of how the experimenters solved the problems they encountered.

Gray, S. W., et al. *Before first grade.* New York: Teachers College Press, 1966. (A paperback.) Describes the procedures, techniques, and activities used by the Gray-Klaus group in conducting the Early Training Project.

Lindgren, H. C., and Lindgren, F. (eds.) *Readings in educational psychology,* 2nd ed. New York: Wiley, 1972. See section 9 for research and comment on the problems of disadvantaged children.

Maccoby, E. E., and Zellner, M. (eds.) *Experiments in primary education: Aspects of Project Follow-Through.* New York: Harcourt, Brace, and Jovanovich, 1970. A paperback collection of two-page descriptions of programs which pick up where Project Head Start leaves off and follow children during the first four years of elementary school. Reports describe the philosophies of their sponsors, and a summary details the difficulties encountered in any kind of compensatory program, especially political pressures.

Payne, J. S., et al. *Head Start: A tragicomedy with epilogue.* New York: Behavioral Publications, 1973. A paperback analyzing Head Start problems, describing a number of innovative programs, and making suggestions for its betterment.

Tanner, L., and Lindgren, H. C. *Classroom teaching and learning.* New York: Holt, Rinehart, and Winston, 1971. See Chapter 9, "The disadvantaged learner."

Psychological Services:
Individual Help
for the Learner

The Shortcomings of Mass Education

With all its faults, mass education, as exemplified by modern educational systems, has produced immense benefits for all mankind. For one thing, it makes available to virtually everyone within reach of a school a common body of the skills and information that are essential for functioning in a civilized world. Furthermore, it puts within everyone's grasp the means for finding a place in the social order and for realizing his potentialities.

On the other hand, mass education has undeniable shortcomings. It does lend itself to the control of a few people at the top, particularly in those countries or communities where political power is the monopoly of an elite group. In such societies, well-organized school systems become all-too-convenient channels for political propaganda and provide only limited opportunities for mental growth. Even in the more democratic societies systems of mass education tend to produce a kind of educational bureaucracy that acts to prevent educational change and restricts the freedom of the classroom teacher. Such weaknesses are not due so much to any basic flaw in the idea of organized mass education, as they are due to apathy, ineptitude, or a lack of understanding of educational goals and processes on the part of the citizenry. What we are concerned about in this chapter, however, is still another kind of deficiency: the danger, and even the probability, that some very important educational needs will go unmet in even the most efficiently organized system of mass education.

The Need for Individualized Attention

There are, for example, the needs of the children whom we have described in the last two chapters—children who need special help because they have special problems. These problems cannot be handled easily and successfully on a mass basis. To be sure, we can organize special programs for groups of children who are socially disadvantaged, hard-of-hearing, or mentally retarded, but such group treatment is only a partial solution to the problem. At some point, we must intervene as individuals and work with students as individuals. As we noted in Chapter 16, most deprived children must be given individual attention, because they, unlike middle-class children, are relatively unable to respond to social reinforcement and ego rewards. Hard-of-hearing and mentally retarded children not only need a great deal of personal care on the part of teachers, but specialized professional people, such as physicians and psychologists, must give them individual diagnostic attention as well.

The way in which a hard-of-hearing child gets into the special program is an example. Perhaps the teacher is the first person to spot him. He notices that the child does not understand his assignments correctly; he raises questions that are irrelevant; he is continually asking people to repeat what they say; at times he appears to be concentrating on a task

and is unaware that someone is speaking to him. As the teacher notes these symptoms, he is not reacting as a mass educator, as someone who is concerned only with classes and groups. He is responding to the needs of an individual child. As a next step, he may refer the child to the school nurse, who satisfies herself that the child needs a hearing test. She may then refer him to the school physician and consult with the parents. If it is decided to assign the child to a special class, several other people—administrators, supervisors, special teachers, psychologists, audiologists—may be involved, each dealing with the problem of an individual child. This is not mass education; this is individualized education. In a system that operated only on a mass-education basis, the problems of the individual child would be ignored or would be handled administratively in accordance with policies for whatever classification the child might fall into.

The kind of child that we discussed in the preceding two chapters is one who needs *continuing* or *frequent* special attention, and there is every reason why we might want to individualize education on his behalf. His needs for special treatment are dramatic and urgent; when we try to meet them through the methods of mass education, it just does not work. His slowness in learning and the continual problems this creates remind us that we are not meeting the needs of this child. Hence we make special provisions for satisfying them.

The fact that we make special arrangements for the exceptional or the disadvantaged child does not mean, however, that the needs of the rest of the student population can be met by the procedures and provisions of mass education alone. Every student needs some special and individualized attention at some time or other during his educational career. Some need it at frequent intervals, others need it less often, but everyone needs it on occasion. Sometimes this help is needed for a special problem that has arisen, such as an illness that has taken a student out of school for several weeks. Sometimes a student needs to talk to someone about a personal problem that is causing so much anxiety that his ability to learn is momentarily impaired. And sometimes what is needed is merely some kind of personal attention, which should remind us that the need for attention is a basic psychological need that must be satisfied if the human organism is to develop and mature normally. The fact that a system of mass education is operating efficiently should not blind us to the fact that whatever learning the individual student accomplishes under ordinary classroom conditions can be increased by giving him a little personal attention. Some of this special help and attention can be given by teachers in the classroom during the instructional period; some of it can be given by teachers during free periods, after school, or at other odd times. But much of it can be provided more efficiently and effectively by persons who are specialists in psychological services: persons who are referred to as student personnel workers or guidance workers.

PSYCHOLOGICAL OR GUIDANCE SPECIALISTS

The School Counselor

The school counselor is perhaps the least specialized of the several kinds of guidance workers. Most counselors are teachers or former teachers who have a strong interest in working with students on a person-to-person basis and who have developed some special skills in interviewing and testing. There is a growing trend to require teachers to take professional training in counseling and guidance before being appointed to counselor positions. Some states prescribe special credentials for counselors.

A generation or so ago counselors were inclined to specialize in problems of vocational choice—helping adolescents select their life work and advising them about appropriate courses. Inevitably, vocational counseling came to include educational counseling as well, because students changed their minds about their decisions or failed in their courses and had to be readvised or had to be helped to make decisions when two required courses came at the same time of the day. Inevitably, too, counselors became involved with problems

of personal and social adjustment. The necessity of making an occupational choice often arouses confusion and anxiety; sometimes parents and children disagree as to which career should be followed; and the ability of a student to succeed in the course of his choice depends, in part, on his attitudes, his motivation, and his ability to make progress in spite of the frustrations and distractions of everyday life.

The clients of the counselor come to him for help in making decisions about *choices* or *changes*, according to Leona E. Tyler (1969). The student typically has a number of options open to him—academic majors, courses, and careers—and he needs help in making the *choices* that best express his self-concept. Or, the student does not like the options that are available to him; for some reason or other they are inconsistent with his aspirations. He therefore wants to make *changes* in himself or in his situation to the end that he will have better options from which to choose.

The choices and changes students want to make inevitably involve the school program both in its curricular as well as in its extracurricular phases. As a psychological worker in a school setting, the counselor is in a position to involve a variety of agents—teachers, administrators, parents, employers, legal authorities—in helping the student and the system adapt to each other. The elementary school counselor, according to Martha Ellison (1968), "may serve as therapist, focusing on problems and adjustment; as liaison between school and home; as administrator and interpreter of tests; or as coordinator and planner of a broad guidance program involving all faculty and staff." He may also serve as a consultant to teachers, a resource person for curricular units based on occupations, a team contributor for case conferences, or a coordinator for sex education. In the secondary school setting, the counselor may do many of these things and, in addition, will assist students in matters of vocational choice and will organize related group activities: career days, college nights, and assembly programs. Michael A. Ciavarella (1970) also stresses the counselor's role as a mental health consultant, working with teachers, administrators, other specialists, and parents. He sees the counselor as one who keeps his finger on the school's "mental health pulse." He is suited for this role by virtue of his training in psychology, his availability, his freedom of movement, and the information he possesses, through his counseling interviews, regarding students' concerns about school.

The work of the school counselor is likely to have strong support in the community, as well as among students. In a nationwide poll, 79 percent of parents and 83 percent of high-school students said that they felt that guidance counselors were worth the extra cost (Gallup, 1970). A nationwide poll of high-school students indicated that about half of them wanted counseling to help with decisions about colleges and universities and almost as many wanted information about future careers. Only about 20 percent said they were not in need of counseling (Erlick, 1974).

The School Psychologist

The school psychologist's role is similar in many ways to the role of the counselor. Both help students with their problems and serve as consultants. There are some important differences and distinctions, however. Most counselors are educators with some additional training in dealing with school problems. A master's degree in psychology is usually considered to be minimum training for a school psychologist, and many secure a Ph.D. or Ed.D. as well. School psychologists have in the past tended to spend their time working with children of elementary school age, whereas most counselors are in secondary schools. As a consequence, school psychologists are less involved in helping children with problems of vocational choice and more concerned with learning difficulties and emotional problems. School counselors are members of the teaching or the administrative staff of the school where they work; most of them teach some classes. School psychologists very seldom teach classes. Furthermore, they either work in a clinic or serve schools on an itinerant basis. This is partly because they need special equipment and facilities that are best kept separate from the hustle and bustle of school buildings and partly because elementary schools have smaller enrollments than secondary schools and are unable to afford or may not require the services of a full-time psychologist.

There has been a trend in the last decade to expand the professional role of the school psychologist. It is now generally recognized, at least by the leadership of the profession, that it may be more economical to use school psychologists in the in-service education of teachers than on specific interactions with a single child or a single teacher. A number of school psychologists are also becoming involved in administration and research in programs concerned with disadvantaged, emotionally disturbed, or physically handicapped children. In recent years, clincial psychologists have been moving into the field of community psychology, and many school psychologists have also begun to function in this area. The doctoral program in clinical psychology and public practice at Harvard University is an indication of how the roles and areas of concern of the clinical and the school psychologists are merging. The Harvard program emphasizes efforts to understand and change social institutions and notes that "attitudes expressed in the structure of school systems affect the cognitive and creative potential of virtually every child, as do the feelings and personalities of teachers and their supervisors." The program recognizes that, because of the magnitude and deficiencies of social institutions, for example, the school, the effectiveness of individual psychotherapy has serious limitations. The faculty staffing Harvard's program have therefore developed a problem-centered orientation "in which faculty and students pursue the origins of broadly defined educational, social, and political disabilities"[1] and are concerned with topics such as early childhood education and school failure. To educators, these may seem to be obvious topics for clinical psychologists to study, but their inclusion in a Ph.D. program amounts to a drastic change from the model that prevailed a decade ago.

[1] Quotations are from the *Program in clinical psychology and public practice,* Harvard University, 1970–1971.

Although the position held by the school psychologist offers opportunities to work in the field of community relations, most school psychologists perform tasks and provide services that are closely tied to the immediate needs of children and teachers. Robert D. Roberts (1970) conducted a survey of the activities of school psychologists, and found that much of their time was taken up with the administration of psychological tests. Half the respondents reported that they wished they could spend less time on such duties. This feeling was in contrast to the one expressed by a sampling of elementary teachers who stated that they wished school psychologists would spend more, not less, time on this task. Teachers also wished them to do more psychotherapy, but psychologists wished to play the consultant role with teachers more than teachers wanted them to. In general, psychologists wished to become more involved with educational functions than they were currently, whereas teachers preferred that they spend more time on the traditional functions of the clinical psychologist.

The School Social Worker

School social workers or visiting teachers usually work in guidance clinics or out of the central offices of school systems. Most social workers have received training in a graduate school of social work and have a master's degree in that field. They may provide counseling or psychotherapy for disturbed children or their parents in much the same way as the school or clinical psychologist, except that the giving of tests is primarily a responsibility of the psychologist. The social worker is also more likely to interview parents and to work with family service agencies, the juvenile court, and other community agencies and organizations.

In some states and in many communities, the work of the attendance officer is becoming recognized as a branch of child welfare, and training in social work is being recommended or required increasingly as preparation for this position. Attendance officers are often concerned with contacting parents and in maintaining liaison with the courts,

although there is a great deal of counseling and referral that is carried on as a necessary function of the job. This is a far cry from the traditional role of the "hookey cop."

Medical Specialists

Another role that is growing in importance is that of the psychiatrist. Psychiatrists are medical doctors who have received specialized training in the diagnosis and treatment of psychopathology. They are usually included in the guidance programs as part-time members of the psychological clinic staff, where they serve as consultants or as key members of psychiatric teams consisting of psychologists and social workers. A small portion of the children referred to a guidance clinic will be so seriously disturbed or so retarded mentally that placement in an institution is indicated. Inasmuch as the work of school psychologists and social workers involves problems of mental and physical health, the presence of a medical doctor on the staff of a clinic is highly desirable.

In actuality, there is a considerable overlap in the roles of counselor, school psychologist, school social worker, and psychiatrist. They all may deal with emotional problems, they may all make referrals, and they may all serve as consultants to teachers and administrative personnel. Here is a quotation from a paper written by Irving N. Berlin (1956), drawn from his experiences as a psychiatrist member of a consultation team:

At the beginning of the fourth year of school consultation, we met with a group of new teachers who were having difficulties with their classes. This experiment was approached with caution by our team because we had learned our lesson about the difficulties involved in such group sessions. We thought we would try this because these teachers all had similar, acute problems and anxieties and it seemed the only way to reach more than one teacher at a time during a period of need. The teachers were surprised to find that there were others in the same predicament and as troubled as they. Most of them, after some initial hesitation, talked freely about their difficulties. They all seemed bewildered that the precepts taught in education courses and fairly easily carried out in their practice teaching seemed so ineffectual in their overcrowded classrooms, with many tense, overactive, disinterested, and rebellious children, many from minority groups and many in marginal economic circumstances. The team's concern with these teachers, and the team's verbalization of the kinds of feelings these new teachers might have seemed to help them talk more freely. During the meeting several teachers began to express the feeling that perhaps they expected too much of themselves—maybe they didn't need to love all their pupils. They all seemed easier as the team gave examples to illustrate that as teachers were able to be more direct and firm and less afraid that setting limits in the classroom would be "traumatic" to their pupils, they felt better, the children felt better, and more learning in a more agreeable classroom atmosphere occurred. After this meeting we heard that several new teachers on the verge of resigning their positions took a new lease on life and most of the group felt more relaxed and better able to handle their classroom situation.

There are other kinds of specialists who have important functions in the guidance program, although the amount and kind of participation varies from school to school and from community to community. The school nurse and the school physician often play key roles, particularly when it comes to making contacts with parents and making referrals to clinics. One great difficulty is to get parents to see that the behavior of a disturbed child is probably not something he will "grow out of," and that he needs psychological help. Parents can often accept such recommendations more easily from a school nurse because she is a medical person than from a teacher or principal.

Administrative Personnel

In some schools, particularly in rural areas, the principal or his assistant may provide guidance services. One disadvantage of this system is that these individuals are the same persons responsible for the enforcement of school regulations; hence it is difficult for them to establish the comfortable, permissive kind of relationship with boys and girls that is basic to good counseling. There are certain exceptions to this, of course. In some schools the assistant principal devotes himself entirely to counseling and guidance, and infractions of school regulations come under the jurisdiction of the principal. In other schools, the principal or assistant principal just happens to be the kind of person who can convey the warmth, sympathy, and genuine interest in the problems that young people bring to him and thus is able to dispel some of the fear and anxiety that most students associate with a visit to the principal's office.

INDIVIDUALIZED ATTENTION FROM TEACHERS

The chief function of the specialists whom we have described is that of giving help to individual students—help that could not be provided if schools operated completely on a mass-education basis. Although some needs can be met by teachers, a great many of them require the attention of the specialist. Let us see what some of these needs are, giving particular attention to the needs that all children are likely to have from time to time.

The Need for Special Instruction

The need for special instruction is perhaps the first that comes to the mind of most teachers.

Lucy cannot seem to understand what it means to "carry" a number when you add two or more columns of figures. Miss Brandon, her teacher, gives Lucy what time she can during the arithmetic period. If this does not suffice, she may ask her to stay after school or give her some special assignments. Ford Galvin, in the fifth grade, is at about the third-grade level in his reading ability. He is very worried about this deficiency and wants to do something about it. Mr. Marshall, his teacher, has asked the school librarian for a list of books that are fifth grade in interest level but are at the third grade in vocabulary. There are two other children in the class who also read at Ford's level, and Mr. Marshall will give them an opportunity to read by themselves from their special list. Mr. Marshall is using the librarian in still another way. Frank and Rudolfo have shown a tendency to engage in horseplay and practical jokes during class period. Mr. Marshall is not sure whether this is preadolescent high spirits and rebelliousness or whether their disruptive behavior is symptomatic of deeper disturbances. While he is studying their problem, he wants to make some adjustment in the curriculum which will involve them more deeply in school work. Since both the boys are fascinated with airplanes, he has assigned them a project of finding out why airplanes can fly and reporting their findings to the class. So far this approach has worked very well. The librarian was able to supply the boys with books and pamphlets dealing with airplanes, and they seem completely absorbed in their task.

Meeting the individualized needs of students for instruction, then, is chiefly a function of the classroom teacher's role. Teachers are limited in this respect only by their ability to diagnose special needs and by the time they can devote to the giving of this help. Very often teachers can get assistance in special instructional problems of the kind just described by discussing their problems among themselves and by consulting with supervisors and administrators. Most teachers are aware of a need for more help than they can readily give, which is one of the reasons why smaller classes are so important in meeting the needs of individual students. The larger the class, the less time the teacher can spend on special problems of learning.

Personal Adjustment Problems

The second kind of need likely to be overlooked in a system geared entirely to provide mass education is what we might call the "personal need," that is, the need stemming from personal problems. In some ways, these problems resemble those of the emotionally disturbed child that we discussed in Chapter 15. But the difference here lies in the severity of the problem and the extent to which it dominates the life of the child. The learning capacity of a child in the "emotionally disturbed" category is continually threatened or impaired by the problems he must face in his everyday life. Only a few children in the average classroom will need continuing psychological help over a long period of time. On the other hand, virtually all children have to deal with psychological problems at some time or other. The very unpredictability of life is bound to cause some anxiety.

Most children learn how to cope with most of the recurring problems in their lives as a matter of course, as a part of growing up. But every child (and adult, too) must occasionally deal with problems that are temporarily more than he can easily handle. Some of the critical situations that produce problems are obvious—a new brother or sister is born, the family decides to move, Mother has to go to work, Father is called for military service, and so forth. These are the crises of everyday living. Children survive them, of course, and are perhaps stronger for having lived through them, but while they are in the process of adjusting to the demands that life makes on them, it is not surprising that they should become less attentive in class, unusually quarrelsome, quiet and withdrawn, or whatever their customary and individual mode of dealing with crisis and anxiety happens to be.

As a way of discussing the teacher's role in easing such problems, let us consider some of the problems of adjustment that are not so obvious and dramatic but that may seem crucial to the child.

Billy is genuinely upset because he has lost his eraser. Now there is nothing particularly serious about a second-grader losing his eraser, but Billy is so disturbed that he cannot concentrate on his number problems. Back of Billy's concern is the fact that this is the fifth eraser he has lost in two weeks. Erasers cost only a nickel, but his father got very angry when Billy asked him for the money for the one he just lost. He is troubled not only because he is afraid to go to his father and ask for another nickel, but because he also wonders what is *wrong* with him: Why *can't* he keep from losing erasers? Maybe he is *no good.*

When biology class started, Mrs. Desmond became aware that Charmaine was behaving in a very silly manner. To be sure, teenagers are awfully silly at times, but Charmaine was acting sillier than most. Furthermore, this wasn't like her. She was working with a couple of boys who were dissecting a frog and was making remarks that were supposed to be funny and giggling at them. The boys didn't seem to think they were very funny. A couple of the other groups looked up to see what was going on, so Mrs. Desmond moved across the laboratory toward Charmaine's table. Charmaine saw her out of the corner of her eye and quieted down. However, a minute later the giggles started again, so Mrs. Desmond decided that something must be done.

"Charmaine," she said, pleasantly, "will you give me a hand in the storeroom?"

Charmaine's face fell as she turned and walked toward the storeroom door, and Mrs. Desmond knew she had seen through the ruse.

The two of them said nothing while Mrs. Desmond stood on a ladder and put plaster models on the top shelf as Charmaine handed them to her. Then, when they were finished, Charmaine said, in a small voice: "I'll try to keep quiet now, Mrs. Desmond."

Mrs. Desmond did not answer her directly but asked: "Is there something bothering you, Charmaine?"

Charmaine bit her lip and shook her head "No," while two tears welled up in her eyes. She turned and started to leave the room.

"Just a moment, Charmaine," Mrs. Desmond said gently. "Would you drop in and see me after school for a little while?"

Charmaine looked apprehensive, then relieved, and said she would come. Then she turned and went back to the frogs. She was quiet during the rest of the period.

In her conversations with Charmaine during the following week, Mrs. Desmond found the cause of Charmaine's disruptive behavior. It appeared that Charmaine had been going with a small clique of girls who had suddenly decided to exclude her from their plans and activities. Charmaine wasn't sure why, unless it was because of something she had said. The girls had been talking about their ancestry and the famous families and names they counted among their forebears, when Charmaine had said, with some pride, that her great-grandmother was a Hawaiian princess. The girls had said little about this at the time, but her exclusion from the group started shortly thereafter.

The troubles faced by Billy and Charmaine appear somewhat trivial, perhaps. There is nothing particularly crucial or vital about losing an eraser or being excluded from a group of snobbish girls. Yet as far as these two individuals are concerned, the world looks black indeed, and their ability to function normally is impaired, at least temporarily. Hence we must consider problems of this type together with those that are more obvious and more dramatic. It should be noted, in passing, that children often seem to be able to stand up under difficult crises but break down in situations that seem relatively unimportant. We mention this point as a reminder that it is how the problem appears to the individual student that counts with him, not how it appears to teachers and other adults.

INDIVIDUALIZED ATTENTION FROM PSYCHOLOGICAL SPECIALISTS

Emotional Disturbances

Emotional problems that disturb the functioning of individual students are not the kind of difficulties that can generally be treated by changes in curriculum, better methods of instruction, or special tutoring, yet they are a proper concern for the teacher because they interfere with the capacity to learn. Usually the disturbance is temporary; after a while, the difficult situation rights itself or the student learns how to adjust to the problem and accept it. Occasionally, things do not work out well; the situation does not improve or the child continues to feel defeated and upset, whereupon we have a chronically disturbed child on our hands, a child who needs more help that we can give him in our role as a teacher.

The extent to which teachers can help children with their emotional problems will depend on the amount of time they can spend as well as on the kind of training or preparation they have for the task. There are other factors that are important, of course—the emotional climate of the school, which will govern the extent to which children will feel encouraged to talk to teachers about their problems; the conflict that sometimes arises between the role of helping students talk about their problems and that of giving the same students grades and marks; the extent to which an individual teacher enjoys counseling students; and the question of whether it is fair to the rest of the students to spend so much time with one or two.

Guidance workers can help in various ways with the problem of what to do about the student who is temporarily disturbed. The teacher can refer the student directly to a counselor or school psychologist. Sometimes, however, the teacher feels that he would like to continue the task he has already begun. Perhaps he does not want to disturb the counseling relationship that has grown up between him and the student but is not sure how to proceed or whether the student needs more help than he can give. If so, he may be able to use the guidance worker as a consultant.

Teachers are sometimes afraid that the guidance worker may interfere in the relationship they have developed with their students. They point out that students *do* come to teachers with their problems, and should they, in effect *reject* these students by sending them on to guidance workers? No one intends, of course, that guidance workers interfere with sound teacher-student relationships. The purpose of having guidance workers in school is to get more individualized attention to more students, not to reduce any help they may now be getting from teachers. As we noted above, however, there are students who are reluctant to take their problems to teachers, and there are some students whose problems are so complex that most teachers have neither the time nor the training to do justice to them. In the final analysis, a properly functioning guidance service will help teachers do their main job of classroom instruction more effectively. Some of the ways in which such a service can help will be discussed a few pages hence.

Problems of Choosing a Career

We have thus far discussed two major kinds of problems that require individualized attention and that may be overlooked in a system of mass education: learning problems and emotional problems. A third kind of problem or need is one that we have already mentioned in connection with our discussion of the duties of the school counselor: the need for vocational counseling.

The need to choose and prepare for a vocation is one of the key developmental needs of adolescence. Vocational adjustment looms large on the horizon of adult life ahead. In our culture it is perhaps the most crucial adjustment of life because it is so closely identified with the self-concept of the individual. When a youth talks about what he wants to be, we know that he is not so much talking about the kind of personality he expects to have as he is about the kind of work he wants to do. When we talk about "success" in life, we are usually thinking of *vocational* success. Therefore most adolescents are aware that vocational choice and preparation cannot be undertaken casually. To be sure, many of them adopt a casual attitude as a mask for their real anxieties—just one more reason why school counselors are unable to limit themselves solely to educational and vocational problems.

This does not mean that career counseling has become less important as a counselor function. Harold L. Wilensky (1967) maintains that career counselors are very much needed by youth today in order to "convey a sense of the wondrous variety of work worlds. . . " and to guide teenagers through "the maze of school curricula, training programs, jobs, and employment services." The rapidly changing complexity of today's world calls for expertise in collecting and communicating occupational information.

There is a great deal of detailed work involved in vocational counseling that a guidance worker can handle more efficiently and effectively than a classroom teacher. The counselor who teaches part-time and who is assigned, say, two hundred advisees, will interview them once a year or oftener, if necessary; he will administer and interpret appropriate

INDIVIDUALIZED ATTENTION FROM
PSYCHOLOGICAL SPECIALISTS

psychological tests, such as the Kuder Preference Record or the Bennett Mechanical Aptitude; he will maintain a file of occupational information; he will keep in touch with local employers and the admissions officers of nearby colleges and universities; and he will arrange for speakers representing various occupations to meet with groups of interested students. In addition, he may help students plan their programs each semester, see that they get placed in part-time jobs or summer jobs that provide valuable vocational experience, advise the school librarian on the purchase of books dealing with the major occupational fields, and maintain a file of pamphlets and other materials providing vocational information.

The Guidance Worker and the "Dropout"

Some of the inadequacies of a system of mass education are reflected in what is called the "dropout rate"—the proportion of students who leave school before graduation. At first glance, it seems a rather strange paradox that in a land where education is the key to opportunity, and where education is more or less free for the asking, almost a third of those who start school at age 6 fail to graduate from high school. One of the first explanations that comes to mind is that those who drop out are the ones who cannot benefit from education. There is some basis for this impression. As Figure 17-1 indicates, the average young person who drops out of high school reads at about the sixth-grade level and hence is likely to have difficulty in coping with the demands of the curriculum. Yet an uncomfortably high proportion of the school leavers have above-average to superior aptitude. Furthermore, we do not know at what point or at what level young people really become uneducable. Probably few students, if any with IQs between 80 and 90 can benefit from the college-preparatory curriculum that is standard fare at most of the high schools in this country, but it is very likely that we could provide many different kinds of educational experiences that would be of great benefit to these students, as well as to the society in which they will live.

Although it is impossible to measure the direct social cost of an incomplete high-school education,

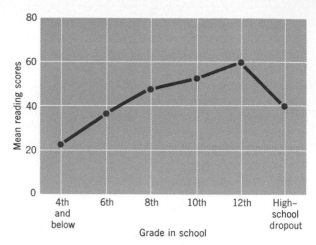

FIG. 17-1. Mean scores on the reading section of Wide Range Achievement test for youths twelve to seventeen years of age by grade in school (U. S. Department of Health, Education, and Welfare, 1974).

statistical studies show that the "holding power" of high schools is related to a number of indices of economic, social, and political viability. Donald G. Barker and Paul R. Hensarling (1965) computed correlations for each of the fifty states between high-school retention rates and a number of variables. The high-school retention rate was calculated in terms of the percentage of eighth-grade students in 1958 who graduated in 1962. As Figure 17-2 shows, states with high retention rates had low percentages of selective service registrants failing mental and literacy tests. They also had low rates of infant mortality and a lower number of pupils per teacher. Furthermore, citizens of states with high retention rates were more likely to vote in national elections. They tended to have higher income and paid higher teacher salaries as well. Somewhat similar results were reported by Lindgren (1974) some years later. He found that states in which the high-school dropout rate was high also tended to have high homicide rates. In such states, the percentages of young people volunteering for the Peace Corps tended to be low.

A large number of students drop out of school because they have come to feel that further efforts are useless. Their morale is low, and they are obsessed by a sense of personal failure. Many of them

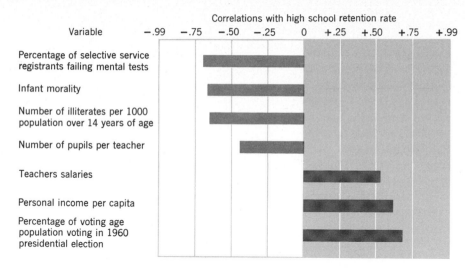

Correlations with high school retention rate

| Variable | −.99 | −.75 | −.50 | −.25 | 0 | +.25 | +.50 | +.75 | +.99 |

Percentage of selective service registrants failing mental tests

Infant morality

Number of illiterates per 1000 population over 14 years of age

Number of pupils per teacher

Teachers salaries

Personal income per capita

Percentage of voting age population voting in 1960 presidential election

FIG. 17-2. Relationship between the "holding power" or retention rate of high schools and various indices of mental, physical, economic, and political health in each of the fifty states (Barker and Hensarling, 1965).

view the school, rather than themselves, as the cause of their failure and can hardly wait to escape. Lucius F. Cervantes (1965), in his study of high-school dropouts, told of four youths who were charged with a series of burglaries and were found guilty by a South Carolina general sessions court. The judge, on learning that they had quit school, gave them the choice of returning to school or being sentenced to "do time" on the county chain gang. Without hesitation, all four youths elected the chain gang. To these boys, school was obviously worse than jail.

Although we might think that students who are having difficulties in school would be inclined to seek help and thus improve their chances for success, the opposite seems to be true. A nationwide survey of students' attitudes toward school showed that those whose grades were in the bottom 5 percent of the distribution, in contrast to those who were in the top 7 percent, were more inclined to say that they were not in need of counseling. Figure 17-3 indicates the differences between the perceived counseling needs of the two groups. It is especially interesting to note that only 19 percent of the failing students wanted counseling on school problems in contrast to 35 percent of the successful group.

There are several ways in which school guidance

workers can help reduce the number of students who drop out of school. Many schools require students to have at least one interview a term with a counselor. Although such contacts are likely to be brief, a sensitive and alert counselor can often pick up cues that indicate the presence of serious difficulties which can be discussed in follow-up interviews. In order to provide this kind of help, a counselor must listen sympathetically to whatever complaints and problems students bring to him. Attending school, like any other kind of group activity, is an experience likely to be characterized by frustrations and disappointments which arouse hostility and/or anxiety. Many students are able to get over these feelings or at least to push them into the background, keeping in mind their main objective of finishing high school. But some students brood about the wrongs they have suffered and permit their resentment to accumulate to the point where they can no longer tolerate life in school, whereupon they leave. A counselor can keep matters from going too far by providing a kind of emotional safety valve. It is difficult for anyone to maintain his resentment at a high pitch if he has a chance to talk out the problems that trouble him. Indeed, talking through personal problems with a counselor who is a "good listener" is an effective way of developing

INDIVIDUALIZED ATTENTION FROM
PSYCHOLOGICAL SPECIALISTS

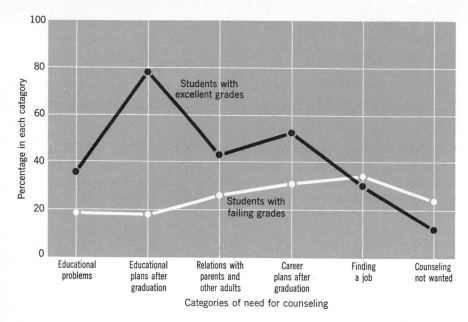

FIG. 17-3. Percentages of high-school students reporting a need for counseling help with various categories of problems (data from Erlick, 1974).

an objective point of view—a prerequisite to sensible decisions.

A large number of students drop out of school because they come to feel that further efforts to succeed are useless. Their morale is low, and they are obsessed by a sense of failure. Sometimes these students need to have someone show interest in their progress, sometimes they need an objective appraisal of their abilities, and sometimes they need to be reassured about the advantages to be gained through continuing in school.

Actually, it is impossible to outline all the ways in which counselors and other guidance workers can help students who are potential dropouts to make the adjustments that will keep them in school. Perhaps it can be summed up by saying that their chief function is to make the school more of a human institution, more interested in the welfare of each individual student. If they can make students aware that the school is interested in them as individuals, they should be able not only to lower the dropout rate but also to give all students a better feeling about the school, one that will improve their morale and general attitude, thus enabling them to gain greater benefits from their educational experiences.

Research studies generally show that students who are counseled are less likely to drop out of school than students who are not counseled, but there is some question whether merely making contact with a counselor is sufficient to act as a deterrent. In one study, counselors were instructed in the use of behavior modification methods before instituting an experimental program of "contingency counseling" with high-school students whose absenteeism was running about 30 percent, a rate that suggested that they were potential dropouts. Inasmuch as the counselors had little control over the kinds of things that could reinforce the behavior of these students, they contacted persons outside the school (parents, girl and boy friends) who would cooperate in giving or withholding reinforcements. The counselor than negotiated a "deal" between the outside agent and the student whereby the latter's school attendance would be reinforced. The results, as shown by Figure 17-4 showed that the program was successful in bringing about a significant improvement in the students' attendance. The change cannot be attributed to the fact that the counselors were now making contact with students they had previously overlooked, because other stu-

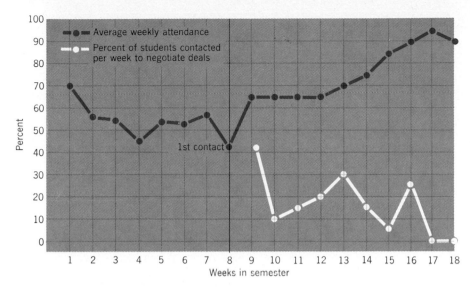

FIG. 17-4. Average weekly attendance of twenty high-school students who initially had poor attendance records and who participated in a contingency counseling program (MacDonald, Gallimore, and MacDonald, 1970).

dents with poor attendance records who were merely contacted by the counselor showed no such improvement, even though they were seen three times as often (MacDonald, Gallimore, and Mac-Donald, 1970).

One approach that has met with some success in keeping students in school is that of the work-study program, an arrangement that enables students to work part of the day and go to school part of the day. These programs are most successful when they are supervised by counselors, who approve the kinds and places of employment, help to make adjustments between work and school schedules, and lend sympathetic ears to the problems that inevitably arise in any kind of experimental undertaking. Daniel Schreiber (1963) reported on the first year's operation of a work-study program at McKinley High School in St. Louis. The actual dropout rate of students enrolled in the program was 11.6 percent, as contrasted with 35.2 percent in a comparable control group. Another project in New York City that combined study, work, and guidance for fifty-three academic failures who had truancy and discipline records enjoyed similar success. Sixty-four percent of the group graduated, as contrasted

with 36 percent of a matched control group (Slotkin, 1963).

Group Counseling of Students with Problems

There are numerous demands made on the time of the school guidance worker. In many schools he advises two hundred or more students when they select and schedule courses at the start of each term, talks to students who have been designated as discipline problem cases, serves as liaison with the juvenile court, makes referral of students to community agencies, consults with teachers and administrators, conducts case conferences, and advises students on personal, educational, and career-choice problems. Often he has a part-time teaching load in addition to these duties and functions. Perhaps the commonest complaint of school counselors is that they never have enough time for their main role: helping students with problems.

One partial answer to this complaint is group counseling, a technique that enables a guidance worker to work with as many as ten or fifteen students simultaneously. On the face of it, group counseling appears to be a second-rate method of treating adjustment problems that are unique for each student. In actuality, however, group counseling possesses a number of advantages and, for many students, may actually be preferable to individual counseling. For one thing, a student is likely to discover, in the context of group discussion, that his problems are not so unique, and that other students also cannot concentrate when trying to study, do not get along with their parents, feel that others do not like them, are unable to meet deadlines for homework and term papers, forget all they have learned when taking exams, and so forth. For another, many students find it easier to tell their peers about their difficulties than to recount them to an adult, no matter how sympathetic and friendly he

may be. Furthermore, students tend to accept advice given them by peers more readily than that given by adults.

Ben C. Finney and Elizabeth Van Dalsem (1969) have described a group counseling program for gifted underachievers which was instituted on an experimental basis in a California high-school district. Counselors who were to lead the groups received special training from psychological consultants in the use of group methods. Groups averaged about twelve students of the same sex, who met in one-hour sessions once a week over the greater part of two school years.

Group counseling is like many worthwhile human undertakings in that it often seems to be a waste of

GROUP COUNSELING
The emotional needs of teenagers are especially attuned to group counseling. Within the context of a group of peers they feel more secure in examining feelings and emotional problems and in dealing with the interpretations that adults place on their behavior. Conclusions and decisions reached in group settings often have a more lasting influence than those attained in individual counseling sessions.

time and more detrimental than helpful. For instance, group leaders in this program observed that the students were inclined to deal with group counseling situations much as they did other school requirements and responsibilities, for they continually tried to avoid the kind of involvement needed for making progress in the group sessions by shifting responsibility to other students or to the group leader. "Typically at the beginning of the experiment they spent much group time criticizing—often with devastating accuracy—teachers, parents, adults, the school, the social system, etc., but delicately avoiding any inspection of the part which they played in their academic difficulties—or the feelings behind the actions."

After this initial phase, students started to take on more responsibility for seeing that the time of the group was taken up constructively. They began to share more personal feelings and experiences and to probe some of the attitudes that lay behind their behavior. "Characteristically the course of the group movement was erratic with long periods of trivial or confused discussion or anxious silence, which would suddenly be interrupted with brief periods of warm sharing of feelings and exploration of feelings and motives."

A number of variables were used by the investigators in order to assess the effect the experimental treatment had on student behavior: grade-point average, number of absences from school, number of referrals to a school dean for deportment problems, teacher appraisal of students' classroom behavior, and scores on a personality test—the California Psychological Inventory or CPI. As compared to a control group of underachievers who had received no treatment, the students who had received group counseling attained a slightly higher grade-point average, but the difference was not a significant one. At the end of the first year of counseling, there was no difference between control and experimental students in number of absences from school, but by the end of the second year, the experimental students had considerably fewer absences. They also had fewer disciplinary referrals, although the difference (24 percent, in contrast to 33 percent, over the two-year period) was not statistically significant. The experimental students made a considerably better impression on their teachers. In contrast to the control-group students, they were perceived as being more attentive, more task-oriented, less disruptive, less often tardy to class, more accepting of teachers' suggestions, and demonstrating more pleasure in learning. An analysis of scores made on the CPI also indicated that the counseled students showed significant improvement in poise, social adequacy, confidence in directing and initiating their own actions, and resourcefulness in dealing with stress.

In other words, although the nonsignificant gain in grade-point average was somewhat of a disappointment to the investigators and the group leaders, other measures of students' behavior and attitudes showed satisfying indications of improvement.

The Problem of Academic Pressure

An obvious solution to the problem of how to get students of all levels of ability to realize more of their potentiality for learning is that of increasing the academic pressure on them—urge them to do better, exhort them, and threaten them with academic failure if they do not do their best. This is a solution that ranks very high in the preferences of teachers and parents who are confronted with the student who "will not work up to capacity." Sometimes such measures will work, but more often they will not. Usually they only serve to aggravate the sense of failure that already troubles such a student. Often the guidance worker can make a positive contribution to the problem by counseling the student or by interpreting the situation to teachers and parents or both.

Gerry, an eighth-grader, was one of the youngest in his class. In spite of being concerned about his immaturity and lack of confidence, teachers had promoted him each year, yielding to the insistence of the parents that Gerry not be held back. Gerry's family was continually comparing him with a more successful cousin, presumably to encourage him to try harder. This tactic, however, only undermined Gerry's self-confidence and probably contributed to his stuttering and his withdrawal from activities involving reading. His parents required him to go to summer school each year. Instead of helping him, this experience made Gerry all the more conscious of his inadequacies.

Gerry's teachers referred him to the school psychologist for diagnostic appraisal. The psychologist reported him to be average in intelligence, but reading at about the third-grade level. Personality testing showed feelings of inadequacy, aggravated by unsuccessful attempts to compete academically with a successful younger sister. Gerry saw himself as someone who tried constantly to please, who always failed whatever he attempted, and who was forced to live with problems that were more than he could solve. In addition, he was very dependent on his mother.

Treatment in Gerry's case consisted of having his teachers give him materials with reading difficulty at about the second-grade level but interest level appropriate for the teen years. The psychologist told Gerry that he was confident that Gerry could do the job but left the decision up to him as to whether it was worth the effort. Gerry took home some self-testing materials and in a short time confirmed the psychologist's analysis. At his next therapy session he reported that he was quite pleased and encouraged by his ability to read and understand the material given him and asked for more homework. As therapy progressed, Gerry's reading continued to improve and teachers reported that he was able to participate successfully in some of the regular classroom work. This, in turn, led to greater acceptance on the part of his classmates (Dinkmeyer and Dreikurs, 1963).

Helping Schools Adjust to the Psychological Needs of Students

The case we have described shows how psychological workers and teachers, working together, can aid children in adjusting more successfully to the demands of the school. This is the first major contribution the psychological worker makes. In the secondary schools, according to Joyce Slayton Mitchell (1970), helping students to adjust to the school will involve aiding them with such problems as; "I can't get along with Miss Power," "Why do I need to take Algebra II?", and "I can't concentrate when I study." These problems, Mitchell says, are largely surface manifestations of the student's basic question: "Who am I?" She comments further:

The purpose of high school is not to prepare for after high school. Today's students have been very clear about the irrelevance of this purpose. To be meaningful to them, the purpose of high school must be to find out about themselves.

The second contribution that counselors can make is that of helping (and this usually means prodding) the school to adjust itself to the demands of students. Any counselor who has a good relationship with students will hear them saying things like the following:

"I learned how to bake a cake in home economics, but I still don't know how to shop."

"Half the kids in our algebra class got Fs. I was one of them. Maybe I deserved it, but what I want to know is: Why do I have to take algebra anyhow?"

"I wanted to take auto shop or metalcraft, but the classes were full."

"When I worked up in the woods last summer, the boss and all the fellows treated me like one of the gang. Here they treat me like a little kid."

"The English teacher spends all her time on rules and parts of speech, the same stuff we had in grammar school. I guess I know the rules all right, because I got a 'B,' but I can't write good enough to get on the school paper. I wish we would learn how to write."

Perhaps we are inclined to discount such remarks as perfectly normal "griping"—something that all students do. However, if we are serious about finding out why students have difficulties or drop out of school, we must find out where *we* are failing. And the students themselves are the best source of such information.

It is difficult for teachers and administrators to evaluate an isolated complaint about the school, but a counselor who has an intimate, face-to-face relationship with a sizable number of students is in an excellent position to give a clear report about the way in which the school is failing to help students.

Michael A. Ciavarella (1968) says that a major responsibility of the school counselor is that of minimizing the frustration of students in order to "make school achievement more possible and school life more satisfying." He observes that one type of frustration needing constant counselor attention is "curricular conflict frustration," a reaction to "an inflexible, narrow, lifeless, and undifferentiated curriculum." He continues:

Ideally, the curriculum is the vehicle by which a student tries out exploratory experiences or tasks which meet his own developmental needs, desires, and interests. Yet this same vehicle, which is presumably designed to move a student toward healthy goal-attainment in school, can become an obstacle or source of frustration that inhibits healthy school adjustment.

In order to prevent this from occurring, says Ciavarella, the counselor must become involved in curriculum revision. Dugald Arbuckle (1970) has the following to say about the counselor's role:

The counselor, more than anyone else, is the one who can help revolutionize the educational experience—so that the school can become a relevant institution, so that the educational experience it provides can be centered in the young for whom it was created, so that the young can come to feel, all of them, of worth, and thus be able to play their parts as free members of a free society.

Although the counselor can serve as a resource person and may initiate moves that will lead to changes in the school program, he cannot bring about the changes alone. The responsibility for making these changes is shared by the school administration and the faculty, as well as by the school board and the community. The counselor plays his part by keeping the school informed and by encouraging the kind of action that needs to be taken. This is not an easy task; it is often a thankless one. People seldom like to be reminded of their deficiencies, and teachers and administrators are no exception. Therefore the counselor has to play his active role of consultant and critic with much skill and sensitivity, continuing to remind his colleagues of the problem of the dropout but not carrying his campaign to the point at which he arouses hostility and resistance.

Some schools simplify this task of the guidance worker by including him on committees charged with responsibilities for curriculum revision. Sometimes he plays a major part in the in-service training of teachers. The schools where counselors have status and respect, where they are listened to and consulted by their colleagues, are the schools that

(Ford Button, *Phi Delta Kappan*, September 1974)

"It might help if we stopped referring to the faculty as 'us' and the students as 'them'"

INDIVIDUALIZED ATTENTION FROM
PSYCHOLOGICAL SPECIALISTS

are getting the greatest value from their guidance workers.

The Case Conference

One of the most effective approaches to pupil personnel problems is the case conference, in which the guidance worker who has been working closely with a certain student sits down with teachers, administrators, and other staff members to discuss the problems the student is encountering. Such conferences are valuable for a number of reasons. In the first place, they bring together several sources of information. Usually the guidance worker has the results of his interviews with the student, as well as psychological test data, interviews with parents, and cumulative records. But he also needs to have the thoughts and feelings of the other people who have worked with the child or have met with his parents. It is one thing to read a few terse statements in a cumulative file and quite another to have a teacher describe what it is like to deal with the student in the classroom.

In the second place, case conferences help teachers who have a child in a classroom to gain some new insights and understandings into his behavior. These insights are valuable not only because they help teachers to understand this particular child, but also because seeing what lies behind the behavior of one child helps in understanding the behavior of other children.

In the third place, a case conference is a cooperative venture in communication. Each staff member participates on an equal basis; each is there to share information and points of view; each has something to give and something to gain. The conference provides teachers and guidance staff with an opportunity to collaborate, to tackle a problem together.

The fourth advantage to the case conference is that it gives the guidance worker a chance to share some of his findings about students in general. This not only helps teachers develop different perspectives on students, but it also stimulates thinking about changes in the school program that would be helpful in promoting the general educational plan of the school. This is quite different from having the guidance worker get up in faculty meetings and say what is wrong with the program and what needs changing. His arguments are far more eloquent when he tells the teachers participating in a case conference about the problems faced by a child in trouble. Over a period of time, case conferences are bound to touch on a cross section of the inadequacies of the school program. The guidance worker may not even have to point them out as inadequacies, for one of the things that is likely to happen in the cooperative atmosphere of a well-managed case conference is that staff members become more objective and less defensive about the school's deficiencies. It is as a consulting participant in a case conference that the guidance worker can do some of his most effective work in helping the school adjust to the needs of the individual student.

"Life-space" or "Crisis" Interviewing

One approach that William C. Morse (1963) has found to be useful in helping teachers gain a better understanding of the world in which children and young people live consists of a technique of interviewing which he had used to good effect in a camp for disturbed, hostile-aggressive boys. This method of interviewing is used at a time when there is a crisis or a problem. A boy has been hitting a smaller child, or a girl has failed for the third time to come through with an assignment that she had promised to turn in. The teacher or guidance worker feels that this calls for some serious talk with the student, not only because he is interested in helping the student control the behavior in question, but also because he feels the need to understand what is leading the student to behave in this negative way.

In training teachers in life-space interviewing, Morse begins by having them describe the way the world looks to the child under study and what results are likely to eventuate. This, of course, calls for a great deal of empathy on the part of the teacher, not only with the child in question, but also with children in general. The steps used in life-space interviewing are as follows:

1. The teacher begins his conversation with the student in an interested, accepting, nonjudg-

mental way, allowing him to describe the situation or problem in his own terms, just as he sees it, even though it may be distorted or incorrect.

2. The teacher explores the possibility that there may be other, related problems. Perhaps the problem of the moment is merely a side issue. In what way is the problem an expression of the pupil's personality? "Children frequently give deep and meaningful material at this stage, and teachers can learn to listen without probing or accepting responsibility for resolving that which is beyond their sphere of influence."

3. The teacher then raises the question: "What do you think ought to be done about it?" The pupil's system of values comes into play at this point, and he is likely to reveal any anxiety he has about committing himself to any course of behavior that might change things. Sometimes the problem "solves itself" at this stage.

4. The teacher becomes somewhat more active in the interview at the next stage, in that he indicates any features of the real world that the student may have overlooked and that might have implications for the problem at hand. This is done in a factual manner, without any change from the accepting attitudes the teacher has expressed from the beginning.

5. At this point, pupil motivation for change is explored. How does he think he might be helped? What role should the teacher play in supporting and encouraging a reasonable degree of management of the behavior in question?

6. Finally, the teacher develops a follow-through plan with the pupil. What must we do if this happens again? The plan should be realistic and relevant, must be kept within the limitations of the school resources, and must take cognizance of any possible "escape hatches." If there is any pretense within the school or any reluctance on the part of teachers or the administration to come to grips with issues, this must also be faced frankly. For example, the teacher cannot suggest the possibility of suspension if it is against school policy to suspend any student, or

to suggest referral to psychotherapy, if no such referral is possible.

Before using such techniques the teacher must begin with a recognized group or individual problem he is trying to work with. Morse also suggests that techniques like these should be learned under adequate supervision. During the initial stages, it may be a good idea for the teacher to interview the child in the presence of a supervisor or, at second best, tape-record the interview or take notes afterward.

It should be kept in mind that life-space interviewing has two aims: (1) to improve the understanding and empathy of the teacher, and (2) to help the student with an emotional or social problem that is causing difficulties. Morse is optimistic about the attainment of both objectives. He believes that a great many teachers have empathic and intuitive resources that will enable them to develop skill at using the method, and that children generally will respond to it. He says:

Pupils do not await perfection in their teachers. They often respond well to moderation or mitigation of negative forces. This is not to say that the course is always smooth, for at times there are outcroppings of human relations that make one wince. However, in our experience most teachers are reasonable and when they respond in poor fashion it is usually our of frustration regarding their inability. . . .

Collaboration of Teachers and Guidance Workers

Most of the day-by-day work with the emotional problems of school children is the responsibility of the classroom teacher. Linda cries because Derek keeps taking her crayons, so Mrs. Henley moves her to another table where she will be in more congenial company. Cissy copied another child's work during an arithmetic quiz. Miss Crane decides to fail her on the quiz and to have a talk with her after school. Gino counted on going to the state capital with the glee club. It was quite a disappointment to him when he didn't make it. Mr. Hines, the club's sponsor, decides that he'd better buy Gino a coke after practice to give him a chance to talk it out. Mr. Lennon notices that Mac, the new boy from out of state, had been in a fight. It occurs to him that the boy seemed to have a chip on his shoulder. He wonders what he can do to help him become better integrated with the class.

This is a rough sampling of the kinds of personal and emotional problems teachers deal with every day. Some of them turn out to be quite serious and should eventually be referred to a specialist. But even the children who are receiving treatment from specialists remain in the classroom. Hence, for better or worse, the teacher is in the position of being his own guidance worker much of the time. His effectiveness in this role will depend upon his training and experience, his flexibility, his willingness to try to understand the behavior of children, and the amount and kind of help he gets from the guidance staff. If he can develop his own skills and personal resources and coordinate them with the help the school can provide, he should have a great deal more success with his "problem children." As he develops his competencies along these lines, he will discover new ways in which members of the guidance staff can help him. In general, the more teachers develop their ability to understand and cope with the emotional problems of the classroom, the more likely they are to make use of the psychological services available in the school guidance department.

SUMMARY

Although mass education is a necessary and desirable part of our civilization, it does not supply the answers to all educational problems. If the learning needs of all students are to be met, the methods of mass education must be supplemented by arrangements for providing individualized help when needed. Much of this individualized help comes from the teacher, particularly when the problems involve classroom learning. However, teachers also help students with personal problems, and even with emotional disturbances, provided, of course, that they have the necessary background, the proper relationships with students, and the time.

Nevertheless there will always be special and individual needs that are beyond the scope of the teacher's ability to serve. These needs generally require the attention of specialists—counselors, psychologists, social workers, nurses, physicians, and administrators—persons who provide psychological guidance or student personnel services for the school. Sometimes these specialists help by working with students who are referred to them. Sometimes their task is to see every student from time to time in the course of helping him with his educational and vocational plans. Sometimes they work with teachers on a consulting basis. And sometimes they participate with teachers and administrators in case conferences.

The guidance specialist is specifically charged with the task of helping the individual student—with individualizing education. Much of what he does is concerned with aiding the student to make an adjustment to the demands of everyday life, including those of the school. However, by working with teachers individually and collectively, he also helps the school to adjust to the needs of students. Perhaps he may present data that indicate a need for curriculum revision; perhaps he helps an individual teacher to get a better understanding of the problems of a student and thus is instrumental in bringing about a change in a classroom situation.

One of the major educational problems is that of the student who drops out of high school before graduation. Often such students are so discouraged by their inability to cope with the demands of teachers that they have no interest in seeking help from counselors. The problems of bright underachievers are also difficult and complex. They can be resolved in part by group counseling, if school authorities are willing to arrange for special training of group leaders and plan for sessions that meet weekly over a two-year period. Increasing the academic pressure on less successful students appears to do little good and may aggravate problems. The guidance worker may be of assistance here by working with the dissatisfied, apathetic, and overly tense student. Perhaps the student needs help in adjusting to the program of the school; perhaps there are changes that should be made in the curriculum or perhaps the parents need to be brought into the situation.

In short, the guidance worker makes his best contribution by "humanizing" the school, by making it less impersonal, less detached and remote from the problems and needs of the students.

Suggested Problems

1. At the start of the chapter, the author mentioned only two of the advantages of mass education. What are some of the other advantages? What are additional disadvantages he did not mention?

2. What are some of the ways in which guidance specialists can promote better relations between schools and parents? Between schools and communities?

3. If two or three boys in your class were disruptive, at what point in your dealings with them would you use a guidance worker? How would you use him? What kind of help would you expect from him.

4. Every student has had several experiences which involve some kind of counseling relationship with a guidance specialist or a teacher. Describe an experience of your own (or that of a friend, if you prefer). How would you evaluate it? Do you think it helped you (or your friend) to make a better adjustment to the school? In what ways could the relationship have been better or more helpful?

5. Locate a college or university catalogue and make a brief list of the course titles required as preparation for counselors, psychologists, school social workers, or attendance officers. Write a sentence or two justifying each course. Are there any courses that could easily be omitted? Are there any courses not included that should be added?

6. Some school administrators insist that the school psychologists they hire have completed a year or more of classroom teaching. Psychologists often object to meeting such requirements. What do you suppose are the arguments for and against such requirements?

7. Read over the brief case description of Gerry's problem on pages 453-454. How do you think he regards the significant people (parents, teacher, siblings, classmates) in his world?

Suggested Readings

Adams, J. F. (ed.) *Counseling and guidance.* New York: Macmillan, 1965.

Amos, W. E., and Grambs, J. D. (eds.) *Counseling the disadvantaged youth.* Englewood Cliffs, N. J.: Prentice-Hall, 1968.

Bordin, E. S. *Psychological counseling,* 2nd ed. Englewood Cliffs, N. J.: Prentice-Hall, 1968.

Campbell, D. P. *The results of counseling: twenty-five years later.* Philadelphia: Saunders, 1965. A group of University of Minnesota alumni who were counseled as freshmen in the 1930s are compared with another group who were freshmen at the same time but who were not counseled.

Eiserer, P. E. *The school psychologist.* New York: Center for Applied Research in Psychology, 1963. A brief, straightforward description of the roles and functions of school psychologists.

Gray, S. W. *The psychologist in the schools.* New York: Holt, Rinehart, and Winston, 1963. A well-written description of the duties, training, and problems of the school psychologist.

Hansen, J. C., and Stevic, R. R. *Elementary school guidance.* New York: Macmillan, 1969.

Milard, C. V., and Rothney, J. W. M. *The elementary school child: A book of cases.* New York: Dryden, 1957. A broad sampling of cases, including anecdotal data, test scores, and a range of background material.

Mortensen, D. G., and Schmuller, A. M. *Guidance in today's schools,* 2nd ed. New York: Wiley, 1966.

Sprinthall, N. A., and Tiedeman, D. V. "Guidance and the pupil." In J. I. Goodlad (ed.), *The changing American school,* 65th Yearbook of the National Society for the Study of Education, Part II. Chicago: University of Chicago Press, 1966.

Strang, R., and Morris, G. *Guidance in the classroom.* New York: Macmillan, 1964. A brief paperback describing guidance services in schools, with some discussion of how teachers can participate.

Tyler, L. E. *The work of the counselor,* 3rd ed. Englewood Cliffs, N. J.: Prentice-Hall, 1969.

See also the following journals: *Journal of Counseling Psychology, Journal of the National Association of Deans of Women, Personnel and Guidance Journal, The School Counselor.*

18

The Psychology of Being a Teacher

The Importance of Self-understanding

As we study the psychological factors that affect the learning process and the learning situation—that is, as we study the psychological aspects of being a learner—we cannot help but be impressed by their complexity. Indeed, it is easy to become so lost in wonder at the complexity of the psychology of the learner that we are likely to forget that the psychology of the teacher is equally complex. And we also

tend to forget that teachers ·need to understand their own behavior just as much as they need to understand the behavior of the students they teach.

What goes on in the classroom may be described as a process of interaction between pupil and teacher, and between the individual student and the classroom group. The teacher is as much a part of this process of interaction as is the group or the individual student. Developing an understanding of children is essentially a problem of understanding human motivation. And the human being to whom the teacher is closest and with whom he is most familiar is he himself. Indeed, a fairly reasonable hypothesis would be that a teacher's insight into and understanding of his students are in approximate proportion to the insight and understanding that he possesses regarding himself.

The understanding of defense mechanisms may serve as an example. It is one thing to study a catalogue of the devious ways in which people avoid anxiety and responsibility by the little psychological tricks that they play on themselves. It is quite another to discover the same interesting quirks in our own behavior. If we advance no further than the first stage—that of cataloguing the defense mechanisms of others—we are inclined to become somewhat judgmental, moralistic, superior, or unsympathetic when we catch one of our students or a colleague using a defense mechanism. But if we have experienced the second stage—that of understanding how *we ourselves* use such mechanisms—we are in a better position to work *with* the student or colleague, rather than against him. There is a feeling of acceptance and respect for others that comes with self-understanding.

In this book we have said much about the psychological factors and forces that affect the lives of students and, to a significant extent, make them the kinds of individuals they are and lead them to behave the way they do. Actually, the same kinds of forces affect the lives and behavior of teachers. Teachers and students alike are affected by the norms and standards of the culture and the community and experience the stresses and strains of balancing their personal needs with the demands of the group. Teachers experience a sense of freedom and heightened morale under democratic leadership or, conversely, feel rebellious or apathetic under authoritarian leadership, just as students do.

Hence we say that one of the first things a teacher must do to understand what goes on in the classroom is to understand himself and the psychological factors and forces in his environment.

INSTRUCTIONAL AND ADMINISTRATIVE ROLES

Let us begin our discussion of the psychology of teachers with an analysis of some of the roles they play. Roles are bits or sequences of patterned behavior that we have developed into familiar routines. Roles are based on the expectations we have of ourselves, which, in turn, stem from the expectations that others have of us. For example, we stand before the class and lead our pupils in the morning ''Pledge of Allegiance to the Flag'' because everyone expects us to do so, and we have come to expect this of ourselves. It is one of the many roles that makes us a teacher—and not a geologist, an accountant, or a social worker. Our roles contribute to our social identity, and our identity determines our roles.

Teachers play many roles. The roles interlock and overlap. Some are complementary and some are contradictory. They differ with the kind of school and the subject, and they differ, of course, with the individual teacher. What we shall try to do in this discussion is to select some of the roles that are common to most teachers and teaching situations, recognizing that our catalogue is by no means mutually exclusive. Some of these categories are covered in Table 18-1, which shows the percentages of teachers who reported involvement in various kinds of noninstructional duties and activities, together with the average number of hours devoted to such duties outside the regular school hours (which average about thirty-five hours a week). It may be well to keep this list of activities in mind in reading the next few pages.

The Instructor

The first and most obvious role performed by teachers is that of the *instructor:* the person who initiates, directs, and evaluates learning. Presumably, this is the chief reason why teachers are employed—to see that learning takes place. This role serves as a kind of nucleus or ''core role'' for other subordinate roles—not all of them but most of them.

In recent years there has been a shift in the focus of this role and the way in which it is played by

TABLE 18-1. Percentages of Teachers Participating in Activities Other than Classroom Instruction, Together with Number of Hours per Week Devoted to School Duties Outside the Regular School Hours[a,b]

Activity	Men	Women	Elementary	Secondary	Rural	Urban
Monitorial duties (keeping order in halls and on playgrounds, etc.)	78	81	86	72	83	79
Administrative duties (library, traffic squads, etc.)	49	43	45	45	44	45
Coaching athletics	32	9	15	17	20	13
Noncoaching duties related to athletics	49	18	14	46	34	23
Directing plays, concerts, and other public performances	49	55	58	46	63	47
Sponsoring class organizations, clubs, student government, etc.	56	38	24	70	44	42
Committees and lectures related to professional improvement	50	49	47	52	38	56
Keeping records	81	88	87	85	84	87
Individual out-of-class assistance for one's own pupils	74	74	68	83	72	75
Working with parents of own pupils	64	78	79	66	69	76
No. of hours spent in school duties and activities outside of school hours	11.3	9.7	9.8	10.7	10.7	9.8

[a] NEA, 1957.
[b] Although this study was conducted twenty years ago, more recent surveys show little change in the amount of time teachers spend on nonteaching duties (McQueen, 1968).

teachers. Gordon C. Lee (1966), Dean of the College of Education, University of Washington, states that there has been a tendency for teachers to become specialists, to some degree, in a basic field of learning. This has been true of elementary, as well as of secondary, teachers. Such a trend is in contrast to earlier patterns in which teachers were supposed to be able to teach anything and everything. Another change that he notes is the tendency for teachers to become less involved in being exclusively and predominantly sources of data and dispensers of information. There has been a growing stress on "learning how to learn" and on strategies for motivating and facilitating learning. Still another trend is for teachers to become resource people to a much greater degree. In other words, teachers today are more likely to answer students' queries by telling them how and where to find answers, instead of giving them information directly.

The Teacher as Model

In the introduction to Chapter 10 we noted that a teacher serves an important function as a model who exposes students to adult forms of behavior. This exposure is necessary if social learning through imitation is to take place. Although this learning is usually incidental to the main focus of instruction, it may nevertheless have a significant long-range effect on student behavior. Fritz Redl and William W. Wattenberg (1959) observed that when the teacher plays the role of social model he is serving as the *representative of society,* the person who is charged with the task of transmitting the values and standards of the community and of the culture in general and who is perceived by students as representing or embodying these values. "By precept and example, we try to develop the moral attitudes, the thinking patterns, the life goals which we feel make for good citizens living a good life. In this role, we are more or less faithful mirrors of the society in which we live."

The teacher also serves as a model in terms of his attitudes toward the subject he teaches and toward learning in general. The teacher who has an enthusiasm for his subject and for learning in general is more likely to reinforce similar attitudes on the part of his students. The opposite is also true. It is only the rare and unusual student who can work up any enthusiasm for a subject when his teacher's approach to it is reluctant, apathetic, and lifeless.

The Classroom Manager

Another subordinate role is that of ordering or structuring the learning situation, laying down rules and procedures for learning tasks. Sometimes this role becomes that of the *disciplinarian,* the person who must see that the classroom group and its individual members stay within the limits set by society, the school, and the tasks at hand. In its best sense, the role of the manager calls for teachers to help students and classroom groups to become self-disciplining—to the end that they learn to control and limit their own behavior in the absence of adults. In its worst form, this role may lead to the nagging pettiness of the martinet and to abject apathy on the part of the class, or it may lead to a preoccupation with classroom control and a consequent reduction in learning-task involvement. Irving N. Berlin (1964) tells of an incident involving a young and inexperienced teacher who had been assigned to an unruly class of socially disadvantaged children. When a supervisor criticized her for poor curriculum planning, she burst into tears and said: "What curriculum? Most of these fourth-graders haven't even learned to read, and I'm just a policeman."

As we have stated previously, most teachers find that their initial worries about discipline tend to diminish as they become more effective in their teaching. Teachers who have a feeling of adequacy and competence, and who are able to convey a corresponding sense of security to their classes, find that their main problems become those of how to *teach* better, not of finding better ways to handle discipline problems. If the role of the classroom manager take precedence over that of guiding learning experiences, this is a sign that teaching is not very effective. The reasons why it is not effective may lie within the attitudes and methods of the teacher or within the attitudes of the community or the teaching staff. In either event, the problem calls for careful study and analysis.

In recent years, teachers have become classroom managers in another sense. Increasingly, especially in elementary schools, their services as instructors are being supplemented by paid or volunteer helpers designated as paraprofessionals, clerical aides, or educational materials assistants, to name some of the more common titles and functions (Canady, 1973). Needless to say, this extra assistance can be a major resource to the harassed teacher who is trying to involve some thirty or so children in projects that have been more or less individualized to meet their special needs. Like other rewards in life, however, these advantages have their costs. One of them is that the teacher must not only supervise his thirty-odd students, he must also supervise and even train his paraprofessional staff. This calls for considerable preplanning, staff conferences, and, on occasion, some confusion and even friction. Fred G. Esposito (1970) has observed the following kinds of problems with respect to volunteer aides:

> Some teachers complain that aides spend so little time working directly with children or only do so sporadically. In other cases, teachers have been put on the defensive because aides demonstrate more skill and imagination than they do. In still other instances, teachers have complained that aides have literally folded their arms, leaned against the wall, and observed the classroom scene, without offering to contribute anything of themselves. When challenged, their defense is that no one told them what to do or what was expected of them.

Other problems occur when the aide or paraprofessional lives in the inner city, considers herself an expert on ghetto psychology, and dispenses a steady stream of advice on how to handle certain situations and certain children. Such expertise is often welcome, but a steady diet can take its toll in the form of tense teacher-paraprofessional relations.

Another problem occurs when a teacher wants a paraprofessional to perform clerical and monitorial tasks, but the paraprofessional sees tutoring and other instructional duties as more consistent with her role. The opposite also occurs.

The point is that a teacher who is responsible for the supervision of paraprofessionals and other aides cannot take for granted that they will perceive their functions as he sees them, and an understanding must be reached, preferably in advance, of what can reasonably be expected of them.

Clerk

Another of the roles subordinate to that of instructor is that of *clerk*. Most professional jobs require a large amount of clerical work, and teaching is no exception. There are papers to be read and graded, tests to be scored, marks to be entered, reports to be made, letters and notes to be written, files to be maintained, and so on ad infinitum. Teachers tend to rate their clerical role at the lowest level of esteem, partly because it gives them less time and energy to spend on their chief role of helping children learn, and partly because they see it as incompatible with their professional role—after all, they are *teachers,* not clerks! Nevertheless, workers in every profession have to devote a large portion of their time to tedious details, often of a clerical nature. Note that the category of "keeping records" accounted for the largest percentage of teachers in the group whose replies were reported in Table 18-1. As we observed above, some school districts provide teachers with paraprofessionals or aides whose task it is to relieve the teacher of some of his more routine duties. Some high schools also provide aides to grade students' assignments in English, as well as in other subjects.

Youth Group Worker

Most teachers participate in one or more school activities outside of class—in what are sometimes called *extracurricular* or *cocurricular activities*. Under this heading come the directing of plays and operettas, coaching basketball, advising clubs, sponsoring Scout troops, and the like. The survey conducted by the Research Division of the National Education Association and reported in Table 18-1 showed that more than half of the teachers included in the survey said they spent some time in such activity. This role roughly corresponds to what might be called a *youth group worker*. Writers in the field of education commonly consider this function to be part of the teacher's main role of "initiating, guiding, and evaluating learning experiences," on the grounds that much of the important learning for which the school is responsible takes place in extracurricular activities. However, many teachers see this role as something separate and distinct, perhaps because they are not physically in the classroom, because they are not "instructing" in the more formal sense, because it seems to be an

(Mal Gordon, *NEA Journal*)

"When they said that the hours were from 9 to 3, I didn't know they meant 3 A.M."

A DAY IN THE LIFE OF A TEACHER
There is virtually no limit to the variety of activities
that are crowded into a teacher's day. In addition to
the obvious one of instruction, there are tasks such
as correcting papers, dealing with emergencies,
advising on extracurricular activities, and participating
in meetings.

added burden, or because they do not recognize it as a learning experience. Or perhaps, as with clerical duties, they see this role as somehow incompatible with that of "being a teacher," that is, it does not fit their concept of what a teacher is or should be. Nevertheless, in spite of their misgivings about the appropriateness of their functioning as youth group leaders, most teachers feel a high degree of responsibility to their students and to the school that employs them, and they know that if they did not serve as leaders and advisers to these groups, there would be no one else to take their places. Perhaps teachers would be even more effective as youth group leaders if they could see this role in perspective as an important function of their major role as guiders of learning.

In recent years there has been an increasing tendency for school districts to pay supplemental allowances for after-school duties. A National Education Association (1970b) survey reported that teachers who coached football teams were paid an additional $1050 per year, on the average. In the largest school systems, directors of bands made $600 and directors of school plays, $309. Other nonathletic activities for which teachers received extra pay included debating, yearbook, and newspaper.

Public Relations Person

Every teacher plays this role to a greater or lesser degree and probably oftener than he realizes. In this role the teacher helps the public to arrive at a better understanding of the community's schools and what they are attempting to accomplish. The chief actor in this role is, of course, the school administrator because he has direct access to the community through the school board and the newspapers. Furthermore, official pronouncements come from him rather than from individual teachers. What often happens, therefore, is that the responsibility for communicating with the public is more or less abdicated by teachers in favor of the administrator or is preempted by him. Unfortunately, this policy tends to isolate teachers from the community and leads to misunderstanding of the school and its

goals, loss of public support, and lower status and morale among the teaching staff.

Many teachers show reluctance when it comes to carrying out the duties of this role because they are not clear as to what their functions actually are. Nevertheless, the role of public interpreter is inescapable. Parents and other members of the community are continually asking teachers to comment on some aspect of the school program, and the teacher who is not familiar with the main concerns that laymen have regarding education, who is not informed about school policies, and who has not even done any thinking about the major issues in education makes a poor impression.

One opportunity to play the public relations role lies in the relationship between teachers and parents. Some teachers make contact with parents during Parent-Teacher Association meetings, some make home visits, and some invite parents to meet with them at school. Almost three-fourths of the teachers in the survey reported in Table 18-1 said that they spent some time working with parents. Although such contacts usually occur because of the need to discuss the progress of individual children and the problems they are encountering, a great deal of incidental learning and communication can take place. For instance, the parent can learn that the teacher is a person who is sympathetically inclined toward the problems encountered by children in the classroom, as well as toward the problems that parents face. He learns that the school is concerned about learning in the broader sense— the ability to work cooperatively with other students, as well as the ability to read, write, and cipher. Or he may learn about the kind of help the school is giving students in choosing and preparing for a vocation. The teacher helps parents to learn more about the schools by being a good listener, refraining from judgmental statements as much as possible, and avoiding the role of an advice giver. This means that the teacher will not be able to spend much time *telling* parents about the school and its goals, at least not in the initial phases of their relationship. However, as parents come to realize that teachers are interested in working cooperatively with them for the welfare of the children, they will be more receptive to what teachers have to say, but will be interested inquirers about information relating to the school.

Teachers also have opportunities to carry out their function as public interpreters through participation in community organizations, where they interact with members who are outside the teaching profession. The NEA survey referred to in Table 18-1 found that half the teachers belonged to three or more different kinds of community groups, and only 7 percent belonged to no groups at all. It is within such voluntary organizations as churches, service clubs, the League of Women Voters, and "Y" groups that many of the vital decisions affecting the community and its schools are made. In a survey of school superintendents, Neal Gross (1958) found that the PTA was mentioned most frequently (by 69 percent) as a source of public support for the school program, but local service clubs (such as Rotary, Kiwanis, and Lions) were also mentioned by a sizable number (23 percent). There seems to be a relationship between the public spirit shown by a community and the quality of the school leadership. Gross found that the most effective superintendents tended to be appointed by school boards who were interested in and supportive of public education, and the best school boards and school superintendents were in communities that strongly supported the Community Chest. It appears, therefore, that those communities that show an active concern in public welfare are the ones most likely to have the best schools.

PSYCHOLOGICALLY ORIENTED ROLES

The second group of teachers' roles might easily have been included under the first category we discussed, for many would consider them a part of being an "effective guider of learning experiences." Although there is much to be said for including them under the first category, we are treating them separately because they are roles in which the teacher becomes the *educational psychologist*— the psychological worker in an educational setting. These roles are relatively new ones for teachers to play. The teacher of today is taking on these roles because he realizes that the more traditional roles of subject-matter expert and disciplinarian are too limiting and do not provide an adequate base for the effective promotion of learning.

The Artist in Human Relations

One of the chief roles teachers play as educational psychologists is that of the *artist in human relations*—the person who works with a variety of techniques and forces to produce situations that will stimulate learning. We use the term "artist" because the work of an effective teacher is much more than using the "right techniques." It involves sensitivity for the needs and feelings of the group, as well as for knowing how to introduce a new topic into the discussion, when to end the discussion of a given subject, how to change pace and emphasis, and the like. We also use the term "artist" as a way of indicating that no two teachers will teach the same subject or the same class in the same way. They may be equally successful, but their approaches will vary with the differences in their personalities, with their background, and with the conditions under which they teach. Professional workers in all fields are to some degree artists, at least to the extent that they blend both scientific lore and personal experience in carrying out the functions of their profession.

On another occasion, the present writer expressed himself as follows:

> Essentially, any person who works with such dynamic, changeable, and complex media as human relationships is, or ought to be, an artist. An artist may use formulas and techniques to help him with his work, but he uses them in a highly individualized manner. A technician decides what to do about a problem because of what his rule book or his manual tells him. An artist makes his *decisions on the basis of what feels like the right thing to do. He may be aided by scientific knowledge, but he knows better than to operate through the rigid application of formulas (Lindgren, 1954).

The Social Psychologist

The artist in human relations who works in an educational setting must be a social psychologist, at least to some degree. The traditional teacher gives no great thought to the classroom group as such, except perhaps to regard it as a menace. As we indicated in Chapter 12, he thinks of teaching in terms of a relationship between himself and individual pupils. The teacher who is a serious student of the psychology of the classroom, however, knows that the *group* can knowingly or unknowingly block the progress of learning, and that there are factors or forces *within the group* that can be used to stimulate learning. And he knows, furthermore, that groups that have high morale and are cohesive are more receptive to learning than groups that are poorly integrated. Therefore he sees his job as a teacher, at least to some extent, as one of building the classroom group by helping students understand and accept one another, work together cooperatively, share experiences and materials, and communicate more effectively both with one another and with the teacher. Indeed, promoting effective communication will be one of the chief tasks of the teacher who carries out his professional role as a part-time social psychologist.

The Catalyst

Another way to look at the many-layered role of a teacher as educational psychologist, artist in human relations, or social psychologist is to think of him as a *catalytic agent*. In the physical sciences, a catalyst is an element of substance that helps to bring about a change. Water is commonly used as a catalytic agent, inasmuch as many compounds will not react unless they are in solution. A teacher may be thought of as a psychological catalyst because many changes occur merely because he is there. He may not be actively or personally involved in the changes, but they would not occur if he were absent. All teachers have a catalytic effect of some kind on their classes; the problem is to produce changes that are integrative and group-building, rather than disintegrative.

The Clinician

This role includes all the functions a teacher performs in helping students learn more effective patterns of living, in reducing neurotic anxiety or in arousing normal anxiety, in helping them meet their psychological needs, in guiding them through the developmental tasks that lead to greater maturity, and the like. In this role he may function as a referral agent to a counselor or some other guidance worker, he may give reassurance or emotional support, he may restrain or limit—there is an endless list of things he can do or may do to improve the mental health of the classroom group or of the individual student.

Like other roles we have described, that of the clinician or mental-health worker may be played incidentally and simultaneously with other roles. Irving N. Berlin (1964), speaking from his experience as a psychiatrist consultant to a number of school systems, gives one example of how a teacher played this kind of a role in the course of instruction in arithmetic. We cite this incident not only because it is a good example of a teacher playing a mental-health role, but also because it shows how success in this role depends on being natural, "real," and, most of all, persistent:

> I observed a teacher of delinquent adolescents return day after day to helping a hulking, sullen, hostile, loud-mouthed delinquent boy learn the fundamentals of addition and subtraction. Despite threat of physical violence, sullen negativism, feigned illness, and emergency trips to the toilet by the youth, the teacher spent a designated twenty minutes (a day) with him. Thus, he slowly convinced the youngster that he felt the boy could learn, that he could teach him, and that this kid was important to him. I can recall now with the same spine-tingling excitement, the day when this boy got the first real glimmering of understanding of arithmetic, as his veiled eyes began to glow with pleasure. This occurred after weeks of persistent effort. Toughness, not sweet offers of love from the teacher, seemed to do the trick. This teacher, in discussions about this boy

and his stubborn refusal to learn, many times expressed feelings of anger and hatred because the youngster was frustrating his best efforts. As you read of these events, I am sure you recognize the kind of love that was there—love which has as its focus the well-being of someone else, such as the parent whose love is revealed by the time he is willing to spend with his children to help them acquire the fun of learning and subsequently the pleasure of effective living as a useful citizen.

Being a mental-health worker is perhaps not the chief role of a teacher, unless we consider the education of children essentially a process of improving their mental health. At any rate, most teachers do not see this as their chief role. Yet if a teacher ignores the clinical aspects of his work, he will be much less effective than he should be. He will fail to help his students at crucial times and with crucial problems, and he will ignore some of the more basic goals and objectives of education. If education is to do its part in developing healthy citizens for a healthy society, teachers must become aware of the responsibilities of their roles as mental-health workers.

SELF-EXPRESSIVE ROLES

Thus so far we have been discussing the roles that teachers play in their attempts to serve the needs of the community in general and the child in particular. But much of what we do as teachers is an attempt to meet our *own* needs—our personal needs, as contrasted with the needs of those we serve. Teachers are sometimes unwilling to admit that there is any motive but concern for others in their work. Yet all behavior occurs at least partly in response to our own psychological needs; even when we are ministering to the needs of other people, we are simultaneously meeting our own needs to help others. The needs related to "self-expressive roles" are the needs that teachers have because they are the kind of people they are, the needs that make them different from people who perform other professional roles.

The Need to Help Others

Most teacher chose their profession at least partly because it offered an opportunity to help others, to build a better world, or to give something of themselves to further the common good. On the Strong Vocational Interest Blank for Men, for example, social science high-school teachers and school administrators reveal themselves to have interests that are similar to those of YMCA secretaries and physical directors, clergymen, personnel directors, and public administrators—people who spend their professional lives in helping others (Strong, 1943). Teachers score higher than most people on the social service scale of the Kuder Preference Record (Kuder, 1951). In carrying out the role of helper the teacher often makes adjustments in his personal life, and even sacrifices, in response to the ideal of "the greatest good for the greatest number." It is this dedication to helping others, even at some personal cost, that has led many teachers to spend months and years abroad under difficult and primitive conditions as members of the Peace Corps, VISTA, and other groups extending aid to people who are in need.

The Learner and Scholar

Although these two roles are different in some respects, they overlap and merge into each other; hence we link them together in this discussion. Scholars are people who are interested in learning; they have an interest in and respect for ideas. Many a person has been drawn into teaching through his enjoyment of reading and his interest in some field of subject matter. Some of the really outstanding teachers in our schools are people who have an enthusiasm for their subject and are able to communicate in such a way that students are somehow infected with their enthusiasm and are stimulated into learning for themselves. Other teachers, unfortunately, contain their enthusiasm within themselves and stimulate nothing in their students but boredom and apathy.

Irving N. Berlin (1960) once observed that the teachers who have the most difficulty in learning are the ones also who seem to have the most difficulty in coping with problems of all kinds. He said:

> *I have been most interested in . . . teachers who appear to derive little satisfaction from learning. Since they themselves have not acquired the capacity to obtain pleasure and satisfaction from learning, from working effectively and mastering their job, they seem to be especially vulnerable to situations where their students manifest similar problems. . . . Thus they are caught in the dilemma of trying to help others do what they themselves cannot do. Many of them turned to education in the hope that they could get by with little effort or knowledge, only to find themselves increasingly disorganized, harried, frantic, and unable to control their classes. If the administrator tries to help by making the job easier, by expecting less of the teacher or doing some of it for the teacher, the problems usually are compounded. These teachers tend to regress the more their work is done for them. They are most difficult for administrators, and I feel they are their most troublesome problems.*
>
> *For such teachers classroom control is extremely difficult. They often lose their tempers and resort to corporal punishment in a desperate effort to maintain some control of their pupils. The substitute of force for teaching skills and knowledge occurs frequently with these teachers and presents recurrent problems to the administrator.*

The most effective teachers are those who are able to grow not only in knowledge of their subject but in their understanding of life both in and out of the classroom. For some teachers, the classroom is a rut that they erode deeper as the years go by, but for others it is a fascinating laboratory of life, in which they grow in their ability to understand more about their subject, more about children and how they learn, and more about themselves as teachers and as individuals.

The Parent-figure

Still another role that distinguishes teachers from persons in other occupations is that of the *parent-figure*. Children tend to look upon teachers somewhat as they would upon a substitute parent.[1] Their attitudes toward teachers tend to be somewhat similar to the attitudes they have toward their own parents, and they expect teachers to react and behave more or less as their parents do. For their part, teachers tend to reciprocate because they, too, see themselves in a parental relationship to their students. Perhaps teachers are more conscious of their roles as social service workers and scholar-learners than they are of their roles as parent-figures. Yet there is a fairly steady undercurrent of parentlike behavior in many of the relationships between teacher and child. The importance of the parental role in teaching is highlighted when we compare teaching with other professions—accountant, engineer, chemist, journalist—occupations from which the parental element is largely absent. Observations of teachers in classroom situations lead us to believe that most, if not all, effective teachers are people who can accept their role as part-time parents and play it with ease and grace, without overstressing it or understressing it. And we are led to the further belief that many people who enter teaching and find it a satisfying profession are people who need to express themselves through parental roles, people who rather enjoy being parent-figures.

This is probably as good a place as any to comment on a very interesting difference between parents and teachers. Although a teacher may play a parental role for a child, his psychological effect on the child is quite different from that obtained by his real parent. As a matter of fact, the teacher may

---

[1] This attitude is reflected in the laws relating to schools that designate them in *loco parentis*—as parent-substitutes—during the portion of the day that children are in school.

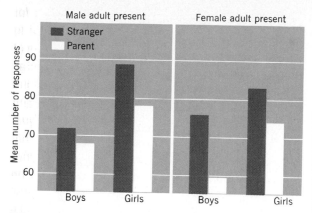

FIG. 18-1. Differences in the performance of nursery school children obtained when a strange adult was present, as contrasted with that obtained when a parent was present (Stevenson, Keen, and Knights, 1963).

have an advantage in the fact that he is not the parent. Parents often fail at the task of trying to teach their children even simple skills, perhaps because the parent-child relationship makes it difficult to institute an effective teacher-pupil relationship. The two relationships may not be very compatible. Indeed, the question can be raised as to whether parents are really the best teachers of academic skills for their children. One experiment suggests that children actually perform more poorly for their parents than for strangers. Nursery school children were asked to play a very simple game in the presence of a stranger or one of their parents. As Figure 18-1 shows, their performance was higher when the adult was a stranger rather than a parent (Stevenson, Keen, and Knights, 1963). Somehow, being watched by an adult who was not a parent gave the task a degree of importance or excitement that led the child to put out more effort. The significant point here is that teachers may be able to make unique contributions to the lives of children simply *because they are not their parents.*

The Power Seeker

There is another role related to that of the parent-figure, one that may be more sinister—at least it is more provocative or controversial in its implica-tions. It is the role that the teacher plays as a *power seeker*. This is the role of the person who enjoys controlling and directing other people, the role of the person who "knows best" and wants to impose that best on the lives of others. Undoubtedly, most teachers do not think of themselves as power seekers, yet there is no doubt that teaching is a job that is concerned with power wielding, that is, with directing, controlling, judging, rewarding, punishing, and limiting. Teachers are, of course, not alone in their search for power, since workers in all professional fields are to some extent seeking power over people, forces, or things. And teachers certainly need some power in order to cope with the problems of the classroom.

The search for power, however, is likely to create two problems. One is that power seeking complicates and many even negate our attempts to improve human relations in the classroom. The goals of power seeking and of creating democratic classrooms are basically and mutually incompatible. Indeed, the conflict between the search for power and the desire to develop a democratic atmosphere in the classroom is a common source of guilt feelings, dilemmas, and anxieties. The relationship between democratic attitudes and effectiveness in teaching is shown by an analysis of the letters of fourteen thousand students from the first through the twelfth grade who wrote on the topic, "The teacher who helped me most." When these letters were analyzed, it appeared that the personality trait that was most characteristic of the helpful teacher was "cooperative, democratic attitude," with "kindliness and consideration for the individual" coming second. These two traits ranked higher than traits that are more commonly identified with the instructional aspect of teaching behavior, such as "use of recognition and praise" and "unusual proficiency in teaching." The latter two traits ranked eleventh and twelfth in the list. In other words, the traits which students recognize as most characteristic of an effective teacher are those which are associated with democratic behavior and concern for the individual student (Witty, 1951).

Ned A. Flanders (1970) took these findings a step further. After reviewing a large number of studies of teacher effectiveness, Flanders concluded that students tend to achieve best in classes in which teachers made use of ideas and attitudes expressed by students, were not critical, and did not dominate discussion. In other words, students were inclined to learn better when teachers behaved more democratically. Students also tended to express a higher degree of acceptance for teachers whose classroom behavior was more democratic.

Individuals who are power-oriented are likely to score high on scales measuring preferences for authoritarian rather than democratic solutions in problems involving human relations. One study found that student teachers with authoritarian leanings had "very few warm accepting attitudes toward children" (Ofchus and Gnagey, 1963). Another set of studies showed that teachers with strong authoritarian attitudes tended to be less willing to endorse educational practices that were based on students' psychological needs and that embodied democratic principles. The research also showed that such teachers scored low on tests measuring attitudes associated with independence in thought and behavior. Although most people tend to think of authoritarian individuals as being free and independent because of their willingness to use power in arbitrary, decisive, and often punitive ways, this research makes the point that authoritarian individuals are likely to be more conforming, less independent, and more afraid of being different than are individuals who subscribe to democratic ideals and who favor child-centered programs. One interpretation of such findings is that it takes a great deal of independence to maintain one's faith in democratic classroom procedures in the face of unfavorable public opinion. (Lindgren, 1961, 1962; Lindgren and Singer, 1963; Al Omar, Eid, Majdalani, and Lindgren, 1965.)

A second problem that teachers encounter in their search for power is that of determining how much power they really need. There is a rather common tendency to feel that we do not have the power to do the things we need to do, and this feeling persists no matter how much power we may

have. And it is commonly observed that those persons who are most concerned about power are the ones least capable of using it.

The Security Seeker

Related to the search for power is the search for security. Many teachers have become attracted to the profession because it promises a high degree of financial and psychological security. In general, teachers are people who like life to be stable and predictable; hence they avoid taking chances and making changes that would disrupt the *status quo*, even when they feel there are some changes that should be taken and some things that need changing. This does not mean that teachers tend to be against progress but, instead, that they feel changes should come slowly. This attitude finds its fullest expression in the larger school systems, which often become rigid bureaucracies that are threatened by any form of innovation, no matter how desirable or well conceived.

The role of the *security seeker* is not without its problems. Just as it is difficult to decide how much power is enough, so it is equally difficult to decide how much security is enough because there is always the chance that the unexpected may happen. And one of the chief difficulties in pursuing power and security is that we can become so absorbed in our pursuit that we easily lose sight of our main job of teaching. In that connection, it is worthwhile noting that persons who are psychologically secure seem to be able to achieve this goal at least in part by their ability to give security to others. The very act of reassuring others can itself be a source of personal security.

DISINTEGRATIVE AND INTEGRATIVE FORCES IN TEACHING

Bureaucratic Restrictions

A survey conducted by Malcolm Provus (1966) turned up five major areas of teacher frustration: poor organization of the instructional program, inadequate curriculum planning and material selection, excessive nonteaching duties, insufficient time for working with individual students, and administrative interference. These frustrations seem to be related to teachers' desires to find satisfaction in their work, motives that are characteristic of professional workers in other fields. Provus (1969) noted an increasing tendency for teachers to deal with these frustrations through collective action and predicted that teachers would exercise a greater amount of control in determining policy and practice in their schools.

Conflicts in Roles

Even the task of managing and directing activities in a single classroom has its built-in frustrations, however. Classroom teaching is strenuous work. Some of the strain comes from the necessity to play many different roles, particularly roles that are in conflict with one another. One of the key problems that faces the teacher, therefore, is that of integrating his roles, organizing them around the values in life that are most important to him, and playing them in ways that are not in basic conflict with his self-concept or his self-ideal. The need for developing an integrated and reasonably consistent approach to life, on the job and off, is one that every adult faces. When we are continually forced to behave in ways that are mutually inconsistent and that open up gaps, so to speak, between our self-ideals and our self-concepts (between what we think we should be and what we think we are), we are likely to be dissatisfied, unhappy, and ineffective in our work. Feelings of optimism, satisfaction, and happiness are not only pleasurable in and of themselves, but they are also indicative of and basic to good mental health. Therefore we need to be aware of the factors and forces in our professional lives that help us to develop integrity and strength of personality, as well as those factors that impede integration or are disintegrative and dangerous to our morale and sense of well-being.

Even as there are many roles performed by teachers, so is there also a wide range of factors that impede or aid integration. These factors differ, of course, with each teacher's personality and situation. Furthermore, factors that disturb one teacher may not affect another in the slightest. However, there are some factors and forces that tend to be present in every teaching situation and that are consistently integrative or disintegrative. Let us first consider the ones that are disintegrative.

One has only to follow a teacher through a typical working day to realize how many tensions, pressures, and frustrations he must cope with. Let us examine a small sample of the kind of problems teachers must face by following one teacher through the first few hours of her day.

When Miss Frank faced her sixth-grade class that Monday morning, she had a neatly typed schedule before her of the things she expected to do that day and when she expected to do them. It really wasn't necessary to type the daily schedule, but Miss Frank liked things neat and efficient.

Everything ran according to plan at first. As the 8:50 bell finished ringing, the class stood at attention and recited the "Pledge of Allegiance." While Jane Kitagawa, the news-committee chairman for the day, hurriedly collected items from her committee members, Miss Frank entered the names of two absentees on the daily report and placed the form in the clip near the door. By the time she had finished, Jane was standing before the class, ready to give her report. The time was 8:55.

This morning's news was especially interesting, if somewhat grim. An airliner had been hijacked by members of an extremist group. Even one or two of the more retiring students wanted to have their say on how the incident should have been handled, and Miss Frank let the discussion run on because she felt that it was a good thing for students to get involved in thinking about problems that had an international scope. After the discussion had gone on for twelve minutes beyond the time she had scheduled for it, she reluctantly brought it to a halt and began to summarize the important points students had made, intending also to bring out some issues they had overlooked. She had hardly finished the first sentence when a monitor from the office opened the door, collected the attendance report, and brought a mimeographed notice to her desk for her to read.

Miss Frank sighed; it seemed as though she was always being interrupted at crucial points.

She read the announcement to the class. It told of the exhibit of student art work in the cafeteria during the noon period and gave directions on how students could vote for paintings to be entered in the city-wide art contest. The directions were a little complex and there were a few questions to be clarified.

As the monitor left, Miss Frank glanced at the clock. It was 9:30, and she was twenty minutes behind schedule. She had wanted to have a short spelling lesson, based on the news presentation, but that would put her even farther behind schedule unless she took the time out of the free-reading period. It always seemed that the free-reading period was the victim when something happened to the schedule. This was too bad because the children enjoyed the reading period and seemed to get a lot out of it. Besides, the reading period was her chance to work with Gene and Clarence, her two slow readers. She hadn't been able to give them any help for more than a week.

She decided to let the spelling go for the day and to go on to the history lesson, which was supposed to cover the Monroe Doctrine. The interest of the class had been reasonably high when they studied the War of 1812, during the preceding weeks, but these sixth-graders seemed to be able to focus more easily on wars than on other historical events that Miss Frank felt were just as important. To be sure, wars had drama and excitement, something that was lacking from political pronouncements like the Monroe Doctrine. In order to bring the subject to life, Miss Frank had secured a short historical film. The projector was being used by another teacher during the first hour of school, and she was to get it at 9:45.

She began to talk to the class about the international situation that led to President Monroe's pronouncement, trying to give them some background for the film. She would have preferred an approach that would have involved the participation of the class, but it seemed important for them to get a brief synopsis of events, and she felt that she could do this herself more quickly and efficiently.

She had barely warmed up to her subject when Mr. Whitehead, the principal, appeared at the back door with Mrs. Eliason, the assistant superintendent for elementary education. They both smiled at her, asked her to go on, and took seats at the back of the room. Miss Frank knew that she had nothing to worry about; she had always got along well with the administration. Besides she had tenure. But she never felt at ease when people watched her at work in front of a class. She had a sinking feeling in the pit of her stomach, and she always expected that she would commit some horrible error. She never had, really, and the principal had always complimented her on her work, but she wondered whether he wasn't just being nice.

She continued her discussion of the Monroe Doctrine, leading up to the things the children were to watch for in the film. She was aware that the class was less attentive than it had been before the two adults had entered the room. Several children were giving them sidewise glances, and there was an air of restlessness and uneasiness. Hence she was relieved when she finished her short presentation and was able to send two of the bigger boys down to the office to get the film and projector. As she started to pull down the shades to darken the room, both Mr. Whitehead and Mrs. Eliason came up to her, thanked her for letting them sit in her class, said that she certainly knew her subject and her class, and left.

Nine forty-five came and went, but there was no sign of the boys with the audio-visual equipment. Miss Frank told the class they could talk quietly till the film was ready to begin. When 9:50 came, she decided to investigate. She left the class and hurried down to the office, arriving just as the teacher who had had it during the first hour was turning it in. The other teacher was apologetic, saying that it had taken her longer to thread the machine than she had expected. Miss Frank said that she sometimes had that trouble, too.

It was almost 10:00 by the time she got back to the room with the two boys and the equipment. By 10:05 she had the film threaded through the machine. The boys had set up the screen, and plugged in the speaker. The class settled down to watch the picture. Two words appeared on the screen, upside down: "The End." Miss Frank set her teeth, to keep from saying what she felt like saying, and stopped the machine. Someone had forgotten to rewind the film. The class laughed and then started to talk, everybody all at once. Miss Frank had to speak to them sharply to remind them to keep their voices down.

By the time she had the film rewound and rethreaded, it was 10:15. She was in a quandary. The film would take twenty minutes to run and would not be over till 10:35. But at 10:30 the bell would ring for a ten-minute recess, and recess was followed by a twenty-minute period of directed play. She wished that she had not got involved with a film that morning and she began to regret that she had ever heard of audio-visual aids. Sometimes they were more trouble than they were worth. But the children were expecting a film, and it was probably best to go through with it. She decided to show fifteen minutes of the film, stop it when the bell rang for recess, and finish it when they came back from their physical education class. Then they would have their discussion. Miss Frank felt strongly about having discussions after films: There was really no point in using them unless you had some kind of discussion to tie the loose ends together. Goodness knows, stopping a film in the middle and picking up again after a half-hour lapse wasn't the best way to do things, but once you are committed to a film, it's better to go through with it. She hoped that no other teacher wanted the projector during the next hour, but that was a chance she would have to take. She would have to dash down to the office to check on this between doing hall duty at the beginning and end of recess. She'd just have to keep her fingers crossed till then. Teaching was wonderful when things were going right, but it was nerve-racking when things went wrong. Trouble was, there were too many days like today.

These thoughts flashed through her mind in rapid sequence as she flipped the projector switch on and watched the film title and credits appear on the screen. She would have to make some more adjustments in her schedule. It looked as though the free-reading period would be a casualty again today. . . .

Of course, matters do not always go as badly for Miss Frank as they have during the first two hours of the day we have described, but such days are not unusual. There is hardly a day without its interruptions, frustrations, and emergencies. There are announcements, assemblies, hall duty, yard duty, cafeteria duty, faculty meetings, conferences with parents, talks with individual children, last-minute preparations—all to be fitted into an overcrowded schedule. This is what makes teaching a demanding, tiring job. When teachers find themselves shifting from one role to another with barely a moment's notice, it is not surprising that some of the roles become incompatible and contradictory.

Conflicts in Expectations

During the last few decades, the teacher has become the focal point for an ever-broadening range of expectations. Inasmuch as roles and expectations bear a close relationship to each other, the greater the variety of expectations focused on the teacher, the greater the variety of roles he must play. It is inevitable, under such circumstances, that conflicts should develop among these roles and expectations. For example, there is often a discrepancy between what people expect of teachers and what teachers expect of themselves. The administration may expect the teacher to follow the prescribed curriculum to the letter, without deviations, but at the same time to make adjustments for certain students who have difficulties. Or the teacher may be expected to maintain high academic standards in his classes, but not to give any grades below a C. Parents may expect the teacher to be a strict disciplinarian, but also to be a person who loves children and is loved by them in return. The teacher is expected by some to be a paragon of all virtues, even to the point of never losing his temper or raising his voice, but still to be a very human kind of person.

Unfortunately, the teacher cannot succeed in all of those roles. He cannot be both a stern dispenser of justice and also someone who is liked by children as a friend. Perhaps one of the reasons he is inclined to play roles that are contradictory is that he tries to live up to too many expectations. He does not want to disappoint anyone; he would like to satisfy everybody. What he really wants to do is to avoid trouble and go about his business of helping children learn.

The Teacher and the Public: Conflicts in Priorities

Because the schools belong to the community, and because the community is composed of so many different people and groups with varied interests, teachers are almost certain to disappoint someone. Very often the basis for the public's disappointment may be formed of a fundamental difference between the way the public views educational processes and the views held by teachers.

A survey of teachers' opinions conducted in Delaware illustrates the problem. Joseph R. Jenkins and R. Barker Bausell (1974) asked 264 teachers and administrators to rate, using a nine-point scale, the importance of sixteen criteria for judging teacher effectiveness. Their ratings, ranked according to the relative importance assigned each criterion, are listed in Table 18-2.

There are a number of interesting aspects to the rankings. One is that the six criteria that are given the highest ratings are largely psychological in nature, in that they draw heavily on the teacher's understanding of students' needs and motives, of the dynamics of the classroom, and of his own motives and needs. The teacher's competence as a clinician and a social psychologist figures strongly in these top six criteria, as well as in Criteria 8 and 9.

What is particularly interesting, in the context of our present discussion, is that the criterion that most laymen would rate at the top of the list, "Amount students learn," is far down the list in eleventh place. Jenkins and Bausell quite rightly point to this low priority as a major cause of friction between teachers and the lay public. From the public's point of view, schools exist only to produce learning in students; hence it follows that teacher competency should be measured in terms of the amount of learning that has been produced. It is this concept that lies behind the demands for accountability and the computerized management-assessment programs that have been imposed on schools in recent years.

It does little good for teachers to explain that the outcome of the complex psycho-social processes which take place in the schools cannot be adequately assessed by such simplistic means, and that a preoccupation with achievement test scores can produce serious distortion and displacement in the

TABLE 18-2. Teachers' Perceptions of the Relative Importance of Sixteen Criteria of Teaching Effectiveness[a]

Criteria	Mean Rating[b]
1. Relationship with class (good rapport)	8.3
2. Willingness to be flexible, to be direct or indirect as situation demands	8.2
3. Effectiveness in controlling class	7.9
4. Capacity to perceive world from student's point of view	7.8
5. Personal adjustment and character	7.7
6. Influence on student's behavior	7.6
7. Knowledge of subject matter and related areas	7.6
8. Ability to personalize teaching	7.6
9. Extent to which verbal behavior in classroom is student-centered	7.3
10. Extent to which inductive (discovery) methods are used	7.0
11. Amount students learn	6.9
12. General knowledge and understanding of educational facts	6.4
13. Civic responsibility (patriotism)	6.2
14. Performance in student teaching	5.7
15. Participation in community and professional activities	4.9
16. Years of teaching experience	3.9

[a] After Jenkin and Bausell, 1974.
[b] Rating was done on a nine-point scale, ranging from 9—"extremely important," to 1—"completely unimportant." Any rating over 5, therefore, would indicate that a criterion was perceived as more important than unimportant.

educational program. The fact that attempts to increase achievement test scores rapidly by introducing large-scale performance contracting into schools have been disastrous does not seem to have deterred the public's demand for accountability.

What all this means is that many people will come to feel that school people are uncooperative or even devious, that teachers and administrators are letting them down, and that the educational system is failing because some high-school graduates cannot read, students are unmannerly or even delinquent, or whatever.

Teachers would be peculiar indeed if they did not react negatively to being the focal point for disappointment and disapproval. To be accused of having failed arouses anxieties. Even though a teacher may be deriving deep satisfactions from the kind of work he is doing, he cannot help but wonder whether his critics are right. Some teachers, especially those whose faith in themselves is not very strong, are made very anxious by accusations of this sort. It is therefore not surprising that teachers and teachers' organizations become oversensitive and defensive about criticism, even constructive, reasonable criticism.

Teachers are inclined to set high standards for themselves. They are likely to be people who never quite achieve what they expect of themselves, that is, there tends to be a gap between their self-ideal and their self-concept. Therefore when they find themselves the focal point for criticism, their sense of failure and guilt is heightened. A probable result of these pressures is the relatively high rate of neurosis that is found among teachers, in contrast to individuals in other occupations (Smith and Hightower, 1948). This raises the question of whether people should go into teaching if they are not already free of emotional problems and conflicts. Percival M. Symonds (1950) conducted a clinical study of successful and unsuccessful teachers which is as relevant today as when he made it many years ago. Here are some of his observations:

It is a common belief that only normal, well-adjusted persons should be teachers. But some of the successful teachers observed were definitely neurotic, and their neuroticism contributed to their success as teachers. Here is a teacher who is obviously compulsive-obsessional. She puts great emphasis on order, accuracy, precision, and she is teaching children to order their lives. Here is another teacher with an overdeveloped conscience who teaches her pupils to distinguish right from wrong. Here is another teacher with a need to dominate who vigorously carries children along with her own high standards of achievement. Here is a teacher with masochistic tendencies who whips herself by the long hours and hard work she puts into the job. These neurotic teachers may not fit every type of situation but if they can find the right place they can be high constructive influences.

None of this means, of course, that successful teaching and neurotic tendencies are necessarily related. On the contrary, the most successful teachers, and the ones that are best liked by their students, tend to be those who are the best adjusted. Most of us, however, have a few neurotic tendencies, and Symonds' point was that such traits alone should not be the prime determinant in hiring and tenure decisions.

Conflicts in Loyalties and Responsibilities

A problem related to the incompatible expectations teachers feel they must satisfy is that of split or divided loyalties. A teacher's first and primary loyalty is said to be to the children for whose learning he is responsible. We use the phrase "is said" because teachers are so often put in the position of having to subordinate this responsibility to other responsibilities.

Mr. Dexter was supposed to send Rodney to the principal because he found him smoking in the boys' lavatory. That was the school rule, and there was no other course he could take. Mr. Dexter somehow wished that he could talk to Rodney alone, because he felt that his smoking was related to the fact that his parents were in the throes of divorce. Rodney had always been a well-behaved boy, but during the last two weeks, while the divorce proceedings were being reported in lurid detail on the front page of the local newspaper, Rodney had been sullen and rebellious. Mrs. Henderson, the principal, handled all smoking violations the same way—they got the paddle. Mr. Dexter decided he would have to talk to her about Rodney, but he felt that it wouldn't do much good. Who knows, perhaps a paddling would help the boy. It seemed to straighten out some kids. . . .

Mr. Dexter has a conflict in loyalties, a conflict he will probably resolve in favor of the administration. Psychologically, it will cost him something to make the decision, for no matter whether he reports Rodney or not, he will experience some feelings of guilt.

Teachers also have loyalties to themselves as professional workers and as individuals. Part of Mr. Dexter's conflict stems from the fact that he feels, as a professional worker, that there are better ways of dealing with Rodney's problems than strapping him; it also goes against the grain for him to "tell" on Rodney. He feels that Rodney's problem is one that he could handle himself, and he rather resents the regulations that take it out of his hands.

Conflicts involving divided loyalties are sometimes aggravated by an administration that is calloused or apathetic in matters that concern the morale of teachers. The crucial role played by administrators in determining the psychological climate of the school is eloquently described by a psychiatrist who participated in a mental-health institute for teachers and who later studied the transcripts of the group meetings:

> Authoritarian administration adversely affects interpersonal relations among colleagues. Often there is a resentment against authority for unfair distribution of teaching load. Professional jealousy becomes a festering sore, insidiously operating to the detriment of the school program. In this hostile atmosphere, no teacher can work closely with the administrator for fear of being thought by his colleagues as an "apple-polisher."
>
> One factor clearly emerged . . . . The pattern or tone for the human relationships in the school is distinctly set up by the administrator, and this pattern frequently extends to the community.

> This is especially evident when frustrated teachers express their aggression against parents, making fruitful parent-teacher relations very difficult or well-nigh impossible . . . . Authority relationships constitute the fulcrum upon which levers can be applied for transmitting forces that lead to a good or bad mental-hygiene practice in the school.

On the positive side, teachers felt that the kind of interpersonal relations fostered by democratic relationships with administrators made teaching an enriching experience. Administrators, they said, should permit teachers to plan with them: "Sharing in decisions encourages closer working relationships essential to effective administration. Teachers . . . feel the need to be regarded and respected as individuals in their own right. Creativity in teaching depends greatly upon the administrator's respect for individual differences" (Margolin, 1953).

These comments were made a quarter of a century ago, but that does not make them irrelevant. The fact that they are equally appropriate in the context of today's schools shows that the relationships between teachers and administrators have changed but little in the intervening years.

The problem of getting administrators to behave in ways that are more democratic is not an easy one, however. For one thing, many of them do not seem to have any awareness of how democratic or undemocratic their behavior is. Robert E. Cummins (1957) found, in a study of a teacher and administrator attitudes, that three out of four school principals gave themselves higher ratings in democratic behavior than their staffs did. The principal whose behavior was rated as least democratic of all the principals gave himself the highest self-rating.

Teachers also owe a certain loyalty to the community that employs them. Because of this, they sometimes feel uneasy when they teach or discuss certain topics that some people in the community want excluded from the curriculum, or, even more likely, when they omit certain topics because of community pressures. What is involved here is a conflict between what teachers think children should learn and what some groups in the community think they should learn (or not learn). Teachers are highly sensitive and vulnerable to these pressures, not only because they are employees of the community, but because they are a part of the community itself. It is difficult for them to run counter even to a minority opinion when they are continually hearing their fellow citizens say: "I think that something ought to be done about the things that go on in schools these days!" And so teachers stop and ask themselves whether anyone will be upset if they follow their own judgment in deciding what topics should be taught or discussed. In many communities, teachers have learned to avoid discussing Darwin's *Origin of Species*, the facts of human reproduction, the role of this country in international affairs, the history and function of labor unions, racial segregation, or any other area of human experience that happens to be touched by controversy.

In this connection, there is some indication that teachers are inclined to be overly sensitive when it comes to public opinion. In Chapter 1 we noted some research suggesting that teachers tend to be more concerned about the opinions of persons outside their profession than about those of their peers and colleagues (Rettig and Pasamanick, 1959; Jacobson, Rettig, and Pasamanick, 1959).

In recent years, teachers' attitudes have shifted with respect to some of these problems. Today there is a greater tendency for teachers to be less plastic with respect to the expectations and demands of the community. During the 1969–1970 school year there were 180 teacher strikes, in contrast with only three ten years before. The proportion of teachers endorsing strikes under some or any circumstances rose from 53 percent in 1965 to 73 percent in 1970 (National Education Association, 1970c). Irrespective of whether one approves of striking as a tactic, the figures indicate a stronger tendency on the part of teachers to take collective action in making themselves heard.

Teachers as Targets for Hostility

Although the willingness to strike may have earned teachers a degree of public respect they did not have previously, it has not improved the public's attitude in other ways. Some feel that the recent inclination on the part of voters to reject tax increases

and bonds for schools (Gallup, 1970) is a kind of retaliation for teacher strikes, although this interpretation is beclouded somewhat by the fact that the public has become less willing to pay increased costs for *any* public services, not merely education. There is little doubt, however, that the threat posed by some of the more militant teachers has stirred up other preexisting sources of hostility.

Some of this antipathy undoubtedly stems from disappointments at the schools' inability to satisfy the public's demands for accountability with respect to unrealistic standards of performance, as we have indicated, but there are other sources of hostility as well, particularly of the type that is more pervasive and less obvious and that has always been an underlying factor in the relations between teachers and the public. Teachers sometimes become the targets for hostility because their education and professional position give them a higher status than that enjoyed by most people. People who are sensitive about such differences sometimes make the teacher the target for malicious gossip; at other times, this feeling is expressed through an undercurrent of resentment. For example, a school board composed largely of people who have high-school education or less might be unduly critical and uncooperative because of feeling unduly defensive or inferior about the differences in educational level. Some insecure parents become jealous when their chidren express a fondness for their teachers; others are upset when their children contradict them, quoting the teacher as an authority. Other parents become angry when a teacher wishes to discuss their child's difficulties with them because they believe that the entire problem of the child, his discipline and his behavior, is the responsibility of the school, not theirs. Often such parents had difficulties in school when they were youngsters and now have consistently negative attitudes toward the school and toward teachers. And then there is the resistance and resentment that teachers all too frequently find in their own classrooms. By the very nature of their jobs, teachers often have to stop children from doing things they enjoy and start them doing things they dislike. No one likes to be frustrated, least of all children, and it is to be expected that they may develop some hostile feelings

(Drawing by Saxon; © 1975 The New Yorker Magazine, Inc.)

"Christopher has never been treated unkindly by adults. He trusts us implicitly. I hope, Miss Forbes, you won't in any way betray that trust."

as a result. Even teachers who are able to operate democratic classrooms find that their relations with students are not free from hostility; hostility is something that every person encounters who performs a leadership role.

Psychological Effects of Disintegrative Factors

It is difficult to say, with any degree of exactness, what the net effect of the disintegrative factors has been on the teaching profession. It may show up in the studies that report that older teachers are less effective than younger ones. Perhaps with years of teaching the need to cope with disintegrative factors tends to dampen the enthusiasm and drive that are essential to good teaching. Robert N. Bush (1970a) maintains that the seniority system that prevails in most school systems is responsible for the attrition of dedicated and enthusiastic young teachers. It is common practice to give beginning teachers, who are least experienced, the most difficult classes and the most difficult children. "Unless we can fundamentally change what happens to the beginning teacher during the first one, two or three years," he states "I don't think we are going to make any really fundamental inroad on the teacher dropout problem." Arthur F. Corey (1970) observes that salary differences may be a factor in recruiting new teachers, but that they seldom are important in decisions to leave the profession. On the other hand, psychological factors, such as "negative human relationships," have a more significant effect. The net effect of these disintegrative forces is that a good many very able teachers decide, after a few years of teaching, that they will go into other fields of work, where the opportunities for self-expression and advancement are better, and the disintegrative factors fewer.

This loss of talent is no mere supposition. A United States Office of Education study by Robert L. Thorndike and Elizabeth Hagen (1959) of the careers of 658 men who had been engaged in teaching and educational administration for some period of time, showed that the individuals who left teaching were intellectually superior to those who remained. Another survey found that men who dropped out of teaching had made higher grades in college than those who stayed in the profession, although the opposite was true for women (Levin, Hilton, and Leiderman, 1957).

The study by Levin, Hilton, and Leiderman found that administrators were cited as a major source of dissatisfaction by persons who had left the teaching profession, and it is a common complaint among teachers who wish to make use of innovative methods that they get little administrative encouragement and support.

An interesting sidelight to this dissatisfaction with administrators is provided by a study of teacher behavior as reported by students. Students in junior and senior high schools in Texas were asked to rate 554 student teachers on a number of characteristics. When supervisors were asked to rate the same teachers on their effectiveness, they tended to favor the ones that students had also rated high on three factors: (1) being friendly and cheerful, (2) being knowledgeable and poised, and (3) exercising strict control over their classes. However, teachers whom students *preferred,* who were more interesting, and who used democratic procedure tended to be ignored by supervisors (Veldman and Peck, 1963). Such findings help explain why it is that the profession continues to lose its more creative teachers. Apparently, this will continue until supervisors, and other persons who make judgments of teachers, become more encouraging of creative and experimental approaches to teaching.

The disintegrative forces and factors in teaching make heavy demands on teachers. There is no question but that they constitute a serious threat to the mental health of both teachers and the children who are placed in their charge. Indeed, if it were not for counterbalancing factors and forces that are of even greater importance, the education profession would not be able to attract and hold the two-and-one-half million individuals who serve as teachers in the United States and Canada.

Integrative Factors in Teaching

In spite of the annoyances, tensions, and anxieties that constitute the disintegrative forces in teaching, most teachers like their jobs and would not change. In the NEA survey we referred to earlier, 54 percent of the men and 81 percent of the women said that if they had the chance to start over again, they would still go into teaching.

There are many studies that indicate the kinds of satisfactions teachers find in their profession. J. C. Gowan (1957) approached twenty teachers rated as best out of 3000 women elementary teachers and asked them what they thought were the main satisfactions and appeals in teaching. Eleven said that being with children was the most important reward; eight mentioned watching change and growth; and three mentioned changing the attitudes of children. A study by George G. Stern and Joseph M. Masling (1958) of the unconscious factors in the motivation of teachers produced an interesting list of attitudes and gratifications, which is presented in a somewhat modified form in Table 18-3.

TABLE 18-3. Psychological Rewards in Teaching, Based on an Analysis of Teacher Statements Regarding Sources of Gratification[a]

Gratifications	Mode of Expression
1. Instrumental rewards	1. Detachment; a "practical approach" to life
2. Prestige	2. Maintenance of professional dignity
3. Children's affection	3. Providing love
4. Children's autonomy	4. Encouraging self-actualization, self-direction, and independence in children
5. Promoting teachers' rights	5. Organizational activity; reforming the schools
6. Vicarious participation	6. Identification with children; enjoying children's experiences
7. Neatness and orderliness	7. Developing good pupil habits
8. Support from superiors	8. Cooperating with persons in authority
9. Children's admiration	9. Showmanship in teaching
10. Children's obedience	10. Maintaining discipline and order

[a] Stern and Masling, 1958.

An examination of the items in Table 18-3 shows that there is a wide range of satisfactions that are to be found in teaching. Probably few other occupations can satisfy such a variety of motives. Even on the score of economic returns, teachers are better off than most employed persons. Although the pay in teaching is not high, in most communities it is, at least, up to the average income received by all employed persons. Because their work is steadier and is less responsive to seasonal fluctuations and business cycles, teachers are generally able to maintain a consistently higher standard of living than most employed persons over a lifetime period.

The significant rewards in teaching are, however, more psychological than economic. It is difficult to say which one of the several satisfactions that we have mentioned is of greatest importance as an integrative factor because motives are highly personalized and vary with each individual. It is most likely that the opportunity to serve humanity is very significant for most teachers. The idea that one is making a contribution to the lives of young people, helping them even a little in their task of growing up to achieve the best that is in them, has great potential as an integrative force. Teachers can accept a high degree of frustration and disappointment if they feel that they are making some positive contribution to the citizens and the community of tomorrow. There is some data to show that appreciation of teachers' contributions may be on the increase. One opinion survey showed that junior high students in the 1960s felt considerably more positive toward their teachers and also studied harder than did students at the same school in the 1930s (Greenfeld and Finkelstein, 1970).

Teacher education students who eventually stay in the profession (as indicated by a later follow-up) have better psychological adjustment than students who later turn out to be weakly committed to teaching and are dropout candidates, according to a study by Donald J. Veldman and Shirley L. Menaker (1969). When asked to write stories for TAT pictures, the more committed teacher trainees tended to be more optimistic about the outcome of their stories, and their characters coped more actively with problems, employed more appropriate actions,

and resolved their problems more fully. Another survey compared attitudes of a large sample of teachers of both sexes, all ages, married and unmarried, with a similar sample of nonteachers. In general, teachers tended to be better adjusted and to have more positive attitudes toward various phases of their lives than did nonteachers. Furthermore, unlike the nonteachers, the mental health of teachers tended to improve well into the middle years of life and beyond (Horrocks and Mussman, 1970). These findings are consistent with other research showing that teachers tend to emphasize the pleasant and optimistic side of their experiences, rather than the unpleasant and pessimistic (Jackson, Silberman, and Wolfson, 1969).

A major characteristic of teaching that undoubtedly has an effect on results such as the above is the fact that it offers unlimited opportunities for personal growth and exploration. Relatively few teachers feel that they have reached the limits of their professional skill. The opportunity to innovate, experiment, and to learn better ways of teaching is an attraction that keeps many teachers in the profession in spite of the disintegrating and frustrating experiences they encounter in their daily work.

Although teachers often think that their status is low, in relative terms it is actually quite high. A nationwide survey conducted in 1963 found that in a list of ninety jobs, ranging from Supreme Court justice to shoeshiner, "instructor in public schools" rated 27th in status and "public school teacher," 29th. These ratings were higher than the ones given to "county agricultural agent" (39th), "newspaper columnist" (46th), "newspaper reporter" (48th), and "radio announcer" (50th). The 1963 ratings for teachers were, furthermore, about six or seven status levels higher than those made in a similar survey conducted seventeen years earlier (Hodge, Siegel, and Rossi, 1964).

One gets the impression that the status of the educational profession has continued to rise since the survey was conducted. More teachers today have graduate degrees, and teachers are more likely to be appointed or elected to prestigious positions in community groups. Teachers are also likely to receive more help today in the form of paraprofessionals and teacher aides, while the average class size, over the last thirty years, has dropped from more than thirty to twenty-three.[2] Still other evidence of higher status is the fact that teachers have more personal freedom both in and out of the classroom than they did a generation ago. There is also a greater tendency for teachers to stand up for their rights, as we noted earlier. Teachers' associations and unions today are much more likely to intervene on behalf of a teacher whose professional or personal rights have been placed in jeopardy and to take positive steps in maintaining educational standards in communities where they have been threatened. The willingness of teachers both in the United States and in Canada to support higher credential standards in terms of general education and professional training is also winning them respect. Even the negative attention directed toward teachers today is evidence of the importance placed on the value of education and the role and function of the teacher. As teachers contribute to and become aware of the increasing status and importance of their profession, they will be helped to outgrow the all-too-common feeling of being on the fringes of life.

Still another integrative factor lies in the opportunities teachers have to work together with other like-minded persons for a common cause. As the teacher realizes that he is part of a large movement—of something that is bigger than he is, that is bigger than his classroom or the school system in which he works—he gets the sense of participating in a grand enterprise. As he works with other educators in pursuit of their common goals, he is able to share his ideas and skills, to help others and be helped by them, to accept and be accepted as a member of a large professional fraternity. Such experiences are integrative, strengthening, and reassuring. To be sure, collaborating with others also brings frustrations and disappointments, but as teachers continue to work together and have successes in overcoming obstacles and solving the problems that are bound to occur, the forces that unite them will grow stronger.

[2] NEA Research Bulletin, 1970, **48**(2), 35, 38.

SUMMARY

The effectiveness of a teacher depends as much on his understanding of himself as it does on his understanding of his students. Hence it is essential that teachers study and try to understand the psychologial factors in their own lives.

The varied duties, functions, and problems for which the teacher is responsible require him to enact a number of psychological roles, which in this book are grouped under the heading of instructional and administrative roles, psychologically oriented roles, and self-oriented roles.

Instructional and administrative roles include the subordinate roles of instructor, model, representative of society, classroom manager, clerk, youth group worker, and interpreter to the public. Teachers take most of these roles for granted, for they are obviously and traditionally an inherent part of being a teacher. Some of the roles, such as those of youth group worker and interpreter to the public, are less obvious and more likely to be slighted.

The psychologically oriented roles of the teacher include those of the educational psychologist, artist in human relations, group builder, catalytic agent, and mental-hygiene worker. Teachers carry out these roles whenever they make use of the techniques and theories developed by psychologists, particularly those techniques and theories that are related to mental hygiene and the dynamics of group processes. These roles also serve to broaden the function of teaching beyond the relatively narrow limits of traditional concepts of education.

There is a third category of roles that are largely "self-oriented"—roles that are functions of the self-concepts of teachers. Among these roles are those of the social service worker, learner and scholar, parent-figure, power seeker, and security seeker. Some of these roles are positive forces; others are negative. However, they have much to do with the kinds of individuals who are attracted to teaching and who find satisfactions therein.

Bureaucratic restrictions and conflicts in roles and expectations make teaching difficult work at times. The public served by the teacher may expect things of him that are mutually inconsistent; the teacher, too, may have expectations of himself that are mutually inconsistent. Because of these inconsistencies, the teacher is bound to disappoint someone. When he is aware that he is not living up to expectations, he is likely to develop anxieties. Public demands for greater accountability have in recent years aggravated these anxieties.

Teachers are likely to be troubled by conflicting loyalties—loyalties to students, to administrators, to the community, and to their own principles and standards. Sometimes pressures force them to behave in ways that compromise some of their loyalties, thus adding to their burden of anxiety and guilt. Teachers also become the targets for hostility. Some of this may be because of their greater willingness to organize and even to strike, when they consider it necessary, but some hostility results from the fact that they are better educated than the average person. Some parents become jealous when children use teachers as models, and students may express hostility merely because teachers are persons in authority. Some of these disintegrative factors lead some of the more able teachers to leave the profession.

For most teachers, the psychologically integrative factors in their work far outweigh the disintegrative ones. Teaching provides a broad range of satisfactions, ranging from satisfactions that are personal and practical to those that are idealistic and humanitarian. Teachers tend to be happier and better adjusted than the average person, perhaps because teaching provides opportunities to do work that is creative and important, to achieve status and prestige, to give something of oneself, to attain financial security, to contribute something of value to the lives of children and youth, and to attain greater personal growth. Teaching provides opportunities, too, for individuals to work together in common cause with like-minded people.

Suggested Problems

1. Why should our understanding of students depend on our understanding of ourselves?

2. In what way would the defense mechanisms employed by teachers interfere with their understanding of children or of themselves?

3. What are some of the psychological reasons why teachers usually dislike clerical work more than most other phases of their duties?

4. Why might teachers object to the public relations aspect of their professional roles?

5. Judging from your own school experiences, to what extent do teachers today play psychologically oriented roles?

6. Are there any self-oriented roles, other than those listed in the text, that figure importantly in teaching?

7. Some writers hold that many individuals find teaching a way of rising from lower-middle-class status to upper-middle-class status. If this is so, which of the several roles discussed in this book would play an important part in this process? Which of them might be particularly attractive to persons interested in improving their social status?

8. In what ways might the interests and satisfactions of teachers *differ* from those that are characteristic of people in medicine, law, social work, and engineering? How might they *resemble* the interests and satisfactions of people in each of these professions?

9. What can teachers do to increase the area of freedom that is available to them to experiment with finding new and better ways of teaching?

Suggested Readings

Combs, A. W. *The professional education of teachers: a perceptual view of teacher preparation.* Boston: Allyn and Bacon, 1965. Some of the more intriguing chapters are "What is a good teacher?", "The teacher's self," and "The personal discovery of ways to teach."

Dunkin, M. J., and Biddle, B. J. *The study of teaching.* New York: Holt, Rinehart, and Winston, 1974. A textbook that attempts to review concepts and procedures as they relate to the classroom environment.

Gage, N. L. *Teacher effectiveness and teacher education: The search for a scientific basis.* Palo Alto, Calif.: Pacific Books, 1972. Examines, among other aspects of teacher behavior, the personality traits that seem to be associated with effective teaching.

Hunter, E., and Amidon, E. J. *Student teaching: Cases and comments.* New York: Holt, Rinehart, and Winston, 1964. Presents thirty-six cases, each illustrating a problem or a dilemma encountered by student teachers and new teachers, together with discussions of alternative solutions.

Lindgren, H. C., and Lindgren, F. (eds.) *Readings in educational psychology,* 2nd ed. New York: Wiley, 1972. See Section 10 for discussions of teacher psychology.

Mitchell, L. S. *Two lives: The story of Wesley Clair Mitchell and myself.* New York: Simon and Schuster, 1953. The story of two effective, creative individuals and their happy and successful marriage. The careers described are those of a leader in the development of education for young children and an original thinker in the field of economics.

Morrison, A., and McIntyre, D. *Teachers and teaching.* Baltimore: Penguin, 1969. (A paperback.) Focuses on research studies of teachers and teaching in school settings. Although a large part of the material is British, a great deal of it is relevant to the American scene.

Stinnett, T. M. *The teacher dropout.* Itasca, Ill.: Peacock, 1970.

Tanner, L. N., and Lindgren, H. C. *Classroom teaching and learning: A mental health approach.* New York: Holt, Rinehart, and Winston, 1971. See especially the last four chapters: "Relations with parents and community," "The teacher's classroom behavior: Principles and problems," "The teacher as a learner," and "Personal satisfaction in teaching."

Person to person. Washington: National Education Association, no date. A pamphlet issued by the National School Public Relations Association, in cooperation with the Department of Classroom Teachers, for the purpose of providing teachers with some suggestions on how they can best represent their school and their profession to the public.

The following journals often contain material relevant to the subject of this chapter: *Education, Educational Administration and Supervision, Educational Leadership, Educational Theory, Journal of the National Education Association, Peabody Journal of Education, Phi Delta Kappan.*

Photo Credits

References and Author Index

Works cited in this book are listed alphabetically by author and year of publication. Numbers in **boldface type** following each citation refer to the pages in this book on which the works are cited.

Abbot, L., *see* Wilson et al.

Aboloon, W. D., *see* Zigler et al.

Adams, J. F., ed. (1965). *Counseling and guidance.* New York: Macmillan. **459**

Adelson, J., *see* Douvan and Adelson.

Ahlstrom, W. M., and Havighurst, R. J. (1971). *Four hundred losers.* San Francisco: Jossey-Bass. **403–404**

Aiken, L. R., Jr. (1970). Attitudes toward mathematics. *Rev. educ. Res.,* 40:551–596. **218**

Aiker, H. A., Carlson, J. A., and Hermann, M. F. (1969). Multiple-choice questions and student characteristics. *J. educ. Psychol.,* 60:231–243. **327, 328**

Ainsworth, M., *see* Butcher et al.

Airasian, P. W., and Madaus, G. F. (1972). Criterion-referenced testing in the classroom. *Measmt. in Educ.,* 3(4):1–8. **341**

Akeju, S. A. (1972). The reliability of General Certificate of Education Examination English composition papers in West Africa. *J. educ. Measmt.,* 9:175–180. **324**

Allebrand, G. N., *see* Zimmerman and Allebrand.

Allen, K. E., and Harris, F. R. (1966). Elimination of a child's excessive scratching by training the mother in reinforcement procedures. *Behav. Res. and Therapy.* 4:79–84. **277**

Allen, L., *see* Macfarlane et al.; *and* Honzik et al.

Al Omar, N., Eid, S. K., Majdalani, M., and Lindgren, H. C. (1965). Tendermindedness in education, independence, and authoritarianism: a cross-cultural study. *Psychol. Rep.,* 17:230. **474**

Alpert, D., and Bitzer, D. L. (1970). Advances in computer-based education. *Science,* 167:1582–1590. **290**

Amante, D., et al. (1970). The epidemiological distribution of CNS dysfunction. *J. soc. Issues,* 26(4):105–136. **386**

Ames, L. B., and Walker, R. N. (1964). Prediction of later reading ability from kindergarten Rorschach and IQ scores. *J. educ. Res.,* 55:309–313. **225**

Amidon, E. J., *see* Hunter and Amidon.

Amos, W. E., and Grambs, J. D., eds. (1968). *Counseling the disadvantaged youth.* Englewood Cliffs, N.J.: Prentice-Hall. **459**

Anastasi, A. (1968). *Psychological testing,* 3rd ed. New York: Macmillan. **373**

Anderson, C. C. (1962). A developmental study of dogmatism during adolescence with reference to sex differences. *J. abnorm. soc. Psychol.,* 65:132–135. **62**

Anderson, C. M. (1950). The anatomy, physiology, and pathology of the psyche: a new concept of the dynamics of behavior. *Amer. Practitioner Dig. Treatment,* 1:400–405. **28**

Anderson, G., *see* Anderson and Anderson.

Anderson, G. J., *see* Walberg and Anderson.

Anderson, H., and Anderson, G. (1956). Cultural reactions to conflict: A study of adolescent children in seven countries. In G. M. Gilbert, ed., *Psychological* approaches to intergroup and international understanding, *a symposium of the Third Interamerican Congress of Psychology,* Austin, Tex. **83**

Anderson, J. E. (1942). The relation of emotional behavior to learning. In N. B. Henry, ed., *The psychology of learning,* 41st Yearbook of the National Society for the Study of Education, Part II. Chicago: Univ. of Chicago Press. **219**

Anderson, R. C. (1965). Can first-graders learn an advanced problem-solving skill? *J. educ. Psychol.,* 56:283–294. **54**

Andreas, B. G. (1968). *Psychological science and the educational enterprise.* New York: Wiley. **16**

Arbuckle, D. S. (1970). Does the school really need counselors? *School Counselor,* 17:325–330. **455**

Armel, S., *see* Taffel et al.

Armstrong, W. H. (1974). *The education of Abraham Lincoln.* New York: Coward, McCann, and Geohegan. **167**

Arnold, J. M., *see* Randazzo and Arnold.

Aschner, M. J. M., *see* Gallagher and Aschner.

Ashcraft, C. (1970). Later school achievement of treated and untreated emotionally handicapped children. *Amer. Psychol. Assn. Proceedings,* 5:651–652. **404**

Asher, S. R., and Markell, R. A. (1974). Sex differences in comprehension of high- and low-interest reading material. *J. educ. Psychol.,* 66:680–687. **222–223, 361**

Ashton-Warner, S. (1963). *Teacher.* New York: Simon and Schuster. **312**

Asker, W. (1923). Does knowledge of formal grammar function? *School and Society,* 17:109–111. **167**

Assn. for Supervision and Curriculum Dept. (1964). *Individualizing instruction.* Washington: Natl. Educ. Assn. **312**

Atkinson, R. C. (1968). Computerized instruction and the learning process. *Amer. Psychologist,* 23:225–239. **192**

Austin, D. B. (1969). Secondary education. In Ebel, Noll, and Bauer, eds., *Encyclopedia of educational research,* 4th ed. New York: Macmillan. **291**

Ausubel, D. P. (1961). A new look at classroom discipline. *Phi Delta Kappan,* 43:25–30. **264**

Ausubel, D. P. (1962). Can children learn anything that adults can—and more efficiently? *El. School J.,* 62:270–272. **227**

Ausubel, D. P. (1969). A cognitive theory of school learning. *Psychol. in the Schools,* 6:331–335. **198, 200**

Bahnmuller, M., *see* Zweibelson et al.

Baker, C. T., *see* Sontag et al.

Baldwin, A. L., and Levin, H. (1970). How can we intervene "massively"? *Science,* 167:123. **355**

Ball, S., and Bogatz, G. A. (1970). *The first year of Sesame Street: an evaluation.* Princeton, N.J.: Educ. Testing Service. **57**

Baller, W. R., Charles, D. C., and Miller, E. L. (1967). Mid-

life attainment of the mentally retarded: a longitudinal study. *Genet. Psychol. Monogr.,* 75:235–329. **387**

Bandura, A. (1969). Social-learning theory of identificatory processes. In D. A. Goslin, ed., *Handbook of socialization theory and research.* Chicago: Rand McNally. **60**

Bandura, A., and Huston, A. C. (1961). Identification as a process of incidental learning. *J. abnorm. soc. Psychol.,* 63:311–318. **77**

Bandura, A., and McDonald, F. J. (1963). Influence of social reinforcement in the behavior of models in shaping children's moral judgments. *J. abnorm. soc. Psychol.,* 67:274–281. **61**

Bandura, A., and Walters, R. H. (1963). *Social learning and personality development.* New York: Holt, Rinehart, and Winston. **86, 141**

Bankes, J., *see* Long et al.

Baratz, S. S., *see* Rosenthal et al.

Barbrack, C. R., and Horton, D. M. (1970). Educational intervention in the home and paraprofessional career development; a second generation mother study with an emphasis on costs and benefits. *Darcee Papers and Reports,* 4(4). John F. Kennedy Center for Res. on Educ. and Human Devpt, Geo. Peabody Coll. for Teachers, Nashville, Tenn. **429**

Barker, D. G., and Hensarling, P. R. (1965). Correlates of high school retention rates by states. *J. exper. Educ.,* 58:298–299. **448–449**

Barr, R. D. (1973). What ever happened to the Free School Movement? *Phi Delta Kappan,* 54:454–457. **305**

Barth, R. S. (1971). So you want to change to an open classroom. *Phi Delta Kappan,* 53:97–99. **287**

Barth, R. S. (1974). *Open education and the American school.* New York: Schocken. **287**

Barthell, C. N., and Holmes, D. S. (1968). High school yearbooks: a nonreactive measure of social isolation in graduates who later became schizophrenic. *J. abnorm. soc. Psychol.,* 73:313–316. **131**

Bassett, S. J., *see* Brooks and Bassett.

Battle, H. (1957). Relation between personal value and scholastic achievement. *J. exper. Educ.,* 26:27–41. **237**

Bauernfeind, R. H. (1951). *Guidance at the elementary school level.* Div. Educ. Reference, Purdue Univ. **299**

Baumrind, D. (1967). Child care practices anteceding three patterns of preschool behavior. *Genet. Psychol. Monogr.,* 75:43–88. **80–81**

Bausell, R. B., *see* Jenkins and Bausell.

Bavary, J., *see* Schwenn et al.

Bayles, E. E. (1960). *Democratic educational theory.* New York: Harper. **178**

Bayley, N. (1964). Consistency of maternal and child behaviors in the Berkeley Growth Study. *Vita Humana,* 7:73–95. **80**

Beatty, W. H., and Clark, R. (1972). A self-concept theory of learning: a learning theory for teachers. In Lindgren and Lindgren, eds., *Current readings in educational psychology,* 2d ed. New York: Wiley. **187, 219, 232**

Beck, J. M., and Saxe, R. W., eds. (1965). *Teaching the culturally disadvantaged pupil.* Springfield, Ill.: Charles C Thomas. **437**

Becker, W. C., et al. (1967). The contingent use of teacher attention and praise in reducing classroom behavior problems. *J. spec. Educ.,* 1:287–307. **277**

Beckman, L. (1970). Effects of students' performance on teachers' and observers' attributions of causality. *J. educ. Psychol.,* 61:76–82. **241**

Bedoian, V. H. (1953). Mental health analysis of socially overaccepted, socially underaccepted, overage and underage pupils in the sixth grade. *J. educ. Psychol.,* 44:366–371. **392**

Bedoian, V. H. (1954). Social acceptability and social rejection of the underage, at-age, and overage pupils in the sixth grade. *J. educ. Res.,* 47:513–520. **392**

Bell, M., *see* Kreitman et al.

Bell, R. Q., *see* Waldrop and Bell.

Belmont, L., and Marolla, F. A. (1973). Birth order, family size, and intelligence. *Science,* 182:1096–1101. **32**

Benjamin, H. (1939). *The sabre-tooth curriculum.* New York: McGraw-Hill. **178**

Bennell, E. L., et al. (1964). Chemical and anatomical plasticity of the brain. *Science,* 146:610–619. **30**

Bennett, G. K., *see* Doppelt and Bennett.

Berlin, I. N. (1956). Some learning experiences and psychiatric consultant in the schools. *Mental Hyg.,* 40:215–236. **443**

Berlin, I. N. (1960). From teachers' problems to problem teachers. *Mental Hyg.,* 44:80–83. **472**

Berlin, I. N. (1964). Unrealities in teacher education. *Sat. Rev.,* 47(51): 56–58, 65. **464, 470**

Berlin, I. N. (1965). Mental health consultation in the schools: who can do it and why. *Community Health J.,* 1:19–22. **404**

Bestor, A. (1956). *The restoration of learning.* New York: Knopf. **2**

Biddle, B. J., *see* Dunkin and Biddle, *and* Kounin et al.

Bingham, A. (1958). *Improving children's facility in problem solving.* New York: Bureau of Publ., Teachers Coll., Columbia Univ. **175, 294**

Birns, B. (1965). Individual differences in human neonates' responses to stimuli. *Child Develpm.,* 36:249–259. **67**

Bitzer, D. L., *see* Alpert and Bitzer.

Blakely, W. P. (1958). A study of seventh grade children's reading of comic books as related to other variables. *J. genet. Psychol.,* 93:291–301. **183**

Blommers, P., *see* Coffield and Blommers.

Bloom, B. S., ed. (1956). *Taxonomy of educational objectives. Handbook 1: Cognitive domain.* New York: McKay. **215, 221, 232**

Bloom, B. S. (1964). *Stability and change in human characteristics.* New York: Wiley. **420–421**

Bloom, B. S. (1971). Learning for mastery. In B. S. Bloom et al., *Formative and summative evaluation of student learning.* New York: McGraw-Hill. **201**

Bloom, B. S. (1974). An introduction to mastery learning theory. In J. H. Block, ed., *Schools, society, and the mastery of learning.* New York: Holt, Rinehart, and Winston. **289**

Bloom, B. S., Davis, A., and Hess, R. (1965). *Compensatory education for cultural deprivation.* New York: Holt, Rinehart, and Winston. **437**

Bloom, B. S., *see also* Kratwohl et al.

Bloom, R. D., *see* Dunn et al.

Bogatz, G. A., *see* Ball and Bogatz.

Bond, B. W. (1956). *Group discussion-decision: an appraisal of its use in health education.* Minneapolis: Minn. Dept. of Health. **246**

Bordin, E. S. (1968). *Psychological counseling,* 2nd ed. New York: Appleton-Century-Crofts. **459**

Borg, W. R. (1964). *An evaluation of ability grouping.* Cooperative Res. Project, No. 577. Logan: Utah State Univ. **394, 407**

Borg, W. R. (1972). The minicourse as a vehicle for changing teacher behavior: a three-year follow-up. *J. educ. Psychol.,* 63:572–579. **243, 250**

Borgman, R. D., *see* Polansky et al.

Bossard, J. H. S. (1954). *The sociology of child development,* rev. ed. New York: Harper. **82**

Brackbill, Y. (1970). Continuous stimulation and arousal level in infants: additive effects. *Amer. Psychol. Assn. Proceedings,* 5:271–272. **30–31**

Brackbill, Y. (1973). Continuous stimulation reduces arousal level: stability of effect over time. *Child Develpm.,* 44:43–46. **30**

Bradshaw, C. E. (1968). *Relationship between maternal behavior and infant performance in environmentally disadvantaged homes.* Unpubl. Ed. D. dissertation, Univ. of Fla. **87**

Brenner, M. H. (1968). Use of high school data to predict work performance. *J. appl. Psychol.,* 52:29–30. **344**

Bridger, W. H., *see* Golden et al.

Britton, J. H., Britton, J. O., and Fisher, C. F. (1969). Perceptions of children's moral and emotional behavior: a comparison of Finnish and American children. *Human Develpm.,* 12:55–63. **105**

Britton, J. O., *see* Britton et al.

Bronfenbrenner, U. (1970). Reaction to social pressure from adults versus peers among Soviet day school and boarding school pupils in the perspective of an American sample. *J. Pers. soc. Psychol.,* 15:179–189. **83, 105, 148**

Brooks, F. D., and Bassett, S. J. (1928). The retention of

REFERENCES AND AUTHOR INDEX

American history in the junior high school. *J. educ. Res.,* 18:195–202. **166**

Brophy, J. E. (1974). Some good five cent cigars. *Educ. Psychologist,* 11:46–51. **424**

Brophy, J. E., and Good, T. L. (1972). Teacher expectations: beyond the Pygmalion controversy. *Phi Delta Kappan,* 54:276–278. **239**

Brophy, J. E., *see also* Good and Brophy; Laosa and Brophy; *and* Veldman and Brophy.

Brown, B., *see* Deutsch and Brown.

Brown, R. D., *see* Newton and Brown.

Bruner, J. S. (1960). *The process of education.* Cambridge: Harvard Univ. Press. **206, 219, 226, 232**

Bruner, J. S. (1961). The act of discovery. *Harvard educ. Rev.,* 31:21–32. **53, 197, 213**

Bruner, J. S. (1964a). The course of cognitive thought. *Amer. Psychologist,* 19:1–15. **53**

Bruner, J. S. (1964b). Some theories on instruction illustrated with reference to mathematics. In E. R. Hilgard, ed., *Theories of learning and instruction,* 63rd Yearbook, Natl. Soc. for the Study of Educ., Part 1. Chicago: Univ. of Chicago. **198**

Bruner, J. S., et al. (1966). *Studies in cognitive growth.* New York: Wiley. **72**

Bryant, B. K. (1974). Locus of control related to teacher-child interperceptual experiences. *Child Develpm.,* 45:157–164. **227**

Buchanan, L. J., Jr., and Lindgren, H. C. (1973). Brainstorming in large groups as a facilitator of children's creative responses. *J. Psychol.,* 83:117–122. **299**

Bugelski, B. R. (1956). *The psychology of learning.* New York: Holt. **228, 242**

Bugelski, B. R. (1964). *The psychology of learning applied to teaching.* Indianapolis: Bobbs-Merrill. **228**

Bundy, R. F. (1974). Accountability: a new Disneyland fantasy. *Phi Delta Kappan,* 56:176–180. **338**

Burchinal, L., Gardner, B., and Hawkins, G. R. (1958). Children's personality adjustment and the socio-economic status of their families. *J. genet. Psychol.,* 92:49–59. **144**

Burnham, J. (1960). *The managerial revolution.* Bloomington: Univ. of Ind. Press. **337**

Buros, O. K. (1965). *Sixth mental measurements yearbook.* Highland Park, N.J.: Gryphon Press. **374**

Burton, R. V., *see* Yarrow et al.

Bush, R. N. (1970). Microteaching enters second generation of research. *Teaching,* Stanford Center for R&D in Teaching, April, No. 1. **11**

Bush, R. N. (1970a). The status of the career teacher: its effect upon the teacher dropout problem. In T. M. Stinnett, ed., *The teacher dropout.* Bloomington, Ind.: Phi Delta Kappa. **482**

Busk, P. L., Ford, R. C., and Schulman, J. L. (1973). Stability of sociometric responses in classrooms. *J. genet. Psychol.,* 123:69–84. **102**

Butcher, H. J., Ainsworth, M., and Nesbitt, J. E. (1963). Personality factors and school achievement: a comparison of British and American children. *Brit. J. educ. Psychol.,* 33:276–285. **105**

Byrne, D., *see* Lindgren and Byrne.

Callahan, O. D., and Robin, S. S. (1969). A social system analysis of preferred leadership role characteristics in high school. *Sociol. of Educ.,* 42:251–260. **108**

Campbell, D. P. (1965). *The results of counseling: twenty-five years later.* Philadelphia: Saunders. **459**

Campbell, J., *see* Dunnette et al.

Campbell, J. D., *see* Yarrow et al.

Canady, R. L. (1973). Paraprofessionals: should roles be differentiated? *Phi Delta Kappan,* 55:206. **464**

Canning, R. R. (1956). Does an honor system reduce classroom cheating? An experimental answer. *J. exper. Educ.,* 24:291–296. **150**

Cantor, G. N., and Paternite, C. E. (1973). A follow-up study of race awareness using a conflict paradigm. *Child Develpm.,* 44:859–861. **122**

Cantor, N. (1946). *Dynamics of learning.* Buffalo, N.Y.: Foster and Stewart. **242**

Carey, G. L. (1958). Sex differences in problem-solving performance as a function of attitude differences. *J. abnorm. soc. Psychol.,* 56:250–256. **223**

Carlson, J. A., *see* Aiker et al.

Castenada, A., *see* McCandless et al.

Caterall, C. D., *see* Chamberlin and Caterall.

Cervantes, L. F. (1965). *The dropout: causes and cures.* Ann Arbor, Mich.: Univ. of Mich. Press. **449**

Chabassol, D. (1970). Prejudice and personality in adolescence. *Alberta J. educ. Res.,* 16:3–12. **122**

Chamberlin, G. L., and Caterall, C. D. (1965). Acceleration for the overage potential dropout? *Phi Delta Kappan,* 45:98–99. **388**

Chambers, G. S., and Zabarenko, R. N. (1956). Effects of glutamic acid and social stimulation in mental deficiency. *J. abnorm. soc. Psychol.,* 53:315–320. **387**

Chambers, J. A. (1973). College teachers: their effect on the creativity of students. *J. educ. Psychol.,* 65:326–334. **246**

Charles, D. C. (1953). Ability and accomplishment of persons earlier judged mentally deficient. *Genet. Psychol. Monogr.,* 47:39–71. **386**

Charles, D. C., *see also* Baller et al.

Charters, W. W., and Gage, N. L., eds. (1963). *Readings in the social psychology of education.* Boston: Allyn and Bacon. **126**

Chatterjee, B. B., *see* Gage et al.

Cherlin, D. L. *see* Schwebel and Cherlin.

Ciavarella, M. A. (1968). The counselor as a participant in minimizing curricular frustrations. *Counselor Educ. and Supervision,* 7:132–136. **454–455**

Clavarella, M. A., (1970). The counselor as a mental health consultant. *School Counselor,* 18:121–125. **441**

Clarizio, H. F., and McCoy, G. F. (1970). *Behavior disorders in school-aged children.* Scranton, Pa.: Intext. **143, 154**

Clark, K. B. (1972). As cited in J. McV. Hunt, ed., *Human intelligence.* New Brunswick, N.J.: Transaction Books. **359**

Clark, R., *see* Beatty and Clark.

Clarke, H. H., and Olson, A. L. (1965). Characteristics of 15-year-old boys who demonstrate various accomplishments or difficulties. *Child Developm.,* 36:559–567. **355–356**

Cleary, T. A., *see* Clifford and Cleary.

Clifford, C., *see* Wattenberg and Clifford.

Clifford, M. M., and Cleary, T. A. (1970). Effect of competition on fifth and sixth graders. Unpubl. paper, Amer. Psychol. Assn. Convention, Miami Beach. **121**

Cloward, R. (1967). Studies in tutoring. *J. exper. Educ.,* 36:14–25. **295**

Coe, J., *see* Elkind et al.

Coffield, W. H., and Blommers, P. (1956). Effects of non-promotion on educational achievement in the elementary school. *J. educ. Psychol.,* 47:135–150. **388**

Coffman, W. E. (1974). A moratorium? What kind? *Special Reports of the Natl. Council on Measmt. in Educ.,* 5(2). **342**

Cogan, M. L. (1954). The relation of the behavior of teachers to the productive behavior of their pupils. Unpublished Ed.D. dissertation, Harvard Univ. **237**

Cohen, R. (1969). The effects of group interaction and progressive hierarchy presentation on desensitization of test anxiety. *Behav. Res. and Therapy,* 7:15–26. **277**

Coladarci, A. P. (1959). The teacher as hypothesis-maker. *Calif. J. for Instructional Improvement,* 2:3–6. **13–14**

Cole, M., *see* Scribner and Cole.

Cole, R. W., Jr. (1974). Ribbin', jivin', and playin' the dozens. *Phi Delta Kappan,* 56:171–175. **434**

Coleman, J. S. (1961). *The adolescent society.* New York: Free Press. **108**

Coleman, J. S. (1965). *Adolescents and the schools.* New York: Basic Books. **108**

Coleman, J. S., et al. (1966). *Equality of educational opportunity.* Washington: Natl. Center for Educational Statistics. **2, 235, 410**

Collister, E. C., *see* Kuhlen and Collister.

Combs, A. W. (1965). *The professional education of teachers: a perceptual view of teacher preparation.* Boston: Allyn and Bacon. **250, 368, 486**

Combs, A. W. (1973). Educational accountability from a humanistic perspective. *Educ. Researcher,* 2(9):19–21. **339**

Combs, A. W., and Snygg, D. (1959). *Individual behavior: a perceptual approach to behavior,* rev. ed. New York: Harper. **21, 34, 41, 200**

Combs, A. W., *see also* Snygg and Combs.

Conger, J. J., *see* Mussen et al.

Cooley, W. W., and Glasser, R. (1969). The computer and individualized instruction. *Science,* 166:574–582. **291, 293**

Coon, C. L. (1915). *North Carolina schools and academies (1790–1840).* Raleigh, N. C.: Edwards and Broughton. **151**

Coons, A. E., *see* Stogdill and Coons.

Cooper, C. J. (1964). Some relationships between paired-associates learning and foreign-language aptitude. *J. educ. Psychol.,* 55:132–138. **225**

Coopersmith, S. (1967). *The antecedents of self-esteem.* San Francisco: Freeman. **35, 96**

Corbin, G., *see* Kreitman et al.

Corey, A. F. (1970). Overview of factors affecting the holding power of the teaching profession. In T. M. Stinnett, ed., *The teacher dropout.* Bloomington, Ind.: Phi Delta Kappa. **482**

Cowen, E. L., et al. (1965). The relation of anxiety in school children to school record, achievement and behavioral measures. *Child Develpm.,* 36:685–695. **138**

Cox, F. N. (1960). Correlates of general and test anxiety in children. *Austral. J. Psychol.,* 12:169–177. **229**

Cox, R. C., *see* Lindvall and Cox.

Crandall, V. J., *see* Walters and Crandall.

Cratty, B. J. (1970). *Perceptual and motor development in infants and children.* New York: Macmillan. **72**

Cronbach, L. J. (1969). Environment, heredity, and intelligence. Reprint Series No. 2, *Harvard Educ. Rev.* **374**

Cronbach, L. J. (1970). *Essentials of psychological testing,* 3rd ed. New York: Harper. **374**

Cronbach, L. J. (1975). Five decades of public controversy over mental testing. *Amer. Psychologist,* 30:1–14. **239**

Cronbach, L. J. (1975). Beyond the two disciplines of scientific psychology. *Amer. Psychologist,* 30:116–127. **172**

Crowl, T. K., and Macginitie, W. H. (1974). The influence of students' speech patterns on teachers' evaluation of oral answers. *J. educ. Psychol.,* 66:304–308. **423**

Cumming, J., *see* McCaffrey and Cumming.

Cummings, W. (1975). Checklist of criteria to be used for the identification of candidates for the gifted student program. San Francisco Unified School District, mimeographed. **390**

Cummins, R. E. (1957). An evaluative study of certain teacher perceptions related to professional growth. Unpublished doctoral dissertation, Univ. of Ala. **480**

Davis, A. (1948). *Social-class influences upon learning.* Cambridge: Harvard Univ. Press. **399**

Davis, A. (1951). Socio-economic influences upon children's learning. *Understanding the Child,* 20:10–16. **359**

Davis, A., and Havighurst, R. J. (1947). *Father of the man.* Boston: Houghton Mifflin. **32**

Davis, A., *see also* Bloom et al.

Davis, G. A., and Warren, T. F., eds. (1974). *Psychology of education: new looks.* Lexington, Mass.: Heath. **16**

de Lara, H. C., *see* Friedlander and de Lara.

Dellinger, W. S., *see* Naeye et al.

Delp, H. A. (1949). Mental health problems in the elementary school. Unpublished paper, Institute on Mental Health for School Administrators, Center for Continuation Study, Univ. of Minn. **260–261**

Dennis, W. (1960). Causes of retardation among institutional children: Iran. *J. genet. Psychol.,* 96: 47–59. **68–69**

Dennis, W. (1973). *Children of the creche.* Englewood Cliffs, N. J.: Prentice-Hall. **55, 69, 357**

Denniston, C. (1975). Accounting for differences in mean IQ. *Science,* 187:161–162. **358**

Denny, B. C. (1974). The decline of merit. *Science,* 186:875. **2**

Denny, T., Paterson, J., and Feldhusen, J. (1964). Anxiety and achievement as functions of daily testing. *J. educ. Measmt.,* 1:143–147. **355**

de Saix, C., *see* Polansky et al.

Deutsch, M., and Brown, B. (1964). Social influences in Negro-white intelligence differences. *J. soc. Issues,* 20(2):24–35. **422**

Deutsch, M., *see also* Katz and Deutsch.

Dewey, J. (1903). *Ethical principles underlying education.* Chicago: Univ. of Chicago Press. **197**

Dewey, J. (1910). *How we think.* Boston: Heath. **206**

Dewey, J. (1940). My pedagogic creed (originally published in 1897). In *Education today.* New York: Putnam. **178, 197**

Diaz-Guerrero, R., and Holtzman, W. H. (1974). Learning by televised "Plaza Sesamo" in Mexico. *J. educ. Psychol.,* 66:632–643. **57–58**

Diaz-Guerrero, R., *see also* Maslow and Diaz-Guerrero.

Diedrich, P. B., and Link, F. R. (1967). Cooperative evaluation in English. In F. T. Wilhelms, ed., *Evaluation as feedback and guide.* Washington: Assn. for Supervision and Curric. Develpm., NEA. **325**

Diedrich, P. B., *see also* Link and Diedrich.

Diener, M. N., *see* Naeye et al.

DiNapoli, P. J. (1937). *Homework in the New York City elementary schools.* New York: Bureau of Publ., Teachers Coll., Columbia Univ. **244**

Dinkmeyer, D. C. (1965). *Child development: the emerging self.* Englewood Cliffs, N.J.: Prentice-Hall. **72**

Dinkmeyer, D., and Dreikurs, R. (1963). *Encouraging children to learn.* Englewood Cliffs, N.J.: Prentice-Hall. **255, 454**

Dohrenwend, B. S., and Dohrenwend, B. P. (1966). Stress situations, birth order, and psychological symptoms. *J. abnorm. soc. Psychol.,* 71:215–223. **32**

Donahue, G. T., and Nichtern, S. (1965). *Teaching the troubled child.* Glencoe, Ill.: Free Press. **407**

Doppelt, J. E., and Bennett, G. K. (1967). Testing job applicants from disadvantaged groups. *Test Bull.* (Psychological Corp.), May, No. 57. **359**

Doris, S., *see* Sarason and Doris.

Douvan, E., and Adelson, J. (1965). *The adolescent experience.* New York: Wiley. **126**

Dowart, W., et al. (1965). The effect of brief social deprivation on social and nonsocial reinforcement. *J. Pers. soc. Psychol.,* 2:111–115. **100**

Doxiadis, C. A. (1970). Ekistics: the science of human settlements. *Science,* 170:393–404. **29**

Dreikurs, R. (1951). *Understanding the child: a manual for teachers.* Chicago: mimeographed publ. by author. **266**

Dreikurs, R. (1952a). *Character values and spiritual education in an anxious world.* Boston: Beacon Press. **434**

Dreikurs, R. (1952b). Understanding the exceptional child. In *Music therapy.* Chicago: Natl. Assn. for Music Therapy. **385, 389, 401, 405**

Dreikurs, R. (1957). *Psychology in the classroom.* New York: Harper. **148**

Dreikurs, R., *see also* Dinkmeyer and Dreikurs.

Dubois, P. H., ed. (1961). Toward a theory of achievement measurement. *Proceedings of the 1961 Invitational Conference on Testing Problems.* Princeton: Educ. Testing Service. **347**

Dunkin, M. J., and Biddle, B. J. (1974). *The study of teaching.* New York: Holt, Rinehart, and Winston. **486**

Dunn, J. A. (1968). The approach-approach paradigm as a model for the analysis of school anxiety. *J. educ. Psychol.,* 59:388–394. **107**

Dunn, J. A., Bloom, R. D., and Morse, W. C. (1964). Multiple descriptions of classroom behavior via pupil report. *Psychol. Rep.,* 14:651–656. **310**

Dunnette, M. D., Campbell, J., and Jaastad, K. (1963). The effect of group participation on brainstorming effectiveness for two industrial samples. *J. appl. Psychol.,* 47:30–37. **298**

Durell, D. D. (1961). Implementing and evaluating pupil-team learning plans. *J. educ. Sociol.,* 34:360–365. **295**

Durflinger, G. W. (1956). The fundamentals forgotten by college students. *J. educ. Res.,* 49:571–579. **167**

Early, C. J. (1968). Attitude learning in children. *J. educ. Psychol.,* 59:176–180. **124, 187**

Ebbinghaus, H. (1913). *Memory: a contribution to experimental psychology.* (Translated by H. A. Ruger and C. E. Bussenius.) New York: Teachers Coll., Columbia Univ. **167, 200**

Ebel, R. L. (1951). Writing the test item. In E. F. Lindquist, ed., *Educational measurement.* Washington: Amer. Council on Educ. **326**

Ebel, R. L., ed. (1960). Inventories and tests. *Education,* 81:67–99. **332**

Ebel, R. L. (1968). Standardized achievement tests: uses and limitations. In W. L. Barnette, ed., *Readings in*

Friedenberg, E. Z. (1965). *Coming of age in America.* New York: Random House. **1**

Friedlander, B. Z., and de Lara, H. C. (1973). Receptive language anomoly and language/reading dysfunction in "normal" primary-grade children. *Psychol. in the Schools,* 10:12–18. **396**

Friesen, W. V., *see* Kounin et al.

Frierson, E. C. (1969). The gifted. *Rev. educ. Res.,* 39:25–37. **391**

Frisch, H. E., and Revelle, R. (1970). Height and weight and a hypothesis of critical body weights and adolescent events. *Science,* 169:397–399. **66**

Froelich, C. P., and Moser, W. E. (1954). Do counselees remember test scores? *J. counsel. Psychol.,* 1:149–152. **169**

Gage, N. L. (1972). *Teacher effectiveness and teacher education.* Palo Alto: Pacific Books. **486**

Gage, N. L., Runkle, P. J., and Chatterjee, B. B. (1960). *Equilibrium theory and behavior change: an experiment in feedback from pupils to teachers.* Urbana: Bureau of Educational Res., Univ. of Ill. **321**

Gage, N. L., *see also* Charters and Gage.

Gagné, R. M. (1968). Contributions of learning to human development. *Psychol. Rev.,* 75:177–191. **49**

Gagné, R. M. (1970). *The conditions of learning.* New York: Holt, Rinehart, and Winston. **49, 53, 215**

Gagné, R. M., and Rohwer, W. D. (1969). Instructional psychology. In P. H. Mussen and W. W. Rosenzweig, eds., *Annual Review of Psychology,* 20:381–418. **192**

Gaier, E. L., *see* Morgan and Gaier.

Gale, R. F. (1969). *Developmental behavior: a humanistic approach.* New York: Macmillan. **411**

Gall, M. D., and Ward, B. A., eds. (1974). *Critical issues in educational psychology.* Boston: Little, Brown. **16**

Gallagher, J. J. (1974). Phenomenal growth and new problems characterize special education. *Phi Delta Kappan,* 55:516–520. **381**

Gallagher, J. J., and Aschner, M. J. M. (1963). A preliminary report: analysis of classroom interaction. *Merrill-Palmer Quart.,* 9:183–194. **237**

Gallimore, R., Tharp, R. G., and Kemp, B. (1969). Positive reinforcing function of "negative attention." *J. exper. Child Psychol.,* 8: 140–146. **162**

Gallimore, R., *see also* MacDonald et al.; *and* Sloggett et al.

Gallup, G. (1970). Second annual survey of the public's attitude toward the public schools. *Phi Delta Kappan,* 52:97–112. **257, 339, 442, 481**

Gallup, G. (1973). Fifth annual Gallup Poll of public attitudes toward education. *Phi Delta Kappan,* 55:38–51. **280**

Gallup, G. H. (1974). Sixth annual Gallup Poll of public attitudes toward education. *Phi Delta Kappan,* 56:20–32. **244, 257**

Garai, J., and Scheinfeld, A. (1968). Sex differences in mental and behavioral traits. *Genet. Psychol. Monogr.,* 77:169–299. **146, 222**

Garber, H., and Heber, R. (1973). *The Milwaukee Project: early intervention as a technique to prevent mental retardation.* Natl. Leadership Institute in Teacher Education/Early Childhood. Univ. of Conn. Technical Paper. **357**

Gardner, B., *see* Burchinal et al.

Gardner, W. I. (1969). Use of punishment with the severely retarded: a review. *Amer. J. ment. Deficiency,* 74:86–103. **263**

Gartner, A., *see* Riessman and Gartner.

Garverick, C. M., *see* Sassenrath and Garverick.

Geer, J. H., and Turteltaub, A. (1967). Fear reduction following observation of a model. *J. Pers. soc. Psychol.,* 6:327–331. **236**

Gelfond, A. (1952). The relationship of the onset of pubescence to certain interpersonal attitudes in girls. Unpubl. doctoral dissertation, New York Univ. **110**

Gesell, A., et al. (1940). *The first five years of life.* New York: Harper. **47, 353**

Gesell, A. (1943). *Infant and child in the culture of today.* New York: Harper. **47, 353**

Getzels, J. W., and Jackson, P. W. (1962). *Creativity and intelligence.* New York: Wiley. **369**

Ginsburg, H., and Opper, S. (1969). *Piaget's theory of intellectual development: an introduction.* Englewood Cliffs, N.J.: Prentice-Hall. **72**

Glaser, R., *see* Cooley and Glaser.

Glasser, W. (1969). *Schools without failure.* New York: Harper and Row. **313**

Glavin, J. P., and Quay, H. C. (1969). Behavior disorders. *Rev. educ. Res.,* 39:83–102. **130**

Glueck, E. T., *see* Glueck and Glueck.

Glueck, S. (1953). The home, the school, and delinquency. *Harvard educ. Rev.,* 23:17–32. **400**

Glueck, S., and Glueck, E. T. (1950). *Unravelling juvenile delinquency.* New York: Commonwealth Fund. **400**

Gnagey, T. (1970). Let's individualize discipline. *Adolescence,* 5:101–108. **265**

Gnagey, W. J., *see* Ofchus and Gnagey.

Goldberg, M. H., and Maccoby, E. H. (1965). Children's acquisition of skill in performing a group task under two conditions of group formation. *J. Pers. soc. Psychol.,* 2:898–902. **106**

Goldberg, M. L., Passow, A. H., and Justman, J. (1966). *The effects of ability grouping.* New York: Teachers Coll. Press. **395, 407**

Golden, M., Bridger, W. H., and Montare, A. (1974). Social class differences in the ability of young children to use verbal information to facilitate learning. *Amer. J. Orthopsychiat.,* 44:86–91. **90**

Goldman, B. A. (1969). Effect of classroom experience and video tape self-observation upon undergraduate attitudes toward self and toward teaching. *Amer. Psychol. Assn. Proceedings,* 4:647–648. **11**

Goldman, R. D., and Richards, R. (1974). The SAT prediction of grades for Mexican-American versus Anglo-American students at the University of California, Riverside. *J. educ. Measmt.,* 11:129–135. **355**

Goldschmid, M. L. (1968). Role of experience in the acquisition of conservation. *Amer. Psychol. Assn. Proceedings,* 3:361–362. **54**

Good, T. L., and Brophy, J. E. (1973). *Looking in classrooms.* New York: Harper and Row. **12, 313**

Good, T. L., *see also* Brophy and Good.

Goodlad, J. I. (1960). Classroom organization. In C. W. Harris, ed., *Encyclopedia of educational research,* 3rd ed. New York: Macmillan. **393**

Goodlad, J. I. (1968). To promote or not to promote? Several answers: short-term and long-term. In V. H. Noll and R. P. Noll, eds., *Readings in educational psychology,* 2nd ed. New York: Macmillan. **388**

Goodman, P. (1966). *Compulsory miseducation and the community of scholars.* New York: Vintage. **1**

Gordon, H. (1923). *Mental and scholastic tests among retarded children: an inquiry into the effects of schooling on various tests.* Educational Pamphlet No. 44. London: Board of Educ. **421**

Gordon, I. J. (1966). *Studying the child in school.* New York: Wiley. **72**

Gordon, L. V., *see* Mooney and Gordon.

Gottesman, I. (1968). Beyond the fringe—personality and psychopathology. In D. Glass, ed., *Genetics.* New York: Rockefeller Univ. Press. **358**

Gough, H. G. (1964). Academic achievement in high school as predicted from the California Psychological Inventory. *J. educ. Psychol.,* 55:174–180. **225–226**

Gould, E., *see* Sheehan et al.

Gowan, J. C. (1957). A summary of the intensive study of twenty highly selected elementary women teachers. *J. exper. Educ.,* 26:115–124. **483**

Gozali, H., et al. (1973). Relationship between the internal-external control construct and achievement. *J. educ. Psychol.,* 64:9–14. **227**

Grambs, J. D. (1952). *Group processes in intergroup education.* New York: Natl. Conf. of Christians and Jews. **297**

Grambs, J. D., *see also* Amos and Grambs.

Gray, S. W. (1963). *The psychologist in the schools.* New York: Holt, Rinehart, and Winston. **459**

Gray, S. W., and Klaus, R. A. (1965a). An experimental preschool program for culturally deprived children. *Child Develpm.,* 36:887–898. **425–431**

Gray, S. W., and Klaus, R. A., et al. (1965b). *The early training project: a handbook of aims and activities.* Nashville and Murfreesboro, Tenn.: George Peabody Coll. and Murfreesboro City Schools. **425–431, 437**

Gray, S. W., and Klaus, R. A. (1970). The Early Training Project: a seventh year report. *Child Develpm.,* 41:909–924. **425–431**

Gray, S. W., et al. (1966). *Before first grade.* New York: Teachers College Press. **437**

Gray, S. W., *see also* Klaus and Gray.

Green, D. R. (1954). Teaching methods and performance on a test of cancer knowledge in medical schools. *Calif. J. educ. Res.,* 5:188. **248**

Green, R. L., and Farquhar, W. W. (1965). Negro achievement motivation and scholastic achievement. *J. educ. Psychol.,* 56:241–243. **355, 422**

Green, R. L., and Hofmann, L. J. (1965). A case study of educational deprivation on Southern rural Negro children. *J. Negro Educ.,* 34:327–341. **421–422, 429**

Greenfeld, N., and Finkelstein, E. L. (1970). A comparison of the characteristics of junior high school students. *J. genet. Psychol.,* 117:37–50. **484**

Greenfield, P. M., Reich, L. C., and Olver, R. R. (1966). On culture and equivalence. In J. S. Bruner et al., eds., *Studies in cognitive growth.* New York: Wiley. **55**

Greenwood, G. E., and Soar, R. S. (1973). Some relationships between teacher morale and teacher behavior. *J. educ. Psychol.,* 64:105–108. **247**

Grobman, H. (1973). In A. C. Ornstein, ed., *Accountability for teachers and administrators.* Belmont, Calif.: Fearon. **339**

Gronlund, N. E. (1951). *The accuracy of teachers' judgments concerning the sociometric status of sixth grade pupils.* Beacon, N.Y.: Beacon House. **113**

Gronlund, N. E. (1959). *Sociometry in the classroom.* New York: Harper. **126**

Gronlund, N. E. (1970). *Stating behavioral objectives for classroom instruction.* New York: Macmillan. **347**

Gronlund, N. E. (1971). *Measurement and evaluation in teaching,* 2nd ed. New York: Macmillan. **347**

Gronlund, N. E. (1974). *Determining accountability for classroom instruction.* New York: Macmillan. **347**

Gross, N. (1958). *Who runs our schools?* New York: Wiley. **469**

Grossack, M. M. (1954). Some effects of cooperation and competition upon small group behavior. *J. abnorm. soc. Psychol.,* 49:341–348. **121**

Grosswald, J. (1970). Testing perspectives in the large cities. *Natl. Council on Measmt. in Educ. News,* 13(3). **239**

Grotberg, E. H. (1965). The Washington program in action. *Education,* 85:490–494. **432**

Guedes, H. de A., *see* Lindgren and Guedes.

Guerney, B. G., Jr., ed. (1969). *Psychotherapeutic roles for nonprofessionals, parents, and teachers.* New York: Holt, Rinehart, and Winston. **154, 282**

Guilford, J. P. (1959). Three faces of intellect. *Amer. Psychologist,* 14:469–479. **369**

Gump, P. V., and Kounin, J. S. (1957). Effects of teachers' methods of controlling misbehavior upon kindergarten children. *Amer. Psychologist,* 12:296 (abstract). **265**

Gump, P. V., *see also* Kounin and Gump; *and* Kounin et al.

Hadley, R., *see* Sheehan et al.

Hagen, E., *see* Thorndike and Hagen.

Haggard, E. A. (1954). The proper concern of educational psychologists. *Amer. Psychologist,* 9:539–543. **192**

Hall, C. M., *see* Rosenthal et al.

Hall, V. C., and Turner, R. R. (1974). The validity of the "different language explanation" for poor scholastic performance by black students. *Rev. educ. Res.,* 44:69–81. **423**

Hamblin, R. L., et al. (1969). Changing the game from "get the teacher" to "learn." *Trans-action,* 6(3):20–31. **276–277**

Hansen, D. N., *see* O'Neil et al.

Hansen, J. C., and Stevic, R. R. (1969). *Elementary school guidance.* New York: Macmillan. **459**

Harlow, H. F. (1962). The heterosexual affectional system in monkeys. *Amer. Psychologist,* 17:1–9. **31**

Harris, F. R., *see* Allen and Harris.

Hartley, R. E. (1959). Sex-role pressures and the socialization of the male child. *Psychol. Rep.,* 5:457–468. **146**

Haselrud, G. M., and Meyers, S. (1969). The transfer value of given and individually derived principles. *J. educ. Psychol.,* 49:293–296. **200**

Hausdorff, H., and Farr, S. D. (1965). The effects of grading practices on the marks of sixth grade children. *J. educ. Res.,* 59:169–172. **393**

Havighurst, R. J. (1970). Minority subcultures and the law of effect. In Korten, Cook, and Lacey, eds., *Psychology and the problems of society.* Washington: Amer. Psychol. Assn. **411**

Havighurst, R. J., and Neugarten, B. L. (1957). *Society and education.* Boston: Allyn and Bacon. **85**

Havighurst, R. J., et al. (1962). *Growing up in River City.* New York: Wiley. **96**

Havighurst, R. J., *see also* Ahlstrom and Havighurst, *and* Davis and Havighurst.

Havumaki, S., *see* Flanders and Havumaki.

Hawkins, G. R., *see* Burchinal et al.

Hawkins, R. P., *see* Surratt et al.

Heal, L. W., *see* Israel and Heal.

Hebb, D. O. (1955). The mammal and his environment. *Amer. J. Psychiat.,* 111:826–831. **30**

Heber, R., et al. (1972). *Rehabilitation of families at risk for mental retardation: a progress report.* Madison: Rehab. Res. and Training Center in Mental Retardation, Univ. of Wisc. **55–56**

Hechninger, G. (1973). Does education for all lead to mediocrity? *Wall St. J.,* July 25, 1973. **3**

Hecht, J. T., *see* Mouw and Hecht.

Heinstein, M. (1965). *Child rearing in California: a study of mothers with young children.* Berkeley: Calif. State Dept. of Public Health. **81**

Henning, C. J. (1949). Discipline: are school practices changing? *Clearing House,* 23:266–273. **263**

Henry, J. (1963). *Culture against man.* New York: Random House. **415**

Henry, N. B., ed. (1961). *Social forces influencing American education.* 60th Yearbook of the Natl. Soc. for the Study of Educ., Part II. Chicago: Univ. of Chicago Press. **255**

Hensarling, P. R., *see* Barker and Hensarling.

Hentoff, N. (1970). The schools we want. *Sat. Rev.,* 53(38):74, 77. **286**

Hermann, M. F., *see* Aiker et al.

Herndon, J. (1968). *The way it spozed to be.* New York: Simon and Schuster. **282**

Hess, R. D. (1964). Educability and rehabilitation: the future of the welfare class. *J. Marriage Faml.,* 26:422–429. **87**

Hess, R. D., *see also* Bloom et al.

Hetzel, D., *see* Elkind et al.

Hewitt, F. (1968). *The emotionally disturbed child in the classroom.* Boston: Allyn and Bacon. **407**

Highet, G. (1950). *The art of teaching.* New York: Knopf. **178**

Hightower, N. C., *see* Smith and Hightower.

Hilgard, E. R. (1956). *Theories of learning,* 2nd ed. New York: Appleton-Century-Crofts. **191**

Hilgard, E. R., ed. (1964). *Theories of learning and instruction.* 63rd Yearbook of the Natl. Soc. for the Study of Educ., Part I. Chicago: Univ. of Chicago Press. **206**

Hilgard, E. R., and Bower, G. H. (1966). *Theories of learning,* 3rd ed. New York: Appleton-Century-Crofts. **192**

Hilgard, E. R., *see also* Sears and Hilgard.

Hill, J. P., *see* Shelton and Hill.

Hilton, T. L., *see* Levin et al.

Hobbs, N., et al. (1974). *The futures of children.* San Francisco: Jossey-Bass. **385, 401, 407**

Hobson, J. R. (1963). High school performance of under-age pupils initially admitted to kindergarten on the basis of physical and psychological examinations. *Educ. psychol. Measmt.,* 23:159–170. **392**

Hodge, R. W., Siegel, P. M., and Rossi, P. H. (1964). Occupational prestige in the United States. *Amer. J. Sociol.,* 70:286–302. **484**

Hoffman, L. W. (1974). Effects of maternal employment on the child—a review of the research. *Developmental Psychol.,* 10:205–228. **79**

Hoffmann, B., (1962). *The tyranny of testing.* New York: Crowell-Collier. **327**

Hofmann, L. J., *see* Green and Hofmann.

Hollingshead, A. B. (1949). *Elmtown's youth.* New York: Wiley. **86**

Hollister, W. G. (1959). Current trends in mental health programming in the classroom. *J. soc. Issues,* 15(1):50–58. **152**

Holmes, D. S., *see* Barthell and Holmes.

Holt, J. (1964). *How children fail.* New York: Dell. **1, 179, 255**

Holt, J. (1972). *Freedom and beyond.* New York: Dutton. **1**

Holtzman, W. H., *see* Diaz-Guerrero and Holtzman.

Honzik, M. P., Macfarlane, J. W., and Allen, L. (1971). The stability of mental test performance between two and eighteen years. In M. C. Jones et al., eds., *The course of human development.* Waltham, Mass.: Xerox, 1971. **356**

Honzik, M. P., *see also* Macfarlane et al.

Horowitz, M. M. (1959). The teacher utilizes group forces. In *Learning and the teacher,* Yearbook of the Assn. for Supervision and Curric. Develpm. Washington: Natl. Educ. Assn. **313**

Horrocks, J. E., and Mussman, M. C. (1970). Middlescence: age-related stress periods during adult years. *Genet. Psychol. Monogr.,* 82:119–159. **484**

Horton, D. M., *see* Barbrack and Horton.

Horton, R. E., and Remmers, H. H. (1953). *Youth views current issues in education.* Purdue Opinion Panel, 12(1), November. **149**

House, E. R., *see* Walberg et al.

Hoyt, F. S. (1906). Studies in the teaching of English grammar. *Teachers Coll. Record,* 7:467–500. **167**

Hudgins, B. B. (1966). *Problem solving in the classroom.* New York: Macmillan. **179**

Hunnicutt, C. W. (1949). Selecting tomorrow's experience: liberal or authoritarian? The J. Richard Street Lecture for 1949. Syracuse, N.Y.: Syracuse Univ. Press. **258–259**

Hunter, E., and Amidon, E. J. (1964). *Student teaching: cases and comments.* New York: Holt, Rinehart, and Winston. **486**

Huntley, M. S. (1973). Alcohol influences upon closed-course driving performance. *J. Safety Res.,* 5:149–164. **3**

Huston, A. C., *see* Bandura and Huston.

Illich, I. (1971). *Deschooling society.* New York: Harper & Row. **1, 54**

Inhelder, B., and Piaget, J. (1958). *The growth of logical thinking from childhood to adolescence.* New York: Basic Books. **49**

Israel, L. J., and Heal, L. W. (1971). A developmental study of the subject matter choices in the free drawing of trainable mentally retarded subjects. *Exceptional Children,* 37:597–600. **222**

Iscoe, I., *see* Semler and Iscoe.

Jaastad, K., *see* Dunnette et al.

Jackson, P. W., and Lahaderne, H. M. (1967). Scholastic success and attitude toward school in a population of sixth graders. *J. educ. Psychol.,* 58:15–18. **174**

Jackson, P. W., Silberman, M. L., and Wolfson, B. J. (1969). Signs of personal involvement in teachers'
descriptions of their students. *J. educ. Psychol.,* 60:22–27. **484**

Jackson, P. W., *see also* Lahaderne and Jackson; *and* Getzels and Jackson.

Jacob, P. E., *see* Riesman et al.

Jacobson, F. N., Rettig, S., and Pasamanick, B. (1959). Status, job satisfaction, and factors of job satisfaction of state institution and clinic psychologists. *Amer. Psychologist,* 14:144–150. **481**

Jacobson, L., *see* Rosenthal and Jacobson.

James, L. R., Ellison, R. L., McDonald, B. W., and Taylor, C. W. (1968). Effectiveness of biographical information in predicting teacher assessments of creativity and leadership. *Amer. Psychol. Assn. Proceedings,* 3:231–232. **370**

Jencks, C. S., et al. (1972). *Inequality: a reassessment of the effect of family and schooling in America.* New York: Basic Books. **2, 358**

Jenkins, J. R., and Bausell, R. B. (1974). How teachers view the effective teacher: student learning is not the top criterion. *Phi Delta Kappan,* 55:572–573. **478**

Jennings, H. H. (1959). *Sociometry in group relations.* Washington: Amer. Council on Educ. **126**

Jensen, A. C. (1969). How much can we boost IQ and scholastic achievement? *Harvard Educ. Rev.,* 39:1–123. **357–359**

Jensen, A. R. (1974). Interaction of Level I and Level II abilities with race and socioeconomic status. *J. educ. Psychol.,* 66:99–111. **358**

Jex, F. B. (1963). Negative validities for two different ingenuity tests. In C. W. Taylor and F. Barron, eds., *Scientific creativity: its recognition and development.* New York: Wiley. **372**

Johnson, D. W., *see* Litcher and Johnson.

Johnson, R. A. (1974). Differential effects of reward versus no-reward instructions on the creative thinking of two economic levels of elementary school children. *J. educ. Psychol.,* 66:530–533. **418**

Johnson, R. E., *see* Steininger et al.

Johnson, W. (1946). *People in quandaries.* New York: Harper. **396**

Jones, H. E., *see* Pinneau and Jones.

Jones, M. C., et al., eds. (1971). *The course of human development.* Waltham, MA: Xerox. **68, 126**

Jones, P. A., and McMillan, W. B. (1973). Speech characteristics as a function of social class and situational factors. *Child Develpm.,* 44:117–121. **91**

Judy, C. J. (1969). Educational background information versus aptitude measures in the selection and classification of airmen. *Amer. Psychol. Assn. Proceedings,* 4:705–706. **344**

Justman, J., *see* Goldberg et al.

Kagan, J., and Freeman, M. (1963). Relation of childhood intelligence, maternal behaviors, and social class to behavior during adolescence. *Child Develpm.,* 34:899–911. **80**

Kagan, J., *see* Tulkin and Kagan; *and* Mussen et al.

Kagan, J. S. (1969). Inadequate evidence and illogical conclusions. *Harvard Educ. Rev.,* 39:126–129. **358**

Kahana, B., and Kahana, E. (1970). Roles of delay of gratification and motor control in the attainment of conceptual thought. *Amer. Psychol. Assn. Proceedings,* 5:287–288. **62**

Kammeyer, K. (1967). Birth order as a research variable. *Social Forces,* 46:71–80. **32**

Kandel, D. (1973). Adolescent marihuana use: role of parents and peers. *Science,* 181:1067–1070. **102, 113**

Kanfer, F. H., and Zich, J. (1974). Self-control training: the effects of external control on children's resistance to temptation. *Developmental Psychol.,* 10:108–115. **147**

Kanzer, P., *see* Zigler and Kanzer.

Karmel, L. H. (1970). *Measurement and evaluation in the schools.* New York: Macmillan. **347**

Katz, I. (1967). The socialization of academic motivation in minority group children. In D. Levine, ed., *Nebraska symposium on motivation.* Lincoln: Univ. of Nebraska Press. **433**

Katz, P., and Deutsch, M. (1967). The relationships of auditory and visual functioning to reading achievement in disadvantaged children. In M. Deutsch, ed., *The disadvantaged child.* New York: Basic Books. **53**

Katz, P. A., and Zalk, S. R. (1974). Doll References: an index of racial attitudes. *J. educ. Psychol.,* 66:663–668. **122**

Keen, R., *see* Stevenson et al.

Keliher, A. V. (1936). Some developmental factors in children . . . two to eight. In *Growth and development: the basis for educational programs.* New York: Progressive Educ. Assn. **250**

Keliher, A. V. (1938). *Life and growth.* New York: Appelton-Century-Crofts. **65**

Kelley, E. A. (1974). Implementing the IGE model: impact on teachers. *Phi Delta Kappan,* 55:570. **290**

Kelley, E. C. (1947). *Education for what is real.* New York: Harper. **177, 179**

Kemp, B., *see* Gallimore et al.

Kent, R. N., *see* Serbin et al.

Kersh, B. Y. (1958). The adequacy of "meaning" as an explanation for the superiority of learning by independent discovery. *J. educ. Psychol.,* 49:282–292. **171**

Kersh, B. Y. (1962). The motivating effect of learning by directed discovery. *J. educ. Psychol.,* 53:65–71. **171**

Kessen, W., ed. (1965). *The child.* New York: Wiley. **72**

Kirk, S. A. (1972). *Educating exceptional children,* 2nd ed. Boston: Houghton Mifflin. **379, 407**

Kirtz, D. D., *see* Steininger et al.

Kitzhaber, A. R. (1963). *Themes, theories, and therapy: the teaching of writing in college.* New York: McGraw-Hill. **167**

Klaus, R. A., and Gray, S. W. (1968). The early training project for disadvantaged children: a report after five years. *Soc. for Res. in Child Developm. Monogr.,* 33(4), Serial No. 120. **425–431**

Klaus, R. A., *see* Gray and Klaus.

Klausmeier, H. J., Morrow, R., and Walter, J. E. (1968). *Individually guided education in the multiunit elementary school: guidelines for implementation.* Madison, WI: Wisconsin Res. & Develpm. Center for Cognitive Learning. **289**

Kline, M. (1973). *Why Johnny can't add: the failure of the new math.* New York: St. Martin's Press. **218**

Kluckhohn, C. (1949). *Mirror for man.* New York: McGraw-Hill. **32**

Knapp, R. R. (1960). The effect of time limits on the intelligence test performance of Mexican and American subjects. *J. educ. Psychol.,* 51:14–20. **360**

Knights, R. M., *see* Stevenson et al.

Koch, H. L. (1955). Some personality correlates of sex, sibling position, and sex of sibling among five- and six-year-old children. *Genet. Psychol. Monogr.,* 52:3–50. **32**

Kodman, F., Jr. (1970). Effects of preschool enrichment on intellectual performance of Appalachian children. *Exceptional Children,* 36:503–507. **430**

Kodman, F., Jr., *see* Whipple and Kodman.

Kogan, N., and Pankove, E. (1974). Long-term predictive validity of divergent-thinking tests: some negative evidence. *J. educ. Psychol.,* 66:802–810. **370**

Kogan, N., *see* Ward et al.

Kohlberg, L. (1958). The development of modes of moral thinking and choice in the years ten to sixteen. Unpubl. doctoral dissertation Univ. of Chicago. **147**

Kohlberg, L. (1969). Stage and sequence: the cognitive-developmental approach to socialization. In D. Goslin, ed., *Handbook of socialization theory and research.* Chicago: Rand McNally. **59**

Kohlberg, L. (1973). The development of children's orientations toward a moral order. I. Sequence in the development of moral thought. *Vita Humana,* 6:11–33. **60**

Kohn, M. L. (1959). Social class and parental values. *Amer. J. Sociol.,* 64:337–351. **87**

Kolb, D. A. (1965). Achievement motivation for under-achieving high-school boys. *J. Pers. soc. Psychol.,* 2:783–792. **362**

Korchin, S. J., and Levine, S. (1957). Anxiety and verbal learning. *J. abnorm. soc. Psychol.,* 54:234–240. **229**

Kounin, J. S. (1970). *Discipline and group management in classrooms.* New York: Holt, Rinehart, and Winston. **242, 247, 255, 261, 282**

Kounin, J. S. (1970b). Relationship between activity signal-system and children's involvement. Unpubl. research. **293**

Kounin, J. B., Friesen, W. V., and Norton, A. E. (1966). Managing emotionally disturbed children in regular classrooms. *J. educ. Psychol.*, 57:1-13. **404**

Kounin, J. S., and Gump, P. V. (1961). The comparative influence of punitive and non-punitive teachers upon children's concepts of school misconduct. *J. educ. Psychol.*, 52:44-49. **265**

Kounin, J. S., Gump, P. V., and Biddle, B. J. (1957). The comparative influence of home, school, and camp upon children's concepts of misconduct. *Amer. Psychologist*, 12:396-397. **275**

Kounin, J. S., *see also* Gump and Kounin.

Kozol, J. (1972). *Free schools*. Boston: Houghton Mifflin. **305**

Kraus, P. E. (1973). *Yesterday's children: a longitudinal study of children from kindergarten into the adult years*. New York: Wiley-Interscience. **388, 392**

Kratwohl, D. R., Bloom, B. S., and Masia, B. B. (1964). *Taxonomy of educational objectives. Handbook II: Affective domain*. New York: McKay. **232**

Krech, D. (1969). Psychoneurobiochemeducation. *Phi Delta Kappan*, 50:370-375. **211**

Kreitman, L., Corbin, G., and Bell, M. (1969). The use of operant learning principles with retarded children. *Educ. Train. mental. Retard.*, 4:109-112. **277**

Kuder, G. F. (1951). *Examiner manual for the Kuder Preference Record Vocational-Form C*. Chicago: Science Research Associates. **471**

Kuethe, J. L. (1968). *The teaching-learning process*. Glenview, IL: Scott-Foresman. **206**

Kuhlen, R. G., and Collister, E. C. (1952). Sociometric status of sixth and ninth-graders who fail to finish high school. *Educ. psychol. Measmt.*, 12:632-637. **111**

LaCrosse, E. R., Jr. (1970). Psychologist and teacher: cooperation and conflict. *Young children*, 25:223-229. **12, 14**

Ladd, E. T. (1970). Pills for classroom peace? *Sat. Rev.*, 53(Nov. 21): 66-68, 81-83. **145**

Lahaderne, H. M., *see* Jackson and Lahaderne.

Landers, J. (1973). Accountability and progress by nomenclature: old ideas in new bottles. *Phi Delta Kappan*, 54:539-541. **339**

Lane, P. A., *see* Tolor et al.

Laosa, L. M., and Brophy, J. E. (1970). Sex and birth order interaction in measures of sex typing and affiliation in kindergarten children. *Amer. Psychol. Assn. Proceedings*, 5:363-364. **32**

Law, A. I. (1974). *Basic objectives for California State Reading Tests for grades 2, 3, 6, and 12: California assessment program*. Sacramento: California State Dept. of Educ. **318**

Layzer, D. (1974). Heritability analyses of IQ scores: science or numerology? *Science*, 183:1259-1266. **358**

Lebo, D., *see* Smith and Lebo.

Lee, E. A., and Thorpe, L. P. (1956). *Occupational interest inventory*. Monterey, CA: CTB/McGraw-Hill. **364**

Lee, E. S. (1951). Negro intelligence and selective migration: a Philadelphia test of the Klineberg hypothesis. *Amer. sociol. Rev.*, 16:227-233. **421**

Lee, G. C. (1966). The changing role of the teacher. In J. I. Goodlad, ed., *The changing American school*, 65th yearbook of the Natl. Soc. for the Study of Educ., Part II. Chicago: Univ. of Chicago Press. **463**

LeFurgy, W. G., and Woloshin, G. W. (1968). Modification of children's moral judgments through experimentally induced social influence. *Amer. Psychol. Assn. Proceedings*, 3:347-348. **61**

Leiderman, G. F., *see* Levin et al.

Leonard, G. B. (1968). *Education and ecstasty*. New York: Dell. **1, 313**

Lessinger, L. M., and Tyler, R. W. eds. (1971). *Accountability in education*. Worthington, Oh.: Jones. **347**

Leton, D. A. (1962). Assessment of school phobia. *Mental Hyg.*, 46:256-264. **143**

Levin, H., Hilton, T. L., and Leiderman, G. F. (1957). Studies of teacher behavior. *J. exper. Educ.*, 26:81-91. **482**

Levin, H., *see* Baldwin and Levin.

Levin, L. A., *see* Triandis et al.

Levine, S., *see* Korchin and Levine.

Levison, B. (1962). Understanding the child with school phobia. *Except Child*, 28:393-398. **143**

Levitt, E. E. (1967). *The psychology of anxiety*. Indianapolis: Bobbs-Merrill. **232**

Lewin, K. (1935). *A dynamic theory of personality: selected papers*. (Translated by D. D. Adams and K. E. Zener.) New York: McGraw-Hill. **194**

Lewin, K. (1951). *Field theory in social science*. New York: Harper. **194**

Lewin, K. (1958). Group decision and social change. In E. E. Maccoby et al., eds., *Readings in social psychology*, 3rd ed. New York: Holt. **169, 246**

Lewin, K., Lippitt, R., and White, R. K. (1939). Patterns of aggressive behavior in experimentally created "social climates." *J. soc. Psychol.*, 10:271-299. **119, 195, 237**

Lewis, H. H. (1951). A county guidance department looks at its problem behavior children. *Calif. J. educ. Res.*, 2:32-35. **135**

Liberman, D., *see* Wohlford and Liberman.

Liddle, G. (1958b). Overlap among desirable and undesirable characteristics in gifted children. *J. educ. Psychol.*, 49:219-223. **335**

Lindgren, F., *see* Lindgren and Lindgren.

Lindgren, H. C. (1954). *Mental health in education*. New York: Holt. **469**

Lindgren, H. C. (1961). Correlates of attitudes toward child-centered practices in education. *Psychol. Rep.*, 9:440. **474**

Lindgren, H. C. (1962). Authoritarianism, independence,

and child-centered practices in education. *Psychol. Rep.*, 10:747–750. **474**

Lindgren, H. C. (1966). Unpublished survey of the cheating. San Francisco State College. **149**

Lindgren, H. C. (1967). Brainstorming and the facilitation of creativity expressed in drawing. *Percept. Mot. Skills*, 24:350. **298**

Lindgren, H. C. (1973). *Introduction to social psychology*, 2nd ed. New York: Wiley. **96**

Lindgren, H. C. (1974). Political conservatism and its social environment: an appraisal of the American presidential election of 1972. *Psychol. Rep.*, 34:55–62. **3, 448**

Lindgren, H. C., and Byrne, D. (1975). *Psychology: an introduction to a behavioral science*, 4th ed. New York: Wiley. **206**

Lindgren, H. C., and Fisk, L. W., Jr. (1976). *Psychology of personal development*, 3rd ed. New York: Wiley. **41**

Lindgren, H. C., and Guedes, H. de A. (1963). Social status, intelligence, and educational achievement among elementary and secondary students in Sao Paulo, Brazil. *J. soc. Psychol.*, 60:9–14. **92**

Lindgren, H. C., and Lindgren, F. (1965a). Brainstorming and orneriness as facilitators of creativity. *Psychol. Rep.*, 16:577–583. **298, 369**

Lindgren, H. C., and Lindgren, F. (1965b). Creativity, brainstorming and orneriness: a cross-cultural study. *J. soc. Psychol.*, 67:23–30. **298, 369**

Lindgren, H. C., and Lindgren, F. (1972). *Current research in educational psychology*, 2nd ed. New York: Wiley. **16**

Lindgren, H. C., and Patton, G. M. (1958). Attitudes of high school and other teachers toward children and current educational methodology. *Calif. J. educ. Res.*, 9:80–85. **264, 309**

Lindgren, H. C., and Singer, E. (1963). Correlates of Brazilian and North American attitudes toward child-centered practices in education. *J. soc. Psychol.*, 60:3–7. **474**

Lindgren, H. C., *see also* Al Omar et al., Buchanan and Lindgren, Fisk and Lindgren, Tanner and Lindgren, *and* Watson and Lindgren.

Lindvall, C. M., and Cox, R. C. (1969). The role of evaluation in progress for individualized instruction. In R. W. Tyler, ed., *Educational evaluation: new roles, new means*. 68th yearbook, Natl. Soc. for the Study of Educ., Part II. Chicago: Univ. of Chicago Press. **323**

Link, F. R., and Diedrich, P. B. (1967). A cooperative evaluation program. In F. T. Wilhelms, ed., *Evaluation as feedback and guide*. Washington: Assn. for Supervision and Curric. Devpt., NEA. **326**

Link, F. R., *see* Diedrich and Link.

Lippitt, R., *see* Lewin et al., *and* White and Lippitt.

Litcher, J. H., and Johnson, D. W. (1969). Changes in attitudes toward Negroes of white elementary school students after use of multi-ethnic readers. *J. educ. Psychol.*, 60:148–152. **124**

Lodge, W. J. (1951). Classroom cheating—a measure of children's character or teacher attitudes? *Calif. J. educ. Res.*, 2:63–66. **245**

Loh, W. D., *see* Triandis et al.

Long, B. H., Ziller, R. C., and Bankes, J. (1968). Self-other orientations of institutionalized behavior-problem adolescents. *Amer. Psychol. Assn. Proceedings*, 3:483–484. **100**

Long, N. J., Morse, W. C., and Newman, R. G., eds. (1965). *Conflict in the classroom: the education of emotionally disturbed children*. Belmont, CA: Wadsworth. **155, 283, 407**

Lott, A. J., and Lott, B. E. (1970). Some indirect measures of interpersonal attraction among children. *J. educ. Psychol.*, 61:124–135. **113**

Lott, B. E., *see* Lott and Lott.

Lovos, G., and Norton, V. (1962). Teaching the barely educable: the Cupertino story. *Phi Delta Kappan*, 43:391–394. **388**

Lubin, S. C. (1965). Reinforcement schedules, scholastic aptitude, autonomy need, and achievement in a programmed course. *J. educ. Psychol.*, 56:295–302. **191**

Lunt, P. S., *see* Warner and Lunt.

Lyman, L., *see* Zweibelson et al.

Lytton, H. (1968). Some psychological and sociological characteristics of "good" and "poor" achievers (boys) in remedial reading groups: clinical case studies. *Hum. Develpm.*, 11:260–276. **398**

McCaffrey, L., and Cumming, J. (1967). *Behavior patterns associated with persistent emotional disturbances of school children in regular classes of elementary grades*. Syracuse, NY: Onondago County Mental Health Res. Unit, New York State Dept. of Ment. Hyg. **134**

McCandless, B. R. (1970). *Adolescents: behavior and development*. New York: Dryden. **127**

McCandless, B. R., Castenada, A., and Palermo, D. S. (1956). Anxiety in children and social status. *Child Develpm.*, 27:385–391. **138**

McCandless, B. R., Roberts, A., and Starnes, T. (1972). Teachers' marks, achievement test scores, and aptitude relations with respect to social class, race, and sex. *J. educ. Psychol.*, 63:153–159. **343**

McCandless, B. R. *see also* Pusser and McCandless.

McCarthy, D. (1953). Some possible explanations of sex differences in language development and disorders. *J. Psychol.*, 35:155–160. **146, 398**

Maccoby, E. E. (1975). Socialization of children. Unpubl. presidential address, WPA, Sacramento, CA, April, 1975. **222**

Maccoby, E. E., and Zellner, M., eds. (1970). *Experiments in primary education: aspects of Project Follow-through*. New York: Harcourt Brace Jovanovich. **437**

Maccoby, E. H., *see* Goldberg and Maccoby.

McCoy, G. F., *see* Clarizio and McCoy.

McDaniel, E. D., and Feldhusen, J. F. (1970). Relationships between faculty ratings and indexes of service and scholarship. *Amer. Psychol. Assn. Proceedings*, 5:619–620. **13, 211**

MacDonald, A. P., Jr. (1969). Manifestations of differential levels of socialization by birth order. *Develpm. Psychol.*, 1:485–492. **32**

McDonald, B. W., *see* James et al.

McDonald, F. J., *see* Bandura and McDonald.

MacDonald, G., *see* Macdonald, W. S., et al.

MacDonald, W. S., Gallimore, R., and MacDonald, G. (1970). Contingency-counseling by school personnel: an economical model of intervention. *J. appl. behav. Anal.*, 3:175–182. **451**

McEvoy, J., *see* Stark and McEvoy.

Macfarlane, J. W. (1971). From infancy to adulthood. In M. C. Jones et al., eds., *The course of human development*. Waltham, MA: Xerox. **135**

Macfarlane, J. W., Allen, L., and Honzik, M. P. (1971). A developmental study of the behavior problems of normal children between twenty-one months and fourteen years. In M. C. Jones et al., eds., *The course of human development*. Waltham, MA: Xerox. **135**

Macfarlane, J. W., *see also* Honzik et al.

McGehee, F. (1952). *Please excuse Johnny*. New York. Macmillan. **92**

McGinnies, E., *see* Mitnick and McGinnies.

MacGinitie, W. H., *see* Crowl and MacGinitie.

McGuire, D., *see* Zimmerman et al.

McIntyre, D., *see* Morrison and McIntyre.

McLaughlin, K. F., ed. (1960). *Understanding testing: purposes and interpretations for pupil development*. (Pamphlet of OE-25003) Washington: U.S. Office of Educ. **347**

McLaughlin, K. F. (1964). *Interpretation of test results*. Washington: U.S. Office of Educ. **347**

Macmillan, D. L., Forness, S. R., and Trumbull, B. M. (1973). The role of punishment in the classroom. *Excep. Children*, 40:85–96. **267, 278**

McMillan, W. B., *see* Jones and McMillan.

McQueen, M. (1968). Are teachers' roles changing? *Educ. Digest*, 34:8–11. **463**

Madaus, G. F., *see* Airasian and Madaus.

Madsen, C. H., *see* Muller and Madsen.

Mager, R. F. (1962). *Preparing instructional objectives*. Palo Alto: Fearon. **318**

Mager, R. F. (1968). *Developing attitudes toward learning*. Belmont, Calif.: Fearon. **232**

Maher, B., *see* Spence and Maher.

Mahler, C., and Smallenburg, H. (1963). Effects of testing programs on the attitudes of students, teachers, parents, and the community. In N. B. Henry and H. G. Richey, eds., *The impact and improvement of school testing programs*. 62nd yearbook of the Natl. Soc. for the study of Educ., Part II. Chicago: Univ. of Chicago Press. **342**

Majdalani, M., *see* Al Omar et al.

Margolin, R. J. (1953). New Perspectives for teachers—an evaluation of a mental-health institute. *Ment. Hyg.*, 37:394–424. **480**

Markell, R. A., *see* Asher and Markell.

Marolla, F. A., *see* Belmont and Marolla.

Marshall, H. H. (1969). Learning as a function of task interest, reinforcement, and social class variables. *J. educ. Psychol.*, 60:133–137, **94**

Marwit, S. J., and Neumann, G. (1974). Black and white children's comprehension of standard and nonstandard English passages. *J. educ. Psychol.*, 66:329–332. **423–424**

Masia, B. B., *see* Kratwohl et al.

Masling, J. M., *see* Stern and Masling.

Maslow, A. H. (1954). *Motivation and personality*. New York: Harper. **24, 41**

Maslow, A. H., and Diaz-Guerrero, R. (1960). Adolescence and juvenile delinquency in two different cultures. In Peatman and Hartley, eds., *Festschrift for Gardner Murphy*. New York: Harper. **83**

Massimo, J. L., *see* Shore and Massimo.

May, R. (1950). *The meaning of anxiety*. New York: Ronald. **99**

Meier, G. W. (1961). Infantile handling and development in Siamese kittens. *J. comp. physiol. Psychol.*, 54:284–286. **30**

Menaker, S. L., *see* Veldman and Menaker.

Mensh, I. N., et al. (1959). Children's behavior symptoms and their relationship to school adjustment, sex, and social class. *J. soc. Issues*, 15(1):8–15. **135–136, 144**

Metfessel, N. S., and Foster, J. T. (1965). Twenty-one research findings re culturally disadvantaged youth supported by information obtained from preschool critical incident observation records. Unpubl. paper. **413–414**

Meyer, S., *see* Haselrud and Meyers.

Millard, C. V., and Rothney, J. W. M. (1957). *The elementary school child: a book of cases*. New York: Dryden. **459**

Miller, E. L., *see* Baller et al.

Miller, H. R. (1951). What if they don't know grammar? *English J.*, 40:525–526. **167**

Miller, N. (1969). Learning of visceral and glandular responses. *Science*, 163:434–445. **185**

Mintz, A. (1951). Non-adaptive group behavior. *J. abnorm. soc. Psychol.*, 46:150–159. **120**

Minuchin, S. et al. (1967). *Families of the slums: an exploration of their structure and treatment*. New York: Basic Books. **413**

Mischel, W. (1958). Preference for delayed reinforcement: an experimental study of a cultural observation. *J. abnorm. soc. Psychol.*, 56:57–61. **78, 419**

Mitchell, J. S. (1970). High school: relevant? *School Counselor*, 17:345–349. **454**

Mitchell, L. S. (1953). *Two lives: the story of Wesley Clair Mitchell and myself.* New York: Simon and Schuster. **487**

Mitnick, L. L., and McGinnies, E. (1958). Influencing ethnocentrism in small discussion groups through film communication. *J. abnorm. soc. Psychol.,* 56:82–90. **302**

Montare, A., *see* Golden et al.

Montessori, M. (1964). *The Montessori method.* New York: Schocken. **49**

Mooney, R. L., and Gordon, L. V. (1950). *Mooney problem checklists.* New York: Psychological Corp. **366**

Moore, T. (1969). Stress in normal childhood. *Hum. Relat.,* 22:235–250. **175**

Morgan, P. K., and Gaier, E. L. (1956). The direction of aggression in the mother-child punishment situation. *Child Develpm.,* 27:447–457. **366**

Morris, G., *see* Strang and Morris.

Morrison, A., and McIntyre, D. (1969). *Teachers and teaching.* Baltimore: Penguin. **487**

Morrison, E. (1969). Underachievement among preadolescent boys considered in relation to passive aggression. *J. educ. Psychol.,* 60:168–173. **360**

Morrow, R., *see* Klausmeier et al.

Morse, W. C. (1961). A study of school classroom behavior from diverse evaluative frameworks: developmental, mental health, substantive learning, and group process. Cooperative res. proj. No. 753. Ann Arbor: School of Educ., Univ. of Mich. **310**

Morse W. C. (1962). Perceptions of classroom mental health, group process, and learning from diverse points of view. *Percept. Mot. Skills,* 14:390. **310**

Morse, W. C. (1963). Working paper: training teachers in life space interviewing. *Amer. J. Orthopsychiat.,* 33:727–730. **456–457**

Morse, W. C., *see also* Dunn et al.; *and* Long et al.

Mortensen, D. G., and Schmuller, A. M. (1966). *Guidance in today's schools,* 2nd ed. New York: Wiley. **459**

Moser, W. E., *see* Froelich and Moser.

Mosher, D. L., and Scodel, A. (1960). Relationships between ethnocentrism in children and ethnocentrism and authoritarian rearing practices of their mothers. *Child Develpm.,* 31:369–376. **122**

Mouw, J. T., and Hecht, J. T. (1973). Transfer of the "concept" of class inclusion. *J. educ. Psychol.,* 64:57–62. **53**

Muller, S. D., and Madsen, C. H., Jr. (1970). Group sensitization for "anxious" children with reading problems. *Psychol. in the Schools,* 7:184–189. **277**

Murphy, L. B. (1956). *Personality in young children. Vol. 1. Methods for the study of personality in young children.* New York: Basic Books. **136**

Murray, H. A. (1938). *Explorations in personality.* Cambridge: Harvard Univ. Press. **25**

Mussen, P. H., Conger, J. J., and Kagan, J. (1974). *Child development and personality,* 4th ed. New York: Harper and Row. **73**

Mussman, M. C., *see* Horrocks and Mussman.

Myerson, D. W. (1970). Student-operated token economy system. Unpublished paper, Western Psychol. Assn. Convention, Los Angeles, April, 1970. **293**

Naeye, R. L., Diener, M. M., and Dellinger, W. S. (1969). Urban poverty: effects on prenatal nutrition. *Science,* 166:1026. **414**

National Education Association (1957). The status of the American public-school teacher. *Nat. Educ. Assn. Res. Bull.,* 35: No. 1. **463**

National Education Association (1970a). Corporal punishment: teacher opinion. *Nat. Educ. Assn. Res. Bull.,* 48(2):48–49. **264**

National Education Association (1970b). Salary supplements for extra duties. *Nat. Educ. Assn. Res. Bull.,* 48(2):42–46. **468**

National Education Association (1970c). Teacher strikes, 1960–61 to 1969–70. *Nat. Educ. Assn. Res. Bull.,* 48(3):69–73. **481**

National Education Association (1970d). School marks and reporting to parents. *Nat. Educ. Assn. Res. Bull.,* 48(3):76–81. **342**

Nelson, C. H. (1970). *Measurement and evaluation in the classroom.* New York: Macmillan. **347**

Nelson, V. L., *see* Sontag et al.

Nesbitt, J. E., *see* Butcher et al.

Neugarten, B. L. (1946). Social class and friendship among school children. *Amer. J. Sociol.,* 51:305–313. **92**

Neugarten, B. L., *see* Havighurst and Neugarten.

Neumann, G., *see* Marwit and Neumann

Newman, R. G., *see* Long et al.

Newton, M. R., and Brown, R. D. (1967). A preventive approach to developmental problems in school children. In W. G. Hollister and E. M. Brower, eds. *Behavioral science frontiers in education.* New York: Wiley. **155**

Nisbett, R. E. (1968). Birth order and participation in dangerous sports. *J. Pers. soc. Psychol.,* 8:351–353. **32**

Norton, A. E., *see* Kounin et al.

Norton, B., *see* Lovos and Norton.

Nye, F. I. (1958). *Family relationships and delinquent behavior.* New York: Wiley. **79**

Oberholtzer, K. E., *see* Schramm and Oberholtzer.

Oden, M. H. (1968). The fulfillment of promise: 40-year follow-up of the Terman Gifted Group. *Genet. Psychol. Monogr.,* 77:3–93. **391**

Ofchus, L. T., and Gnagey, W. J. (1963). Factors related to the shift of professional attitudes of students in teacher education. *J. educ. Psychol.,* 54:149–153. **474**

Ogletree, E. J. (1970). Ability grouping: its effect on attitudes. *J. soc. Psychol.,* 82:137–138. **394**

Ohio State University and Westinghouse Learning Corporation (1969). *The impact of Head Start: an evaluation of the effects of Head Start on children's cognitive and af-*

fective development. Springfield, Va.: Clearinghouse for Federal Scientific and Technical Information, 2 vols. **57**

O'Leary, K. D., *see* Serbin et al.; Toffel et al.

Olsen, J. (1965). Challenge of the poor to the schools. *Phi Delta Kappan*, 47:79–84. **418**

Olson, A. L., *see* Clarke and Olson.

Olson, W. C. (1949). *Child development*. Boston: Heath. **67**

Olver, R. R., *see* Greenfield et al.

O'Neil, H. F., Jr., Spiegelberger, C. D., and Hansen, D. N. (1969). Effects of state anxiety and task difficulty on computer-assisted learning. *J. educ. Psychol.,* 60:343–350. **228**

Opper, S., *see* Ginsburg and Opper.

Osborn, A. F. (1957). *Applied imagination*, rev. ed. New York: Scribner. **298**

Page, E. B. (1958). Teacher comments and student performance: a seventy-four classroom experiment in school motivation. *J. educ. Psychol.*, 49:173–181. **189, 211, 320**

Paivio, A. (1964). Childrearing antecedents of audience sensitivity. *Child Develpm.*, 35:397–416. **140–141**

Palermo, D. S., *see* McCandless et al.

Palmer, F. H. (1970). Socioeconomic status and intellective performance among Negro preschool boys. *Develpm. Psychol.*, 3:1–9. **358**

Palmer, R. D. (1966). Birth order and identification. *J. consult. Psychol.*, 30:129–135. **32**

Panda, K. C. (1971). Effects of social reinforcement, locus of control, and cognitive style on concept learning among educable mentally retarded children. *APA Experimental Publ. System*, June, 12, Ms. No. 475–34. **163**

Pankove, E., *see* Kagan and Pankove; *and* Ward et al.

Parnes, S. J. (1966). Programming creative behavior. U.S. Office of Educ., Coop. Res. Proj., No. 5–0716. Buffalo: State Univ. of New York at Buffalo. **371**

Parten, M. L. (1932). Social participation among preschool children. *J. abnorm. soc. Psychol.*, 27:243–269. **102–104**

Pasamanick, B., *see* Rettig and Pasamanick; *and* Jacobson et al.

Passow, A. H., *see* Goldberg et al.

Paternite, C. E., *see* Cantor and Paternite.

Paterson, J., *see* Denny et al.

Patterson, J. L. (1974). How popular is the paddle? *Phi Delta Kappan*, 55:707. **264**

Patton, G. M., *see* Lindgren and Patton.

Payne, J. S., et al. (1973). *Head Start: a tragicomedy with epilogue*. New York: Behavioral Publ. **437**

Peck, R. F., *see* Veldman and Peck.

Perkins, H. V. (1965). Classroom behavior and underachievement. *Amer. educ. Res. J.*, 2:1–2. **360**

Phenix, P. H., ed. (1961). *Philosophies of education*. New York: Wiley. **179**

Piaget, J. (1948). *The moral judgment of the child.* (Orig. published in 1932.) Glencoe, IL: Free Press. **59, 147**

Piaget, J., *see* Inhelder and Piaget.

Pickrel, E. W. (1958). The differential effect of manifest anxiety on test performance. *J. educ. Psychol.,* 49:43–46. **229**

Pinneau, S. R. (1955). The infantile disorders of hospitalism and anaclitic depression. *Psychol. Bull.*, 52:429–452. **24**

Pinneau, S. R., and Jones, H. E. (1959). A longitudinal study of the consistency of behavior between three and ten years. *Calif. J. educ. Res.*, 10:119–120. **67**

Polansky, N. A., Borgman, R. D., and de Saix, C. (1972). *Roots of futility*. San Francisco: Jossey-Bass. **96**

Popham, W. J. (1973). In A. C. Ornstein, ed., *Accountability for teachers and administrators*. Belmont, Calif.: Fearon. **339**

Postman, N., and Weingartner, C. (1969). *Teaching as a subversive activity*. New York: Delacorte. **13**

Pressey, S. L. (1926). A simple device for teaching, testing, and research in learning. *School and Society,* 23:373–376. **189**

Proctor, J. H., and Smith, K. (1974). IGE and open education: are they compatible? *Phi Delta Kappan,* 55:564–566. **290**

Provus, M. (1966). *Time to teach: action report*. Washington: Natl. Educ. Assn. **474**

Provus, M. (1969). Collective action by teachers. In Ebel, Noll, and Bauer, eds., *Encyclopedia of educational research*, 4th ed. New York: Macmillan. **475**

Pusser, H. E., and McCandless, B. R. (1974). Socialization dimensions among inner-city five-year-olds and later school success: a follow-up. *J. educ. Psychol.,* 66:285–290. **431–432**

Quay, H. C. and Quay, L. C. (1965). Behavior problems in early adolescence. *Child Develpm.*, 36:215–220. **134**

Quay, H. C., *see* Glavin and Quay.

Rasher, S. P., *see* Walberg and Rasher.

Radin, N. (1973). Observed parental behaviors as antecedents of intellectual functioning in young boys. *Develpm. Psychol.*, 8:369–376. **87**

Rainwater, L. (1970). The problem of lower class culture. *J. soc. Issues*, 26(2):133–148. **410**

Rajpal, P. L. (1972). What behavior problems do teachers regard as serious? *Phi Delta Kappan*, 53:591–592. **131**

Randazzo, J. D., and Arnold, J. M. (1972). Does open education really work in an urban setting? *Phi Delta Kappan*, 54:107–110. **306**

Redl, F., and Wattenberg, W. W. (1959). *Mental hygiene in teaching*, rev. ed. Boston: Houghton Mifflin. **463**

Rees, J., *see* Tizard and Rees.

Reich, L. C., *see* Greenfield et al.

Reid, J. B., *see* Sutter and Reid.

Remmers, H. H., *see* Horton and Remmers.

Rettig, S., and Pasamanick, B. (1959). Status and job satisfaction of public school teachers. *School and Society,* 87:113–116. **12, 481**

Rettig, S., *see* Jacobson et al.

Revelle, R., *see* Frisch and Revelle.

Reynolds, M., and Davis, M., eds. (1971). *Exceptional children in regular classrooms.* Minneapolis: Univ. of Minnesota Press. **407**

Ricciuti, H. N. (1970). Malnutrition, learning, and intellectual development: research and remediation. In Korten, Cook, and Lacey, eds., *Psychology and the problems of society.* Washington: Amer. Psychol. Assn. **66**

Rice, J. M. (1897). The futility of the spelling grind. *Forum,* 23:163–172. **173, 176**

Richards, R., *see* Goldman and Richards.

Ricklefs, R. (1974). More public systems open schools allowing pupils independence. *Wall Street J.,* 110, No. 106, May 31, pp. 1, 27. **308**

Rickover, H. G. (1963). *American education—a national failure.* New York: Dutton. **2**

Riesman, D., Jacob, P. E., and Sanford, N. (1959). *Spotlight on the college student.* Washington: Amer. Council on Educ. **240**

Riessman, F., and Gartner, A. (1969). New careers and pupil learning. *Calif. Teachers Assn. J.,* 65(2):6–9. **434–435**

Ringness, T. A. (1967). Identification patterns, motivation, and school achievement of bright junior high school boys. *J. educ. Psychol.,* 58:93–102. **107**

Roberts, A., *see* McCandless et al.

Roberts, R. D. (1970). Perceptions of actual and desired role functions of school psychologists by psychologists and teachers. *Psychol. in the Schools,* 7:175–178. **443**

Robin, S. S., *see* Callahan and Robin.

Rodriguez, A., Rodriguez, M., and Eisenberg, L. (1959). The outcome of school phobia: a follow-up study based on 41 cases. *Amer. J. Psychiat.,* 116:540–544. **143**

Roff, M., and Sells, S. B. (1965). Relations between intelligence and sociometric status in groups differing in sex and socioeconomic background. *Psychol. Rep.,* 16:511–516. **114–115**

Rogers, C. R. (1951). *Client-centered therapy.* Boston: Houghton Mifflin. **21, 24, 33, 41**

Rogers, C. R. (1961). *On becoming a person.* Boston: Houghton Mifflin. **241**

Rogers, C. R. (1969). *Freedom to learn.* Columbus, O.: Merrill. **255**

Rogers, C. R. (1970). It is my observation . . . *Newsletter, Assn. for Humanistic Psychol.,* 7(1):1,7. **242**

Rohwer, W. D., *see* Gagné and Rohwer.

Roman, M. (1957). *Teaching delinquents through reading.* Springfield, Ill. Thomas. **398**

Rosenthal, R., and Jacobson, L. (1968). *Pygmalion in the classroom.* New York: Holt, Rinehart, and Winston. **233**

Rosenthal, R., Baratz, S. S., and Hall, C. M. (1974). Teacher behavior, teacher expectations, and gains in pupils' rated creativity. *J. Genet. Psychol.,* 124:115–121. **239**

Rossi, P. H., *see* Hodge et al.

Rothney, J. W. M., *see* Millard and Rothney.

Rowley, V. N., *see* Stone and Rowley.

Rubin, L. F., ed. (1969). *Life skills in school and society.* Washington: Assn. for Supervision and Curric. Develpm., Natl. Educ. Assn. **232**

Runkle, P. J., *see* Gage et al.

Rust, R. M. (1958). Personality and academic achievement: a questionnaire approach. In B. M. Wedge, ed., *Psychosocial problems of college men.* New Haven: Yale Univ. Press. **144**

Ryan, T. J. (1968). Effects of observer, instructional set, and reward schedule upon instrumental performance. *Amer. Psychol. Assn. Proceedings,* 3:363–364. **188**

Rychlak, J. F., and Tobin, T. J. (1971). Order effects in the affective learning styles of overachievers and underachievers. *J. educ. Psychol.,* 62:141–147. **361**

St. John, N. H. (1970). Desegregation and minority group performance. *Rev. educ. Res.,* 40:111–133. **410**

Samuels, S. J., and Turnure, J. E. (1974). Attention and reading achievement in first-grade boys and girls. *J. educ. Psychol.,* 66:29–32. **222**

Sanford, N., *see* Riesman et al.

Sarason, S. B., and Doris, S. (1969). *Psychological problems in mental deficiency,* 4th ed. New York: Harper and Row. **407**

Sassenrath, J. M., and Garverick, C. M. (1965). Effects of differential feedback from examinations on retention and transfer. *J. educ. Psychol.,* 56:259–263. **320**

Sexe, R. W., *see* Beck and Saxe.

Scarpetti, W. L., *see* Tolor et al.

Scarr-Salapatek, S. (1971). Race, social class, and IQ. *Science,* 174:1285–1295. **358**

Scarr-Salapatek, S., and Williams, M. L. (1973). The effects of early stimulation on low-birth-weight infants. *Child Develpm.,* 44:94–101. **30**

Schaefer, E. A. (1969). The need for early and continuing education. Unpublished paper, Amer. Assn. for the Advancement of Science, Chevy Chase, Md.: December. **358**

Scheinfeld, A., *see* Garai and Scheinfeld.

Schiamberg, L. (1969). Some socio-cultural factors in adolescent-parent conflict: a cross-cultural comparison of selected cultures. *Adolescence,* 4:333–360. **110**

Schmidt, G. W., and Ulrich, R. E. (1969). Effects of group contingent events upon classroom noise. *J. appl. Behav. Anal.,* 2:171–179. **277**

Schmuller, A. M., *see* Mortensen and Schmuller, *and* Thorpe and Schmuller.

Schramm, W., and Oberholtzer, K. E. (1964). (No title) *Phi Delta Kappan,* 46:133. **293**

Schreiber, D. (1962). Finding and developing talent. Unpublished address delivered at the Univ. of San Francisco, March 13. **432**

Schreiber, D. (1963). The dropout and the delinquent: promising practices gleaned from a year of study. *Phi Delta Kappan*, 44: 215–221. **432, 451**

Schulman, J. S., *see* Busk et al.

Schunert, J. (1951). The association of mathematical achievement with certain factors resident in the teacher, in the pupil, and in the school. *J. exp. Educ.*, 19:219–238. **244**

Schwartz, B. (1959). An investigation of the effects of a seventh and eighth grade core program. *J. educ. Res.*, 53:149–152. **292**

Schwebel, A. I., and Cherlin, D. L. (1972). Physical and social distancing in teacher-pupil relationships. *J. educ. Psychol.*, 63:543–550. **272**

Schwenn, E. A., Sorenson, J. S., and Bavary, J. (1970). *The effects of individual adult-child conferences on the independent reading of elementary school children.* Wisconsin Research and Development Center for Cognitive Learning, Univ. of Wisconsin Tech. Report No. 125, March. **212**

Scodel, A., *see* Mosher and Scodel.

Scribner, S., and Cole, M. (1973). Cognitive consequences of formal and informal education. *Science*, 183:553–559. **54**

Sears, P. S., and Hilgard, E. R. (1964). The teacher's role in the motivation of the learner. In E. R. Hilgard, ed., *Theories of learning and instruction*, 63rd Yearbook. Chicago: Nat. Soc. for the Study of Educ. **225**

Sechrest, L. (1963). Implicit reinforcement of responses. *J. educ. Psychol.*, 54:197–201. **121**

Seitz, T. L. (1964). The relationship between creativity and intelligence, personality, and value patterns in adolescence. Unpublished doctoral dissertation, Univ. of Denver. **370**

Seitz, V., *see* Zigler et al.

Sells, S. B., *see* Roff and Sells.

Semler, I. J., and Iscoe, I. (1963). Comparative and developmental study of the learning abilities of Negro and white children under four conditions. *J. educ. Psychol.*, 54:38–44. **422**

Serbin, L. A., O'Leary, K. D., and Kent, R. N. (1973). A comparison of teacher response to the preacademic and problem behavior of boys and girls. *Child Develpm.*, 44:796–804. **147**

Shanker, A. (1971). Accountability: possible effects on instructional programs. In L. M. Lessinger and R. W. Tyler, eds., *Accountability in education.* Worthington, O.: Jones. **305**

Shaw, M. C. (1964). Note on parent attitudes toward independence training and the academic achievement of their children. *J. educ. Psychol.*, 55:371–374. **361**

Sheehan, J., Hadley, R., and Gould, E. (1967). Impact of authority on stuttering. *J. abnorm. Psychol.*, 72:290–293. **397**

Shelton, J., and Hill, J. P. (1968). Effects on cheating of achievement anxiety and knowledge of peer performance. *Amer. Psychol. Assn. Proceedings.* 3:349–350. **149**

Sherif, M. (1936). *The psychology of social norms.* New York: Harper. **299**

Shore, M. F., and Massimo, J. L. (1967). Verbalization, stimulus relevance, and personality change. *J. consult. Psychol.*, 31:423–424. **399**

Siegel, P. M., *see* Hodge et al.

Silberman, C. E. (1970). *Crisis in the classroom.* New York: Random House. **1**

Silberman, M. L., *see* Jackson et al.

Singer, E., *see* Lindgren and Singer.

Skidelsky, R. (1969). *English progressive schools.* Baltimore: Penguin. **305, 313**

Skinner, B. F. (1953). *Science and human behavior.* New York: Macmillan. **161, 188**

Skinner, B. F. (1958). Teaching machines. *Science,* 128:969–977. **190**

Skinner, B. F. (1961). The design of cultures. *Daedulus,* 90:534–546. **188**

Skinner, B. F. (1968). *The technology of teaching.* New York: Meredith. **207**

Skinner, B. F. (1973). Some implications of making education more efficient. In C. E. Thoresen, ed., *Behavior modification in education.* 72nd Yearbook of the Natl. Soc. for the Study of Educ., Part 1. Chicago: Univ. of Chicago Press. **278**

Slotkin, H. (1963). New program for dropouts. *Voc. guid. Quart.*, 12:127–132. **451**

Smallenburg, H., *see* Mahler and Smallenburg.

Smelser, W. T., and Stewart, L. H. (1968). Where are the siblings: a re-evaluation of the relationship between birth order and college attendance. *Sociometry,* 31:294–303. **32**

Smith, G. M. (1969). Personality correlates of academic performance in three dissimilar populations. *Amer. Psychol. Assn. Proceedings,* 4:303–304. **115**

Smith, H. L., and Hightower, N. C. (1948). Incidence of functional disease (neurosis) among patients of various occupations. *Occup. Med.*, 5:182–185. **479**

Smith, K., *see* Proctor and Smith.

Smith, M., ed. (1966). *A decade of comment on education.* Washington: Council for Basic Educ. **2**

Smith, T. S., *see* Walls and Smith.

Smith, W. D., and Lebo, D. (1956). Some changing aspects of the self-concept in pubescent males. *J. genet. Psychol.*, 88:61–75. **66**

Snow, R. H. (1963). Anxieties and discontents in teaching. *Phi Delta Kappan*, 44:318–321. **279**

REFERENCES AND AUTHOR INDEX

Snyder, E. E. (1969). A longitudinal analysis of the relationship between high school student values, social participation, and educational-occupational achievement. *Sociol. of Educ.*, 42:261–270. **108**

Snygg, D., and Combs (1949). *Individual behavior.* New York: Harper. **21, 200, 214, 217**

Snygg, D., *see also* Combs and Snygg.

Solomon, M. D. (1951). The personality factor of rigidity as an element in the teaching of the scientific method. Unpublished doctoral dissertation, Michigan State College. **123**

Sontag, L. W., Baker, C. T., and Nelson, V. L. (1958). Mental growth and personality development: a longitudinal study. *Monographs of the Society for Research in Child Develpm.*, 23: No. 68. **357**

Sorenson, J. S., *see* Schwenn et al.

Spaulding, R. L. (1963). What teacher attitudes bring out the best in gifted children? *Gifted Children Quart.*, 7:150–156. **371**

Spence, J. T., and Maher, B. (1962). Handling and noxious stimulation of the albino rat: II. Effects on subsequent performance in a learning situation. *J. comp. physiol. Psychol.*, 55:252–255. **30**

Spiegelberger, C. D. (1966). *Anxiety and behavior.* New York: Academic. **227**

Spiegelberger, C. D., *see* O'Neil et al.

Spitz, R. A. (1945). Hospitalism. An inquiry into the genesis of psychiatric conditions in early childhood. *Psychoanalytic Study of the Child*, vol. 1. New York: International Universities Press. **24**

Spitz, R. A. (1945). Hospitalism: a follow up report on investigation described in Vol. 1. *Psychoanalytic Study of the Child*, 2:113–117. **24**

Spring, C. (1971). Perceptual speed in poor readers. *J. educ. Psychol.*, 62:492–500 **146**

Sprinthall, N.A., and Tiedman, D. V. (1966). Guidance and the pupil. In J. I. Goodlad, ed., *The changing American school*, 65th Yearbook of the Natl. Soc. for the Study of Educ., Part II. Chicago: Univ. of Chicago Press. **459**

SPSSI Council (1960). Statement dated January 31, 1960, on the New York City Youth Board's report: "An experiment in predicting juvenile delinquency." *Newsletter of the Soc. for the Psychological Study of Soc. Issues.* **401**

Staats, A. W., and Staats, C. K. (1963). *Complex human behavior: a systematic extension of learning principles.* New York: Holt, Rinehart, and Winston. **41**

Staats, C. K., *see* Staats and Staats.

Stacey, B. (1969). Achievement motivation, occupational choice and inter-generation occupational mobility. *Hum. Relat.*, 22:275–281. **25**

Starch, D. (1927). *Educational psychology*, rev. ed. New York: Macmillan. **324**

Stark, R., and McEvoy, J., III. (1970). Middleclass violence. *Psychology Today*, 4(6):52–54. **264**

Starmes, T., *see* McCandless et al.

Starry, A. R., *see* Erlick and Starry.

Steele, J. M., *see* Walberg et al.

Steininger, M., Johnson, R. E., and Kirts, D. K. (1964). Cheating on college examinations as a function of situationally aroused anxiety and hostility. *J. educ. Psychol.*, 55:317–324. **149**

Stennett, R. G. (1966). Emotional handicap in the elementary years: phase or disease? *Amer. J. Orthopsychiat.*, 36:444–449. **134**

Stennett, R. G. (1969). The relationship of sex and socioeconomic status to IQ changes. *Psychology in the Schools*, 6:385–390. **356–357**

Stern, G. G., and Masling, J. M. (1958). *Unconscious factors in career motivation for teaching.* (SAE6459) Washington : Office of Educ. **483**

Stevenson, H. W., Keen, R., and Knights, R. M. (1963). Parents and strangers as reinforcing agents for children's performance. *J. abnorm. soc. Psychol.*, 67:183–186. **473**

Stevic, R. R., *see* Hansen and Stevic.

Stewart, L. H., *see* Smelser and Stewart.

Stinnett, T. M. (1970). *The teacher dropout.* Itasca, Ill.: Peacock. **487**

Stogdill, R. M. (1969). Validity of leader descriptions. *Personnel Psychol.*, 22:153–158. **260**

Stogdill, R. M., and Coons, A. E. (1957). *Leader behavior: its description and measurement.* Research Monogr. No. 88. Columbus: Bureau of Business Research, Ohio State Univ. **260**

Stone, F. B., and Rowley, V. N. (1964). Educational disability in emotionally disturbed children. *Except. Children*, 30:423–426. **403**

Stovall, T. F. (1958). Lecture vs. discussion. *Phi Delta Kappan*, 39:255–258. **246**

Strang, R. (1937). *Behavior and background of students in college and secondary school.* New York: Harper. **244**

Strang, R., and Morris, G. (1964). *Guidance in the classroom.* New York: Macmillan. **459**

Stringer, L. A. (1959). Academic progress as an index of mental health. *J. soc. Issues*, 15(1):16–29. **132**

Strobel, D. A., *see* Zimmerman et al.

Strommen, E. A. (1973). Verbal self-regulation in a children's game: impulsive errors on "Simon says." *Child Developm.*, 44:849–853. **146–147**

Strong, E. K., Jr. (1943). *Vocational interests of men and women.* Stanford: Stanford Univ. Press. **471**

Studholme, J. M. (1964). Group guidance with mothers of retarded readers. *Reading Teacher*, 17:234–239. **398**

Sullivan, H. S. (1947). *Conceptions of modern psychiatry.* Washington: William Alanson White Psychiatric Foundation. **27**

Superintendent of Public instruction, State of California (1965). Results of the California State Testing Program for 1964–65. Unpublished memorandum to the Calif. State Board of Educ., dated October 12, 1965. **340**

Suppes, P. (1964). Modern learning theory and the elementary school curriculum. *Amer. educ. Res. J.*, 1:79–93. **378–379**

Surratt, P. R., Ulrich, R. E., and Hawkins, R. P. (1969). An elementary student as a behavioral engineer. *J. appl. Beh. Anal.*, 2:85–92. **277**

Sutter, E. G., and Reid, J. B. (1969). Learner variables and interpersonal conditions in computer-assisted instruction. *J. educ. Psychol.*, 60:153–157. **290**

Swaim, E. E. (1972). B. F. Skinner and Carl R. Rogers on behavior and education. Unpublished doctoral dissertation, Univ. of Oregon. **203**

Symonds, P. M. (1950). Reflections on observations of teachers. *J. educ. Psychol.*, 43:688–696. **479**

Symonds, P. M. (1955). What education has to learn from psychology. II. Reward. *Teachers College Record*, 57:15–25. **219**

Symonds, P. M. (1956). What education has to learn from psychology. III. Punishment. *Teachers College Record*, 57:449–462. **266**

Symonds, P. M. (1957). What education has to learn from psychology. IV. Whole versus part learning. *Teachers College Record*, 58:329–339. **224**

Taba, H. (1951). Generalizing, summarizing, and developing group methods. Unpublished paper, Conference on Group Processes, San Francisco State College, June. **304**

Taba, H. (1955). *With perspective on human relations.* Washington: Amer. Council on Educ. **313**

Taba, H. (1955). In G. D. Spindler, ed., *Educational anthropology.* Stanford: Stanford Univ. Press. **109, 118**

Taeuber, C. (1972). Population trends in the 1960s. *Science*, 176:773–777. **78**

Taffel, S. J., O'Leary, K. D., and Armel, S. (1974). Reasoning and praise: their effects on academic behavior. *J. educ. Psychol.*, 66:291–296. **213**

Tanner, J. M. (1970). Physical growth. In P. H. Mussen, ed., *Carmichael's manual of child psychology*, 3rd ed. New York: Wiley. **66**

Tanner, L. N., and Lindgren, H. C. (1971). *Classroom teaching and learning: a mental health approach.* New York: Holt, Rinehart, and Winston. **16, 155**

Taylor, C. S., and Ellison, R. L. (1967). Biographical predictors of scientific performance. *Science*, 155:1075–1080. **344**

Taylor, C. S., *see* James et al.

Tenenbaum, S. (1963). The teacher, the middle class, the lower class. *Phi Delta Kappan*, 45:82–86. **411–412**

Tharp, R. G., *see* Gallimore et al.

Thelen, H. A. (1954). *Dynamics of groups at work.* Chicago: Univ. of Chicago Press. **313**

Thelen, H. A. (1960). *Education and the human quest.* New York: Harper. **41**

Thelen, H. J. (1969). The evaluation of group instruction. In R. W. Tyler, ed., *Educational evaluation: new roles, new means*, 68th Yearbook, Part II. Chicago: Natl. Society for the Study of Educ. **316**

Thistlethwaite, D. L. (1959). Effects of social recognition upon the educational motivation of talented youth. *J. educ. Psychol.*, 50:111–116. **211**

Thomas, J. (1970). Tutoring strategies and effectiveness: a comparison of elementary age tutors and college tutors. Unpublished doctoral dissertation, Univ. of Texas. **295**

Thorndike, E. L. (1923). The gains made in ability by pupils who study Latin and by pupils who do not. *School and Soc.*, 18:690. **183**

Thorndike, E. L. (1924). Mental discipline in high school studies. *J. educ. Psychol.*, 15:1–22; 83–98. **173**

Thorndike, R. L. (1966). *Thorndike dimensions of temperament: manual.* New York: Psychol. Corp. **365**

Thorndike, R. L., and Hagen, E. (1959). *Characteristics of men who remained in and left teaching.* Coop. Res. Proj., No. 574 (SAE 8189). Washington: U.S. Office of Educ. **482**

Thorndike, R. L., and Hagen, E. (1969). *Measurement and evaluation in psychology and education*, 3rd ed. New York: Wiley. **319**

Thorpe, L. P., *see* Lee and Thorpe.

Tiedeman, D. V., *see* Sprinthall and Tiedeman.

Tift, K. F. (1968). The disturbed child in the classroom. *NEA J.* (March), 12–14. **137**

Tiger, L. (1969). *Men in groups.* New York: Random House. Paperback, 1970. **31**

Tizard, J. (1964). *Community services for the mentally handicapped.* London: Oxford Univ. Press. **24**

Tizard, R., and Rees, J. A. (1974). A comparison of the effects of adoption, restoration to the natural mother, and continued institutionalization on the cognitive development of four-year-old children. *Child Develpm.*, 45:92–99. **55, 357**

Tobias, J. J. (1970). Counseling the affluent suburban male delinquent. *Natl. Catholic Guid. Conference J.*, 14:80–85. **401**

Tobin, T. J., *see* Rychlak and Tobin.

Toffler, A. (1970). *Future shock.* New York: Random House. **78**

Tolor, A. (1969). Children's popularity and psychological distance. *Amer. Psychol. Assn. Proceedings*, 4:545–546. **113**

Tolor, A., Scarpetti, W. L., and Lane, P. A. (1967). Teachers' attitudes toward children's behavior revisited. *J. educ. Psychol.*, 58:175–180. **131**

Torrance, E. P. (1963). *Creativity.* Washington: Natl. Educ. Assn. **374**

Torrance, E. P. (1964). Education and creativity. In C. W. Taylor, ed., *Creativity: progress and potential.* New York: McGraw-Hill. **371**

Torrance, E. P. (1965). *Rewarding creative behavior.* Englewood Cliffs, N.J.: Prentice Hall. **298**

Torrance, E. P. (1970a). Stimulation, enjoyment, and originality. *Experimental Publications System, Amer. Psychol. Assn.,* Issue No. 7, Ms. 246–234. **298**

Torrance, E. P. (1970b). Influence of dyadic interaction on creative functioning. *Psychol. Rep.,* 26:391–394. **298**

Triandis, H. C., Loh, W. D., and Levin, L. A. (1966). Race, status, quality of spoken English, and opinions about civil rights as determinants of interpersonal attitudes. *J. Pers. soc. Psychol.,* 3:468–472. **423**

Trotter, S. (1975). Labeling: it hurts more than it helps. *Amer. Psychol. Assn. Monitor,* 6(1), 5. **384**

Trumbull, B. M., *see* Macmillan et al.

Tulkin, S. R., and Kagan, J. (1970). Mother-child interaction: social class differences in the first year of life. *Amer. Psychol. Assn. Proceedings,* 5:261–263. **415**

Tulkin, S. R., and Kagan, J. (1972). Mother-infant interaction in the first year of life. *Child Develpm.,* 43:31–41. **89**

Turner, R. R., *see* Hall and Turner.

Turner, R. V., *see* Fisher and Turner.

Turnure, J. E., *see* Samuels and Turnure.

Turtletaub, A., *see* Geer and Turtletaub.

Tyler, L. E. (1969). *The work of the counselor,* 3rd ed. New York: Appleton-Century-Crofts. **441, 459**

Tyler, L. E. (1972). Human abilities. *Annual Rev. Psychol.,* 23:177–206. **354**

Tyler, L. (1974). *Individual differences.* Englewood Cliffs, N.J.: Prentice Hall. **374**

Tyler, R. W. (1948). Cooperation and conflict in the mental development of the child. *Ment. Hyg.,* 32:253–260. **175**

Tyler, R. W., ed. (1969). *Educational evaluation: new roles, new means,* 68th Yearbook, Part II. Chicago: Natl. Soc. for the Study of Educ. **347**

Tyler, R. W., *see also* Lessinger and Tyler.

Ulibarri, H. (1966). Social and attitudinal characteristics of Spanish-speaking migrant and ex-migrant workers in the Southwest. *Sociol. Soc. Res.,* 30:361–370. **93**

Ulrich, R. E., *see* Schmidt and Ulrich; Surratt et al.

U.S. Dept. of Health, Education, and Welfare (1973). *Age at menarche.* DHEW Publ. (HRA) 74–1615, November. **65**

U. S. Dept. of Health, Education, and Welfare (1973). *Literacy among youths 12–17 years.* U.S. DHEW Publ. No. (HRA) 74–1613, December. **2**

U. S. Dept. of Health, Education, and Welfare (1974). *Reading and arithmetic achievement among youths 12–17 years, as measured by the Wide Range Achievement Test.* DHEW Publ. (HRA) 74–1618, February. **448**

U. S. Dept. of Health, Education, and Welfare (1974). *Family background, early development, and intelligence of children 6–11 years,* U.S. DHEW Publ. (HRA) 75–1624, August. **32**

U.S. Office of Education (1964). The education of handicapped children. *School Life,* 46(6):10. **379–380**

U. S. Office of Education (1969). *Educational research and development in the United States.* Washington: Government Printing Office. **380, 395**

U. S. Office of Education (1973). *Digest of educational statistics.* Washington: Government Printing Office. **380**

Valin, E. (1961). La valeur des examens: étude docimologique realisée au Liban. *Études et documents d'éducation,* No. 40. Paris: UNESCO. **324–325**

Van Dalsem, E., *see* Finney and Van Dalsem.

van de Riet, H. (1964). Effects of praise and reproof on paired-associate learning in educationally retarded children. *J. educ. Psychol.,* 55:139–143. **163**

Veldman, D. J., and Brophy, J. E. (1974). Measuring teacher effects on pupil achievement. *J. educ. Psychol.,* 66:319–324. **236**

Veldman, D. J., and Menaker, S. L. (1969). Directed imagination method for projective assessment of teacher candidates. *J. educ. Psychol.,* 60:178–187. **484**

Veldman, D. T., and Peck, R. F. (1963). Student teacher characteristics from the pupil's point of view. *J. educ. Psychol.,* 54:346–355. **483**

Walberg, H. J., and Anderson, G. J. (1968). Classroom climate and individual learning. *J. educ. Psychol.,* 59:414–419. **237**

Walberg, H. J., House, E. R., and Steele, J. M. (1973). Grade level, cognition, and affect: a cross-section of classroom perceptions. *J. educ. Psychol.,* 64:142–146. **221–222**

Walberg, H. J., and Rasher, S. P. (1974). Public school effectiveness and equality: new evidence and its implications. *Phi Delta Kappan,* 56:3–9. **2**

Waldrop, M. F., and Bell, R. Q. (1964). Relation of preschool dependency behavior to family size and density. *Child Develpm.,* 35:1187–195. **143**

Walker, R. N., *see* Ames and Walker.

Wallace, P. (1974), Complex environments: effects on brain development. *Science,* 185:1035–1037. **30**

Wallen, N. E., et al. (1963). Relationship between teacher needs and teacher behavior in the classroom. *J. educ. Psychol.,* 54:23–32. **262**

Walls, R. T., and Smith, T. S. (1970). Development of preference for delayed reinforcement in disadvantaged children. *J. educ. Psychol.,* 61:118–123. **419**

Walter, J. E., *see* Klausmeier et al.

Walters, C. E. (1965). Prediction of postnatal development from fetal activity. *Child Develpm.,* 36:801–808. **31**

Walters, R. H., *see* Bandura and Walters.

Ward, B. A., *see* Gall and Ward.

Ward, W. C., Kogan, N., and Pankove, E. (1970). Motivation and ability in children's creativity. *Amer. Psychol. Assn. Proceedings,* 5:285–286. **371**

Warner, W. L., and Lunt, P. S. (1941). *Social life of a modern community.* New Haven: Yale Univ. Press. **85**

Warren, J. M., *see* Wilson et al.

Warren, T. F., *see* Davis and Warren.

Washburne, N. F. (1959). Sociometric status, urbanism, and academic performance in college. *J. educ. Res.*, 53:130–137. **93**

Waters, E., and Crandall, V. J. (1964). Social class and observed maternal behavior from 1940 to 1960. *Child Develpm.*, 35:1021–1032. **86**

Watson, R. I., and Lindgren, H. C. (1973). *Psychology of the child.*, 3rd ed. New York: Wiley. **73**

Wattenberg, W. W., and Clifford, C. (1962). *Relationship of self-concept to beginning achievement in reading.* U.S. Office of Educ. Coop. Res. Proj., No. 377. Detroit: Wayne State Univ. **225**

Wattenberg, W. W., and Clifford, C. (1964). Relations of self-concepts to beginning achievement in reading. *Child Develpm.*, 35:461–467. **424**

Wattenberg, W. W., *see* Redl and Wattenberg.

Weiner, I. B. (1970). *Psychological disturbance in adolescence.* New York: Wiley. **155**

Weingartner, C., *see* Postman and Weingartner.

Westinghouse Learning Corp., *see* Ohio State Univ. and Westinghouse Learning Corp.

Westley, W. A., and Epstein, N. B. (1969). *The silent majority: families of emotionally healthy college students.* San Francisco: Jossey-Bass. **96**

Whipple, C. I., and Kodman, F., Jr. (1969). A study of discrimination and perceptual learning with retarded readers. *J. educ. Psychol.*, 60:1–5. **53**

White, R. K., *see* Lewin et al.

White, R. W. (1959). Motivation reconsidered: the concept of competence. *Psychol. Rev.*, 66:297–333. **21**

Whiting, A. (1970). Parental expectations for independent behaviors and achievement of elementary school boys. Unpubl. paper, Western Psychol. Assn., Los Angeles, April. **77, 80**

Wickman, E. K. (1928). *Children's behavior and teachers' attitudes.* New York: Commonwealth Fund. **130–131**

Widdowson, E. M. (1951). Mental contentment and physical growth. *Lancet*, 260:1316–1318. **69**

Wilensky, H. L. (1967). Careers, counseling, and the curriculum. *J. human Resources*, 2:19–40. **447**

Wilhelms, F. T., ed. (1967). *Evaluation as feedback and guide.* Washington: Assn. for Supervision and Curric. Develpm., NEA. **347**

Willoughby, S. S. (1969). Mathematics. In R. L. Ebel, et al., eds., *Encyclopedia of educational research*, 4th ed. New York: Macmillan. **311**

Wilson, J. A. R. (1959). Some results of an enrichment program for gifted ninth graders. *J. educ. Res.*, 53:157–160. **391**

Wilson, M., Warren, J. M., and Abbott, L. (1966). Infantile stimulation, activity, and learning by cats. *Child Develpm.*, 36:843–853. **30**

Witherspoon, P. (1960). A comparison of the problems of certain Anglo- and Latin-American junior high school students. *J. educ. Res.*, 53:295–299. **83–84**

Witty, P. A. (1951). The teacher who has helped me the most. *Studies in higher educ.*, No. 76. Lafayette, Ind.: Div. of Educ. Reference, Purdue Univ. **473**

Witty, P. A., ed. (1967). *The educationally retarded and disadvantaged.* 66th Yearbook, Part I. Chicago: Natl. Soc. for the Study of Educ. **407**

Wohlford, P., and Liberman, D. (1970). Effect of father absence on personal time, field independence, and anxiety. *Amer. Psychol. Assn. Proceedings*, 5:263–264. **78**

Wolf, W., et al. (1965). How do children look at television? *Phi Delta Kappan*, 46:537–540. **356**

Wolff, P. H., and Hurwitz, I. (1973). Functional implications of the minimal brain damage syndrome. *Seminars in Psychiat.*, 5:105–115. **145**

Wolfson, B. J., *see* Jackson et al.

Woloshin, G. W., *see* Le Furgy and Woloshin.

Woodring, M. N. (1925). *The study of the quality of English in Latin translations.* New York: Bureau of Publ., Teachers Coll., Columbia Univ. **183**

Woodward, R. G. (1973). Title VIII and the Oglala Sioux. *Phi Delta Kappan*, 55:249–251. **152**

Woody, R. H. (1969). *Behavioral problem children in the schools.* New York: Appleton-Century-Crofts. **155, 407**

Woolman, M. (1964). *Evaluations of the Progressive Choice Reading Method.* Washington: Inst. of Educ. Res. **432**

Worcester, D. A. (1966). *The education of children of above-average mentality.* Lincoln: Univ. of Nebr. Press. **392**

Worcester, E. E. (1974). Louisiana studies reading skills. *NAEP Newsletter*, 7(6):4. **340**

Worthen, B. R. (1968). Discovery and expository task presentation in elementary mathematics. *J. educ. Psychol.*, 59, No. 1 (Part II) Monograph suppl. **170**

Yarrow, M. R., Campbell, J. D., and Burton, R. V. (1968). *Child rearing: an inquiry into research and methods.* San Francisco: Jossey-Bass. **96**

Yates, A. B. (1970). *Behavior therapy.* New York: Wiley. **283**

Yee, A. H. (1968). Source and direction of casual influence in teacher-pupil relationships. *J. educ. Psychol.*, 59:275–282. **419**

Zabarenko, R. N., *see* Chambers and Zabarenko.

Zalk, S. R., *see* Katz and Zalk.

Zich, J., *see* Kanfer and Zich.

Zigler, E. (1967). Familial mental retardation: a continuing dilemma. *Science*, 155:292–298. **386**

Zigler, E., Abelson, W. D., and Zeitz, V. (1973). Motivational factors in the performance of economically disadvantaged children on the Peabody Picture Vocabulary Test. *Child Develpm.*, 44:294–303. **360**

513

Zigler, E., and Kanzer, P. (1962). The effectiveness of two classes of verbal reinforcers on the performance of middle- and lower-class children. *J. Pers.*, 30:157–163. **94**

Ziller, R. C., *see* Long et al.

Zellner, M., *see* Maccoby and Zellner.

Zimmerman, I. L. (1965). Personal communication to the author. **431**

Zimmerman, I. L., and Allebrand, G. N. (1965). Personality characteristics and attitudes toward achievement of good and poor readers. *J. educ. Res.*, 59:28–30. **397–398**

Zimmerman, R. R., Strobel, D. A., and McGuire, D. (1970). Neophobic reactions in protein malnourished infant monkeys. *Amer. Psychol. Assn. Proceedings*, 5:197–198. **415**

Zweibelson, I., Bahnmuller, M., and Lyman, L. (1965). Team teaching and flexible grouping in the junior high school studies. *J. exper. Educ.*, 43:20–32. **292**

Subject Index

reinforcement techniques at, 426–427

relations with mothers, 429

Edison, T. A., 54

Education, laymen's concepts of, 12

Educational measurements, interpreting, 14–15

Educational psychology, as empirical foundation of education, 13–14

focal areas of, 12–14

Ego rewards, 418–419

"Eleven-plus" examinations, in Britain, 68

Emotional adjustment, and IQ, 355

Emotional climate, in the classroom, 118–125

Emotional conflict, and problem behavior, 141–142

Emotional development, 61–64

Emotional disturbance, severe, 402–404

Emotional maturity, 61–62

Emotions, and behavior, 26–28

English grammar, students' retention of, 166

Environment, and human organism, 29–30

stimulus-enriched and stimulus-deprived, 30

Ethnic language, instruction in, 252

Ethnic prejudice, 121–122

European schools, attitudes toward peer groups in, 105

Evaluation, and anxiety, 244–246

attitudes toward, 321–322

as distinguished from measurement, 318

as feedback, 317–318, 320–321

of learning, 315–344

teachers' role in, 316–317

teachers' conflicts regarding, 316–317

Exceptional children, 377–405

categorizing of, 384–385

failure experiences of, 385–386

overprotection of, 385–386

percentages of, 379–380

programs for, 380

school adaptations needed for, 381

Experimental psychology, and teaching practices, 191–193

Experimentation, in the classroom, 310–311

Expository method, in teaching, 169–172

Extracurricular activities, and social class, 92

Eysenck, H. J., 358

Failure in school, and parental discipline, 81

Failures, in learning, 173–175

Family, emotional climate of, 79

influence of children's behavior, 75–94

single-parent, 78

Father absence, influence of, 78

Feedback, and evaluation, 317–318, 320–321

and learning, 244–246

Field theory, and learning, 194–195

Films, and group discussion, 302

Finnish children, 83

Firstborns, personality of, 32

Foreign languages, learning of, 225

Forgetting, and learning, 165–168

"Free schools," 49

Free-School Movement, 304–306

Freud, S., 62, 305

Friendship patterns, in childhood, 105–106, 111–113

Frustration, in learning, 173–175

Future orientation, of deprived children, 419

Gagné's "conditions of learning," 215–216

German children, 83

Gestalt psychology, 193–194

Gifted students, 388–395

criteria for identifying, 390

"double promotion" of, 391–392

special programs for, 390–391

Goals, educational, 317–318

Goddard, H. H., 350

"Good behavior," lower-class parents' expectations regarding, 420

Grade-point average, relationship to popularity of, 115–116

Grading practices, 342–344

Grammatical errors, of university students, 166–167

Group counseling, 451–453

Group discussion, 298–303

Group methods, best uses of, 304

of teaching/learning, 296–304

Group norms, in adolescence, 110–111

in childhood, 101, 105

Guidance workers, 447–458

and collaboration with teachers, 457–458

and school dropouts, 448–451

Hartmann, G. W., 193

Hawaiian-English dialect, 423

Head Start Program, 57

Herrnstein, R., 358

Homework, and learning, 243–244

Homicide rate, and illiteracy, 2–3

Honors courses, and the gifted, 393

Hopi families, 81

Hostility, among peer groups, 121–125

displaced, 139

Human organism, as energy system, 28–29

Humanist-behaviorist controversy, 201–203

Humanistic views, research supporting, 213

Hyperactivity, in children, 144–145

Illiteracy, 2

Immaturity, and problem behavior, 134

Impulsivity, and problem behavior, 146–147

Independence, and creativity, 369–370

Individual differences, measurement of, 349–372

providing for, 70

Individualized attention, need for, 440–441

from psychological specialists, 446–457

from teachers, 444–446

Individualized instruction, 212

Individually Guided Instruction (IGE), 289–290, 322

Individually Prescribed Instruction (IPI), 293, 322

Inductive approaches, to teaching/learning, 169–172

Infant schools, British, 49

Information, learning of, 216–217

Inhelder, B., 48

Input, as stimuli, 28–29

Insight, defined, 10–11

and learning, 194

Institutions, children in, 55
  effect on children, 68–69
Instruction, defined, 8
Intelligence tests, history of, 350–355
  legal limits to use of, 354
  reliability of, 356–357
  validity of, 355–356
Interests tests, 363–364
Interest in learning tasks, and social
  class, 94
International Association for the
  Evaluation of Education, 3
"Intervention programs," for
  adolescents, 432–434
  for deprived children, 424–435
IQ, formula for, 350
  meaning of, 355–356
  and relationship to popularity,
  114–115
  stability and change in, 356–357
IQs, of black students, 421–422

Koffka, K., 193
Köhler, W., 193
Kuder Preference Record, 363
Kuhlmann, F., 350

Latin courses, effect on competence
  in English, 183
Leadership, and IQ, 355
Learner, maturation of, 43–70
  understanding the, 6–7
Learner-centered methods, 285–311
  characteristics of, 287–289
  experimentation in, 310–311
  in group settings, 296–304
  innovations in, 291–292
  and peer tutoring, 294–295
  resistance to, 308–310
  student involvement in, 292–293
Learning, and anxiety, 227–230
  additive theory of, 164–165
  of attitudes, 218–223
  and "being told," 168–169
  "carrot-and-stick" approaches to,
  160–164
  cognitive and affective factors in,
  209–230
  of concepts, 217–218
  as conditioning, 187–189
  deductive approaches to, 169–172
  through discovery, 170–172,
  197–198
  enjoyment of, 174–176
  evaluation of, 244–246, 315–344

factors that interfere with, 214–215
and feedback, 244–246
Gagné's and Bloom's concepts
  compared, 215–216
Gestaltist approaches to, 193–194
and homework, 243–244
through imitation, 210
inductive approaches to, 169–172
and learner-centered methods, 246
and locus of control, 227
management of, 235–253
for mastery, 201
and the "mind as a storehouse"
  approach, 164–165
motivation underlying, 19–39
and normal anxiety, 229–230
and peer-group norms, 240–241
persistence of
  traditional/conventional beliefs
  regarding, 176–177
personality factors in, 225–230
phenomenological concepts of,
  198–201
and practice, 167–168
as problem solving, 195–198
readiness for, 226–227
and reinforcement, 174, 188–191
and retention, 165–168
reward-and-punishment
  approaches to, 175–176
and self-concept, 217, 219
of skills and information, 216–218
social view of, 203–204
"stress-and-strain" theories of,
  172–174
and teacher guidance, 242–243
teacher-centered approaches to,
  238–246
and teacher-expectancy effects,
  238–240
and teachers' anxieties, 241–242
teachers' influence on, 236
traditional/conventional views of,
  157–177
transfer of, 172–174
use of punishment in, 161
use of rewards in, 161
of wholes and parts, 223–225
Learning process, understanding, 7
Learning situation, understanding,
  7–8
Learning styles, social-class
  differences in, 172

Learning theory, as based on
  scientific research, 182–183
  necessity of, 181–182
  and teaching experience, 191–193
"Life space" interviewing, 456–457
Limits, to misbehavior, 265
Locke, J., 170
Locus of control, 35, 38
  and learning, 227
Louisiana, achievement of pupils in,
  340
Love, need for, 24
Lower-class subculture,
  characteristics of, 86

Maladjustments, of children, 129–153
  social and emotional, 395–404
Management assessment model,
  337–338
Managerial approach, to teaching-
  learning situation, 286–287
Manipulation, in teaching-learning
  process, 242–243
Mann, H., 324
Marihuana, and attitudes toward
  authority, 109
  and peer-group relations, 102
Mastery, teaching for, 201
Maternal employment, influence on
  children, 79
Mathematical skills, retention of, 166
Mathematics, learning of, 226–227
  teachers' and students' attitudes
  toward, 218–219
Maturation, 43–70
Maturity, and changes in percepts, 35
  contrasted with concept of age,
  45–46
Measurements, skepticism about, 322
Medical specialists, in schools,
  443–444
Memory, and learning, 165–168
Menarche, age decline in, 66
Mental age, 350
Mental discipline, theories of, 172–174
Mental health, and school policies,
  150–153
Mental retardation, 386–388
Mexican-Americans, 410
Mexican children, 57–58, 83–84
Middle-class children, verbal
  experiences of, 415–418
Middle-class subculture,
  characteristics of, 86

emphasis on verbal activity in, 88–91

Middle-class values, and delinquency, 399

Migrant farm workers, and attitudes toward school, 92

"Mind as a storehouse," as an approach to teaching/learning, 164–165

Minimal brain damage (MBD), 145

Moral development, 59–61
stages of (Kohlberg), 60

Morale, in classroom groups, 118

Mothers, influence of employed, 79

Motivation, and awareness, 36–38
below awareness level, 210
and genetics, 30–31
and goals, 38–39
as "internal" cause of behavior, 19–20
and learning, 19–39
and multiple causation of behavior, 39
and purposes, 38–39
and social class attitudes toward learning, 93–94

Modeling, see Social learning

Montessori, M., 170

Mooney Problem Checklist, 365

National Assessment of Educational Progress, 340–341

Need, to be competent and effective, 20–21
defined, 20–21
for stimulation and arousal, 29–30

Needs, for achievement, see Achievement need
for affiliation, see Affiliation need
basic, 21–26, 210
deficiency, 24
maintenance, 24
normative, 240
physical, 24
psychological, 240
self-actualization, 25
social, 24

Neill, A. S., 304–305

"New math," failure of, 218

Nonconformity, and creativity, 369–370

Nonpromotion, of slow learners, 388

Nonteaching activities, of teachers, 463

Normal anxiety, and learning, 229–230

Normal curve, of probability, 336

Norms, of peer group, 240–241

Nutritional deficiencies, 66

Obedience, 258–259

Objectives, behavioral statements of, 317–318
educational, 317–318

Occupational Interest Inventory, 363–364

"Open classroom" methods, characteristics of, 287–289

"Open classrooms," 49

"Open schools," 203

Operant conditioning, 188–191

Output, as response, 29

"Overdwelling," by teachers, 246–247

Overprotection, by teachers, 175

Paraprofessionals, in inner-city schools, 434–435
and relations with teachers, 464–465

Parent-Teacher Association, 469

Parental attitudes, and homework, 243–244
influence of, 75–83

Parental permissiveness, 80–81

Peabody Picture Vocabulary Test, 360

Peace Corps, 2–3, 448

Peer acceptance, and relation to IQ, 114–115
teachers' ability to determine, 113–114

Peer group, influence of, 83, 105–106, 110–111
relations with, 99–125

Peer-group norms, and teacher expectancies, 240–241

Percentile scores, 336

Perception, and personality, 33–35
and maturity, 35–36

Permissiveness, of parents, 80–81

Personal adjustment problems, and help from teachers, 445–446

Personality, and perception, 33

Personality factors, and learning, 225–230

Personality problems, as contrasted with conduct problems, 133–134

Personality testing, 364–367
legal restrictions on, 367
public criticism of, 366–367

Pestalozzi, H., 170

Phenomenal field, and school curriculum, 217

Physical development, 64–66

Physiological processes, and learning, 185–186

Piaget, J., 62, 170, 226
developmental stages described by, 48–54
and John Dewey, 197

Play patterns, in preschool children, 102–104

Plaza Sesamo, 57

Possessiveness, in preschool children, 45–46

Poverty, and social deprivation, 409–411

Probability, normal curve of, 336

Problem behavior, and anxiety, 137–142
and discouragement, 148–149
and emotional conflict, 141–142
and learning progress, 131–133
of middle-class and upper-class children, 143–144
among "normal" children, 135–136
prevalence of, 134–136
psychologists' attitudes toward, 130–131
and pupils' environments, 142–144
and reading problems, 146
sex differences in, 146–148
and social class, 142–144
of students, 129–153
teachers' attitudes toward, 130–131
understanding, 136–137

Problem solving, in learning, 170–172
sex differences in, 222–223

Programmed learning, 189–191, 290–291

Progressive Education movement, 304

Project PLAN, 322–323

Projective tests, 365–366

Psychiatrists, in schools, 443–444

Psychological climate, 195, 237
in the classroom, 118–125

Psychological services, in the schools, 439–458

Psychologists, teachers' attitudes toward, 12–13

Puerto Ricans, 410

Punishment, 262–267
effects on learning, 161–163
and negative reinforcement, 188
physical, 257, 264

as public-relations persons,
468–469
as question posers, 237
and relations with
paraprofessionals, 464–465
roles of, 462–474
as security seekers, 474
self-expressive roles of, 471–474
self-ideal conflicts of, 479
as social psychologists, 470
status and prestige of, 5–6, 484–485
and strikes, 481
students' attitudes toward, 484
as targets for hostility, 481–482
as youth group workers, 465–468
Teaching, and accountability,
338–339
bureaucratic restrictions in,
474–475
deductive and inductive
approaches to, 169–172
disintegrative forces in, 474–483
economic status of, 484
effect of disintegrative factors in,
482–483
group methods of, 296–304
innovations in, 291–292
integrative factors in, 483–485
learner-centered, 285–311
and overprotection of children, 175
psychological rewards in, 483
psychological status of, 484–485
role conflict in, 475–477
social status of, 484–485
structure and organization in,
247–249
traditional/conservative views of,
157–177
Teaching effectiveness, teachers' and
laymen's views of, 478
Teaching-learning problems,
increasing complexity of, 253

Teaching-learning process,
psychological concepts of,
157–175
traditional/conventional concepts
of, 157–175
Teaching-learning theory,
requirements of, 184–186
and students' motives, 186–187
Teaching machines, 189–191
Teaching methods, and effect on
classroom behavior, 262
and students' ratings, 221
Team teaching, 292
Television viewing, and social-class
differences, 89
"Telling," and learning, 168–169
Terman, L. M., 350, 389
Territoriality, 45
Test anxiety, 360
and IQ, 355
Tests, achievement, 332–334
aptitude, 362–363
choice-type or objective, 326–329
completion, 328
criterion-referenced, 232, 341–342
essay, 324–326
of intelligence, 350–360
interpreting results of, 334–337
matching type, 329
multiple-choice type, 327
norm-referenced, 332
objective, 326–329
of personal and social adjustment,
364–367
projective, 365–366
reliability and validity of, 329–331
standardized, 331–336
teacher-made, 323–331
true-false, 327
of vocational interests, 363–364
use of, 318–320
Thematic Apperception Test (TAT),
397–398

Thorndike Dimensions of
Temperament (TDOT), 365
Thorndike, E. L., 195
Token economies, 293–294
Torrance Tests of Creative Thinking,
418
Traditional/conventional methods,
deficiencies and strengths of, 286
Traditional/conventional views,
scientific tests of, 183
of teaching-learning process,
157–177
Tutoring, by peers, 294–295, 433

Underachievers, 360
"Understanding," as an aim of
psychology, 4
defined, 8–12
of educational processes, 4–5
prescientific, 5
Upper-class subculture,
characteristics of, 86

Validity, of tests, 329–331
Values, as learned from family, 77
Verbal facility, as predictor of school
success, 431–432
Vocational counseling, 441–442,
447–448

War on Poverty, 410
Wechsler, D., 352
Wechsler Intelligence Scales, 352
Wholes versus parts, in learning,
223–225
Winnetka Plan, 293
Work-study programs, 451
for delinquency-prone boys,
403–404

Zuñi children, 32
Zuñi families, 81